The Negro in America: A Bibliography

The Negro in America: A Bibliography

Compiled by Elizabeth W. Miller

Second Edition, Revised and Enlarged

Compiled by Mary L. Fisher

With a New Foreword by Thomas F. Pettigrew

Harvard University Press, Cambridge, Massachusetts   1970

Foreword

This volume constitutes an important and overdue contribution to the understanding of American race relations. Not since the definitive treatment of the issue by Gunnar Myrdal in *An American Dilemma,* now a generation old, have we had such an extensive and searching bibliographical collection. In addition to its obvious value as a sourcebook for information and references, this modern bibliography chronicles the latest chapter in the long and curious history of American thinking about the Negro—a history that deserves brief mention in order to place this work in temporal perspective.

American racial thought was initially shaped by slavery. The peculiar institution posed a serious dilemma for early America: How could slaveholders treat human beings as mere property and at the same time uphold the lofty American ideal of human equality? The answer is that many never did rest easily with this glaring contradiction, though they tried as best they could to rationalize and excuse the conflict. Built around the firm insistence that slavery was a "positive good," these rationalizations took three basic forms: religious, cultural, and racial.

First, slavery was defended as a religiously ordained system—an effective method to Christianize and civilize African heathen. But, in time, this claim lost most of its potency. To begin with, it conflicted with the racist notion that the Negro was incapable of acculturation. And by the nineteenth century it was seriously undermined by the increasing numbers of slaves who had become Christians and thus no longer needed to be converted. More enduring were the biblical defenses of slavery. Virtually all pro-slavery spokesmen employed literal interpretations of the Old Testament to prove that the institution had Christian sanction. God had willed that the black man forever serve the white man, according to the especially popular interpretation of a drunken man's curse in Genesis 9. In fact, the whole array of Old Testament arguments assembled in the defense of slavery is still heard in the South today as a defense of segregation.

Second, slavery was justified as a cultural necessity. As fiery anti-slavery attacks from the North began to find their mark in the 1820's and 1830's, slave interests countered that the system fostered a superior culture. Great scholars, great writers, great statesmen were made possible, contended slaveholders, when an institution such as slavery gave them the wealth and leisure to develop their talents. After all, the South was only following the examples set by the slaveholding societies of ancient Greece and Rome. Already the results of this noble experiment were evident. Did not the planter class possess a patrician charm and gentility not to be found in the hustle and bustle of the crudely materialistic, urbanizing North? Indeed, an angry finger could be pointed at the labor evils right under the sensitive noses of the Abolitionists. Was it not true that the factory workers in the North and in England were mere "wage slaves"? Could the critics of the South deny that their own laborers suffered from miserable living and working conditions without even the "security" provided by chattel slavery? How could Northern and English Abolitionists dare to question the "benign" system of slavery upon which the South was building a great culture at precisely the time when their own societies were deep in the quagmire of cultural decay?

This cultural argument encountered two major obstacles. Any glorification of a despotic system directed by a special elite had to come to terms with the American dream. Most slavery spokesmen avoided meeting this conflict head on; they tried to maintain both the rationalization and the dream by claiming that only in a slave society could real freedom and opportunity exist for them. Moreover, the analogy with ancient Greece and Rome suffered from a fundamental difference between modern and earlier forms of slavery, for in the New World the institution was totally identified with one specific group. And, as Frank Tannenbaum comments in his *Slave and Citizen,* this difference "spelled the death knell of slavery itself within the European cultural area." Previously, slavery had been a condition anyone might suffer, and so it was regarded as a misfortune, but when the slave status came to be occupied solely by Negroes, the question naturally arose: Why the Negro? This query made slavery a moral problem for the first time.

Why the Negro? The cultural arguments did not provide a straightforward reply to this question; consequently, the slaveholders still relied on the Bible. By the 1830's, however, a third defense for slavery began to appear, a defense clothed in the respectability of "science." Rather than depend upon biblical revelation, the new ethnological arguments relied upon "natural law." Negroes were slaves because they comprised a separate, inferior species; their lowly rank was merely a reflection of the natural relations among the "races" of man. The basic tenet of this theory was that the various races had had distinctly different origins, for a common origin was assumed to mean equal endowment for all races. And unequal racial endowments were substantiated by an odd variety of historical and anatomical data ranging from Egyptology to the size and shape of skulls. The leaders in this thinking were actually such prominent Northern scientists as Samuel Morton and Louis Agassiz, though the most vocal and vociferous proponents were pro-slavery Southerners.

Yet two features of this early "scientific" doctrine kept it from gaining critical importance in the slavery debate. First, the more technical features of the theory were too complex to be widely read and understood. And, second, the full doctrine flew in the face of the South's most cherished religious beliefs. In particular, the concept of diverse origins conflicted with the insistent scriptural interpretation that all men arose from a common Adam-and-Eve beginning. Attractive as it was, "The theory of the diversity of man," writes William Stanton in *The Leopard's Spots,* "tossed the religious into a theological bramble patch." Thus, most Southern spokesmen rejected the full "scientific" theory of race. Only those who liked both to dabble in "science" and engage in "parson-skinning" consistently made use of the most intellectually respectable defense of slavery.

The crowning irony came in 1859 with the publication of *On the Origin of Species.* Going over much of the same ethnological ground, Charles Darwin arrived at the conclusion of the Church—the common origin of man. Religion had been vindicated by a man whose acceptance by it would require generations. And the "scientists" had been proven wrong by one of their own. Our chief interest today in this historical backwater is that it marks the national beginning of a formal, articulate doctrine of white superiority. Even more than the other rationalizations of slavery, aspects of this doctrine are with us today. In fact, though repeatedly repudiated by modern research, portions of the antebellum "evidence" for Negro inferiority are still to be found in the popular racist tracts of our own times listed in this volume (see references to the work of Garrett, George, Putnam, Shuey, and Weyl).

At the popular level these elaborate theories about racial origins and scientific proofs were not appreciated or needed, but the general ideas of "race" and Negro "racial" inferiority were accepted and utilized. In the early days slaveowners had simply assumed Negro inferiority and the new doctrine comfortably supported this view. Only a few thoughtful men such as James Bowdoin, mentioned in the Preface which follows, raised the possibility of environmental influences. By the early nineteenth century, increasing numbers of white Americans accepted the idea that Negroes formed a distinct and lower type of humanity. Thus, in 1857, Chief Justice Roger Taney could confidently claim in his *Dred Scott* opinion that Negroes were ". . . so far inferior, that they had no rights which the white man was bound to respect . . ."

Naive and vicious as this doctrine appears today in the light of the vast advances of recent years in the biological and social sciences, Taney's racist reasoning seemed logical to many of his contemporaries. All one had to do was to look around. Were not slaves obviously inferior to their masters in intelligence and manners? And if such things were all biologically determined, was this not proof that whites were racially superior to Negroes? Such was the simple argument, for the sweeping importance of environment and opportunity were not well understood by the scientists of this period much less the laymen.

Despite Emancipation and Reconstruction, the late nineteenth century witnessed little fundamental change in the prevailing ideas about race. To be sure, as C. Vann Woodward and others have documented, there were notable, if brief, instances of biracial egalitarianism during these times—in the Reconstruction state governments, even occasionally in the Redeemer state governments, and in some segments of the Populist revolt. Nevertheless, this period culminated in the most explicitly racist era of American history, 1890 to 1910. This is the period Rayford Logan calls the "nadir" of Negro-American history. These years marked the establishment of the modern form of *de jure* racial segregation, a trend sanctioned by such key Supreme Court decisions as *Louisville, New Orleans, and Texas Railroad v. Mississippi* (1890), *Plessy v. Ferguson* (1896), and *Cumming v. Board of Education* (1899). This was also the period of American colonialism. Indeed, it was the expansion of the United States into the Philippines that led to the unhappy phrase, "our little brown brothers."

Intellectual thought about race at the turn of the century reflected these events. Had the American Academy of Arts and Sciences commissioned a racial bibliography in 1910, it would have bulged with articles and books written from a heavily Darwinistic viewpoint. Undaunted by Darwin's blow to earlier racist notions, many believers in white racial superiority utilized biological Darwinism to argue that Negroes had evolved later than Caucasians and were therefore less "advanced." Social Darwinism, led by Yale's William Graham Sumner, completed the dominant reasoning of the period. In essence, Social Darwinists claimed government was in large part helpless to correct the desperate situation in which the Negro found himself. Stateways could not change folkways; if national traditions placed the Negro in a status of social inferiority, there was little that law and decree could do about it.

World War I shook the nation violently and sharply altered the racial scene. The mass movement of Negroes from the rural South to the nation's largest urban areas began; and "the Harlem Renaissance" of the 1920's signaled a new era of American race relations, an era in which the sophisticated and militant Negro of the cities began to replace the backward and subservient Negro of the open country. The psychological literature of the period, however, did not reflect the shift. World War I had shown the utility of intelligence tests, and many psychologists found themselves with an instrument more developed than their abilities to interpret its results. With few exceptions, the large majority of racial studies in psychology during the 1920's supported racist theories of white superiority. Empirically inadequate and theoretically naive, the racial literature of the decade was characterized by intelligence-test studies of white and Negro Americans that uncritically interpreted the usually higher white I.Q. means as evidence of inherent intellectual differences between the races.

The 1930's, however, witnessed a remarkable change in the dominant interpretation of such findings. Psychologists began to consider systematically the effects of environment and opportunity upon performance in their tests.

Though still crude in some respects, a new series of more rigorous racial studies appeared in the social science literature. Certainly one of the most important and influential landmarks among these newer investigations was Otto Klineberg's *Negro Intelligence and Selective Migration* (1935). Do Negro children who migrate from the South improve their test performance as they remain in the North? This was the basic question Klineberg answered affirmatively, together with a demonstration that selective migration of brighter Negroes to the North was not an explanation of his critical results.

More carefully controlled research on Negro Americans over the past generation has duplicated and confirmed the fundamental findings and conclusions of the 1930's. The critical significance of environmental factors in shaping and altering human behavior is now clearly recognized. Indeed, social scientists are no longer interested in testing environmental *versus* heredity questions. The new conception requires a specification of how environment *and* heredity complexly interact to produce behavior. "Race" and all of the distorted notions surrounding this concept are simply not productive ways to approach the central scientific issues. Inherent differences between Negro and white Americans may exist, but superiority-inferiority claims have no validity in modern scientific thinking. In addition, users of this volume are cautioned that just because many differences are discernible among "races" does not necessarily mean that such differences are *due* to "race."

Interestingly, this advance in American social science thought appears to have been both a cause and a result of a comparable general shift in American racial thought. Consider the data collected by the National Opinion Research Center in reply to the question: "In general, do you think that Negroes are as intelligent as white people—that is, can they learn things just as well if they are given the same education and training?" In 1942, only two out of five white Americans thought Negroes equal in intelligence to whites; by 1956, almost four out of five thought so. Even more dramatic has been the change in the white South. In 1942, only one in five white Southerners agreed that Negroes were of equal intelligence to whites; by 1963, three out of five agreed.

The full force of these sweeping alterations in American thought on race will impress those who utilize this bibliography. The books and articles cited herein serve as definitive documentation of this new and refreshing look at Negro Americans. The reader will note, too, that this view pervades material of all kinds—from fiction and biography through sociology and psychology. Indeed, this modern conception requires for its understanding insights from many diverse directions; and this need is comprehensively met in this significant volume.

Thomas F. Pettigrew
Harvard University
December 1965

Foreword to the Second Edition

If anything, the need for this invaluable and popular bibliography has heightened in the four years since its initial appearance. The United States has moved during these few years into yet another race relations era, a confusing time of such ideologically-charged cross-currents that the necessity for an informed perspective was never greater. It is an era tragically triggered by the assassin of Dr. Martin Luther King, Jr. in April of 1968, and marked by imperceptible gains and conspicuous losses. And, most important of all, it is an era dominated by the background of an unpopular war.

But this "post-movement" period, novel as it may first appear, is not without its roots in the nation's 350 years of racial history nor beyond analysis and understanding. Indeed, as C. Vann Woodward has indicated, this period was even predicted by a number of astute observers as a type of "second post-Reconstruction." And the old racist theme traced in the earlier foreword has emerged from under the rocks once again. Accurately spotlighted by the 1968 *Report of the National Advisory Commission on Civil Disorders* ("the Kerner Commission Report") as the key to the entire issue, racist theories received their latest revival from ostensibly "scientific" papers which chose to ignore the progress on the subject of the past four decades in both genetics and social science. And, strangely, much of the mass media excitedly greeted the revival as if racist notions were new.

As a consequence of these eventful years, a mass of new and relevant material has appeared since *The Negro in America* was first issued. This situation posed both opportunities and problems for the new editor. But the focus throughout has been to aid its users in formulating their own analyses and understandings of this new era upon which we have embarked. It succeeds in direct proportion to its usefulness in helping its readers to acquire a broad perspective on American race relations. I believe that this carefully-prepared new edition will admirably fulfill its goal.

Thomas F. Pettigrew
Harvard University
February 1970

Contents

Preface

When James Bowdoin was inducted into office as the first president of the American Academy of Arts and Sciences, he presented "A Philosophical Discourse Publickly Addressed" to that body on the eighth of November, 1780. He recited many reasons why the members should find, in the new nation, rich materials for their investigations. In common with other patriots of the day, he celebrated the unique advantages enjoyed by the citizens of the Republic, where, unfettered by tradition, by feudal forms, by the chains of custom, a new kind of society would make its contributions to mankind. Among his speculations on that occasion was one as to the "greater or less degree of natural knowledge and improvements" to be distinguished in the inhabitants of various parts of the globe. Referring to the difference between Europeans and Africans, he raised the question whether, if an inequality of "natural faculties" were observed between them, it might not "in a great measure be accounted for, by the operation of natural causes." He suggested that "there may be a variety of things, on which . . . [equality of capacity] . . . may depend: such as education, religion, government, and other circumstances," and that "the human faculties, by reason of sameness of situation and other circumstances, might in general be equal." During the years between the Supreme Court decision of May 17, 1954, and the enactment of the Voting Rights bill in August 1965, his question has assumed dimensions as extensive as the nation itself, and the Negro citizens of America now demand that they at last be allowed to enjoy a "sameness of situation" with their white fellow Americans . . .

It is now two years since *Daedalus,* the journal of the American Academy of Arts and Sciences, under the editorship of Stephen R. Graubard embarked on preparatory work for the publication of two issues on the Negro in America, which appeared in the Autumn of 1965 and the Winter of 1966. The compilation of the bibliography was originally initiated by Mr. Graubard as a part of a study of the Negro in America undertaken by the Academy and eventuating in the *Daedalus* issues. The Carnegie Corporation of America generously supported this entire project, for which the deepest appreciation of everyone associated with the enterprise is here expressed. My personal indebtednesses are many, to members of the faculties of Harvard University who have answered appeals, to the reference librarians of the several Harvard libraries who have resolved many queries out of the riches of the Harvard collections. A number of Harvard and Radcliffe students at various times scanned periodicals and verified references. I should particularly like to thank Daniel Horowitz for his resourceful and highly knowledgeable contributions in the early stages of the task. Susanne Bodenheimer, at a later stage, gave dedicated assistance. Members of the staff of *Daedalus* have furnished unfailing support. Finally, Ann Orlov of the Harvard University Press so quickly transcended her role as editor that I can only express my warmest gratitude to her as collaborator.

Elizabeth W. Miller
Cambridge, Massachusetts
December 1965

Preface to the Second Edition

Since the first edition of this bibliography was published, important developments, marking both progression and regression in the course toward the legitimate goal of black equality, have occurred and been recorded. New studies have been undertaken in the search for a better understanding of the educational, employment, health, and social factors which bear upon the continued intractability of the racial problem. The exigency and pace of events demand serious examination and reflection. As a nation we must consider new interpretations of our history and of the role of all people in it. For a deeper knowledge of ourselves, black or white, we must reevaluate our history to include a proper measure of the contributions and achievements of black people, no less in past times than at the present. Moreover, the message and impetus of the black nationalist movement, as one aspect of the over-all problem of black-white interrelationships, compels the thoughtful attention of us all.

References to materials published for the most part since 1954 have been brought together in this bibliography. Older sources chosen for their seminal value or to illumine historical background, attitudes, and trends have also been included. The plethora of reprints of works from this century and the last, by and about the black man, makes their over-all inclusion neither possible nor useful. However, certain of these titles which have been reprinted with noteworthy new critical introductions or which, as classics within their disciplines, have been reissued frequently, will be found within the bibliography.

Embracing several disciplines, this bibliography provides intensive coverage of many different English language monographs and serials, with emphasis on those published in the United States. In content, it encompasses the clinical, empirical, prescriptive, and polemic, the scholarly and the journalistic. It seeks to make accessible to both layman and scholar significant writings and, at the same time, to identify the problems and mark the urgency of their solutions.

The scope of this revised edition is considerably enlarged. Greater coverage is given to black history and social institutions, and to economic, political, and educational conditions. New sections on music, literature, and the arts are introduced. The last chapter, a guide to further research, has been expanded.

The bibliography is a selective one. News items appearing in many weekly periodicals and newspapers are not cited herein. When of import, the substance of their content is invariably discussed elsewhere, often with critical evaluation or commentary, and it is to these references that this bibliography is directed. References to dissertations have been omitted; the author and subject indexes to *Dissertation Abstracts* will suffice. Although titles first appearing in paperback are included as appropriate, the paperback imprint for other titles is not given; the reader is referred to current issues of *Paperbound Books in Print* for the availability of titles in softcover editions. Annotations are made as necessary to clarify titles which are not self-explanatory or to indicate the scope or significance of individual items. An author index serves to make the classified entries more accessible.

Omissions of some references will be questioned by the reader. Some stem from intention, others from negligence or oversight. The compiler will always appreciate any specific suggestions or areas for inclusion in a subsequent edition. While acknowledging that errors are unwittingly mine, I am deeply indebted to Sally C. Nesson for her unflagging support and secretarial skill and to Beth R. Petrow for her counsel and research in the music section of this edition.

Mary L. Fisher
February 1970

The Negro in America: A Bibliography

1   General Background

Berelson, Bernard, and Gary A. Steiner. *Human Behavior: An Inventory of Scientific Findings.* New York: Harcourt, Brace, 1964. A convenient summation of findings in the main areas of psychological research, including a chapter on ethnic relations, with references to classic and recent studies. One conclusion: "All races possess the abilities to participate. . .in modern technological civilization."

Berry, Brewton. *Race and Ethnic Relations.* 1951. 3d ed. Boston: Houghton Mifflin, 1965. A comparative view of racial and ethnic interaction which examines recent events in the United States and abroad from a sociological point of view.

Blair, Lewis H. *A Southern Prophecy: The Prosperity of the South Dependent upon the Elevation of the Negro.* 1889. Boston: Little, Brown, 1964. The book was written by a Southern businessman who had served in the Confederate Army. C. Vann Woodward has edited the reissue and provides an introduction presenting the work as a strong and realistic argument for civil rights.

Bontemps, Arna, and Jack Conroy. *Anyplace But Here.* New York: Hill and Wang, 1966. A revised and enlarged version of their 1945 book published by Doubleday entitled *They Seek a City.* New material on Negro nationalism, and the Watts, Chicago, and Detroit riots is added. Extensive bibliography.

Broderick, Francis L., and August Meier, eds. *Negro Protest in the Twentieth Century.* Indianapolis: Bobbs-Merrill, 1965. Fifty-four statements of Negro leaders from Booker T. Washington to James Farmer addressing a CORE convention. Useful as background source material of the civil rights movement.

Broom, Leonard, and Norval D. Glenn. *Transformation of the Negro American.* New York: Harper, 1965. A summary, drawn chiefly from other sources, of information about the present position of the Negro in the U.S.

Brotz, Howard, ed. *Negro Social and Political Thought, 1850-1920.* New York: Basic Books, 1966. Selections with the stated purpose "to bring within view the range of thought and opinion of Negroes about the future of their race in this country."

Brown, Ina Corinne. *The Story of the American Negro.* 1936. 2d rev. ed. New York: Friendship Press, 1957.

Caldwell, Erskine. *In Search of Bisco.* New York: Farrar, 1965. Southern life and attitudes as presented in conversations with both black and white Southerners.

Carawan, Guy, and Candie Carawan. *Ain't You Got a Right to the Tree of Life? The People of Johns Island, South Carolina—Their Faces, Their Words and Their Songs.* New York: Simon & Schuster, 1966. Notable photographs by Robert Yellin accompany brief text about descendants of plantation slaves who, isolated from the mainland, preserve much of the Afro-American folk traditions.

Cash, W. J. *The Mind of the South.* New York: Knopf, 1941. An extraordinarily penetrating picture of the origins of the Southern point of view, the background of Southern romanticism, the growth of violence as an instrument of legality. Author's approach is literary and psychological, but the book is more rather than less illuminating for that reason.

Chametzky, Jules, and Sidney Kaplan, eds. *Black and White in American Culture: An Anthology of the "Massachusetts Review."* Amherst: University of Massachusetts Press, 1969. Literary and critical commentaries on the interaction of black and white culture. Essays on civil rights protest, blues and jazz, and literature.

Clark, Thomas D. *The Emerging South.* 1961. 2d ed. New York: Oxford University Press, 1968. The author reviews economic and cultural changes that have occurred, the shift from a rural to an industrialized society, the impact of federal aid, and then proceeds to a discussion of Southern strategies of resistance and the techniques of Negro civil rights protest. Revised edition adds final chapter, "The Way of the Transgressor." Revised and expanded bibliography.

Clarke, John Henrik, ed. *Harlem: A Community in Transition.* New York: Citadel, 1964. Essays on the social, economic, political and literary, and musical aspects of this black community. Many articles drawn from *Freedomways.*

Clytus, John, with Jane Rieker. *Black Man in Red Cuba: The first Complete Account of a Black American's Experiences in Castro's Cuba.* Coral Gables, Fla.: University of Miami Press, 1970.

Cole, Stewart G., and Mildred Wiese Cole. *Minorities and the American Promise.* New York: Harper, 1954.

Coleman, James. "Race Relations and Social Change," in Irwin Katz and Patricia Gurin, eds., *Race and the Social Sciences.* New York: Basic Books, 1969, pp. 274-341.

Commager, Henry Steele, ed. *Documents of American History.* 8th ed. New York: Appleton-Century-Crofts, 1968. Several documents pertinent to the Negro including the Black Codes of Mississippi and Louisiana, Truman's civil rights message, February 2, 1948, texts of the Freedmen's Bureau bill, and the several civil rights bills.

Cox, Oliver Cromwell. *Caste, Class and Race.* Garden City, N.Y.: Doubleday, 1948. A Marxist criticism of the caste-class interpretation of American race relations.

Cruse, Harold. *The Crisis of the Negro Intellectual.* New York: Morrow, 1967. A readable examination of Negro intellectual development in America from the 1920's to the present. Bibliography.

Curtis, James C., and Lewis L. Gould, eds. *The Black Experience in America.* Austin: University of Texas Press, 1970.

Daedalus. The Negro American. Edited by Talcott Parsons and Kenneth B. Clark. Cambridge, Mass.: Houghton Mifflin, 1966. Essays by civil rights leaders and scholars, with two exceptions originally published in the Fall 1965 and Winter 1966 issues of *Daedalus,* are analyzed herein in the appropriate sections. This volume contains a lengthy introduction by the editors and a 32-page portfolio of photographs.

Davie, Maurice. *Negroes in American Society.* New York: McGraw-Hill, 1949. A comprehensive volume, with bibliography, covering all aspects of the experience of the Negro in America.

Davis, John P., ed. *The American Negro Reference Book.* Englewood Cliffs, N. J.: Prentice-Hall, 1966. Essay format with a detailed index.

Degler, Carl N. "Negro in America: Where Myrdal Went Wrong," *New York Times Magazine,* December 7, 1969, pp. 64-65 + .

Dollard, John. *Caste and Class in a Southern Town.* New Haven: Yale University Press, 1937. The third edition of this important study was published by Doubleday Anchor Books in 1957. In his preface to that edition, the author, while reiterating that "the caste device for placing Negroes must be abandoned," and acknowledging present dangers, maintains that, "If white men can solve the color problem, the United States is in an excellent position to do it."

Drake, St. Clair. "Recent Trends in Research on the Negro in the United States," *International Social Science Bulletin,* UNESCO, 9, no.4 (1957):475-492. Evaluative summaries of developments in sociological research.

Drake, St. Clair. "The Social and Economic Status of the Negro in the United States," *Daedalus* 94 (Fall 1965):771-814. A survey of the extent of the victimization experienced by the Negro in America today.

DuBois, W. E. B. *W. E. B. DuBois: A Reader.* Edited by Meyer Weinberg. New York: Harper & Row, 1970.

Dunbar, Ernest, ed. *The Black Expatriates: A Study of American Negroes in Exile.* New York: Dutton, 1968. Interviews with United States expatriates by an editor of *Look.*

Eaton, Clement. *The Growth of Southern Civilization.* New York: Harper, 1961. The author demonstrates the growing pressure of race relations on public affairs.

Emerson, Rupert, and Martin Kilson. "The American Dilemma in a Changing World: The Rise of Africa and the Negro American," *Daedalus* 94 (Fall 1965):1055-1084.

Frazier, E. Franklin. *The Negro in the United States.* 1949. Rev. ed. New York: Macmillan, 1957. A major work, of wide historical understanding. Extensive bibliography.

Frazier, E. Franklin. *Race and Culture Contacts in the Modern World.* New York: Knopf, 1957. An analysis of racial relations with a worldwide perspective. In his treatment of the Negro in America the author discusses patterns of migration, economic status, political status, the caste system of the South, prejudice, and problems of assimilation.

Furnas, J. C. *Goodbye to Uncle Tom.* New York: Sloane, 1956. Partly an attack on *Uncle Tom's Cabin,* partly a documentary social history on what conditions and customs were really like, the author's conclusion is that the only practical solution to the interracial problem is to let the Negro find his own level in society, without "caste pressures." Bibliography.

Gibson, Donald B. "The Negro: An Essay on Definition," *Yale Review* 57 (Spring 1968):337-345.

Ginzberg, Eli, and Alfred S. Eichner. *The Troublesome Presence: American Democracy and the Negro.* New York: Free Press, 1964. A fact-crammed work which surveys the impact of the Negro on America and of America on the Negro, and assesses the cost to the nation of continuing to deny the Negro his rights.

Grimes, Alan P. *Equality in America.* New York: Oxford University Press, 1964. See especially chapter 2, "Race," which discusses reasons for the difficulty of solving racial problems, traces the history of white supremacist theories, analyzes the rise of civil rights movement, the effect of *Brown v. Board of Education,* protest tactics, and related matters.

Handlin, Oscar. *Race and Nationality in American Life.* Boston: Little, Brown, 1957.

Harris, Fred R. "The American Negro Today," *William and Mary Law Review* 10 (1969):550-578. Includes a prefatory historical synopsis.

Henderson, George. "Negroes into Americans: A Dialectical Development," *Journal of Human Relations* 14 (Fourth quarter 1966):535-549.

Hero, Alfred O., Jr. "American Negroes and U.S. Foreign Policy: 1937-1967," *Journal of Conflict Resolution* 13 (June 1969):220-251. A sampling of Negro attitudes towards issues of U.S. foreign policy. Based on secondary sources.

Hero, Alfred O., Jr. *The Southerner and World Affairs.* Baton Rouge: Louisiana State University Press, 1965. An examination of changing Southern attitudes toward participation by the U.S. in international undertakings, which at the same time constitutes a profile of the Southerner, both black and white, and of developing relationships, interregional as well as interracial. Extensive "Observations on Selected Sources."

Herskovits, Melville J. *The Myth of the Negro Past.* New York: Harper, 1941. Reissued, Boston: Beacon, 1958, with new preface by the author. The outstanding work on Africanisms in the New World.

Herskovits, Melville J. *The New World Negro.* Edited by Frances S. Herskovits. Bloomington: Indiana University Press, 1966.

Highsaw, Robert B., ed. *The Deep South in Transformation.* University of Alabama Press, 1965. Discussions of social, political, economic, and cultural problems. Contributors include O. C. Carmichael, Everett C. Hughes, Louis Rubin, and Luther H. Hodges.

Hughes, Everett C. "Anomalies and Projections," *Daedalus* 94 (Fall 1965):1133-1147. The author considers, "at this time of actual and impending great change in the relations of Negro with other Americans, what is likely to be the general effect on our institutions and conduct."

Hughes, Everett C. "Race Relations and the Sociological Imagination," *American Sociological Review* 28 (December 1963):879-890.

Isaacs, Harold R. *The New World of Negro Americans*. New York: Day, 1963. Subtitled, "The impact of world affairs on the race problem in the United States and particularly on the Negro, his view of himself, his country, and Africa." Based on 107 interviews with American Negroes, the author provides an impressive analysis of the ways in which the growing importance and power of nonwhite, particularly African, nations has affected the life and thinking of American Negroes.

Isaacs, Harold R. "World Affairs and U.S. Race Relations: A Note on Little Rock," *Public Opinion Quarterly* 22 (Fall 1958):364-396.

Jones, LeRoi. *Home: Social Essays*. New York: Morrow, 1966. Twenty-four polemical essays on racism, politics, and the role of the black artist.

Katz, Irwin, and Patricia Gurin, eds. *Race and the Social Sciences*. New York: Basic Books, 1969. Scholarly inquiries of the current research issues in race relations in the United States. Individual articles are analyzed under the appropriate section.

Krueger, Thomas A. *And Promises to Keep—The Southern Conference for Human Welfare, 1938-1948*. Nashville: Vanderbilt University Press, 1967. Bibliography.

Margolis, Joseph, and Clorinda Margolis. "Black and White on Black and White," *Humanist* 29 (July-August 1969):unpaged center section. The theology of Blackness.

Morris, Willie, ed. *The South Today: 100 Years After Appomattox*. New York: Harper, 1965. A composite picture of Southern life, developed from a *Harper's* supplement.

Mphahlele, Ezekiel. *The African Image*. New York: Praeger, 1962. The author, a South African-born poet and novelist, writes about how Africans and Americans feel about each other, as well as about intergroup relationships in general. He also discusses the black nationalists.

Murray, Albert. *The Omni-Americans: New Perspectives on Black Experience and American Culture*. New York: Outerbridge & Dienstfrey, 1970.

Myrdal, Gunnar. *An American Dilemma*. 2 vols. New York: Harper, 1944; 20th anniversary ed., 1963. With a new preface by Myrdal and a 10,000 1-word "Postscript Twenty Years Later" by Arnold Rose. This monumental work, with the basic theme of inequality and its impact on every phase of Negro life and personality, has not forfeited its classic dimensions despite inevitable modifications and injection of new factors during intervening years.

The Negro Handbook. Compiled by the editors of *Ebony*. Chicago: Johnson, 1966. A comprehensive fact book, current up to the end of 1965, of information and brief articles arranged under 18 broad classifications. A complement to the *American Negro Reference Book*.

Nicholls, William H. *Southern Tradition and Regional Progress*. Chapel Hill: University of North Carolina Press, 1960. The effect of developing industrialization on Southern values and behavior, including a comparison of the attitudes of the rural elites and the new urban managerial, commercial, and professional classes.

"Notes From the Academy: Transcript of the American Academy Conference--May 14-15, 1965," *Daedalus* 95 (Winter 1966):287-441. Contributors to Fall 1965 and Winter 1966 issues of *Daedalus* on the Negro in America met with specialists from several fields to discuss and criticize drafts of papers in advance of publication.

Odum, Howard W. *Folk, Region, and Society: Selected Papers of Howard W. Odum*. Edited by Katherine Jocher et al. Chapel Hill: University of North Carolina Press, 1964. Excellent collection of Odum's papers. Odum had arrived at the conviction that "the earlier verdict of organic and composite race difference was wrong," and in his "Agenda for Integration" (1954) declared "'gradualism' is out." Also contains a collection of Negro folk songs, and a trilogy on Left-Wing Gordon.

Odum, Howard W. *Southern Regions of the United States*. Chapel Hill: University of North Carolina Press, 1936. Presented as an index of regional culture, this monumental study has as its principal focus the economic deficiencies of the South, its essentially "colonial" economy, that progressively exploited natural resources and cheap labor without any appreciable accumulation of capital.

"One Tenth of a Nation," *Reporter* 22 (March 31, 1960):14-22. Special section.

Osofsky, Gilbert. *The Burden of Race: A Documentary History of Negro-White Relations in America.* New York: Harper & Row, 1967. Chronologically arranged from the period of slave trade to black power; with most emphasis on the twentieth century. Introductory notes to each section. Bibliography.

Park, Robert Ezra. *Race and Culture.* Glencoe, Ill.: Free Press, 1950. On the whole, the papers of this distinguished scholar and teacher take a more optimistic view of a parallel Negro and white rise than has been proved by the event.

Parsons, Talcott. "Full Citizenship for the Negro American: A Sociological Problem," *Daedalus* 94 (Fall 1965):1009-1054. The author suggests that the resolution of the Negro's predicament as the most stigmatized American minority group lies in his inclusion as a full participant in a pluralistic societal situation.

Pinkney, Alphonso. *Black Americans.* Englewood Cliffs, N.J.: Prentice-Hall, 1969. An objective overview. Extensive chapter bibliographies.

Ploski, Harry A., and Roscoe C. Brown, comps. *The Negro Almanac.* New York: Bellweather, 1967. Popularly written, concise essays covering the historical, political, and social aspects of the American Negro. Short biographies. Illustrated.

Preu, James, ed. *The Negro in American Society.* Tallahassee: Florida State University, 1958.

Proctor, Samuel D. *The Young Negro in America: 1960-1980.* New York: Association Press, 1966. A concise, optimistic prognosis for the young Negro in the forthcoming decade. Jacket subtitle: Where he is and where he seeks to go in education, employment, social and political status; what he must do to get there.

"Race in America," *Christianity and Crisis* 21 (May 29, 1961):83-100.

Reid, Ira de A. "The American Negro," in Joseph B. Gittler, ed., *Understanding Minority Groups.* New York: Wiley, 1956. Traces changing relation to the white majority, and outlines major movements through which the Negro has sought to improve his status.

"The Relative Status of the Negro in the United States," *Journal of Negro Education* 22 (Summer 1953):221-451. Entire issue.

Roche, John P. *The Quest for the Dream: The Development of Civil Rights and Human Relations in Modern America.* New York: Macmillan, 1963. A social history, in which the author examines the development of—and threats to—American liberties since 1900. Ethnic and religious intolerance, the Negroes' awakening sense of identity and community, the confrontation of the American conscience concerning the Negro are among the themes treated.

Rose, Arnold M. *The Negro in America.* New York: Harper, 1948. A condensation of Myrdal's *American Dilemma.*

Schermerhorn, R. A. "Minorities: European and American," *Phylon* 20 (Summer 1959):178-185.

Schermerhorn, R. A. "Power as a Primary Concept in the Study of Minorities," *Social Forces* 35 (October 1956):53-56.

Sloan, Irving J. *The American Negro: A Chronology and Fact Book.* 2d ed. Dobbs Ferry, N.Y.: Oceana Publications, 1968. Significant events in Negro life from Spanish explorations to the present.

Thorpe, Earl E. *The Mind of the Negro: An Intellectual History of Afro-Americans.* Baton Rouge, La.: Ortlieb Press, 1961. A social as well as an intellectual history, this book has as its thesis the proposition that the central theme of Negro thought has been the quest for freedom and equality. The author ranges from cultural ties with Africa, through nineteenth-century protest movements, the Washington-DuBois controversy, patterns of political behavior, down to contemporary Negro cultural life.

U.S. Bureau of the Census. *Statistical Abstract of the United States.* Washington: U.S. Govt. Print. Off. Annual. Useful for comparative data of White-Negro (or sometimes non-white) aspects of population, education and desegregation thereof, achievement scores, family income and work experience, minority group employment, selective service draftees examined, narcotic addiction, voting by state.

Wagley, Charles W., and Marvin Harris. *Minorities in the New World.* New York: Columbia University Press, 1958. Prepared for UNESCO, this book offers a comparative analysis of six minority groups in the Western Hemisphere. Included is a study of the historical development of barriers to the integration of Negroes into U.S. society.

Wagley, Charles W. "The Situation of the Negro in the United States," *International Social Science Bulletin,* UNESCO, vol. 9, no. 4 (1957):427-438. Comparison of the caste system in the United States with the freer Latin American system.

Walker, H. J. "Changes in the Status of the Negro in American Society," *International Social Science Bulletin,* UNESCO, vol. 9, no. 4 (1957):438-474. Covers economic developments, changes in politics and government, urbanization, increased voter registration, etc.

Walters, Ronald. "Political Strategies of the Reconstruction," *Current History* 57 (November 1969):263-268. Draws parallels between the political, social, and economic climate of the Negro in the United States during Reconstruction and at present.

Watters, Pat. *The South and the Nation.* New York: Pantheon, 1970.

Weyl, Nathaniel. *The Negro in American Civilization.* Washington: Public Affairs Press, 1960. Beginning with an examination of the historical background of American efforts to define relationship of the Negro to the nation, the author concludes that the Supreme Court decisions of 1875-1900 were liberal on racial matters. He finds significant differences between the African and European brain which he accounts for by speculations about man in torrid climates, and insists that the issue in the present "crisis" is one of individual liberty rather than of equality.

"The White Problem in America," *Ebony* 20 (August 1965):27 + . Special issue. Statement by John H. Johnson, editor and publisher: "The white man has been trying to solve the race problem through studying the Negro. We feel the answer lies in a more thorough study of the man who created the problem. In this issue we, as Negroes, look at the white man today with the hope that our effort will tempt him to look at himself more thoroughly."

Woofter, Thomas J. *Southern Race Progress: The Wavering Color Line.* Washington: Public Affairs Press, 1957. Autobiography of a Southerner covering racial events since the 1890's. The story of changing race relations, with emphasis on racial cooperation for regional progress.

Worsnop, Richard L. "Black Pride," *Editorial Research Reports* 2 (September 11, 1968):663-680. Contents: Changing goals of the Negro in America. His image in arts and education. Decline of the Negro rights movement.

2   History

General

American Convention for Promoting the Abolition of Slavery and Improving the Condition of the African Race. *Minutes, Constitution, Addresses, Memorials, Resolutions, Reports, Committees and Anti-Slavery Tracts.* 3 vols. New York: Bergman, 1969. Vol. 1: first to the tenth convention, 1794-1805; vol. 2: eleventh to the seventeenth, 1806-1821; vol. 3: eighteenth to the twenty-first, 1823-1829. A reprint; limited by the lack of name index.

Appel, John J. "The American Negro and Immigrant Experience: Similarities and Differences," *American Quarterly* 18 (Spring 1966):95-103.

Aptheker, Herbert, ed. *A Documentary History of the Negro People in the United States.* 2 vols. New York: Citadel, 1951. A readable selection from a wide variety of sources. Vol. I covers the period through the Civil War; vol. II, from Reconstruction to 1910. See also his *Afro-American History: The Modern Period.*

Aptheker, Herbert. *Essays in the History of the American Negro.* New York: International Publishers, 1945.

Aptheker, Herbert. *Nat Turner's Slave Rebellion; Together with the Full Text of the So-called 'Confessions' of Nat Turner Made in Prison in 1831.* New York: Humanities Press, 1966. Background and evidence of the rebellion. The author's master's thesis submitted in 1937.

Aptheker, Herbert. *To Be Free: Studies in American Negro History.* 1948. 2d ed. New York: International Publishers, 1968.

Baldwin, James. "The Nigger We Invent," *Integrated Education* 7 (March-April 1969):15-23. Author's statement before a Congressional hearing to establish a National Commission on Negro History and Culture.

Bennett, Lerone, Jr. *Before the Mayflower: A History of the Negro in America, 1619-1966.* 1962. Rev. ed. Chicago: Johnson, 1966. A popularized history, based on a series of articles originally published in *Ebony.*

Bergman, Peter M., and Mort N. Bergman. *The Chronological History of the Negro in America.* New York: Bergman, 1968.

Bergman, Peter M., and Jean McCarroll, comps. *The Negro in the 'Congressional Record'.* New York: Bergman, 1969— . 10 vols. projected. References made to the Negro in official Congressional records are extracted and annotated. Vols. 1-2 analyze the *Journals* (1774-1789) and the *Annals,* covering the first through the sixth Congress (1789-1801).

Binder, Frederick M. *The Color Problem in Early National America As Viewed by John Adams, Jefferson and Jackson.* The Hague: Mouton, 1969.

Blaustein, Albert P., and Robert L. Zangrando, comps. *Civil Rights and the American Negro: A Documentary History.* New York: Trident, 1968. Significant documents from 1619 to 1968. A short introductory explanation precedes each section.

Bolt, Christine. *The Anti-Slavery Movement and Reconstruction: A Study of Anglo-American Cooperation, 1833-1877.* London: Published for the Institute of Race Relations by Oxford University Press, 1969. Attention is given to the efforts of English philanthropists and religious groups who protested against slavery and collected money for the American freedmen.

Ciba Foundation. *Caste and Race: Comparative Approaches.* Edited by Anthony de Reuck and Julie Knight. Boston: Little, Brown, 1967. A symposium devoted to interpretations and comparisons of slavery in the western hemisphere.

Drimmer, Melvin, comp. *Black History: A Reappraisal.* Garden City, N. Y.: Doubleday, 1968. Essays (some previously published) by black and white writers and historians. Selections emphasize the revisionist viewpoint.

Drotning, Phillip T. *A Guide to Negro History in America.* Garden City, N.Y.: Doubleday, 1968. A geographic guide of the Negro's contribution to American cultural history from the pre-colonial period to the present.

Fishel, Leslie H., and Benjamin Quarles, eds. *The Black American: A Documentary History.* New York: Morrow, 1970. A revised edition of *The Negro American*, 1967. Traces the history of the black American from his African heritage to the present, drawing heavily from primary source materials. Illustrations.

Flexner, Eleanor. *Century of Struggle: The Women's Rights Movement in the United States.* Cambridge, Mass.: Harvard University Press, 1959. Information on Negro women as abolitionists, on their education, patterns of voting, and organizations. Also a note on bibliographical sources on the history of Negro women.

Forbes, Jack D. "Black Pioneers: The Spanish-speaking Afro-Americans of the Southwest," *Phylon* 27 (Fall 1966):233-246.

Franklin, John Hope. "History of Racial Segregation in the United States," *Annals of the American Academy of Political and Social Science* 304 (March 1956):1-9.

Franklin, John Hope. *The Militant South.* Cambridge, Mass.: Harvard University Press, 1956. Reissued with a new preface, 1970. While primarily concerned with the period 1800-1861, the author delineates persisting traits and patterns of violence that have continued into the present.

Franklin, John Hope. "The New Negro History," *Journal of Negro History* 42 (April 1957):89-97.

Franklin, John Hope. "The Two Worlds of Race: A Historical View," *Daedalus* 94 (Fall 1965):899-920.

Garraty, John A., ed. *Quarrels That Have Shaped the Constitution.* New York: Harper, 1964. Included: C. Vann Woodward (*Plessy v. Ferguson*); Bruce Catton (*Dred Scott*); Alfred H. Kelly (*Brown v. Board of Education*).

Goldston, Robert. *The Negro Revolution.* New York: Macmillan, 1968. A synthesis of the Negro's struggle from the time of African slavery to the summer of 1967. Bibliography.

Gottschalk, Jane. "The Rhetorical Strategy of Booker T. Washington," *Phylon* 27 (Winter 1966):388-395. His speeches viewed as a strategic and convincing social argument during the period, 1880-1915.

Grant, Joanne, ed. *Black Protest: History, Documents, and Analyses, 1619 to the Present.* Greenwich, Conn.: Fawcett, 1968. Documents, speeches, and other material illustrating "verbal and violent reaction" of the Negro to slavery, segregation, and discrimination in the United States to 1966. Emphasis is given to the period since 1954.

Hill, Roy L., ed. *Rhetoric of Racial Revolt.* Denver, Colo.: Golden Bell Press, 1964. Speeches, arranged historically, often followed by editorial commentary delineating the Negro's quest for equality—from Frederick Douglass to Martin Luther King. Emphasis is on the twentieth century.

Hill, Stuart L. "Are Negroes Just Another Immigrant Group?" *Discourse* 11 (Autumn 1969):450-459.

Hoover, Dwight W., ed. *Understanding Negro History.* Chicago: Quadrangle, 1968. Articles previously published in the *Journal of Negro History* and the *Journal of Southern History.*

Katz, William Loren. *Eyewitness: The Negro in American History.* New York: Pitman, 1967. Describes contribution of Negroes. Well illustrated with text and documentary extracts.

Katz, William Loren. *Teachers' Guide to American Negro History.* Chicago: Quadrangle, 1968. Annotated bibliography.

Kristol, Irving. "The Negro Today Is Like the Immigrant Yesterday," *New York Times Magazine,* September 11, 1969, 50-51 +. An examination of the extent to which problems of Negro migrants into large cities have relevant precedents in American history.

Lincoln, C. Eric. *The Negro Pilgrimage in America.* 1967. Rev. ed. New York: Praeger, 1969.

Little, Malcolm. *Malcolm X on Afro-American History.* New York: Merit, 1967.

Logan, Rayford W., and Irving S. Cohen. *The American Negro: Old World Background and New World Experience.* Boston: Houghton Mifflin, 1967. An historical overview.

Logan, Rayford W. *The Negro in the United States: A Brief Review.* Princeton, N.J.: Van Nostrand, 1957. Part I consists of a concise history of the Negro from 1619. Part II is a useful compilation of 25 documents of significance for that history, mostly key court decisions and executive orders from 1873 to 1954.

Meier, August, and Elliott M. Rudwick. *From Plantation to Ghetto: An Interpretative History of American Negroes.* New York: Hill & Wang, 1966. A notable, incisive final chapter on the civil rights revolution. Bibliography.

Meier, August, and Elliot M. Rudwick, eds. *The Making of Black America: Essays in Negro Life and History.* New York: Atheneum, 1969. Essays previously published in scholarly journals, by sociologists, historians, and political scientists, covering the span from slavery to the present militancy. Reflects the black man's thinking.

Meltzer, Milton, ed. *In Their Own Words—A History of the American Negro.* Vol. I: *1619-1865.* Vol. II: *1865-1916.* Vol. III: *1916-1966.* New York: Apollo Editions, 1964-1967.

Murray, Andrew E. *Presbyterians and the Negro—A History.* Philadelphia: The Presbyterian Historical Society, 1966. Exceptional bibliographic essay appended.

Negro Protest Pamphlets: A Compendium. New York: Arno Press, 1969. (The American Negro, His History and Literature)

"NYPL Sees New Life for Harlem Collection," *Library Journal* 94 (November 15, 1969):4094-4095. Increased financing and plans for the Schomburg Collection.

Ottley, Roi, and William J. Weatherby, eds. *The Negro in New York: An Informal Social History.* New York: Oceana, 1967. Edited from manuscripts in the Schomburg Collection; originally prepared under the Federal Writers' Project. Covers Harlem history from 1626-1940. Selective bibliography.

Perry, Charlotte Bronte. *The History of Coloured Canadians in Windsor, Ontario, 1867-1967.* 1967. 2d ed. Windsor, Ontario: Sumner Printing and Publishing, 1969. Bibliography.

Philadelphia. Library Company. *Negro History, 1553-1903: An Exhibition of Books, Prints, and Manuscripts from the Shelves of the Library Company of Philadelphia and the Historical Society of Pennsylvania.* Philadelphia, 1969.

Record, Wilson. "The Development of the Communist Position on the Negro Question in the United States," *Phylon* 19 (Fall 1958):306-326.

Redding, Saunders. *The Negro.* Washington: Potomac Books, 1967. A sound overview of history of the Negro in the United States up to but not including the black power movement. Annotated bibliography.

Reimers, David M. *White Protestantism and the Negro.* New York: Oxford University Press, 1965. Covers the period from the nineteenth century to early 1960's.

Ruchames, Louis., ed. *Racial Thought in America.* Vol. I: *From the Puritans to Abraham Lincoln, A Documentary History.* Amherst: University of Massachusetts Press, 1969. Seventy-five essays, only four of which record the opinions of black writers on their own condition. A biographical sketch of contributors places each item in historical perspective.

Seabrook, Isaac DuBose. *Before and After, or The Relations of the Races at the South.* Edited with an introduction by John Hamilton Moore. Baton Rouge: Louisiana State University Press, 1967. Essay written by a Southern aristocrat in 1895—hitherto unpublished. Its significance is to be considered in the political context of period when written.

Sellers, Charles Grier, ed. *The Southerner as American.* Chapel Hill: University of North Carolina Press, 1960. Saunders Redding: "In this group of essays, the reevaluation of Southern history and of the Southern mind, which W. J. Cash began and Vann Woodward has lifted to academic excellence, begins to prove its influence on historical thought and scholarship in the South."

Shade, William G., and Roy C. Herrenkohl, eds. *Seven on Black: Reflections on the Negro Experience in America.* Philadelphia: Lippincott, 1969. Essays ranging from a discussion of the Reconstruction period by James McPherson to an evaluation of black power by Charles V. Hamilton. Annotated bibliography.

Tannenbaum, Frank. *Slave and Citizen: The Negro in the Americas.* New York: Knopf, 1947. An analysis of differences in treatment and development of Negroes in North and South America, effectively employing the comparative method.

Tourgee, Albion W. *A Fool's Errand.* 1879. Edited by John Hope Franklin. Cambridge, Mass.: Harvard University Press, 1961. The 1961 edition carries a lengthy critical introduction of the novel describing the author as a perceptive social critic of Southern intolerance, the treatment of the Negro, and Reconstruction.

U. S. Congress. Senate. *A Commission on Negro History and Culture.* Washington, D.C., 1968. (90th Congress, 2d Session) Text of Senate bill S2979. Also printed in *Integrated Education* 7 (March–April 1969):13–14.

Ury, Claude M. "Commission on Negro History and Culture: Implications for Education," *Phi Delta Kappan* 50 (January 1969):289–290.

Wesley, Charles Harris. *Neglected History: Essays in Negro History by a College President.* Wilberforce, Ohio: Central State College Press, 1965.

Woodson, Carter G., and Charles H. Wesley. *The Negro in Our History.* 1922. 10th ed. rev. and enl. Washington: Associated Publishers, 1962. A work which remains extremely useful.

Woodward, C. Vann. "Flight From History: The Heritage of the Negro," *Nation* 201 (September 20, 1965):142–146. In 100th anniversary issue.

Wright, Richard. *Twelve Million Black Voices.* New York: Viking, 1941. Informal folk history.

See also Education—Historical Background.

Ante-Bellum

Bailey, Hugh C. *Hinton Rowan Helper: Abolitionist-Racist.* University: University of Alabama Press, 1965. Biography of a militant racist whose anti-Negro writings were in opposition to the radical programs first offered during the Reconstruction. Bibliography.

Bell, Howard H. "Negroes in California, 1849–1859," *Phylon* 28 (Summer 1967):151–160.

Berns, Walter. "The Constitution and the Migration of Slaves," *Yale Law Journal* 78 (December 1968):198–228.

Bernstein, Barton J. "Southern Politics and Attempts to Reopen the American Slave Trade," *Journal of Negro History* 51 (January 1966):16–35. In the decade before the Civil War.

Berwanger, Eugene H. "The 'Black Law' Question in Ante-Bellum California," *Journal of the West* 6 (April 1967):205–220. Traces the pattern of civil restrictions upon the Negro from 1818 to the Civil War, and their effect on migrations.

Berwanger, Eugene H. *The Frontier Against Slavery: Western and Anti-Negro Prejudice and the Slavery Extension Controversy.* Urbana: University of Illinois Press, 1967. Bibliography includes manuscript and published sources and documents.

Bryce-LaPorte, Roy Simón. "The American Slave Plantation and Our Heritage of Communal Deprivation," *American Behavioral Scientist* 12 (March–April 1969):2–7.

Calligaro, Lee. "The Negro's Legal Status in Pre-Civil War New Jersey," *New Jersey History* 85 (April 1967):167–180.

Cobb, Henry E. "The African Background of the American Negro: Myth and Reality," *Bulletin of the Southern University and A & M College* 55 (June 1969):9–19.

Cohen, William. "Thomas Jefferson and the Problem of Slavery," *American Historical Review* 61 (December 1969):503–526.

Davis, David B. *The Problem of Slavery in Western Culture.* Ithaca: Cornell University Press, 1966. Various sections pertinent to the American slavery controversy in the eighteenth and nineteenth centuries. Pulitzer prize winner.

Delany, M. R., and Robert Campbell. *Search for a Place: Black Separatism and Africa, 1860.* 1861. Introduction by Howard H. Bell. Ann Arbor: University of Michigan Press, 1969. A Negro abolitionist who, having rejected the panaceas offered to his race prior to the Civil War, outlines a program of emigration.

Dillon, Merton L. *Benjamin Lundy and the Struggle for Negro Freedom.* Urbana: University of Illinois Press, 1966. The American anti-slavery movement. A bibliographical essay is appended.

Drew, Benjamin. *The Refugee: A Northside View of Slavery.* 1856. With an introduction by Tilden G. Edelstein. Reading, Mass.: Addison-Wesley, 1969. Countering a book entitled *A Northside View of Slavery,* a Boston editor recorded the narratives of 116 freedmen who emigrated to Canada.

Duberman, Martin, ed. *The Antislavery Vanguard: New Essays on the Abolitionists.* Princeton, N.J.: Princeton University Press, 1965.

Eighmy, John Lee. "The Baptists and Slavery: An Examination of the Origins and Benefits of Segregation," *Social Science Quarterly* 49 (December 1968):666-673.

Epps, Archie. "A Negro Separatist Movement of the 19th Century," *Harvard Review* 4 (Summer-Fall 1966):69-87.

Filler, Louis. "Dynamics of Reform: The Antislavery Crusade, and Others; With Something about the Negro," *Antioch Review* 27 (Fall 1967):362-378.

Finnie, Gordon E. "The Antislavery Movement in the Upper South before 1840," *Journal of Southern History* 35 (August 1969):319-342.

Fischer, Roger A. "Racial Segregation in Ante Bellum New Orleans," *American Historical Review* 74 (February 1969):926-937.

Foner, Eric. "Politics and Prejudice: The Free Soil Party and the Negro, 1849-1852," *Journal of Negro History* 50 (October 1965):239-256.

Franklin, John Hope. *From Slavery to Freedom: A History of Negro Americans.* 1947. 3d ed. New York: Knopf, 1967. A comprehensive historical work with a classified bibliographical essay. The new edition reflects the author's new perspectives.

Frederickson, George M., and Christopher Lasch. "Resistance to Slavery," *Civil War History* 13 (December 1967):315-329.

Gara, Larry. *The Liberty Line: The Legend of the Under-Ground Railroad.* Lexington: University of Kentucky Press, 1961. The legend is revealed as largely melodrama. The work of rescue was chiefly carried out by free Negroes, not abolitionists. Valuable as showing how the legend grew.

Garvin, Russell. "The Free Negro in Florida before the Civil War," *Florida History Quarterly* 46 (July 1967):1-17.

Greene, Lorenzo J. *The Negro in Colonial New England, 1620-1776.* New York: Columbia University Press, 1942. Bibliography.

Hart, Charles Desmond. "Slavery Expansion to the Territories, 1850: A Forgotten Speech by Truman Smith," *New Mexico Historical Review* 41 (October 1966):269-287.

Hast, Adele. "The Legal Status of the Negro in Virginia, 1705-1765," *Journal of Negro History* 54 (July 1969):217-239.

Helper, Hinton R. *The Impending Crisis of the South: How To Meet It.* 1857. Cambridge, Mass.: Harvard University Press, 1968. With a lengthy critical introduction by George M. Frederickson.

Johnson, Frank Roy. *The Nat Turner Slave Insurrection.* Murfreesboro, N.C.: Johnson, 1966. Bound with *The Confession, Trial and Execution of Nat Turner* by Thomas R. Gray.

Jordan, Winthrop D. *White Over Black: American Attitudes Toward the Negro, 1530-1812.* Chapel Hill: University of North Carolina Press, 1968. Learned work on attitudes and ideas about the Negro antedating the English founding of Jamestown settlement. It effectively explores the ambivalence of the white conscience. A bibliographical essay is appended. Winner of the 1969 National Book Award.

Kates, Don B., Jr. "Abolition, Deportation, Integration: Attitudes toward Slavery in the Early Republic," *Journal of Negro History* 53 (January 1968):33-47.

Kemble, Frances Anne. *Journal of a Residence on a Georgia Plantation in 1838-1839.* New York: Harper, 1863. Reprinted with a new introduction by John A. Scott. New York: Knopf, 1961. The British actress Fanny Kemble gave a detailed and intimate account of the day-to-day functioning of Southern slave economy at the plantation level.

Kilson, Marion D. "Toward Freedom: An Analysis of Slave Revolts in the United States," *Phylon* 25 (Summer 1964):175-187.

Klein, Herbert S. "Anglicanism, Catholicism and the Negro Slave," *Comparative Studies in Society and History.* 8 (April 1966):295-327. With a rejoinder by E. V. Goveia, *ibid.,* 328-330.

Klein, Herbert S. *Slavery in the Americas: A Comparative Study of Virginia and Cuba.* Chicago: University of Chicago Press, 1967.

Levy, Ronald. "Bishop Hopkins and the Dilemma of Slavery," *Pennsylvania Magazine of History and Biography* 97 (January 1967):56-71. Of particular interest in the context of the current dilemma of the churches.

Litwack, Leon F. *North of Slavery: The Negro in the Free States, 1790-1860.* University of Chicago Press, 1961. How the North resolved, or failed to resolve, its integration problems in the ante-bellum period. The author effectually shows that the haven to which the North Star beckoned the fugitive slave was a Jim Crow haven. Contains a bibliographical essay.

Lofton, John. *Insurrection in South Carolina: The Turbulent World of Denmark Vesey.* Yellow Springs, Ohio: Antioch Press, 1964.

Long, Durward. "The Methodist Church and Negro Slavery in America, 1784-1844," *Wesleyan Quarterly Review* 3 (February 1966):3-17.

Loveland, Amy C. "Evangelicalism and 'Immediate Emancipation' in American Antislavery Thought," *Journal of Southern History* 32 (May 1966):172-188.

Lumpkin, Katherine DuPre. "'The General Plan Was Freedom': A Negro Secret Order on the Underground Railway," *Phylon* 28 (Spring 1967):63-77.

Lythgoe, Dennis L. "Negro Slavery and Mormon Doctrine," *Western Humanities Review* 21 (Fall 1967):327-338.

McManus, Edgar J. *A History of Negro Slavery in New York.* Syracuse: Syracuse University Press, 1966. A bibliographical essay is appended.

McPherson, James M. *The Struggle for Equality: Abolitionists and the Negro in the Civil War and Reconstruction.* Princeton, N.J.: Princeton University Press, 1964.

Mannix, Daniel P. *Black Cargoes: The Story of the Atlantic Slave Trade: 1518-1865.* New York: Viking, 1962. Critical bibliography.

Mathews, Donald. "Abolitionists on Slavery: The Critique Behind the Social Movement," *Journal of Southern History* 33 (May 1967):163-182.

Mathews, Donald G. *Slavery and Methodism: A Chapter in American Morality, 1780-1845.* Princeton, N.J.: Princeton University Press, 1965. A careful study of agitation about slavery within the Methodist Church. Useful comparisons are made to other denominations.

Mellon, Matthew Taylor. *Early American Views on Negro Slavery from the Letters and Papers of the Founders of the Republic.* 1934. New ed. With an introduction by Richard B. Morris. New York: Bergman Publishers, 1969. First edition with variant title.

Miles, Edwin A. "The Mississippi Slave Insurrection Score of 1835," *Journal of Negro History* 42 (January 1957):48-61.

Moulton, Phillips. "John Woolman's Approach to Social Action—as Exemplified in Relation to Slavery," *Church History* 35 (December 1966):399-410. A Quaker minister's influence on the elimination of slavery.

Myers, John L. "American Antislavery Society Agents and the Free Negro, 1833-1838," *Journal of Negro History* 52 (July 1967):200-219.

Nadelhaft, Jerome. "Somerset Case and Slavery: Myth, Reality, and Repercussions," *Journal of Negro History* 51 (July 1966):193-208. Somerset decision in 1772 and its influence in American courts for the next 70 years.

Norvill, Stanley B. "Views of a Negro during 'The Red Summer' of 1919," edited by William M. Tuttle, Jr. *Journal of Negro History* 51 (July 1966):209-218. Norvill was a Negro war veteran from Chicago.

Palmer, Paul C. "Servant into Slave: The Evolution of the Legal Status of the Negro Laborer in Colonial Virginia," *South Atlantic Quarterly* 65 (Summer 1966):355-370.

Payne, Daniel Alexander. "Document: Bishop Daniel Alexander Payne's Protestation of American Slavery," edited by Douglas C. Stange. *Journal of Negro History* 52 (January 1967):59-64. An ordained Lutheran clergyman who became a bishop of the African Methodist Church and President of Wilberforce University.

Pease, William H., and Jane H. Pease. "Antislavery Ambivalence: Immediatism, Expediency, Race," *American Quarterly* 17 (Winter 1965):682-695.

Pease, William H., and Jane H. Pease. "Boston Garrisonians and the Problem of Frederick Douglass," *Canadian Journal of History* 2 (September 1967):29-48. Outlines the subtle prejudice against Douglass exhibited by the Boston group. Based on evidence drawn from the abolitionist press and unpublished papers.

Pilcher, George William. "Samuel Davies and the Instruction of Negroes in Virginia," *Virginia Magazine of History and Biography* 74 (July 1966):293-300. The pastoral labors of an eighteenth-century Presbyterian minister.

Price, John Milton. "Slavery in Winn Parish," *Louisiana History* 8 (Spring 1967):137-148.

Proctor, William G., Jr. "Slavery in Southwest Georgia," *Georgia Historical Quarterly* 49 (March 1965):1-22.

Purifoy, Lewis M. "The Southern Methodist Church and the Proslavery Arguement," *Journal of Southern History* 32 (August 1966):325-341.

Quarles, Benjamin. *Black Abolitionists.* New York: Oxford University Press, 1969. Treats black writers, preachers, and agitators, those who operated the underground railroad and the effects of their activities, and of the fugitive slave law on many facets of public life. A bibliographical note on sources is appended.

Quarles, Benjamin, comp. *Frederick Douglass.* Englewood Cliffs, N.J.: Prentice-Hall, 1968. Includes excerpts from the speeches and writings of Douglass and evaluations by his contemporaries as well as by present century historians.

Quarles, Benjamin. *The Negro in the American Revolution.* Chapel Hill: University of North Carolina Press, 1961.

Ratner, Lorman. *Powder Keg: Northern Opposition to the Antislavery Movement, 1831-1840.* New York: Basic Books, 1968.

Rogers, Tommy W. "Dr. Frederick A. Ross and the Presbyterian Defense of Slavery," *Journal of Presbyterian History* 45 (June 1967):112-124.

Schnell, Kempes. "Anti-Slavery Influence on the Status of Slaves in a Free State," *Journal of Negro History* 50 (October 1965):255-273.

Scott, Kenneth. "The Slave Insurrection in New York in 1712," *New York Historical Society Quarterly* 45 (January 1961):43-74.

Seip, Terry L. "Slaves and Free Negroes in Alexandria," *Louisiana History* 10 (Spring 1969):147-165. A sketch of the Negro population in a town in Rapides Parish, Louisiana in the decade prior to the Civil War.

Senese, Donald J. "The Free Negro and the South Carolina Courts, 1790-1860," *South Carolina Historical Magazine* 68 (July 1967):140-153.

Sewell, Samuel. *The Selling of Joseph: A Memorial.* 1700. Edited by Sidney Kaplan. Amherst: University of Massachusetts Press, 1969. An early important anti-slavery tract to which the editor of this edition adds important notes.

Simms, L. Moody, Jr. "Charles Francis Adams, Jr. and the Negro Question," *New England Quarterly* 41 (September 1968):436-438.

Simms, L. Moody, Jr. "Philip Alexander Bruce and the Negro Problem, 1884-1930," *Virginia Magazine of History and Biography* 75 (July 1967):349-362. An evaluation of the views of a Virginia aristocrat towards the Negro as a freeman.

Smith, Elbert B. *The Death of Slavery: United States, 1837-1865.* Chicago: University of Chicago Press, 1967. Bibliography.

Spector, Robert M. "The Quock Walker Cases (1781-83)—Slavery, Its Abolition and Negro Citizenship in Early Massachusetts," *Journal of Negro History* 53 (January 1968):12-32.

Stafford, Frances J. "Illegal Importations: Enforcement of the Slave Trade Laws along the Florida Coast, 1810-1828," *Florida Historical Quarterly* 46 (October 1967):124-133.

Stange, Douglas C. "Compassionate Mother to Her Poor Negro Slaves: The Lutheran Church and Negro Slavery in Early America," *Phylon* 29 (Fall 1968):272-281.

Stange, Douglas C. "Lutheran Involvement in the American Colonization Society," *Mid-America* 49 (April 1967):140-151.

Starobin, Robert. "Disciplining Industrial Slaves in the Old South," *Journal of Negro History* 53 (April 1968):111-128.

Staudenrauss, P. *The African Colonization Movement, 1816-1865.* New York: Columbia University Press, 1961.

Szasz, Ferenc M. "The New York Slave Revolt of 1741: A Re-Examination," *New York History* 48 (June 1967):215-231.

Tate, Thaddeus W. *The Negro in Eighteenth-Century Williamsburg.* Charlottesville: Distributed by the University of Virginia Press, 1965.

Thorpe, Earl E. *Eros and Freedom in Southern Life and Thought.* Durham, N.C.: Printed by Seeman Printery, 1967. The nature of Southern culture and Negro-White relations in the ante-bellum South.

Toplin, Robert Brent. "Peter Still Versus the Peculiar Institution," *Civil War History* 13 (December 1969):340-349. Records experiences of a divided slave family.

Twombly, Robert C., and Robert H. Moore. "Black Puritan: The Negro in Seventeenth-Century Massachusetts," *William and Mary Quarterly* 24 (April 1967):224-242. Covers the period 1630-1710.

Tyler, Ronnie C. "The Callahan Expedition of 1855: Indians or Negroes?" *Southwestern Historical Quarterly* 70 (April 1967):574-585. Forcible recovery of fugitive slaves from northern Mexico.

Wade, Richard C. *Slavery in the Cities: The South, 1820-1860.* New York: Oxford University Press, 1965. The author demonstrates that while slavery in urban areas was vastly different from that on the plantation, it was equally degrading, enforced by harsh municipal codes, restrictions on Negro association (e.g., in their churches), segregation, and fear. The majority were household slaves, but hotels, factories, railroads, and municipalities maintained large holdings whom they hired out for short-term jobs.

Wade, Richard C. "The Vesey Plot: A Reconsideration," *Journal of Southern History* 30 (May 1964):143-161. Uprising in 1822.

Wamble, Gaston Hugh. "Negroes and Missouri Protestant Churches before the Civil War," *Missouri Historical Review* 61 (April 1967):321-347. Includes a bibliography of church records.

Wax, Darold D. "The Demand for Slave Labor in Colonial Pennsylvania," *Pennsylvania History* 34 (1967):331-345.

Wax, Darold D. "Georgia and the Negro before the American Revolution," *Georgia Historical Quarterly* 51 (March 1967):63-77.

Wax, Darold D. "Negro Resistance to the Early American Slave Trade," *Journal of Negro History* 51 (January 1966):1-15.

Weisbord, Robert J. "The Back-to-Africa Idea," *History Today* 18 (January 1968):30-37. Discusses proposals of whites and prominent Negroes such as Turner, Delaney, and Garvey for immigration to Africa from America.

Wilson, Prince E. "Black Men before the Civil War," *Current History* 57 (November 1969):257-262+.

Woolfolk, George R. "Turner's Safety-Valve and Free Negro Westward Migration," *Journal of Negro History* 50 (July 1965):185-197. The Free Negro migration to Texas up to the Civil War. Also appears in *Pacific Northwest Quarterly* 56 (1965):125-130.

Wright, Conrad. *Liberal Christians.* Boston: Beacon, 1970. Includes a section on the role of Unitarian ministers in the antislavery movement.

Wright, J. Leitch, Jr. "Note on the First Seminole War as Seen by the Indians, Negroes, and their British Advisers," *Journal of Southern History* 34 (November 1968):565-575.

Zilversmit, Arthur. *The First Emancipation; The Abolition of Slavery in the North.* Chicago:

University of Chicago Press, 1967. Interpretations of northern ante-bellum slavery, drawn from primary sources. Bibliographical essay.

Zilversmit, Arthur. "Quock Walker, Mumbet, and the Abolition of Slavery in Massachusetts," *William and Mary Quarterly* 25 (October 1968):614-624.

Civil War to Present

Abbott, Martin. *Freedmen's Bureau in South Carolina, 1865-1872.* Chapel Hill: University of North Carolina Press, 1967. Bibliography.

Andrews, Thomas F. "Freedmen in Indian Territory: A Post Civil-War Dilemma," *Journal of the West* 4 (July 1965):367-376. Relations with the Choctaw and Chickasaw tribes.

Aptheker, Herbert. *Afro-American History: The Modern Period.* New York: International, 1970. From the end of the nineteenth century to the present.

Armstrong, William M. "Freedmen's Movement and the Founding of the Nation," *Journal of American History* 53 (March 1967):708-726.

Beals, Carleton. *War Within a War: The Confederacy Against Itself.* Philadelphia: Chilton, 1965. A revisionary treatment of the legend of Confederate gallantry, fidelity, and unity, which brings together evidence of disaffection and desertion within the South during the Civil War.

Bell, John L., Jr. "Baptists and the Negro in North Carolina during Reconstruction," *North Carolina Historical Review* 42 (October 1965):391-409.

Bell, John L., Jr. "The Presbyterian Church and the Negro in North Carolina during Reconstruction," *North Carolina Historical Review* 40 (January 1963):15-36.

Bennett, Lerone. *Black Power U.S.A.: The Human Side of Reconstruction, 1867-1877.* Chicago: Johnson, 1967. Recounts the struggle to attain political and economic power during the period of Reconstruction. An expanded version of a study published in *Ebony,* November 1965-January 1967. Bibliography.

Bentley, George R. *A History of the Freedmen's Bureau.* Philadelphia: University of Pennsylvania Press, 1955.

Berrier, G. Gail. "The Negro Suffrage Issue in Iowa, 1865-1868," *Annals of Iowa* 39 (1968):241-261.

Betts, John R. "Negro and the New England Conscience in the Days of John Boyle O'Reilly," *Journal of Negro History* 51 (October 1966):246-261. Roman Catholic editor of Boston's *Pilot* championed the Negro cause.

Blodgett, Geoffrey. "John Mercer Langston and the Case of Edmonia Lewis; Oberlin, 1862," *Journal of Negro History* 53 (July 1968):201-218.

Brewer, James H. *The Confederate Negro: Virginia's Craftsmen and Military Laborers, 1861-1865.* Durham, N.C.: Duke University Press, 1969.

Calista, Donald J. "Booker T. Washington: Another Look," *Journal of Negro History* 49 (October 1964):240-255.

Carter, Dan T. *Scottsboro: A Tragedy of the American South.* Baton Rouge: Louisiana State University Press, 1969. Definitive account of nine Negro youths falsely accused and arrested in 1931, the miscarriage of justice, their subsequent pardon in 1950. Illustrated. See also: H. Murray's article in *Phylon* 28 (Fall 1967):276-287.

Castel, Albert. "Civil War Kansas and the Negro," *Journal of Negro History* 51 (April 1966):125-138.

"A Century of Struggle," *Progressive* 26 (December 1962):3-58. Entire issue in celebration of the anniversary of the Emancipation Proclamation with articles by Adlai Stevenson, James Baldwin, Harry Golden, Martin Luther King, C. Vann Woodward, Murray Kempton.

Christman, Henry M., ed. *The South As It Is 1865-1866.* New York: Viking, 1965. Republication of a report by John Richard Dennett to *Nation* on life in seven Southern states at the beginning of Reconstruction. Documents Southern hopes of keeping Negroes in condition resembling slavery.

Conway, Alan. "Georgia's Black Legacy," in *The Reconstruction of Georgia.* Minneapolis: University of Minnesota Press, 1966, pp. 61–99.

Coulter, E. Merton. "Henry M. Turner: Georgia Negro Preacher during the Reconstruction Era," *Georgia Historical Quarterly* 48 (December 1964):371–410.

Cox, La Wanda, and John H. Cox. *Politics, Principle and Prejudice, 1865–1866: Dilemma of Reconstruction America.* New York: Free Press, 1963. A detailed study of the early Reconstruction, including party congressional politics on civil rights issues.

Cox, La Wanda. "The Promise of Land for the Freedmen," *Mississippi Valley Historical Review* 45 (December 1958):413–440.

Crowe, Charles. "Racial Massacre in Atlanta, September 22, 1906," *Journal of Negro History* 54 (April 1969):150–173.

Cruden, Robert L. *The Negro in Reconstruction.* Englewood Cliffs, N.J.: Prentice-Hall, 1969. Covers political, social, and historical aspects with a retrospective assessment of the impact of the Reconstruction on the Negro then and now.

Dalfiume, Richard M. "The Forgotten Years of the Negro Revolution," *Journal of American History* 55 (June 1968):90–106. The Negro and World War II.

Daniel, W. Harrison. *"Virginia Baptists and the Negro, 1865–1902," Virginia Magazine of History and Biography* 76 (July 1968):340–363.

Donald, David. *The Politics of Reconstruction, 1863–1867.* Baton Rouge: Louisiana State University Press, 1965.

Douglas, William O. *Mr. Lincoln and the Negroes.* New York: Atheneum, 1963.

Duberman, Martin B. *In White America: A Documentary Play.* Boston: Houghton Mifflin, 1964. A dramatized representation of historical episodes in American Negro history.

DuBois, W. E. B. *Black Reconstruction.* New York: Harcourt, Brace, 1935. From a Marxian point of view.

Durden, Robert Franklin. *James Shepherd Pike: Republicanism and the American Negro, 1850–1882.* Durham, North Carolina: Duke University Press, 1957. Bibliography.

Edelstein, Tilden G. *Strange Enthusiasm: A Life of Thomas Wentworth Higginson.* New Haven: Yale University Press, 1968. A critical appraisal of the white abolitionist and an important contribution towards an understanding of the social and political tenets of the post-bellum era.

Elkins, W. F. "Unrest among the Negroes: A British Document of 1919," [with text] *Science and Society* 32 (Winter 1968):66–79. British government expresses apprehension of Afro-American radicalism in intelligence report, October 1919.

Evans, W. McKee. *Ballots and Fence Rails: Reconstruction on the Lower Cape Fear.* Chapel Hill: University of North Carolina Press, 1966.

Fischer, Roger A. "Pioneer Protest: The New Orleans Street-Car Controversy of 1867," *Journal of Negro History* 53 (July 1968):219–233.

Franklin, John Hope. *The Emancipation Proclamation.* Garden City, N.Y.: Doubleday, 1963. By placing the Proclamation in its historical setting, the author seeks to give proper evaluation to a document of American freedom which he believes has been greatly neglected.

Franklin, John Hope, and Isidore Starr, eds. *The Negro in Twentieth Century America: A Reader on the Struggle for Civil Rights.* New York: Vintage, 1967. Bibliography.

Franklin, John Hope. *Reconstruction After the Civil War.* Chicago: University of Chicago Press, 1961.

Friedel, Frank, ed. *Union Pamphlets of the Civil War, 1861–1865.* 2 vols. Cambridge, Mass.: Harvard University Press, 1967. Several pamphlets pertinent to slavery and the Negro's political rights can be found easily through the detailed index.

Gatewood, Willard B. "Theodore Roosevelt and the Indianola Affair," *Journal of Negro History* 53 (January 1968):48–69. The President's defense of a Negro postmistress and the political aftermath.

Greenbaum, Fred. "The Anti-Lynching Bill of 1935: The Irony of 'Equal Justice—Under Law'," *Journal of Human Relations* 15 (Third Quarter 1967):72–85. Politics of the bill. Justice aborted.

Gutman, Herbert G. "Documents on Negro Seamen During the Reconstruction Period," *Labor History* 7 (Fall 1966):307–311.

Hancock, Harold B. "The Status of the Negro in Delaware After the Civil War, 1865-1875," *Delaware History* 13 (April 1968):57-66.

Harding, Leonard. "The Cincinnati Riots of 1862," *Cincinnati Historical Society Bulletin* 25 (October 1967):229-239.

Harlan, Louis R. "Booker T. Washington and the White Man's Burden," *American Historical Review* 71 (January 1966):441-467.

Harris, William C. "Formulation of the First Mississippi Plan: The Black Code of 1865," *Journal of Mississippi History* 29 (August 1967):181-201.

Hart, Charles Desmond. "Why Lincoln Said 'No'; Congressional Attitudes on Slavery Expansion, 1860-1861," *Social Science Quarterly* 49 (December 1968):732-741.

Hixson, William B., Jr. "Moorfield Storey and the Defense of the Dyer Anti-Lynching Bill," *New England Quarterly* 42 (March 1969):65-81. In part, a summary of the NAACP's long-term campaign against lynching. Arguments for federal action against denial of civil rights to the Negro.

Hixson, William B., Jr. "Moorfield Storey and the Struggle for Equality," *Journal of American History* 55 (December 1968):533-554. The impetus of a white reformer in the formation of the NAACP.

Jackson, Kenneth T. *The Ku Klux Klan in the City, 1915-1930.* New York: Oxford University Press, 1967. Bibliography.

James, Parthena Louise. "Reconstruction in the Chickasaw Nation: The Freedman Problem," *Chronicles of Oklahoma* 45 (Spring 1967):44-57.

Kellogg, Charles Flint. *NAACP: A History of the National Association for the Advancement of Colored People.* Vol. I: *1909-1920.* Baltimore: John Hopkins Press, 1967. First of a projected 2 volume series. Includes bibliographical notes.

Kirby, Jack Temple. "Clarence Poe's Vision of a Segregated Great Rural Civilization," *South Atlantic Quarterly* 68 (Winter 1969):27-38.

Kirwan, Albert D. *Revolt of the Rednecks: Mississippi Politics, 1876-1925.* Lexington: University of Kentucky Press, 1951. Demonstrates, among other themes, how the rise of white democracy of the "rednecks" in the Lower South was regularly accompanied by the rise of racism.

Lang, Jane, and Harry N. Scheiber. "The Wilson Administration and the Wartime Mobilization of Black Americans," *Labor History* 10 (Summer 1969):433-458.

Livesay, Harold C. "The Delaware Negro, 1865-1915," *Delaware History* 13 (October 1968):87-123.

Logan, Frenise A. *The Negro in North Carolina, 1876-1894.* Chapel Hill: University of North Carolina Press, 1964. Includes a bibliography of primary and secondary sources.

Logan, Rayford W. *The Betrayal of the Negro.* New York: Collier Books, 1965. A reissue, with limited revision or enlargement, of *The Negro in American Life and Thought: The Nadir, 1877-1901,* published in 1954.

Logan, Rayford W. *The Negro in American Life and Thought: The Nadir, 1877-1901.* New York: Dial, 1954. Concerned chiefly with political and economic developments in the post-Reconstruction period, the author follows the steps by which Northern desires for peace with the South and for a free hand in Northern economic expansion were realized at the expense of relegating the Negro to second-class citizenship. Bibliographical references in footnotes.

McFeely, William S. *Yankee Stepfather: General O. Howard and the Freedmen.* New Haven: Yale University Press, 1968. A study of the Freedmen's Bureau as a tool of Southern containment of the Negro, with the compliance of the first and only commissioner.

McGhee, Reginald, ed. *The World of James Van Derzee: A Visual Record of Black Americans.* New York: Grove Press, 1969. A historical photographic collection of Harlem since 1908.

McLaughlin, Tom L. "Sectional Responses of Free Negroes to the Idea of Colonization," *Washington State University Research Studies* 34 (September 1966):123-134.

McPherson, James M. "Abolitionist and Negro Opposition to Colonization During the Civil War," *Phylon* 26 (Winter 1965):391-399.

McPherson, James M. *The Negro's Civil War: How American Negroes Felt and Acted During the War for the Union.* New York: Pantheon, 1965. Impressive marshaling of evidence from which the Negroes emerge as vigorous participants on both the battle and intellectual fronts.

May, J. Thomas. "The Freedmen's Bureau at the Local Level: A Study of a Louisiana Agent," *Louisiana History* 9 (Winter 1968):5-19.

Meier, August. *Negro Thought in America, 1880-1915: Racial Ideologies in the Age of Booker T. Washington.* Ann Arbor: University of Michigan Press, 1964. In this period, as a result of the conflict between adherents of DuBois and of Washington, Negro thought became dichotomized into an ideology of integration and an ideology of separation. Bibliography.

Meier, August. "Negroes in the First and Second Reconstructions of the South," *Civil War History* 13 (June 1967):114-130.

Moore, John Hammond. "The Negro and Prohibition in Atlanta, 1885-1887," *South Atlantic Quarterly* 69 (Winter 1970):38-57.

Murray, Hugh T., Jr. "The NAACP versus the Communist Party: The Scottsboro Rape Cases, 1931-1932," *Phylon* 28 (Fall 1967):276-287. For a fuller treatment of the subject, see also Dan T. Carter's *Scottsboro: A Tragedy of the American South.*

Norris, Marjorie M. "An Early Instance of Non-Violence: The Louisville Demonstrations of 1870-71," *Journal of Southern History* 32 (November 1965):487-504.

Olsen, Otto H., ed. *The Thin Disguise: Turning Point in Negro History, A Documentary Presentation (1864-1896).* New York: Humanities Press, 1967. Background and litigation in the Plessy v. Ferguson case. Includes the argument before the court, heretofore unpublished, of Plessy's attorney, A. W. Tourgee.

Pease, William H., and Jane H. Pease. *Black Utopia: Negro Communal Experiments in America.* The State Historical Society of Wisconsin, 1963. Includes a bibliography of manuscript and special collections, government documents, and other published material.

Phillips, Paul David. "White Reaction to the Freedmen's Bureau in Tennessee," *Tennessee Historical Quarterly* 25 (Spring 1966):50-62.

Quarles, Benjamin. *Lincoln and the Negro.* New York: Oxford University Press, 1962.

Record, Wilson. *Race and Radicalism: The NAACP and the Communist Party in Conflict.* Ithaca: Cornell University Press, 1964. The author demonstrates that the Communist line in the 1930's had no more appeal to the Negroes than the back-to-Africa movement had in the 1830's, and that what the Negro wants is simply to be part of America.

Redkey, Edwin S. "Bishop Turner's African Dream," *Journal of American History* 54 (September 1967):271-290. The spokesman for black nationalism in the period between Reconstruction and World War I.

Richardson, Joe M. *The Negro in the Reconstruction of Florida, 1865-1877.* Tallahassee: Florida State University Press, 1965.

Rose, Willie Lee Nichols. *Rehearsal for Reconstruction; The Port Royal Experiment.* With an introduction by C. Vann Woodward. Indianapolis: Bobbs-Merrill, 1964. Extensive bibliographical essay appended.

Rudwick, Elliott M., and August Meier. "Black Man in the White City: Negroes and the Columbian Exposition, 1893," *Phylon* 26 (Winter 1965):354-361.

Rudwick, Elliott. "The Niagara Movement," *Journal of Negro History* 42 (July 1957):177-200.

Sanders, Albert N. "Jim Crow Comes to South Carolina," *Proceedings of the South Carolina Historical Association* (1966):27-39. Outlines the Hamptonite solution, 1876-1898 and the Jim Crow legislation which followed it.

Scheiner, Seth M. *Negro Mecca: A History of the Negro in New York City, 1865-1920.* New York: New York University Press, 1965. Notable bibliography of primary and secondary sources.

Schwendemann, Glen. "Nicodemus: Negro Haven on the Solomon," *Kansas Historical Quarterly* 34 (Spring 1968):10-31. A history of a Kansas community founded by former slaves who had emigrated to Topeka. Includes biographical sketches of some of the settlers.

Seifman, Eli. "Education or Emigration: The Schism within the African Colonization Movement, 1865-1875," *History of Education Quarterly* 7 (Spring 1967):36-57.

Simms, L. Moody, Jr. "Thomas Underwood Dudley: A Forgotten Voice of Dissent," *Mississippi Quarterly* 20 (Fall 1967):217-223. A Southerner's opposition to Negro disfranchisement and segregation.

Singletary, Otis A. *Negro Militia and Reconstruction.* Austin: Texas University Press, 1957.

Strickland, Arvarh E. *History of the Chicago Urban League.* Urbana: University of Illinois Press, 1966. From its establishment in 1817 to early 1960. Bibliography.

Swint, Henry L., ed. *Dear Ones at Home: Letters from Contraband Camps.* Nashville: Vanderbilt University Press, 1966. Letters written by two Northern women describing the conditions and care of the freedmen who came under federal control, 1863-1869, and the white Southern attitudes toward them.

Toppin, Edgar A. "The Negro in America: 1901 to 1956," *Current History* 57 (November 1969):269-274 + .

Vandersee, Charles. "Henry Adams and the Invisible Negro," *South Atlantic Quarterly* 66 (Winter 1967):13-30.

Voegeli, V. Jacque. *Free But Not Equal: The Midwest and the Negro During the Civil War.* Chicago: University of Chicago Press, 1967. Much more than a regional study of the backlash to emancipation, the author proffers evidence of the extent of Union political directives which increased the virulence of racist attitudes.

Wagandt, Charles L. *The Mighty Revolution: Negro Emancipation in Maryland, 1862-1864.* Baltimore: Johns Hopkins, 1964.

Weaver, Valeria W. "The Failure of Civil Rights, 1875-1883 and Its Repercussions," *Journal of Negro History* 54 (October 1969):368-382.

Weiss, Nancy J. "The Negro and the New Freedom: Fighting Wilsonian Segregation," *Political Science Quarterly* 84 (March 1969):61-79.

White, Howard Ashley. *The Freedmen's Bureau in Louisiana.* Baton Rouge: Louisiana State University Press, 1970.

Wiley, Bell Irvin. *Southern Negroes 1861-1865.* New Haven: Yale University Press, 1938. Remains a very useful general treatment.

Wilhoit, Francis M. "An Interpretation of Populism's Impact on the Georgia Negro," *Journal of Negro History* 52 (April 1967):116-127.

Williamson, Joel. *After Slavery: The Negro in South Carolina During Reconstruction, 1861-1877.* Chapel Hill: University of North Carolina Press, 1965. The first three chapters are especially useful toward an understanding of the freedmen in the state. Bibliography of primary and secondary sources.

Wilson, Theodore Brantner. *The Black Codes of the South.* University: University of Alabama Press, 1965. Includes a bibliography of manuscripts, public documents, and newspapers.

Wish, Harvey. *The Negro Since Emancipation.* New York: Prentice-Hall, 1964. A sampler of the writings of Douglass, DuBois, J. W. Johnson, Hughes, Wright, Ellison, and other Negro exponents of their time.

Wood, Forrest G. *Black Scare: The Racist Response to Emancipation and Reconstruction.* Berkeley: University of California Press, 1968. Includes a bibliography with an extensive list of racist pamphlets written during the Civil War and the Reconstruction era.

Woodward, C. Vann. *The Burden of Southern History.* 1960. Rev. ed. Baton Rouge: Louisiana University Press, 1968. Essays on the impact of urbanization and industrialization, the struggle over integration, and the civil rights movement.

Woodward, C. Vann. *Origins of the New South, 1877-1913.* Baton Rouge: Louisiana State University Press, 1951. The growth of the importance of industrial, commercial, and professional elements in Southern urban areas, and the effect on Southern thought and behavior. Extensive bibliography.

Woodward, C. Vann. *The Strange Career of Jim Crow.* 1955. 2d rev. ed. New York: Oxford University Press, 1966. The strangeness of the case residing in the fact that Jim Crow was actually a late comer on the scene and not an immemorial character in the sanctified Southern "way of life." The revised edition contains new material on civil rights legislation, public accommodations and school segregation demonstrations, and racial clashes in Birmingham, Selma, Little Rock, Harlem, Los Angeles. Bibliographical essay appended.

Wynes, Charles E. "Evolution of Jim Crow Laws in Twentieth-Century Virginia," *Phylon* 28
    (Winter 1967):416-425.
Wynes, Charles E., ed. *The Negro in the South Since 1865; Selected Essays in American Negro
    History.* University: University of Alabama Press, 1965.
Zangrando, Robert L. "The NAACP and A Federal Antilynching Bill, 1934-1940," *Journal
    of Negro History* 50 (April 1965):106-117.

See also Employment—Historical Background; Politics and Suffrage—Historical
    Background.

Historiography

Bluestone, Donald M. "Marxism without Marx: The Consensus-Conflict of Eugene Geno-
    vese," *Science and Society* 33 (Spring 1969):231-243. A refutation of Genovese's thesis
    regarding the slave society of the South.
Chew, Peter. "Black History or Black Mythology?" *American Heritage* 20 (August
    1969):4-94.
Cook, Samuel DuBois. "A Tragic Conception of Negro History," *Journal of Negro History*
    45 (October 1960):219-240.
Dillon, Merton L. "The Abolitionists: A Decade of Historiography, 1959-1969," *Journal of
    Southern History* 35 (November 1969):500-522.
Elkins, Stanley. *Slavery: A Problem in American Institutional and Intellectual Life.* 1963. 2d
    ed. Chicago: University of Chicago Press, 1968. Using both comparative and social
    science data, Elkins' major theme is the development of a unique and more thorough
    form of slavery in America because of the lack of structured institutions. Minor themes
    are the influence of this fact on the Negro's personality and the nature of the opposition
    to slavery. The second edition includes two new essays: "Negro Slavery in North Amer-
    ica: A Study in Social Isolation," and "Slavery and Its Aftermath in the Western
    Hemisphere."
Frazier, E. Franklin. "Sociological Theory and Race Relations," in G. Franklin Edwards,
    ed., *On Race Relations: Selected Writings.* Chicago: University of Chicago Press, 1968,
    pp. 30-42. First published in *American Sociological Review* 12 (June 1947):265-271.
Frazier, E. Franklin. "Theoretical Structure of Sociology and Sociological Research," in
    G. Franklin Edwards, ed., *On Race Relations: Selected Writings.* Chicago: University of
    Chicago Press, 1968, pp. 3-29. First published in *British Journal of Sociology* 4 (Decem-
    ber 1953):292-311.
Genovese, Eugene D. *The Political Economy of Slavery: Studies in the Economy and Society of
    the Slave South.* New York: Pantheon, 1965.
Genovese, Eugene D. "Rebelliousness and Docility in the Negro Slave: A Critique of the
    Elkins Thesis," *Civil War History* 13 (December 1967):293-314.
Genovese, Eugene D. *The World the Slaveholders Made.* New York: Pantheon, 1969. Relates
    American slavery to its counterpart in other societies, and attempts to analyze the
    intellectual defense of slavery in the United States.
Handy, Robert T. "Negro History and American Church Historiography," in Jerald C.
    Brauner, *Reinterpretation in American Church History.* Chicago: University of Chicago
    Press, 1968, pp. 91-112.
Hyman, Harold M., ed. *New Frontiers of the American Reconstruction.* Urbana: University of
    Illinois Press, 1966.
Jordan, Winthrop D. "Modern Tensions and the Origins of American Slavery," *Journal of
    Southern History* 28 (February 1962):18-30.
Lewis, Mary Agnes. "Slavery and Personality," *American Quarterly* 19 (Spring
    1967):114-121. A refutation of Elkins's thesis on slavery.
Lynd, Staughton. "Rethinking Slavery and Reconstruction," *Journal of Negro History* 50
    (July 1965):198-209.

Meyer, Howard N. "Overcoming the White Man's History," *Massachusetts Review* 7 (Summer 1966):569-578.

Newby, I. A. "Historians and Negroes," *Journal of Negro History* 54 (January 1969):32-47.

O'Brien, David J. "Black History and Color Blind Men," *Catholic World* 208 (October 1968):29-32.

O'Dell, J. H. "Colonialism and the Negro American Experience," *Freedomways* 6 (Fall 1966):296-308. "A Special Variety of Colonialism," *ibid.,* 7 (Winter 1967):7-14.

Phillips, Ulrich B. *American Negro Slavery.* New York: Appleton, 1918. Frequently reprinted. A classic interpretation of the nature of slavery. For opposing view, see Kenneth Stampp's *The Peculiar Institution.*

Quarles, Benjamin. "What the Historian Owes the Negro," *Saturday Review* 49 (September 3, 1966):10-13.

Rose, Arnold M. "History with a Present Meaning," *Commentary* 24 (December 1957):542-546. A review of recent revisionist works on the Negro.

Roucek, Joseph. "The Changing Relationship of the American Negro to African History and Politics," *Journal of Human Relations* 14 (First Quarter 1966):17-27.

Shepperson, George. "The African Abroad or the African Diaspora," in T. O. Ranger, ed., *Emerging Themes in African History.* Nairobi: East African Publishing House, 1968, pp. 152-176.

Stampp, Kenneth M. *The Era of Reconstruction: 1865-1877.* New York: Knopf, 1965. The author's purpose is to expose the falsehood of the Southern version of Reconstruction and to demonstrate both the discriminatory strategies of the South and the genuine concern of the radical Republicans for Negro rights and welfare.

Stampp, Kenneth M. *The Peculiar Institution: Slavery in the Ante-Bellum South.* New York: Knopf, 1956. The author begins by denying the dogma of the inferiority of the race, and proceeds, using a wide choice of records and documents, to a complete revision of the history of the "peculiar institution."

Stampp, Kenneth M., and Leon F. Litwack, eds. *Reconstruction: An Anthology of Revisionist Writings.* Baton Rouge: Louisiana State University Press, 1969. Includes essays on President Andrew Johnson and the Negro, and the Negro in politics, 1870-1875.

Staroben, Robert. "The Negro: A Central Theme in American History," *Journal of Contemporary History* 3 (April 1968):37-53.

Weinstein, Allen, and Frank Otto Gatell, eds. *American Negro Slavery: A Modern Reader.* New York: Oxford University Press, 1969. Bibliography.

Weisberger, Bernard A. "The Dark and Bloody Ground of Reconstruction Historiography," *Journal of Southern History* 25 (November 1959):427-447. Bibliographical footnotes.

Wesley, Charles H. "W. E. B. DuBois—The Historian," *Journal of Negro History* 50 (July 1965):147-162.

Wood, Forrest G. "On Revising Reconstruction History: Negro Suffrage, White Disenfranchisement, and Common Sense," *Journal of Negro History* 51 (April 1966):98-113.

Woodward, C. Vann. "Clio with Soul," *Journal of American History* 56 (June 1969):5-20.

3 Demography

Beshers, James M. "Delineation of Demographic Areas and the Contiguity Ratio," *Proceedings of the Social Statistics Section, American Statistical Association.* Washington, 1958.

Bogue, Donald J. *The Population of the United States.* Glencoe, Ill.: Free Press, 1959. Deals with period 1940-1958. See particularly chapter 7, "Color-Nativity-Race Composition," and chapter 26 for projections into the future.

Calef, Wesley C., and Howard J. Nelson. "Distribution of Negro Population in the United States," *Geographical Review* 46 (January 1956):82-97.

Campbell, Rex R., and Peter R. Robertson. *Negroes in Missouri: A Compilation of Statistical Data from the 1960 United States Census of Population.* Jefferson City: Missouri Commission on Human Rights, 1967.

Center for Research in Marketing, Inc. *The Negro Population: 1965 Estimates and 1970 Projections.* Peekskill, N.Y., 1966.

Clemence, Theodore G. "Residential Segregation in the Mid-Sixties," *Demography* 4 (1967):562-568. Polarization of white and Negro population in large urban areas.

Cowhig, James D. "The Negro Population of the United States, March 1967," *Welfare in Review* 7 (January-February 1967):14-16.

De Jong, Gordon F., and George A. Hillery, Jr. *Kentucky's Negro Population in 1960.* Lexington: University of Kentucky, Department of Rural Sociology, 1965?

Ezell, John Samuel. *The South Since 1865.* New York: Macmillan, 1963. Geographical, demographic, and social composition of the South.

Farley, Reynolds, and Karl E. Taeuber. "Population Trends and Residential Segregation since 1960: Special Censuses for 13 Cities Reveal Increasing Concentration of Highly Segregated Negroes," *Science* 159 (March 1, 1968):953-956.

Farley, Reynolds. "Recent Changes in Negro Fertility," *Demography* 3 (1966):188-203.

Glick, Paul C. *American Families.* New York: Wiley, 1957. A volume in the Census Monograph Series. A demographic analysis of census data on American families, with most of the information gathered since 1944. Includes differentials between whites and nonwhites in marriage age, family composition, women in the labor force, marriage rates, separation, divorce, and widowhood statistics.

Hauser, Philip M. "Demographic and Social Factors in the Poverty of the Negro," in *The Disadvantaged Poor: Education and Employment.* Washington: Chamber of Commerce of the United States, Task Force on Economic Growth and Opportunity, 1966, pp. 229-261. The demographic background of the Negro in the United States. A comparison of the acculturation process of the Negro with that of other white immigrant groups.

Hauser, Philip M. "Demographic Factors in the Integration of the Negro," *Daedalus* 94 (Fall 1965):847-877.

Jackson, Eureal Grant. "Some Tendencies in Demographic Trends in Maryland, 1950-1956," *Journal of Negro Education* 26 (Fall 1957):514-519.

Lansing, John B., et al. "Negro-White Differences in Geographic Mobility," in *The Geographic Mobility of Labor*. Ann Arbor: Institute for Social Research, University of Michigan, 1967.

Lieberson, Stanley. *Ethnic Patterns in American Cities*. Glencoe, Ill.: Free Press, 1963.

Lyman, S. M. "Spectrum of Color," *Social Research* 31 (Fall 1964):364-373. Concerning racial hybrids who inhabit the Eastern, Midwestern, and Southern United States.

O'Kane, James M. "Ethnic Mobility and the Lower-Income Negro: A Socio-Historical Perspective," *Social Problems* 16 (Winter 1969):302-311.

Palmer, Dewey H. "Moving North: Migration of Negroes during World War I," *Phylon* 28 (Spring 1967):52-62.

"The Relative Status of the Negro Population in the United States," *Journal of Negro Education* 22 (Summer 1953):221-451. Entire issue; a general demographic survey.

Robinson, Henry S. "Some Aspects of the Free Negro Population of Washington, D.C., 1800-1862," *Maryland Historical Magazine* 64 (Spring 1969):43-64.

Rose, Harold M. "The All-Negro Town: Its Evolution and Function," *Geographical Review* 55 (July 1965):362-381. A socioeconomic study of all-Negro towns in the United States. Maps, illustrations.

Smith, T. Lynn. "The Changing Number and Distribution of the Aged Negro Population in the United States," *Phylon* 18 (Fall 1957):339-354.

Smith, T. Lynn. "Redistribution of the Negro Population of the United States, 1910-1960," *Journal of Negro History* 51 (July 1966):155-173.

Social Statistics and the City: Report of a Conference Held in Washington, D.C., June 22-23, 1967, edited by David M. Heer. Cambridge, Mass.: Published by the Joint Center for Urban Studies of the Massachusetts Institute of Technology and Harvard University. Distributed by Harvard University Press, 1968. Implications of lack of complete Census coverage of the nonwhite population.

Stinner, William F., and Gordon F. De Jong. "Southern Negro Migration: Social and Economic Components of an Ecological Model," *Demography* 6 (November 1969):455-471.

Taeuber, Conrad, and Irene B. Taeuber. *The Changing Population of the United States*. New York: Wiley, 1958. A volume in the Census Monograph Series, prepared for the Social Science Research Council in cooperation with the Department of Commerce. With emphasis on the period 1890-1950, white-nonwhite differentials are presented on such matters as rates of growth, migrations and urbanization of nonwhites, marital status, families, education, fertility, and mortality.

Taeuber, Irene B. "Change and Transition in the Black Population of the United States," *Population Index* 34 (April-June 1968):121-151.

Taeuber, Karl E., and Alma F. Taeuber. "Changing Character of Negro Migration," *American Journal of Sociology* 70 (January 1965):429-441.

Taeuber, Karl E. "Negro Population and Housing: Demographic Aspects of a Social Accounting Scheme," in Irwin Katz and Patricia Gurin, eds., *Race and the Social Sciences*. New York: Basic Books, 1969, pp. 145-193. Bibliographical notes.

U.S. Bureau of the Census. *Estimates of the Population of the United States by Age, Race, and Sex: July 1, 1969*. Washington: U.S. Govt. Print. Off., 1969. (Population Report P-25, no. 427). Where available, separate data is shown for Negro population. For statistical summary, consult U.S. Bureau of the Census. *Statistical Abstract of the United States,* latest annual.

U.S. Bureau of the Census. *Negro Population, By County: 1960 and 1950*. Washington: U.S. Govt. Print. Off., 1966.

U.S. Bureau of the Census. *Negro Population of Selected Areas of the United States in Which Special Censuses Have Been Taken: January 1, 1965 to June 30, 1968*. Washington: U.S. Govt. Print. Off., 1968. (Current Population Reports P-28, no. 1476)

Valien, Preston. "General Demographic Characteristics of the Negro Population in the United States," *Journal of Negro Education* 32 (Fall 1963):329-336.

Watson, Franklin J. "A Comparison of Negro and White Populations, Connecticut: 1940-1960," *Phylon* 29 (Summer 1968):142-155.

Wattenberg, Ben. *This U.S.A.: An Unexpected Family Portrait of 194,067,296 Americans Drawn From the Census.* Garden City, N.Y.: Doubleday 1965. Based on 1965 Census Bureau statistics and in collaboration with Richard M. Scammon, Director, U.S. Bureau of the Census. See particularly chapters 15 and 16.

Wheeler, James O., and Stanley D. Brunn. "Agricultural Ghetto: Negroes in Cass County, Michigan, 1845-1968," *Geographical Review* 59 (July 1969):317-329. Maps.

Wheeler, James O., and Stanley D. Brunn. "Negro Migration into Rural Southwestern Michigan," *Geographical Review* 58 (April 1968):214-230. The demographic structure also shown by maps and charts.

Zelnik, Melvin. "Fertility of the American Negro in 1830 and 1850," *Population Studies* (Great Britain) 20 (July 1966):77-83. Compares age distribution of Negroes drawn from the U.S. decennial censuses for the period and projects declining fertility rate.

See also Urban Problems—In-Migration and Population.

4　Definition and Description

The Idea of Race

Alpenfels, Ethel. *Sense and Nonsense About Race.* New York: Friendship Press, 1957.

Barnicot, N. "Coon's Theory of Evolution," *Observer Weekend Review,* May 26, 1963.

Berry, Brewton. *Almost White: A Study of Certain Racial Hybrids in the Eastern United States.* New York: Macmillan, 1963.

Boyd, William C. "Genetics and the Human Race," *Science* 140 (June 7, 1963):1057-1064.

Boyd, William C. *Genetics and the Races of Man.* Boston: Little, Brown, 1954.

Coon, Carleton S., with Edward E. Hunt, Jr. *The Living Races of Man.* New York: Knopf, 1965. Presenting a theory of the division of Man, as he is today, into five races.

Coon, Carleton S. *The Origin of Races.* New York: Knopf, 1962. A work which aroused much controversy for positing a theory of the stage of evolution at which various races have arrived.

Dobzhansky, Theodosius. "A Debatable Account of the Origin of the Races," *Scientific American* 208 (February 1963):169-172.

Dobzhansky, Theodosius. *Heredity and the Nature of Man.* New York: Harcourt, Brace, 1964. A distinguished philosopher of science warns against faddist "science" that presumes to find superiority or inferiority in individuals of one race or another, reminding the reader of scientists' inability to agree on what constitutes a race, and that it is not genes or color that carry the cultural heritage of a society.

Dobzhansky, Theodosius. *Mankind Evolving: The Evolution of the Human Species.* New Haven: Yale University Press, 1962. Chapters on biology and culture in human evolution, environmentalism vs. hereditarianism, natural selection and survival of the fittest, evolution in process and in the future. Includes a discussion of race theories and categories, with critical suggestions as to the need to reformulate our thinking about such concepts.

Frazier, E. Franklin. "Racial Problems in World Society," in Jitsuichi Masuoka and Preston Valien, eds., *Race Relations: Problems and Theory.* Chapel Hill: University of North Carolina Press, 1961.

Garn, Stanley. *Human Races.* Springfield, Ill.: Thomas, 1961.

George, Wesley Critz. *The Biology of the Race Problem.* New York: Putnam Letters Committee, 1962. A work sponsored by a commission appointed by the Governor of Alabama.

Giles, E., and O. Elliot. "Race Identification from Cranial Measurements," *Journal of Forensic Science* 7 (April 1962):147.

Glass, Bentley. "On the Unlikelihood of Significant Admixture of Genes from the North American Indians in the Present Composition of the Negroes of the United States," *American Journal of Human Genetics* 7 (December 1955):368-385.

Gossett, Thomas F. *Race: The History of an Idea in America.* Dallas, Tex.: Southern Methodist University Press, 1963. The author traces the development of ideas on race in the United States from the seventeenth century to the present, drawing on evidence from literature, politics, the social sciences, and religion, and presents a survey both of race theory and of bigotry.

Gould, L. "Negro = Man," *American Anthropology* 67 (October 1965):1281-1282. Reply by A. H. Schultz, *ibid.*, 68 (April 1966):528; rejoinder 69 (February 1967):89.

Haller, Mark H. *Eugenics, Hereditarian Attitudes in American Thought.* New Brunswick, N.J.: Rutgers University Press, 1963. Including attitudes toward Negroes. Bibliography.

Herskovits, Melville J. *The Anthropometry of the American Negro.* New York: Columbia University Press, 1930. Estimates that 71 percent of American Negroes have some white ancestry.

Ingle, Dwight J. "Racial Differences and the Future," *Science* 146 (October 16, 1964):375-379. "There is no sound structure of evidence and logic which compels a conclusion" on the issue of race and intelligence. "The concept of equality is meaningful only as it relates to civil rights and opportunities."

Isaacs, Harold R. "Blackness and Whiteness," *Encounter* 21 (August 1963):8-21.

Karrick, D. B. "What Constitutes a Negro: A Review of Legal Statutes," *Journal of the National Medical Association* 51 (May 1959):211-214.

Landes, Ruth. "Biracialism in American Society: A Comparative View," *American Anthropologist* 57 (December 1955):1253-1263.

"Legal Definition of Race," *Race Relations Law Reporter* 3 (June 1958):571.

Lincoln, C. Eric. "Color and Group Identity in the United States," *Daedalus* 96 (Spring 1967):527-540. References.

Mangum, Charles S., Jr. *The Legal Status of the Negro.* Chapel Hill: University of North Carolina Press, 1940. See particularly chapter 1, "Who Is a Negro."

Mayer, Milton. "The Issue is Miscegenation," *Progressive* 23 (September 1959):8-18.

Mead, Margaret. "The Student of Race Problems Can Say. . .," *Race* 3 (November 1961):3-9. Poses the question of whether our scientific knowledge of race differences is improving.

Morant, D. M. *The Significance of Racial Differences.* Paris: UNESCO, 1952.

Morrison, J. L. "Illegitimacy, Sterilization and Racism: A North Carolina Case History," *Social Service Review* 39 (March 1965):1-10.

The Myths of Racial Integration. New York: American Jewish Congress, 1960?

Newby, I. A. *Jim Crow's Defense: Anti-Negro Thought in America, 1900-1930.* Baton Rouge: Louisiana State University Press, 1965. The rise and fall of the concept of innate Negro inferiority among scientists, social scientists, historians, and theologians.

Pollitzer, W. S. "The Negroes of Charleston: A Study of Hemoglobin Types, Serology, and Morphology," *American Journal of Physical Anthropology* 16 (1958):241.

Putnam, Carleton. *Race and Reality: A Search for Solutions.* Washington: Public Affairs Press, 1967.

Putnam, Carleton. *Race and Reason: A Yankee View.* Washington: Public Affairs Press, 1961. Proclaims the inherent inferiority of Negroes to whites in their capacity for civilization.

Race and Science: The Race Question in Modern Science. New York: Columbia University Press, 1961. Includes a statement prepared by a conference convened by UNESCO on "The Nature of Race and Race Differences."

Schneider, Louis. "Race, Reason and Rubbish Again," *Phylon* 23 (Summer 1962):149-155. Review of Putnam's *Race and Reason.*

"Science and the Race Problem: A Report of the AAAS Committee on Science in the Promotion of Human Welfare," *Science* 142 (November 1963):558-561. In refutation of racism and specifically of Putnam's *Race and Reason,* the report concludes "that the available evidence on the measurable differences among racial groups cannot properly support a challenge to the principle of human equality which is assured by the Constitution of the United States."

Shapiro, M. "Blood Groups and Skin Colour in Human Anthropology," *Journal of Forensic Medicine* 1 (July-September 1953):2-10.

Smith, Samuel Stanhope. *An Essay on the Causes of the Variety of Complexion and Figure in the Human Species.* 1787. Cambridge, Mass.: Harvard University Press, 1965. Edited with an introduction by Winthrop D. Jordan, this essay by a Presbyterian clergyman and president of the College of New Jersey (now Princeton University) was an attempt to show that physical variety among the peoples of the world was due to natural causes, and that all men belong to a single creation.

Snyder, Louis L. *The Idea of Racialism: Its Meaning and History.* Princeton, N.J.: Van Nostrand, 1962. History of theories of racial differences.

Stanton, William. *The Leopard's Spots: Scientific Attitudes Toward Race in America, 1815-1859.* Chicago: University of Chicago Press, 1960.

Thompson, Edgar T., and Everett C. Hughes, eds. *Race: Individual and Collective Behavior.* Glencoe, Ill.: Free Press, 1958. An anthology of readings directed to "the problem of understanding and dealing with an idea, the idea of race" as related to "concrete social, political, demographic, and biological problems." An extensive bibliography of great value.

Tyler, Leona E. *The Psychology of Human Differences.* New York: Appleton, 1956. A textbook which deals to some extent with race and nationality differences, especially in chapter 5.

Van Den Berghe, Pierre L. "Hypergamy, Hypergenation, and Miscegenation," *Human Relations* 13 (February 1960):83-91.

Washburn, Sherwood L. "The Study of Race," *American Anthropologist* 65 (June 1963):521-531.

"Who is a Negro?" *University of Florida Law Review* 11 (Summer 1958):235.

Wirth, Louis, and Herbert Goldhamer. "The Hybrid and the Problem of Miscegenation," in Otto Klineberg, ed., *Characteristics of the American Negro.* New York: Harper, 1944.

Workman, P. L., B. S. Blumberg, and A. J. Cooper. "Selection, Gene Migration and Polymorphic Stability in a U.S. White and Negro Population," *American Journal of Human Genetics* 15 (December 1963):429-437.

See also Individual Characteristics—Intelligence; Health—Genetic.

Social Institutions and Conditions

Family and Child Rearing

Andrew, Gwen. "Determinants of Negro Family Decisions in Management of Retardation," *Journal of Marriage and the Family* 30 (November 1968):612-617. Comparison of the determinants of Negro and White families to institutionalize their retarded children.

Andrews, Roberta G. "Permanent Placement of Negro Children through Quasi-Adoption," *Child Welfare* 47 (December 1968):583-586.

Barker, Howard F. "The Family Names of American Negroes," *American Speech* 14 (October 1939):163-174.

Baughman, Earl, and W. Grant Dahlstrom. *Negro and White Children. A Psychological Study in the Rural South.* New York: Academic Press, 1968. Winner of Anisfield-Wolf Award in race relations for the "Best scholarly book in the field of race relations published in 1968." Book based on 14-year study of racially segregated students in a rural, economically deprived area of North Carolina.

Bell, Robert R. "The Lower-Class Negro Family in the United States and Great Britain: Some Comparisons," *Race* 11 (October 1969):173-181.

Bell, R. R. "Lower Class Negro Mothers' Aspirations for Their Children," *Social Forces* 43 (May 1965):493-500.

Bernard, Jessie. *Marriage and Family Among Negroes.* Englewood Cliffs, N.J.: Prentice-Hall, 1966. Conflicting opinions of reviewers as to the value of this study.

Bieler, Henry B. "Note on Father Absence and Masculine Development in Lower-Class Negro and White Boys," *Child Development* 39 (September 1968):1003-1006.

Billingsley, Andrew, with the assistance of Amy Tate Billingsley. *Black Families in White America.* Englewood Cliffs, N.J.: Prentice-Hall, 1968. Seeks to contravene the Moynihan thesis of social disorganization of lower-class Negro families. Attention also to the small percentage of upper-class Negro families, the present Negro elite.

Billingsley, Andrew. "Family Functioning in the Low-Income Black Community," *Social Casework* 50 (December 1969):563-572.

Billingsley, Andrew. "Illegitimacy Problems of Negro Family Life," in Robert W. Roberts, ed., *The Unwed Mother.* New York: Harper, 1966, pp. 133-158.

Billingsley, Andrew, and Amy Tate Billingsley. "Negro Family Life in America," *Social Service Review* 39 (September 1965):310-319.

Billingsley, Andrew. "New Approaches for Expanding Services to Negro Unwed Mothers," in *Mobilizing for Community-Wide Services to Unwed Parents.* Chicago: Florence Crittenton Association of America, 1968, pp. 40-48.

Blau, Zena Smith. "Exposure to Child-Rearing Experts: A Structural Interpretation of Class-Color Differences," *American Journal of Sociology* 69 (May 1964):596-608.

Blood, Robert O., and Donald M. Wolfe. *Husbands and Wives: The Dynamics of Married Living.* New York: Free Press, 1963. An investigation of the differences between white and Negro families in respect of the relative "power" of men and women.

Brody, Eugene B. "Color and Identity Conflict in Young Boys: Observations of Negro Mothers and Sons in Urban Baltimore," *Psychiatry* 26 (May 1963):188-201.

Buffalo and Erie County Community Welfare Council. "Report and Recommendations of the Committee for Negro Adoptions." Buffalo, N.Y., 1961. Mimeographed.

Burton, R. V., and J. W. M. Whiting. "The Absent Father and Cross-Sex Identity," *Merrill-Palmer Quarterly* 7 (April 1961):85-95.

Cavan, Ruth Shonle. "Negro Family Disorganization and Juvenile Delinquency," *Journal of Negro Education* 28 (Summer 1959):230-239.

Coles, Robert. *Children of Crisis: A Study of Courage and Fear.* Boston: Little, Brown, 1967. A psychiatrist discusses effects of desegregation on both Negro and White children.

Davis, Allison W., and Robert J. Havighurst. *The Father of the Man: How Your Child Gets His Personality.* Boston: Houghton Mifflin, 1947. Study of child-rearing practices among Negroes at the lower-class and middle-class levels in Chicago.

Davis, Elizabeth B. "The American Negro: From Family Membership to Personal and Social Identity," *Journal of the National Medical Association* 60 (March 1968):72-99.

Deasy, Leila C., and Olive W. Quinn. "The Urban Negro and Adoption of Children," *Child Welfare* 41 (November 1962):400-407.

Derbyshire, R. L., et al. "Family Structure of Young Adult Negro Male Mental Patients: Preliminary Observations from Urban Baltimore," *Journal of Nervous and Mental Disease* 136 (March 1963):245-251.

DuBois, W. E. B. *The Negro American Family.* 1908. New York: Negro Universities Press, 1969. Originally published by the Atlanta University Press, a social study made by the classes of 1909 and 1910 of Atlanta University, together with the proceedings of the 1908 Conference for the Study of the Negro Problems.

Dukette, Rita, and Thelma G. Thompson. *Adoptive Resources for Negro Children: The Use of Community Organization and Social Casework in Recruitment and Development.* New York: Child Welfare League of America, 1959.

Duncan, Beverly, and Otis D. Duncan. "Family Stability and Occupational Success," *Social Problems* 16 (Winter 1969):273-285. The comparative effects of family stability in the parental generation on Negro and non-Negro males.

Edwards, G. Franklin. "Marriage and Family Life among Negroes," *Journal of Negro Education* 32 (Fall 1963):451-465.

Edwards, Harry. "Black Muslim and Negro Christian Family Relationships," *Journal of Marriage and the Family* 30 (November 1968):604-611.

Epstein, Ralph, and S. S. Komorita. "Prejudice among Negro Children as Related to Parental Ethnocentrism and Punitiveness," *Journal of Personality and Social Psychology* 4 (December 1966):643-647. References appended.

Erikson, Erik. "Memorandum on Identity and Negro Youth," *Journal of Social Issues* 20 (October 1964):29-42.

Fanshel, David. *A Study in Negro Adoption.* New York: Child Welfare League of America, 1957.

Farmer, James. "The Plight of Negro Children in America Today," *Child Welfare* 47 (November 1968):508-515.

Feagin, Joe R. "The Kinship Ties of Negro Urbanites," *Social Science Quarterly* 49 (December 1968):660-665. Based on an evaluation study done in Boston's Roxbury-Dorchester ghetto.

Fischer, Ann, Joseph D. Beasley, and Carl L. Harter. "The Occurrence of the Extended Family at the Origin of the Family of Procreation: A Developmental Approach to Negro Family Structure," *Journal of Marriage and the Family* 30 (May 1968):290-300.

Fowler, Irving A. "The Urban Middle-Class Negro and Adoption: Two Series of Studies and Their Implications for Action," *Child Welfare* 45 (November 1966):522-525.

Frazier, E. Franklin. "Ethnic Family Patterns: The Negro Family in the United States," *American Journal of Sociology* 54 (May 1948):432-438.

Frazier, E. Franklin. "The Impact of Urban Civilization upon Negro Family Life," "Certain Aspects of Conflict in the Negro Family," and "Problems and Needs of Negro Children and Youth Resulting from Family Disorganization," in G. Franklin Edwards, ed., *On Race Relations: Selected Writings.* Chicago: University of Chicago Press, 1968, pp. 161-174; 210-224; 225-235. Articles firt published in 1937, 1931, and 1950 respectively.

Frazier, E. Franklin. "The Negro Family in Chicago," in E. W. Burgess and D. J. Bogue, eds., *Contributions to Urban Sociology.* Chicago: University of Chicago Press, 1964, pp. 404-418.

Frazier, E. Franklin. *The Negro Family in the United States.* 1939. Revised and abridged edition, with a new introduction by Nathan Glazer. Chicago: University of Chicago Press, 1966. Vivid accounts of the lower-class Negro world and the family system. Published in many editions since 1939, it is still a major work on the subject.

Frazier, E. Franklin. *Negro Youth at the Crossways.* 1940. New York: Schocken Books, 1967. First sponsored by American Council on Education. This edition contains new introductions by St. Clair Drake and the author.

Frazier, E. Franklin. "Problems and Needs of Negro Children," *Journal of Negro Education* 19 (Summer 1950):269-277.

Frumkin, Robert M. "Attitudes of Negro College Students Toward Intrafamily Leadership and Control," *Marriage and Family Living* 16 (August 1954):252-253.

Ginzberg, Eli, ed. *The Nation's Children.* Vol. I: *The Family and Social Change;* Vol. II: *Development and Education;* Vol. III: *Problems and Prospects.* New York: Columbia University Press, 1960. Essays and articles written for Golden Anniversary White House Conference on Children and Youth.

Gipson, Theodore H. "Educational Status of the Negro Family in Louisiana," *Journal of Educational Sociology* 32 (October 1958):83-89.

Gould, Flo, and Richard K. Kerckhoff. "Family Life Education for the Biracial Community," *Journal of Negro Education* 29 (Spring 1960):187-190.

"Growing Up Negro," *American Child* (January 1963):entire issue.

Hallow, Ralph Z. "The Blacks Cry Genocide," *Nation* 208 (April 28, 1969):535-537. Opinion pro and con about family planning program.

Herzog, Elizabeth, and Cecelia S. Sudia. "Family Structure and Composition," in Roger R. Miller, ed., *Race, Research, and Reason: Social Work Perspectives.* New York: National Association of Social Workers, 1969, pp. 145-164. Study concerns a fatherless low-income family.

Herzog, Elizabeth. "Is There a 'Breakdown' of the Negro Family?" *Social Work* 11 (January 1966):3-10.

Herzog, Elizabeth, and Rose Bernstein. "Why So Few Negro Adoptions," *Children* 12 (January-February 1965):14-18.

Hill, Adelaide Cromwell, and Frederick S. Jaffe. "Negro Fertility and Family Size Preferences: Implications for Programing of Health and Social Services," in *Daedalus.*

The Negro American, edited by Talcott Parsons and Kenneth B. Clark. Cambridge, Mass.: Houghton Mifflin, 1966, pp. 205-224.

Himes, Joseph S. "Interrelation of Occupational and Spousal Roles in a Middle Class Negro Neighborhood," *Marriage and Family Living* 22 (November 1960):362.

Hyman, Herbert H., and John Shelton Reed. "'Black Matriarchy' Reconsidered: Evidence from Secondary Analysis of Sample Surveys," *Public Opinion Quarterly* 33 (Fall 1969):346-354.

Illegitimacy and its Impact on the Aid to Dependent Children Program. Washington: Bureau of Public Assistance, U. S. Department of Health, Education and Welfare, 1960.

Jenkins, Wesley W. "An Experimental Study of the Relationship of Legitimate and Illegitimate Birth Status to School and Personal and Social Adjustment of Negro Children," *American Journal of Sociology* 64 (September 1958):169-173.

Kamii, Constance K., and Norma L. Radin. "Class Differences in the Socialization Practices of Negro Mothers," *Journal of Marriage and the Family* 29 (May 1967):302-310. Within the context of their child-rearing goals.

King, Karl. "Adolescent Perception of Power Structure in the Negro Family," *Journal of Marriage and the Family* 31 (November 1969):751-755.

King, Karl. "A Comparison of the Negro and White Family Power Structure in Low-Income Families," *Child and Family* 6 (Fall 1967):65-74.

Kunstadter, Peter. "A Survey of the Consanguine or Matrifocal Family," *American Anthropologist* 65 (February 1963):56-66.

Lawder, Elizabeth A. "Quasi-Adoption," *Children* 13 (January 1966):11-12. Service of the Children's Aid Society of Pennsylvania providing uninterrupted care for young Negro children for whom renewal of family living is unlikely.

Lefcowitz, Myron J. *Differences between Negro and White Women in Marital Stability and Family Structure: A Multiple Regression Analysis.* Madison, Wis.:Institute for Research on Poverty, 1968.

Lewis, Hylan. "The Changing Negro Family," in Eli Ginzberg, ed., *The Nation's Children.* Vol. I. New York: Columbia University Press, 1960. Points out that the new task of the Negro family is to prepare its members to live in a desegregated world. Also appears in Joan I. Roberts, ed., *School Children in the Urban Slum.* New York: Free Press, 1967, pp. 397-405.

Lincoln, C. Eric, "The Absent Father Haunts the Negro Family," *New York Times Magazine,* November 28, 1965, p. 60+.

Madison, Bernice, and Michael Shapiro. "Long-Term Foster Family Care: What Is Its Potential for Minority Group Children," *Public Welfare* 27 (April 1969):167-175.

Manning, Seaton W. "The Changing Negro Family: Implications for the Adoption of Children," *Child Welfare* 43 (November 1964):480-485.

Maxwell, Joseph W. "Rural Negro Father Participation in Family Activities," *Rural Sociology* 33 (March 1968):80-83.

Middleton, Russel, and Snell Putney. "Dominance in Decisions in the Family: Race and Class Differences," *American Journal of Sociology* 65 (May 1960):605-609.

Minuchin, Salvador, et. al. *Families of the Slums: An Exploration of Their Structure and Treatment.* New York: Basic Books, 1967. An inter-disciplinary research study of Negro and Puerto Rican families in New York City with one or more delinquent children.

Moynihan, Daniel Patrick. "Employment, Income, and the Ordeal of the Negro Family," *Daedalus* 94 (Fall 1965):745-770.

Moynihan, Daniel Patrick. *The Negro Family: The Case for National Action.* Washington: U.S. Govt. Print. Off., 1965. Prepared for Office of Policy Planning and Research of the Department of Labor, the author documents and describes the destructive effects of the breakdown of the Negro family, particularly in urban ghettos.

Moynihan, Daniel P. "The President and the Negro: The Moment Lost," *Commentary* 43 (February 1967):31-45.

"Negro Families in Rural Wisconsin: A Study of their Community Life." Madison, Wis.: Governor's Commission on Human Rights, 1959. Mimeographed.

North, George E., and O. Lee Buchanan. "Maternal Attitudes in a Poverty Era," *Journal of*

Negro Education 37 (Fall 1968):418–425. Study involved parents with nursery and kinder-garten children in an impoverished area of Phoenix, Arizona.

Opler, Marvin K. "The Influence of Ethnic and Class Structures on Child Care," *Social Problems* 3 (July 1955):12–21.

Parker, Seymour, and Robert J. Kleiner. "Characteristics of Negro Mothers in Single-Headed Households," *Journal of Marriage and the Family* 28 (November 1966):507–513. Contrasts the adjustment and attitudes of mothers in broken and intact families. Implications for achievement attitudes of their children.

Parker, Seymour, and Robert J. Kleiner. "Social and Psychological Dimensions of the Family Role Performance of the Negro Male," *Journal of Marriage and the Family* 31 (August 1969):500–506.

Pavenstedt, Eleanor, et al. *Drifters: Children of Disorganized Lower-Class Families.* Boston: Little, Brown, 1967.

Perry, Martha. "An Experiment in Recruitment of Negro Adoptive Parents," *Social Case-work* 39 (May 1958):292–297.

Pierce, Chester M. "Problems of the Negro Adolescent in the Next Decade," in Eugene B. Brody, ed., *Minority Group Adolescents in the United States.* Baltimore: Williams and Wilkins, 1968, pp. 17–47.

Pope, Hallowell. "Negro-White Differences in Decisions Regarding Illegitimate Children," *Journal of Marriage and the Family* (November 1969):756–764.

Queen, Stuart A., and Robert W. Habenstein. "The Contemporary American Negro Family in the U.S.," in *The Family in Various Cultures.* 1952. 3d ed. New York: Lippincott, 1967.

Radin, Norma, and Constance K. Kamii. "The Child-Rearing Attitudes of Disadvantaged Negro Mothers and Some Educational Implications," *Journal of Negro Education* 34 (Spring 1965):138–146.

Rainwater, Lee. "Crucible of Identity: The Negro Lower-Class Family," *Daedalus* 95 (Winter 1966):172–216.

Rainwater, Lee, and William L. Yancey. *The Moynihan Report and the Politics of Contro-versy.* Cambridge, Mass.: M. I. T. Press, 1967. A systematic review of the response to the report from government, news media, civil rights, and other organizations. Includes the text of Moynihan's *The Negro Family: The Case for National Action* and other related documents.

Reiner, Beatrice Simcox. "The Real World of the Teenage Negro Mother," *Child Welfare* 47 (July 1968):391–396.

Reiss, I. L. "Premarital Sexual Permissiveness Among Negroes and Whites," *American Sociological Review* 29 (October 1964):688–698.

Riese, Hertha. *Heal the Hurt Child: An Approach Through Educational Therapy with Special Reference to the Extremely Deprived Negro Child.* Chicago: University of Chicago Press, 1962.

Rodman, Hyman, and Paul Grams. "Juvenile Delinquency and the Family: A Review and Discussion in the U.S. President's Commission on Law Enforcement and Administration of Justice," *Task Force Report: Juvenile Delinquency and Crime.* Washington: U.S. Govt. Print. Off., 1967, pp. 188–221.

Rousseve, R. J. "Negro Family Structure and the American School Experiences," *National Catholic Guidance Conference Journal* 11 (Fall 1966):22–39.

Ryan, William. "Savage Discovery: The Moynihan Report," *The Nation* 201 (November 22, 1965):380–384.

Safa, Helen Icken. *An Analysis of Upward Mobility in Low-Income Families: A Comparison of Family and Community Life among Negro and Puerto Rican Poor.* Syracuse, N.Y.: Syracuse University, 1967.

Schenck, Mary-Low. "A Southern Negro Girl in a White Northern Family: A Case Study," *Social Work* 14 (July 1969):77–83. Southern Student Project—a program for bringing a deprived Southern Negro high school student into a Northern family.

Schulz, David A. "Variations in the Father Role in Complete Families of the Negro Lower Class," *Social Science Quarterly* 49 (December 1968):651–659.

Schwartz, M. "Northern United States Negro Matriarchy: Status Versus Authority," *Phylon* 26 (Spring 1965):18-24.

Setleis, Lloyd. "Civil Rights and the Rehabilitation of the AFDC [Aid to Families with Dependent Children] Clients," *Social Work* 9 (April 1964):3-9.

Smith, Howard P., and Marcia Abramson. "Racial and Family Experience Correlates of Mobility Aspirations," *Journal of Negro Education* 31 (Spring 1962):117-124.

Smith, Mary. "Birth Control and the Negro Woman," *Ebony* 23 (March 1968):29-32+.

Social Planning Council of Metropolitan Toronto. *The Adoption of Negro Children; A Community-Wide Approach.* Toronto, 1966.

Strodtbeck, Fred L. "The Poverty-Dependency Syndrome of the ADC Female-Based Negro Family," *American Journal of Orthopsychiatry* 34 (March 1964):216-217. Analysis of the "progressive estrangement of indigent female-based Negro families in urban centers."

Taeuber, Karl E. "Negro Population and Housing: Demographic Aspects of a Social Accounting Scheme," in Irwin Katz and Patricia Gurin, eds., *Race and the Social Sciences.* New York: Basic Books, 1969, pp. 145-193. Bibliographical Notes.

Tietze, C., and S. Lewit. "Patterns of Family Limitation in a Rural Negro Community," *American Sociological Review* 18 (October 1953):563-564.

U.S. Department of Labor. Bureau of Labor Statistics. *The Negro in the West: The Negro Family.* San Francisco: U.S. Department of Labor, 1967?

Vincent, Clark. *Unmarried Mothers.* Glencoe, Ill.: Free Press, 1961. Vincent reports that 64 percent of all illicit live births in America are to Negro mothers.

Wakin, Edward. *At the Edge of Harlem: Portrait of a Middle-Class Negro Family.* Photographs by Edward Lettau. New York: Morrow, 1965. A photo documentary.

Wasserman, Herbert L. *Father-Absent and Father-Present Lower-Class Negro Families: A Comparative Study of Family Functioning.* Ann Arbor, Mich.: University Microfilms, 1968. Subjects were 117 Boston Negro families.

Webster, Staten W. "Some Correlates of Reported Academically Supportive Behaviors of Negro Mothers Toward Their Children," *Journal of Negro Education* 34 (Spring 1966):114-120. Bibliography.

Weinstein, E. A., and P. N. Geisel. "Family Decision Making over Desegregation," *Sociometry* 25 (March 1961):21-29.

Weller, Leonard, and Elmer Luchterhand. "Comparing Interviews and Observations on Family Functioning," *Journal of Marriage and the Family* 3 (February 1969):115-122. A sampling of low-income, large Negro families.

Whitehead, John S. *Ida's Family: Adaptations to Poverty in a Suburban Ghetto.* Yellow Springs, Ohio: Antioch College, 1969. Describes a low-income black family in a Washington, D.C. ghetto. Prepared for the National Institute of Mental Health.

Woods, Sister Frances Jerome, and Alice Cunningham Lancaster. "Cultural Factors in Negro Adoptive Parenthood," *Social Work* 7 (October 1962).

See also Intermarriage and Interracial Adoption.

Religious Life and Negro Churches

Bardolph, Richard. "Negro Religious and Educational Leaders in 'Who's Who in America,' 1936-1955," *Journal of Negro Education* 26 (Spring 1957):182-192.

Beynon, Erdmann Doane. "The Voodoo Cult among Negro Migrants in Detroit," *American Journal of Sociology* 43 (May 1938):894-907.

Bock, E. Wilbur. "The Decline of the Negro Clergy: Changes in Formal Religious Leadership in the United States in the Twentieth Century," *Phylon* 29 (Spring 1968):48-64.

Bontemps, Arna. "Rock, Church, Rock," in Sylvester C. Watkins, ed., *Anthology of American Negro Literature.* New York: Random, 1944. On Gospel singers and their religious orientation.

Brewer, J. Mason. *The Word on the Brazos.* Austin: University of Texas Press, 1953. Negroes' reactions to their preachers.

Cantril, Hadley. *The Psychology of Social Movements.* New York: Wiley, 1941. Good section on Father Divine and his "kingdom."

Clark, Elmer T. *The Small Sects in America.* 1937. Rev. ed. Nashville, Tenn.: Abingdon, 1949. Chapter 4 deals in detail with Negro sects, distinguishing five types of "charismatic" sects, most of them offshoots of regular churches, and all of them characterized by revivalism, emotionalism, and evangelism.

Cleage, Albert B., Jr. *The Black Messiah.* New York: Sheed & Ward, 1968. Black power and theology.

Cone, James H. "Failure of the Black Church," *Liberator* (May 1969):15-17+.

Daniel, Vattel E. "Ritual and Stratification in Chicago Negro Churches," *American Sociological Review* 7 (June 1942):353-358. Describes types of behavior in ecstatic cults.

Davies, Everett F.S. "Negro Protest Movement: The Religious Way," *Journal of Religious Thought* 24, no. 2(1967-1968): 13-25.

Dillard, J. L. "On the Grammar of Afro-American Naming Practices," *Names* 16 (September 1968):230-237. Comparison of ghetto church names with those of white, middle-class churches.

Drake, St. Clair, and Horace Cayton. *Black Metropolis.* New York: Harcourt, Brace, 1945. Rev. and enl. ed. New York: Harper, 1963. This Harper Torchbook edition, in two volumes, includes a new chapter, "Bronzeville 1961," an appendix, "Black Metropolis 1961," and "Suggestions for Collateral Reading, 1962." A chapter on religion has good descriptive material, as well as discussion of Negro ministers in a Northern urban community.

Elder, John Dixon. "Meeting the Crisis of Negro Leadership in the Church," *Harvard Divinity Bulletin* (new series) no. 1 (Autumn 1967):17-18. The role of Negro clergymen and the responsibility of theological educators.

Faulkner, William J. "Influence of Folklore upon the Religious Experience of the Ante-Bellum Negro," *Journal of Religious Thought* 24 (1967-1968):26-28.

Fauset, Arthur H. *Black Gods of the Metropolis.* Philadelphia: University of Pennsylvania Press, 1944. Most valuable study of Negro cults in the city.

Feagin, Joe R. "Black Catholics in the United States: An Exploratory Analysis," *Sociological Analysis* 29 (Winter 1968):186-192. Examines growth and distribution trends of Negro Catholics.

Frazier, E. Franklin. *The Negro Church in America.* New York: Schocken, 1963. Gunnar Myrdal: "His posthumous work on the Negro is a brief but brilliant analysis of the historical origin and the present situation of a crucially important institution of the American Negro people." Wise and humane.

Gillard, John T. *Colored Catholics in the United States.* Baltimore, Md.: The Josephite Press, 1941.

Glenn, Norval D. "Negro Religion and Negro Status in the United States," in Louis Schneider, ed., *Religion, Culture, and Society.* New York: Wiley, 1964.

Gustafson, James M. "The Clergy in the United States," *Daedalus* 92 (Fall 1963):724-744. Includes material on the unsatisfactory state of Negro Protestant ministry and their inadequate education.

Harper, Howard V. "Richard Allen," in *Profiles of Protestant Saints.* New York: Fleet Press, 1968, pp. 56-76. Biography of the first Negro bishop in America (1760-1831).

Haughey, John C. "Black Sisters Become Soul Sisters," *America* 121 (August 2, 1969):67. The Black Sisters' Conference.

Haynes, Leonard L. *The Negro Community within American Protestantism.* Boston: Christopher, 1953.

Herskovits, Melville J. "The Contemporary Scene: Africanisms in Religious Life," in *The Myth of the Negro Past.* New York: Harper, 1941.

Herskovits, Melville J. "Social History of the Negro," in C. Murchison, ed., *Handbook of Social Psychology.* Worcester, Mass.: Clark University Press, 1935. Contains material on place of song in Negro religious service.

Jackson, James Conroy. "The Religious Education of the Negro in South Carolina Prior to 1850," *Historical Magazine of the Protestant Episcopal Church* 36 (March 1967):35-61.

James, Willis Laurence. "The Romance of the Negro Folk Cry in America," *Phylon* 16 (Spring 1955):15-30. An essay on the religious expression of folk music and on the gospel singers.

Johnson, Benton, "Do Holiness Sects Socialize in Dominant Values?" *Social Forces* 39 (May 1961):309-316.

Johnson, Charles S. *Growing Up in the Black Belt*. Washington: American Council on Education, 1941. Contains excellent section on the rural church.

Johnson, James Weldon. *God's Trombones*. New York: Viking, 1927. Contains striking descriptions of Negro sermons.

Johnson, Ruby F. *The Development of Negro Religion*. New York: Philosophical Library, 1954.

Johnson, Ruby F. *The Religion of Negro Protestants*. New York: Philosophical Library, 1956.

Jones, Major J. "Black Awareness: Theological Implications of the Concept," *Religion in Life* 38 (Autumn 1969):389-403. Traditional Christianity of the black church must assume an active role in the search for black identity if it is to survive.

Jones, Raymond J. *A Comparative Study of Religious Cult Behavior Among Negroes with Special Reference to Emotional Conditioning Factors*. (Howard University Studies in the Social Sciences, vol. 2, no. 2). Washington: Howard University Graduate School, 1940. Classifies different types of cults from standpoint of whether they are faith-healing, or holiness, or claiming Islamic origins, etc.

Jones, William A., Jr. "The Negro Church," *Foundations* 10 (April-June 1967):108-110. Why the Negro church is outside the mainstream of (white) American Protestantism and is viewed as its foster child.

Kiely, Pat. "A Cry for Black Nun Power," *Commonweal* 88 (September 27, 1968):650. First National Black Sisters' Conference held August 17-24 at Mt. Mercy College, Pittsburgh.

Lee, J. Oscar. "Religion Among Ethnic and Racial Minorities," *Annals of the American Academy of Political and Social Science* 332 (November 1960):112-124.

Lenski, Gerhard. *The Religious Factor: A Sociologist's Inquiry*. Garden City, N.Y.: Doubleday, 1961. Religion and ethnic factors.

Le Mone, A. "Afro-American Churches," *Ecumenical Review* 20 (January 1968):44-52.

McLaughlin, Wayman B. "Symbolism and Mysticism in the Spirituals," *Phylon* 24 (Spring 1963):69-77.

Mays, Benjamin E., and Joseph W. Nicholson. *The Negro's Church*. New York: Institute of Social and Religious Research, 1933. A thorough and searching account not only of the Negro's church but of its role in the Negro community.

Moss, James A. "The Negro Church and Black Power," *Journal of Human Relations* 17 (First Quarter 1968):119-128.

Muelder, Walter. "Recruitment of Negroes for Theological Studies," *Review of Religious Research* 5 (Spring 1964):152-156.

National Committee of Black Churchmen. "Black Theology," *Christian Century* 86 (October 15, 1969):1310. A statement of the National Committee prepared by the (Sub-) Committee on Theological Prospectus. See also P. N. William's article, *ibid.*, pp. 1311-1312.

Niebuhr, H. Richard. *The Social Sources of Denominationalism*. New York: Holt, 1929. Contains material on early Negro churches in America.

Parker, Robert A. *The Incredible Messiah*. Boston: Little, Brown, 1937. Father Divine. *New Day* was the weekly publication of the movement.

Patterson, Bernardin J., O. S. B. "Reflections of a Negro Priest," *Catholic World* 200 (February 1965):269-276.

Pope, Liston. *The Kingdom Beyond Caste*. New York: Friendship Press, 1957. Contains material on religious affiliations of American Negroes.

Pope, Liston. "The Negro and Religion in America," *Review of Religious Research* 5 (Spring 1964):142-152.

Powdermaker, Hortense. *After Freedom: A Cultural Study in the Deep South*. New York: Viking, 1939. Contains interesting accounts of Negro revivals.

"Racist Church? Black Clergy Conference," *Commonweal* 88 (May 10, 1968):222.

Rasky, Frank. "Harlem's Religious Zealots," *Tomorrow* 9 (November 1949):11-17. Elder

Lightfoot Solomon Michaux, "Happy Am I Prophet," and Mother Rosa Artimus Horne, "Pray for Me Priestess."

Reid, Ira De Augustine. "Let Us Prey!" *Opportunity* 4 (September 1926):274-278. On Negro churches in the city.

Reimers, David M. "Negro Leadership in the Methodist Episcopal Church, 1900-1920: A Plea for Research in Negro Church History," *Wesleyan Quarterly Review* 3 (November 1966):243-251.

Reuther, Rosemary. "Black Theology and Black Church," *America* 120 (June 14, 1969):684-687. Poses the question: Is black theology a subterfuge for racial propaganda, or is it a sensitive Christian concern? Author is professor of theology at Howard University.

Root, Robert, and Shirley W. Hall. *Struggle for Decency: Religion and Race in Modern America.* New York: Friendship Press, 1965. Authors, one black, one white, view the race question from a Protestant perspective.

"Seminaries Urged: Enlist, Train Black Clergy," *Christian Advocate* 12 (September 5, 1968):22.

Shockley, Grant S. "Ultimatum and Hope: The Black Churchmen's Convocation, An Interpretation," *Christian Century* 86 (February 12, 1969):217-219. National Committee of Black Churchmen's commitment to the black revolution.

Spalding, D. "The Negro Catholic Congresses, 1889-1894," *Catholic Historical Review* 55 (October 1969):337-357.

Stange, Douglas C. "The Trials and Tribulations of One Jehu Jones, Jr., The First Ordained Negro Lutheran Clergyman in America," *Una Sancta* 24 (Pentacost 1967):52-55.

Sweet, William W. *The American Churches.* Nashville, Tenn.: Abingdon, 1948. Contains material on the religious affiliations of American Negroes.

Thurman, Howard. *Deep River: Reflections on the Religious Insight of Certain of the Negro Spirituals.* New York: Harper, 1955.

Tyms, J. D. *The Rise of Religious Education among Negro Baptists: A Historical Case Study.* New York: Exposition Press, 1966.

Washington, Joseph R., Jr. "Are American Negro Churches Christian?" *Theology Today* 20(April 1963):76-86.

Washington, Joseph R., Jr. *Black Religion: The Negro and Christianity in the United States.* Boston: Beacon, 1964. This book is a combination of empirical and historical data concerning the churches of the Negro in America and a tract for the times urging the "assimilation" of the Negro into the "mainstream" of the Christian "mission."

Washington, Joseph R., Jr. *The Politics of God: The Future of the Black Churches.* Boston: Beacon Press, 1967. Introduces concept of the Negro church as having potential for marshalling power to achieve political goals for its people. Author considers this a sequel to earlier volume.

Watts, Leon. "A Modern Black Looks at His Outdated Church," *Renewal* 7 (December 1967):3-6.

Weatherford, Willis Duke. *American Churches and the Negro: An Historical Study from Early Slave Days to the Present.* Boston: Christopher, 1957.

Williams, Ethel L. *Biographical Directory of Negro Ministers.* New York: Scarecrow, 1965.

Willoughby, William. "Storefront Churches: Social Stabilizers," *Christianity Today* 13 (May 9, 1969):44-45.

Winter, Gibson. *The Suburban Captivity of the Churches.* Garden City, N.Y.: Doubleday, 1961. Contains section on middle-class Negro churches.

Witheridge, David E. "Why Neglect the Negro Churches?" *Christian Century* 85 (October 16, 1968):1303-1304.

Woodson, Carter G. *The History of the Negro Church.* Washington: Associated Publishers, 1921. A most important general study. Continues to be basic to study of the Negro church.

For gospel singing *see also* Music.

Social Class

Antonovsky, Aaron. "Aspiration, Class and Racial-Ethnic Membership," *Journal of Negro Education* 36 (Fall 1967):385-393.

Antonovsky, Aaron. "A Study of Some Moderately Successful Negroes in New York City," *Phylon* 28 (Fall 1967):246-260.

Bloom, R., et al. "Race and Social Class as Separate Factors Related to Social Environment," *American Journal of Sociology* 70 (January 1965):471-476.

Blue, John J., Jr. "Patterns of Racial Stratification: A Categoric Typology," *Phylon* 20 (Winter 1959):364-371.

Cagle, Laurence T., and Jerome Beker. "Social Characteristics and Educational Aspirations of Northern, Lower-class, Predominantly Negro Parents Who Accepted and Declined a School Integration Opportunity," *Journal of Negro Education* 37 (Fall 1968): 406-417.

Cordtz, Dan. "The Negro Middle Class Is Right in the Middle," *Fortune* 74 (November 1966):174-180+.

Davidson, William. "Our Negro Aristocracy," *Saturday Evening Post* 235 (January 13, 1962):9-16.

Davis, Allison W., and John Dollard. *Children of Bondage.* Washington: American Council on Education, 1940. A detailed examination of the social classes into which Negroes are divided in the South within the Negro caste.

Dollard, John. *Caste and Class in a Southern Town.* New Haven: Yale University Press, 1937. 3d ed. Garden City, N.Y.: Doubleday, 1957. In the preface to the third edition, the author, while reiterating that "the caste device for placing Negroes must be abandoned," and acknowledging present dangers, maintains that, "If white men can solve the color problem, the United States is in an excellent position to do it."

Dykeman, Wilma, and James Stokely. "New Southerner: The Middle Class Negro," *New York Times Magazine,* August 9, 1959, p. 11 +.

Edwards, G. Franklin. "The Changing Status and Self-Image of Negroes in the District of Columbia," *Journal of Intergroup Relations* 3 (Winter 1962-1963).

Edwards, G. Franklin. *The Negro Professional Class.* Glencoe, Ill.: Free Press, 1959. A study of occupational mobility among Negroes in professions and its influence on development of a differentiated middle class. Emphasis on generational picture and occupational goals.

Fein, Rashi. "An Economic and Social Profile of the Negro American," *Daedalus* 94 (Fall 1965):815-846. A profile based on comparison between the Negro and other Americans, using data as to the positions of the two groups at different moments in time. Extremely useful concluding note on sources, particularly U.S. government publications.

Fisher, Sethard. "Essay Review—Negro Life and Social Process," *Social Problems* 13 (Winter 1966):343-353.

Frazier, E. Franklin. *Black Bourgeoisie.* 1957. Reissued with new preface by author, New York: Collier, 1962. A social and political tract in which the author castigates the Negro middle class.

Frazier, E. Franklin. "The Negro Middle Class and Desegregation," *Social Problems* 4 (April 1957):291-301.

Frazier, E. Franklin. "The Status of the Negro in the American Social Order," *Journal of Negro Education* 4 (July 1935):293-307.

Frumkin, Robert M. "Race, Occupation, and Social Class in New York," *Journal of Negro Education* 27 (Winter 1958):62-65.

Gaier, Eugene L. "Current Attitudes and Socialization Patterns of White and Negro Students Entering College," *Journal of Negro Education* 38 (Fall 1969):342-350.

Geisnar, Ludwig L., and Ursula C. Gerhart. "Social class, Ethnicity, and Family Functioning: Exploring Some Issues Raised by the Moynihan Report," *Journal of Marriage and the Family* 30 (August 1968):480-487. Reply by W. L. Parish, Jr. *ibid.*, 31 (August 1969):429-431. The effect of social status and ethnic patterns on family behavior. A study of White, Negro, and Puerto Rican families.

Glenn, Norval D. "Negro Population Concentration and Negro Status," *Journal of Negro Education* 36 (Fall 1967):353-361.

Glenn, Norval D. "Negro Prestige Criteria: A Case Study in the Bases of Prestige," *American Journal of Sociology* 68 (November 1963):645-657. Education the most important prestige criterion.

Glenn, Norval D. "Some Changes in the Relative Status of American Negroes," *Phylon* 24 (Summer 1963):109-122.

Hill, M. C., and T. D. Ackiss. "Social Classes: A Frame of Reference for the Study of Negro Society," *Social Forces* 22 (October 1943):92-98.

Himes, Joseph, and Margaret L. Hamelett. "The Assessment of Adjustment of Aged Negro Women in a Southern City," *Phylon* 23 (Summer 1962):139-147.

King, Charles E. "The Process of Social Stratification among an Urban Southern Minority Population," *Social Forces* 31 (May 1953):352-355. How urban Negroes in a North Carolina city (21 percent Negro) stratify themselves socially.

Kleiner, R. J., and H. Taylor. *Social Status and Aspirations in Philadelphia's Negro Population.* Philadelphia: Commission on Human Relations, 1962.

Lees, Hannah. "The Making of a Negro Middle Class," *Reporter* 31 (October 8, 1964):41-44.

Leggett, John C. *Class, Race, and Labor—Working-Class Consciousness in Detroit.* New York: Oxford University Press, 1968. Bibliography.

Levinson, Boris M. "A Comparative Study of Northern and Southern Negro Homeless Men," *Journal of Negro Education* 35 (Spring 1966):144-160.

Lewis, Hylan. "Innovations and Trends in the Contemporary Southern Community," *Journal of Social Issues.* 10 (January 1954):19-27. A class analysis of Southern Negroes emphasizing the changes brought about by increasing urbanization.

Lewis, Hylan. "Race, Class and Culture in the Sociopolitics of Social Welfare," in Roger R. Miller, ed., *Race, Research and Reason: Social Work Perspectives.* New York: National Association of Social Workers, 1969, pp. 35-44.

Liebow, Elliot. *Tally's Corner: A Study of Negro Streetcorner Men.* Boston: Little, Brown, 1967. Washington, D.C. based study. References appended.

Lincoln, C. Eric. "The Negro's Middle-Class Dream," *New York Times Magazine,* October 25, 1964, p. 35+.

Luchterhand, Elmer, and Leonard Weller. "Social Class and the Desegregation Movement: A Study of Parents' Decisions in a Negro Ghetto," *Social Problems* 13 (Summer 1965):83-88.New Rochelle, N.Y.

Meier, August, and David Lewis. "History of the Negro Upper Class in Atlanta, Georgia, 1890-1958," *Journal of Negro Education* 28 (Spring 1959):128-139.

Meier, August. "Negro Class Structure and Ideology in the Age of Booker T. Washington," *Phylon* 23 (Fall 1962):258-266.

Montague, Joel B., and Edgar G. Epps. "Attitudes Toward Social Mobility as Revealed by Samples of Negro and White Boys," *Pacific Sociological Review* 1 (Fall 1958):81-84.

Noel, Donald L. "A Theory of the Origin of Ethnic Stratification," *Social Problems* 16 (Fall 1968):157-172. As reflected in the emergence of slavery in seventeenth-century colonial America.

Orum, Anthony M., and Amy W. Orum. "The Class and Status Bases of Negro Student Protest," *Social Science Quarterly* 49 (December 1968):521-533.

Parker, Seymour, and Robert J. Kleiner. "Status Position, Mobility, and Ethnic Identification of the Negro," *Journal of Social Issues* 20 (April 1964):85-102.

Rainwater, Lee. "The Problem of Lower-Class Culture and Poverty-War Strategy," in Daniel P. Moynihan, ed., *On Understanding Poverty.* New York: Basic Books, 1969, pp. 229-259.

Record, Wilson. "Social Stratification and Intellectual Roles in the Negro Community," *British Journal of Sociology* 8 (September 1957):235-255. Bibliography.

Richard, Michael P. "The Ideology of Negro Physicians: A Test of Mobility and Status Crystallization Theory," *Social Problems* 17 (Summer 1969):20-29.

Rohrer, J. H., and M. S. Edmonson. *The Eighth Generation.* New York: Harper, 1960. This study is a follow-up twenty years later of the people described by Davis and Dollard in *Children of Bondage.*

Schulz, David A. *Coming Up Black: Patterns of Negro Socialization.* Englewood Cliffs, N.J.:
Prentice-Hall, 1969. Case studies of ten Negro families. Bibliography.
Simon, Julian L., and Rita James Simon. "Class, Status, and Savings of Negroes," *American
Sociologist* 3 (August 1968):218-219.
Solzbacher, Regina. "Occupational Prestige in a Negro Community," *American Catholic
Sociological Review* 22 (Fall 1961):250-257.
Warner, W. Lloyd. "Social Class and Color Caste in America," in *American Life: Dream and
Reality.* Rev. ed. Chicago: University of Chicago Press, 1962. Presents a general formula-
tion of the problem as well as results from widely contrasting field studies.
Wilson, Alan B. "Social Class and Educational Opportunity," in *Equal Educational Opportunity.* Cambridge, Mass.: Harvard University Press, 1969, pp. 80-87. Originally appeared
in the *Harvard Educational Review,* Winter 1968.
Young, Whitney M., Jr. "The Role of the Middle-Class Negro, " *Ebony* 18 (September
1963):66-71. The author gives his specifications for future Negro leaders. They must be
equipped "to understand and cope with the complex psychological, socio-economic factors in our society that create poverty, ignorance, prejudice, and deprivation. Social
scientists can best fulfill this role."

See also Employment—The Negro in the Professions.

Community Life, Leaders, and Organizations

"The Adam Clayton Powell Case: A Test for Christian Ethics; A Report to the Presbytery
of New York City. . . ," *Social Progress* 57 (March-April 1967):39-46.
Alex, Nicholas. *Black is Blue: A Study of the Negro Policeman.* New York: Appleton-Cen-
tury-Crofts, 1969.
"America's One Hundred Most Influential Negroes," *Ebony* 18 (September 1963):228-232.
Babchuk, Nicholas, and Ralph V. Thompson. "The Voluntary Associations of Negroes,"
American Sociological Review 27 (October 1962):647-655.
Bardolph, Richard. *The Negro Vanguard.* New York: Rinehart, 1959. An historical study of
leading Negroes, emphasizing their origins and careers. Organized chronologically, the
final section, 1936-1959, describes the acculturation process of large numbers of
achieving Negroes, their approach to white middle-class values, attitudes, and behavior.
Barth, Ernest A. T., and Baha Abu-Laban. "Power Structure and the Negro Sub-Com-
munity," *American Sociological Review* 24 (February 1959):69-76.
Beattie, Walter M., Jr. "The Aging Negro: Some Implications for Social Welfare Services,"
Phylon 21 (Summer 1960):131-135.
Bell, Daniel. *The End of Ideology.* Glencoe, Ill.: Free Press, 1959. An eminently readable as
well as illuminating work which, although only incidentally concerned with the Negro,
casts important light on the relation of the Negro community to the whole society.
Bennett, Lerone, Jr. "The Black Establishment," in *The Negro Mood.* Chicago: Johnson,
1964. The author considers the Negro elites, their social organization, their community
roles, and the relationships of this establishment to the world of white power.
Bittle, William E., and Gilbert Geis. "Racial Self-Fulfillment and the Rise of an All-Negro
Community in Oklahoma," *Phylon* 18 (Fall 1957):247-260.
"Black Priority," *Saturday Review* 52 (November 15, 1969):90. Formation of the National
Association of Black Students which broke from the National Students Association at
the latter's fall convocation.
Blalock, H. M., and Ann B. Blalock. "Situational Factors and Negro Leadership Activity in
a Medium-Sized Community," *Journal of Negro Education* 29 (Winter 1960):85-90.
Bowman, Lewis. "Racial Discrimination and Negro Leadership Problems: The Case of a
Northern Community," *Social Forces* 44 (December 1965):173-186.
Brazier, Arthur M. *Black Self-Determination: The Story of the Woodlawn Organization.*
Grand Rapids, Mich.: Eerdmans, 1969. Thesis that blacks must seize the initiative and
exercise their power to force the white establishment to yield a rightful place to the black
minority. A final chapter suggests a positive role for the white churches.

Breed, Warren. "Group Structure and Resistance to Desegregation in the Deep South," *Social Problems* 10 (Summer 1962):84-94.

Burgess, M. Elaine. *Negro Leadership in a Southern City.* Chapel Hill: University of North Carolina Press, 1962. Case histories of public issues and of Negro participation in them. In general, Negro civic leaders in the South tend to be in greater agreement on goals and to receive greater support from their followers than in the North.

Carter, Robert L. "The Black Lawyer," *Humanist* 29 (September-October 1969):12-16. Calls for leadership from the black bar and Howard University Law School in the areas of civil rights and social redress.

Claye, Clifton M. "Leadership Behavior Among Negro School Principals," *Journal of Negro Education* 31 (Fall 1962):521-526.

Coleman, J. S. "Community Disorganization," in R. K. Merton and R. A. Nisbet, eds., *Contemporary Social Problems.* New York: Harcourt, Brace, 1961.

Craig, William W. "Weekend and Vacation Recreational Behavior of a Negro Community in Louisiana—A Spatial Study," *Bulletin of the Southern University and A & M College* 55 (June 1969):63-75.

Cuban, Larry. "Strategy for Racial Peace: Negro Leadership in Cleveland, 1900-1919," *Phylon* 28 (Fall, 1967):299-311.

Diggs, C., Jr. "Negro Congressmen," *Negro History Bulletin* 27 (February 1964):114+.

Dove, Adrian. "Soul Story," *New York Times Magazine,* December 8, 1968, pp. 82-96.

DuBois, W. E. B. *Economic Cooperation among American Negroes.* Atlanta: Atlanta University Press, 1907. For historical retrospect. Economic cooperation among Negroes began with church groups after the Civil War.

DuBois, W. E. B. *The Philadelphia Negro: A Social Study.* 1899. New York: Schocken, 1967. Sociological study of a black community at end of nineteenth century. Introduction to 1967 issue by E. Digby Baltzell places book in the intellectual atmosphere of the period. Updated supplementary bibliography.

Edwards, G. Franklin. "Community and Class Realities: The Ordeal of Change," *Daedalus* 95 (Winter 1966):1-23.

Ellis, William W. *White Ethics and Black Power: The Emergence of the West Side Organization.* Chicago: Aldine, 1969. A study of a black independent community organization in Chicago; a case analysis of the achievement and use of power in a black community.

Gerber, Irwin. "The Effects of the Supreme Court's Desegregation Decision on the Group Cohesion of New York City's Negroes," *Journal of Social Psychology* 58 (December 1962):295-303.

Geschwender, J. A. "Social Structure and the Negro Revolt: An Examination of Some Hypotheses," *Social Forces* 43 (December 1964):248-256.

Gulley, William H. "Relative Effectiveness in Negro and White Voluntary Associations," *Phylon* 24 (Summer 1963):172-183.

Handlin, Oscar. *The Newcomers: Negroes and Puerto Ricans in a Changing Metropolis.* Cambridge, Mass.: Harvard University Press, 1959. See especially the chapter on the "Forms of Social Action" for discussion of problem of leadership and social action in Negro (and Puerto Rican) groups.

Hannerz, Ulf. "The Rhetoric of Soul: Identification in Negro Society," *Race* 9 (April 1968):543-566. The social and cultural ramifications of the "soul" concept, and its potential usefulness to a black nationalist political movement.

Harell, James A. "Negro Leadership in the Election Year 1936," *Journal of Southern History* 34 (November 1968):546-564.

Heer, David M. "The Attractiveness of the South to Whites and Nonwhites: An Ecological Study," *American Sociological Review* 28 (February 1963):101-108.

Henderson, E. B. "Washington Who's Who: Pigskin Club," *Negro History Bulletin* 26 (March 1963):190-195. On Negro clubs.

Himes, Joseph. "Changing Social Roles in the New South," *Southwestern Social Science Quarterly* 37 (December 1956):234-242. Because of growing Negro militancy.

Himes, Joseph. "Negro Teen-Age Culture," *Annals of the American Academy of Political and Social Science* 338 (November 1961):91-101.

Hughes, Langston. *Fight for Freedom: The Story of the NAACP.* New York: Norton, 1962.

Hunter, Floyd. *Community Power Structure: A Study of Decision Makers.* Chapel Hill: University of North Carolina Press, 1953. The "Regional City" which the author studies is Atlanta, Ga.; his conclusion, that "none of the leaders in the Negro community may operate in the same echelons of power as the top leaders in the total community."

Jackman, Norman, and Jack Dodson. "Negro Youth and Direct Action," *Phylon* 28 (Spring 1967):5-15. Organization, recruitment, and leadership of CORE.

Jarmon, Charles. "The Sploe House: A Drinking Place of Lower Socio-Economic Status Negroes in a Southern City," *Bulletin of the Southern University and A & M College* 55 (June 1969):53-61.References appended.

Johnson, Charles S. "A Southern Negro's View of the South," *Journal of Negro Education* 26 (Winter 1957):4-9.

Kellogg, Charles Flint. *NAACP: A History of the National Association for the Advancement of Colored People.* Vol. I: *1909-1920.* Baltimore: Johns Hopkins Press, 1967. The first of a projected two-volume series. Includes bibliographical notes.

Killian, Lewis M., and Charles Grigg. "Negro Perceptions of Organizational Effectiveness," *Social Problems* 11 (Spring 1964):380-388. Organizations Negroes prefer to look to for help are, according to Florida sample: NAACP, Democratic Party, federal government, Urban League, Negro church, labor unions, in that order.

Killian, Lewis M., and Charles U. Smith. "Negro Protest Leaders in a Southern Community," *Social Forces* 38 (March 1960):253-257.

Killian, Lewis M., and Charles Grigg. *Racial Crisis in America: Leadership in Conflict.* Englewood, N.J.: Prentice-Hall, 1964. With Southern cities as their setting, the authors examine the attitudes of both white and Negro leaders, the operation and effectiveness of community biracial committees, and the significance of the Negro repudiation of accommodation in favor of militant protest under new, young leaders.

Kirkhart, Robert O. "Minority Group Identification and Group Leadership," *Journal of Social Psychology* 59 (February 1963):111-117.

Larkins, John R. *Patterns of Leadership Among Negroes in North Carolina.* Raleigh, N.C.: Irving-Stone, 1959.

Levi, Julian H. "The Greatest Domestic Challenge," *Chicago Today* 5 (Summer 1968):2-9. Notes on the Woodlawn communities.

Lewis, Hylan. *Blackways of Kent.* Chapel Hill: University of North Carolina Press, 1955. A distinguished study of Negroes in a small South Carolina mill town. The author has done some of the most creative work in the area of racial culture patterns. Rejecting the idea that there is such a thing as a distinctively "Negro culture," he finds class status and economic status the more powerful determinants.

Lewis Hylan, and Mozell Hill. "Desegregation, Integration, and the Negro Community," *Annals of the American Academy of Political and Social Science* 304 (March 1956):116-123.

Lohman, Joseph D., and D. C. Reitzes. "Deliberately Organized Groups and Racial Behavior," *American Sociological Review* 19 (June 1954):342-344.

McPherson, James Alan. "And What Does That Mean," *Atlantic* 223 (May 1969):74-84; *ibid.,* (June 1969):92-100. A two-part study of South Side Chicago's Blackstone Rangers, their organization, activities, and relation to the black community.

McWorter, Gerald A., and Robert L. Crain. "Subcommunity Gladiatorial Competition: Civil Rights Leadership as a Competitive Process," *Social Forces* 46 (September 1967):8-21. A study of the degree and character of Negro leadership competition in 14 urban areas.

Miller, Kenneth H. "Community Organizations in the Ghetto," in Richard S. Rosenbloom and Robin Marris, eds., *Social Innovation in the City: New Enterprises for Community Development.* Cambridge, Mass.: Harvard University Press, 1969, pp. 97-108. Examines and contrasts two model community organizations: The East Central Citizens Organization in Columbia, Ohio and the West Side Organization in Chicago, Illinois.

"The Negro in Atlanta: An Analysis of the Facts, Forces, and Frustrations That Shape the Lives and Future of Atlanta's Negro Community," *Atlanta Magazine* 6 (June 1966):25-30.

O Reilly, Charles T., Willard E. Downing, and Steven I. Pflanczer. *The People of the Inner*

Core-North: A Study of Milwaukee's Negro Community. New York: LePlay Research, 1965.

Ottenburg, Simon. "Leadership and Change in a Coastal Georgia Negro Community," *Phylon* 20 (Spring 1962):7–18.

Pfautz, Harold W. "The New 'New Negro': Emerging American," *Phylon* 24 (Winter 1963):360–368.

Pfautz, Harold W. "The Power Structure of the Negro Sub-Community: A Case Study and a Comparative View," *Phylon* 23 (Summer 1962):156–166.

Poinsett, Alex. "Negro Officer," *Ebony* 23 (August 1968):136–141.

Record, Wilson. "American Racial Ideologies and Organizations in Transition," *Phylon* 26 (Winter 1965):315–329. The structure, influence, and flexibility of the NAACP.

Roemele, Victoria, and Henry Greenebaum. "Helping the Helpers," *International Journal of Psychotherapy* 17 (July 1967):343–355. Adolescent Negroes employed as teachers in a church-sponsored educational program for young disadvantaged children.

Rose, Arnold M. "New and Emerging Negro Problems," *Journal of Intergroup Relations* 1 (Spring 1960):71–75. The author considers that gaining acceptance, training for higher types of employment, and acculturation are the newer problems for Negroes, especially in the North.

Rose, Arnold M. "Voluntary Associations Under Conditions of Competition and Conflict," *Social Forces* 34 (December 1955):159–163.

Rudwick, Elliott M. *The Unequal Badge: Negro Policemen in the South.* Atlanta: Southern Regional Council, 1962.

Safa, Helen Icken. *An Analysis of Upward Mobility in Low-Income Families: A Comparison of Family and Community Life among Negro and Puerto Rican Poor.* Syracuse, N.Y.: Syracuse University, 1967.

Safa, Helen Icken. "The Case for Negro Separatism: The Crisis of Identity in the Black Community," *Urban Affairs Quarterly* 4 (September 1968):45–63.

St. James, Warren D. *The National Association for the Advancement of Colored People: A Case Study in Pressure Groups.* New York: Exposition Press, 1958. Most useful portions are the addenda: NAACP constitutions, bibliography, and summary of cases.

Smuts, Robert W. "The Negro Community and the Development of Negro Potential," *Journal of Negro Education* 26 (Fall 1957):456–465. The chief responsibility of the Negro community is to broaden the horizon of Negro youth by fighting for better education and thus stimulating their motivation.

Stinchcombe, Jean L. "The Civic and Political Role of Negro Leaders," in *Reform and Reaction: City Politics in Toledo.* Belmont, Calif.: Wadsworth, 1968, pp. 177–204.

Strickland, Arvarh E. *History of the Chicago Urban League.* Urbana: University of Illinois Press, 1966. From its establishment in 1917 to the early 1960's. Bibliography.

Suttles, Gerald. *The Social Order of the Slums: Ethnicity and Territory in the Inner City.* Chicago: University of Chicago Press, 1968. References to Negro churches, culture, and intergroup relations. Special attention is called to chapter 7, entitled, "The Projects and the Negroes."

Thompson, Daniel C. *The Negro Leadership Class.* Englewood Cliffs, N.J.: Prentice-Hall, 1963. With his focus on New Orleans from 1940 to 1960, the author traces the origins of Negro leaders, the influences that have formed the leadership class, and the rapidly changing patterns of that leadership, and furnishes detailed and candid data on the problems of the Negro leader both within and outside his own society.

Walker, Jack L. "The Functions of Disunity: Negro Leadership in a Southern City," *Journal of Negro Education* 32 (Summer 1963):227–236.

Walter, Ingo, and John F. Kramer. "Political Autonomy and Economic Dependence in an All-Negro Municipality," *American Journal of Economics* 28 (July 1969):225–248.

Warner, W. Lloyd, and Leo Srole. *The Social Systems of American Ethnic Groups.* New Haven: Yale University Press, 1946.

Weaver, Robert C. "The NAACP Today," *Journal of Negro Education* 29 (Fall 1960):421–425.

Williams, Avon. "Negro Subculture, The White Man's Problem," *New South* 16 (October 1961):7–9.

Williams, Preston N. "The Black Experience and Black Religion," *Theology Today* 26 (October 1969):246–261.

Wilson, James Q. *Negro Politics: The Search for Leadership.* Glencoe, Ill.: Free Press, 1960. A valuable study of contemporary Negro politics in Northern cities, this volume is an examination of the leadership level of Negro community life, with the main emphasis on Chicago.

Wilson, James Q. "The Strategy of Protest: Problems of Negro Civic Action," *Journal of Conflict Resolution* 5 (September 1961):291–303. The author examines 17 issues involving Negroes in Chicago between 1958 and 1960.

Woodson, Carter G. *The Negro Professional Man and the Community.* Washington: Association for the Study of Negro Life and History, 1934. Most comprehensive study in this field up to date of publication, and still very useful.

See also Biography and Letters.

Language and Idiom

Abrahams, Roger D. *Deep Down in the Jungle. . . :Negro Narrative Folklore from the Streets of Philadelphia.* Hatboro, Penna.: Folklore Associates, 1964. An expansion of his study of "Playing the Dozens."

Abrahams, Roger D. "'Playing the Dozens,'" *Journal of American Folklore* 75 (July–September 1962):209–220. Description and analysis of a Negro verbal insult game.

Ayoub, Millicent R., and Stephen A. Barnett. "Ritualized Verbal Insult in White High School Culture," *Journal of American Folklore* 78 (October–December 1965):337–344. Function of Negro verbal game, playing the dozens, as played by black and white students. Reply and rejoinder: *ibid.,* 79 (April–June 1966):374–377; 80 (January–March 1967):89–90.

Bailey, Beryl Loftman. "Toward a New Perspective in Negro English Dialectology," *American Speech* 40 (October 1965):171–177.

Baratz, Joan C. "A Bi-Dialectal Task for Determining Language Proficiency in Economically Disadvantaged Negro Children," *Child Development* 40 (September 1969):889–901.

Barth, Ernest A. T. "The Language Behavior of Negroes and Whites," *Pacific Sociological Review* 4 (Fall 1961):69–72. Language behavior reinforces social distance.

Berdie, R. F. B. "Playing the Dozens," *Journal of Abnormal and Social Psychology* 42 (January 1947):120–121. Examination of an aggressive type of behavior, especially characteristic of Negroes, which follows a formalized pattern of exchange of insults.

Brown, Claude. "Language of Soul," *Esquire* 69 (April 1968):88 + .

Bruce, Beverlee. "The Social and Psychological Implications of Language Changing," *American Behavioral Scientist* 12 (March–April 1969):34–37. Implications of language in racial identification.

Butler, Melvin Arthur. "African Linguistic Remnants in the Speech of Black Louisianians," *Bulletin of the Southern University and A & M College* 55 (June 1969):45–52.

DeCoy, Robert H. *The Nigger Bible.* Los Angeles: Holloway House, 1967.

Dillard, J. L. "Negro Children's Dialect in the Inner City," *Florida Foreign Language Reporter* 5, no. 4 (1967):7–10.

Dillard, J. L. "Non-Standard Negro Dialects—Convergence or Divergence?" *Florida Foreign Language Reporter* 6, no. 2 (1968):9–12.

Fasold, Ralph W. "Some Grammatical Features of Negro Dialect." Washington: Center for Applied Linguistics, 1969. Mimeographed.

Fasold, Ralph W. "Tense and the Form *be* in Black English," *Language* 45 (December 1969):763–776.

Gold, Robert S. *A Jazz Lexicon.* New York: Knopf, 1964. Dictionary of jazz vernacular which evolved from Negro language and jazz slang. Bibliography.

Hannerz, Ulf. "What Negroes Mean By 'Soul,'" *Trans-action* 5 (July–August 1968):57–58 + .

As an idiom of the urban ghetto: the essence of Negroness, an attempt to establish a self-image.

Kochman, Thomas. "Language Behavior in the Negro Ghetto." Chicago: Northeastern Illinois State College, Center for Inner City Studies, 1968. Mimeographed.

Kochman, Thomas. "'Rapping' in the Black Ghetto," *Trans-action* 6 (February 1969):26–34. Verbal idiom in the ghetto.

Labov, William, et al. *A Study of the Non-Standard English of Negro and Puerto Rican Speakers in New York City.* 2 vols. Washington: U.S. Office of Education, 1968. (Cooperative Research Project no. 3288). Volume one is an analysis of phonology and grammar; volume two is a detailed study of the use of the language in the communities.

Ledvinka, James David. *Race of Employment Interviewer and the Language Elaboration of Black Job-Seekers.* Ann Arbor, Mich.: University Microfilms, 1969.

Loman, Bengt. *Conversations in a Negro American Dialect.* Washington: Center for Applied Linguistics, 1967.

Major, Clarence, ed. *A Short Dictionary of Afro-American Idioms.* New York: International, 1970.

Middleton, Russell, and John Moland. "Humor in Negro and White Sub-Cultures: A Study of Jokes among University Students," *American Sociological Review* 24 (February 1959):61–69.

Millstein, Gilbert. "A Negro Says It With Jokes," *New York Times Magazine,* April 30, 1961, p. 34+.

Olim, Ellis G., Robert D. Hess, and Virginia C. Shipman. "The Role of Mothers' Language Styles in Mediating Their Preschool Children's Cognitive Development," *School Review* 75 (Winter 1967):414–424. Research based on 163 urban Negro mothers from variant social status groups.

Pederson, Lee A. "Non-Standard Negro Speech in Chicago," in William A. Stewart, ed., *Nonstandard Speech and the Teaching of English.* Washington: Center for Applied Linguistics, 1964, pp. 16–23.

Stewart, William A. "Continuity and Change in American Negro Dialects," *Florida Foreign Language Reporter* 6, no. 1 (1968):3–4+.

Stewart, William A. "Sociolinguistic Factors in the History of American Negro Dialects," *Florida Foreign Language Reporter* 5, no. 2 (1967):11+.

Stewart, William A. "Urban Negro Speech: Sociolinguistic Factors Affecting English Teaching," in Roger W. Shury, ed., *Social Dialects and Language Learning.* Champaign, Ill.: National Council of Teachers of English, 1965, pp. 10–19.

Torrey, Jane W. "Illiteracy in the Ghetto," *Harvard Educational Review* 40 (May 1970):253–259. And dialectal differences.

Wolfram, Walter A. *A Sociolinguistic Description of Detroit Negro Speech.* Washington: Center for Applied Linguistics, 1969.

Yancey, William, and Bonne Hammond. "Glossary of Negro Jive." St. Louis: Washington University, Social Science Institute, 1965. Mimeographed.

Intermarriage and Interracial Adoption

Annella, Sister M. "Some Aspects of Interracial Marriage in Washington, D.C.," *Journal of Negro Education* 25 (Fall 1956):380–391.

Avins, Alfred. "Anti-Miscegenation Laws and the Fourteenth Amendment: The Original Intent," *Virginia Law Review* 52 (October 1966):1224–1255. Opines that the amendment does not forbid state laws from preventing interracial marriage.

Barron, Milton L. *People Who Intermarry.* Syracuse, N.Y.: Syracuse University Press, 1948.

Barron, Milton L. "Research on Intermarriage: A Survey of Accomplishments and Prospects," *American Journal of Sociology* 57 (November 1951):249–255.

Bernard, Jessie. "Note on Educational Homogamy in Negro-White and White-Negro Marriages, 1960," *Journal of Marriage and the Family* 28 (August 1966):274–276.

Billingsley, Andrew, and Jean Giovannoni. "Research Perspectives on Interracial Adoptions," in Roger R. Miller, ed., *Race, Research, and Reason: Social Work Perspectives.* New York: National Association of Social Workers, 1967, pp. 55-77.

Broderick, C. B. "Social Heterosexual Development Among Urban Negroes and Whites," *Journal of Marriage and the Family* 27 (May 1965):200-203.

Burma, John H. "Interethnic Marriage in Los Angeles, 1948-1959," *Social Forces* 42 (December 1963):156-165. Study of marriage license records of Los Angeles County: Negro-White and Filipino-White most common. Rates at the end of the period triple those at beginning.

Burma, John H. "Research Note on the Measurement of Interracial Marriage," *American Journal of Sociology* 57 (May 1952):587-589. In California after annulment of anti-miscegenation law.

Cahnman, Werner J. "Interracial Jewish Children," *Reconstructionist* 33 (June 9, 1967):7-12.

Carse, James P. "Interracial Marriage: A Christian View," *Christian Century* 84 (June 14, 1967):779-782. Concludes from a survey of biblical texts and writings of theologians that the church should take a stand to eradicate racial separateness. Reply, *ibid.,* 84 (July 5, 1967):859-860.

Clark, Henry. "Thinking About the Unthinkable in Race Relations," *Social Action* 30 (May 1964):17-22.

"The Constitutionality of Miscegenation Statutes," *Howard Law Journal* 1 (January 1955):87-100.

Cummins, J. D., and J. L. Kane, Jr. "Miscegenation, the Constitution, and Science," *Dicta* 38 (February 1961):24.

Doherty, J. F. *Moral Problems of Interracial Marriage.* Washington: Catholic University of America Press, 1949.

Drinan, Robert F. "The Loving Decision and the Freedom to Marry," *Ohio State Law Journal* 29 (Spring 1968):358-398. Analysis of the U.S. Supreme Court decision affirming that a Virginia anti-miscegenation statute violated constitutional rights.

Ehrenzweig, A. A. "Miscegenation in the Conflict of Laws," *Cornell Law Quarterly* 45 (Summer 1960):659.

Feinstein, Phylis. "Report on Interracial Adoption," *Parents Magazine* 43 (December 1968):48-49+.

Fricke, Harriet. "Interracial Adoption: The Little Revolution," *Social Work* 10 (July 1965):92-97.

Furlong, William Barry. "Interracial Marriage Is a Sometime Thing," *New York Times Magazine,* June 9, 1968, pp. 44-45+.

Golden, Joseph. "Characteristics of the Negro-White Intermarried in Philadelphia," *American Sociological Review* 18 (April 1953):177-183.

Golden, Joseph. "Facilitating Factors in Negro-White Intermarriage," *Phylon* 20 (Fall 1959):273-284.

Golden, Joseph. "Patterns of Negro-White Intermarriage," *American Sociological Review* 19 (April 1954):144-147.

Golden, Joseph. "Social Control of Negro-White Intermarriage," *Social Forces* 36 (March 1958):267-269.

Gordon, Albert I. *Intermarriage: Interfaith, Interracial, Interethnic.* Boston: Beacon, 1964. A survey dealing with prospects and problems of intermarriage in America.

Grossman, Susan J. "A Child of a Different Color: Race as a Factor in Adoption and Custody Proceedings," *Buffalo Law Review* 17 (Fall 1967):303-347.

Harte, Thomas J. "Trends in Mate Selection in a Tri-Racial Isolate," *Social Forces* 37 (March 1959):215-221.

Heer, David M. "Negro-white Marriage in the United States," *Journal of Marriage and the Family* 28 (August 1966):262-273.

"Intermarriage and the Race Problem," *U.S. News and World Report* 55 (November 18, 1963):84-93.

Larsson, Clotye M., ed. *Marriage across the Color Line.* Chicago: Johnson, 1965.

Lewis, Anthony. "Race, Sex and the Supreme Court," *New York Times Magazine,* November 22, 1964, p. 30 +. On sex and the Southern caste system as exemplified in the case, *McLaughlin v. Florida.*

"Marriage Across Racial Lines." Statement of the Council for Christian Social Action, United Church of Christ. New York, 1960. Mimeographed.

Mitchell, Marion M. "Transracial Adoptions: Philosophy and Practice," *Child Welfare* 48 (December 1969):613-619.

Nordlie, Esther B., and Sheldon C. Reed. "Follow-up Adoption Counseling for Children of Possible Racial Admixture," *Child Welfare* 41 (September 1962).

Phillips, Cyrus E. "Miscegenation: The Courts and the Constitution," *William and Mary Law Review* 8 (Fall 1966):133-142. Constitutional justification of miscegenation statutes in state courts; the position of the federal judiciary.

Pope William F. "Interracial Adoption," *South Carolina Law Quarterly* 9 (Summer 1957):630-632. Review of legal decisions.

"Racial Intermarriage—A Constitutional Problem," *Western Reserve Law Review* 11 (December 1959):93.

"Racial Intermarriage—A Symposium," *Social Progress* 4 (February 1960):3-35. Presented by the United Presbyterian Church.

Riley, L. H. "Miscegenation Statutes: A Re-evaluation of their Constitutionality in Light of Changing Social and Political Conditions," *Southern California Law Review* 32 (Fall 1958):28.

Schuhmann, George. "Miscegenation: An Example of Judicial Recidivism," *Journal of Family Law* 69 (Spring 1968):69-78. Review of recent legal changes in anti-miscegenation laws.

Seidelson, David E. "Miscegenation Statutes and the Supreme Court: A Brief Prediction of What the Court Will Do and Why," *Catholic University Law Review* 15 (January 1966):156-170.

Shaffer, Helen B. "Mixed Marriage," *Editorial Research Reports* 1 (May 24, 1961):381-398.

Shepherd, Elizabeth. "Adopting Negro Children: White Families Find It Can Be Done," *New Republic* 150 (June 20, 1964):10-12.

Teicher, Joseph D. "Some Observations on Identity Problems in Children of Negro-White Marriages," *Journal of Nervous and Mental Disease* 146 (March 1968):249-256.

Wadlington, Walter. "The Loving Case: Virginia's Anti-Miscegenation Statute in Historical Perspective," *Virgina Law Review* 52 (October 1966):1189-1223.

Walton, Edmund L., Jr. "Present Status of Miscegenation Statutes," *William and Mary Law Review* 4 (January 1963):28-35.

Weinberger, Andrew D. "A Reappraisal of the Constitutionality of Miscegenation Statutes," *Cornell Law Quarterly* 42 (Winter 1957):208-222.

Wilharm, John H., Jr. "Racial Intermarriage—A Constitutional Problem," *Western Reserve Law Review* 11 (December 1959):93 +.

Zabel, William D. "Interracial Marriage and the Law," *Atlantic* 216 (October 1965):75-79.

See also Family and Child Rearing.

Press, Radio, and TV

Bain, George W. "How Negro Editors Viewed the New Deal," *Journalism Quarterly* 44 (Autumn 1967):552-554. Drawn from a content analysis of four Negro newspapers, 1933-1938. Concludes that the Negro press reacted as an institution seeking evolutionary improvement for its people through New Deal programs.

Bayton, J. A., and E. Bell. "An Exploratory Study of the Role of the Negro Press," *Journal of Negro Education* 20 (Winter 1951):8-15.

Beard, Richard L., and Cyril E. Zoerner. "Associated Negro Press: Its Founding, Ascendancy and Demise," *Journalism Quarterly* 46 (Spring 1969):47-52. The period, 1917-1966.

Bennett, Lerone, Jr. "Founder of the Negro Press," *Ebony* 19 (July 1964):96-98+.

Berkman, Dave. "The Segregated Medium: Why Should Negro-Oriented Radio Continue to Exist in the 1960s?" *Columbia Journalism Review* 5 (Fall 1966):29-32.

Boyd, D. E. "Black Radio: A Direct and Personal Invitation," *Media/Scope* 13 (August 1969):14-15.

Boyenton, William H. "The Negro Turns to Advertising," *Journalism Quarterly* 42 (Spring 1965):227-235. Some reasons advanced for slow progress of integration in this area.

Brooks, Maxwell R. *The Negro Press Re-examined: Political Content of Leading Negro Newspapers.* Boston: Christopher, 1959.

Brown, Warren, comp. *Check List of Negro Newspapers in the United States, 1827-1946.* Jefferson City, Mo.: School of Journalism, Lincoln University, 1946.

Buckley, Richard Dale. "Negro Periodicals: Historical Notes and Suggestions for Use," *Social Education* 33 (April 1969):426-428. Includes a representative list (by state) of Negro newspapers. Bibliography.

Christopher, M. "4 As and ANA Study Greater Use of Minority Groups in TV Commercials, " *Advertising Age* 39 (July 1, 1968):1+.

Fain, M. A. "Straight With No Cop-Outs," *Social Problems* 16 (Spring 1969):525-527. Negroes in American films.

Fisher, Paul L., and Ralph L. Lowenstein, eds. *Race and the News Media.* New York:Praeger, 1967. Papers and discussions of the 1965 annual conference of the Freedom of Information Center of the University of Missouri. The role of the Negro press in the civil rights movement is noteworthy.

Hirsch, Paul M. "An Analysis of *Ebony*: The Magazine and Its Readers," *Journalism Quarterly* 45 (Summer 1968):261-270.

Kassarjian, Harold H. "Negro and American Advertising, 1946-1965," *Journal of Marketing Research* 6 (February 1969):29-39. Survey of selected mass media titles to determine extent and frequency of use of Negro models.

Lyle, Jack, ed. *The Black American and the Press.* Los Angeles: Ward Ritchie, 1968. Post-Watts symposium in Los Angeles in 1967. The function and social responsibilites of the white news media vis-a-vis black America.

McCombs, Maxwell E. "Negro Use of Television and Newspapers for Political Information, 1952-1964," *Journal of Broadcasting* 12 (Summer 1968):261-266.

Malec, Michael A. "Some Observations on the Content of *Crisis*: 1932-1962," *Phylon* 28 (Summer 1967):161-167. A content analysis of the NAACP's journal, *Crisis,* as reflecting shifting moods and tensions.

"Negro Admen Point Finger at G A P," *Media/Scope* 12 (July 1968):56-59.

"Negro Press Marks 135th Anniversary," *Editor and Publisher* 95 (March 17, 1962):13.

Ottley, Roi. *The Lonely Warrior: The Life and Times of Robert S. Abbott.* Chicago: Regnery, 1955. Vivid picture of a Negro newspaperman, founder of the Chicago *Defender,* with some discussion of the role of the Negro press in strengthening Negro racial consciousness.

"Radio Could Reach the Rural South, Negro Owner Feels," *Broadcasting* 75 (October 28, 1968):97. A. R. Carter, President of Kansas City station.

Rinder, Irwin D. "A Sociological Look into the Negro Pictorial," *Phylon* 20 (Summer 1959):169-177.

Rosen, Bernard C. "Attitude Changes within the Negro Press toward Segregation and Discrimination," *Journal of Social Psychology* 62 (February 1964):77-84.

Roshco, Bernard. "The Negro Press Views the Riots," *Interplay* 1 (February 1968):9-11.

Sargeant, Leslie, Wiley Carr, and Elizabeth McDonald. "Significant Coverage of Integration by Minority Group Magazines," *Journal of Human Relations* 13 (Fourth Quarter 1965):484-491.

Schmidt, David C., and Ivan L. Preston. "How NAACP Leaders View Integrated Advertising," *Journal of Advertising Research* 9 (September 1969):13-16.

Spaulding, Norman W. "Bridging the Color Gap: Effective Communication with the Black Community Calls for an Understanding of Its Media and Leading Organizations," *Public Relations Journal* 25 (April 1969):8-11.

Thornbrough, Emma Lou. "American Negro Newspapers, 1880–1914," *Business Historical Review* 40 (First Quarter 1966):467–490. The organizational and financial aspects.
Waters, Enoc P. "The Negro Press: A Call for Change," *Editor and Publisher* 95 (May 12, 1962):67–68.

Individual Characteristics

Personality

Allport, Gordon W. *Pattern and Growth in Personality.* New York: Holt, 1961.
Anastasi, Anne. "Psychological Research and Educational Desegregation," *Thought* 35 (Fall 1960):421–429.
Ausubel, David P., and Pearl Ausubel. "Ego Development among Segregated Negro Children," in A. Harry Passow, ed., *Education in Depressed Areas.* New York: Bureau of Publications, Columbia University, 1963, pp. 109–141. Bibliography.
Axline, Virginia M. "Play Therapy and Race Conflict in Young Children," *Journal of Abnormal and Social Psychology* 18 (July 1948):300–310.
Axline, Virginia M. "Play Therapy Procedures and Results," *American Journal of Orthopsychiatry* 25 (July 1955):618–626.
Ball, J. C. "Comparison of MMPI Profile Differences among Negro-White Adolescents," *Journal of Clinical Psychology* 16 (July 1960):304–307.
Bandura, A., and R. H. Walters. *Adolescent Aggression.* New York: Ronald, 1959.
Baratz, Stephen S. "Effect of Race of Experimenter, Instructions, and Comparison Population upon Level of Reported Anxiety in Negro Subjects," *Journal of Personality and Social Psychology* 7 (October 1967):194–196.
Bayton, James A., and Tressie W. Muldrow. "Interacting Variables in the Perception of Racial Personality Traits," *Journal of Experimental Research in Personality* 3 (June 1968):39–44.
Beck, Samuel J., et al. "Segregation-Integration: Some Psychological Realities," *American Journal of Orthopsychiatry* 28 (January 1958):12–35. In order to remedy the damages of segregation, "the indicated pattern of therapeutic intervention is prompt and effective action for integration."
Beisser, Arnold R., and Hiawatha Harris. "Psychological Aspects of the Civil Rights Movement and the Negro Professional Man," *American Journal of Psychiatry* 123 (December 1966):733–737.
Bixenstine, V. Edwin, and Ralph L. Buterbaugh. "Integrative Behavior in Adolescent Boys as a Function of Delinquency and Race," *Journal of Consulting Psychology* 31 (October 1967):471–476.
Blalock, Hubert M. *Toward a Theory of Minority-Group Relations.* New York: Wiley, 1967.
Bloom, Robert, and John R. Barry. "Determinants of Work Attitudes among Negroes," *Journal of Applied Psychology* 51 (June 1967):291–294.
Brewster, Edward E., and Martelle D. Trigg. "Moral Values Among Negro College Students: A Study of Cultural and Racial Determinants," *Phylon* 23 (Fall 1962):286–293.
Brody, Eugene B. "Color and Identity Conflict in Young Boys, II," *Archives of General Psychiatry* 10 (April 1964):354–360.
Bronfenbrenner, Urie. "The Psychological Costs of Quality and Equality in Education," in Conference on Quality and Equality in Education. *Proceedings,* edited by Melvin M. Tumin and Marvin Bressler. Princeton, N.J.: Princeton University Press, 1966. The sources of psychological inadequacy; countermeasures and consequences in the behavior of the Negro child. Bibliography. Also appears in *Child Development* 38 (December 1967):909–925.
Broom, Leonard, and Norval D. Glenn. "Negro-White Differences in Reported Attitudes and Behavior," *Sociology and Social Research* 50 (January 1966):187–200.
Burton, R. V., and J. W. M. Whiting. "The Absent Father and Cross-Sex Identity," *Merrill-Palmer Quarterly* 7 (April 1961):85–95.

Butcher, James, Brenda Ball, and Eva Ray. "Effects of Socio-Economic Level on MMPI Differences in Negro-White College Students," *Journal of Counseling Psychology* 11 (Spring 1964):83-87.

Butts, Hugh F. "Skin Color Perception and Self-Esteem," *Journal of Negro Education* 32 (Spring 1963):122-128.

Cameron, Howard. "A Review of Research and an Investigation of Emotional Dependency among Negro Youth," *Journal of Negro Education* 36 (Spring 1967):111-120. Bibliography.

Carpenter, Thomas R., and Thomas V. Busse. "Development of Self Concept in Negro and White Welfare Children," *Child Development* 40 (September 1969):935-939.

Chein, Isidor. "What Are the Psychological Effects of Segregation Under Conditions of Equal Facilities?" *International Journal of Opinion and Attitude Research* 3 (1949):229. Cited in 1954 decision *Brown v. Board of Education.*

Clark, Edward T., and Kenneth F. Misa. "Peers' Perceptions of Negro and White Occupational Preferences," *Personnel and Guidance Journal* 46 (November 1967):288-291.

Clark, Kenneth B. "Color, Class, Personality and Juvenile Delinquency," *Journal of Negro Education* 28 (Summer 1959):240-251.

Clark, Kenneth B. "Effect of Prejudice and Discrimination on Personality Development." Midcentury White House Conference on Children and Youth, 1950. Cited in 1954 decision *Brown v. Board of Education.*

Clark, Kenneth B. *Prejudice and Your Child.* 1955. 2d ed. enl. Boston: Beacon, 1963.

Clark, Kenneth B., and Mamie P. Clark. "Racial Identification and Preference in Negro Children," in Eleanor Maccoby, et al., eds., *Readings in Social Psychology.* New York: Holt, 1958.

Clark, Kenneth B., and J. Barker. "The Zoot Effect in Personality: A Race Riot Participant," *Journal of Abnormal and Social Psychology* 40 (April 1945):143-148.

Clinard, Marshall B., and Donald L. Noel. "Role Behavior of Students from Negro Colleges in a Non-Segregated University Situation," *Journal of Negro Education* 27 (Spring 1958):182-188.

Coles, Robert. *Children of Crisis: A Study of Courage and Fear.* Boston: Little, Brown, 1967. A psychiatrist discusses effects of desegregation on both Negro and White children.

Conyers, James E., and William J. Farmer. *Black Youth in a Southern Metropolis.* Atlanta: Southern Regional Council, 1968. Socioeconomic characteristics and attitudes of 688 Atlanta Negro high school students; based on questionnaire.

Conyers, James E., and T. H. Kennedy. "Negro Passing: To Pass or Not To Pass," *Phylon* 24 (Fall 1963):215-223.

Cook, Stuart W. "Desegregation: A Psychological Analysis," *American Psychologist* 12 (January 1957):1-13.

Dai, Bingham. "Problems of Personality Development among Negro Children," in Clyde Kluckhohn and Harry A. Murray, eds., *Personality in Nature, Society and Culture.* New York: Knopf, 1953.

Datta, Lois-Ellin, Earl Schaefer, and Malcolm Davis. "Sex and Scholastic Aptitude as Variables in Teacher Ratings of the Adjustment and Classroom Behavior of Negro and Other Seventh-Grade Students," *Journal of Educational Psychology* 59 (April 1968):94-101.

Davis, Allison W., and John Dollard. *Children of Bondage.* Washington: American Council on Education, 1940. A detailed examination of the social classes into which Negroes are divided in the South within the Negro caste.

Davis, Arthur P. "Jesse B. Semple: Negro American," *Phylon* 15 (Spring 1954):21-28. Semple is Langston Hughes's "Simple." He exemplifies the pressures of Jim Crow living, and his responses show his confused racial thinking, his inconsistent role playing, etc.

Davis, Elizabeth B. "The American Negro: From Family Membership to Personal and Social Identity," *Journal of the National Medical Association* 60 (March 1968): 92-99.

Dennis, Wayne. "Racial Change in Negro Drawings," *Journal of Psychology* 69 (May 1968): 129-130.

Derbyshire, Robert L., and Eugene B. Brody. "Social Distance and Identity Conflict in Negro College Students," *Sociology and Social Research* 48 (April 1964):301-314.

Derbyshire, Robert L. "United States Negro Identity Conflict, " *Sociology and Social Research* 51 (October 1966):63-77. Results of 102 Negro college students tested for associative meanings with a series of ethnic concepts.

Deutscher, Isaac, and Isidor Chein. "The Psychological Effects of Enforced Segregation: A Survey of Social Science Opinion," *Journal of Psychology* 26 (October 1948):259-287. Cited in 1954 decision *Brown v. Board of Education.*

Dreger, Ralph M., and Kent S. Miller. "Comparative Psychological Studies of Negroes and Whites in the United States: 1959-1965," *Psychological Bulletin* Monograph Supplement 70 (September 1968):1-58.

Epps, Edgar G., Irwin Katz, and Leland Axelson. "Relation of Mother's Employment to Intellectual Performance of Negro College Students," *Social Problems* 11 (Spring 1964):414-418. Among Southern Negro college students, sons of working mothers are more strongly motivated and achieve more highly.

Erikson, Erik H. "The Concept of Identity in Race Relations: Notes and Queries," *Daedalus* 95 (Winter 1966):145-171.

Fishman, Jacob R., and Frederic Solomon. "Youth and Social Action, I: Perspectives on the Student Sit-in Movement," *American Journal of Orthopsychiatry* 33 (October 1963):872-882. The effects of social change and crisis on personality and identity formation.

Fishman, Jacob R., and Frederic Solomon. "Youth and Social Action, II: Action and Identity Formation in the First Student Sit-in Demonstration," *Journal of Social Issues* 20 (April 1964):36-45. A case study of one student.

Fishman, Joshua A. "Childhood Indoctrination for Minority Group Membership," *Daedalus* 90 (Spring 1961):329-349.

Flannagan, John, and George Lewis. "Comparison of Negro and White Lower-Class Men on the General Aptitude Testattery and the Minnesota Multiphasic Personality Inventory," *Journal of Social Psychology* 78 (August 1969):289-291. Summary of research.

Fontinell, Eugene. "The Identity of James Baldwin," *Interracial Review* 35 (September 1962):194-199.

Frazier, E. Franklin. *Negro Youth at the Crossways: Their Personality Development in the Middle States. 1940.* New York: Schocken, 1969. First a publication of the American Council on Education. Describes experiences of Negro youths in Washington, D.C. and Louisville, Kentucky, chosen as representative communities. The 1969 issue carries an introduction by St. Clair Drake.

Freeman, Howard E., et al. "Color Gradation and Attitudes Among Middle-Income Negroes," *American Sociological Review* 31 (June 1966):367-374.

Friedman, Neil. "Africa and the Afro-American: The Changing Negro Identity," *Psychiatry* 32 (May 1969):127-136.

Frisch, G. R., et al. "Differences in Negro and White Drawings: A Cultural Interpretation," *Perceptual Motor Skills* 24 (April 1967):667-670.

Gaier, Eugene L., and Helen S. Wambach. "Self-Evaluation of Personality Assets and Liabilities of Southern White and Negro Students," *Journal of Social Psychology* 51 (February 1960):135-143.

Garza, Joseph M. "Race, The Achievement Syndrome, and Perception of Opportunity," *Phylon* 30 (Winter 1969):338-354. Study based on a selected sampling of the population of Lexington, Kentucky.

Gibby, Robert G., and Robert Gabler. "The Self-Concept of Negro and White Children," *Journal of Clinical Psychology* 23 (April 1967):144-148.

Gilliland, Burl E. "Small Group Counseling with Negro Adolescents," *Journal of Counseling Psychology* 15 (March 1968):147-152.

Gochros, Jean S. "Recognition and Use of Anger in Negro Clients," *Social Work* 11 (January 1966):28-34. To effect constructive change.

Gordon, D. N. "Note on Negro Alienation," *American Journal of Sociology* 76 (January 1965):477-478.

Gore, Pearl M., and J. B. Rotter. "A Personality Correlate of Social Action," *Journal of Personality* 31 (March 1963):58-64. An experimental testing of student willingness to participate in protest action.

Greenwald, Herbert J., and Don B. Oppenheim. "Reported Magnitude of Self-Misidentification among Negro Children: Artifact?" *Journal of Personality and Social Psychology* 8 (January 1968):49–52.

Grier, William H., and Price M. Cobbs. *Black Rage.* New York: Basic Books, 1968. Provocative analysis of the Negro personality in a white-dominated culture. Supported with clinical evidence.

Grier, William H. "Some Special Effects of Negroeness on the Oedipal Conflict," *Journal of the National Medical Association* 58 (November 1966):416–418+.

Guggenheim, Fred. "Self-Esteem and Achievement Expectations for White and Negro Children," *Journal of Projective Techniques and Personality Assessment* 33 (February 1969):63–71. References appended.

Gullattee, Alyce C. "The Negro Psyche: Fact, Fiction and Fantasy," *Journal of the National Medical Association* 61 (March 1969):119–129.

Haggstrom, Warren C. "Segregation, Desegregation, and Negro Personality," *Integrated Education* 1 (October–November 1963):19–23.

Hammer, E. F. "Frustration-Aggression Hypothesis Extended to Socioracial Areas: Comparison of Negro and White Children's H-T-P's." *Psychiatric Quarterly* 27 (1953):597–607.

Harris, Edward E. "Family and Student Identities: An Exploratory Study in Self and 'We Group' Attitudes," *Journal of Negro Education* 34 (Winter 1965):17–22. Considers the effect of sex and race on the presence and absence of family and student self and "we-group" identities.

Hatton, John M. "Reactions of Negroes in a Biracial Bargaining Situation," *Journal of Personality and Social Psychology* 7 (November 1967):301–306. Negro high school girls with strong preconceptions of whites as prejudiced against Negroes in a bilateral monopoly bargaining situation.

Hayakawa, S. I. *Symbol, Status, and Personality.* New York: Harcourt, Brace, 1963. Distortion of language for various purposes, among them to encourage suspicion of Negro for white. See especially chapter 6.

Henderson, G. "Role Models for Lower-class Negro Boys," *Personnel and Guidance Journal* 46 (September 1967):6–10. Bibliography.

Henderson, Norman B., Barbara Goffeney, and Bruce V. Butler. "Do Negro Children Project a Self-Image of Helplessness and Inadequacy in Drawing a Person?" *Proceedings of the American Psychological Association* 4, pt. 1 (1969):437–438.

Hetherington, E. Mavis. "Effects of Paternal Absence on Sex-Typed Behaviors in Negro and White Preadolescent Males," *Journal of Personality and Social Psychology* 4 (July 1966):87–91.

Himes, Joseph S. "Some Work-Related Cultural Deprivations of Lower-Class Negro Youths," *Journal of Marriage and the Family* 26 (November 1964):447–449.

Hindman, Baker M. "The Emotional Problems of Negro High School Youth Which are Related to Segregation and Discrimination in a Southern Urban Community," *Journal of Educational Sociology* 27 (September 1953):115–127.

Hines, Ralph H. "Social Distance Components in Integration Attitudes of Negro College Students," *Journal of Negro Education* 37 (Winter 1968):23–30. An analysis of reciprocity of feeling between Negroes and other racial groups.

Hodgkins, Benjamin J., and Robert G. Stakenas. "A Study of Self-Concepts of Negro and White Youth in Segregated Environments," *Journal of Negro Education* 38 (Fall 1969):370–377.

Hokanson, J. E., and G. Calden. "Negro-White Differences on the MMPI," *Journal of Clinical Psychology* 16 (January 1960):32–33.

Hughes, J. H., and G. C. Thompson. "A Comparison of the Value Systems of Southern Negro and Northern White Youth," *Journal of Educational Psychology* 45 (July 1954):300–309.

Iscoe, Ira, Martha Williams, and Jerry Harvey. "Age, Intelligence, and Sex as Variables in the Conformity Behavior of Negro and White Children," *Child Development* 35 (June 1964):451–460.

Johnson, David W. "Racial Attitudes of Negro Freedom School Participants and Negro and White Civil Rights Participants," *Social Forces* 45 (December 1966):266-273. Results suggest need for a finer delineation of "self-attitudes" to be drawn between Negroes of varying backgrounds.

Johnson, Edwina C. "The Child in the Prestige Vacuum," *Integrated Education* 1 (December 1963-January 1964):13-26.

Johnson, Robert B. "Negro Reactions to Minority Group Status," in Milton L. Barron, ed., *American Minorities.* New York: Knopf, 1957. A study of upstate New York community of 60,000 population, 3 percent Negro.

Jones, Beau Fly. "James Baldwin: The Struggle for Identity," *British Journal of Sociology* 17 (June 1966):107-121.

Kardiner, Abram, and Lionel Ovesey. *The Mark of Oppression: Explorations in the Personality of the American Negro.* New York: Norton, 1951. A study of Negro personality based on psychoanalytic investigation of 25 Negroes.

Katz, Irwin, and Charles Greenbaum. "Effects of Anxiety, Threat, and Racial Environment on Task Performance of Negro College Students," *Journal of Abnormal and Social Psychology* 66 (June 1963):562-567.

Kerckhoff, A. C., and T. C. McCormick. "Marginal Status and Marginal Personality," *Social Forces* 34 (October 1955):48-55.

Kincaid, Marylou. "Identity and Therapy in the Black Community," *Personnel and Guidance Journal* 47 (May 1969):884-890.

Kvaraceus, William C. *Negro Self-Concept: Implications for School and Citizenship.* Medford, Mass.: Lincoln Filene Center for Citizenship and Public Affairs, Tufts University, 1964.

Lapouse, Rema, and Mary A. Monk. "Behavior Deviations in a Representative Sample of Children: Variation by Sex, Age, Race, Social Class and Family Size," *American Journal of Orthopsychiatry* 34 (April 1964):436-446.

Lefcowitz, Myron J. *Differences between Negro and White Women in Marital Stability and Family Structure: A Multiple Regression Analysis.* Madison, Wis.: Institute for Research on Poverty, 1968.

Lessing, Elsie E., and Susan W. Zagorin. "Some Demographic, Value, and Personality Correlates of Endorsement of Negro Militancy by Negro and White Youth," *Proceedings of the American Psychological Association* 4, Pt. 1 (1969):295-296.

Levin, David. "James Baldwin's Autobiographical Essays: The Problem of Negro Identity," *Massachusetts Review* 5 (Winter 1964):239-247.

Littig, Lawrence W. "Negro Personality Correlates of Aspiration to Traditionally Open and Closed Occupations," *Journal of Negro Education* 37 (Winter 1968):31-36.

Luchins, Abraham S., and Edith H. Luchins. "Personality Impressions from Communications Reflecting Attitudes Toward Segregation," *Journal of Social Psychology* 58 (December 1962):315-330.

McClain, Edwin W. "Personality Characteristics of Negro College Students in the South; A Recent Appraisal," *Journal of Negro Education* 36 (Summer 1967):320-325.

Middleton, Russell. "Alienation, Race, and Education," *American Sociological Review* 28 (December 1963):973-977.

Miller, C., C. Wertz, and S. Counts. "Racial Differences on the MMPI," *Journal of Clinical Psychology* 17 (April 1961):159-161.

Milner, Esther. "Some Hypotheses Concerning the Influence of Segregation on Negro Personality Development," *Psychiatry* 16 (August 1953):291-297.

Mischel, W. "Delay of Gratification, Need for Achievement, and Acquiescence in Another Culture," *Journal of Abnormal and Social Psychology* 62 (May 1961):543-552.

Mischel, W. "Father-Absence and Delay of Gratification: Cross-Cultural Comparisons," *Journal of Abnormal and Social Psychology* 63 (July 1961):116-124.

Mischel, W. "Preference for Delayed Reinforcement and Social Responsibility," *Journal of Abnormal and Social Psychology* 62 (January 1961):1-7.

Morland, J. Kenneth. "Racial Recognition by Nursery School Children in Lynchburg, Virginia," *Social Forces* 37 (December 1958):132-137.

Morland, J. Kenneth. "Racial Self-Identification: A Study of Nursery School Children," *American Catholic Sociological Review* 24 (Fall 1963):231-242.

Mussen, Paul, and Luther Distler. "Masculinity, Identification, and Father-Son Relationships," *Journal of Abnormal and Social Psychology* 59 (September 1959):350-356.

Myers, Henry J., and Leon Yochelson. "Color Denial in the Negro," *Psychiatry* 11 (February 1948):39-46.

"Negro American Personality," *Journal of Social Issues* 20 (April 1964):1-145. Entire issue, edited by Thomas F. Pettigrew and Daniel C. Thompson. See particularly Pettigrew's article, "Negro American Personality: Why Isn't More Known?" for exposition of problem.

Palermo, D. S. "Racial Comparisons and Additional Normative Data on the Children's Manifest Anxiety Scale," *Child Development* 30 (March 1959):53-57.

Pennington, Stewart, and Lonnie E. Mitchell. "Sex Differences in Reactions to Minority Group Status," *Journal of Negro Education* 28 (Winter 1959):35-41.

Pettigrew, Thomas F. *A Profile of the Negro American.* Princeton, N.J.: Van Nostrand, 1964. A work which brings together an impressive amount of clinical material on the Negro personality, together with studies of behavioral traits. The author demonstrates the need for the development of a broad social psychological theory of Negro American personality. Extensive bibliography.

Phillips, Romeo Eldridge. "Student Activities and Self-Concept," *Journal of Negro Education* 38 (Winter 1969):32-37. A summary of author's unpublished dissertation which was based on a study in a suburban Detroit high school.

Poussaint, Alvin F. "The Negro American: His Self-Image and Integration," *Journal of the National Medical Association* 58 (November 1966):419-423.

Poussaint, Alvin F. "A Negro Psychiatrist Explains the Negro Psyche," *New York Times Magazine,* August 20, 1967 pp. 52-58 +.

Poussaint, Alvin F. "Negro Youth and Psychological Motivation," *Journal of Negro Education* 37 (Summer 1968):241-251. With reference to the individual's self-concept, achievement, and the rewards of society.

Powdermaker, Hortense. "The Channeling of Negro Aggression by the Cultural Process," *American Journal of Sociology* 48 (May 1943):750-758. Discusses concealment of aggression by two nonaggressive roles Negroes have been assigned: the faithful slave and the faithful, meek Negro.

Price, Arthur Cooper. "A Rorschach Study of the Development of Personality Structure in White and Negro Children in a Southeastern Community," *Genetic Psychology Monographs* 65 (1962):3-52.

Proshansky, Harold, and Peggy Newton. "The Nature and Meaning of Negro Self-Identity," in Martin Deutsch, Irwin Katz, and Arthur R. Jensen, eds., *Social Class, Race, and Psychological Development.* New York: Holt, Rinehart & Winston, 1968, pp. 178-218.

Prothro, James W., and Charles U. Smith. "Ethnic Differences in Authoritarian Personality," *Social Forces* 35 (May 1957):334-338. Bibliography.

Prothro, James W., and Charles U. Smith. "The Psychic Cost of Segregation," *Adult Education* 5 (1955):179-181.

Psychiatric Aspects of School Desegregation: Report No. 37. New York: Group for the Advancement of Psychiatry Publications Office, 1957.

Rohrer, J. H., and M. S. Edmonson. *The Eighth Generation.* New York: Harper, 1960. This study is a follow-up twenty years later of the people described by Davis and Dollard in *Children of Bondage.* Problems of racial identification and individual identity stressed throughout.

Rosen, Bernard C. "Race, Ethnicity, and the Achievement Syndrome," *American Sociological Review* 24 (February 1959):47-60.

Rosenberg, Marvin Leonard. *An Experiment to Change Attitudes of Powerlessness among Low-Income Negro Youth.* Cleveland, Ohio: School of Applied Social Sciences, Case Western Reserve University, 1968.

Rosenhan, David L. "Effects of Social Class and Race on Responsiveness to Approval and Disapproval," *Journal of Personality and Social Psychology* 4 (September 1966):253-259. An experiment with lower-class children, Negro and White.

Rowe, Allen S., and Willard E. Caldwell. "The Somatic Apperception Test," *Journal of General Psychology* 68 (January 1963):59-69. Perception of their own size by a group of Negro adolescents.

Schab, Fred. "Adolescence in the South: A Comparison of White and Negro Attitudes about Home, School, Religion, and Morality," *Adolescence* 3 (Spring 1968):33-38.

Scher, Maryonda. "Negro Group Dynamics," *Archives of General Psychiatry* 17 (December 1967):646-651.

Secord, P. F., and E. S. Berscheid. "Stereotyping and the Generality of Implicit Personality Theory," *Journal of Personality* 31 (March 1963):65-78.

Seeman, Melvin. "Intellectual Perspective and Adjustment to Minority Status," *Social Problems* 4 (January 1956):142-153.

Shaw, Marvin E. "Negro-White Differences in Attribution of Responsibility as a Function of Age," *Psychonomic Science* 16 (September 1969):289-291.

Shemberg, K. M., D. B. Leventhal, and L. Allman. "Aggression Machine Performance and Rate Aggression," *Journal of Experimental Research in Personality* 3 (1968):117-119. Test subjects: Negro high school students in an Upward Bound program.

Sigel, Irving E., Larry M. Anderson, and Howard Shapiro. "Categorization Behavior of Lower and Middle-Class Negro Preschool Children: Differences in Dealing with Representation of Familiar Objects," *Journal of Negro Education* 35 (Summer 1966):218-229. Bibliography.

Singer, S. L., and B. Stefflre. "A Note on Racial Differences in Job Values and Desires," *Journal of Social Psychology* 43 (May 1956):333-337.

Smith, Charles U., and James W. Prothro. "Ethnic Differences in Authoritarian Personality," *Social Forces* 35 (May 1957):334-338.

Solkoff, Norman. "Reactions to Frustration in Negro and White Children," *Journal of Negro Education* 38 (Fall 1969):412-418.

Solomon, Daniel, Robert J. Parelius, and Thomas V. Busse. "Dimensions of Achievement-Related Behavior among Lower-Class Negro Parents," *Genetic Psychology Monographs* 79 (May 1969):163-190. References appended.

Spock, Benjamin. "Children and Discrimination," *Redbook* 123 (September 1964):30+.

Steckler, G. A. "Authoritarian Ideology in Negro College Students," *Journal of Abnormal and Social Psychology* 54 (May 1957):396-399.

Stevenson, H. W., and E. C. Stewart. "A Developmental Study of Racial Awareness in Young Children," *Child Development* 29 (September 1958):399-409.

Taylor, Dalmas A. "The Relationship Between Authoritarianism and Ethnocentrism in Negro College Students," *Journal of Negro Education* 31 (Fall 1962):455-459.

Teicher, Joseph D. "Some Observations on Identity Problems in Children of Negro-White Marriages," *Journal of Nervous and Mental Disease* 146 (March 1968):249-256.

Trent, Richard D. "The Relation Between Expressed Self-Acceptance and Expressed Attitudes Toward Negroes and Whites Among Negro Children," *Journal of Genetic Psychology* 91 (September 1957):25-31.

Vaughan, Graham M. "Concept Formation and the Development of Ethnic Awareness," *Journal of Genetic Psychology* 103 (September 1963):93-103.

Vaughan, Graham M. "Ethnic Awareness in Relation to Minority Group Membership," *Journal of Genetic Psychology* 105 (September 1964):119-130.

Veroff, J., et al. "The Use of Thematic Apperception to Assess Motivation in a Nationwide Interview Study," *Psychological Monographs* 74 (1960):1-12.

Vittenson, Lillian. "Areas of Concern to Negro College Students as Indicated by Their Responses to the Mooney Problem Check List," *Journal of Negro Education* 36 (Winter 1967):51-57.

Volkan, U. "Five Poems by Negro Youngsters Who Faced a Sudden Desegregation," *Psychiatric Quarterly* 37 (October 1963):607-617.

Vontress, Clemmont E. "The Negro Against Himself," *Journal of Negro Education* 32 (Summer 1963):237-242.

Vontress, Clemmont E. "The Negro Personality Reconsidered," *Journal of Negro Education* 35 (Summer 1966):210-217.

Webster, Staten W., and Marie N. Kroger. "A Comparative Study of Selected Perceptions and Feelings of Negro Adolescents with and without White Friends in Integrated Urban High Schools," *Journal of Negro Education* 35 (Winter 1966):55-61.

Weinberg, Carl. "Social Attitudes of Negro and White Student Leaders," *Journal of Negro Education* 35 (Spring 1966):161-167.

Weller, Leonard, and Elmer Luchterhand. "Interviewer-Respondent Interaction in Negro and White Family Life Research," *Human Organization* 27 (Spring 1968):50-55.

Williams, Robert L., and Harry Byars. "Negro Self Esteem in a Transitional Society," *Personnel and Guidance Journal* 47 (October 1968):120-125. Study of Negro adolescents in a Southern community undergoing desegregation in the schools and in public accommodations. References appended.

Wise, James H. "Self-Reports by Negro and White Adolescents to the Draw-a-Person," *Perceptual and Motor Skills* 28 (February 1969):193-194. Testing an economic and cultural value preference hypothesis.

Witmer, Helen, and Ruth Kotinsky, eds. *Personality in the Making.* New York: Harper, 1952. Fact-finding report of the Midcentury White House Conference on Children and Youth. Chapter 6 was cited in 1954 decision *Brown v. Board of Education.*

Woronoff, Israel. "Negro Male Identification Problems," *Journal of Educational Sociology* 36 (September 1962):30-32.

Yarrow, Marian R., and Bernard Lande. "Personality Correlates of Differential Reactions to Minority Group-Belonging," *Journal of Social Psychology* 38 (November 1953):253-272.

Intelligence

Ashbury, Charles A. "Some Selected Problems Involved in Assessing the Intelligence and Achievement of Disadvantaged Groups: With Emphasis on the Negro," *Quarterly Review of Higher Education among Negroes* 36 (July 1968):133-144.

Baratz, J. C. "Language and Cognitive Assessment of Negro Children: Assumptions and Research Needs," *Journal of the American Speech and Hearing Association* 11 (March 1969):87-91.

Belcher, Leon H., and Joel T. Campbell. "An Exploratory Study of Word Associations of Negro College Students," *Psychological Reports* 23 (August 1968):119-134. References.

Bloom, Benjamin S. *Stability and Change in Human Characteristics.* New York: Wiley, 1964. See review by Bruno Bettelheim in *New York Review,* September 10, 1964, and flurry of rejoinders by Dr. Robert Coles, Susan Bove, and Dr. Melvin Rubenstein in issue of October 22. At issue: whether deprived child's achievement levels can be altered after four or five years.

Bond, Horace Mann. "Cat on a Hot Tin Roof," *Journal of Negro Education* 27 (Fall 1958):519-523. A review of Audrey Shuey's judgments on Negro intelligence and a general consideration of intelligence tests and the Negro.

Bourisseau, Whitfield, O. L. Davis, and Kaoru Yamamoto. "Sense-Impression Responses of Negro and White Children to Verbal and Pictorial Stimuli," *AV Communication Review* 15 (Fall 1967):259-268. Bibliography.

Caldwell, Marcus B., and Timothy A. Smith. "Intellectual Structure of Southern Negro Children," *Psychological Reports* 23 (August 1968):63-71. References.

Carson, Arnold S., and A. I. Rabin. "Verbal Comprehension and Communication in Negro and White Children," *Journal of Educational Psychology* 51 (April 1960):47-51.

Cartwright, Walter J., and Thomas R. Burtis. "Race and Intelligence: Changing Opinions in Social Science," *Social Science Quarterly* 49 (December 1968):603-618. Surveys the shift in emphasis from racial to social causation of intelligence differences.

Cleary, T. Anne. *Test Bias: Validity of the Scholastic Aptitude Test for Negro and White Students in Integrated Colleges.* Princeton, N.J.: Educational Testing Service, 1966. (College Entrance Examination Board Research and Development Reports no. 18.)

Cooper, G. David, et al. "Porteus Test and Various Measures of Intelligence with Southern Negro Adolescents," *American Journal of Mental Deficiency* 71 (March 1967):787-792.

Deutsch, Martin. "The Disadvantaged Child and the Learning Process: Some Social, Psychological, and Developmental Considerations," in A. H. Passow, ed., *Education in*

Depressed Areas. New York: Bureau of Publications, Teachers College, Columbia University, 1963.

Deutsch, Martin, Irwin Katz, and Arthur Jensen. *Social Class, Race, and Psychological Development.* New York: Holt, 1968.

"Did You Find That There Was Much Difference in the Ability of Negro Children to Receive and Profit by Instruction?" *Southern Regional Council Report No. L-13, December 15, 1959.*

"Discussion: How Much Can We Boost I Q Scholastic Achievement," *Harvard Educational Review* 39 (Spring 1969):273-356. Response to A. R. Jensen's article by the following psychologists and a geneticist: Jerome S. Kagan, J. McV. Hunt, James F. Crow, Carl Bereiter, David Elkind, Lee J. Cronbach, and William F. Brazziel.

Dubin, Jerry A., Hobart Osburn, and David M. Wineck. "Speed and Practice: Effects on Negro and White Test Performance," *Journal of Applied Psychology* 53 (February 1969):19-23.

Edmonds, William S. "Oh, That Median Score—The Bane of Negro Pupils," *Journal of Negro Education* 31 (Winter 1962):75-77.

Edson, Lee. "Jensenism n. the Theory that IQ Is Largely Determined by the Genes," *New York Times Magazine,* August 31, 1969, pp. 10-11 +. With replies and rejoinder, *ibid.,* September 21, 1969.

Eisenberg, Leon, et al. "Class and Race Effects on the Intelligibility of Monosyllables," *Child Development* 39 (December 1968):1077-1089. Bibliography.

Fulk, Byron E., and Thomas W. Harrell. "Negro-White Army Test Scores and Last School Grade," *Journal of Applied Psychology* 36 (February 1952):34-35.

Garfunkel, F., and B. Blatt. "Standardization of Intelligence Tests on Southern Negro School Children," *Training School Bulletin* 60 (August 1963):94-99.

Garrett, Henry E. "The Equalitarian Dogma," *Mankind Quarterly* 1 (1961):253-257. The "equalitarian dogma" is a hoax, embraced for purely ideological purposes, and its supporters ignore the "scientific facts that would prove Negroes as a group are intellectually inferior to whites."

Garrett, Henry E. "Klineberg's Chapter on Race and Psychology: A Review," *Mankind Quarterly* 1 (1960):15-22.

Garrett, Henry E. "The Relative Intelligence of Whites and Negroes: The Armed Forces Tests," *Mankind Quarterly* 8 (October-December 1967):64-79. An example of contemporary racism at its worst.

Garrett, Henry E. "The SPSSI and Racial Differences," *American Psychologist* 17 (May 1962):260-263.

Green, Robert L., and Robert F. Morgan. "The Effects of Resumed Schooling on the Measured Intelligence of Prince Edward County's Black Children," *Journal of Negro Education* 38 (Spring 1969):147-155.

Green, Robert L., Louis J. Hoffman, and Robert F. Morgan. "Some Effects of Deprivation on Intelligence, Achievement and Cognitive Growth," *Journal of Negro Education* 36 (Winter 1967):5-14. Bibliography. Assessment of empirical research.

Gustafson, Lucille. "Relationship Between Ethnic Group Membership and the Retention of Selected Facts Pertaining to American History and Culture," *Journal of Educational Sociology* 31 (October 1957):49-56. The minority group will remain unretentive to the extent that it is kept outside the larger group.

Hammer, E. F. "Comparison of the Performances of Negro Children and Adolescents on Two Tests of Intelligence, One an Emergency Scale," *Journal of Genetic Psychology* 84 (March 1954):85-93.

Harris, Albert J., and Robert J. Lovinger. "Longitudinal Measures of the Intelligence of Disadvantaged Negro Adolescents," *School Review* 76 (March 1968):60-66.

Harrison, Robert H., and Edward H. Kass. "MMPI Correlates of Negro Acculturation in a Northern City," *Journal of Personality and Social Psychology* 10 (November 1968):262-270.

Henning, John J., and Russell H. Levy. "Verbal-Performance IQ Differences of White and Negro Delinquents on the WISC and WAIS," *Journal of Clinical Psychology* 23 (April 1967):164-168. References.

Herskovits, Melville. *The Anthropometry of the American Negro.* 1930. New York: AMS Press, 1969.

Higgins, C., and Cathryne Sivers. "A Comparison of Stanford-Binet and Colored Raven Progressive Matrices I.Q.'s for Children with Low Socioeconomic Status," *Journal of Consulting Psychology* 22 (December 1958):465-468.

Hobart, Charles W. "Underachievement among Minority Group Students: An Analysis and a Proposal," *Phylon* 24 (Summer 1963):184-196.

Horton, Carrell P., and E. Perry Crump. "Growth and Development XI. Descriptive Analysis of the Backgrounds of 76 Negro Children Whose Scores Are Above or Below Average on the Merrill-Palmer Scale of Mental Tests at Three Years of Age," *Journal of Genetic Psychology* 100 (June 1962):225-265.

Humphreys, Lloyd G., and Hans Peter Dachler. "Jensen's Theory of Intelligence," *Journal of Educational Psychology* 60 (December 1969):419-426. See also Jensen's reply and the authors' rejoinder, *ibid.,* 427-433.

Hunt, J. McVicker. "Black Genes—White Environment," *Trans-action* 6 (June 1969):12-22.

Hunt, J. M. *Intelligence and Experience.* New York: Ronald, 1951. Intelligence not an inherited capacity, genetically fixed, but a set of processes that, within wide hereditary limits, is subject to experiential factors.

Iscoe, Ira, and John Pierce-Jones. "Divergent Thinking, Age, and Intelligence in White and Negro Children," *Child Development* 35 (September 1964):785-798.

Jencks, Christopher. "Intelligence and Race," *New Republic* 161 (September 6 & 13, 1969):25-29.

Jensen, Arthur R. "How Much Can We Boost IQ and Scholastic Achievements?" *Harvard Educational Review* 39 (Winter 1969):1-123. Extensive Bibliography. See also replies, *ibid.,* 39 (Spring 1969):273-356.

Jensen, Arthur R. "Jensen's Theory of Intelligence: A Reply," *Journal of Educational Psychology* 60 (December 1969):427-433. See also Lloyd G. Humphrey's and Hans Peter Dachler's initial article to which Jensen herein replies, and their rejoinder, *ibid.,* 419-426.

Jensen, Arthur R. "Social Class, Race, and Genetics. Implications for Education," *American Educational Research Journal* 5 (1968):1-42. Bibliography.

Jensen, Arthur R. "A Statistical Note on Racial Differences in the Progressive Matrices," *Journal of Consulting Psychology* 23 (June 1959):273-274. With a reply by Gerald Sperrazzo and Walter L. Wilkins.

John, Vera P. "The Intellectual Development of Slum Children: Some Preliminary Findings," *American Journal of Orthopsychiatry* 33 (October 1963):813-822. Patterns of linguistic and cognitive behavior.

Johnson, Granville B., Jr. "A Comparison of Two Evaluation Instruments for the Analysis of Academic Potential of Negro Children," *Phylon* 20 (Spring 1959):44-47.

Kaplan, Henry K., and Anthony J. Matkom. "Peer Status and Intellectual Functioning of Negro Children," *Psychology in the Schools* 4 (April 1967):181-184.

Katz, Irwin, Thomas Henchy, and Harvey Allen. "Effects of Race of Tester, Approval-Disapproval, and Need on Negro Children's Learning," *Journal of Personality and Social Psychology* 8 (January 1968):38-42.

Katz, Irwin. "Some Motivational Determinants of Racial Differences in Intellectual Achievement," *International Journal of Psychology* 2, no. 1 (1967):1-12.

Kennedy, Wallace A. "A Follow-up Normative Study of Negro Intelligence and Achievement," *Child Development* 34 (March-April 1969):1-40. Entire issue.

Kennedy, Wallace A., et al. "A Normative Sample of Intelligence and Achievement of Negro Elementary School Children in the Southeastern United States," *Monographs of the Society for Research in Child Development* 28 (1963):1-112.

Kennedy, Wallace A., and Ronald S. Lindner. "A Normative Study of the Goodenough Draw-a-Man Test on Southeastern Negro Elementary School Children," *Child Development* 35 (March 1964):33-62.

Kennedy, Wallace A., et al. "Use of the Terman-Merrill Abbreviated Scale on the 1960 Stanford-Binet Form L-M on Negro Elementary School Children of the Southeastern United States," *Journal of Consulting Psychology* 27 (October 1963):456-457.

Klineberg, Otto, ed. *Characteristics of the American Negro.* New York: Harper, 1944. Although dated, these six essays present useful summaries of psychological studies up to 1944, and indicate techniques out of which later, and more accurate, methods have developed.

Klineberg, Otto. "Negro-White Differences in Intelligence Test Performance: A New Look at an Old Problem," *American Psychologist* 18 (April 1963):198-203. "The science of psychology can offer no support to those who see in the accident of inherited skin color or other physical characteristics any excuse for denying to individuals the right to full participation in American democracy."

Klineberg, Otto, et al. "On Race and Intelligence: A Joint Statement," *American Journal of Orthopsychiatry* 27 (April 1957):420-422. On the untenability of any theory of inherent racial inequality.

Knobloch, Hilda, and B. Pasamanick. "Further Observations on the Behavioral Development of Negro Children," *Journal of Genetic Psychology* 83 (September 1953):137-157.

Krech, David, and Richard Crutchfield. *Elements of Psychology.* New York: Knopf, 1958. Includes some discussion of racial differences in intelligence.

Lee, Everett S. "Negro Intelligence and Selective Migration: A Philadelphia Test of the Klineberg Hypothesis," *American Sociological Review* 16 (April 1951):227-233. In the main, substantiated by independent evidence in Philadelphia.

"Legal Implications of the Use of Standardized Ability Tests in Employment and Education," *Columbia Law Review* 68 (April 1968):691-744.

Long, Howard Hale. "The Relative Learning Capacities of Negroes and Whites," *Journal of Negro Education* 26 (Spring 1957):121-134.

McCord, William M., and Nicholas J. Demerath. "Negro versus White Intelligence: A Continuing Controversy," *Harvard Educational Review* 28 (Spring 1958):120-135. Bibliography.

McGurk, Frank. "Negro vs. White Intelligence—An Answer," *Harvard Educational Review* 29 (Winter 1959):54-62. The author, professor of psychology at Villanova University, attempts to show that "Negroes as a group do not possess as much capacity as whites as a group."

McGurk, Frank. "On White and Negro Test Performance and Socio-economic Factors," *Journal of Abnormal and Social Psychology* 48 (July 1953):448-450.

McGurk, Frank. "Psychological Test Score Differences and the 'Culture Hypothesis,'" *Mankind Quarterly* 1 (January 1961):165-175.

McGurk, Frank. "Psychological Tests: A Scientist's Report on Race Differences," *U.S. News and World Report* 41 (September 21, 1956):92-96.

McGurk, Frank. "Socio-economic Status and Culturally Weighted Test Scores of Negro Subjects," *Journal of Applied Psychology* 37 (August 1953):276-277.

McNamara, J. R., C. L. Porterfield, and L. E. Miller. "The Relationship of the Wechsler Preschool and Primary Scale of Intelligence with the Coloured Progressive Matrices (1956) and the Bender Gestalt Test," *Journal of Clinical Psychology* 25 (January 1969):65-68.

McQueen, Robert, and Browning Churn. "The Intelligence and Educational Achievement of a Matched Sample of White and Negro Students," *School and Society* 88 (September 24, 1960):327-329.

Mathis, Harold I. "Relating Environmental Factors to Aptitude and Race," *Journal of Counseling Psychology* 15 (November 1968):563-568.

Milgram, Norman A., and Mark N. Ozer. "Peabody Picture Vocabulary Test Scores of Preschool Children," *Psychological Reports* 20 (1967):779-784. Indicates PPVT test may be more susceptible to environmental impoverishment than the Stanford-Binet.

Mitchell, Blythe C. "Predictive Validity of the Metropolitan Readiness Tests and the Murphy-Durrell Reading Readiness Analysis for White and for Negro Pupils," *Educational and Psychological Measurement* 27 (Winter 1967):1047-1054.

National Academy of Science. "Racial Studies: Academy States Position on Call for New Research," *Science* 158 (November 17, 1967):892-893. An official statement of the Academy's position concerning research to evaluate the relative effects of heredity and environment on human intelligence.

Norman, Arthur. "A New Approach to Negro Education," *Journal of Negro Education* 30 (Winter 1961):35–40. On the relation between cultural enrichment and IQ.

North, Robert D. "The Intelligence of American Negroes," *Anti-Defamation League Research Reports* 3, no. 2 (November 1956). A scholarly evaluation of the research literature. Includes a bibliography of published research dealing with Negro-White intelligence differentials.

Osborne, R. T., and A. James Gregor. "Racial Differences in Heritability Estimates for Tests of Spatial Ability," *Perceptual and Motor Skills* 27 (December 1968):735–739.

Osborne, R. T. "Racial Differences in Mental Growth and School Achievement: A Longitudinal Study," *Psychological Reports* 7 (1960):233–239.

Pasamanick, Benjamin. "A Comparative Study of the Behavioral Development of Negro Infants," *Journal of Genetic Psychology* 69 (September 1946):3–44.

Pasamanick, Benjamin, and Hilda Knobloch. "The Contribution of Some Organic Factors to School Retardation in Negro Children," *Journal of Negro Education* 27 (Winter 1958):4–9.

Pasamanick, Benjamin, and Hilda Knobloch. "Early Language Behavior in Negro Children and the Testing of Intelligence," *Journal of Abnormal and Social Psychology* 50 (May 1955):401–402.

Pasamanick, Benjamin. "A Tract for the Times: Some Sociobiologic Aspects of Science, Race, and Racism," *American Journal of Orthopsychiatry* 39 (January 1969):7–15.

Peters, James S., II. "A Study of the Wechsler-Bellevue Verbal Scores of Negro and White Males," *Journal of Negro Education* 29 (Winter 1960):7–16. Extensive Bibliography.

Peterson, J., and L. H. Lanier. "Studies in the Comparative Abilities of Whites and Negroes," *Mental Measurement Monograph* no. 5, 1929.

Pettigrew, Thomas F. "Negro American Intelligence: A New Look at an Old Controversy," *Journal of Negro Education* 32 (Winter 1963):6–25.

Plotkin, Lawrence. "Racial Differences in Intelligence," *American Psychologist* 14 (August 1959):526–527.

Roberts, S. Oliver, Carroll P. Horton, and Barbara T. Roberts. "SAT vs. GRE Performance of Negro American College Students," *Proceedings of the American Psychological Association* 4, Pt. 1 (1969):177–178.

Rosen, S. R. "Personality and Negro-White Intelligence," *Journal of Abnormal and Social Psychology* 61 (July 1960):148–160.

Schultz, Raymond E. "A Comparison of Negro Pupils' Ranking with Those Ranking Low in Educational Achievement," *Journal of Educational Sociology* 31 (March 1958):265–270.

Scott, Ralph. "First to Ninth Grade IQ Changes of Northern Negro Students," *Psychology in the Schools* 3 (April 1966):159–160. Summary analysis of the impact of a Northern environment on the patterning of Negro IQ.

Semler, Ira J., and Ira Iscoe. "Comparative and Developmental Study of the Learning Abilities of Negro and White Children Under Four Conditions," *Journal of Educational Psychology* 54 (February 1963):38–44.

Semler, Ira J., and Ira Iscoe. "Structure of Intelligence in Negro and White Children," *Journal of Educational Psychology* 56 (December 1966):326–336.

Shuey, Audrey M. *The Testing of Negro Intelligence.* 1958. 2d ed. New York: Social Science Press, 1966. Author, chairman of the psychology department at Randolph-Macon College, marshalls further evidence which "inevitably points to the presence of native differences between Negroes and Whites as determined by intelligence tests."

Smart, Mollie S. "Confirming Klineberg's Suspicion," *American Psychologist* 18 (September 1963):621.

Smith, Herbert W., W. Theodore May, and Leon Lebovitz. "Testing Experience and Stanford-Binet Scores," *Journal of Educational Measurement* 3 (Fall 1966):229–233. Negro urban children in Southeastern United States as subjects.

Stanley, Julian C., and Andrew C. Porter. "Correlation of Scholastic Aptitude Test Scores with College Grades for Negroes versus Whites," *Journal of Educational Measurement* 4 (Winter 1967):199–218.

Teahan, John E., and Elizabeth M. Drews. "A Comparison of Northern and Southern Negro Children on the WISC," *Journal of Consulting Psychology* 26 (June 1962):292.

Thumin, F., and Sue Goldman. "Comparative Test Performance of Negro and White Job Applicants," *Journal of Clinical Psychology* 24 (October 1968):455-457.

Tuddenham, R. D. "The Nature and Measurement of Intelligence," in L. Postman, ed., *Psychology in the Making.* New York: Knopf, 1962.

Vane, Julia R., Jonathan Weitzman, and Adrian P. Applebaum. "Performance of Negro and White Children and Problem and Nonproblem Children on the Stanford-Binet Scale," *Journal of Clinical Psychology* 22 (October 1966):431-435.

Voyat, Gilbert. "IQ: God-Given or Man-Made?" *Saturday Review* 52 (May 17, 1969): 73-75+. Response to A. R. Jensen's thesis. The Piagetian approach.

Whiteman, Martin, and Martin Deutsch. "Social Disadvantage as Related to Intellective and Language Development," in Martin Deutsch, Irwin Katz, and Arthur R. Jensen, eds., *Social Class, Race, and Psychological Development.* New York: Holt, Rinehart & Winston, 1968, pp. 86-114. Discussion of research on children differing in socioeconomic status and race.

Willard, Louisa S. "A Comparison of Culture Fair Test Scores with Group and Individual Intelligence Test Scores of Disadvantaged Negro Children," *Journal of Learning Disabilities* 1 (October 1968):584-589.

Woods, Walter, and Robert Toal. "Subtest Disparity of Negro and White Groups Matched for I. Q.'s on the Revised Beta Test," *Journal of Consulting Psychology* 21 (April 1957):136-138.

See also Health—Genetic; Education—Elementary and Secondary—Aspiration and Achievement.

Health

Genetic

Allen, R. L., and David L. Nickel. "The Negro and Learning to Swim: The Buoyancy Problem Related to Reported Biological Differences," *Journal of Negro Education* 38 (Fall 1969):404-412. References appended.

Baker, P. T. "American Negro-White Differences in the Thermal Insulative Aspects of Body Fat," *Human Biology* 31 (December 1959):316-324.

Bass, L. N., and H. B. Yaghmai. "Report of a Case of Hemophilia in a Negroid Infant," *Journal of the National Medical Association* 54 (September 1962):561-562.

Blumberg, B. S., ed. *Genetic Polymorphisms and Geographic Variations in Disease.* New York: Grune and Stratton, 1961.

Bullock, W. H., J. B. Johnson, and T. W. Davis. "Hemophilia in Negro Subjects," *American Medical Association Archives of Internal Medicine* 100 (November 1957):759-764.

Cooper, A. J., et al. "Biochemical Polymorphic Traits in a U.S. White and Negro Population," *American Journal of Human Genetics* 15 (December 1963):420-428.

Damon, Albert. "Race, Ethnic Group, and Disease," *Social Biology* 16 (June 1969):69-80. References appended.

Dublin, T. R., and B. S. Blumberg. "An Epidemiologic Approach to Inherited Disease Susceptibility," *Public Health Reports* 76 (June 1961):499-505. On possession of hemoglobin S trait.

Fuller, J. L., and W. B. Thompson. *Behavior Genetics.* New York: Wiley, 1960.

Goldstein, Marcus S. "Longevity and Health Status of the Negro American," *Journal of Negro Education* 32 (Fall 1963):337-348.

Goldstein, Marcus S. "Longevity and Health Status of Whites and Non-Whites in the United States," *Journal of the National Medical Association* 46 (March 1954):83-104.

Gottesman, I. I. "Biogenetics of Race and Class," in Martin Deutsch, Irwin Katz, and Arthur R. Jensen, eds., *Social Class, Race, and Psychological Development.* New York: Holt, Rinehart & Winston, 1968, pp. 11-51. Genetic factors in black-white social-class and intellectual differences.

Grabill, Wilson H., Clyde V. Kiser, and Pascal K. Whelpton. *The Fertility of American*

Women. New York: Wiley, 1958. Based on censuses of 1950 and earlier, this book is basically a statistical study of population as related to race, age, mobility, etc.

Guralnick, Lillian. *Mortality by Occupation and Industry among Men 20 to 64 Years of Age: United States, 1950.* Vital Statistics Special Reports, Vol. 52, no. 2. Washington: U.S. Govt. Print. Off. 1962.

Harper, P. A., L. K. Fischer, and R. V. Rider. "Neurological and Intellectual Status of Prematures at Three to Five Years of Age," *Journal of Pediatrics* 55 (December 1959):679-690. Includes data on Negro cases.

Horton, C. P., and E. P. Crump. "Changes in Skin Color of Fifty-one Negro Infants from Birth Through Three Years of Age, as Related to Skin Color of Parents, Socioeconomic Status, and Developmental Quotient," *American Medical Association Archives of Dermatology* 80 (October 1959):421-426.

Iampietro, P. F., R. F. Goldman, E. R. Buskirk, and D. E. Bass. "Response of Negro and White Males to Cold," *Journal of Applied Physiology* 14 (September 1959):798-800.

"Improved Mortality Among Colored Policyholders," *Statistical Bulletin, Metropolitan Life Insurance Company* 43 (August 1962):6-8. This company insures about one-fifth of the entire Negro population.

Karpinos, B. D. "Racial Differences in Visual Acuity," *Public Health Reports* 95 (November 1960):1045-1050. Negro Americans, on average, have superior visual acuity.

Kitagawa, Evelyn M., and Philip M. Hauser. "Trends in Differential Fertility and Mortality in a Metropolis—Chicago," in E. W. Burgess and D. J. Bogue, eds., *Contributions to Urban Sociology.* Chicago: University of Chicago Press, 1964. A summary of five studies of fertility and mortality in Chicago made over a period of 40 years, pp. 59-85.

Lee, Everett S., and Anne S. Lee. "The Differential Fertility of the American Negro," *American Sociological Review* 17 (August 1952):437-447.

Lee, Everett S., and Anne S. Lee. "The Future Fertility of the American Negro," *Social Forces* 37 (March 1959):228-231.

Malina, Robert M. "Patterns of Development in Skinfolds of Negro and White Philadelphia Children," *Human Biology* 38 (May 1966):89-103.

Malina, Robert M. "Skeletal Maturation Rate in North American Negro and White Children," *Nature* (London) 223 (September 6, 1969):1075.

Pettigrew, Thomas F., and Ronald L. Nuttall. "Negro American Perception of the Irradiation Illusion," *Perceptual and Motor Skills* 17 (August 1963):98.

Reed, T. Edward. "Caucasian Genes in American Negroes," *Science* 165 (August 22, 1969):762-768. Reply and rejoinder *ibid.,* 166 (December 12, 1969):353.

Reed, T. Edward. "Research on Blood Groups and Selection from the Child Health and Development Studies, Oakland California," *American Journal of Human Genetics* 19 (November 1967):732-746.

Scott, R. B., et al. "Growth and Development of Negro Infants: V. Neuromuscular Patterns of Behavior during the First Year of Life," *Pediatrics* 16 (July 1955):24-30.

Seale, R. U. "The Weight of the Fat-Free Skeleton of American Whites and Negroes," *American Journal of Physical Anthropology* 17 (1959):37-48.

Stern, Curt. "The Biology of the Negro," *Scientific American* 191 (October 1954):81-85.

Taeuber, Karl E. "Negro Population and Housing: Demographic Aspects of a Social Accounting Scheme," in Irwin Katz and Patricia Gurin, eds., *Race and the Social Sciences.* New York: Basic Books, 1969. pp. 145-193. Bibliographical notes.

Vincent, M., and J. Hugon. "Relationships between Various Criteria of Maturity at Birth," *Biologica Neonatorum* (Basel) 4 (1962):223-279.

Walters, C. Etta. "Comparative Development of Negro and White Infants," *Journal of Genetic Psychology* 110 (June 1967):243-251. Results of Gesell Developmental Schedules Tests indicate that factors other than racial ones account for differences in the two groups.

Willie, Charles V., and William B. Rothney. "Racial, Ethnic, and Income Factors in the Epidemiology in Neonatal Mortality," *American Sociological Review* 27 (August 1962):522-526.

Zelnik, Melvin. "Fertility of the American Negro in 1830 and 1850," *Population Studies*

(Great Britain) 20 (July 1966):77–83. Compares age distribution of Negroes drawn from the decennial censuses for the period, and projects declining fertility rate.

Mental

Barglow, Peter, et al. "Some Psychiatric Aspects of Illegitimate Pregnancy in Early Adolescence," *American Journal of Orthopsychiatry* 38 (July 1968):672–687. Data gathered from a study of 78 Negro unwed mothers.

Bernard, Viola W. "Psychoanalysis and Members of Minority Groups," *Journal of the American Psychoanalytic Association* 1 (April 1953):256–267.

Block, Julia B. "The White Worker and the Negro Client in Psychotherapy," *Social Work* 13 (April 1968):37–42.

Breed, Warren. "Suicide, Migration, and Race: A Study of Cases in New Orleans," *Journal of Social Issues* 20 (January 1966):30–43.

Brody, Eugene, Robert L. Derbyshire, and Carl B. Schleifer. "How the Young Adult Baltimore Negro Male Becomes a Maryland Mental Hospital Statistic," in *Psychiatric and Mental Health Planning.* Washington: American Psychiatric Association, 1967, pp. 206–219.

Brody, Eugene B. "Social Conflict and Schizophrenic Behavior in Young Adult Negro Males," *Psychiatry* 24 (November 1961):337–346.

Chethik, Morton, et al. "A Quest for Identity: Treatment of Disturbed Negro Children in a Predominantly White Treatment Center," *American Journal of Orthopsychiatry* 37 (January 1967):71–77.

Christmas, June Jackson. "Sociopsychiatric Rehabilitation in a Black Urban Ghetto: Conflicts, Issues, and Directions," *American Journal of Orthopsychiatry* 39 (July 1969):651–661. Represents a view of a professional militant Negro and staff member in the Division of Rehabilitation Services, Harlem Hospital Center. See also articles by Wade and Hilda Richards, *ibid.*

Crawford, F. R., G. W. Hellins, and R. L. Sutherland. "Variations between Negroes and Whites in Concepts of Mental Illness and Its Treatment," *Annals of the New York Academy of Science* 84 (December 8, 1960):918–937.

Cutting, Allan R. "Segregation, Integration, and Mental Health in an Alabama Community," in Alan B. Tulipan and Saul Feldman, eds., *Psychiatric Clinics in Transition.* New York: Brunner-Mazel, 1969, pp. 53–68.

Derbyshire, R. L., et al. "Family Structure of Young Adult Negro Male Mental Patients: Preliminary Observations from Urban Baltimore," *Journal of Nervous and Mental Disease* 136 (March 1963):245–251.

Deutsch, A. "The First U.S. Census of the Insane (1840) and Its Use as Pro-Slavery Propaganda," *Bulletin of the History of Medicine* 15 (December 1944):469–482. Presented data that the rate of mental illness among Negroes was much higher in the North than in the South.

Dorfman, Elaine, and Robert J. Kleiner. "Race of Examiner and Patient in Psychiatric Diagnosis and Recommendations," *Journal of Consulting Psychology* 26 (August 1962):393.

Dreger, Ralph Mason, and Kent S. Miller. "Comparative Psychological Studies of Negroes and Whites in the United States, 1959–1965," *Psychological Bulletin.* Monograph Supplement (September 1968): entire issue.

Faris, R. E. L., and H. W. Dunham. *Mental Disorder in Urban Areas.* Chicago: University of Chicago Press, 1939. Negroes have higher rates of schizophrenia than manic depression.

Fein, Rashi. *Economics of Mental Illness.* Joint Commission on Mental Illness and Health, Monograph Series, no. 2. New York: Basic Books, 1958. An economist estimates and discusses the significance of direct and indirect costs of mental illness in the U.S. Not specifically concerned with the Negro, it nonetheless has relevance in view of the high incidence of Negro mental illness.

Fischer, Joel. "Negroes and Whites and Rates of Mental Illness: Reconsideration of a Myth," *Psychiatry* 32 (November 1969):411–427. References appended.

Friedman, Neil. "James Baldwin and Psychotherapy," *Psychotherapy: Theory, Research and Practice* 3 (September 1966):177-183. Use of Baldwin's literary insights in the treatment of a disturbed Negro woman.

Grier, William H. "When the Therapist Is Negro: Some Effects on the Treatment Process," *American Journal of Psychiatry* 123 (June 1967):1587-1592.

Grossack, Martin M., ed. *Mental Health and Segregation.* New York: Springer, 1963. Included are studies of the consequences of segregation on personality, school adjustment, mental health in both Northern and Southern states, problems of guidance and treatment, experimental studies, and case reports.

Hansen, Carl F. "Mental Health Aspects of Desegregation," *Journal of the National Medical Association* 51 (November 1959):450-456.

Hendin, Herbert. *Black Suicide.* New York: Basic Books, 1969.

Henton, C. L. "The Effect of Socio-Economic and Emotional Factors on the Onset of Menarche among Negro and White Girls," *Journal of Genetic Psychology* 98 (June 1961):255-264. Negro girls experienced more severe emotional reaction; their mothers were less alert to their needs.

Hollingshead, A. B., and F. C. Redlich. *Social Class and Mental Illness: A Community Study.* New York: Wiley, 1958. Study conducted in New Haven, Conn.

Ivins, S. P. "Psychoses in the Negro: A Preliminary Study," *Delaware State Medical Journal* 22 (August 1950):212-213.

Jaco, E. G. *The Social Epidemiology of Mental Disorders.* New York: Russell Sage Foundation, 1960.

Jahoda, Marie. *Race Relations and Mental Health.* New York: Columbia University Press, 1960.

Keeler, Martin H., and Mintauts M. Vitols. "Migration and Schizophrenia in North Carolina Negroes," *American Journal of Orthopsychiatry* 33 (April 1963):554-557.

Kellam, Sheppard G., and Sheldon K. Schiff. "The Woodlawn Mental Health Center: A Community Mental Health Center Model," *Social Service Review* 40 (September 1966):255-263.

King, Lucy Jane, et al. "Alcohol Abuse: A Crucial Factor in the Social Problems of Negro Men," *American Journal of Psychiatry* 125 (June 1969):1682-1690.

Kleiner, Robert J., and Seymour Parker. "Goal-striving, Social Status, and Mental Disorder: A Research Review," *American Sociological Review* 28 (April 1963):189-203.

Kleiner, Robert J., Jacob Tuckman, and Martha Lavell. "Mental Disorder and Status Based on Race," *Psychiatry* 23 (August 1960):271-274.

Kleiner, Robert J., Jacob Tuckman, and Martha Lavell. "Mental Disorder and Status Based on Religious Affiliation," *Human Relations* 12 (August 1959):273-276.

Kleiner, Robert J., and Seymour Parker. "Migration and Mental Illness: A New Look," *American Sociological Review* 24 (October 1959):687-690.

Knight, Octavia B. "The Self Concept of Negro and White Educable Mentally Retarded Boys," *Journal of Negro Education* 38 (Spring 1969):143-146.

Lachman, Sheldon J., and Thomas F. Waters. "Psychosocial Profile of Riot Arrestees," *Psychological Report* 24 (February 1969):171-181. One hundred male Negroes involved in Detroit riots of July 1967 were studied.

Lalli, Michael, and Stanley H. Turner. "Suicide and Homicide: A Comparative Analysis by Race and Occupation Levels," *Journal of Criminal Law, Criminology and Police Science* 59 (June 1968):191-200.

Lane, Ellen A. "The Influence of Sex and Race on Process-Reactive Ratings of Schizophrenics," *Journal of Psychology* 68 (January 1968):15-20.

Leventman, Seymour. "Race and Mental Illness in Mass Society," *Social Problems* 16 (Summer 1968):73-78.

Levinson, D. A., et al. "Assertive versus Passive Group and Negro Schizophrenic Hospital Patients," *International Journal of Group Psychotherapy* 17 (July 1967):328-335.

Maas, Jeannette P. "Incidence and Treatment: Variations between Negroes and Caucasians in Mental Illness," *Community Mental Health Journal* 3 (Spring 1967):61-65.

Mackler, Bernard. "The '600' Schools: Dilemmas, Problems, and Solutions," *Urban Review,* June 1966, pp. 8-15. The author questions the number of Negroes and Puerto Ricans in these special New York schools for socially maladjusted and emotionally disturbed children. Rebuttals by Albert Budnick and David N. Shapiro, and a rejoinder by the author *ibid.,* November 1966, 28-30.

Malzberg, Benjamin. "Mental Disease among Native and Foreign-Born Negroes in New York State," *Journal of Negro Education* 25 (Spring 1956):175-181.

Malzberg, Benjamin. *The Mental Health of the Negro: A Study of First Admissions to Hospitals for Mental Disease in New York State, 1949-1951.* Albany, N.Y.: Research Foundation for Mental Hygiene, 1963.

Malzberg, Benjamin. *New Data on Mental Disease among Negroes in New York State, 1960-1961.* Albany, N.Y.: Research Foundation for Mental Hygiene, 1965.

Mann, Philip H. "Modifying the Behavior of Negro Educable Mentally Retarded Boys through Group Counseling Procedures," *Journal of Negro Education* 38 (Spring 1969):135-142. References appended.

Parker, Seymour, and Robert J. Kleiner. *Mental Illness in the Urban Negro Community.* New York: Free Press, 1966. Comparative study of selected Negroes in Philadelphia on basis of goal-striving techniques. Bibliography.

Pasamanick, Benjamin. "Mental Subnormality," *New England Journal of Medicine* 266 (May 24, 1962):1092-1097.

Pasamanick, Benjamin. "Myths Regarding Prevalence of Mental Disease in the American Negro: A Century of Misuse of Mental Hospital Data and Some New Findings," *Journal of the National Medical Association* 56 (January 1964):6-17.

Pasamanick, Benjamin, and Hilda Knobloch. "Race, Complications of Pregnancy, and Neuropsychiatric Disorders," *Social Problems* 5 (Winter 1957-1958):267-278.

Pasamanick, Benjamin. "Some Misconceptions Concerning Differences in the Racial Prevalence of Mental Disease," *American Journal of Orthopsychiatry* 33 (January 1963):72-86. The author is sceptical of conclusions that Negroes have higher rates of psychoses.

Popkin, D. R. "Resurrection City, U.S.A.: Social Action and Mental Health," *Perspectives in Psychiatric Care* 6 (September-October 1968):198-204.

Prange, A. J., Jr., and M. M. Vitols. "Jokes among Southern Negroes: The Revelation of Conflict," *Journal of Nervous and Mental Disease* 136 (February 1963):162-167.

Richards, Hilda, and Marionette S. Daniels. "Sociopsychiatric Rehabilitation in a Black Urban Ghetto: Innovative Treatment Roles and Approaches," *American Journal of Orthopsychiatry* 39 (July 1969):662-676.

Riese, H. "Group Therapeutical Experience with Antisocial and Prepsychotic Negro Children," *Acta Psychotherapeutica et Psychosomatica* (Basel), Supplement to 7 (1959):319-327.

Robins, Lee N., and George E. Murphy. "Drug Use in a Normal Population of Young Negro Men," *American Journal of Public Health* 57 (September 1967):1580-1596.

Rose, Arnold M. "Psychoneurotic Breakdown among Negro Soldiers in Combat," *Phylon* 17 (Spring 1956):61-69.

Rosen, H., and J. D. Frank. "Negroes in Psychotherapy," *American Journal of Psychiatry* 119 (November 1962):456-460.

Rosenbaum, Max, Alvin Sandowsky, and Eugene Hartley. "Group Psychotherapy and the Integration of the Negro," *International Journal of Group Psychotherapy* 16 (January 1966):86-90. The effectiveness of group therapy as an instrument of social change.

Rushing, William A. "Suicide and the Interaction of Alcoholism (Liver Cirrhosis) with the Social Situation," *Quarterly Journal of Studies on Alcohol* 30 (March 1969):93-103.

Sabagh, Georges, et al. "Social Class and Ethnic Status of Patients Admitted to a State Hospital for the Retarded," *Pacific Sociological Review* 2 (Fall 1959):76-80.

Scher, Maryonda. "Negro Group Dynamics," *Archives of General Psychiatry* 17 (December 1967):646-651. Summary of a seminar of predominantly economically-deprived, religious, urban, adult, Negro participants.

Schermerhorn, R. A. "Psychiatric Disorders among Negroes: A Sociological Note," *American Journal of Psychiatry* 112 (1956):878-882.

Sclare, A. "Cultural Determinants in the Neurotic Negro," *British Journal of Medical Psychology* 26 (Part 4 1953):278-288.

Shane, M. "Some Subcultural Consideration in the Psychotherapy of a Negro Patient," *Psychiatric Quarterly* 34 (January 1960):9-27.

Stewart, D. D. "Posthospital Social Adjustment of Former Mental Patients from Two Arkansas Counties," *Southwestern Social Sciences Quarterly* 35 (March 1955):317-323.

Vitols, Mintauts M., H. G. Waters, and Martin H. Keeler. "Hallucinations and Delusions in White and Negro Schizophrenics," *American Journal of Psychiatry* 120 (November 1963):472-476. The incidence of hallucinations is greater among Negroes.

Vitols, Mintauts M. "The Significance of the Higher Incidence of Schizophrenia in the Negro Race in North Carolina," *North Carolina Medical Journal* 22 (April 1961):147-158.

Waite, Richard R. "The Negro Patient and Clinical Theory," *Journal of Consulting and Clinical Psychology* 32 (August 1968):427-433. Questions the need for "New" clinical theories for the successful therapeutic treatment of Negro patients.

Wilson, D. C., and Edna M. Lantz. "The Effect of Culture Change on the Negro Race in Virginia as Indicated by a Study of State [Mental] Hospital Admissions," *American Journal of Psychiatry* 114 (July 1957):25-32.

Zegans, Leonard S., Martin S. Schwartz, and Rhetaugh Dumas. "A Mental Health Center's Response to Racial Crisis in an Urban High School," *Psychiatry* 32 (August 1969):252-264. The role of the Connecticut Mental Health Center in a racially-tense integrated high school.

Patterns and Diseases

Adams, M. S., et al. "Iron-Deficiency Anemia in Negro Infants and Children in the Metropolitan Area of the District of Columbia," *Medical Annals of the District of Columbia* 32 (October 1963):391-393.

Alter, S. M. "Multiple Sclerosis in the Negro," *Archives of Neurology* 7 (August 1962):83-91.

Anderson, R. S., and Laurie M. Gunter. "Sex and Diabetes Mellitus: A Comparative Study of 26 Negro Males and 26 Negro Females Matched for Age," *American Journal of the Medical Sciences* 242 (October 1961):481-486.

Bates, William M. "Narcotics, Negroes and the South," *Social Forces* 45 (September 1966):61-67. Analysis of study of addicted males admitted to two U.S. Public Health Hospitals, 1935-1964.

Baumgartner, Leona. "Urban Reservoirs of Tuberculosis," *American Review of Tuberculosis* 79 (May 1959):687-689.

Berry, L. H. "Black Men and Malignant Fevers," *Journal of the National Medical Association* 56 (January 1964):43-47.

Cavusoglu, M., and L. H. Levine. "Gout in the Negro Female," *New York Journal of Medicine* 60 (August 15, 1960):2597-2600.

"Centennial Conference on the Health Status of the Negro Today and in the Future, March 13-14, 1967." Washington, Howard University College of Medicine, 1967. Mimeographed.

Christopherson, W. M., and J. E. Parker. "A Study of the Relative Frequency of Carcinoma of the Cervix in the Negro," *Cancer* 13 (July-August 1960):711-713.

Clausen, J. A. "Drug Addiction," in R. K. Morton and R. A. Nisbet, eds., *Contemporary Social Problems*. New York: Harcourt, Brace, 1961. Negroes constitute 60 percent of addicts.

Comstock, G. W. "An Epidemiologic Study of Blood Pressure Levels in a Biracial Community in the Southern United States," *American Journal of Hygiene* 65 (May 1957):271-315.

Cornely, Paul B. "The Health Status of the Negro Today and in the Future," *American Journal of Public Health* 58 (April 1968):647-654.

Cultural Considerations in Changing Health Attitudes. Washington: Department of Preventive Medicine and Public Health, Howard University, 1961.

Damon, Albert. "Negro-White Differences in Pulmonary Function (Vital Capacity, Timed

Vital Capacity, and Expiratory Flow Rate)," *Human Biology* 38 (December 1966):380-393.

Damon, Albert. "Race, Ethnic Group, and Disease," *Social Biology* 16 (June 1969):69-80. References appended.

Deschin, Celia S. *Teen-Agers and Venereal Disease.* Atlanta, Ga.: U.S. Department of Health, Education, and Welfare, 1961.

Globetti, Gerald A. "A Comparative Study of White and Negro Teenage Drinking in Two Mississippi Communities," *Phylon* 28 (Summer 1967):131-138.

Goldstein, M. S. "Longevity and Health Status of the Negro American," *Journal of Negro Education* 32 (Fall 1963):337-348.

Grant, F. W., and D. Groom. "A Dietary Study among a Group of Southern Negroes," *Journal of the American Dietetic Association* 35 (September 1959):910-918.

Groom, D., et al. "Coronary and Aortic Artereosclerosis in the Negroes of Haiti and the United States," *Annals of Internal Medicine* 51 (August 1959):270-289.

Hanissian, A. "Cystic Fibrosis in Negro Children," *Memphis and Mid-South Medical Journal* 43 (1968):261-262.

Hernandez, Francis A., Robert H. Miller and George L. Schiebler. "Rarity of Coarctation of the Aorta in the American Negro," *Journal of Pediatrics* 74 (April 1969):623-625.

Herring, B. D. "Pernicious Anemia and the American Negro," *American Practitioner* 13 (August 1962):544-548.

Hilleboe, H. E., and B. W. Larimore, eds. *Preventive Medicine.* Philadelphia: Saunders, 1962. Includes data on parasitic diseases of Negro Southerners.

Hingson, R. A. "Comparative Negro and White Mortality During Anesthesia, Obstetrics and Surgery," *Journal of the National Medical Association* 49 (July 1957):203-211.

Kiser, Clyde V. "Trends in Fertility Differentials by Color and Socioeconomic Status in the United States," *Eugenics Quarterly* 15 (December 1968):221-226.

Kitagawa, Evelyn M., and Philip M. Hauser. "Trends in Differential Fertility and Mortality in a Metropolis—Chicago," in E. W. Burgess and D. J. Bogue, eds., *Contributions to Urban Sociology.* Chicago: University of Chicago Press, 1964, pp. 59-85. By 1950 most of the difference between white and nonwhite fertility rates could be attributed to differences in socioeconomic status. As for differential mortality, gradual convergence in mortality differentials by color and socioeconomic status indicates rising accessibility of all groups to good medical care.

Maddox, George L. "Drinking among Negroes: Inferences from the Drinking Patterns of Selected Negro Male Collegians," *Journal of Health and Social Behavior* 9 (June 1968):114-120. Bibliography.

Maddox, George L., and Jay R. Williams. "Drinking Behavior of Negro Collegians," *Quarterly Journal of Studies on Alcohol* 29 (March 1968):117-129. Includes a review of the literature on drinking against which the samplings of this survey are compared and analyzed.

Matsuda, R. "Relative Growth of Negro and White Children in Philadelphia," *Growth* 27 (December 1963):271-284.

Moosbruker, Jane, and Anthony Jong. "Racial Similarities and Differences in Family Dental-care Patterns," *Public Health Reports* 84 (August 1969):721-727. Negro and White subjects drawn from a Boston Head Start Program of 1967.

Newman, Russell W. "Cold Acclimation in Negro Americans," *Journal of Applied Physiology* 27 (September 1969):316-319.

Nichaman, M. Z., E. Boyle, Jr., T. P. Lesesne, and H. I. Sauer. "Cardiovascular Disease Mortality by Race, Based on a Statistical Study in Charleston, South Carolina," *Geriatrics* 17 (November 1962):724-737.

Oh, Shin Joony, and Calvin L. Calhoun. "Multiple Sclerosis in the Negro," *Journal of the National Medical Association* 61 (September 1969): 388-392.

Payton, E., E. P. Crump, and C. P. Horton. "Growth and Development VII: Dietary Habits of 571 Pregnant Southern Negro Women," *Journal of the American Dietetic Association* 37 (August 1960):129-136.

Pettigrew, Ann Hallman, and Thomas F. Pettigrew. "Race, Disease, and Desegregation: A
    New Look," *Phylon* 24 (Winter 1963):315-333. A valuable survey leading to the con-
    clusion that "the 'racial diferences' in health that do exist provide further evidence of the
    societal need for desegregation and improved living conditions for all Americans." Ex-
    tensive bibliographical footnotes.
Phillips, J. H., and G. E. Burch. "Cardiovascular Diseases in the White and Negro Races,"
    American Journal of the Medical Sciences 238 (July 1959):97-124.
Reitzes, Dietrich C. *Negroes and Medicine.* Cambridge, Mass.: Harvard University Press,
    1958. Part I is a study of medical education for Negro students, with emphasis on factors
    limiting their entry into the profession. Part II covers care by and for Negroes in fourteen
    communities, with emphasis on factors affecting integration of Negro doctors into the
    larger medical community. A substantial work on medical services for and by Negroes.
Roberts, H. J. "The Syndrome of Narcolepsy and Diabetogenic Hyperinsulinism in the
    American Negro: Its Relationship to the Pathogenesis of Diabetes Mellitus, Obesity,
    Dysrhythmias, and Accelerated Cardiovascular Disease," *Journal of the National Medical
    Association* 56 (January 1964):18-42.
Robins, Lee N., George E. Murphy, and Mary B. Breckenridge. "Drinking Behavior of
    Young Urban Negro Men," *Quarterly Journal of Studies on Alcohol* 29 (September
    1968):657-684.
Rose, G. "Cardiovascular Mortality among American Negroes," *Archives of Environmental
    Health* 5 (November 1962):412-414.
Rosner, Fred, and Florence S. Steinberg. "Dermatoglyphic Patterns of Negro Men with
    Schizophrenia," *Diseases of the Nervous System* 29 (November 1968):739-743.
Russell, A. L., and P. Ayres. "Periodontal Disease and Socioeconomic Status in Birming-
    ham, Ala.," *American Journal of Public Health* 50 (February 1960):206-214.
Seltzer, A. P. "The Incidence of Otosclerosis among Negroes," *Journal of the National Medi-
    cal Association* 53 (September 1961):502-503.
Southern Rural Research Project. *Black Farm Families—Hunger and Malnutrition in Rural
    Alabama: A Survey by Southern Research Project of Living Conditions in Eight Counties.*
    Selma, Ala., 1968.
Stamler, J., et al. "Racial Patterns of Coronary Heart Disease," *Geriatrics* 16 (August
    1961):382-396.
Steiner, P. E. "Cancer and Race, with Emphasis on the American and African Negroes and
    on the Mexican," *Unio Internationalis Contra Cancrum* (Louvain) 13 (1957):959-966.
Sterne, M. W. *Drinking Patterns and Alcoholism among American Negroes.* St. Louis: Social
    Science Institute, Washington University, 1966.
Strayer, R. "A Study of the Negro Alcoholic," *Quarterly Journal of Studies on Alcohol* 22
    (March 1961):111-123.
Tuberculosis in White and Negro Children. Vol. I: *The Roentgenologic Aspects of the Harriet
    Lane Study,* by Janet B. Hardy. Vol. II: *The Epidemiologic Aspects of the Harriet Lane
    Study,* by Miriam E. Brailey. Cambridge, Mass.: Published for the Commonwealth Fund
    by Harvard University Press, 1958.
Vitols, Mintauts M. "Culture Patterns of Drinking in Negro and White Alcoholics,"
    Diseases of the Nervous System 29 (June 1968):391-394.

Services

Babow, Irving. "Minority Group Integration in Hospitals: A Sample Survey," *Hospitals* 35
    (February 1961):47-48.
Brown, L. G. "Experience with Racial Attitudes of the Medical Profession in New Jersey,"
    Journal of the National Medical Association 55 (January 1963):66-68.
Calvet, Ivis. "Integration in Hospitals," *Interracial Review* 35 (July 1962):163+.
Carnegie, M. E. "Impact of Integration on the Nursing Profession: Historical Sketch,"
    Negro History Bulletin 28 (April 1965):154-155+.

Clark, M. Ferdinand. "A Hospital for the Black Ghetto," *Hospital Progress* 50 (February 1969):49-51. Mercy Hospital in Pittsburgh.

Cobb, W. M., ed. "Integration in Medicine: A National Need," *Journal of the National Medical Association* 49 (January 1957): entire issue. Articles listed separately.

Cobb, W. M. "The Negro Physician and Hospital Staffs," *Hospital Management* 89 (March 1960):22-24.

Cornely, P. B. "Trend in Racial Integration in Hospitals in the United States," *Journal of the National Medical Association* 49 (January 1957):8-10.

Cowles, Wylda, et al. "Health and Communication in a Negro Census Tract," *Social Problems* 10 (Winter 1963):228-236.

Dummett, C. O. "Dental Health Problems of the Negro Population," *Journal of the American Dental Association* 61 (September 1960):308-314.

Engel, Leonard. "We Could Save 40,000 Babies a Year," *New York Times Magazine*, November 17, 1963, p. 31 +. On high U.S. infant mortality rate. High rate for Negroes based on New York Health Department records.

Foster, J. T. "Survey: What's Ahead for Negro Hospitals?" *Modern Hospital* 109 (November 1967):114-116.

Friedsam, N. J., C. D. Whatley, and A. L. Rhodes. "Some Selected Aspects of Judicial Commitments of the Mentally Ill in Texas," *Texas Journal of Science* 6 (1954):27-30. Negroes are more quickly committed to mental institutions than whites. Once committed, they are less likely to receive advanced therapy.

Goldstein, R. L. "Negro Nurses in Hospitals," *American Journal of Nursing* 60 (February 1960):215-217.

Grannum, E. S. "Medical Economics and the Negro Physician," *Journal of the National Medical Association* 55 (September 1963):426-429.

Gunter, L. M. "The Effect of Segregation on Nursing Students," *Nursing Outlook* 9 (February 1961):74-76.

Hentoff, Nat. "Doctor Nyswander," *New Yorker* 41 (June 26, 1965):32-34 +; 41 (July 3, 1965):32-34 +. Account of one woman's effective, if unorthodox, efforts to aid narcotics addicts.

Hill, Adelaide Cromwell, and Frederick S. Jaffe. "Negro Fertility and Family Size Preferences: Implications for Programing of Health and Social Services," in *Daedalus. The Negro American*. Edited by Talcott Parsons and Kenneth B. Clark. Cambridge, Mass.: Houghton Mifflin, 1966, pp. 205-224.

Hirsch, E. F. "The Hospital Care of Negroes and the Appointment of Negro Physicians to Medical Staffs of Hospitals in Chicago," *Proceedings of the Institute of Medicine of Chicago* 23 (November 15, 1960):156-159.

Kenney, J. A., Jr. "Medical Civil Rights," *Journal of the National Medical Association* 55 (September 1963):430-432.

Kenney, J. A., Jr. "What the NMA Can Do About the Shortage of Physicians," *Journal of the National Medical Association* 55 (January 1963):46-48.

Kosa, John, Aaron Antonovsky, and Irving Kenneth Zola, eds. *Poverty and Health: A Sociological Analysis*. Cambridge, Mass.: Harvard University Press, 1969. A joint venture of 13 scholars, this book is a systematic and exhaustive study of one of the crucial problems of present day American society.

Langer, E. "Hospital Discrimination: HEW Criticized by Civil Rights Groups," *Science* 149 (September 17, 1965):355-357.

Lees, Hannah. "Negro Response to Birth Control," *Reporter* 34 (May 19, 1966):46-48.

Liamer, Laurence. "The New Ghetto Medicine," *New Leader* 52 (August 18, 1969):9-12. Harlem Hospital.

McLean, F. C. "Negroes and Medicine in Chicago," *Proceedings of the Institute of Medicine of Chicago* 23 (January 15, 1960):2-6.

Melton, Marli Schenck. "Health Manpower and Negro Health: The Negro Physician," *Journal of Medical Education* 43 (July 1968):798-814. Characteristics of the Negro physician and his relationship to the community.

Milio, Nancy. "Project in a Negro Ghetto," *American Journal of Nursing* 67 (May 1967):1006–1009. Successful health care must relate to the people served.

Morais, Herbert M. *The History of the Negro in Medicine.* 2d ed. New York: Publishers Co., 1968. (International Library of Negro Life and History)

Morris, H. H., Jr., K. E. Appel, and J. L. Procope. "Psychiatric, Community, and Racial Integration in a General Hospital," *American Journal of Psychiatry* 119 (May 1963):1049–1054.

Motley, C. B. "Desegregation: What It Means to the Medical Professions and the Responsibilities It Places on the Negro Professionals," *Journal of the National Medical Association* 55 (September 1963):441–443.

Nash, Robert M. "The Concern of a Health Professional for Negroes in a Segregated Society," *American Journal of Public Health* 59 (February 1969):209–210.

National Urban League. *Health Care and the Negro Population.* New York, 1965.

Peters, Ann DeHuff, and Charles L. Chase. "Patterns of Health Care in Infancy in a Rural Southern County," *American Journal of Public Health* 57 (March 1967):409–423. Describes differences in health care for white and Negro infants. Prescriptions for positive action.

Pierce, H. E., Jr. "Surgical Planning for Cosmetic Defects in the Negro," *Journal of the National Medical Association* 51 (May 1959):190–198.

Robertson, Leon S., et al. "Race, Status and Medical Care," *Phylon* 28 (Winter 1967):353–360. Results of a Boston, Mass. study indicate differences in use of medical resources: Negroes making greater use of impersonal clinics for routine and acute illnesses.

Scholz, B. W. "Medicine in the Slums," *New York State Journal of Medicine* 63 (July 15, 1963):2132–2138.

Shaw, Bynum. "Let Us Now Praise Dr. Gatch," *Esquire* 69 (June 1968):108–111. Hunger, poverty, and inadequate health services for Negroes in Beaufort County, South Carolina as found by a white physician in his daily practice.

Smith, Earl B. "Medical Justice and Injustice," *Interracial Review* 35 (November 1962):254–255.

Smith, Earl B. "Practical Aspects of Hospital Integration," *Journal of the National Medical Association* 52 (September 1960):367–368.

Snyder, J. D. "Race Bias in Hospitals: What the Civil Rights Commission Found," *Hospital Management* 96 (November 1963):52–54.

Stevens, Rutherford B. "Interracial Practices in Mental Hospitals," *Mental Hygiene* 36 (January 1952):56–65.

Stewart, William F., and Louise M. Okaka. *Differential Participation of Low-Income Urban Negroes in a Public Health Birth-Control Program.* Paper presented at the 1967 meeting of the Population Association of America, April 27–29, 1967, in Cincinnati. Abstracted in *Population Index* 33 (July–September 1967):331–332. Based on a program instituted by the District of Columbia Department of Health.

Swift, David W. "Interracial Effectiveness of Sub-professional Aides," *Phylon* 30 (Winter 1969):394–397. Negro health aides in lower-class neighborhoods.

Thompson, W. A., et al. "The Negro in Medicine in Detroit," *Journal of the National Medical Association* 55 (November 1963):475–481.

U.S. Commission on Civil Rights. *Title VI, One Year After: A Survey of Desegregation of Health and Welfare Services in the South.* Washington, 1966.

Watkins, Elizabeth L. "Low-Income Negro Mothers—Their Decision to Seek Pre-Natal Care," *American Journal of Public Health* 58 (April 1968):655–667.

5 Biography and Letters

Collections

Adams, Russell L. *Great Negroes, Past and Present.* Chicago: Afro-American Publishing Co., 1963.

Bennett, Lerone. *Pioneers In Protest.* Chicago: Johnson, 1968.

Bontemps, Arna, ed. *Great Slave Narratives.* Boston: Beacon, 1969. Contents: "The Life of Olandah Equianor, or Gustavus Vassa, the African," "The Fugitive Blacksmith, or Events in the History of James W. C. Pennington, Pastor of A Presbyterian Church, Formerly A Slave in the State of Maryland," and "Running a Thousand Miles for Freedom, or the Escape of William and Ellen Craft from Slavery."

Bontemps, Arna. *One Hundred Years of Negro Freedom.* New York: Dodd, Mead, 1961. Presented through the lives of Negro leaders from the Civil War to the present.

Cherry, Gwendolyn, Ruby Thomas, and Pauline Willis. *Portraits in Color: The Lives of Colorful Negro Women.* Paterson, N.J.: Pageant, 1962.

David, Jay, ed. *Growing Up Black.* New York: Morrow, 1968. Autobiographical selections of 19 negroes whose maturity was shaped by the America of the last two centuries.

Durham, Philip, and Everett L. Jones. *The Negro Cowboys.* New York: Dodd Mead, 1965.

Ginzberg, Eli, and Hyman Berman. *The American Worker in the Twentieth Century: A History Through Biographies.* New York: Free Press, 1963. An attempt to portray American labor history through the words of the workers themselves. Includes some life histories of Negro workers, especially from the years since 1941.

Jones, J. Ralph. "Portraits of Georgia Slaves," *Georgia Review* 21 (Spring 1967):126–132; (Summer 1967):268–273; (Fall 1967):407–411; (Winter 1967):521–525. A collection of interviews with ex-slaves amassed 30 or more years prior to publication.

Metcalf, George R. *Black Profiles.* 1968. Rev. ed. New York: McGraw-Hill, 1970. M. L. King, W. E. B. DuBois, Roy Wilkins, T. Marshall, J. Robinson, H. Tubman, M. Evers, J. Meredith, R. Parks, E. Brooke, W. M. Young, Jr. Revision includes biographies of Malcolm X and E. Cleaver.

Nichols, Charles H. *Many Thousand Gone: The Ex-slaves Account of Their Bondage and Freedom.* Leiden: Brill, 1963. Bloomington: Indiana University Press, 1969.

Osofsky, Gilbert, ed. *Puttin' on Ole Massa: The Slave Narratives of Henry Bibb, William Wells Brown and Solomon Northup.* New York: Harper, 1969. A lengthy introduction by the editor gives added perspective and significance to the autobiographies.

Redding, Jay Saunders. *The Lonesome Road.* Garden City, N.Y.: Doubleday, 1958. The story of the Negro's part in America told through the life stories of a number of Negroes, from Daniel Payne to Thurgood Marshall.

Robinson, Wilhelmena A. *Historical Negro Biographies.* 2d ed. New York: Publishers Co., 1968. Popularly written. Useful for the period of coverage. (International Library of Negro Life and History)

Who's Who in Colored America. 1927. 7th (and last ed.) New York: Who's Who in Colored America Corp., 1950.

Williams, Ethel L. *Biographical Directory of Negro Ministers.* New York: Scarecrow, 1965.
Yetman, Norman R. "The Background of the Slave Narrative Collection," *American Quar-*
terly 19 (Fall 1967):534-553. The slave narrative collection as a Federal Writers' Project.

Individual Biography

ABBOTT, ROBERT S.
Ottley, Roi. *The Lonely Warrior: The Life and Times of Robert S. Abbott.* Chicago: Regnery,
1955. Journalist; founder of the *Chicago Defender.*

ALLEN, RICHARD
Harper, Howard V., ed. "Richard Allen," in *Profiles of Protestant Saints.* New York: Fleet
Press, 1968, pp. 56-76. Biography of the first Negro bishop in America (1760-1831).

BETHUNE, MARY MCLEOD
Holt, Rackham. *Mary McLeod Bethune, A Biography.* Garden City, N.Y.: Doubleday, 1964.

BETHUNE, THOMAS GREENE
Robinson, Norbonne T. N., III. "Blind Tom, Musical Prodigy," *Georgia Historical Quarterly*
51 (September 1967):336-358.

BROWNE, CLAUDE
Brown, Claude. *Manchild in the Promised Land.* New York: Macmillan, 1965. The autobiography of a young man whose Harlem childhood and "education" included belonging
to a gang, being sent to a school for "emotionally disturbed" boys and subsequently to a
reform school, and who now, just graduated from Howard University, plans to study
law. Good writing.

BROWN, H. RAP
Brown, H. Rap. *Die, Nigger, Die.* New York: Dial, 1969. Political autobiography.

BROWN, WILLIAM WELLS
Brown, William W. *Narrative of William W. Brown, A Fugitive Slave.* 1848. Introduction by
Larry Gara. Reading, Mass.: Addison-Wesley, 1969. Experiences of a slave in St. Louis
and following.
Farrison, William Edward. *William Wells Brown: Author and Reformer.* Chicago: University
of Chicago Press, 1969. Literary portrait of a novelist and historian and one of the first
Negro abolitionists.

BROWNE, ROSE BUTLER
Browne, Rose Butler, and James English. *Love My Children: An Autobiography.* Des Moines,
Iowa: Meredith, 1969. A sensitive recounting of upbringing in a Northern ghetto coupled
with specific proposals for teaching young disadvantaged Negro children.

CARVER, GEORGE WASHINGTON
Holt, Rackham. *George Washington Carver.* Garden City, N.Y.: Doubleday, 1943.

CAYTON, HORACE R.
Cayton, Horace R. *Long Old Road: An Autobiography.* New York: Trident, 1965. Life of a
distinguished sociologist, co-author of *Black Metropolis* and *Black Workers.*

CLEAGE, ALBERT B., JR.
Ward, Hiley H. *Prophet of the Black Nation: A Biography of the Reverend Albert B. Cleage,*
Jr. Philadelphia: United Church Press, 1969.

CLEAVER, ELDRIDGE
Cleaver, Eldridge. *Soul on Ice.* New York: McGraw-Hill, 1968. Essays and letters written

from prison reflecting the author's spiritual and intellectual conversion from apathy to militancy.

CULLEN, COUNTEE

Ferguson, Blanche E. *Countee Cullen and the Negro Renaissance.* New York: Dodd Mead, 1966.

DANCY, JOHN C.

Dancy, John C. *Sand Against the Wind.* Detroit: Wayne State University Press, 1966. Blends account of his long association with the Detroit Urban League with a social perspective of the Negro and thoughtful comments on race relations.

DAVIS, BENJAMIN J.

Davis, Benjamin J. *Communist Councilman from Harlem: Autobiographical Notes Written from a Federal Penitentiary.* New York: International, 1969.

DAVIS, SAMMY, JR.

Davis, Sammy, Jr., with Jane and Burt Boyar. *Yes I Can.* New York: Farrar, 1965. Autobiography of a highly successful entertainer who has both surmounted his own racial struggles and contributed greatly to the cause of his fellow Negroes.

DOUGLASS, FREDERICK

Douglass, Frederick. *Narrative of the Life of Frederick Douglass, an American Slave, Written by Himself.* Boston: Anti-Slavery Office, 1845. Edited by Benjamin Quarles. Cambridge, Mass.: Harvard University Press, 1960. The reissue includes a lengthy critical introduction by the editor.

Foner, Philip S. *Frederick Douglass.* New York: Citadel, 1964.

Hale, Frank W. "Frederick Douglass: Antislavery Crusader and Lecturer," *Journal of Human Relations* 14 (First Quarter 1966):100-111.

DUBOIS, W. E. B.

Broderick, Francis L. *W. E. B. DuBois, Negro Leader in a Time of Crisis.* Stanford, Calif.: Stanford University Press, 1959.

DuBois, W. E. B. *The Autobiography of W. E. B. DuBois; A Soliloquy on Viewing My Life from the Last Decade of Its First Century.* Edited by Herbert Aptheker. New York: International Publishers, 1968. Third volume of autobiography of the elderly black leader. Completed in 1960. Portraits. A selected bibliography of the published writings of DuBois is appended.

Howe, I. "Remarkable Man, Ambiguous Legacy," *Harper* 236 (March 1968):143-149.

"The Problem of Color in the Twentieth Century: A Memorial to W. E. B. DuBois," *Journal of Human Relations* 14 (First Quarter 1966):1-84.

Rudwick, Elliott M. *W. E. B. DuBois: Propagandist of the Negro Protest.* New York: Atheneum, 1968. First published in 1960 under the title *W. E. B. DuBois: A Study in Minority Group Leadership* by the University of Pennsylvania Press. Reissued with a new preface by Louis R. Harlan and an epilogue by the author as part of the series, Studies in American Negro Life.

EVERS, MEDGAR H.

Evers, Mrs. Medgar, with William Peters. *For Us the Living.* Garden City, N.Y.: Doubleday, 1967. Biography of her husband, with important autobiographical aspects.

GARVEY, MARCUS.

Cronon, E. D. *Black Moses.* Madison, Wis.: University of Wisconsin Press, 1955. Biography of Marcus Garvey.

GREGORY, DICK

Gregory, Dick, with Robert Lipsyte. *Nigger: An Autobiography.* New York: Dutton, 1964. The vivid life story of a Negro entertainer who has actively engaged in the Negro protest movement.

HENSON, JOSIAH

Henson, Josiah. *An Autobiography of the Reverend Josiah Henson.* 1881. With an introduction by Robin W. Winks. Reading, Mass.: Addison-Wesley, 1969. Narrative of a Kentucky fugitive slave and the "Dawn" attempt to establish a free all-Negro Canadian community. Henson became identified as "Uncle Tom" of Stowe's novel. The introduction traces the use of the narrative by the abolitionists.

HUGHES, LANGSTON

Meltzer, Milton. *Langston Hughes: A Biography.* New York: Crowell, 1968.

JOHNSON, JAMES WELDON

Adelman, Lynn. "A Study of James Weldon Johnson," *Journal of Negro History* 52 (April 1967):128-145.

Johnson, James Weldon. *Along My Way.* New York: Viking, 1933. Memoirs.

JONES, J. RAYMOND.

Connable, Alfred, and Edward Silverfarb. "J. Raymond Jones," in *Tigers of Tammany.* New York: Holt, 1967, pp. 334-364. Profile of a black political leader.

KING, MARTIN LUTHER, JR.

Atlanta. Ebenezer Baptist Church. *Obsequies, Martin Luther King, Jr. Tuesday, April 9, 1968, 10:30 A.M. . . .* Atlanta, 1968.

Bennett, Lerone, Jr. *What Manner of Man: A Biography of Martin Luther King, Jr.* Chicago: Johnson, 1964. Assesses the King achievement through 1964, and considers various criticisms of his tactics.

King, Coretta Scott. *My Life with Martin Luther King, Jr.* New York: Holt, Rinehart & Winston, 1969.

Lewis, David. *King: A Critical Biography.* New York: Praeger, 1970. Based on extensive research by the author, a Georgia black historian. Notable bibliography of primary and secondary sources.

Lincoln, C. Eric. *Martin Luther King, Jr.: A Profile.* New York: Hill & Wang, 1970. Thirteen essays by black and white contributors including Carl Rowan, Vincent Harding, August Meier, and David Halberstam. The collection is introduced with an unusually moving piece by Rev. Abernathy.

Miller, William Robert. *Martin Luther King: His Life, Martyrdom, and Meaning.* New York: Webright & Talley, 1968. With a partially annotated bibliography. Maps, portraits.

Reddick, Lawrence D. *Crusader Without Violence.* New York: Harper, 1959. Biography of Martin Luther King by a member of the faculty of Alabama State College and a witness of the Montgomery bus boycott.

LITTLE, MALCOLM

Breitman, George. *The Last Year of Malcolm X.* New York: Merit Publishers, 1967. Bibliography.

Clark, John Henrik, ed. *Malcolm X: The Man and His Time.* New York: Macmillan, 1969. A gathering of festschrift and critical appraisals of the black leader, as well as some of his own speeches. Complements his autobiography.

Little, Malcolm. *The Autobiography of Malcolm X.* New York: Grove, 1965. The life story and spiritual evolution of an extraordinary man—from rootless hipster to fiercely racist Black Muslim leader, who, by the time of his assassination in 1965, had adopted a world view of Islam and was moving towards a position of understanding and toleration for all men. One of the most powerful, influential books of the 1960's.

MALCOLM X *see* LITTLE, MALCOLM

MALVIN, JOHN

Malvin, John. *North Into Freedom: The Autobiography of John Malvin, Free Negro, 1795-1880.* Edited with an introduction by Allan Peskin. Cleveland: Case Western Reserve University Press, 1966.

MOODY, ANNE

Moody, Anne. *Coming of Age in Mississippi.* New York: Dial Press, 1968. A stimulating
autobiography of a 28-year-old black girl tracing her life from a rural poverty childhood
to an activist position in the civil rights movement. The narration ends in 1964.

NORTHUP, SOLOMON

Northup, Solomon. *Twelve Years A Slave.* 1853. Edited by Sue Eakin and Joseph Logsdon.
Baton Rouge: Louisiana State University Press, 1968. A New York free Negro, lured
and sold into slavery in 1841. This edition is presented with a scholarly introduction by
the editors.

POWELL, ADAM CLAYTON

Hickey, Neil, and Ed Edwin. *Adam Clayton Powell and the Politics of Race.* New York:
Fleet, 1965.

RAPIER, JAMES T.

Feldman, Eugene Pieter Romayn. *Black Power in Old Alabama: The Life and Stirring Times
of James T. Rapier, Afro-American Congressman from Alabama, 1839-1883.* Chicago:
Museum of African History, 1968. Illustrated.

REDDING, JAY SAUNDERS

Redding, Jay Saunders. *On Being Negro in America.* Indianapolis: Bobbs-Merrill, 1951.

REED, JOHN WILLIE

Weltner, Charles Longstreet. *John Willie Reed: An Epitaph.* Atlanta: Southern Regional
Council, 1969. Biography of a rural black migrant who moved to Atlanta. It graphically
illustrates the hopelessness stemming from rural poverty and urban deprivation.

ROBESON, PAUL

Robeson, Paul. *Here I Stand.* New York: Othello Associates, 1958.

ROWAN, CARL

Rowan, Carl. *Go South to Sorrow.* New York: Random, 1957. Life of a Negro journalist and
diplomat.

SANDERSON, JEREMIAH B.

Lapp, Rudolph M. "Jeremiah B. Sanderson: Early California Negro Leader," *Journal of
Negro History* 53 (October 1968):321-333. His political involvement and role as
educator.

SCHUYLER, GEORGE S.

Schuyler, George S. *Black and Conservative.* New York: Arlington House, 1966.
Autobiography.

SHAW, ROBERT GOULD

Burchard, Peter. *One Gallant Rush.* New York: St. Martin's, 1963. Leader of a Negro
regiment of Massachusetts volunteers in the Union army.

STEWARD, AUSTIN

Steward, Austin. *Twenty-Two Years a Slave and Forty Years a Freeman.* 1856. With an
Introduction by Jane H. and William H. Pease. Reading, Mass.: Addison-Wesley, 1969.

STILL, PETER

Toplin, Robert Brent. "Peter Still versus the Peculiar Institution," *Civil War History* 13
(December 1967):340-349. Records experiences of a divided slave family.

TEAGUE, ROBERT

Teague, Bob. *Letters to a Black Boy.* New York: Walker & Co., 1968. Letters to his infant
son preparing him for being black in a white society. Dedication page reads: "You are
not the target, my son. They don't even know you are there."

THISTLE, TAYLOR

O'Donnell, James H., III, ed. "Freedman Thanks His Patrons: Letters of Taylor Thistle, 1872-1873," *Journal of Southern History* 33 (February 1967):68-84. The thought and experience of a Negro from Missouri who attended the Nashville Normal and Theological Institute to train for the ministry.

O'Donnell, James H., III, ed. "Taylor Thistle: A Student at the Nashville Institute, 1871-1880," *Tennessee Historical Quarterly* 26 (Winter 1967):387-395. The biographical sketch of a Freedman.

TOMM, JIM

Wilson, L. D., ed. "Reminiscences of Jim Tomm," *Chronicles of Oklahoma* 44 (Fall 1966):290-306. Short biography of a Negro slave, born near Muskogee, Oklahoma in 1859.

TROTTER, WILLIAM MONROE

Fox, Stephen R. *The Guardian of Boston: William Monroe Trotter.* New York: Atheneum, 1970.

TRUTH, SOJOURNER

Bernard, Jacqueline. *Journey Toward Freedom: The Story of Sojourner Truth.* New York: Norton, 1967. Includes a select bibliography with several titles pertinent to Negro slavery and social conditions in the nineteenth century, and the freedmen.

WASHINGTON, BOOKER T.

Abramowitz, Jack. "Emergence of Booker T. Washington as a National Negro Leader," *Social Education* 32 (May 1968):445-451.

Flynn, John P. "Booker T. Washington: Uncle Tom or Wooden Horse," *Journal of Negro History* 54 (July 1969):262-274.

Harlan, Louis R. "Booker T. Washington and the White Man's Burden," *American Historical Review* 71 (January 1966):441-467.

Hawkins, Hugh. *Booker T. Washington and His Critics: Problem of Negro Leadership.* Boston: Heath, 1962. Bibliography.

Thornbrough, Emma Lou, ed. *Booker T. Washington.* Englewood Cliffs, N.J.: Prentice-Hall, 1967. Selections from Washington's writings. The leader as viewed comtemporaneously, and essays currently appraising his place in history. A useful bibliography is appended.

Thornbrough, Emma L. "Booker T. Washington as Seen by His White Contemporaries," *Journal of Negro History* 53 (April 1968):161-182.

Washington, Booker T. *Up From Slavery.* 1902, frequently reissued. Washington's theme is the need for the Negro to seek economic rather than social advancement.

WEATHERFORD, W. D.

Dykeman, Wilma. *Prophet of Plenty: The First Ninety Years of W. D. Weatherford.* Knoxville: University of Tennessee Press, 1966. A legacy of service as educator and leader of southern Negroes.

WHITE, WALTER

White, Walter. *How Far the Promised Land?* New York: Viking, 1955. White's two most notable campaigns as executive secretary of the NAACP were for federal anti-lynching legislation and against President Hoover's nomination of anti-Negro Judge John J. Parker to the Supreme Court.

WILLIAMS, DANIEL HALE

Buckler, Helen. *Daniel Hale Williams: Negro Surgeon.* 2d ed. New York: Pitman, 1968.

WRIGHT, RICHARD

Webb, Constance. *Richard Wright.* New York: Putnam, 1968. Biography. Portraits.

6 Folklore and Literature

Folklore

Abrahams, Roger D. *Deep Down in the Jungle . . .: Negro Narrative Folklore from the Streets of Philadelphia.* Hatboro, Penna.: Folklore Associates, 1964.

Abrahams, Roger D. *Positively Black.* Englewood Cliffs, N.J.: Prentice-Hall, 1970.

Brewer, John Mason. *American Negro Folklore.* Chicago: Quadrangle, 1968. A wide sampling of animal, ghost, cowboy, and religious tales from both North and South as well as tales of folk figures, sermons, superstitions, proverbs, and rhymes, culled from such folklorists as Joel Chandler Harris, Zore Hurston, Richard Dorson, and a sampling of Brewer's own works.

Brewer, J. Mason. *Worser Days and Better Times: The Folklore of the North Carolina Negro.* Chicago: Quadrangle, 1965. Preface and notes by Warren E. Roberts, drawings by R. L. Toben.

Brown, Sterling A. "Negro Folk Expression," *Phylon* 14 (Spring 1953):50-60. Observations on the uniqueness of Negro spirituals, seculars, and work-songs.

Dorson, Richard M., ed. *Negro Folktales in Michigan.* Cambridge, Mass.: Harvard University Press, 1956.

Dorson, Richard M. "Negro Tales," *Western Folklore* 13 (April 1954):77-97 and 13 (July 1954):160-169. Dorson has considerable skill in describing his storytellers, their surroundings and circumstances, with the result that the reader learns much of how his Negro subjects live.

Dorson, Richard M., ed. *Negro Tales from Pine Bluff, Arkansas, and Calvin, Michigan.* Bloomington: Indiana University Press, 1958.

Dorson, Richard M. "Negro Witch Stories on Tape," *Midwest Folklore* 2 (Winter 1952):229-241 and "A Negro Storytelling Session on Tape," *ibid.,* 3 (Winter 1953):201-212. Stories heard in Calvin Township, Cass County, Michigan, in a Negro enclave within a white farm area, where Negroes have lived and owned farms since 1840.

Dundes, Alan. "African Tales among the North American Indians," *Southern Folklore Quarterly* 29 (September 1965):207-219. The borrowing of tale types from American Negro slaves.

Hampton, Bill R. "On Identification and Negro Tricksters," *Southern Folklore Quarterly* 31 (March 1967):55-65. The "trickster" figure in Negro folklore.

Hughes, Langston, and Arna Bontemps, eds. *The Book of Negro Folklore.* New York: Dodd Mead, 1958.

Jackson, Bruce, ed. *The Negro and His Folklore in Nineteenth-Century Periodicals.* Austin: Published for the American Folklore Society by the University of Texas Press, 1967. An anthology of letters and articles published between 1838 and 1900, reflecting diverse viewpoints: from abolitionist to ardent slaveholder. Bibliography, chronologically arranged.

Jackson, Bruce. "Prison Folklore," *Journal of American Folklore* 78 (October-December 1965):317-329. See especially section on "Toasts."

Jackson, Bruce. "What Happened to Jody," *Journal of American Folklore* 80 (October 1967):387-396.

Lester, Julius. *Black Folktales.* New York: Baron, 1969.

Melnick, Mimi Clar. " 'I Can Peep Through Muddy Water and Spy Dry Land': Boasts in the Blues," in D. K. Wilgus and C. Sommer, eds., *Folklore International: Essays in Traditional Literature, Belief, and Custom in Honor of Wayland Debs Hand.* Hatboro, Penna.: Folklore Associates, 1967, pp. 139-149.

Mullen, Patrick B. "The Function of Folk Belief among Negro Fishermen of the Texas Coast," *Southern Folklore Quarterly* 33 (June 1969):80-91.

Stuckey, Sterling. "Through the Prism of Folklore: The Black Ethos in Slavery," *Massachusetts Review* 9 (Summer 1968):417-437.

For folk traditions in music *see also* Music.

Negro Authors

Abramson, Doris E. *Negro Playwrights in the American Theater, 1925-1959.* New York: Columbia University Press, 1969. An historical survey, followed by a detailed examination of 18 plays and an added chapter on the theater in the 1960s.

Adoff, Arnold, comp. *I Am the Darker Brother.* New York: Macmillan, 1968. An anthology of modern Negro poetry.

Austin, Edmund O. *The Black Challenge.* New York: Vantage Press, 1958. Novel.

Baldwin, James. *The Amen Corner.* New York: Dial Press, 1968. Publication of the author's first drama, produced in 1955 at Howard University, on Broadway in 1965.

Baldwin, James. *Another Country.* New York: Dial, 1962. Novel with New York as setting.

Baldwin, James. *Blues for Mister Charlie.* New York: Dial, 1964. Play about a young Negro who is slain by a white Southern bigot. Baldwin has said that the play is based "distantly" on the case of Emmet Till.

Baldwin, James. *Giovanni's Room.* New York: Dial, 1956. Novel set in Paris concerning conflicting heterosexual and homosexual relations.

Baldwin, James. *Go Tell It on the Mountain.* New York: Dial, 1963. Novel about growing up in Harlem.

Baldwin, James. *Going to Meet the Man.* New York: Dial, 1965. Eight short stories.

Baldwin, James. *Nobody Knows My Name.* New York: Dial, 1961. Essays.

Baldwin, James. *Notes of a Native Son.* Boston: Beacon, 1955. Essays.

Baldwin, James. *Tell Me How Long the Train's Been Gone.* New York: Dial, 1968. Novel.

Bennett, Hal. *The Black Wine.* Garden City, N.Y.: Doubleday, 1968. Novel.

Boles, Robert. *Curling.* Boston: Houghton Mifflin, 1968. Novel.

Boles, Robert. *The People One Knows.* Boston: Houghton Mifflin, 1964. Novel.

Bontemps, Arna, ed. *American Negro Poetry.* New York: Hill & Wang, 1963. Biographical sketches of contributor-poets are included.

Bontemps, Arna. *Personals.* London: Paul Breman, 1963. Poems.

Breman, Paul, ed. *Sixes and Sevens.* London: Paul Breman, 1962. Poems by 13 Negro poets.

Brooks, Gwendolyn. *Annie Allen.* New York: Harper, 1949. Poems. Miss Brooks received the Pulitzer Prize for poetry in 1950.

Brooks, Gwendolyn. *The Bean Eaters.* New York: Harper, 1960. Poems.

Brooks, Gwendolyn. *In the Mecca: Poems.* New York: Harper, 1968.

Brooks, Gwendolyn. *Maud Martha.* New York: Harper, 1953. Novel.

Brooks, Gwendolyn. *Selected Poems.* New York: Harper, 1963. Selections from earlier volumes of verse, plus a number of new poems.

Brooks, Gwendolyn. *A Street in Bronzeville.* New York: Harper, 1945. Poems which convey with great success the authentic flavor of Negro community life in Chicago.

Brown, Cecil. *The Life and Loves of Mr. Jiveass Nigger.* New York: Farrar, Straus & Giroux, 1969.

Brown, Frank L. *Trumbull Park*. Chicago: Regnery, 1959. A novel of race conflict which powerfully conveys the mood of tension developing in a public housing project.

Brown, Sterling A., Arthur P. Davis, and Ulysses Lee, eds. *The Negro Caravan*. New York: Dryden, 1941. Still a very useful source book, with an excellent introduction.

Brown, William Wells. *Clotel: Or the President's Daughter, A Narrative of Slave Life in the United States*. 1867. New York: Citadel, 1969. The first known novel by an American Negro. A concise biography by William Edward Farrison introduces the text of this edition.

Bullins, Ed. *Five Plays: Goin' a Buffalo, In the Wine Time, A Son Come Home, The Electronic Nigger, Clara's Ole Man*. Indianapolis: Bobbs-Merrill, 1969. The first two mentioned are in three acts; the remaining three are one-act pieces. "Clara's Ole Man" is also included in the anthology *Best Short Plays, 1969*.

Bullins, Ed. *How Do You Do*. Mill Valley, Calif.: Illuminations Press, 1968.

Chapman, Abraham, ed. *Black Voices: An Anthology of Afro-American Literature*. New York: New American Library, 1968. With biographical notes.

Clarke, John Henrik, ed. *American Negro Short Stories*. New York: Hill & Wang, 1966. Thirty-one stories and excerpts from novels. Selections are undated. Includes short biographical sketches of authors represented.

Cooper, Clarence. *Black! Two Short Novels*. Evanston, Ill.: Regency, 1963.

Cooper, Clarence L. *The Scene*. New York: Crown, 1960. Fiction.

Couch, William, Jr., ed. *New Black Playwrights: An Anthology*. Baton Rouge: Louisiana State University Press, 1968. Six Negro avant-garde plays by five young authors: Douglas Turner Ward, Adrienne Kennedy, Lonne Elder, Ed Bullins, and William Wellington Mackey.

Cullen, Countee. *On These I Stand*. New York: Harper, 1947. An anthology of poems selected by the author. Includes six previously unpublished pieces.

Cuney, Waring, Langston Hughes, and Bruce McM. Wright, eds. *Lincoln University Poets: Centennial Anthology*. With an introduction by J. Saunders Redding. New York: Fine Editions Press, 1954.

Davis, Ossie. *Purlie Victorious*. New York: French, 1961. Play which ridicules both Negro and Southern stereotypes.

Davis, Russell F. *Anything for a Friend*. New York: Crown, 1963. A "hip" first-person novel, the discovery of love, life, and integration at the high school level.

Demby, William. *The Catacombs*. New York: Pantheon, 1965. Autobiographical novel of the return of a Negro writer from Rome to America to seek his true identity.

Ellison, Ralph. *The Invisible Man*. New York: Random, 1952. A distinguished and angry novel about what white society does to the Negro in America.

Ellison, Ralph. "On Becoming a Writer," *Commentary* 38 (October 1964):57-60. An essay by a writer who has from the beginning refused to think of himself only as a Negro writer.

Ellison, Ralph. *Shadow and Act*. New York: Random, 1964. Twenty essays (and two interviews) written 1945-1964, the best and most personal of which show a writer concerned to understand and to make the reader understand what it is to be an American Negro today.

Emanuel, James A., and Theodore L. Gross, eds. *Dark Symphony: Negro Literature in America*. New York: Free Press, 1968. Poems, essays, and short stories of 34 contributors; selected for their intrinsic merit and to reflect the historical and literary evolution and the complexity of the Negro experience.

Fair, Ronald L. *Many Thousand Gone*. New York: Harcourt, Brace, 1965. Subtitled *An American Fable*, this short novel tells a savage and yet compassionate tale of Negro revolt in an imaginary Mississippi county.

Gaines, Ernest J. *Bloodline*. New York: Dial Press, 1969. Five short stories.

Gaines, Ernest J. *Catherine Carmier*. New York: Atheneum, 1964. A young Negro returns to teach in the South after ten years in the North. A creditable first novel.

Gordone, Charles. *No Place to Be Somebody: A Black-Black Comedy*. Indianapolis: Bobbs-Merrill, 1969.

Goyen, William. *The Fair Sister*. Garden City, N.Y.: Doubleday, 1963. Novel about a
  female evangelist with a night-club background.
Guy, Rosa. *Bird at My Window*. Philadelphia: Lippincott, 1966. A first novel, in memory of
  Malcolm X.
Hansberry, Lorraine. *A Raisin in the Sun*. New York: Random, 1959. Text of the Broadway
  play, which received the New York Critics Circle Award.
Hansberry, Lorraine. *The Sign in Sidney Burnstein's Window*. New York: Random, 1965.
  Drama.
Hansberry, Lorraine. *To Be Young, Gifted and Black: Lorraine Hansberry in Her Own Words*.
  Edited by Robert Nemiroff. Englewood Cliffs, N.J.: Prentice-Hall, 1969.
Hayden, Robert. *A Ballad of Remembrance*. London: Paul Breman, 1962. Poems.
Hayden, Robert, ed. *Kaleidoscope: Poems by American Negro Poets*. New York: Harcourt,
  Brace & World, 1967. An anthology emphasizing twentieth-century poets.
Heard, Nathan C. *Howard Street*. New York: Dial Press, 1968. A penetrating glimpse of the
  ghetto and the hatred it generates. Fiction.
Hill, Herbert, ed. *Soon, One Morning: New Writing by American Writers, 1940-1962*. New
  York: Knopf, 1963. A collection of essays, fiction, poems, "to display the range of
  contemporary writing."
Himes, Chester. *Blind Man with a Pistol*. New York: Morrow, 1969. Satire in a Harlem
  setting. Fiction.
Himes, Chester. *The Heat's On*. New York: Putnam, 1966. Novel.
Himes, Chester. *Run Man Run*. New York: Putnam, 1966. Novel.
Himes, Chester B. *Third Generation*. Cleveland: World, 1954. Novel.
Horne, Frank. *Haverstraw*. London: Paul Breman, 1963. Poems.
Hughes, Langston. *Ask Your Mama*. New York: Knopf, 1961. Poems set in a pattern of jazz
  music.
Hughes, Langston. *The Best of Simple*. New York: Hill & Wang, 1961. Selections from a
  number of Hughes's "Simple" tales.
Hughes, Langston, ed. *The Best Short Stories by Negro Writers: An Anthology from 1899 to
  the Present*. Boston: Little, Brown, 1967.
Hughes, Langston, ed. *The Book of Negro Humor*. New York: Dodd, Mead, 1966.
Hughes, Langston. *Five Plays*. Edited by Webster Smalley. Bloomington: Indiana University
  Press, 1963. Includes "Mulatto," "Soul Gone Home," "Little Ham," "Simply Heavenly,"
  "Tambourines to Glory."
Hughes, Langston. *Montage of a Dream Deferred*. New York: Holt, 1951.
Hughes, Langston, ed. *New Negro Poets U.S.A.* Bloomington: Indiana University Press,
  1964. Thirty-seven poets are represented, few in more than one or two poems. Their
  verses are widely various, from deeply personal lyric to harsh protest.
Hughes, Langston. *The Panther and the Lash: Poems of Our Times*. New York: Knopf, 1967.
Hughes, Langston, and Arna Bontemps, eds. *The Poetry of the Negro, 1746-1949*. Garden
  City, N.Y.: Doubleday, 1949.
Hughes, Langston. *Selected Poems*. New York: Knopf, 1959.
Hughes, Langston. *Simple Stakes a Claim*. New York: Rinehart, 1957. The Simple stories
  have repeatedly been highly praised.
Hughes, Langston. *Simple's Uncle Sam*. New York: Hill & Wang, 1965. Forty-six stories
  about Hughes's famous character, Jesse B. Semple, which bring his observations up to
  date on current affairs.
Hughes, Langston. *Something in Common and Other Stories*. New York: Hill & Wang, 1963.
Hunter, Kristin. *God Bless the Child*. New York: Scribner's, 1964.
Hunter, Kristin. *The Landlord*. New York: Scribner's, 1966. Novel.
Iman, Yusef. *Something Black: Freedom Poetry*. Newark, 1967.
Joans, Ted. *Black Pow-Wow*. New York: Hill & Wang, 1969. Poems.
Johnson, James Weldon, ed. *The Book of American Negro Poetry*. New York: Harcourt,
  Brace, 1922.
Johnson, James Weldon. *God's Trombones*. New York: Viking, 1927.
Johnston, Percy. *Concerto for Girl and Convertible*. Washington: Centennial Press, 1961.
  Poems.

Jones, LeRoi, and Larry Neal, eds. *Black Fire: An Anthology of Afro-American Writing*. New York: Morrow, 1968. Pieces, previously published, which give vent to their authors' anger and contempt for white culture. Includes brief biographical sketches of the contributors.

Jones, LeRoi. *Black Magic Poetry*. Indianapolis: Bobbs-Merrill, 1969. Poems run gamut from early expressions of love and goodness to black hatred of white society.

Jones, LeRoi. *The Dead Lecturer*. New York: Grove, 1964. Poems.

Jones, LeRoi. *Dutchman and the Slave*. New York: Morrow, 1964. Two plays.

Jones, LeRoi. *Four Black Revolutionary Plays*. Indianapolis: Bobbs-Merrill, 1969. Experimental Death Unite #1; A Black Mass; Great Goodness of Life; Madheart. Each is a one-act play, written in poetic form, expressing polemically an aspect of black life.

Jones, LeRoi. *The System of Dante's Hell*. New York: Grove, 1965. A novel about youth in the Negro slums of Newark.

Jones, LeRoi. *Tales*. New York: Grove, 1967.

Kearns, Francis E., ed. *The Black Experience: An Anthology of American Literature for the 1970's*. New York: Viking, 1969.

Kelley, William Melvin. *Dancers on the Shore*. Garden City, N.Y.: Doubleday, 1964. Sixteen short stories which, in spite of firm writing and control of form, are not quite up to the quality of his *A Different Drummer*.

Kelley, William Melvin. *Dem*. Garden City, N.Y.: Doubleday, 1967. Fiction.

Kelley, William Melvin. *A Different Drummer*. Garden City, N.Y.: Doubleday, 1962. A novel about the effect of a mass Negro exodus from the South on the lives of the white Southerners left behind.

Kelley, William Melvin. *A Drop of Patience*. New York: Doubleday, 1965. A novel portraying the world of Negro jazz musicians. It is intended as a bitter commentary on society's human callousness.

Killens, John O. *And Then We Heard the Thunder*. New York: Knopf, 1963. Story of a Negro soldier in World War II who becomes progressively more involved in the battle for equality. An impressive novel.

Killens, John. *'Sippi*. New York: Trident Press, 1967. Novel.

Killens, John O. *Youngblood*. New York: Dial, 1954. Novel of a Georgia Negro family during the early twentieth century.

Lee, Don L. *Don't Cry, Scream*. Detroit: Broadside Press, 1969. Poems.

Locke, Alain. *The New Negro*. New York: Boni, 1925. Author was guiding figure in Negro Renaissance of the 1920's.

Lomax, Alan, and Raoul Abdul, eds. *Three Thousand Years of Black Poetry*. New York: Dodd, Mead, 1969. Black poets from fourteenth-century Egypt to contemporary black America are represented.

Lowenfels, Walter, ed. *The Writing on the Wall: American Poems of Protest*. Garden City, N.Y.: Doubleday, 1969. Includes a wide sampling of poems by black writers.

McKay, Claude. *Home to Harlem*. New York: Harper, 1928.

McKay, Claude. *Selected Poems*. New York: Bookman, 1953.

McPherson, James Alan. *Hue and Cry*. Boston: Little, Brown, 1969. First short-story collection of a young writer.

Major, Clarence, ed. *The New Black Poetry*. New York: International, 1969. Includes some poems previously published and a brief biography of each of the 76 contributors.

Marshall, Paule. *The Chosen Place, The Timeless People*. New York: Harcourt, Brace & World, 1969. Novel.

Marshall, Paule. *Soul Clap Hands and Sing*. New York: Atheneum, 1961. Four short stories with settings in Barbados, Brooklyn, British Guiana, and Brazil.

Mayfield, Julian. *The Grand Parade*. New York: Vanguard, 1961. Novel of politics in a city along the Mason-Dixon line.

Mayfield, Julian. *The Hit*. New York: Vanguard, 1957. Novel about a Harlem Negro and the policy racket.

Mayfield, Julian. *Long Night*. New York: Vanguard, 1958. Novel of a youth in Harlem.

Miller, Warren. *Cool World*. Boston: Little, Brown, 1959. Vivid and powerful novel of the depths of Harlem life; subsequently made into a movie.

Miller, Warren. *The Siege of Harlem*. New York: McGraw-Hill, 1964. A novel describing the organization of a separate Harlem government sometime in the future.

Motley, Willard. *Let Noon Be Fair*. New York: Putnam, 1966. Posthumously published. Motley was the author of at least four earlier novels.

Neugeboren, Jay. *Big Man*. Boston: Houghton Mifflin, 1966. Fiction.

Ottley, Roi. *White Marble Lady*. New York: Farrar, Straus & Giroux, 1965. Fiction; posthumously published.

Parks, Gordon. *The Learning Tree*. New York: Harper, 1963. Novel of a Negro youth growing up in a small Kansas town during the 1920's.

Polite, Charlene Harcher. *The Flagellants*. New York: Farrar, Straus, 1967. Novel.

Pool, Rosey, ed. *Beyond the Blues: New Poems by American Negroes*. London: Headley, 1962. Collection of poems, chiefly by younger poets.

Randall, Dudley, ed. *Black Poetry: A Supplement to Anthologies which Exclude Black Poets*. Detroit: Broadside Press, 1969. Poems of more than a score of black poets are represented.

Redding, Jay Saunders. *Stranger and Alone*. New York: Harcourt, Brace, 1950. Sensitive novel of the education of a young Negro intellectual.

Reed, Ishmael. *The Free-Lance Pall Bearers*. Garden City, N.Y.: Doubleday, 1967. Novel.

Rivers, Conrad Kent. *Perchance to Dream, Othello*. Wilberforce, Ohio: Wilberforce University, 1959. Poems.

Schulberg, Budd, ed. *From the Ashes: Voices of Watts*. New York: New American Library, 1967. An anthology of poems, short stories, essays, and drama by some of the participants of the Watts Writers' Workshop, founded in 1965 by the editor.

Shuman, R. Baird, ed. *Nine Black Poets*. Durham, N.C.: Moore, 1968. Introduces Charles Cooper and other lesser-known talented poets.

Simmons, Herbert. *Corner Boy*. Boston: Houghton Mifflin, 1957. Novel of juvenile delinquency.

Simmons, Herbert. *Man Walking on Eggshells*. Boston: Houghton Mifflin, 1962.

Smith, Arthur Lee. *Break of Dawn*. Philadelphia: Dorrance, 1964. Fiction.

Smith, William Gardner. *South Street*. New York: Farrar, Straus, 1954. Novel of Philadelphia Negroes.

Smith, William Gardner. *The Stone Face*. New York: Farrar, Straus, 1963. Novel.

Tolson, M. B. *Harlem Gallery: Book I—The Curator*. New York: Twayne, 1965. Poems.

Van Dyke, Henry. *Ladies of the Rachmaninoff Eyes*. New York: Farrar, Straus & Giroux, 1965. A novel creating a viable Negro-White relationship devoid of contrived racial considerations.

Vronman, May Elizabeth. *Esther*. New York: Bantam Books, 1963. Fiction.

Walker, Margaret. *Jubilee*. Boston: Houghton Mifflin, 1966. Admirably describes the bondage of slavery in Georgia in the ante-bellum years and life during the Reconstruction.

Watkins, Sylvester C., ed. *Anthology of American Negro Literature*. New York: Random, 1944.

Wheatley, Phyllis. *Poems*. Edited with an introduction by Julian D. Mason, Jr. Chapel Hill: University of North Carolina Press, 1966. Poems selected from *Poems on Various Subjects, Religious and Moral, 1773*, as well as from periodicals and manuscripts of the author. A biographical sketch of the poet and a critical commentary is included.

Williams, John A. *Beyond the Angry Black*. 2d ed. New York: Cooper Square, 1968. A reissue with new material of *The Angry Black*, 1962. Essays, fiction, and poetry.

Williams, John A. *The Man Who Cried I Am*. Boston: Little, Brown, 1967. Novel.

Williams, John A. *Night Song*. New York: Farrar, Straus, 1961. Novel of the jazz world.

Williams, John A. *Sissie*. New York: Farrar, Straus, 1963. Novel of Negro family life.

Williams, John A. *Sons of Darkness Sons of Light: A Novel of Some Probability*. Boston: Little, Brown, 1969.

Wright, Charles. *The Messenger*. New York: Farrar, Straus, 1963. Novel of a messenger's experiences on every level of New York life, from Wall Street to the Bowery.

Wright, Charles. *The Wig, a Mirror Image*. London: Souvenir Press, 1968. Fiction.

Wright, Richard. *Black Boy*. New York: Harper, 1945. Harrowing record of the author's childhood and youth in Chicago.

Wright, Richard. *Eight Men*. Cleveland: World, 1961. Short stories, published posthumously, on the theme of the Negro's conflict with white society.

Wright, Richard. *Lawd Today*. New York: Walker, 1963. Novel, written before *Native Son*, about one sordid day in the life of a Negro postal clerk in depression Chicago. Similar to *Native Son* in atmosphere, but weaker as a novel.

Wright, Richard. *Long Dream*. Garden City, N.Y.: Doubleday, 1958. Novel of a Mississippi Negro who seeks salvation by expatriation in France.

Wright, Richard. *Native Son*. New York: Harper 1940. Titanic story of Bigger Thomas from the Chicago ghetto, his struggle to survive, and his doom.

Wright, Richard. *White Man—Listen!* Garden City, N.Y.: Doubleday, 1957. A personal interpretation of how the white man looks to nonwhite eyes.

Wright, Sarah E. *The Child's Gonna Live*. New York: Delacorte, 1969. Novel.

Young, Al. *Snakes*. New York: Holt, Rinehart & Winston, 1970. Novel.

Literary Criticism

Anderson, Jervis. "Black Writing: The Other Side," *Dissent* 15 (May-June 1968):233-242.

Arnez, Nancy L., and Clara B. Anthony. "Contemporary Negro Humor as Social Satire," *Phylon* 29 (Winter 1968):339-346.

"Baldwin: Gray Flannel Muslim?" *Christian Century* 80 (June 12, 1963):791. An examination of the extent to which Baldwin inclines toward repudiation of the white world.

Barksdale, Richard K. "Trends in Contemporary Poetry," *Phylon* 19 (Winter 1958):408-416.

Bigsby, C. W. E. "The Committed Writer: James Baldwin as Dramatist," *Twentieth Century Literature* 13 (April 1967):39-48.

Bluestein, Gene. "Blues as a Literary Theme," *Massachusetts Review* 8 (Autumn 1967):593-617.

Bone, Robert A. "American Negro Poetry: On the Stage and in the Schools," *Teachers College Record* 68 (February 1967):435-440. Laments one and applauds another presentation of Negro poetry to New York audiences.

Bone, Robert A. *The Negro Novel in America*. 1958. Rev. ed. New Haven: Yale University Press, 1965. A history of novels by Negroes since 1953. Bone favors "art-centered novels" like Ellison's *Invisible Man* rather than more socially inspired materials.

Bone, Robert. *Richard Wright*. Minneapolis: University of Minnesota Press, 1969.

Braithwaite, William S. "Alain Locke's Relationship to the Negro in American Literature," *Phylon* 18 (Summer 1957):166-173. A eulogy of Locke and his gift of "soul" to Negro writers of the twenties and thirties.

Bronz, Stephen H. *Roots of Negro Racial Consciousness; The 1920's: Three Harlem Renaissance Authors*. New York: Libra, 1964.

Brown, Sterling A. *Negro Poetry and Drama*. Washington: Associates in Negro Folk Education, 1937. One of the "Bronze Booklets." An excellent study of the development of Negro poetry from the eighteenth century. In the section on drama, Brown discusses white characterizations of the Negro as well as plays by Negroes.

Butcher, Margaret Just. *The Negro in American Culture, Based on Materials Left by Alain Locke*. New York: Knopf, 1956. Basic survey of contribution of Negroes to the arts in America.

Chapman, Abraham. "The Harlem Renaissance in Literary History," *College Language Association Journal* 11 (September 1967):38-58.

Clairmonte, Glenn. "He Made American Writers Famous," *Phylon* 30 (Summer 1969):184-190. A testimony to William Stanley Braithwaite. A chronology of his works is appended.

Clarke, John Henrik. "The Origin and Growth of Afro-American Literature," *Journal of Human Relations* 16 (Third Quarter 1968):368-384.

Clarke, John Henrik. "Transition in the American Negro Short Story," *Phylon* 21 (Winter 1960):360-366. Shallow in its interpretation, this article is a list of short-story writers from slave narratives to the present.

Clum, John M. "Ridgely Torrence's Negro Plays: A Noble Beginning," *South Atlantic Quarterly* 68 (Winter 1969):96-108.

Coles, Robert. "Baldwin's Burden," *Partisan Review* 31 (Summer 1964):409-416. Critical of Baldwin's romanticism and of his contradictory generalizations about love and hate, this is an impressively probing essay.

Collier, Eugenia W. "James Weldon Johnson: Mirror of Change," *Phylon* 21 (Winter 1960):351-359. An intelligent, if not too detailed, discussion of Johnson's development away from the use of Negro dialect in his poetry while still retaining his folk subject. Central to the piece is a comparison with Paul Dunbar.

Cook, Mercer, and Stephen E. Henderson. *The Militant Black Writer in Africa and the United States.* Oshkosh: University of Wisconsin Press, 1969. Two essays drawn from a symposium "Anger and Beyond: The Black Writer and a World in Revolution," held in 1968 at the University. Henderson analyzes the "soul" and "negritude" concepts in the American works.

Cothran, Tilman C. "White Stereotypes in Fiction by Negroes," *Phylon* 11 (Autumn 1950):252-256. An analysis of novels of the 1940 vintage, demonstrating the Negro response to white conceptions of the Negro.

Davis, Arthur P. "The Alien-and-Exile Theme in Countee Cullen's Racial Poems," *Phylon* 14 (Winter 1953):390-400. A study of poems of the Renaissance of the 1920's, with particular emphasis on African themes.

Davis, Arthur P. "Integration and Race Literature," *Phylon* 17 (Summer 1956):141-146. A discussion of the effect of integration in turning the Negro author away from protest literature immediately after 1954 Supreme Court decision.

Echeruo, M. J. C. "American Negro Poetry," *Phylon* 24 (Spring 1963):62-68. Interesting, though slight account of the effect of race conflict upon the poetry of the Negro. Compares American Negro and African poetry.

Eckman, Fern Morja. *The Furious Passage of James Baldwin.* New York: M. Evans, 1966.

Ellison, Ralph. "Hidden Name and Complex Fate: A Writer's Experience in the U.S.," in *The Writer's Experience.* Washington: U.S. Library of Congress, 1964.

Ellison, Ralph, " 'Tell It Like It Is, Baby,' " *Nation* 201 (September 21, 1965):129-136. In 100th anniversary issue.

Emanuel, James A. *Langston Hughes.* New York: Twayne, 1967. A literary examination.

Ferguson, Blanche E. *Countee Cullen and the Negro Renaissance.* New York: Dodd, Mead, 1966. A mediocre biography, but useful as an insight into the literary period of the 1920's.

Fontaine, William T. "Toward a Philosophy of the American Negro Literature," *Présence Africaine*, (English ed.) no's. 24-25 (February-May 1959):164-176. Impressionistic but interesting glance at Negro literature, especially at Wright's *Native Son.*

Ford, Nick Aaron. "Battle of the Books: A Critical Survey of Books by and about Negroes Published in1960," *Phylon* 22 (Summer 1961):119-134.

Ford, Nick Aaron. "The Fire Next Time? A Critical Survey of Belles Lettres by and about Negroes Published in 1963," *Phylon* 25 (Summer 1964):123-134.

Friedenberg, Edgar Z. "Another Country for an Arkansas Traveler," *New Republic* 147 (August 27, 1962):23-26. Observations on Baldwin's *Another Country* and its implications for the South.

Gayle, Addison, Jr. "Cultural Nationalism: The Black Novel and the City," *Liberator* 9 (July 1969):14-17.

Gayle, Addison, Jr. "A Defense of James Baldwin," *College Language Association Journal* 10 (June 1967):201-208.

Gayle, Addison, Jr. "The Negro Critic: Invisible Man in American Literature; *Record* 70 (November 1968):165-171.

Gilman, Richard. "White Standards and Negro Writing," *New Republic* 158 (March 9, 1968):25-30; "More on Negro Writing," *ibid.,* (April 13, 1968):25-28.

Gloster, Hugh M. *Negro Voices in American Fiction.* Chapel Hill: University of North Carolina Press, 1948. Valuable survey of literature through World War II; often concerned with the social setting of the writer rather than strictly with his literary output.

Golde, William J. "Jean Toomer's Ralph Kabnis: Portrait of the Negro Artist As a Young Man," *Phylon* 30 (Spring 1969):73-85.

Gross, Theodore L. "The Idealism of Negro Literature in America," *Phylon* 30 (Spring 1969):5-10.

Gross, Theodore L. "Our Mutual Estate: The Literature of the American Negro," *Antioch Review* 28 (Fall 1968):293-303.

Heermance, J. Noel. *William Wells Brown and Clotelle: A Portrait of the Artist in the First Negro Novel.* Hamden, Conn.: Archon, 1969. An analysis of the author and his work by an English instructor at Howard University. The rewritten version of the novel is appended. Bibliography.

Hill, Hamlin. "Black Humor: Its Cause and Cure," *Colorado Quarterly* 17 (Summer 1968):57-64.

Hill, Herbert, ed. *Anger and Beyond: The Negro Writer in the United States.* New York: Harper & Row, 1966. The collection includes general historical essays of Negro literature and critiques of individual authors—by Negro writers.

Howe, Irving. "Black Boys and Native Sons," *Dissent* 10 (Fall 1963):353-368.

Howe, Irving, and Ralph Ellison. "The Writer and the Critic—An Exchange," *New Leader,* February 3, 1964. The last stage of a running controversy which began with Howe's article in *Dissent,* Fall 1963, followed by Ellison's reply in the *New Leader,* December 9, 1963, as to possibility of the Negro's writing about any subject independently of the protest movement.

Hughes, Carl Milton. *The Negro Novelist: A Discussion of the Writings of American Negro Novelists, 1940-1950.* New York: Citadel, 1953. Basically a sequel to Gloster's *Negro Voices.*

Hughes, Langston, LeRoi Jones, and John A. Williams. "Problems of the Negro Writer," *Saturday Review* 46 (April 20, 1963):19-21, 40. Three short essays.

Hughes, Langston. "The Twenties: Harlem and Its Negritude, *African Forum* 1 (Spring 1966):11-20.

Isaacs, Harold. "Five Writers and their African Ancestors," *Phylon* 21 (Fall 1960):243-265; 21 (Winter 1960):317-336. Fascinating reflections on the African heritage of the American Negro in the works of Langston Hughes, Richard Wright, Ralph Ellison, James Baldwin, and Lorraine Hansberry. The last three were interviewed.

Jackson, Blyden. "The Blithe Newcomers: A Résumé of Negro Literature in 1954," *Phylon* 16 (Spring 1955):5-12.

Jackson, Blyden. "The Continuing Strain: Résumé of Negro Literature in 1955," *Phylon* 17 (Spring 1956):35-40.

Jackson, Kathryn. "LeRoi Jones and the New Black Writers of the Sixties," *Freedomways* 9 (Summer 1969):232-246.

Jackson, Miles M. "Significant Belles Lettres by and about Negroes Published in 1964," *Phylon* 26 (Fall 1965):216-227.

Jacobson, Dan. "James Baldwin as Spokesman," *Commentary* 32 (December 1961):497-502. A study of Baldwin by a South African Jew, who sees Baldwin's reluctance to aim for power in brute terms as characteristically American.

Jahn, Janheinz. *Neo-African Literature: A History of Black Writing.* Translated from the German by Oliver Coburn and Ursula Lehrburger. New York: Grove, 1969. See especially the chapters 7-14 in part 3 entitled "The American Scene."

Jones, Beau Fly. "James Baldwin: The Struggle for Identity," *British Journal of Sociology* 17 (June 1966):107-121.

Jones, LeRoi. "Myth of a Negro Literature," *Saturday Review* 46 (April 20, 1963):20-21.

Keller, Frances Richardson. "The Harlem Literary Renaissance," *North American Review* (new series) 5 (May 1968):29-34.

Killens, John O., et. al. *The American Negro Writer and his Roots.* New York: American Society of African Culture, 1960. Papers from 1959 conference of AMSAC by Killens, Saunders Redding, Samuel Allen, John Henrik Clarke, Julian Mayfield, Arthur Davis, Langston Hughes, William Branch, Arna Bontemps, Loften Mitchell.

Kinnamon, Kenneth. "Native Son: The Personal, Social, and Political Background," *Phylon* 30 (Spring 1969):68-72. The novel seen as a social protest of the 1940's.

Kostelanetz, Richard. "Fiction for a Negro Politics: The Neglected Novels of W. E. B. DuBois," *Xavier University Studies* 7 (June 1968):5-39.

Kostelanetz, Richard. "Politics of Ellison's Booker: Invisible Man as Symbolic History," *Chicago Review* 19, no. 2 (1967):5-26.

Lash, John. "The Conditioning of Servitude: A Critical Summary of Literature by and about Negroes in 1957," *Phylon* 19 (Summer 1958):143-152.

Lash, John. "Dimension in Racial Experience: A Critical Summary of Literature by and about Negroes in 1958," *Phylon* 20 (Summer 1959):115-131.

Lash, John. "Expostulation and Reply: A Critical Summary of Literature by and about Negroes in 1959," *Phylon* 21 (Summer 1960):111-123.

Lash, John. "A Long Hard Look at the Ghetto: A Critical Summary of Literature by and about Negroes in 1956," *Phylon* 18 (Spring 1957):7-24.

Lilliard, Stewart. "Ellison's Ambitious Scope in *Invisible Man*," *English Journal* 58 (September 1969):833-839.

Lindberg, John. "Discovering Black Literature," *North American Review* (new series) 6 (Fall 1969):51-56. Elements of teaching a course in black literature.

Littlejohn, David. *Black on White: A Critical Survey of Writing by American Negroes*. New York: Grossman, 1966. A good survey. However, because of the wealth of recent Negro literary contributions, it is not completely up-to-date.

McCall, Dan. *The Example of Richard Wright*. New York: Harcourt, Brace & World, 1969. Critical assessment of Wright's continuing influence. A complement to Margolies' critical study.

MacInnes, Colin. "Dark Angel: The Writings of James Baldwin," *Encounter* 21 (August 1963):22-33. A thoughtful essay, giving careful attention to each of Baldwin's books.

Marcus, Steven. "The American Negro in Search of Identity," *Commentary* 16 (November 1953):456-463. An early appreciation of the differences among Wright's *The Outsider,* Ellison's *Invisible Man*, and Baldwin's *Go Tell It On The Mountain.*

Margolies, Edward. *The Art of Richard Wright*. Carbondale: Southern Illinois University Press, 1969. Traces the thematic treatment of black nationalism and other concepts in Wright's writings.

Margolies, Edward. *Native Sons: A Critical Study of Twentieth-Century Negro American Authors*. Philadelphia: Lippincott, 1968. A perceptive analysis of some 20 authors' contributions to American literature, and to the understanding of the Negro in American society. Emphasis on writers of importance after 1940.

Mayfield, Julian. "The Negro Writer and the Stickup," *Boston University Journal* 17 (Winter 1969):11-16.

"The Negro in Literature: The Current Scene," *Phylon* 11 (Winter 1950):297-394. The entire issue devoted to the subject, and constituting an important summary of the work of Negro writers through 1950. Articles of special interest are those by Sterling Brown, Nick A. Ford, Ulysses Lee, Charles H. Nichols, Jr., William G. Smith, and Margaret Walker.

"The Negro Woman in American Literature," *Freedomways* 6 (Winter 1966):8-25. Remarks of members of a panel at a conference on "The Negro Writer's Vision of America."

Nelson, Hugh. "LeRoi Jones' Dutchman: A Brief Ride on a Doomed Ship," *Educational Theatre Journal* 20 (March 1968):53-59.

O'Daniel, Therman B. "The Image of Man as Portrayed by Ralph Ellison," *College Language Association Journal* 10 (June 1967):277-284.

Olderman, Raymond M. "Ralph Ellison's Blues and *Invisible Man*," *Wisconsin Studies in Contemporary Literature* 7 (Summer 1966:142-159.

Peterson, Fred. "James Baldwin and Eduardo Mallea: Two Essayists' Search for Identity," *Discourse* 10 (Winter 1967):97-107.

Redding, Saunders. "The Negro Writer: The Road Where," *Boston University Journal 17* (Winter 1969):6-10.

Redding, Saunders. "The Problems of the Negro Writer," *Massachusetts Review* 6 (Autumn-Winter 1964-1965):57-70.

Redding, Saunders. "Since Richard Wright," *African Forum* 1 (Spring 1966):21-31.

Redding, Jay Saunders. *To Make a Poet Black*. Chapel Hill: University of North Carolina Press, 1939. An important study of Negro literature.

Rexroth, Kenneth. "Panelizing Dissent: Report on Conference on the Negro Writer in the United States," *Nation* 199 (September 7, 1964):97-99. Seminar sponsored by University of California.

Rowell, Charles H. "'Against the Blues': Notes on the Poetry of Alvin Aubert," *Bulletin of the Southern University and A & M College* 55 (June 1969):79-83. See also selections of Aubert's poetry which follows the critique.

Schafer, William J. "Ralph Ellison and the Birth of the Anti-Hero," *Critique* 10, no. 2 (1968):81-93.

Schulberg, Budd. "Black Phoenix: An Introduction," *Antioch Review* 27 (Fall 1967):277-284. The Watts Writers Workshop.

Scott, Nathan A., Jr. "Judgement Marked by a Cellar: The American Negro Writer and the Dialectic of Despair," in Harry J. Mooney and Thomas F. Staley, eds., *The Shapeless God: Essays on Modern Fiction.* Pittsburgh, Penna.: University of Pittsburgh Press, 1968, pp. 139-169. Appeared earlier in the *University of Denver Quarterly* 2 (Summer 1967):5-35.

Shih Hsien-Yung. "Impressions of American Negro Literature," *Chinese Literature* no. 4 (1966):107-112.

Standley, Fred L. "James Baldwin: The Crucial Situation," *South Atlantic Quarterly* 65 (Summer 1966):371-381.

Turner, Darwin T. "The Negro Novel in America: In Rebuttal," *College Language Association Journal* 10 (December 1966):122-134.

Turner, Darwin T. "The Negro Novelist and the South," *Southern Humanities Review* 1 (Winter 1967):21-29.

Turner, Darwin T. "Negro Playwrights and the Urban Negro," *College Language Association Journal* 12 (September 1968):19-25.

Turner, Darwin T. "Paul Laurence Dunbar: The Rejected Symbol," *Journal of Negro History* 52 (January 1967):1-13.

Turpin, Waters E. "Four Short Fiction Writers of the Harlem Renaissance: Their Legacy of Achievement," *College Language Association Journal* 11 (September 1967):59-72. Jean Toomer, Rudolph Fisher, Langston Hughes, and Claude McKay.

"'A Very Stern Discipline': An Interview with Ralph Ellison," *Harper's* 234 (March 1967):76-95. Interview conducted by three young Negro writers.

Watkins, Mel. "The Black Revolution in Books," *New York Times Book Review*, August 10, 1969, p. 8+. An overview of black literary ferment, the black experience being provided in the educational field, and black oriented publishing and bookselling ventures.

Weales, Gerald C. *The Jumping-Off Place: American Drama in the 1960's.* New York: Macmillan, 1969. Includes critical descriptions of dramas of Baldwin, Hansberry, and Jones.

Webb, Constance. *Richard Wright.* New York: Putnam, 1968. Includes portraits.

7 Theatre, Dance, and the Arts

Abramson, Doris E. *Negro Playwrights in the American Theatre, 1925-1959.* New York: Columbia University Press, 1969. An historical survey, followed by a detailed examination of 18 plays and an added chapter on the theater in the 1960's.

"Afro-American Art: 1800-1950," *Ebony* 23 (February 1968):116-118+.

Anderson, John Q. "The New Orleans Voodoo Ritual Dance and Its Twentieth-Century Survivals," *Southern Folklore Quarterly* 24 (June 1960):135-143. History of this Negro dance and its influence upon social dances of American whites.

Atkins, Thomas R. "Theater of Possibilities," *Kenyon Review* 30 (1968):274-281. Total Action Against Poverty (TAP) theatre project in Roanoke.

Austin, Gerlyn E. "The Advent of the Negro Actor on the Legitimate Stage in America," *Journal of Negro Education* 35 (Summer 1966):237-245. Bibliography.

"The Black Theater," *Drama Review* 12 (Summer 1968):entire issue.

"Black Theatre at the Crossroads: Old Formulas or New Directions?" *Negro Digest* 17 (April 1968): entire issue.

Bowling, Frank. "Discussion on Black Art," *Arts Magazine* 43 (April 1969):16-20; (May 1969):20-23.

Costello, Donald P. "LeRoi Jones I: Black Man as Victim," *Commonweal* 88 (June 28, 1968):436-440.

Cripps, Thomas R. "The Death of Rastus: Negroes in American Films Since 1945," *Phylon* 28 (Fall 1967):267-275. Concludes that although Negro characterizations have become more multi-faceted and developed, the screen Negro is still greatly segregated.

Dent, Thomas C. "The Free Southern Theater," *Negro Digest* 16 (April 1967):40-44+.

Dent, Thomas C., Richard Schelchner, and Gilbert Moses, eds. *The Free Southern Theatre by the Free Southern Theatre: A Documentary of the South's Radical Black Theatre with Journals, Letters, Poetry, Essays and a Play Written by Those Who Built It.* Indianapolis: Bobbs-Merrill, 1969.

[A Directory of Black Theatre Groups] *Drama Review* 12 (Summer 1968):172-175. Groups listed by state.

Dover, Cedric. *American Negro Art.* 1960. 3d ed. New York: New York Graphic Society, 1965. Author relates painting, sculpture, and crafts to the changing role of the Negro in American life. Bibliography, including a listing of catalogues of exhibits by Negro artists.

Estrada, R. "Three Leading Negro Artists, and How They Feel about Dance in the Community," *Dance Magazine* 42 (November 1968):45-60.

Frederick Douglass Institute. *The Art of Henry O. Turner.* Washington: Smithsonian Institution, 1969. Catalogue of an exhibition organized by the Institute in collaboration with the National Collection of Fine Arts, Smithsonian Institution.

Gaffney, Floyd. "The Black Actor in Central Park," *Negro Digest* 16 (April 1967):28-34.

Gaffney, Floyd. "A Hand Is on the Gate in Athens," *Educational Theatre Journal* 21 (May 1969):196-201.

Gayle, Addison, Jr., ed. *Black Expression: Essays by and about Black Americans in the Creative Arts.* New York: Weybright and Talley, 1969.

Goldin, Amy. "Harlem Out of Mind," *Art News* 68 (March 1969):52-53 + .

"Harlem: A Photographic Report on Harlem By a Group of Young Negro Photographers," *Camera* 45 (July 1966):4-25.

Harris, H. "Building a Black Theatre," *Drama Review* 12 (Summer 1968):157-158.

Haywood, Charles. "Negro Minstrelsy and Shakespearean Burlesque," in Bruce Jackson, ed., *Folklore and Society: Essays in Honor of Benjamin A. Botkin.* Hatboro, Penna.: Folklore Associates, 1966, pp. 77-92. Shakespearean parody in Negro minstrelsy.

"Henry Ossawa Tanner," *Art News* 66 (December 1967):47 + .

Hilliard, Robert L. "Desegregation in Educational Theatre," *Journal of Negro Education* 26 (Fall 1957):509-513.

Hughes, Langston, and Milton Meltzer. *Black Magic: A Pictorial History of the Negro in American Entertainment.* Englewood Cliffs, N.J.: Prentice-Hall, 1967.

Jackson, Esther Merle. "A 'Tragic Sense' of the Negro Experience," *Freedomways* 7 (Winter 1967):16-25.

Janifer, Ellsworth. "Samuel Coleridge-Taylor in Washington," *Phylon* 28 (Summer 1967):185-196. An English Negro composer's achievements and reception before audiences in Washington, Baltimore, New York, and Chicago.

Jefferson, Miles. "The Negro on Broadway, 1954-55," *Phylon* 16 (Fall 1955):303-312. Extent of employment and type of roles (chiefly minor).

Jefferson, Miles. "The Negro on Broadway, 1955-56," *Phylon* 17 (Fall 1956):227-237.

Jerome, Victor Jeremy. *The Negro in Hollywood Films.* New York: Masses & Mainstream, 1950.

Killens, John O. "The Artist and the Black University," *Black Scholar* 1 (November 1969):61-65.

Killens, John Oliver. "Broadway in Black and White," *African Forum* 1 (Winter 1966):66-76. Includes discussion of Lorraine Hansberry, James Baldwin, and Langston Hughes.

King, Woodie, Jr. "Black Theatre: Present Condition," *Drama Review* 12 (Summer 1968):117-124.

Kmen, Henry A. *Music in New Orleans: The Formative Years, 1791-1841.* Baton Rouge: Louisiana State University Press, 1966. Chapters on Negro music and one on Negro social dancing.

Lazier, Gil. "The Next Stage: Youth Theatre for the Ghetto," *Record* 69 (February 1968):465-467.

"The Learning Tree," *America* 121 (September 27, 1969):245. Commentary on the first film which has been produced by a major American studio directed by a black man (Gary Parks).

Lewis, Samella S., and Ruth G. Waddy, eds. *Black Artists on Art.* Los Angeles, Calif.: Contemporary Crafts. Distributed by Ward Ritchie, 1969. Illustrations and excerpts from contemporary artists.

Lewis, T. "Negro Actors in Dramatic Roles," *America* 115 (September 17, 1966):298-300.

Locke, Alain LeRoy. *The Negro in Art: A Pictorial Record of the Negro Artist and of the Negro Theme in Art.* Washington: Associates in Negro Folk Education, 1940.

Locke, Alain LeRoy. *Negro Art Past and Present.* Washington: Associates in Negro Folk Education, 1936.

Loney, G. "The Negro and the Theatre," *Educational Theatre Journal* 20 (May 1968):231-233.

McDonagh, Don. "Negroes in Ballet," *New Republic* 159 (November 2, 1968):41-44.

Marks, Marcia. "Alvin Ailey American Dance Theatre; Hunter College Playhouse," *Dance Magazine* 42 (March 1968):66-67.

Mathews, Marcia M. *Henry Ossawa Tanner, American Artist.* Edited by John Hope Franklin. Chicago: University of Chicago Press, 1969.

Mayor, Robin. "The Art of Henry Tanner: Rediscovered American Artist," *Arts Magazine* 44 (September-October 1969):46-47. Background of the artist and a review of the National Collection of Fine Arts traveling exhibition of his works. Illustrations.

Miller, Adam David. "It's a Long Way to St. Louis: Notes on the Audience for Black Drama," *Drama Review* 12 (Summer 1968):147–150.

Miller, William C., and Stephanie L. Miller. "All Black Showcase: The Effectiveness of a Negro Theatre Production," *Educational Theatre Journal* 21 (May 1969):202–204.

Minneapolis Institute of Arts. *30 Contemporary Black Artists.* Minneapolis, 1968. Exhibition catalogue.

Mitchell, Loften. *Black Drama: The Story of the American Negro in the Theater.* New York: Hawthorn, 1967.

Neal, Larry. "The Black Arts Movement," *Drama Review* 12 (Summer 1968):29–39.

"The Negro in the Theatre," *Drama Critique* 7 (Spring 1964):entire issue.

Nobel, Peter. *The Negro in Films.* London: S. Robinson, 1948. Reprinted Port Washington, N.Y.: Kennikat, 1969.

"On Black Artists," *Art Journal* 28 (Spring 1969):332.

O'Neal, John. "Motion in the Ocean: Some Political Dimensions of the Free Southern Theatre," *Drama Review* 12 (Summer 1968):70–77.

Parks, Gordon. *Gordon Parks, A Poet and His Camera.* New York: Viking, 1968.

Patterson, Lindsay, ed. *Anthology of the American Negro in the Theater: A Critical Approach.* [2d ed.] New York: Publishers, 1967. (International Library of Negro Life and History). Includes materials published between 1926 and 1966. Illustrated.

Patterson, Lindsay, ed. *The Negro in Music and Art.* [2d ed.] New York: Publishers 1967. (International Library of Negro Life and History)

Pittsburgh. Carnegie Institute Museum of Art. *3 Self-Taught Pennsylvania Artists: Hicks, Kane, Pippin.* Pittsburgh? 1966. Catalogue of an exhibition displayed at the Institute January 6–February 19, 1967.

Porter, James Amos. *Modern Negro Art.* 1943. New York: Arno, 1969. With a new preface by the author.

Porter, James Amos. *Ten Afro-American Artists of the Nineteenth Century.* Washington: Gallery of Art, Howard University, 1967.

Riley, Clayton. "The Negro and the Theatre," *Liberator* 7 (June 1967):20–21; (August 1967):21; (October 1967):8–11.

Reed, Ishmael. "Black Artist: 'Calling a Spade a Spade,'" *Arts* 41 (May 1967):48–49. The Black Arts movement.

Rodman, Selden. *Horace Pippin, A Negro Painter in America.* New York: Quadrangle, 1947. Artist, 1888–1946.

Roelof-Lanner, T. V., ed. *Prints by American Negro Artists.* 2d ed. Los Angeles: Cultural Exchange Center, 1967.

Sayre, Nora. "New York's Black Theatre," *New Statesman* 76 (October 25, 1968):556.

Schroeder, R. J. "The Free Southern Theatre," *Commonweal* 83 (March 18, 1966):696–697.

Siegel, Jeanne. "Why Spiral," *Art News* 65 (September 1966):48–49 +. New York Negro artists.

Stearns, Marshall, and Jean Stearns. "Frontiers of Humor: American Vernacular Dance," *Southern Folklore Quarterly* 30 (September 1966):227–235. Negro vaudeville and humor.

Stearns, Marshall, and Jean Stearns. *Jazz Dance: The Story of American Vernacular Dance.* New York: Macmillan, 1968. Influence of Afro-American dances on American dance history from Africa through minstrelsy to Broadway. Selected bibliography. Analysis and notation of basic Afro-American movements.

Stearns, Marshall, and Jean Stearns. "Vernacular Dance in Musical Comedy: Harlem Takes the Lead," *New York Folklore Quarterly* 22 (December 1966):251–261.

Terry, Walter. "Festival in Brooklyn," *Saturday Review* 52 (December 13, 1969):49. Accolades for Judith Jamison, principal dancer with the Alvin Ailey American Dance group.

Terry, Walter. "Man of Dedication and Talent," *Saturday Review* 51 (October 19, 1968): 49–50.

Terry, Walter. "Two Negro Dance Leaders," *Saturday Review* 51 (February 10, 1968): 45–46.

Todd, Arthur. "American Negro Dance: A National Treasure," *Ballet Annual* 16 (1962):92–105.

Trotta, Geri. "Black Theatre," *Harper's Bazaar* 101 (August 1968):150-153. Attention to actor-playwrights Douglas Turner Ward, Michael Shultz, Robert Hooks, and Ed Bullins.

Turner, Sherry. "An Overview of the New Black Arts," *Freedomways* 9 (Spring 1969):156-163. Attention to the visual and performing arts.

Velde, Paul. "LeRoi Jones II: Pursued by the Furies," *Commonweal* 88 (June 28, 1968): 440-441.

White, Charles. *Images of Dignity: The Drawings of Charles White*. Los Angeles, Calif.: Ward Ritchie Press, 1967.

Williams, Jim. "Pieces on Black Theatre and the Black Theatre Worker," *Freedomways* 9 (Spring 1969):146-155.

For minstrelsy *see also* Music

8 The Negro in Literature and the Arts

Arnez, Nancy L. "Racial Understanding Through Literature," *English Journal* 58 (January 1969):56-61.

Bowdoin College. Museum of Art. *The Portrayal of the Negro in American Painting.* Brunswick, Maine, 1964. Catalogue of a distinguished exhibition of works of art covering the period from 1710 to the present. Informative notes by Sidney Kaplan.

Brown, Sterling A. "A Century of Negro Portraiture in American Literature," *Massachusetts Review* 7 (Winter 1966):73-96.

Brown, Sterling A. "Negro Character as Seen by White Authors," *Journal of Negro Education* 2 (January 1933):180-201. An important essay. Brown describes seven stereotypes of the Negro used by white authors, beginning with pre-Civil War literature.

Brown, Sterling A. *The Negro in American Fiction.* Washington: Associates in Negro Folk Education, 1937.

California University, Los Angeles. Art Galleries. *The Negro in American Art.* Los Angeles, 1966. A catalogue of the exhibition jointly sponsored with the California Art Commission.

Cantor, Milton. "The Image of the Negro in Colonial Literature," *New England Quarterly* 26 (December 1963):452-477.

Clarke, John Henrik, ed. *William Styron's "Nat Turner": Ten Black Writers Respond.* Boston: Beacon, 1968. Strongly critical of the novel's distortion of history, its creation of stereotypes, and its inaccurate treatment of slavery. It attacks distortions of Styron's narrative on historical and literary bases.

Constantine, J. Robert. "Ignoble Savage, An Eighteenth-Century Literary Stereotype," *Phylon* 27 (Summer 1966):171-179. Roots of the image employed by white supremacists through the last two centuries.

Davidson, Bruce. "New York—East 100th Street," *Du* 29 (March 1969):155-224. Photographs of Harlem appearing in a Swiss journal are noted here because of their outstanding quality.

Deane, Paul C. "The Persistence of Uncle Tom: An Examination of the Image of the Negro in Children's Fiction Series," *Journal of Negro Education* 37 (Spring 1968):140-145.

Dowty, Alan. "Urban Slavery in Pro-Southern Fiction of the 1850's," *Journal of Southern History* 32 (February 1966):25-41.

Dufner, Angeline. "The Negro in the American Novel," *American Benedictine Review* 18 (March 1967):122-146.

Durden, Robert F. "William Styron and His Black Critics," *South Atlantic Quarterly* 68 (Spring 1969):181-187.

Fishwick, Marshall. "Uncle Remus vs. John Henry: Folk Tension," *Western Folklore* 20 (April 1961):77-85.

Forrey, Robert. "Herman Melville and the Negro Question," *Mainstream* 15 (February 1962):23-32.

Forrey, Robert. "Negroes in the Fiction of F. Scott Fitzgerald," *Phylon* 28 (Fall 1967):293-298.

Freed, Leonard. *Black in White America*. New York: Grossman, 1969. Excellent photographs with brief commentary.

Gross, Seymour L., and John Edward Hardy, eds. *Images of the Negro in American Literature*. Chicago: University of Chicago Press, 1966. Critical retrospective essays. Extensive bibliography.

Holder, Alan. "Styron's Slave: The Confessions of Nat Turner," *South Atlantic Quarterly* 68 (Spring 1969):167-180.

Hughes, Langston, and Milton Meltzer, eds. *A Pictorial History of the Negro in America*. 1963. Rev. ed. by Milton Meltzer and C. Eric Lincoln. New York: Crown, 1968.

Kaplan, Sidney. "The Negro in the Art of Homer and Elkins," *Massachusetts Review* 7 (Winter 1966):105-120. Notes and reproductions originally appeared in the Bowdoin College exhibition catalogue on Negro American painting.

Kaplan, Sidney. "Towards Pip and Daggoo: Footnote on Melville's Youth," *Phylon* 29 (Fall 1968):291-302.

Moore, Jack B. "Images of the Negro in Early American Short Fiction," *Mississippi Quarterly* 32 (Winter 1968-69):47-57.

Nilon, Charles H. *Faulkner and the Negro*. Boulder: University of Colorado Press, 1962. This work presents a restrained, scholarly examination of Faulkner's treatment of the Negro-White community.

Schoener, Allon, ed. *Harlem on My Mind: Cultural Capital of Black America, 1900-1968*. New York: Random, 1969. Photographs and text of seven decades of American Negro life and culture. Supplemented the 1969 exhibition catalogue of the Metropolitan Museum of Art, which has now been withdrawn.

Strout, Cushing. "Uncle Tom's Cabin and the Portent of Millenium," *Yale Review* 57 (Spring 1968):375-385.

Styron, William. *The Confessions of Nat Turner*. New York: Random, 1967. Pulitzer Prize novel of the Virginia slave rebellion.

Thelwell, Michael. "Turner Thesis," *Partisan Review* 35 (Summer 1968):403-414. With a reply by Robert Coles.

Thelwell, Mike. "Mr. William Styron and the Reverend Turner," *Massachusetts Review* 9 (Winter 1968):7-29.

Tischler, Nancy M. *Black Masks: Negro Characters in Modern Southern Fiction*. University Park: Pennsylvania State University Press, 1969. Bibliography.

U.S. Committee for the First World Festival of Negro Arts. *Ten Negro Artists from the United States*. Dakar, Senegal, New York: Distributed by October House, 1966. Exhibitions catalogue; in French and English.

9　Music

Allen, William Francis, Charles P. Ware, and Lucy McKim Garrison, eds. *Slave Songs of the United States.* 1867. Rev. ed. New York: Oak, 1965. The complete original collection of 136 songs, with new piano and guitar accompaniments provided.

Arvey, Verna. *William Grant Still.* New York: J. Fischer, 1939. A comprehensive study of a Negro classical composer.

"Black America," *Jazz* 6 (January 1967):20-25.

Blesh, Rudi. *Shining Trumpets: A History of Jazz.* 1946. Rev. ed. New York: Knopf, 1958. Author stresses affinity of jazz to African Negro music.

Bluestein, Gene. "Blues as a Literary Theme," *Massachusetts Review* 8 (Autumn 1967):593-617.

Bowen, Elbert R. "Negro Minstrels in Early Rural Missouri," *Missouri Historical Review* 47 (January 1953):103-109.

Carawan, Guy. *Ain't You Got a Right to the Tree of Life? The People of Johns Island, South Carolina—Their Faces, Their Words and Their Songs.* New York: Simon and Schuster, 1966.

Carawan, Guy, comp. *Freedom Is a Constant Struggle: Songs of the Freedom Movement.* New York: Oak, 1968. A collection of songs used in the freedom movement, 1960-1966, with musical transcriptions and illustrations emphasizing their social context.

Carawan, Guy, and Candie Carawan, comps. *We Shall Overcome! Songs of the Southern Freedom Movement.* New York: Oak, 1963. Songbook.

Charters, A. R. Danberg. "Negro Folk Elements in Classic Ragtime," *Ethnomusicology* 5 (September 1961):174-183. Includes musical examples and a bibliography.

Charters, Ann, ed. *The Ragtime Songbook.* New York: Oak, 1965. A summary of ragtime scholarship; with musical examples.

Charters, Samuel B. *The Bluesmen: The Story of the Music and the Men Who Made the Blues.* New York: Oak, 1967. The musicians' style of the Delta and Texas up to World War II, considered as musical and social expressions. Musical examples. A discography is appended.

Charters, Samuel B. *Jazz: New Orleans 1885-1963: An Index to the Negro Musicians of New Orleans.* Rev. ed. New York: Oak, 1963. The first edition covered the period up to 1957. Discography appended.

Chase, Gilbert. *America's Music from the Pilgrims to the Present.* 1955. 2d ed. rev. New York: McGraw-Hill, 1966. A scholarly history with musical examples. Note especially chapter 4, "African Exiles," and chapter 12, "The Negro Spirituals;" also chapters 13, 21-23. Discography and bibliography appended.

Chase, Gilbert. "A Note on Negro Spirituals." *Civil War History* 4 (September 1958):261-267.

Courlander, Harold. *Negro Folk Music, U.S.A.* New York: Columbia University Press, 1963. A comprehensive and scholarly work.

Courlander, Harold. *Negro Songs from Alabama.* New York: Oak, 1963.

Cray, Ed. "An Acculturative Continuum for Negro Folk Song in the United States," *Ethno-musicology* 5 (January 1961):10-15. Interaction and effects of white culture on Negro musical traditions.

Darden, Norman. "My Man André: Classical Pianist," *Saturday Review* 52 (July 26, 1969):43-45. André Watts.

Edwall, Harry R. "The Golden Era of Minstrelsy in Memphis: A Reconstruction," *West Tennessee Historical Society Papers* 9 (1955):29-47. Bibliography.

Epstein, Dena J. "Slave Music in the United States before 1860: A Survey of Sources," *Notes of the Music Library Association* 20 (Spring 1963):195-212; (Summer 1963):377-390. Survey of types of Negro vocal and instrumental music as documented in contemporary sources.

Fisher, Miles M. *Negro Slave Songs in the United States.* Ithaca: Cornell University Press, 1953. Spirituals seen as revolutionary protests. Bibliography.

"The Folksong Revival: A Symposium," *New York Folklore Quarterly* 19 (June 1963):83-142. Considers Negro influence on the development of today's folk music.

Garland, Phyl. *The Sound of Soul.* Chicago: Regnery, 1969.

Garrett, Romeo B. "African Survivals in American Culture," *Journal of Negro History* 51 (October 1966):239-245.

Gold, Robert S. *A Jazz Lexicon.* New York: Knopf, 1964. Dictionary of jazz vernacular which evolved from Negro language and jazz slang. Bibliography.

Goodman, John. "Looking for the Black Message," *New Leader* 51 (January 1, 1968):26-28. Comments on the relationship between jazz and black power.

Greenway, John, comp. "Negro Songs of Protest," in *American Folksongs of Protest.* Philadelphia: University of Pennsylvania Press, 1953, pp. 69-120. Textual matter with limited musical examples.

Griffith, Benjamin W. "Longer Version of 'Guinea Negro Song': From a Georgia Frontier Songster," *Southern Folklore Quarterly* 28 (June 1964):116-118. Describes sources and gives all variants.

Hadlock, Richard. *Jazz Masters of the Twenties.* New York: Macmillan, 1966. Chapters devoted to Louis Armstrong, Earl Hines, Fats Waller, and others. Chapter bibliographies.

Heaps, Willard A., and Porter W. Heaps. "The Negro and the Contraband," in *The Singing Sixties: The Spirit of Civil War Days Drawn from the Music of the Times.* Norman: University of Oklahoma Press, 1960, pp. 268-294.

Hedler, Andre. *Jazz: Its Evolution and Essence.* Translated by David Noakes. New York: Grove, 1955. Chapters devoted to Afro-American origins of jazz and to individual jazz musicians. Discography appended.

Hentoff, Nat. "Jazz and Race: Music as Protest," *Commonweal* 81 (January 8, 1965):482-484. Jazz as protest and as a distinctive Negro language.

Howard, Joseph H. *Drums in the Americas.* New York: Oak, 1967. Attention to chapters 10, 11, and 14 which concern African and Afro-American influences. Bibliography.

Jackson, George Pullen. *White and Negro Spirituals: Their Life Span and Kinship.* New York: J. J. Augustin, 1943. An excellent historical overview with musical examples.

Jahn, Janheinz. "The Negro Spiritual," and "Blues and Calypso," in *Neo-African Literature: A History of Black Writing.* Translated from the German by Oliver Coburn and Ursula Lehrburger. New York: Grove, 1969, pp. 155-165; 166-182.

James, Willis Laurence. "The Romance of the Negro Folk Cry in America," *Phylon* 16 (Spring 1955):15-30. Material on the rise and amazing spread of gospel singing.

Johnson, James Weldon, ed. *The Book of American Negro Spirituals.* New York: Viking, 1947.

Jones, LeRoi. *Black Music.* New York: Morrow, 1967. Essays, reviews, and musical analyses of contemporary jazz musicians and their work.

Jones, LeRoi. *Blues People: Negro Music in White America.* New York: Morrow, 1963. Ralph Ellison, in *New York Review,* February 6, 1964, objects that the "tremendous burden of sociology which Jones would place upon this body of music is enough to give even the blues the blues."

Katz, Bernard, ed. *Social Implications of Early Negro Music in the United States.* New York: Arno Press, 1969. A collection of articles and essays on Negro music.

Keil, Charles. *Urban Blues.* Chicago: University of Chicago Press, 1966. A serious study of music as a vehicle toward understanding the Negro in his community. Written by a jazz musician.

Kmen, Henry A. *Music in New Orleans: The Formative Years, 1791-1841.* Baton Rouge: Louisiana State University Press, 1966. Chapters on Negro music and one on Negro social dancing.

Kolinski, Mieczyslaw. "Classification of Tonal Structures Illustrated by a Comparative Chart of American Indian, Afro-American, and English-American Structures," *Studies in Ethnomusicology* 1 (1961):38-76.

Krehbiel, Henry Edward. *Afro-American Folksongs: A Study in Racial and National Music.* 1913. New York: Ungar, 1967.

Landeck, Beatrice. *Echoes of Africa in Folk Songs of the Americas.* New York: McKay, 1961. Songs, with notes on the origin and performance of each. Percussion instrumental arrangements. Bibliography and discography.

Lloyd, Ruth, and Norman Lloyd, comps. *The American Heritage Songbook.* New York: American Heritage, 1969. Includes a wide sampling of music of the American Negro.

Locke, Alain LeRoy. *The Negro and His Music.* Washington: Associates in Negro Folk Education, 1936. A classic, frequently reprinted. Bibliography and discography accompany most chapters.

Lomax, Alan. "Folk Song Texts as Culture Indicators," in *Folk Song Style and Culture.* Washington: American Association for the Advancement of Science, 1968, pp. 276-299.

Lomax, Alan. "Special Features of the Sung Communication," in June Helen, ed., *Proceedings of the 1966 American Ethnological Society: Essays on the Verbal and Visual Arts.* Seattle, 1967, pp. 109-127.

McCarthy, Albert, et al. *Jazz on Record: A Critical Guide to the First 50 Years, 1917-1967.* London: Hanover, 1968. A discography, ordered alphabetically by musician. Includes stylistic comments and sections on Negro blues, work songs, gospel songs, spirituals, and ragtime.

McRae, Barry. *The Jazz Cataclysm.* New York: A. S. Barnes, 1967. Essays on jazz since the mid-1950's. Chapters on Sonny Rollins, John Coltrane, and Ornette Coleman. Note also the chapter entitled "The Racial Issues" and discussions of "soul jazz" and Negro church music. Selected discography by chapter.

Means, Richard L., and Bertha Doleman. "Notes on Negro Jazz: 1920-1950: The Use of Biographical Materials in Sociology," *Sociological Quarterly* 9 (Summer 1968):332-342. Material on 40 Negro jazz artists was studied in order to assess the relevance of the music to the Negro's social aspirations.

Nathan, Hans. *Dan Emmett and the Rise of Early Negro Minstrelsy.* Norman: University of Oklahoma Press, 1962. Includes unaccompanied melodies and a bibliography of Emmett's works.

"Negro Music," in Willi Apel, ed., *Harvard Dictionary of Music.* 2d ed. Cambridge, Mass.: Harvard University Press, 1969, pp. 567-568. An historical synopsis. Bibliography.

Nettl, Bruno. "African and New World Negro Music," in *Music in Primitive Culture.* Cambridge, Mass.: Harvard University Press, 1956, pp. 1-166. Includes an annotated bibliography.

Odum, Howard W. *Folk, Region, and Society: Selected Papers of Howard W. Odum.* Edited by Katherine Jocher, et al. Chapel Hill: University of North Carolina Press, 1964. Excellent collection of Odum's papers. Includes a group of Negro folk songs.

Oliver, Paul. "Negro Blues and Song Forms," in *Screening the Blues: Aspects of the Blues Tradition.* London: Cassell, 1968, pp. 185-207.

Oliver, Paul. *The Story of the Blues.* Philadelphia: Chilton, 1969. A comprehensive history. Traces the migratory patterns of rural and urban blues, marking their regional differences. Bibliography and discography are appended.

Parrish, Lydia. *Slave Songs of the Georgia Sea Islands.* 1942. With an introduction by Olin

Downes. Hatboro, Penna.: Folklore Associates, 1965. Words and unaccompanied folk melodies collected before these islands became accessible from the mainland.

Patterson, C. L. "A Different Drum: The Image of the Negro in the Nineteenth-Century Songster," *College Language Association Journal* 8 (September 1964):44-50.

Patterson, Lindsay, ed. *The Negro in Music and Art.* 2d ed. New York: Publishers, 1968. (International Library of Negro Life and History)

Pleasants, Henry. "The Afro-American Epoch," in *Serious Music—and All That Jazz! An Adventure in Music Criticism.* New York: Simon and Schuster, 1969, pp. 90-111. An attempt to gauge the influence of Negro jazz upon serious contemporary music.

Ramsey, Frederic, Jr. *Been Here and Gone.* New Brunswick, N.J.: Rutgers University Press, 1960. Photographs and text, including many lyrics, describing Southern Negro musical activity during the 1950's.

Rockmore, Noel. *Preservation Hall Portraits.* Baton Rouge: Louisiana State University Press, 1968. History of New Orleans as a jazz center; black and white reproductions of portraits of jazz musicians, with biographical sketches.

Russcol, Herbert. "Can the Negro Overcome the Classical Music Establishment?" *High Fidelity Musical America* 18 (August 1968):42-46. Comments on the dearth of black conductors and musicians in American symphony orchestras.

Sargeant, Winthrop. *Jazz: A History.* New York: McGraw-Hill, 1964. Originally published in 1946 under the title *Jazz Hot and Hybrid.* Several chapters analyze the "Negroid" sources of American jazz. Bibliography.

Scarborough, Dorothy. *On the Trail of Negro Folk-Songs.* Cambridge, Mass.: Harvard University Press, 1925.

Shaw, Arnold. *The World of Soul: The Black Contribution to Pop Music.* New York: Cowles, 1970.

Simms, David McD. "The Negro Spiritual: Origins and Themes," *Journal of Negro Education* 35 (Winter 1966):35-41.

Smith, Hugh L. "George W. Cable and Two Sources of Jazz," *African Music* 2, no. 3 (1961):59-62. A late nineteenth-century American writer describes Creole and Negro slave songs and dance.

Smith, Willie, and George Hoefer. *Music on My Mind: The Memoirs of an American Pianist.* London: MacGibbon & Kee, 1965.

Stearns, Marshall W. "If You Want to Go to Heaven, Shout," *High Fidelity* 9 (August 1959):36-38, 92-93. Describes the evolution and development of the gospel song.

Stearns, Marshall W. *The Story of Jazz.* New York: Oxford University Press, 1956 [Corr. pr. 1962] See especially Part 1: "The Pre-History of Jazz" (African and American Negro origins); Part 3: "The American Background" (worksongs, blues, minstrelsy, spirituals, ragtime); and the concluding chapter on jazz and the Negro's role.

Stevenson, Robert. "Afro-American Musical Legacy to 1800," *Musical Quarterly* 54 (October 1968):475-502.

Stevenson, Robert. "Negro Spirituals: Origins and Present Day Significance," in *Protestant Church Music in America: A Short Survey of Men and Movements from 1564 to the Present.* New York: W. W. Norton, 1966, pp. 92-105.

Szwed, John F. "Musical Adaptation among Afro-Americans," *Journal of American Folklore* 82 (April 1969):112-121.

Szwed, John F. "Musical Style and Racial Conflict," *Phylon* 27 (Winter 1966):358-366.

Tallmadge, William H. "Afro-American Music," *Music Educators' Journal* 44 (September-October 1957):37-39.

Tallmadge, William H. "Dr. Watts and Mahalia Jackson: The Development, Decline and Survival of a Folk Style in America," *Ethnomusicology* 5 (May 1961):95-99. The practice of "lining-out" hymns and psalms is continued today in certain Negro work songs and gospel songs. Musical examples.

Tallmadge, William H. "The Responsorial and Antiphonal Practice in Gospel Song," *Ethnomusicology* 12 (May 1968):219-238. Stylistic analysis of this performance technique. Musical examples.

Thieme, Darius L. "Negro Folksong Scholarship in the United States," *African Music* 2, no. 3 (1961):67-72. Annotated bibliography.

Tracy, Hugh. "Tina's Lullaby," *Journal of the African Music Society* 2 (1961):99-101. Traces a Georgian Negro lullaby to its possible East African origin.

Turner, Frederick W., III. "Black Jazz Artists: The Darker Side of Horatio Alger," *Massachusetts Review* 10 (Spring 1969):341-353.

Van Dam, Theodore. "The Influence of the West African Songs of Derision in the New World," *African Music* 1, no. 1 (1954):53-56. Describes early blues and calypso as two outgrowths of this song form.

Wachsmann, K. P. "Negritude in Music," *Composer* no. 19 (Spring 1966):12-16.

Walker, Wyatt Tee. "The Soulful Journey of the Negro Spiritual," *Negro Digest* 12 (July 1963):84-95.

Waterman, Richard A. "African Influences on the Music of the Americas," in Sol Tax, ed., *Acculturation in the Americas*. Chicago: University of Chicago Press, 1952. (Proceedings of the 29th International Congress of Americanists, Vol. II)

Waterman, Richard A. "On Flogging a Dead Horse: Lessons Learned from the Africanisms Controversy," *Ethnomusicology* 7 (May 1963):83-87. Analysis of the problems in evaluating the influence of African music on American Negro music.

White, Newman I. *American Negro Folksongs*. Cambridge, Mass.: Harvard University Press, 1928.

Wilgus, D. K. "Negro Music," *Journal of American Folklore* 80 (January-March 1967):105-109. Recent Negro music on record.

Wilgus, D. K. "Negro Secular Music," *Journal of American Folklore* 79 (April-June 1966):404-408. Mostly blues music.

Williams, Martin. *Jazz Masters of New Orleans*. New York: Macmillan, 1967. Chapter bibliographies and discographies.

Wilson, John. *Jazz: The Transition Years, 1940-1960*. New York: Appleton-Century-Crofts, 1966. Bibliography and discography.

10　Intergroup Relations

Studies of Prejudice

Adamo, S. J. "White Press: Black Man Distrusts," *America* 119 (October 26, 1968):390-391.

Adoff, Arnold, ed. *Black on Black.* New York, Macmillan, 1968. Excerpts from the works of 23 Negro writers underscore the continual white racial antipathy and the consequent black foment.

Allman, Reva White. "A Study of the Social Attitudes of College Students," *Journal of Social Psychology* 53 (February 1961):33-51.

Allport, Gordon. *The Nature of Prejudice.* Cambridge, Mass.: Addison-Wesley, 1954. A basic work.

Allport, Gordon W., and B. M. Kramer. "Some Roots of Prejudice," *Journal of Psychology* 22 (July 1946):9-39.

Antonovsky, Aaron. "The Social Meaning of Discrimination," *Phylon* 21 (Spring 1960):81-95.

Asher, Steven R., and Vernon L. Allen. "Racial Preference and Social Comparison Processes," *Journal of Social Issues* 25 (January 1969):157-166. An extension of Clark's study (1947) of racial identification and preference by Negro children. References.

Athey, K. R., et al. "Two Experiments Showing the Effect of the Interviewer's Racial Background on Response to Questionnaires Concerning Racial Issues," *Journal of Applied Psychology* 44 (August 1960):244-246.

Axelrod, Morris, Donald R. Matthews and James W. Prothro. "Recruitment for Survey Research on Race Problems in the South," *Public Opinion Quarterly* 26 (Summer 1962):254-262.

"Backlash Semantics," *America* 115 (December 10, 1966):763-764.

Banks, W. S. M., II. "The Rank Order of Sensitivity to Discrimination of Negroes in Columbus, Ohio," *American Sociological Review* 15 (August 1950):529-534. Conclusion: Myrdal's order of discrimination hypothesis is by and large an accurate portrayal of sensitivity of Negroes in Columbus.

Banton, Michael. "Sociology and Race Relations," *Race* 1 (November 1959):3-14.

Baratz, Stephen S., and Joan C. Baratz. "Early Childhood Intervention: The Social Science Base of Institutional Racism," *Harvard Educational Review* 40 (February 1970):29-50.

Berg, Kenneth R. "Ethnic Attitudes and Agreement with a Negro Person," *Journal of Personality and Social Psychology* 4 (August 1966):215-220.

Berry, Brewton. *Race and Ethnic Relations.* Boston: Houghton Mifflin, 1951. 3d ed., 1965. A comparative view of racial and ethnic interaction which examines recent events in the United States and abroad from a sociological point of view.

Bettelheim, Bruno. "Class, Color and Prejudice," *Nation* 197 (October 19, 1963):231-234. Conflict in White-Negro relations stems from unwillingness to separate class problem from race or caste problem.

Bettelheim, Bruno, and Morris Janowitz. *Social Change and Prejudice.* New York: Free Press, 1964. Reissue of *The Dynamics of Prejudice,* together with reassessment as of 1964.

Black, I. "Race and Unreason: Anti-Negro Opinion in Professional and Scientific Literature Since 1954," *Phylon* 26 (Spring 1965):65-79.

Blalock, Hubert M., Jr. "A Note on Adjusting Discrimination Rates for Per Cent Non-White," *Journal of Negro Education* 27 (Winter 1958):66-68.

Blalock, Hubert M., Jr. "Per Cent Non-White and Discrimination," *American Sociological Review* 22 (December 1957):677-682.

Blalock, Hubert M., Jr. "A Power Analysis of Racial Discrimination," *Social Forces* 39 (October 1960):53-59.

Blumer, Herbert. "Race Prejudice as a Sense of Group Position," *Pacific Sociological Review* 1 (Spring 1958):3-7.

Bogue, Grant. "Racial Separation in a Small Northern City," *Interracial Review* 39 (January 1966):15-22. Meadville, Pennsylvania.

Boylan, Francis T., and O'Meara Byrns. "Stereotype and Inquiry concerning Southern Born Negro Pupils in Chicago," *Journal of Educational Sociology* 32 (October 1958):76-82.

Breed, Warren, and Thomas Ktsanes. "Pluralistic Ignorance in the Process of Opinion Formation," *Public Opinion Quarterly* 25 (Fall 1961):382-392. Relationship between attitudes to segregation and ignorance.

Brody, Eugene B., et al. "Prejudice in American Negro College Students, Mental, Status, Anti-semitism, and Anti-foreign Prejudice," *Archives of General Psychiatry* 9 (December 1963):619-628.

Brooklyn Association for the Study of Negro Life and History. "A Report on the Treatment of Minorities in Elementary School Textbooks." Brooklyn, N.Y., 1963.

Brophy, Ira N. "The Luxury of Anti-Negro Prejudice," *Public Opinion Quarterly* 9 (Winter 1945-1946):456-466.

Brown, Barry S., and George W. Albee. "The Effect of Integrated Hospital Experiences on Racial Attitudes—A Discordant Note," *Social Problems* 13 (Winter 1966):324-333.

Burnstein, E., and Adie V. McRae. "Some Effects of Shared Threat and Prejudice in Racially Mixed Groups," *Journal of Abnormal and Social Psychology* 64 (April 1962):257-263.

Campbell, Byram. *Race and Social Revolution: Twenty-One Essays on Racial and Social Problems.* New York: Truth Seeker, 1958.

Campbell, Ernest Q. "Moral Discomfort and Racial Segregation—An Examination of the Myrdal Hypothesis," *Social Forces* 39 (March 1961):228-234.

Christie, Richard, and Peggy Cook. "A Guide to Published Literature Relating to the Authoritarian Personality through 1956," *Journal of Psychology* 45 (April 1958):171-199.

Christie, Richard, and Marie Jahoda, eds. *Studies in the Scope and Method of "The Authoritarian Personality."* Glencoe, Ill.: Free Press, 1954.

Clark, John G. "The Racial Legacy of the Nineteenth-Century South," *Midwest Quarterly* 7 (Autumn 1965):11-28.

Clark, Kenneth B. *Prejudice and Your Child.* 1955. 2d ed. enl. Boston: Beacon, 1963.

Cooper, Joseph B. "Prejudicial Attitudes and the Identification of their Stimulus Objects: A Phenomenological Approach," *Journal of Social Psychology* 48 (February 1958):15-23.

Crockett, George W., Jr. "Racism in the Law," *Science and Society* 33 (Spring 1969):223-230.

Curry, Andrew E. "The Negro Worker and the White Client: A Commentary on the Treatment Relationship," *Social Casework* 45 (March 1964):131-136.

Curtis, Richard F., Dianne M. Timbers, and Elton F. Jackson. "Prejudice and Urban Social Participation," *American Journal of Sociology* 73 (September 1967):235-244. An investigation of prejudice toward the Negro as related to frequency and range of contact and barriers to communication.

Degler, Carl N. "Slavery and the Genesis of American Race Prejudice," *Comparative Studies in Society and History* 2 (October 1959):49-66.

De Long, Lloyd. "The Other Bodies in the River," *Psychology Today* 3 (June 1968):26-31. +

Dicks, H. V. "Psychological Factors in Prejudice," *Race* 1 (November 1959):27-40.

Dowling, Ed. "Color Us Black," *New Republic* 158 (June 8, 1968):41-43. Failure of commercial TV to provide a balanced view of race relations.

Drake, St. Clair. *Race Relations in a Time of Rapid Social Change: Report of a Survey.* New York: National Federation of Settlements and Neighborhood Centers, 1966.

Duncan, Otis Dudley. "Discrimination against Negroes," *Annals of the American Academy of Political and Social Science* 371 (May 1967):85-103.

Eboine, Alvin E., and Max Meenes. "Ethnic and Class Preferences among College Negroes," *Journal of Negro Education* 29 (Spring 1960):128-133. Study based on a Howard University sample.

Ebony (Editors). *The White Problem in America.* Chicago: Johnson, 1966. Twenty-one essays first published in the August 1965 issue of *Ebony*. Authors include: J. Baldwin, C. T. Rowan, M. L. King, Jr., and W. Young.

Edmunds, Edwin R. "The Myrdalian Thesis: Rank Order of Discrimination," *Phylon* 15 (Summer 1954):297-313. This study, conducted in Texas and Oklahoma, concludes the Myrdalian hypothesis is not accurate in the Southwest.

Ehrlich, Howard J. "The Study of Prejudice in American Social Science," *Journal of Intergroup Relations* 3 (Spring 1962).

Elshorst, Hansjorg. "Two Years after Integration: Race Relations at a Deep South University," *Phylon* 28 (Spring 1967):41-51. Undergraduate Negro students at Louisiana State University, Baton Rouge.

Engle, Gerald. "Some College Students' Responses Concerning Negroes of Differing Religious Background," *Journal of Social Psychology* 74 (February 1968):275-283. References appended.

Erskine, Hazel G. "The Polls: Race Relations," *Public Opinion Quarterly* 26 (Spring 1962):137-148.

Fineberg, S. Andhil. "Deflating the Professional Bigot," *Journal of Intergroup Relations* 1 (Winter 1959-1960):47-53.

Fishman, Joshua A. "An Examination of the Process and Function of Social Stereotyping," *Journal of Social Psychology* 43 (February 1956):26-64. Including racial stereotyping.

Foster, L. H. "Race Relations in the South, 1960: A Tuskegee Institute Report," *Journal of Negro Education* 30 (Spring 1961):138-149.

Frazier, E. Franklin. "The Present State of Sociological Knowledge concerning Race Relations," "Areas of Research on Race Relations," and "A Comparison of Negro-White Relations in Brazil and in the United States," in G. Franklin Edwards, ed., *On Race Relations: Selected Writings.* Chicago: University of Chicago Press, 1968, pp. 65-74; 75-81; 82-102. First published in 1959, 1958, and 1944 respectively.

Frazier, E. Franklin. "Race Contacts and the Social Structure," in G. Franklin Edwards, ed., *On Race Relations: Selected Writings.* Chicago: University of Chicago Press, 1968, pp. 43-61. First published in the *American Sociological Review* 14 (February 1949):1-11.

Frazier, E. Franklin. "Sociological Theory and Race Relations," *American Sociological Review* 12 (June 1947):265-271.

Froncek, Tom. "American Catholics and the American Negro," *Catholic Mind* 64 (January 1966):4-11. Reprinted from *The Tablet* (London), October 9 and 16, 1965.

Glock, Charles Y., and Ellen Siegelman, eds. *Prejudice U.S.A.* New York: Praeger, 1969. Essays by Dore Schary, Saunders Redding, Seymour Lipset, and others exploring prejudice in education, business, and mass media borne by the Negro and the Puerto Rican.

Goodman, Mary Ellen. *Race Awareness in Young Children.* 1954. Introduction by Kenneth B. Clark. New York: Collier Books, 1964. First published by the Anti-Defamation League of B'nai B'rith.

Graham, Hugh Davis. *Crisis in Print; Desegregation and the Press in Tennessee.* Nashville, Tenn.: Vanderbilt University Press, 1967. Contains bibliographical essays by subject areas.

Gray, J. S., and A. J. Thompson. "Ethnic Prejudices of White and Negro College Students," *Journal of Abnormal and Social Psychology* 48 (April 1953):311-313.

Greenberg, Herbert, Jerome Pierson, and Stanley Sherman. "The Effects of Single-Session Education Techniques on Prejudice Attitudes," *Journal of Educational Sociology* 31 (October 1957):82-86.

"Green's Progress in Agency Field Reveals Problems Facing Blacks in Advertising," *Advertising Age* 40 (September 22, 1969):18.

Gregor, A. James, and D. Angus McPherson. "Racial Attitudes among White and Negro Children in a Deep-South Standard Metropolitan Area," *Journal of Social Psychology* 68 (February 1966):95-106.

Gregory, Dick. *The Shadow That Scares Me.* Edited by James R. McGraw. Garden City, N.Y.: Doubleday, 1968. Ten individualistic satirical essays on black and white attitudes.

Grossack, Martin M. "Perceived Negro Group Belongingness and Social Rejection," *Journal of Psychology* 38 (July 1954):127-130.

Hamblin, Robert L. "The Dynamics of Racial Discrimination," *Social Problems* 10 (Fall 1962):103-120.

Heath, G. Louis. "The Racial Pallor of Cairo," *Nation* 209 (December 22, 1969):692-695.

Hentoff, Nat. "Race Prejudice in Jazz," *Harper's* 218 (June 1959):72-77. Observations on the two-way prejudice in what seems outwardly the most integrated of the performing arts.

Heyer, Robert, ed. *Am I A Racist?* New York: Paulist Press, 1969. Extracts from books and periodicals exemplifying the problem of prejudice deemed prevalent in American society.

Higdon, Hal. "The Troubled Heart of Sigma Chi," *New York Times Magazine,* November 14, 1965, pp. 48-49 +. On the pressure being put on all white-only fraternities to open their doors to Negroes, particularly on Sigma Chi, whose national organization has blocked all efforts to liberalize policies.

Himelstein, P., and J. C. Moore. "Racial Attitudes and the Action of Negro and White Background Figures as Factors in Petition-Signing," *Journal of Social Psychology* 61 (December 1963):267-272.

Hites, Robert W., and Edward P. Kellogg. "The F and Social Maturity Scales in Relation to Racial Attitudes in a Deep South Sample," *Journal of Social Psychology* 62 (April 1964):189-196.

Hodge, Robert W., and Donald J. Treiman. "Occupational Mobility and Attitudes toward Negroes," *American Sociological Review* 31 (February 1966):93-102.

Hope, John, II. "Trends in Patterns of Race Relations in the South since May 17, 1954," *Phylon* 17 (Summer 1956):103-118.

Hyman, Herbert H. "Social Psychology and Race Relations," in Irwin Katz and Patricia Gurin, eds., *Race and the Social Sciences.* New York: Basic Books, 1969, pp. 3-48.

Janowitz, Morris. "Social Change and Prejudice," in E. W. Burgess and D. J. Bogue, eds., *Contributions to Urban Sociology.* Chicago: University of Chicago Press, 1964, pp. 373-388.

Javits, Jacob K. *Discrimination—U.S.A.* New York: Harcourt, Brace, 1960. A detailed and concrete review of discrimination in voting, housing, and schooling, which emphasizes the effectiveness of law as a force for progressive social change in race relations.

Jeffries, Vincent, and Richard T. Morris. "Altruism, Egoism, and Antagonism toward Negroes," *Social Science Quarterly* 49 (December 1968):697-709.

Jeffries, Vincent, and H. Edward Ransford. "Interracial Social Contact and Middle-Class White Reactions to the Watts Riot," *Social Problems* 16 (Winter 1969):312-324.

Johnson, Guy B. "The Course of Race Conflicts and Racial Movements in the South," in Jitsuichi Masuoka and Preston Valien, eds., *Race Relations: Problems and Theory.* Chapel Hill: University of North Carolina Press, 1961.

Johnson, Haynes. "That White Revolt," *Progressive* 33 (December 1969):25-28. A disquieting commentary on increasing racial polarization.

Kasoff, Allen. "The Prejudiced Personality: A Cross Cultural Test," *Social Problems* 6 (Summer 1958):59-67.

Katz, Irwin, and L. Benjamin. "Effects of White Authoritarianism in Biracial Work Groups," *Journal of Abnormal and Social Psychology* 61 (September 1960):448-456.

Kelly, James G., Jean E. Ferson, and Wayne H. Holtzman. "The Measurement of Attitudes toward the Negro in the South," *Journal of Social Psychology* 48 (November 1958):305-317.

Kelman, Herbert C., and Thomas F. Pettigrew. "How to Understand Prejudice," *Commen-*

tary 28 (November 1959):436-441. Reply to William Petersen. "Prejudice in American Society," *ibid.,* 26 (October 1958):342-348.

Killian, Lewis M., and Charles M. Grigg. "Rank Order of Discrimination of Negroes and Whites in a Southern City," *Social Forces* 39 (March 1961):235-239.

Knowles, Louis L., and Kenneth Prewitt, eds. *Institutional Racism in America.* Englewood Cliffs, N.J.: Prentice-Hall, 1969.

Koenig, Frederick W., and Morton B. King, Jr. "Cognitive Simplicity and Out-Group Stereotyping," *Social Forces* 42 (March 1964):324-327.

Koenig, Frederick W., and Morton B. King, Jr. "Cognitive Simplicity and Prejudice," *Social Forces* 40 (March 1962):220-222.

Kutner, Bernard, Carol Wilkins, and Penny R. Yarrow. "Verbal Attitudes and Overt Behavior Involving Racial Prejudice," *Journal of Abnormal and Social Psychology* 47 (July 1952):649-652.

Lee, Frank F. *Negro and White in a Connecticut Town: A Study in Race Relations.* New York: Bookman Associates, 1961.

Lee, Frank F. "The Race Relations Patterns by Areas of Behavior in a Small New England Town," *American Sociological Review* 19 (April 1954):138-143.

Lief, Harold I. "Development of Attitudes in Respect to Discrimination: An Atypical Stereotype of the Negroes' Social Worlds," *American Journal of Orthopsychiatry* 32 (January 1962):86-88.

Livson, Norman, and Thomas F. Nichols. "Social Attitude Configurations in an Adolescent Group," *Journal of Genetic Psychology* 91 (September 1957):3-23.

McDaniel, Paul A., and Nicholas Babchuk. "Negro Conceptions of White People in a Northeastern City," *Phylon* 21 (Spring 1960):7-19.

Mack, Raymond W. "Riot, Revolt, or Responsible Revolution: Of Reference Groups and Racism," *Sociological Quarterly* 10 (Spring 1969):147-156. Consequences of racial discrimination in American society.

Maliver, Bruce L. "Anti-Negro Bias among Negro College Students," *Journal of Personality and Social Psychology* 2 (November 1965):770-775. References.

Mann, John H. "The Influence of Racial Prejudice on Sociometric Choices and Perceptions," *Sociometry* 21 (June 1958):150-158.

Mann, John H. "The Relationship between Cognitive, Affective, and Behavioral Aspects of Racial Prejudice," *Journal of Social Psychology* 49 (May 1959):223-228.

Maranell, Gary M. "An Examination of Some Religious and Political Attitude Correlates of Bigotry," *Social Forces* 45 (March 1967):356-362. A survey of anti-Semitism and anti-Negro attitudes. Analysis shows high correlations between political conservatism and the degree of bigotry in all sectors and strong correlations between religiosity and bigotry in Southern areas.

Marney, Carlyle. *Structures of Prejudice.* Nashville, Tenn.: Abingdon, 1961.

Martin, James G. "Group Discrimination in Organizational Membership Selection," *Phylon* 22 (June 1959):186-192.

Martin, James G. "Intergroup Tolerance—Prejudice," *Journal of Human Relations* 10 (Winter-Spring 1962):197-204.

Marx, Gary T. *Protest and Prejudice: A Study of Belief in the Black Community.* New York: Harper & Row, 1967. Sensitive, scholarly opinion research based on extensive interviews conducted in late 1964.

Mason, Philip. *An Essay on Racial Tension.* New York: Oxford University Press, 1954. What can be learned from biological sciences and other disciplines concerning racial tension.

Medalia, Nahum Z. "Myrdal's Assumptions on Race Relations: A Conceptual Commentary," *Social Forces* 40 (March 1962):223-227.

Mendelson, Wallace. *Discrimination: Based on the Report of the United States Commission on Civil Rights.* Englewood Cliffs, N.J.: Prentice-Hall, 1962.

Merz, Louise E., and Leonard I. Pearlin. "The Influence of Information on Three Dimensions of Prejudice toward Negroes," *Social Forces* 95 (May 1957):344-351.

Middeke, Ralph. "Black and Poor in Cairo," *Commonweal* 90 (July 25, 1969):453-454. A description of militant racism at the confluence of the Ohio and the Mississippi rivers.

Middleton, Russel. "Ethnic Prejudice and Susceptibility to Persuasion," *American Socio-logical Review* 25 (October 1960):679-686.

Miyamoto, S. Frank. "The Process of Intergroup Tension and Conflict," in E. W. Burgess and D. J. Bogue, eds., *Contributions to Urban Sociology.* Chicago: University of Chicago Press, 1964.

Morland, J. Kenneth. "Race Awareness among American and Hong-Kong Chinese Children," *American Journal of Sociology* 75 (November 1969):360-374. Author com-pares racial awareness of Chinese children in Hong Kong with that of American Cau-casian and Negro children.

Nelson, Harold A. "Expressed and Unexpressed Prejudices against Ethnic Groups in a College Community," *Journal of Negro Education* 31 (Spring 1962):125-131.

Neprash, Jerry A. "Minority Group Contacts and Social Distance," *Phylon* 14 (June 1953):207-212. Conclusion: prejudice flourishes in absence of personal contacts. Thus the existence of segregation is a condition of its perpetuation.

Newby, I. A., ed. *The Development of Segregationist Thought.* Homewood, Ill.: Dorsey Press, 1968. Nineteen essays by white supremacists represent segregationist ideas since 1890. With an introduction and epilogue by the editor. Bibliography.

Noel, Donald L., and Alphonso Pinkney. "Correlates of Prejudice: Some Racial Differences and Similarities," *American Journal of Sociology* 69 (May 1964):609-622.

Nolen, Claude H. *The Negro's Image in the South: The Anatomy of White Supremacy.* Lex-ington: University of Kentucky Press, 1967. Drawing heavily from primary sources, author presents history of anti-Negro propaganda. Bibliographical essay appended.

Osborne, William A. *The Segregated Covenant: Race Relations and American Catholics.* New York: Herder & Herder, 1967. A sectional appraisal of Catholic attitudes and actions.

O'Shea, Harriet E., and Gerald Engel. "Some Current Student Attitudes toward Presidential Candidates of Different Categories (Racial and Religious)," *Journal of Psychology* 51 (January 1961):233-246.

Palmer, Roderick. "The Incidence of Race in Social Action," *Journal of Negro Education* 31 (Spring 1962):188-190.

Petersen, William. "Prejudice in American Society: A Critique of Some Recent Formu-lations," *Commentary* 26 (October 1958):342-348.

Phillips, Ulrich Bonnell. *The Slave Economy of the Old South: Selected Essays in Economic and Social History.* 1928. Baton Rouge: Louisiana State University Press, 1968. Reissue includes an important introduction by Eugene D. Genovese. Note also the 1928 credo of white supremacy. Bibliography.

Pinkney, Alphonso. "Prejudice toward Mexican and Negro Americans: A Comparison," *Phylon* 24 (Winter 1963):353-359.

Podhoretz, Norman. "My Negro Problem—and Ours," *Commentary* 35 (February 1963):93-101.

Raab, Earl, ed. *American Race Relations Today.* Garden City, N.Y.: Doubleday, 1962. Ten essays on factors other than discrimination which complicate process of achieving integrated society. Among contributors: Seymour M. Lipset, Morton Grodzins, Nathan Glazer, Joseph Himes, James B. Conant.

Raab, Earl, and Seymour M. Lipset. *Prejudice and Society.* New York: Anti-Defamation League, 1959.

"Racism: American Style," *Social Progress* 58 (May-June 1969):3-47. Entire issue.

Record, Wilson. *Minority Groups and Intergroup Relations in the San Francisco Bay Area.* Berkeley: Institute of Governmental Studies, University of California, 1963.

Redfield, Robert. "Ethnic Relations, Primitive and Civilized," in Jitsuichi Masuoka and Preston Valien, eds., *Race Relations: Problems and Theory.* Chapel Hill: University of North Carolina Press, 1961.

Reitzes, Dietrich C. "Institutional Structure and Race Relations," *Phylon* 20 (Spring 1959):48-66.

Rhyne, Edwin Hoffman. "Racial Prejudice and Personality Scales: An Alternative Ap-proach," *Social Forces* 41 (October 1962):44-53; 42 (December 1963):242-246.

Richmond, Anthony H. "Sociological and Psychological Explanations of Racial Prejudice," *Pacific Sociological Review* 4 (Fall 1961):63-68.

Roberts, Harry W. "Prior-Service Attitudes toward Whites of 219 Negro Veterans," *Journal of Negro Education* 22 (Fall 1953):455-465.

Rokeach, Milton, and Louis Mezei. "Race and Shared Belief as Factors in Social Choice," *Science* 151 (January 14, 1966):167-172.

Rose, Arnold M. "Intergroup Relations vs. Prejudice," *Social Problems* 4 (October 1956):173-176. Suggests attitudes not necessarily related to action patterns.

Rose, Arnold M., and Caroline Rose, eds. *The Minority Problem: A Book of Readings.* New York: Harper, 1965. Such problems as residential segregation, fair employment, intergroup relations examined in the context of theories of prejudice and discrimination.

Rose, Arnold M., ed. *Race Prejudice and Discrimination.* New York: Knopf, 1951. Sections on minority problems in U.S., kinds of discrimination, group identification and minority community, perceptions of the minority and the causes of prejudice, and proposed techniques for eliminating minority problems.

Rose, Peter I. *The Subject Is Race: Traditional Ideologies and the Teaching of Race Relations.* New York: Oxford University Press, 1968. Provides an historical summary of racial concepts and ethnic relations. Correlates data on the teaching aspect providing an insight into the dimensions of American prejudices. Selective bibliography.

Rousseve, Ronald J. *Discord in Brown and White: Nine Essays on Intergroup Relations in the United States, by a Negro-American.* New York: Vantage, 1961.

Rudwick, Elliott M. "Race Labeling and the Press," *Journal of Negro Education* 31 (Spring 1962):177-181.

Schaffer, Ruth C., and Albert Schaffer. "Socialization and the Development of Attitudes toward Negroes in Alabama," *Phylon* 27 (Fall 1966):274-285. An analysis of change in attitudes of selected students in an Alabama University indicates parental teachings as most influential factor.

Schuman, Howard. "Sociological Racism," *Trans-action* 7 (December 1969):44-48.

Schumann, T. E. W. "The Unpreparedness of Civilized Countries for the Twentieth-Century Racial Revolution," *Mankind Quarterly* 8 (October-December 1967):80-93. Another example of the contemporary racist position.

Schwartz, Mildred A. *Trends in White Attitudes toward Negroes.* Chicago: National Opinion Research Center, 1967. Based on surveys conducted 1942-1965.

Scott, Alan. "Twenty-Five Years of Opinion on Integration in Texas," *Southwestern Social Science Quarterly* 48 (September 1967):155-163. Selected findings from published reports of Texas polls, 1946-1965.

Segal, Bernard E. "Racial Perspectives and Attitudes among Negro and White Delinquent Boys: An Empirical Examination," *Phylon* 27 (Spring 1966):27-39.

Sharnik, John. "When Things Go Wrong All Blacks Are Black," *New York Times Magazine,* May 25, 1969, pp. 30-31 +. Norwalk, Connecticut.

Sheatsley, Paul B. "White Attitudes toward the Negro," *Daedalus* 95 (Winter 1966): 217-238.

Simon, W. B. "Race Relations and Class Structures," *Journal of Social Psychology* 60 (August 1963):187-193.

Simpson, George Eaton, and J. Milton Yinger. *Racial and Cultural Minorities: An Analysis of Prejudice and Discrimination.* 1953. 3d ed. New York: Harper, 1965. A study of majority-minority relations in the context of the whole area of sciences of human behavior. A broad and scholarly study. Excellent bibliography.

Skipper, James J., Jr., Powhatan J. Wooldridge, and Robert C. Leonard. "Race, Status, and Interaction between Patients and Hospital Personnel," *Sociological Quarterly* 9 (Winter 1968):35-46. Patient perceptions of low-scale Negro hospital workers compared with patient perceptions of white professional staff.

Smith, Carole R., Lev Williams, and Richard H. Willis. "Race, Sex and Belief as Determinants of Friendship Acceptance," *Journal of Personality and Social Psychology* 5 (February 1967):127-137.

Star, Shirley. "An Approach to the Measurement of Interracial Tension," in E. W. Burgess and D. J. Bogue, eds., *Contributions to Urban Sociology*. Chicago: University of Chicago Press, 1964, pp. 346-372.

Stein, David D., Jane Allyn Hardyck, and M. Brewster Smith. "Race and Belief: An Open and Shut Case," *Journal of Personality and Social Psychology* 1 (April 1965):281-290.

Stouffer, Samuel A. "Quantitative Methods in the Study of Race Relations," in Jitsuichi Masuoka and Preston Valien, eds., *Race Relations: Problems and Theory*. Chapel Hill: University of North Carolina Press, 1961.

Stuart, Irving R. "Minorities vs. Minorities: Cognitive, Affective and Conative Components of Puerto Rican and Negro Acceptance and Rejection," *Journal of Social Psychology* 59 (February 1963):93-99. In labor unions.

Suchman, Edward A., et al. "Hypotheses and Prospects for Opinion Research in Desegregation," *Public Opinion Quarterly* 22 (Summer 1958):190-191.

Summers, Gene F., and Andre D. Hammonds. "Effect of Racial Characteristics of Investigator on Self-Enumerated Responses to a Negro Prejudice Scale," *Social Forces* 44 (June 1966):515-518.

Tabachnick, B. Robert. "Some Correlates of Prejudice toward Negroes in Elementary Age Children," *Journal of Genetic Psychology* 100 (June 1962):193-203.

Thompson, Daniel C. "Development of Attitudes in Respect to Discrimination: The Formation of Social Attitudes," *American Journal of Orthopsychiatry* 32 (January 1962):74-85.

Thompson, Edgar T. "Language and Race Relations," in Jitsuichi Masuoka and Preston Valien, eds., *Race Relations: Problems and Theory*. Chapel Hill: University of North Carolina Press, 1961.

Trent, Richard D. "The Color of the Investigator as a Variable in Experimental Research with Negro Subjects," *Journal of Social Psychology* 40 (November 1954):281-287.

Triandis, Harry C., and Leigh Mintern Triandis. "Race, Social Class, Religion, and Nationality as Determinants of Social Distance," *Journal of Abnormal and Social Psychology* 61 (July 1960):110-118.

Turner, Eugene. "A Heritage of Racism," *Social Progress* 58 (May-June 1968):34-45. An historical overview of U.S. racial relations and the response of the black movement.

Van den Berghe, Pierre L. *Race and Racism: A Comparative Perspective*. New York: Wiley, 1967. Cross-cultural research as a basis of race relations from historical, social, and ethnic approach. Chapter four specifically applicable to the United States. Bibliography.

Vander Zanden, James W. *American Minority Relations: The Sociology of Race and Ethnic Group*. New York: Ronald, 1963. Well-written and well-ordered study drawing on research in many fields. Discusses the operation of prejudice and discrimination in intergroup relations, and the function of social change in affecting dominant-minority group relations.

VanFossen, Beth E. "Variables Related to Resistance to Desegregation in the South," *Social Forces* 47 (September 1968):39-45.

Walters, Pat. *The South and the Nation*. New York: Pantheon, 1970. Excerpt entitled "Society of the Absurd," appears in *Dissent* (January-February 1970):32-37.

Wasserman, Miriam. "The Souls of White Folk: Atlanta, Georgia, 1964-1966," *New Politics* 5 (Summer 1966):46-61. Explores the prevailing racist attitudes of the city.

Watson, Bruce. "The Backlash of White Supremacy: Caste Status and the Negro Revolt," *Journal of Human Relations* 14 (First Quarter 1966):88-99.

Weiss, Walter. "An Examination of Attitude toward Negroes," *Journal of Social Psychology* 55 (October 1961):3-21.

Westie, Frank R., and Margaret L. Westie. "The Social-Distance Pyramid: Relationships between Caste and Class," *American Journal of Sociology* 63 (September 1957):190-196.

Wilkinson, Doris Y. "Status Differences and the Black Hate Stare: 'A Conversation of Gestures,'" *Phylon* 30 (Summer 1969):191-196.

Williams, J. Allen, Jr. "Interviewer Role Performance: A Further Note on Bias in the Information Interview," *Public Opinion Quarterly* 32 (Summer 1968):287-294. Based on a sample of rural and urban Negro respondents.

Williams, J. Allen, and Paul L. Wiener. "A Reexamination of Myrdal's Rank Order of Discriminations," *Social Problems* 14 (Spring 1967):443-454. Results of a questionnaire testing and ranking discrimination against Negroes by white college students.

Williams, John A. *This is My Country Too.* New York: New American Library, 1965. Account of author's trip by automobile back and forth across the country, and of what, as a Negro, he encountered.

Williams, Robin M., Jr., et al. *Strangers Next Door: Ethnic Relations in American Communities.* Englewood Cliffs, N.J.: Prentice-Hall, 1964. Sociological and social-psychological studies made between 1948 and 1956 in Elmira, N.Y.; Steubenville, Ohio; Bakersfield, Calif.; and Savannah, Ga.

Wills, Garry. "In Defense of Uncle Toms: The Semantics of Racism," *Commonweal* 83 (November 1965):178-180.

Wolfe, John B. "Incidents of Friction between Negroes and Whites in Southeastern U.S.A.," *Mankind Quarterly* 2 (October-November 1961):122-127. Catalogue of nearly 2000 interviews to determine what incidents involving a person of the same or of different race are the most irritating.

Works, Ernest. "The Prejudice-Interaction Hypothesis from the Point of View of the Negro Minority Group," *American Journal of Sociology* 67 (July 1961):47-52.

Wright, Richard. *The Outsider.* New York: Harper, 1953. A personal interpretation of how the white man looks to nonwhite eyes.

Negro-Jewish Relations

Balfour, Brickner. *New Jewish Initiatives in the Field of Race.* New York: Union of American Hebrew Congregations, 1963.

Bender, Eugene I. "Reflections on Negro-Jewish Relationships: The Historical Dimension," *Phylon* 30 (Spring 1969):56-65.

Black Anti-Semitism and Jewish Racism. New York: Richard W. Baron, 1969. Essays contributed by Nat Hentoff, James Baldwin, Harold Cruse, and others. A few selections have appeared previously in journals.

Brotz, Howard. "Negro 'Jews' in the United States," *Phylon* 12 (Winter 1952):324-337.

Cohen, Henry. *Justice, Justice: A Jewish View of the Black Revolution.* 1968. Rev. ed. New York: Union of American Hebrew Congregations, 1969. The revised edition contains two additional chapters entitled "Allies or Adversaries" and "A New Look at Black Anti-Semitism."

Conference on Negro-Jewish Relations in the United States, New York, 1964. *Papers and Proceedings.* New York: Citadel, 1966. Also appears in *Jewish Social Studies* 27 (January 1965):3-66. Entire issue. Good bibliography.

Ehrlich, Howard J. "Stereotyping and Negro-Jewish Stereotypes," *Social Forces* 41 (December 1962):171-176.

Featherstone, Joseph. "Inflating the Threat of Black Anti-Semitism," *New Republic* 160 (March 8, 1969):14-15.

Fishman, Joshua A. "Southern City," *Midstream* 7 (Summer 1961):39-63. Jews and civil rights in Montgomery, Alabama.

Friedman, Murray. "Virginia Jewry in the School Crisis: Anti-Semitism and Desegregation," *Commentary* 27 (January 1959):17-22.

Glazer, Nathan. "Blacks, Jews and the Intellectuals," *Commentary* 47 (April 1969):33-39. The issue of black anti-Semitism.

Glazer, Nathan. "Negroes and Jews: The New Challenge to Pluralism," *Commentary* 38 (December 1964):29-34.

Halpern, Ben. "Brandeis University and Ocean Hill-Brownsville," *Midstream* 15 (February 1969):15-21. Seen as two aspects of a confrontation between black militants and Jews.

Himmelfort, Milton. "Negroes, Jews and Muzhiks," *Commentary* 42 (October 1966):83-86.

Hollander, Judith. "Black Consciousness and Jewish Conscience," *Reconstructionist* 32 (February 3, 1967):7-14.

Katz, Schlomo, ed. *Negro and Jew: An Encounter in America*. New York: Macmillan, 1967. A symposium first published in *Midstream* in December 1966.

Kogan, Lawrence A. "The Jewish Conception of Negroes in the North: An Historical Approach," *Phylon* 28 (Winter 1967):376-385. Concludes that being part of a minority group does not preclude prejudice toward another minority group; that minority groups are not natural allies in countering prejudice.

Kopkind, Andrew. "Blacks vs. Jews," *New Statesman* 77 (February 7, 1969):175-176.

Krasner, Barbara. "Jew and Black in Christian America: A Study in Separation," *Renewal* 9 (March 1969):6-9.

Landes, Ruth. "Negro Jews in Harlem," *Jewish Journal of Sociology* 9 (December 1967):175-190. Synthesis of an unpublished essay written in 1933. A history of Black Hebrewism and the relationship of the group to the Universal Negro Improvement Association.

Leo, J. "Black Anti-Semitism," *Commonweal* 89 (February 14, 1969):618-620. Discussion (March 7, 1969):695 + ; 90 (March 21, 1969):3 + .

Malev, William S. "The Jew of the South in Conflict on Segregation," *Conservative Judaism* 13 (Fall 1958):33-46. Strategy considerations for Jewish community.

Mantinband, Charles. "From the Diary of a Mississippi Rabbi," *American Judaism,* Winter 1962-1963.

Pettigrew, Thomas F. "Parallel and Distinctive Changes in Anti-Semitic and Anti-Negro Attitudes," in Charles H. Stember, ed., *Jews in the Mind of America.* New York: Basic Books, 1966, pp. 377-403. A comparison of anti-Jewish and anti-Negro attitudes from the end of World War II to the present.

Raab, Earl. "The Black Revolution and the Jewish Question," *Commentary* 47 (January 1969):23-33.

Ringer, Benjamin B. "Jews and the Desegregation Crisis," in Charles H. Stember, ed., *Jews in the Mind of America.* New York: Basic Books, 1966, pp. 197-207.

Robinson, James H., and Kenneth B. Clark. "What Negroes Think about Jews." *Anti-Defamation League Bulletin* 14 (December 1957):4-8.

Rubenstein, Richard L. "Jews, Negroes and the New Politics," *Reconstructionist* 33 (November 17, 1967):7-16.

Sheppard, Harold L. "The Negro Merchant: A Study of Negro Anti-Semitism," *American Journal of Sociology* 53 (September 1947):96-99.

Simpson, Richard. "Negro-Jewish Prejudice: Authoritarianism and Some Social Variables as Correlates," *Social Problems* 7 (Fall 1959):138-146.

Still, Lawrence A. "Black Anti-Semitism? Realignment or Alienation," *Renewal* 9 (March 1969):4-5.

Teller, J. L. "Negroes and Jews: A Hard Look," *Conservative Judaism* 21 (Fall 1966):13-20.

Waitzkin, Howard. "Black Judaism in New York," *Harvard Journal of Negro Affairs* 1, no. 3 (1967):12-44. A discussion of the religious beliefs and rituals and of Rabbi Wentworth A. Matthew.

Walden, Theodore. "Intervention by a Jewish Community Relations Council in a Negro Ghetto: A Case Illustration," *Journal of Jewish Communal Service* 44 (Fall 1967):49-63.

Wilkins, Roy. "Jewish-Negro Relations: An Evaluation," *American Judaism,* Spring 1963.

Overcoming Prejudice

Adams, James Luther. "The Shock of Recognition: The Black Revolution and Greek Tragedy," *Harvard Divinity Bulletin* (new series) 1 (Spring 1968):9-12. Appeal to whites to recognize "black identity."

Babbit, Thelma W., and Arthur W. Chickering. "The Conference as a Resource," *Journal of Intergroup Relations* 3 (Winter 1961-1962):12-20.

Banks, Waldo R. "Changing Attitudes towards the Negro in the United States: The Primary Causes," *Journal of Negro Education* 30 (Spring 1961):87-93.

Bloch, Herman D. "Recognition of Negro Discrimination: A Solution," *Journal of Social Psychology* 48 (November 1958):291-295.

Bogardus, Emory S. "Stages in White-Negro Relations in the United States: An Outline," *Society and Social Research,* October 1960.

Bond, Marjorie H. "Teenage Attitudes and Attitude Change as Measured by the Q-Technique," *Journal of Educational Sociology* 36 (September 1962):10-15. Description of Brotherhood, U.S.A., intergroup education workshop for southern California youth.

Brodey, S. "In Local Television the Eye Begins to Open on the Ghetto," *Television* 25 (August 1968):37-49+.

Burd, Gene. "The Media: View of the Ghetto," *New City* 6 (January 1968):8-11.

Burgess, Ernest W. "Social Planning and Race Relations," in Jitsuichi Masuoka and Preston Valien, eds., *Race Relations: Problems and Theory.* Chapel Hill: University of North Carolina Press, 1961.

Campbell, Ernest Q. "On Desegregation and Matters Sociological," *Phylon* 22 (Summer 1961):135-145.

Campbell, John D., Leon J. Yarrow, and Marian R. Yarrow. "A Study of Adaptation to a New Social Situation," *Journal of Social Issues* 14 (January 1958):3-7. Group adaptation as observed in a two-weeks' camp of Negro and white children.

Carleton, William G. "Negro Rights in the South: Making Haste Slowly," *Teachers College Record* 62 (October 1960):18-26. Author finds that racial attitudes are softening, and that there have been gains in acceptance of desegregation.

Clark, Dennis. "Leadership Education in an All-White Neighborhood," *Journal of Intergroup Relations* 3 (Winter 1961-1962).

Clark, Kenneth B., ed. "Desegregation: An Appraisal of the Evidence," *Journal of Social Issues* 9 (Fall 1953):2-76.

Clark, Mary T. *Discrimination Today: Guidelines for Civic Action.* New York: Hobbs, Dorman, 1966. Racial discrimination viewed in relation to precepts of Roman Catholicism. Chapter bibliographies.

Coleman, A. Lee. "Social Scientists' Predictions About Desegregation, 1950-1955," *Social Forces* 38 (March 1960):258-262.

Colle, Royal D. "Negro Image in the Mass Media: A Case Study in Social Change," *Journalism Quarterly* 45 (Spring 1968):55-60.

Cook, Lloyd A., and Elaine Cook. *Intergroup Education.* New York: McGraw-Hill, 1954.

Cook, Stuart W. "Desegregation: A Psychological Analysis," *American Psychologist* 12 (January 1957):1-13. Address by the president of the New York State Psychological Association, January 28, 1956.

Dabbs, James McBride. "The South's Man Across the Table," *New South* 12 (June 1957):3-9. Confronting Negroes in community conferences a new experience for Southern whites.

Daly, Victor R. "A Decade of Progress in Race Relations in the Nation's Capital," *Journal of Intergroup Relations* 2 (Summer 1961):252-258.

Davis, James C. "The Organized Bar's Responsibility to Improve Interracial Relations," *American Bar Association Journal* 54 (June 1968):551-554.

Dean, John P., and Alex Rosen. *A Manual of Intergroup Relations.* Chicago: University of Chicago Press, 1955. The authors outline several "propositions" that can be applied in intergroup relations to minimize prejudiced behavior, with special emphasis on changing situations as mechanisms for altering discriminatory actions.

De Fleur, Melvin L., and Frank R. Westie. "The Interpretation of Interracial Situations: An Experiment in Social Perception," *Social Forces* 38 (October 1959):17-23.

Eddy, Elizabeth M. "Attitudes toward Desegregation among Southern Students on a Northern Campus," *Journal of Social Psychology* 62 (April 1964):285-302.

Epstein, Charlotte. "A Plan for Coordination of Intergroup Relations Services," *Journal of Intergroup Relations* 1 (Summer 1960):32-36.

Erskine, Hazel. "The Polls: Speed of Racial Integration," *Public Opinion Quarterly* 32 (Fall 1968):513-524. Based on nationwide samples of opinion. Covers period 1961 to date.

Erskine, Hazel. "The Polls: World Opinion of U.S. Racial Problems," *Public Opinion Quarterly* 32 (Summer 1968):299-312. Includes an opinion sampling of whether United States minorities fare better or worse than abroad and a foreign assessment of United States progress in race relations.

Felton, J. S. "Care, Compassion and Confrontation: The Correctives in the Occupational Mental Health of the Future," *Journal of Occupational Medicine* 10 (July 1968):331-343. Comparative study of black and white social workers in bi-racial situations.

Fen, Sing-Nan. "The Learning of Social Relations in School," *Journal of Negro Education* 32 (Winter 1963):87-91.

Frank, John P. "Legal Developments in Race Relations," in Allan P. Sindler, ed., *Change in the Contemporary South*. Durham, N.C.: Duke University Press, 1963.

Frazier, E. Franklin. "Desegregation as an Object of Sociological Study," in Arnold M. Rose, ed., *Human Behavior and Social Processes*. Boston: Houghton Mifflin, 1962.

Gerson, Walter M. "Mass Media Socialization Behavior: Negro-White Differences," *Social Forces* 45 (September 1966):40-50.

Gibson, D. Parke. "Race Relations: A Plan to Avoid Social Disasters," *Public Relations Journal* 23 (November 1967):12-13. Sees effective Negro immersion into the labor force as a key to avoid further urban unrest.

Gordon, Milton M. *Assimilation in American Life*. New York: Oxford University Press, 1964. The author has "chosen to focus on the nature of group life itself in the United States as constituting the social setting in which relationships among persons of differing race, religion, and national origin take place." He concludes that the American social structure will continue to consist of a series of ethnic subcommunities crisscrossed by social class, and that secondary group relationships across ethnic lines will increasingly occur in urbanized industrial society.

Greenberg, Herbert, and Dolores Hutto. "The Attitudes of West Texas College Students toward School Integration," *Journal of Applied Psychology* 42 (October 1958):301-304. A study indicating that while the attitudes of white students were generally positive, they were influenced by negative attitude toward desegregation by their parents.

Greenberg, Herbert, A. L. Chase, and T. M. Cannon, Jr. "Attitudes of White and Negro High School Students in a West Texas Town toward School Integration," *Journal of Applied Psychology* 41 (February 1957):27-31.

Greene, Robert J. "Some Proposals Looking toward Cooperation among Public and Private Intergroup Relations Agencies," *Journal of Intergroup Relations* 3 (Winter 1961-1962):21-27.

Greer, Colin. "Cultural Pluralism and Racism," *Record* 70 (January 1969):341-345. Provocative essay; a plea for a society not of conformity, but one sensitive to individual differences within cultural pluralism.

Griffin, John H. *Black Like Me*. New York: Signet Books, 1962. The author, white, becomes cosmetically black to discover what it is like to be a Negro in the South.

Hager, Don J. "Social and Psychological Factors in Integration," *Journal of Educational Sociology* 31 (October 1957):57-63. Importance of community-wide efforts in all areas of social contact.

Halsell, Grace. *Soul Sister*. New York: World, 1969. Highly personal experiences of a white author who has colored her skin black.

Henderson, G. "Understanding the Negro Revolt," *Social Studies* 58 (April 1967):145-153. Bibliography appended.

Holmes, Eugene C. "A Philosophical Approach to the Study of Minority Problems," *Journal of Negro Education* 38 (Summer 1969):196-203.

Horn, John. "Television," *Nation* 206 (March 18, 1968):390. Adjures national television for its failure to give adequate coverage to the Negro community and to use its position to ameliorate racial unrest.

Hyman, Herbert H., and Paul B. Sheatsley. "Attitudes toward Desegregation," *Scientific American* 195 (December 1956):26, 35-39.

Hyman, Herbert H., and Paul B. Sheatsley. "Attitudes toward Desegregation—Seven Years Later," *Scientific American* 211 (July 1964):14, 16-23.

Holtzman, W. H. "Attitudes of College Men toward Non-Segregation in Texas Schools," *Public Opinion Quarterly* 20 (Fall 1956):559-569.

Iskander, Michel G. "The Neighborhood Approach," *Journal of Intergroup Relations* 3 (Winter 1961-1962):80-86.

Johnson, Charles S. "Introduction: From Race Relations to Human Relations," in Jitsuichi Masuoka and Preston Valien, eds., *Race Relations: Problems and Theory.* Chapel Hill: University of North Carolina Press, 1961.

Johnson, Guy B. "A Sociologist Looks at Racial Desegregation in the South," *Social Forces* 32 (October 1954):1-10.

Johnson, Oakley C. "The Negro-Caucasian Club: A History," *Michigan Quarterly Review* 8 (Spring 1969):97-105. American students' first inter-racial organization.

Johnson, Robert B. "Changing Status of the Negro in American Life," *Journal of Intergroup Relations* 1 (Spring 1960):56-70.

Kaplan, John. "Equal Justice in an Unequal World: Equality for the Negro—The Problem of Special Treatment," *Northwestern University Law Review* 61 (July-August 1966): 363-410. A discussion of the practical and moral problems stemming from special treatment for the Negro in employment, housing, and public education.

Katz, Irwin. *Conflict and Harmony in an Adolescent Interracial Group.* New York: New York University Press, 1955.

Katz, Irwin, and Melvin Cohen. "The Effects of Training Negroes upon Cooperative Problem Solving in Biracial Teams," *Journal of Abnormal and Social Psychology* 64 (May 1964):319-325.

Kinnick, Bernard C., and Stanton D. Plattor. "Attitudinal Change toward Negroes and School Desegregation among Participants in a Summer Training Institute," *Journal of Social Psychology* 73 (December 1967):271-283.

Kohn, M. L., and Robin Williams, Jr. "Situational Patterning in Intergroup Relations," *American Sociological Review* 21 (April 1956):164-174. Report of experiment which consisted in initiating unpatterned situations of integration and studying responses of participants, and processes by which participants redefined or modified responses.

Lamanna, Richard. "Ecological Correlates of Attitude toward Desegregation," *American Catholic Sociological Review* 22 (Fall 1961):242-249.

Levine, Louis S. "The Racial Crisis: Two Suggestions for a National Program," *American Journal of Orthopsychiatry* 37 (March 1967):235-264.

Lippman, Leopold. "Public Relations for Better Race Relations," *Public Relations Journal* 16 (February 1960):18-19. Prepared for Seattle Urban League.

Lombardi, Donald N. "Factors Affecting Changes in Attitudes toward Negroes among High School Students," *Journal of Negro Education* 32 (Spring 1963):129-136.

Long, Heiman. "Community Research and Intergroup Adjustment," in Jitsuichi Masuoka and Preston Valien, eds., *Race Relations: Problems and Theory.* Chapel Hill: University of North Carolina Press, 1961.

Long, Herman H. "Some Major Issues of Intergroup Relations for the Sixties," *Journal of Intergroup Relations* 1 (Fall 1960):5-11. Objectives: equal opportunities in all areas and eradication of group victimization of Negroes.

Loth, David, and Harold C. Fleming. *Integration North and South.* Santa Barbara, Calif.: Fund for the Republic, 1956. Survey of desegregation progress.

Lott, Bernice E., and Albert J. Lott. *Negro and White Youth: A Psychological Study in a Border State Community.* New York: Holt, 1963. A study of high school students in a Kentucky community tending to demonstrate there is a "community culture" which penetrates the barrier of segregation.

McArdle, Clare G. "Classroom Discussion of Racial Identity or How Can We Make It without Acting White?" *American Journal of Orthopsychiatry* 40 (January 1970):135-141. Interracial meeting of high school students.

McKee, James B. "Community Power and Strategies in Race Relations: Some Critical Observations," *Social Problems* 6 (Winter 1958-1959):195-203.

Mann, John H. "The Effect of Inter-Racial Contact on Sociometric Choices and Perceptions," *Journal of Social Psychology* 50 (August 1959):143-152.

Marciniak, Edward. "Interracial Councils in Chicago," *America* 99 (September 20, 1958):640-642.

Marrow, Alfred J. *Changing Patterns of Prejudice: A New Look at Today's Racial, Religious, and Cultural Tensions.* Philadelphia: Chilton, 1962. Former chairman of New York City's Commission on Intergroup Relations (1955-1960) presents his views on work of municipal intergroup commission, relates examples of how effective one in New York was, and discusses intergroup problems in United States in general.

Marsh, B. L. "Easing Community Tensions," *Public Management* 45 (September 1963):194-198. In a suburban community.

Mason, Philip. "An Approach to Race Relations," *Race* 1 (November 1959):41-52.

Mausner, Bernard. "Desegregation and Integration," *American Psychologist* 16 (June 1961):317-318.

Maxey, Alva. "The Block Club Movement in Chicago," *Phylon* 18 (Summer 1957):124-131. How community activities within small areas can foster an integrative spirit.

Mays, Benjamin E. "A Plea for Straight Talk between the Races," *Atlantic* 206 (December 1960):85-86. Author is president of Atlanta's Morehouse College, and an authority on the Negro church.

Molotch, Harvey. "Racial Integration in a Transition Community," *American Sociological Review* 34 (December 1969):878-893. South Shore community of Chicago.

Nichols, Lee. *Breakthrough on the Color Front.* New York: Random, 1954. History of the integration of the armed forces. Conclusion: military was a spearhead toward integration in the United States at large.

Ogburn, William Fielding. "Social Change and Race Relations," in Jitsuichi Masuoka and Preston Valien, eds., *Race Relations: Problems and Theory.* Chapel Hill: University of North Carolina Press, 1961.

Organizations and Personnel Engaged in Human Relations Activities in the South: Special Report. Atlanta: Southern Regional Council, May 1, 1957.

Peck, Marshall H., Jr. "Man in the Middle," *Rockefeller Foundation Quarterly* no. 1 (1968):4-21. Efforts of the Washington, D.C. Urban League to assist the Negro.

Pettigrew, Thomas F. "Complexity and Change in American Racial Patterns: A Social Psychological View," *Daedalus* 94 (Fall 1965):974-1008. The author's prognosis for 1984 is that racial patterns will most differ from today's "in the employment realm and least in the areas of housing and family." He points out that "The whole issue of de facto segregation in schools, churches, and other neighborhood-based institutions revolves around residential segregation," and that this is the most difficult problem to solve.

Pettigrew, Thomas F. "Demographic Correlates of Border-State Desegregation," *American Sociological Review* 22 (December 1957):683-689.

Pettigrew, Thomas F., and Richard M. Cramer. "The Demography of Desegregation," *Journal of Social Issues* 15 (October 1959):61-71.

Pettigrew, Thomas F. "Social Psychology and Desegregation Research," *American Psychologist* 16 (March 1961):105-112. On the importance of directing research to the attitudes of the "latent liberal," "one who has the personality potentiality of becoming liberal once the norms of the culture change."

Piedmont, Eugene B. "Changing Racial Attitudes at a Southern University: 1947-1964," *Journal of Negro Education* 36 (Winter 1967):32-41.

Pierce, C. M. "A Psychiatric Approach to Present Day Racial Problems," *Journal of the National Medical Association* 51 (May 1959):207-210.

"Racial Desegregation and Integration," *Annals of the American Academy of Political and Social Science* 304 (March 1956):1-143. Entire issue. Articles listed separately.

Robbins, Richard. "Local Strategy in Race Relations: The Illinois Experience With Community Human Relations Commissions and Councils," *Journal of Intergroup Relations* 2 (Fall 1961):311-324.

Roberts, Harry W. "The Impact of Military Service upon the Racial Attitudes of Negro Servicemen in World War II," *Social Problems* 1 (October 1953):65-69.

Root, Robert. *Progress against Prejudice.* New York: Friendship Press, 1965. Reports of recent developments in improving race relations, principally in the North and border states.

Rubington, Earl. "Race Relations in a Psychiatric Hospital," *Human Organization* 28 (Summer 1969):128-132. Study of housing and eating conditions of Negro and white patients in a non-segregated facility.

Schermer, George. *Guidelines: A Manual for Bi-Racial Committees.* New York: Anti-Defamation League of B'nai B'rith, 1964?

Shelley, J. "Biracial Citizens' Committee Works toward Integration," *Public Management* 45 (December 1963):277.

Sherif, Muzafer, and Carolyn Sherif. *Groups in Harmony and Tension.* New York: Harper, 1953. Largely theoretical. Chapters 2, 4, and 5 more particularly directed to problems concerning Negroes.

Sherif, Muzafer, ed. *Intergroup Relations and Leadership.* New York: Wiley, 1962.

Simpson, George Eaton, and J. Milton Yinger. "The Changing Patterns of Race Relations," *Phylon* 15 (December 1954):327-345. The authors predict that changes in economic conditions in the South, increased Negro voting, legal changes, and increased opportunities for higher education will be most effective means of advancing the Negro and spurring desegregation rather than efforts to decrease prejudice.

Smith, Charles U. "Race, Human Relations and the Changing South," *Phylon* 23 (Spring 1962):66-72.

Smith, Lillian. *Now is the Time.* New York: Viking, 1955. Both a polemic and an account of race relations since the 1954 Supreme Court decision. The author gives a list of what whites can do to improve race relations. A bibliography "for the layman."

Spaulding, Norman W. "Bridging the Color Gap: Effective Communication with the Black Community Calls for an Understanding of Its Media and Leading Organizations," *Public Relations Journal* 25 (April 1969):8-11.

"Sports Integration is Setting Example," *New South* 13 (April 1958):3-9. On the basis of a survey of professional and college sports, the evidence is that when barriers fall in sport, other barriers give way.

Stahl, David, Frederick B. Sussmann, and Neil J. Bloomfield, eds. *The Community and Racial Crises.* New York: Practising Law Institute, 1966. Papers and summaries from a 1964 forum on racial relations in the United States. Most useful to public officials concerned with this subject.

"Statement on Integration," *American Journal of Orthopsychiatry* 34 (April 1964):421-422. Prepared by Social Issues Committee of the American Orthopsychiatric Association on the need for joint effort by all behavioral scientists to help Negro solve integration problems.

Stember, Charles Herbert. *Education and Attitude Change: The Effect of Schooling on Prejudice against Minority Groups.* New York: Institute of Human Relations, 1961.

Stetler, Henry G. *Attitudes toward Racial Integration in Connecticut.* Hartford: Commission on Civil Rights of the State of Connecticut, 1961.

"Symposium in Memory of Dr. Martin Luther King, Jr.," *Columbia Law Review* 68 (June 1968):1011-1048. Nine contributors discuss how lawyers can improve intergroup relations.

Teacher Education for Human Relations in the Classroom: A Report from 1,108 College Professors. Chicago: North Central Association, 1962.

Thompson, Richard. *Race and Sport.* London: Oxford University Press, 1964. Issued under the auspices of Institute of Race Relations.

Thurne, Jeanne M. "Racial Attitudes of Older Adults," *Gerontologist* 7 (September 1967):172-182. Report of the first phase of a study of the racial attitudes of 320 older Negro and white adults in a Southern city. An attempt to determine if current social change has a marked effect on their attitudes.

Traxler, Margaret Ellen. "American Catholics and Negroes," *Phylon* 30 (Winter 1969):355-366.

Tumin, Melvin M. *Desegregation: Resistance and Readiness.* Princeton, N.J.: Princeton

University Press, 1958. Suggests that propensities to unlawfulness bear an inverse relationship to improvements in social class and occupational status.

Walker, E. Jerry. "The WASPS and Self-Awareness," *Religion in Life* 38 (Autumn 1969):421-426.

Warner, W. Lloyd, and Leo Srole. "Differential Assimilation of American Ethnic Groups," in Milton L. Barron, ed., *American Minorities.* New York: Knopf, 1957.

Watts, Lewis G. "Social Integration and the Use of Minority Leadership in Seattle, Washington," *Phylon* 21 (Summer 1960):136-143.

Weaver, Robert C. "The Changing Status of Racial Groups," *Journal of Intergroup Relations* 2 (Winter 1960):6-17.

Webster, Staten W. "The Influence of Interracial Contact on Social Acceptance in a Newly Integrated School," *Journal of Educational Psychology* 52 (December 1961):292-296.

Williams, Lorraine A. "The Interracial Conference of the National Council of Negro Women," *Journal of Negro Education* 26 (Spring 1957):204-206.

Williams, Robert L. "Cognitive and Affective Components of Southern Negro Students' Attitude toward Academic Integration," *Journal of Social Psychology* 76 (October 1968):107-111.

Williams, Robin M., Jr. *The Reduction of Inter-Group Tensions.* New York: Social Science Research Council, 1947. Education alone has little effect in reducing deep prejudice. (Bulletin No. 57)

Wilner, Daniel M., Rosabelle Price Walkley, and Stuart W. Cook. *Human Relations in Interracial Housing: A Study of the Contact Hypothesis.* Minneapolis: University of Minnesota Press, 1955.

Winder, Alvin. "White Attitudes toward Negro-White Interaction in a Number of Community Situations," *Journal of Social Psychology* 44 (August 1956):15-32.

Wright, Nathan. *Let's Work Together.* New York: Hawthorn, 1968. An articulate analysis of the basic divided responsibility of white and black people to achieve genuine interracial cooperation. His conclusions contain specific suggestions for a reasoned solution.

Yarrow, Marian R., John D. Campbell, and Leon J. Yarrow. "Acquisition of New Norms: A Study of Racial Desegregation," *Journal of Social Issues* 14 (Winter 1958):8-28.

Yarrow, Marian R., ed. "Interpersonal Dynamics in a Desegregation Process," *Journal of Social Issues* 14 (Winter 1958):3-63.

Young, R. K., W. M. Benson, and W. H. Holtzman. "Changes in Attitudes toward the Negro in a Southern University," *Journal of Abnormal and Social Psychology* 60 (January 1960):131-133.

Young, Whitney M., Jr. "Reason and Responsibility in the Elimination of Bigotry and Poverty," in *Social Welfare Forum, 1968.* New York: Columbia University Press, 1968, pp. 141-168.

11   Rural Problems

Anderson, C. Arnold. "Economic Status Differentials within Southern Agriculture," *Rural Sociology* 19 (March 1954):50-67.

Anderson, C. Arnold, and M. J. Bowman. *Tenure Changes and the Agricultural Ladder in Southern Agriculture.* 1955. (Kentucky Agricultural Experiment Station Bulletin no. 634)

Beardwood, Robert. "Southern Roots of Urban Crisis; Forced Off the Farms into Destitution, Thousands of Negroes Migrate to Northern Slums," *Fortune* 78 (August 1968):80-84. Agricultural policy discussed in relation to economic conditions. Map, illustrations.

Bertrand, Alvin L. *Agricultural Mechanization and Social Change in Rural Louisiana.* Baton Rouge: 1957. (Louisiana State University Agricultural Experiment Station Bulletin no. 458). Result: decreased need for plantation agricultural labor and hence increased Negro migration to cities.

Bird, Alan R. *Poverty in Rural Areas of the United States: Agricultural Economic Report No. 63.* Washington: U.S. Department of Agriculture, June 1965.

Brown, Morgan C. "Selected Characteristics of Southern Rural Negroes Exchanged to a Southern Urban Center," *Rural Sociology* 27 (March 1962):64-70.

Cahn, Edgar S., and Jean Camper Cahn. "The New Sovereign Immunity," *Harvard Law Review* 81 (March 1968):929-991. Child Development Group of Mississippi.

Carter, Hodding. "The Negro Exodus from the Delta Continues," *New York Times Magazine,* March 10, 1968, pp. 26-27 + .

Claspy, Everett. *The Negro in Southwestern Michigan: Negroes in the North in a Rural Environment.* Dowagiac, Michigan, 1967.

Coles, Robert. "What Migrant Farm Children Learn," *Saturday Review* 48 (May 15, 1965):73-74 + .

Cowhig, James D., and Calvin L. Beale. "Socioeconomic Differences between White and Nonwhite Farm Populations of the South," *Social Forces* 42 (March 1964):354-362. Study from census data of 1950 and 1960 shows improvement for both groups, but also difference widening.

Dillingham, Harry C., and David F. Sly. "Mechanical Cotton-Picker, Negro Migration, and the Integration Movement," *Human Organization* 25 (Winter 1966):344-351. The impact of technological change upon the Negro.

Dunbar, Anthony. *The Will to Survive: A Study of a Mississippi Plantation Community Based on the Words of Its Citizens.* Atlanta: Published by the Southern Regional Council and the Mississippi Council on Human Relations, 1969. Negro tenant farmers in the Delta.

"Federal Agricultural Stabilization Program and the Negro," *Columbia Law Review* 67 (June 1967):1121-1136.

Finney, Frederick Marshall. "Delta Tractor Driver and Mr. Charlie," *North American Review* (new series) 3 (Spring 1966):21-22.

Friedland, William H. "Six Migrant Labor Camps," in Cornell University Migrant Labor Project, *2d Annual Report.* Ithaca: New York State School of Industrial and Labor

Relations, Cornell University, 1968, pp. 26-38. The social system, conditions, and culture of the Southern Negro migrants.

Good, Paul. *Cycle to Nowhere.* Washington: U.S. Govt. Print. Off., 1968. (Commerce Clearing House Publication no. 14). Lack of economic opportunity for Negroes in Alabama.

Good, Paul. "The Thorntons of Mississippi: Peonage on the Plantation," *Atlantic* 218 (September 1966):95-100. Describes a rural Negro Mississippi family, a case of abject poverty.

Greenberg, Polly. *The Devil Has Slippery Shoes; A Biased Biography of the Child Development Group of Mississippi.* London: Macmillan, 1969. Combines an account of the educational program with the intricate political struggle for survival of the project.

Hesslink, George K. *Black Neighbors: Negroes in a Northern Rural Community.* Indianapolis: Bobbs-Merrill, 1968. Cass County, Michigan. An historical and sociological examination.

Hill, Herbert. *No Harvest for the Reaper: The Story of the Migratory Agricultural Worker in the United States.* New York: NAACP, 1960.

Hilsheimer, G. von. "Child Care and the Migrant Farm Hand," *Journal of Nursing Education* 18 (September 1963):262-266.

Holmes, William G. "Whitecapping: Agrarian Violence in Mississippi 1902-1906," *Journal of Southern History* 35 (May 1969):165-185. Movement of white dirt-farmers' organization to terrorize and drive Negroes from property they rented or owned.

Johnson, Charles S. *Growing Up in the Black Belt.* Washington: American Council on Education, 1941. A study of the personality development of rural Negro youth as affected by their cultural environment in the South. Part I consists of ten brief sketches of youths from different rural settings. Part II examines the rural South which makes up their environment, economic institutions, patterns of social life, family life.

Johnson, Louise A. *Follow-Up Study of MDTA E & D Project Conducted by Tuskegee Institute.* Washington: Bureau of Social Science, 1967. See also the Silverman article.

Jones, Lewis W. "The Negro Farmer," *Journal of Negro Education* 22 (Summer 1953):322-332.

Marcuse, Peter. "Crop Allotments: Power behind the Cotton," *Nation* 206 (January 8, 1968):43-46. Decries the lack of black representation on the Agricultural Stabilization and Conservation Service in rural Alabama.

Maxwell, Joseph W. "Rural Negro Father Participation in Family Activities," *Rural Sociology* 33 (March 1968):80-83.

Mayo, Selz C., and C. Horace Hamilton. "Current Population Trends in the South," *Social Forces* 42 (October 1963):77-88.

Mayo, Selz C., and C. Horace Hamilton. "The Rural Negro Population of the South in Transition," *Phylon* 24 (Summer 1963):160-171. The authors examine population growth rates and distribution, Negro fertility rates, age groups, occupations, education. Their data show that 43 percent of rural Negroes have had less than five grades of school and are functional illiterates.

Miles, Michael. "Black Cooperatives," *New Republic* 159 (September 21, 1968):21-23.

Mirel, E. "Rural Negroes Need Help," *Science News Letter* 84 (October 5, 1963):214. Especially Negro youth.

Moore, Truman E. *The Slaves We Rent.* New York: Random, 1965. A description of the life of migrant workers, a vivid picture of rural slum life. Illustrated.

"Negro Families in Rural Wisconsin: A Study of their Community Life," Madison, Wis.: Governor's Commission on Human Rights, 1959.

"Negro Farmers Get Unfair Deal," *Farm Journal* 89 (April 1965):78.

"New Hope for Rural Dixie: Firms in Carolinas Create Jobs for Negroes," *Ebony* 19 (June 1964):50 +.

Ohlendorf, George W., and William P. Kuvlesky. "Racial Differences in the Educational Orientation of Rural Youths," *Social Science Quarterly* 49 (September 1968):274-283. Research data obtained from study of Negro and white youths in rural east central Texas. Extensive footnotes, tables.

Palley, Howard A. "The Migrant Labor Problem—Its State and Interstate Aspects," *Journal of Negro Education* 32 (Winter 1963):35-42.

Payne, Raymond. "Organizational Activities of Rural Negroes in Mississippi," Starkville, Miss., 1953. (Mississippi State College Agricultural Experiment Station Circular no. 192). Southern Negroes unlikely to participate actively in organizations other than churches and fraternal groups.

Pederson, H. A. "Mechanized Agriculture and the Farm Laborer," *Rural Sociology* 19 (June 1954):143-151.

Pellegrin, Roland J., and Vernon J. Parenton. "The Impact of Socio-Economic Change on Racial Groups in a Rural Setting," *Phylon* 23 (Spring 1962):55-60.

Peter, E. "Keeping 'Em Down on the Farm; Negroes as County Agricultural Agents," *New Republic* 159 (October 19, 1968):15-17.

Peter, Emmet, Jr. "On the Outside Looking Out," *New Republic* 152 (June 26, 1965):18. On the position of Negro farmers.

Piore, Michael J. "Changes in the Mississippi Agricultural Economy and the Problems of Displaced Negro Farm Workers," *American Journal of Psychotherapy* 22 (October 1968):592-601.

Piore, Michael J. "Negro Workers in the Mississippi Delta," *Monthly Labor Review* 91 (April 1968):23-25.

Record, C. Wilson. "Negroes in the California Agriculture Labor Force," *Social Problems* 6 (Spring 1959):354-361. Attempt to account for the few Negroes in this field.

Reddick, M. E., and E. C. Pasour, Jr. *Economic Opportunities for Farm Adjustments by Nonwhite Operators in the Southern Coastal Plain, North Carolina.* Raleigh: Department of Economics, North Carolina State University, n.d. (Economic Information Report no. 2). Evaluates opportunities on farms with varying amounts of land, labor, and capital.

Rogers, W. W. "Negro Alliance in Alabama," *Journal of Negro History* 45 (January 1960):38-44. Account of the Colored Farmers' National Alliance and Cooperative Union.

Rubin, Morton. "Localism and Related Values among Negroes in a Southern Rural Community," *Social Forces* 36 (March 1958):263-267.

Rubin, Morton. "Migration Patterns of Negroes from a Rural Northeastern Mississippi Community," *Social Forces* 39 (October 1960):59-66.

Rubin, Morton. *Plantation County.* Chapel Hill: University of North Carolina Press, 1951; New Haven: College and University Press, 1963. Observations on the social structure and cultural values of a typical Southern County, in effect constituting a companion work to *Blackways of Kent,* Hylan Lewis's study of a Southern mill town.

Rubin, Morton. "Social and Cultural Change in the Plantation Area," *Journal of Social Issues* 10 (January 1954):28-35.

Ruttan, Vernon W. "Farm and Non-Farm Employment Opportunities for Low Income Farm Families," *Phylon* 20 (Fall 1959):248-255.

Sargent, F. O. "Economic Adjustments of Negro Farmers in East Texas," *Southwestern Social Science Quarterly* 42 (June 1961):32-39.

Silverman, Leslie J. *Follow-Up of Project Uplift, The MDTA E & D Project Conducted by Florida A & M University.* Washington: Bureau of Social Science Research, 1967. Evaluates program for training of the rural Negro. See also Louise A. Johnson's publication on this topic.

Smith, P. M. "Personal and Social Adjustment of Negro Children in Rural and Urban Areas of the South," *Rural Sociology* 26 (March 1961):73-77.

Smith, Stanley H. "The Older Rural Negro," in E. Grant Youmans, ed., *Older Rural Americans.* Lexington: University of Kentucky Press, 1967, pp. 262-280. Presents demographic, educational, employment, and income data.

Southern Regional Council. *Hungry Children.* Atlanta, 1967. A report of six physicians on the health and living conditions of Negro children in rural Mississippi.

Southern Rural Research Project. *Black Farm Families—Hunger and Malnutrition in Rural*

Alabama: A Survey by Southern Research Project of Living Conditions in Eight Counties.
Selma, Ala., 1968.

Southern Rural Research Project. *The Extinction of the Black Farmer in Alabama.* Selma,
Ala., 1968. Examines the effectiveness of the Agricultural Stabilization and Conservation
Service, the Farmers Home Administration, and the Federal Extension Service.

Steptoe, R., and B. Clark. "The Plight of Rural Southern Blacks and Some Policy Implications," *Bulletin of the Southern University and A & M College.* 55 (June 1969):21-35.

Thelwell, Mike. "Fish Are Jumping an' the Cotton Is High: Notes from the Mississippi
Delta," *Massachusetts Review* 7 (Spring 1966):362-378. Impressions from a SNCC and
Mississippi Freedom Democratic party worker. Black and white illustrations are
appended.

U.S. Commission on Civil Rights. Alabama State Advisory Committee. *The Agricultural
Stabilization and Conservation Service in the Alabama Black Belt.* Washington: U.S. Govt.
Print. Off., 1968.

U.S. Commission on Civil Rights. Georgia State Advisory Committee. *Equal Opportunity in
Federally Assisted Agricultural Programs in Georgia.* Washington, 1967.

U.S. Office of Education. *Better Homes for Negro Farm Families: A Handbook for Teachers
Outlining an Educational Program in Housing.* Washington, 1947. Prepared jointly by
Agricultural Education Service and Home Economics Education Service.

Wasserman, Miriam. "White Power in the Black Belt," *New South* 22 (Winter 1967):27-36.
Describes the inequitable treatment of the Negro sharecroppers in Alabama by the
Agricultural Stabilization and Conservation Service.

Welch, Finis. "Labor-Market Discrimination: An Interpretation of Income Differences in
the Rural South," *Journal of Political Economy* 75 (June 1967):225-240.

Weltner, Charles Longstreet. *John Willie Reed: An Epitaph.* Atlanta: Southern Regional
Council, 1969. Biography of a rural black migrant who moved to Atlanta. It graphically
illustrates the hopelessness stemming from rural poverty and urban deprivation.

Wheeler, James O., and Stanley D. Brunn. "Negro Migration into Rural Southwestern
Michigan," *Geographical Review* 58 (April 1968):214-230.

"White Agriculture," *New Republic* 161 (November 29, 1969):11. Continued discrimination
against the black farmer in Mississippi by the Agricultural Stabilization and Conservation Service.

Wright, Dale. *They Harvest Despair: The Migrant Farm Worker.* Boston: Beacon, 1965.

12   Urban Problems

General

Abbott, David W., Louis H. Gold, and Edward T. Rogowsky. *Police, Politics, and Race: The New York City Referendum on Civilian Review.* Cambridge, Mass.: American Jewish Committee and the Joint Center for Urban Studies of the Massachusetts Institute of Technology and Harvard University. Distributed by Harvard University Press, 1969.

Abrams, Charles. *The City Is the Frontier.* New York: Harper, 1965. A searching analysis of urban renewal in the United States. See particularly chapter 4, "The Racial Upheaval in Cities."

Allen, James Egert. *The Negro in New York.* New York: Exposition Press, 1964. Foreword by Arthur Levitt.

An American City in Transition: The Baltimore Community Self-Survey of Inter-Group Relations. Maryland Commission on Interracial Problems and Relations, and Baltimore Commission on Human Relations, 1955.

Anthony, Daniel S., and Walter D. Chambers. *Newark: A City in Transition.* Newark, N.J.: Mayor's Commission on Group Relations, 1959. Vol. I: Characteristics of the Population; Vol. II: Residents' Views on Inter-Group Relations & Statistical Tables; Vol. III: Summary and Recommendations.

Archibald, Helen A. "Notes on the Culture of the Urban Negro Child," *Religious Education* 62 (July 1967):321-326.

Bailey, Harry A., Jr. "Negro Interest Group Stategies," *Urban Affairs Quarterly* 4 (September 1968):27-38.

Banfield, Edward C. *The Unheavenly City: The Nature and The Future of Our Urban Crisis.* Boston: Little, Brown, 1970.

Banks, Roger W. "Between the Tracks and the Freeway: The Negro in Albuquerque," in Henry Tobias and Charles E. Woodhouse, eds., *Minorities in Politics.* Albuquerque: University of New Mexico Press, 1969, pp. 113-131. An overview of their social, educational, and economic status. The author notes the ineffectiveness of the black minority here in contrast to the larger Spanish-American group.

Berkeley, Ellen Perry. "Workshop in Watts," *Architectural Forum* 130 (January-February 1969):58-63. Structure and accomplishments of a group of black architects and planners.

Berry, Edwin C., et al. *The Racial Aspects of Urban Planning: An Urban League Critique of the Chicago Comprehensive Plan.* Chicago: Chicago Urban League, 1968. Commentaries on the desegregation rate and residential accommodation of Negro families.

Beshers, James M. *Urban Social Structure.* New York: Free Press, 1962. A study of the overall network of social relations which emphasizes social distance. Analysis centers on both belief and behavior and such factors as residence and marriage, and how these have implications for urban social structure.

Black, W. Joseph. "Renewed Negro and Urban Renewal," *Architectural Forum* 128 (June 1968):60-67. Asks for Negro participation in the conceptual and decision-making programs for urban renewal and planning; particular reference is made to the Lawndale section of Chicago.

Blalock, H. M., Jr. "Urbanization and Discrimination in the South," *Social Problems* 7 (Fall 1959):146-152.

Blumberg, Leonard. "Urban Rehabilitation and Problems of Human Relations," *Phylon* 19 (Spring 1958):97-105.

Brooks, Michael P., and Michael A. Stegman. "Urban Social Policy, Race, and the Education of Planners," *Journal of the American Institute of Planners* 34 (September 1968): 275-286. Orientation of planners towards the problems engendered by racial and social discord.

Brown, Claude, Arthur M. Dunmeyer, and Ralph Ellison. "Harlem's America," *The New Leader* 49 (September 26, 1966):entire issue. Transcript of their testimony before a U.S. Senate subcommittee examining the "Federal Role in Urban Problems."

Burgess, E. W., and Donald J. Bogue, eds. *Contributions to Urban Sociology.* Chicago: University of Chicago Press, 1964. Several useful articles on the urban Negro are listed in the appropriate sections.

Carter, Wilmoth A. "Negro Main Street as a Symbol of Discrimination," *Phylon* 21 (Fall 1960):234-242.

Carter, Wilmoth A. *The Urban Negro in the South.* New York: Vantage, 1962. Title misleading since this is an analysis of one street in one city, Raleigh, N.C. The author does not use the 1960 census data, although she does have an appendix on the sit-ins.

Clark, Kenneth B. "The Negro and the Urban Crisis," in Kermit Gordon, ed. *Agenda for the Nation.* Washington: Brookings Institution, 1968, pp. 117-140.

Coke, James G. "The Lesser Metropolitan Areas of Illinois," *Illinois Government* no. 15, November 1962. Urbana: Institute of Government and Public Affairs, University of Illinois. Shows that, with respect to Illinois, large city problems, such as unsatisfactory racial relations, are duplicated in small cities.

Drake, St. Clair, and Horace R. Cayton. *Black Metropolis: A Study of Negro Life in a Northern City.* New York: Harcourt, Brace, 1945; New York: Harper Torchbook, 2 vols., 1963. The Harper edition has been enlarged by a new chapter, "Bronzeville 1961," an appendix, "Black Metropolis 1961," and "Suggestions for Collateral Reading, 1962." The classic study of urban Negro life, it is a great social survey as well as a systematic analysis of social organization.

Dulaney, William L. "The Negro and the City," *Journal of Negro Education* 31 (Spring 1962):198-201.

Egan, John J. "The Human Side of Neighborhoods," *Integrated Education* 1 (June 1963):20-25.

Fact Book on Youth in New York City. Community Council of Greater New York, 1956.

Farley, Reynolds. "The Urbanization of Negroes in the United States," *Journal of Social History* 1 (Spring 1968):241-258.

Frazier, E. Franklin. "Negro Harlem: An Ecological Study," in G. Franklin Edwards, ed., *On Race Relations: Selected Writings.* Chicago: University of Chicago Press, 1968, pp. 142-160. First published in the *American Journal of Sociology* 43 (July 1937):72-88.

Frazier, E. Franklin. "The Urban Ordeal of Negroes," *Negro Digest* 12 (December 1962) 26-32.

Friesema, H. Paul. "Black Control of Central Cities: The Hollow Prize," *Journal of the American Institute of Planners* 35 (March 1969):75-79.

Funnyé, Clarence. "Deghettoization: Choice of the New Militancy." *Architectural Forum* 130 (April 1969):74-77.

Gist, Noel P., and L. A. Halbert. *Urban Society.* New York: Crowell, 1956.

Glazer, Nathan, and Daniel Patrick Moynihan. *Beyond the Melting Pot.* Cambridge, Mass.: M.I.T. Press and Harvard University Press, 1963. A study of the five largest ethnic groups in New York City: Negroes, Puerto Ricans, Jews, Italians, Irish. Full bibliographical notes and index.

Glazer, Nathan. "The Real Task in America's Cities," *New Society* 11 (March 21,

1968):406-408. An appraisal of the report of the U.S. National Commission on Civil Disorders relative to the direction of the present inequal societies.

Green, Constance McLaughlin. *The Rise of Urban America.* New York: Harper, 1965. See particularly last chapter for Negro urban minorities today.

Green, Constance McLaughlin. *The Secret City: A History of Race Relations in the Nation's Capital.* Princeton, N.J.: Princeton University Press, 1967. Period covered: 1791-1960. Bibliography includes public documents, published and unpublished primary sources.

Grier, Eunice, and George Grier. *Negroes in Five New York Cities: A Study of Problems, Achievements, and Trends.* New York State Commission against Discrimination, 1958.

Grodzins, Morton. *The Metropolitan Area as a Racial Problem.* Pittsburgh: University of Pittsburgh Press, 1958.

Horne, Frank S. "The Open City—Threshold to American Maturity," *Phylon* 38 (Summer 1957):133-139.

Jacobs, Paul. *Prelude to Riot: A View of Urban America from the Bottom.* New York: Random, 1967. A critical appraisal of the effect of public administration and institutions which serve the Watts district of Los Angeles. Written by a staff member of the Center for the Study of Democratic Institutions. Bibliography.

John F. Kraft, Inc. *Attitude of Negroes in Various Cities.* New York, 1966. Prepared for the U.S. Senate Sub-committee on Executive Reorganization.

Johnson, James Weldon. *Black Manhattan.* New York: Knopf, 1930. Valuable retrospectively, especially for description of the gradual takeover of Harlem by the Negroes.

Kain, John F. "The Big Cities' Big Problem: The Growth of Huge Racial Ghettos Exacerbates Already Existing Urban Problems Ranging from Finance to Transportation," *Challenge* 15 (September-October 1966):4-8.

Kantrowitz, Nathan. "Ethnic and Racial Segregation in the New York Metropolis, 1960," *American Journal of Sociology* 74 (May 1969):685-693.

Killian, Lewis M., and Charles M. Grigg. "Urbanism, Race, and Anomia," *American Journal of Sociology* 67 (May 1962):661-665.

Lewis, Walter B. *Problems of the Negro in the City.* Washington: U.S. Dept. of Housing and Urban Development, 1968. Address delivered at the Conference of Problems of Negro in Central City of the South, Southern University, Baton Rouge, La. by the Director of the Office of Equal Opportunity.

Lieberson, Stanley. *Ethnic Patterns in American Cities.* Glencoe, Ill.: Free Press, 1963.

Lowi, Theodore J. "Apartheid U.S.A.; Federally Assisted Urban Redevelopment: A Blueprint for Segregation," *Trans-action* 7 (February 1970):32-39.

Marcuse, Peter. "Black Housing: A New Approach for Planners," *Connection* 6 (1969):95-125.

Marcuse, Peter. "Integration and the Planner." *Journal of the American Institute of Planners* 35 (March 1969):113-117. Calls for a commitment by urban planners to foster integration in housing, and their recognition of ghetto residents' participation in renewal planning.

Martin, Roscoe C. *Metropolis in Transition: Local Government Adaptation to Changing Urban Needs.* Washington: U.S. Housing and Home Finance Agency, September 1963.

Meyer, J. R., J. F. Kain, and M. Wohl. "Race and the Urban Transportation Problem," in *The Urban Transportation Problem.* Cambridge, Mass.: Harvard Universtiy Press, 1965, pp. 145-167.

Meyer, Philip. *Miami Negroes: A Study in Depth.* Miami, Fla.: Miami Herald, 1968.

Mitchell, Howard E. "The Urban Crisis and the Search for Identity," *Social Casework* 50 (January 1969):10-15

Moynihan, Daniel P. "Urban Conditions: General," *Annals of the American Academy of Political and Social Science* 321 (May 1967):159-177.

The Negro and the City. New York: Time-Life Books, 1968. Adapted from a special issue [January 1968] of *Fortune* on "Business and the Urban Crisis."

The Negro in Cleveland. Cleveland Urban League, June 1964.

New York City in Crisis: A Study in Depth of Urban Sickness. New York: McKay, 1965. Prepared by the staff of the *New York Herald-Tribune.*

Oppenheimer, Martin. *The Urban Guerrilla.* Chicago: Quadrangle, 1969.

Ratner, Gershon M. "Inter-Neighborhood Denials of Equal Protection in the Provision of Municipal Services," *Harvard Civil Rights-Civil Liberties Law Review* 4 (Fall 1968):1-63. Contends that equal protection clause in the fourteenth amendment is applicable to education, police, and other educational services for Negroes.

Schlivek, Louis B. *Man in Metropolis.* Garden City, N.Y.: Doubleday, 1965. Contains accounts of the difficulties Negroes have in finding homes in suburbia, with the result that Negro workers in suburban plants face long commutes to city ghettos.

Schnore, Leo F. *The Urban Scence: Human Ecology and Demography.* New York: Free Press, 1965.

Silberman, Charles E. "The City and the Negro," *Fortune* 65 (March 1962):88 + .

Stahl, David, Frederick B. Sussmann, and Neil J. Bloomfield, eds. *The Community and Racial Crisis.* New York: Practising Law Institute, 1966.

Stern, Michael L. "Constitutional Law—Equal Protection—Racial Discrimination in Urban Renewal Program, *Arrington v. City of Fairfield,*" *Harvard Civil Rights-Civil Liberties Law Review* 5 (Winter 1970):184-191.

Tucker, Priscilla. "Poor Peoples' Plan," (New York) *Metropolitan Museum Bulletin* 27 (January 1969):265-279. Black city planning, the architect's role.

Vance, Rupert B., and Nicholas J. Demerath, eds. *The Urban South.* Chapel Hill: University of North Carolina Press, 1954. A useful collection. Articles listed separately.

Waller, Peter. "Social Science Seminar: Negro Problem is People Problem," *Public Relations Journal* 24 (May 1968):19-21. Race relations in urban areas.

Weaver, Robert C. *Dilemmas of Urban America.* Cambridge, Mass.: Harvard University Press, 1965. On new trends in suburbia, urban renewal, and problems of racial policy.

Weaver, Robert C. "Urbanization of the Negro," in *The Urban Complex: Human Values in Urban Life.* Garden City, N.Y.: Doubleday, 1964, pp. 223-270. Takes the position that despite glaring evils, the move to the city has resulted in net gain for the Negro.

Weissbourd, Bernard. *Segregation, Subsidies, and Megalopolis.* Santa Barbara, Calif.: Center for the Study of Democratic Institutions, 1964. The effects of federal housing policies.

Weissbourd, Bernard, and Herbert Channick. "An Urban Society," *Center Magazine* 1 (September 1968):56-65.

Whyte, William H., Jr. "Are Cities Un-American?" *Fortune* 56 (September 1957):122-127 + .

Williams, J. Allen, Jr. "The Effects of Urban Renewal upon a Black Community: Evaluation and Recommendations," *Social Science Quarterly* 50 (December 1969):713-722.

Wilson, James Q. *The Metropolitan Enigma: Inquiries into the Nature and Dimensions of America's "Urban Crisis."* Rev. ed. Cambridge, Mass.: Harvard University Press, 1968. First published in 1966 by the Task Force on Economic Growth and Opportunity of the United States Chamber of Commerce. Considerable information on the economic, educational, and social plight of the urban Negro is interspersed throughout.

Wolf, Eleanor P., and Charles N. Lebeaux. "On the Destruction of Poor Neighborhoods by Urban Renewal," *Social Problems* 15 (Summer 1967):3-8. Concludes slum clearance of poor Negro areas presents more losses than gains.

Wright, Nathan, Jr. *Ready to Riot.* New York: Holt, Rinehart & Winston, 1968. The Director of the Department of Urban Work of Newark focuses on the city's malaises in a social analysis of ghetto unrest. Illustrations, maps.

Young, Whitney, Jr. "The Case for Urban Integration," *Social Work* 12 (July 1967):12-17.

See also Housing; Education.

In-Migration and Population

Bahr, Howard M., and Jack P. Gibbs. "Racial Differentiation in American Metropolitan Areas," *Social Forces* 45 (June 1967):521-532.

Bogue, D. J., and D. P. Dandekar. *Population Trends and Prospects for the Chicago-Northwest-*

ern Indiana Consolidated Metropolitan Area: 1960-1990. Population Research and Training Center, University of Chicago, March 1962.

California. Division of Fair Employment Practices. *Negroes and Mexican Americans in South and East Los Angeles: Changes between 1960 and 1965 in Population, Employment, Income, and Family Status.* San Francisco, 1966.

Chapin, F. Stuart, and Shirley F. Weiss, eds. *Urban Growth Dynamics.* New York: Wiley, 1962.

Chicago Commission on Human Relations. *Solving the Problem of Chicago's Population Growth.* 1957. Report on a conference of community leaders.

Coe, Paul F. "Non-White Population Increases in Metropolitan Areas," *Journal of American Statistical Association* 50 (June 1955):283-308. Chiefly on population movements 1940-1950.

Coe, Paul F. "The Nonwhite Population Surge to Our Cities." *Land Economics* 35 (August 1959):195-210. A useful article; see especially footnote references for bibiliography.

Duncan, Otis D., and Beverly Duncan. *Chicago's Negro Population.* Chicago: University of Chicago Press, 1956.

Fried, Marc. "Deprivation and Migration: Dilemmas of Causal Interpretation," in Daniel P. Moynihan, ed., *On Understanding Poverty.* New York: Basic Books, 1969, pp. 111-159.

Grier, Eunice, and George Grier. *Race Relations in Broome County: A Profile for 1958.* New York State Commission against Discrimination, 1958. Race relations in Binghamton, Endicott, Johnson, where Negro influx has been numerically insignificant.

Grier, Eunice S. *Understanding Washington's Changing Population.* Washington: Washington Center for Metropolitan Studies, 1961.

Grier, George, with Eunice Grier. *The Impact of Race on Neighborhood in the Metropolitan Setting.* Washington: Washington Center for Metropolitan Studies, May 1961.

Grier, George, with Eunice Grier. "The Negro Migration: Doubled Populations in a Decade Pose Urgent Problems for Northern Cities," *Housing Yearbook.* Washington: National Housing Conference, 1960.

Hamilton, C. Horace. "Educational Selectivity of Net Migration from the South," *Social Forces* 38 (October 1959):33-42.

Hamilton, C. Horace. "The Negro Leaves the South," *Demography* 1 (1964):273-295.

Hauser, Philip M. *On the Impact of Population and Community Changes on Local Government.* Pittsburgh: Pittsburgh University Press, 1961.

Hauser, Philip M., ed. *Population Dilemma: A Policy for America.* New York: Spectrum-Prentice Hall, 1963.

Hauser, Philip M. *Population Perspectives.* New Brunswick, N.J.: Rutgers University Press, 1961.

Hauser, Philip M. *Rapid Growth: Key to Understanding Metropolitan Problems.* Washington: Washington Center for Metropolitan Studies, 1961.

Hauser, Philip M. *Total and Metropolitan Population of the United States as the Sixties Begin.* New York: Lawrence, 1960. All of these works by Mr. Hauser have great relevance for understanding the problems of Negroes in urban situations.

Hill, Herbert. "Demographic Change and Racial Ghettos: The Crisis of American Cities." *Journal of Urban Law* 44 (Winter 1966):231-285. Contents: Negro population characteristics; housing and the pattern of the segregated slums; public housing programs; governmental power and housing segregation in the 1960s.

Hopkins, Richard J. "Occupational and Geographical Mobility in Atlanta, 1870-1896," *Journal of Southern History* 34 (May 1968):200-213.

Kahl, Joseph A. *The American Class Structure.* New York: Rinehart, 1957. Chapter 8 "Ethnic and Race Barriers," deals with the movement of Negroes into cities and into industry.

Knapp, Robert B. *Social Integration in Urban Communities: A Guide for Educational Planning.* New York: Bureau of Publications, Teachers College, Columbia University, 1960.

Lee, George A. "Negroes in a Medium-Sized Metropolis: Allentown, Pennsylvania—A Case Study," *Journal of Negro Education* 37 (Fall 1968):397-405. Demographic and social characteristics.

Levine, Daniel U., and Robert J. Havighurst. "Negro Population Growth and Enrollment in the Public Schools: A Case Study and Its Implications," *Education and Urban Society* 1 (November 1968):21-46. References.

Meadow, Kathryn P. "Negro-White Differences among Newcomers to a Transitional Urban Area," *Journal of Intergroup Relations* 3 (Fall 1962):320-330.

Miller, Loren. "The Changing Metro-Urban Complex," *Journal of Intergroup Relations* 3 (Winter 1961-1962):55-64.

Mugge, Robert H. "Differentials in Negro Migration to Atlanta," in E. W. Burgess and D. J. Bogue, eds., *Contributions to Urban Sociology*, Chicago: University of Chicago Press, 1964, pp. 459-470.

"Negroes in the City of New York." Commission on Intergroup Relations, City of New York, 1961.

New York State Commission against Discrimination. *Non-Whites in New York's Four "Suburban" Counties: An Analysis of Trends.* New York, 1959.

Newman, Dorothy K. "The Negro's Journey to the City—Part I," *Monthly Labor Review* 88 (May 1965):502-507. Brief survey of what Negro migrant experiences in housing, occupations, earnings and income, education.

Newman, Dorothy K. "The Negro's Journey to the City—Part II," *Monthly Labor Review* 88 (June 1965):644-649. Comparison of Negro experience with that of white immigrant minorities demonstrates tragic discrepancy in their degree of acceptance and inclusion.

Pruitt, Shirley. "Ethnic and Racial Composition of Selected Cleveland Neighborhoods," *Social Science* 43 (June 1968):171-174.

Rames, Jose. "Racial Anatomy of a City," *New University Thought* 3 (September-October 1963):20-34. Detroit.

Reid, Ira De Augustine. *The Negro Immigrant, His Background Characteristics and Social Adjustment, 1899-1937.* New York: Columbia University Press, 1949.

Schmid, Calvin F., and Wayne W. McVey, Jr. *Growth and Distribution of Minority Races in Seattle, Washington.* Seattle: Seattle Public Schools, 1964.

Schnore, Leo F., and Harry Sharp. "Racial Changes in Metropolitan Areas, 1950-1960," *Social Forces* 41 (March 1963):241-253.

Shannon, Lyle W. "The Public's Perception of Social Welfare Agencies and Organizations in an Industrial Community," *Journal of Negro Education* 32 (Summer 1963):276-285.

Straits, Bruce C. "Residential Movement among Negroes and Whites in Chicago," *Social Science Quarterly* 49 (December 1968):573-592. Includes tabular presentation.

Taeuber, Karl E., and Alma F. Taeuber. "Is the Negro an Immigrant Group?" *Integrated Education* 1 (June 1963):25-28. Raises the question whether Negroes who migrate to Northern cities will be assimilated in same way as European immigrant groups have become, or whether the second-generation urban Negro will remain in same relative position as his parents.

Taeuber, Karl E., and Alma F. Taeuber. "The Negro as an Immigrant Group: Recent Trends in Racial and Ethnic Segregation in Chicago," *American Journal of Sociology* 69 (January 1964):374-382.

United Community Services of Metropolitan Boston. *Black and White in Boston: A Report on the Community Research Project.* Boston, 1968. Immigration, population, and housing patterns of black and white families.

Zimmer, Basil G. "The Adjustment of Negroes in a Northern Industrial Community," *Social Problems* 9 (Spring 1962):378-386.

The Ghetto

Allen, Thomas H. "Mass Media Patterns in a Negro Ghetto," *Journalism Quarterly* 45 (Autumn 1968):525-528. Patterns and effects of the media in a metropolitan ghetto as one outlet of racial tension.

Baldwin, James. "The Harlem Ghetto: Winter 1948," *Commentary* 5 (February 1948):165-170.

Banks, William H., Jr. "Land Grants for Black Communities," *Liberator* 9 (October 1968):8-9.

Bell, Wendell. "A Probability Model for the Measurement of Ecological Segregation," *Social Forces* 32 (May 1954):357-364.

Bell, Wendell, and Ernest M. Willis. "The Segregation of Negroes in American Cities," *Social and Economic Studies* 6 (March 1957):59-75.

Bienen, Henry. "Violence in the Ghetto," in *Violence and Social Change.* Chicago: University of Chicago Press, 1968, pp. 13-38.

Blauner, Robert. "Internal Colonialism and Ghetto Revolt," *Social Problems* 16 (Spring 1969):393-408. Consideration of aspects of black protest: urban riots, cultural nationalism, and the seeking of community control within the ghetto.

Blumberg, Leonard, and Michael Lalli. "Little Ghettoes: A Study of Negroes in the Suburbs," *Phylon* 27 (Summer 1966):117-131. Metropolitan Philadelphia.

Boesel, David, et al. "White Institutions and Black Rage," *Trans-action* 6 (March 1969):24-31. Examines some white institutions and attitudes in the ghetto to understand the Negro antagonism to them.

Boskin, Joseph. "The Revolt of the Urban Ghettos, 1964-1967," *Annals of the American Academy of Political and Social Science* 382 (March 1969):1-14.

Brazier, Arthur M. *Black Self-Determination: The Story of the Woodlawn Organization.* Grand Rapids, Mich.: Eerdmans, 1969. Thesis: that blacks must seize the initiative and exercise their power to force the white establishment to yield a rightful place to the black minority. A final chapter suggests a positive role for the white churches.

Brown Claude. "Harlem, My Harlem," *Dissent* 8 (Summer 1961):371-382.

Brown, Thomas Edwards. "Sex Education and Life in the Negro Ghetto," *Pastoral Psychology* 19 (May 1968):45-54.

Bullock, Paul, ed. *Watts: The Aftermath, An Inside View of the Ghetto by the People of Watts.* New York: Grove, 1969.

Bullough, Bonnie. "Alienation in the Ghetto," *American Journal of Sociology* 72 (March 1967):469-478. Comparative sampling of a middle-class Negro living in the traditional ghetto and another living in a predominantly white suburban community.

Clark, Dennis. *The Ghetto Game.* New York: Sheed & Ward, 1962.

Clark, Kenneth B. *Dark Ghetto.* New York: Harper, 1965. Taking his departure from the HARYOU report *Youth in the Ghetto,* the author here goes on to examine the ugly facts of the ghetto everywhere and for all its denizens, and to articulate the minimum requirements for a genuine obliteration of ghetto barriers.

Coles, Robert. *The Image Is You.* Edited by Donald Erceg. Boston: Houghton Mifflin, 1969. A vivid portrayal of the black ghetto is achieved by photographs of their environment taken by Roxbury, Massachusetts young people—with perceptive commentaries by the author.

Coles, Robert. "Like It Is in the Alley," *Daedalus* 97 (Fall 1968):1315-1330. The life of a Negro ghetto child whose parents chose a Boston ghetto over Alabama poverty.

Coles, Robert. "Maybe God Will Come and Clean Up this Mess," *Atlantic* 220 (October 1967):103-106. The squalor of the ghettos and the insensitive and prejudicial attitude of white officialdom.

Curtis, C. Michael. "Travels with Mr. Charlie: Journalists Look at the Black American Ghetto," *Atlantic* 224 (August 1969):31-38. An honest appraisal.

DeMott, Benjamin. "An Unprofessional Eye: Project for Another Country," *American Scholar* 32 (Summer 1963):451-457. On domestic Peace Corps pilot project in Harlem.

Downs, Anthony. "Alternative Futures for the American Ghetto," *Daedalus* 97 (Fall 1968):1331-1378. Develops and supports the concept of dispersal or population diffusion.

Elman, Richard M. *Ill-at-Ease in Compton.* New York: Pantheon, 1967. A social portrait of a predominantly Negro city in Los Angeles County. Map.

English, W. H. "Minority Group Attitudes of Negroes and Implications for Guidance," *Journal of Negro Education* 26 (Spring 1957):99-107. A study of the Negro minority in Springfield, Mass., to determine why the Negroes, as a group, seemed so unwilling "to participate in many activities open to them as residents," why they were so unaggressive. (In 1965, Springfield was the scene of intense Negro protest.)

Etzkowits, Henry, and Gerald M. Schaflander. *Ghetto Crisis: Riots or Reconciliation.* Boston: Little, Brown, 1969. Bedford-Stuyvesant.

Fry, John R. "Mayor Daley and Chicago's Blacks," *Christianity and Crisis* 28 (April 15, 1968):77-80.

Glazer, Nathan. "Ghetto Crisis," *Encounter* 29 (November 1967):15-22.

Glazer, Nathan. "Slums and Ethnicity," in Thomas R. Sherrard, ed., *Social Welfare and Urban Problems.* New York: Columbia University Press, 1968, pp. 84-112. Describes the early ghetto cultures and the transformation of these ethnic groups into interest-status groups. Special emphasis on the Negro.

Grodzins, Morton. *The Metropolitan Area as a Racial Problem.* Pittsburgh: University of Pittsburgh Press, 1958. Development of the central city into a lower-class Negro slum and its consequences.

Grodzins, Morton. "Metropolitan Segregation," *Scientific American* 198 (October 1957):33-41.

Hannerz, Ulf. "Roots of Black Manhood," *Trans-action* 6 (October 1969):13-21. Male role in a ghetto.

Hannerz, Ulf. *Soulside: Inquiries into Ghetto Culture and Community.* New York: Columbia University Press, 1969. Observations from field work in a Washington black neighborhood by a Swedish anthropologist.

Harrington, Michael. "Harlem Today," *Dissent* 8 (Summer 1961):371-382.

Heilbrun, James, and Stanislaw Wellisz. "An Economic Program for the Ghetto," *Academy of Political Science Proceedings* 29 (July 1968):72-85. A proposal for viable ghetto enterprises.

Hill, Richard J., and Calvin J. Larson. "Variability of Ghetto Organization," in Thomas D. Sherrard, ed., *Social Welfare and Urban Problems.* New York: Columbia University Press, 1968, pp. 132-160. Compares and contrasts the Negro ghetto in Harlem with the Old Annex neighborhood in Chicago.

Horton, John. "Time and Cool People," *Trans-action* 4 (April 1967):5-12. The street culture of the poverty ghetto.

Hunter, David R. *The Slums: Challenge and Response.* New York: Free Press, 1964.

Kain, John F., and Joseph J. Persky. "Alternatives to the Gilded Ghetto," *Public Interest* no. 14 (Winter 1969):74-87. Reasons given for rejecting the strengthening of ghettos.

Keller, Suzanne. "The Social World of the Urban Slum Child," *American Journal of Orthopsychiatry* 33 (October 1963):823-831. Comparison of Negro and white children.

Lawrence, Paul R. "Organization Development in the Black Ghetto," in Richard S. Rosenbloom and Robin Marris, eds., *Social Innovation in the City: New Enterprises for Community Development.* Cambridge, Mass.: Harvard University Press, 1969, pp. 109-119.

Lawrence, Paul R. "The Uses of Crisis: Dynamics of Ghetto Organization Development," in Richard S. Rosenbloom and Robin Marris, eds., *Social Innovation in the City: New Enterprises for Community Development.* Cambridge, Mass.: Harvard University Press, pp. 121-126.

Lerner, Max. "The Negro American and His City: Person in Place in Culture," *Daedalus* 97 (Fall 1968):1390-1408.

Levine, Robert A. *Black Power, White Style.* Washington: U.S. Office of Economic Opportunity, 1968.

Lyford, Joseph P. "The Talk of Vandalia," in *The Negro as an American.* Santa Barbara, Calif.: Center for the Study of Democratic Institutions, 1963. Preliminary report of study of Manhattan's West Side, with both Negro and Puerto Rican minorities.

McCord, William, et al., eds. *Life Styles in the Black Ghetto.* New York: Norton, 1969. Based on interviews of black people in Houston, Oakland, and Los Angeles, with opinions ranging from the apathetic to the militant.

McKay, Claude. *Harlem: Negro Metropolis.* New York: Dutton, 1940.

Marx, W. "Watkins of Watts: What One Man Can Do," *Reporter* 38 (January 25, 1968): 36-38. The efforts of Ted Watkins, labor leader.

Millea, Thomas V. *Ghetto Fever.* Milwaukee, Wis.: Bruce, 1966. Negro inequities in Lawndale (West-Side Chicago) are set forth by a white Catholic priest. A pastoral program to aid the black ghetto is presented.

Miller, Kenneth H. "Community Organizations in the Ghetto," in Richard S. Rosenbloom and Robin Marris, eds., *Social Innovation in the City: New Enterprises for Community Development.* Cambridge, Mass.: Harvard University Press, 1969, pp. 97-108. Examines and contrasts two model community organizations: the East Central Citizens Organization in Columbus, Ohio and the West Side Organization in Chicago, Illinois.

Morrill, Richard L. "The Negro Ghetto: Problems and Alternatives," *Geographical Review* 55 (July 1965):339-361.

Nash, Robert J. "A Black Architect Speaks Frankly," *Journal of the American Institute of Architects* 50 (October 1968):36+. Emphasizes the black man's right to exercise a role in rebuilding black ghettos.

Neuwirth, Gertrud. "Weberian Outline of a Theory of Community: Its Application to the Dark Ghetto," *British Journal of Sociology* 20 (June 1969):148-163.

"New Hope for Watts," *IUD Agenda* 3 (February 1967):13-15+. The activities of the Watts Labor Community Action Committee.

Osofsky, Gilbert. "The Enduring Ghetto," *Journal of American History* 55 (September 1968):243-255.

Osofsky, Gilbert. *Harlem: The Making of a Ghetto.* New York: Harper, 1966. Traces the change in Harlem from an elegant white neighborhood to a slum and center of Negro population.

Quinlivan, Francis. "Understanding the Children of the Ghetto," *Catholic Mind* 66 (June 1968):22-28.

Rustin, Bayard. "Way Out of the Exploding Ghetto," *Harvard Review* 4, no. 3 (1968):31-40.

Saunders, Marie Simmons. "The Ghetto: Some Perceptions of a Black Social Worker," *Social Work* 14 (October 1969):84-88. Characteristics of the black ghetto, outlined for the white professional worker.

Scheiner, Seth M. *Negro Mecca: A History of the Negro in New York City, 1865-1920.* New York: New York University Press, 1965. Notable bibliography of primary and secondary sources.

Silberman, Charles E. "Up from Apathy—The Woodlawn Experiment: Self-Help in a Slum Neighborhood," *Commentary* 37 (May 1964):51-58.

Silvers, Arthur H. "Urban Renewal and Black Power," *American Behavioral Scientist* 12 (March-April 1969):43-46.

Smith, Ralph V., et al. *Community Interaction and Racial Integration in the Detroit Area: An Ecological Analysis.* Ypsilanti: Eastern Michigan University, 1967. A study of the forces and patterns which perpetuate the ghetto. Includes tabular data gathered in 1965.

Spear, Allan H. *Black Chicago: The Making of a Negro Ghetto, 1890-1920.* Chicago: University of Chicago Press, 1967.

Stern, Sol. "Trouble in an 'All America City,'" *New York Times Magazine,* July 10, 1966, pp. 20-22. Oakland, California, a city "sagging under the multiple conflicts of race, class, and technological change," with blacks comprising over one quarter of the population.

Stringfellow, William. *My People Is the Enemy: An Autobiographical Polemic.* New York: Holt, 1964. A young white lawyer and Episcopal layman, who lived and worked among the Harlem poor, gives a vivid picture of ghetto life.

Stringfellow, William. "Race, Religion, and Revenge," *Christian Century* 79 (February 14, 1962):192-194.

Suttles, Gerald. *The Social Order of the Slums: Ethnicity and Territory in the Inner City.* Chicago: University of Chicago Press, 1968. Special attention is called to chapter seven entitled "The Projects and the Negroes."

Taeuber, Karl E., and Alma F. Taeuber. *Negroes in Cities.* Chicago: Aldine, 1965. An important study based on calculation of the segregation indices for 207 American cities.

Taeuber, Karl E. "Residential Segregation," *Scientific American* 213 (August 1965):12-19. The author finds that the principal cause of Negro segregation in urban ghettos is discrimination and that there is "no basis for anticipating major changes . . . until patterns of housing discrimination can be altered." An important study based on calculation of the segregation indices for 207 American cities.

Tucker, Sterling. *Beyond the Burning: Life and Death of the Ghetto.* New York: Association Press, 1968. Short-term objectives and long-term goals for the reduction and elimination of gross inequities and exploited conditions—by an Urban League official.

U.S. Commission on Civil Rights. *A Time to Listen, A Time to Act: Voices from the Ghettos of the Nation's Cities.* Washington, 1967.

U.S. Commission on Civil Rights. Massachusetts Advisory Committee. *The Voice of the Ghetto: Report on Two Boston Neighborhood Meetings.* Washington: U.S. Govt. Print. Off., 1967. Negro residents in areas of Roxbury, North Dorchester, and Boston's South End describe the patterns of their lives and work.

U.S. Department of Housing and Urban Development. *The House on W. 114th Street.* Washington: U.S. Govt. Print. Off., 1968. The life of a Harlem Negro family in a reconstructed housing project.

Weaver, Robert C. *The Negro Ghetto.* 1948. New York: Russell & Russell, 1967. Reissued with a new preface by the author.

Weaver, Robert C. "Non-White Population Movements and Urban Ghettos," *Phylon* 20 (Fall 1959):235-241.

Wheeler, James O. "Transportation Problems in Negro Ghettos," *Sociology and Social Research* 53 (January 1969):171-179.

Williams, Walter. "Cleveland's Crisis Ghetto," *Trans-action* 4 (September 1967):33-37. A 1965 census of the city indicates important social changes since 1960 and a sharp economic polarization of the resident Negroes.

Williamson, Stanford W. *With Grief Acquainted.* Chicago: Follett, 1964. Negro life on Chicago's South Side.

Wirth, Louis. *The Ghetto.* Chicago: University of Chicago Press, 1928. Describes ghetto formation as inevitable and product of successive stages.

Youth in the Ghetto: A Study of the Consequences of Powerlessness and a Blueprint for Change. New York: Harlem Youth Opportunities Unlimited, 1964. HARYOU report presented to the President's Committee on Juvenile Delinquency, April 1964.

See also Race Violence and Riots.

Delinquency, Crime, and Police Practices

Axelrad, Sidney. "Negro and White Male Institutionalized Delinquents," *American Journal of Sociology* 62 (May 1952):569-574.

Bacon, Margaret K., I. L. Child, and H. Barry. "A Cross-Cultural Study of Correlates of Crime," *Journal of Abnormal and Social Psychology* 66 (April 1963):291-300.

Barker, Gordon H., and W. Thomas Adams. "Negro Delinquents in Public Training Schools in the West," *Journal of Negro Education* 32 (Summer 1963):294-300.

Bates, William. "Caste, Class and Vandalism," *Social Problems* 9 (Spring 1962):349-353.

Beattie, R. H. "Criminal Statistics in the United States," *Journal of Criminal Law, Criminology and Police Science* 51(May-June 1960):49-65.

Bensing, R. C., and O. Schroeder, Jr. *Homicide in an Urban Community.* Springfield, Ill.: Thomas, 1960.

Brown, L. P. "Black Muslims and the Police," *Journal of Criminal Law, Criminology and Police Science* 56 (March 1965):119-126.

Caldwell, M. G. "Personality Trends in the Youthful Male Offender," *Journal of Criminal Law, Criminology and Police Science* 49 (January-February 1959):405-416.

Cavan, Ruth Shonle. "Negro Family Disorganization and Juvenile Delinquency," *Journal of Negro Education* 28 (Summer 1959):230-239.

Chamdliss, W. J., and R. H. Nagasawa. "On the Validity of Official Statistics: A Comparative Study of White, Black and Japanese High-School Boys," *Journal of Research in Crime and Delinquency* 6 (January 1969):71-77.

Chein, Isidor, et al. *The Road to H: Narcotics, Delinquency and Social Policy.* New York: Basic Books, 1964.

Clark, Kenneth B. "Color, Class, Personality and Juvenile Delinquency," *Journal of Negro Education* 28 (Summer 1959):240-251.

Cloward, Richard A., and Lloyd E. Ohlin. *Delinquency and Opportunity: A Theory of Delinquent Gangs.* Glencoe, Ill.: Free Press, 1960. An important book in the contemporary reconsideration of gangs which is changing the perspective from delinquency as an attribute of individuals to that of a larger social system.

Cohen, A. K. *Delinquent Boys: The Culture of the Gang.* Glencoe, Ill.: Free Press, 1955.

Cohen, A. K., and J. F. Short, Jr. "Juvenile Delinquency," in R. K. Merton and R. A. Nisbet, eds., *Contemporary Social Problems.* New York: Harcourt, Brace, 1961.

Cohen, A. K., and J. F. Short, Jr. "Research in Delinquent Subcultures," *Journal of Social Issues* 14 (Summer 1958):20-37.

Coles, Robert. "The Question of Negro Crime," *Harper's* 228 (April 1964):134-136+.

Cressey, Donald R. "Crime," in R. K. Merton and R. A. Nisbet, eds., *Contemporary Social Problems.* New York: Harcourt, Brace, 1961.

Cressey, Donald R. "Epidemiology and Individual Conduct: A Case from Criminology," *Pacific Sociological Review* 3 (Fall 1960):47-58.

Cross, G. J. "Negro, Prejudice, and the Police," *Journal of Criminal Law, Criminology and Police Science* 55 (September 1964):405.

Daniel, Walter G. "The Role of Youth Character-Building Organizations in Juvenile Delinquency Prevention," *Journal of Negro Education* 28 (Summer 1959):310-317.

Diggs, Mary H. "Some Problems and Needs of Negro Children as Revealed by Comparative Delinquency and Crime Statistics," *Journal of Negro Education* 19 (Summer 1950):290-297.

Dobbins, D. A., and B. M. Bass. "Effects of Unemployment on White and Negro Prison Admissions in Louisiana," *Journal of Criminal Law, Criminology and Police Science* 48 (January-February 1958):522-525.

Douglass, Joseph H. "The Extent and Characteristics of Juvenile Delinquency among Negroes in the United States," *Journal of Negro Education* 28 (Summer 1959):214-229.

Epstein, Charlotte. *Intergroup Relations for Police Officers.* Baltimore: Williams & Wilkins, 1962.

Finestone, Harold. "Cats, Kicks, and Color," *Social Problems* 5 (July 1957):3-13. Suggestions as to the origin and function of a style of life among lower-class Negro heroin users.

Fogelson, Robert M. "From Resentment to Confrontation: The Police, the Negroes, and the Outbreak of the Nineteen-Sixties Riots," *Political Science Quarterly* 83 (June 1968): 217-247. Also published in *Social Action* 35 (February 1969):6-33.

Forslund, Morris A. "Age, Occupation and Conviction Rates of White and Negro Males: A Case Study," *Rocky Mountain Social Science Journal* 6 (April 1969):141-146.

Fox, Vernon, and Joann Volakakis. "The Negro Offender in a Northern Industrial Area," *Journal of Criminal Law, Criminology and Police Science* 46 (January-February 1956):641.

Geis, Gilbert. "Statistics Concerning Race and Crime," *Crime and Delinquency* 11 (April 1965):142-150.

Gold, M. "Suicide, Homicide, and the Socialization of Aggression," *American Journal of Sociology* 63 (May 1958):651-661.

Henry, A. F., and J. F. Short, Jr. *Suicide and Homicide.* Glencoe, Ill.: Free Press, 1954.

Henton, Comradge L., and Charles Washington. "Differential Studies of Recidivism among Negro and White Boys," *Journal of Genetic Psychology* 98 (June 1961):247-253.

Hill, Mozell C. "The Metropolis and Juvenile Delinquency among Negroes," *Journal of Negro Education* 28 (Summer 1959):277-285.

Hypps, Irene C. "The Role of the School in Juvenile Delinquency Presentation (with Especial Reference to Pupil Personnel Services)," *Journal of Negro Education* 28 (Summer 1959):318-328.

Jenkins, Herbert T. "Police, Progress, and Desegregation in Atlanta," *New South* 17 (June 1962):10-13. Author is Atlanta Chief of Police.

Johnson, Guy B. "The Negro and Crime," in Martin E. Wolfgang, Leonard Savitz, and Norman Johnston, eds., *The Sociology of Crime and Delinquency.* New York: Wiley,

1962, pp. 145–153. While based on a prewar study, this paper is still a useful discussion of such factors as subordination and insecurity in Negro crime, as well as of the caste structure of the administration of justice in the South.

Kephart, William M. "Integration of Negroes into the Urban Police Force," *Journal of Criminal Law, Criminology and Police Science* 45 (September–October 1954):325–333.

Kephart, William, M. "The Negro Offender," *American Journal of Sociology* 60 (July 1954):46–50.

Kephart, William M. *Racial Factors and Urban Law Enforcement.* Philadelphia: University of Pennsylvania Press, 1957. Based on extensive research on Philadelphia Police Force.

Kramer, S. A. "Predicting Juvenile Delinquency among Negroes," *Sociology and Social Research* 48 (July 1964):478–489.

Kvaraceus, William C. "The Nature of the Problem of Juvenile Delinquency in the United States," *Journal of Negro Education* 28 (Summer 1959):191–199.

Levy, Burton. "Cops in the Ghetto: A Problem of the Police System," *American Behavioral Scientist* 11 (March 1968):31–34.

Lewis, Hylan. "Juvenile Delinquency among Negroes: A Critical Summary," *Journal of Negro Education* 28 (Summer 1959):371–387.

Lohman, Joseph D. "Juvenile Delinquency: A Social Dimension," *Journal of Negro Education* 28 (Summer 1959):286–299.

London, Nathaniel J., and Jerome K. Myers. "Young Offenders: Psychopathology and Social Factors," *Archives of General Psychiatry* 4 (March 1961):274–282. A report of research conducted by the Connecticut State Department of Mental Health in New Haven County jail on all young white and Negro male offenders in jail for more than ten days. Psychiatric diagnoses, socioeconomic background, and education taken into account for each subject.

Luchterhand, Elmer, and Leonora Weller. "Delinquency Theory and the Middle-Size City: A Study of Problem and Promising Youth," *Sociological Quarterly* 7 (Autumn 1966): 413–422. Causes of delinquency and outstanding differences between problem white and Negro males.

Luther, Beverly. "Group Service Programs and Their Effect on Delinquents," in Harold H. Weissman, *Individual and Group Services in the Mobilization for Youth Experience.* New York: Association Press, 1969, pp. 115–135.

McCloskey, Mark A. "State and Municipal Youth Authorities or Commissions and Their Role in Juvenile Delinquency Prevention," *Journal of Negro Education* 28 (Summer 1959):339–350.

Maccoby, Eleanor E., Joseph P. Johnson, and Russell M. Church. "Community Integration and the Social Control of Juvenile Delinquency," *Journal of Social Issues* 14 (Summer 1958):38–51.

McCormick, Ken. *Sprung: The Release of Willie Calloway.* New York: St. Martin's, 1964. Articles written by the author for the *Detroit Free Press* helped to produce new witnesses and obtain a new trial for Calloway, wrongfully sentenced to life imprisonment.

McManus, George P. "Human Relations Training for Police," *Interracial Review* 35 (April 1962):98–99.

Mays, Benjamin E. "The Role of the 'Negro Community' in Delinquency Prevention among Negro Youth," *Journal of Negro Education* 28 (Summer 1959):366–370.

Miller, Carroll L. "Educational Level and Juvenile Delinquency among Negroes," *Journal of Negro Education* 28 (Summer 1959):268–276.

Morgan, Charles, Jr. "Integration in the Yellow Chair," *New South* 18 (February 1963):11–16. On segregated justice except in the "yellow chair."

Moses, Earl R. "Differentials in Crime Rates between Negroes and Whites," in Marvin E. Wolfgang, Leonard Savitz, and Norman Johnston, eds., *The Sociology of Crime and Delinquency.* New York: Wiley, 1962, pp. 154–162.

Nelson, Harold A. "Defenders: A Case Study of an Informal Police Organization," *Social Problems* 15 (Fall 1967):127–147. Negro residents in a Southern community form a counterforce to a white power monopoly, resulting in a lessening of traditional authority and redistribution of power.

Nelson, Truman. *The Torture of Mothers.* Newburyport, Mass.: Garrison Press, 1965. A retrospective account of the case of the Harlem Six, Negro boys convicted of a 1964 murder in New York. Part of book originally appeared in *Ramparts.*

Neto, Virginia, and Ted Palmer. *Patterns of Conflict among Higher Maturity Urban Negro Delinquents.* Sacramento?: California Youth Authority and the National Institute of Health, 1969. (Community Treatment Project Report no. 3)

Pettigrew, Thomas F., and Rosalind B. Spier. "The Ecological Structure of Negro Homicide," *American Journal of Sociology* 67 (May 1962):621-629.

Pittman, John. "Negroes Challenge the Jackboot in San Francisco," *Freedomways* 7 (Winter 1967):42-53.

Poague, Frank, Jr. "The Truth about Negro Crime," *Negro Digest* 15 (July 1966):15-23.

Porterfield, Austin L., and Robert H. Talbert. "Crime in Southern Cities," in Rupert B. Vance and Nicholas J. Demerath, eds., *The Urban South.* Chapel Hill: University of North Carolina Press, 1954.

Reiss, Albert J., and Albert Lewis Rhodes. "Are Educational Norms and Goals of Conforming, Truant and Delinquent Adolescents Influenced by Group Position in American Society," *Journal of Negro Education* 28 (Summer 1959):252-267.

Rice, Charles E. "The Negro Crime Rate: Its Causes and Cure," *Modern Age* 10 (Fall 1966):343-358.

Robins, Lee N. "Negro Homicide Victims—Who Will They Be?" *Trans-action* 5 (June 1958):15-19. The linkage between school problems and other behavioral factors and high mortality rate.

Robinson, Sophia M. "How Effective Are Current Delinquency Preventive Programs?" *Journal of Negro Education* 28 (Summer 1959):351-365.

Roebuck, Julian B., and M. L. Cadwallader. "The Negro Armed Robber as a Criminal Type: The Construction and Application of a Typology," *Pacific Sociological Review* 4 (Spring 1961):21-26.

Roebuck, Julian B. "The Negro Drug Addict as an Offender Type," *Journal of Criminal Law, Criminology and Police Science* 53 (March 1962):36-43.

Roebuck, Julian B. "Negro Numbers Man as a Criminal Type: The Construction and Application of a Typology," *Journal of Criminal Law, Criminology and Police Science* 54 (March 1963):48-60.

Rudwick, Elliott M. "Negro Police Employment in the Urban South," *Journal of Negro Education* 30 (Spring 1961):102-108.

Rudwick, Elliott M. "Negro Policemen in the South," *Journal of Criminal Law, Criminology and Police Practice* 51 (July-August 1960):273.

Rudwick, Elliott M. "Police Work and the Negro," *Journal of Criminal Law, Criminology and Police Science* 50 (March-April 1960):596-599.

Rudwick, Elliott M. "The Southern Negro Policeman and the White Offender," *Journal of Negro Education* 30 (Fall 1961):426-431.

Salisbury, Harrison. *The Shook-Up Generation.* New York: Harper, 1958. Illuminating study of New York gangs, including Negro gangs.

Samuels, Gertrude. "Who Shall Judge a Policeman?" *New York Times Magazine,* August 2, 1964, pp. 8 +. Following upon 1964 Negro riots, persistent charges of police brutality bring demands for a civilian review board.

Savitz, Leonard. *Delinquency and Migration.* Philadelphia: Commission on Human Relations, 1960.

Schmid, C. F. "Urban Crime Areas, Part I," *American Sociological Review* 25 (August 1960):527-542; "Part II," *ibid.,* 25 (October 1960):655-678.

Schulz, David A. "Some Aspects of the Policeman's Role as It Impinges upon the Lower-Class Negro Family." Mimeographed. Paper presented to the American Sociological Association, Boston, August 1968.

Schultz, Leroy G. "Why the Negro Carries Weapons," *Journal of Criminal Law, Criminology and Police Science* 53 (December 1962):476-481.

Shaw, Clifford R., and Henry D. McKay. *Juvenile Delinquency and Urban Areas.* 1942. Rev. ed. Chicago: University of Chicago Press, 1969. The revised edition contains new chapters updating delinquency data for Chicago and its suburbs by McKay.

Sherif, Muzafer, and Carolyn Sherif. *Reference Groups: Explorations in Conformity and De-viance of Adolescents.* New York: Harper, 1964.

Short, James F., Jr., and Fred L. Strodtbeck. *Group Process and Gang Delinquency.* Chicago: University of Chicago Press, 1965. Negro groups considered *passim.*

Southern Regional Council. *Race Makes the Difference: An Analysis of Sentence Disparity among Black and White Offenders in Southern Prisons.* Atlanta, 1969. Based on 1,200 cases in seven Southern states in 1967.

Spergel, Irving. "Male Young Adult Criminality, Deviant Values, and Differential Oppor-tunities in Two Lower-Class Negro Neighborhoods," *Social Problems* 10 (Winter 1963):237-250.

"A Statement of Recommended Police Policy Resulting from the New York University Graduate School of Public Administration Conference on 'The Challenge of Desegrega-tion for the American Police Executive,'" *Interracial Review* 35 (May 1962):115.

Teeters, Negley K., and David Matza. "The Extent of Delinquency in the United States," *Journal of Negro Education* 28 (Summer 1959):200-213.

Thomas, Rose C. "Family and Child Welfare Agencies and Juvenile Delinquency Pre-vention," *Journal of Negro Education* 28 (Summer 1959):300-309.

Towler, Juby E. *The Police Role in Racial Conflicts.* Springfield, Ill.: Thomas, 1965. A handbook by the Chief of Detectives of Danville, Va., on how to use the law as an instrument by which one race may subject another.

Tufts, Edith Miller. "The Role of the Children's Bureau and Other Federal Agencies in Juvenile Delinquency Prevention," *Journal of Negro Education* 28 (Summer 1959):329-338.

U.S. President's Commission on Law Enforcement and Administration of Justice. *Task Force Report: Crime and Its Impact—An Assessment.* Washington: U.S. Govt. Print. Off., 1967. Special attention is called to the sections on crime and the inner city and the relationship of riots to crime. However, the whole is relevant to causes of crime as applicable to the circumstance of the black man today.

U.S. President's Commission on Law Enforcement and Administration of Justice. *Task Force Report: Juvenile Delinquency and Crime.* Washington: U.S. Govt. Print. Off., 1967.

U.S. President's Commission on Law Enforcement and Administration of Justice. *Task Force Report: The Police.* Washington: U.S. Govt. Print. Off., 1967. Special attention is called to the section entitled "The Police and the Community."

Vontress, Clemmont E. "Patterns of Segregation and Desegregation: Contributing Factors to Crime among Negroes," *Journal of Negro Education* 31 (Spring 1962):108-116.

Waskow, Arthur I. "Community Control of the Police," *Trans-action* 7 (December 1969):4-7. Includes suggestions for black recruiting and empowered precinct commis-sions. The Community Alert Patrols are discussed.

Wilson, C. E. "The System of Police Brutality," *Freedomways* 8 (Winter 1968):45-56. Law enforcement in relation to blacks.

Wilson, James Q. "Arrest Rates for Negroes and Whites," in *Varieties of Police Behavior: The Management of Law and Order in Eight Communities.* Cambridge, Mass.: Harvard University Press, 1968, pp. 159-212.

Wolfgang, Marvin E. *Patterns in Criminal Homicide.* Philadelphia: University of Pennsyl-vania Press, 1958. A valuable study strongly suggesting that racial discrimination exists in both North and South in the conviction and sentencing of those accused of criminal homicide. Careful research on black-white differentials with reference to socioeconomic factors, choice of victim, style.

Zeitz, L. "Survey of Negro Attitudes toward Law," *Rutgers Law Review* 19 (Winter 1965):288-316.

Social Services

Banks, George, Bernard G. Berenson, and Robert R. Corkhuff. "The Effects of Counselor Race and Training upon Counseling Process with Negro Clients in Initial Interviews," *Journal of Clinical Psychology* 23 (January 1967):70-92. A statistical sampling which indicates the desirability of using Negro counselors to whom Negro clients can relate.

Berry, Margaret. "Civil Rights and Social Welfare," in *Social Welfare Forum, 1963.* New York: Columbia University Press, 1963, pp. 84-96.

Bowles, Dorcas D. "Making Casework Relevant to Black People: Approaches, Techniques, Theoretical Implications," *Child Welfare* 48 (October 1969):468-475.

Brieland, Donald. "Black Identity and the Helping Person," *Children* 16 (September-October 1969):171-176. Attitudes of selected Negroes toward social service.

Clark, Leroy D. "Minority Lawyer: Link to the Ghetto," *American Bar Association Journal* 55 (January 1969):61-64. Suggests program for establishing link between black ghetto lawyers and large white firms.

Cohen, Jerome. "Race as a Factor in Social Work Practice," in Roger R. Miller, ed., *Race, Research and Reason: Social Work Perspectives.* New York: National Association of Social Workers, 1969, pp. 99-114.

Collins, LeRoy. "Civil Rights and a Concerned Community," in *Social Welfare Forum, 1965.* New York: Columbia University Press, 1965, pp. 35-42.

Del Valle, Allina, and Alexander Felton. "Effects of the Project [ENABLE] on Family Service Agencies and Urban Leagues," *Social Casework* 48 (December 1967):633-639.

Drake, St. Clair. "Intergroup Relations at the Neighborhood Level," in Roger R. Miller, ed., *Race, Research and Reason: Social Work Perspectives.* New York: National Association of Social Workers, 1969, pp. 123-144.

Fogel, David. "Social Work and Negroes," *Phylon* 18 (Fall 1957):277-285.

Gary, Lawrence. "Social Work Education and the Black Community: A Proposal for Curriculum Revisions," *Social Work Education Reporter* 16 (December 1968):47-50+.

Golden, Joseph. "Desegregation of Social Agencies in the South," *Social Work* 10 (January 1965):58-67.

Jacobs, Paul. "The Lower Depths in Los Angeles," *Midstream* 13 (May 1967):14-23. The chronically unemployed Negro and employment agencies.

Johnson, Mrs. Charles W. "The Black Community Looks at the Welfare System," *Public Welfare* 26 (July 1968):205-208.

Long, H. H. "The Negro as Minority Community," in Roger R. Miller, ed., *Race, Research and Reason: Social Work Perspectives.* New York: National Association of Social Workers, 1969, pp. 25-34.

Luther, Beverly. "Negro Youth and Social Action," in Harold H. Weissman, ed., *Individual and Group Services in the Mobilization for Youth Experience.* New York: Association Press, 1969, pp. 151-161. Seeks to channel frustrated adolescents, mostly Negro, into constructive participation in social and civil rights projects.

Manning, Seaton W. "Cultural and Value Factors Affecting Negro's Use of Agency Services," *Social Work* 5 (October 1960):3-13.

Manser, Ellen, Jewaldean Jones, and Selma Ortof. "An Overview of Project ENABLE," *Social Casework* 48 (July 1967):609-617.

Miller, Henry. "Social Work in the Black Ghetto: The New Colonialism," *Social Work* 14 (July 1969):65-76. Admonishes the social welfare programs as philanthropic colonialism and paternalism. The author presses for the provision of economic opportunity to enable the Negro to enter the social mainstream while he maintains his ethnicity.

"N.E.G.R.O. Charts New Paths to Freedom," *Ebony* 23 (April 1968):49-56. A program for black self-help.

Popkin, Dorothy R. "Resurrection City: Social Action and Mental Health," *Perspectives in Psychiatric Care* 6 (September-October 1968):198-204.

Robinson, William H. "The Relevancy of Church Social Work to the Black Revolution," *Lutheran Social Welfare* 9 (Spring 1969):11-20. The author is a black social worker.

Saunders, Marie Simmons. "The Ghetto: Some Perceptions of a Black Social Worker,"

Social Work 14 (October 1969):84-88. Characteristics of the black ghetto, outlined for the white professional worker.

Shannon, Lyle W., and Elaine Krass. "The Urban Adjustment of Immigrants: The Relationship of Education to Occupation and Total Family Income," *Pacific Sociological Review* 6 (Spring 1963):37-42. Anglos, Mexican-Americans, and Negroes compared.

Simmons, Leonard C. "Crow Jim: Implications for Social Work," *Social Work* 8 (July 1963):24-30.

Specht, Harry. "Community Development in Low-Income Negro Areas," *Social Work* 11 (October 1966):78-91.

Stringfellow, William. "Christianity, Poverty and the Practice of the Law," *Harvard Law School Bulletin* 10 (June 1959):4-7+. On "the need for the law and the lawyer to be really immersed in life as it is." Harlem as case study.

Sykes, O. "Vocational Rehabilitation Services in a Black Community." 1968. Mimeographed. Paper presented at 1968 annual meeting of the American Orthopsychiatric Association in Chicago.

Thomas, Rose C. "Family and Child Welfare Agencies and Juvenile Delinquency Prevention," *Journal of Negro Education* 28 (Summer 1959):300-309.

Wade, Ruth, Garland Jordan, and George Myers. "Sociopsychiatric Ghetto: The View of a Paraprofessional," *American Journal of Orthopsychiatry* 39 (July 1969):677-683.

Yancey, William L. "Intervention as a Strategy of Social Inquiry: An Exploratory Study with Unemployed Negro Men," *Social Science Quarterly* 50 (December 1969):582-588.

Race Violence and Riots

"Anatomy of a Riot," *Journal of Urban Law* 45 (Spring-Summer 1968):entire issue. Attention to the Detroit riot, police brutality and racial prejudice, response of the courts, and efficient methods of riot control.

Anderson, Jervis. "The Voices of Newark," *Commentary* 44 (October 1967):85-90.

Aptheker, Herbert. "The Watts Ghetto Uprising," *Political Affairs* 44 (October 1965):16-29; (November 1965):28-44.

Bernstein, Saul. *Alternatives to Violence: Alienated Youth and Riots, Race, and Poverty.* New York: Association Press, 1967. Bibliography.

Berson, Lenora E. *Case Study of a Riot: The Philadelphia Story.* With commentaries by Alex Rosen and Kenneth B. Clark. New York: Institute of Human Relations Press, 1966.

Blauner, Robert. "Whitewash over Watts," *Trans-action* 3 (March-April 1966):9.

Bloombaum, Milton. "Conditions Underlying Race Riots as Portrayed by Multidimensional Scalogram Analysis: A Reanalysis of Lieberson and Silverman's Data," *American Sociological Review* 33 (February 1968):76-91.

Boskin, Joseph, and Fred Krinsky. *Urban Racial Violence in the Twentieth Century.* Beverly Hills, Calif.: Glencoe Press, 1969.

California. Governor's Commission on the Los Angeles Riots. *Violence in the City—An End or a Beginning?* Los Angeles, 1965. The commission, headed by John McCone, former head of the CIA, found the summer riots symptomatic of a serious urban sickness which, if not attacked with energetic new measures, will become endemic.

Caplan, Nathan S., and J. M. Paige. "Study of Ghetto Rioters," *Scientific American* 219 (August 1968):15-21.

Clark, Kenneth B. "Group Violence: A Preliminary Study of the Attitudinal Pattern of Its Acceptance and Rejection—A Study of the 1943 Harlem Riots," *Journal of Social Psychology* 19 (August 1944):319-337.

Cohen, Jerry, and William S. Murphy. *Burn, Baby, Burn! The Los Angeles Race Riot, August, 1965.* New York: Dutton, 1966.

Conot, Robert. *Rivers of Blood, Years of Darkness: The Unforgettable Classic Account of the Watts Riot.* New York: Morrow, 1967. Bibliography includes pamphlet material, some undated.

Crowe, Charles. "Racial Violence and Social Reform—Origins of the Atlanta Riot of 1906," *Journal of Negro History* 53 (July 1968):234-256.

Crump, Spencer. *Black Riots in Los Angeles: The Story of the Watts Tragedy.* Los Angeles: Trans-Anglo Books, 1966.

Curry, J. E., and Glen D. King. *Race Tensions and the Police.* Springfield Ill.: Thomas, 1962.

Downes, Bryan T. "Social and Political Characteristics of Riot Cities: A Comparative Study," *Social Science Quarterly* 49 (December 1968):504-520. A preliminary examination of social and political urban factors related to the incidence and intensity of riots.

Erskine, Hazel. "Polls: Demonstrations and Race Riots," *Public Opinion Quarterly* 31 (Winter 1967-1968):655-677.

"F.B.I. Report on Racial Disturbances during the Past Summer," *America* 111 (October 10, 1964):414-415.

Feagin, Joe R., and Paul B. Sheatsley. "Ghetto Resident Appraisals of a Riot," *Public Opinion Quarterly* 32 (Fall 1968): 352-362. Based on data gathered from residents of Bedford-Stuyvesant by Negro interviewers.

Feagin, Joe R. "Social Sources of Support for Violence and Non-Violence in a Negro Ghetto," *Social Problems* 15 (Spring 1968): 432-440. Social characteristics of Negroes oriented to violence, or the lack of it, drawn from an opinion sampling in New York's Bedford-Stuyvesant ghetto following the 1964 riot.

Fogelson, Robert M. "Violence as Protest," *Academy of Political Science Proceedings* 29 (July 1968):25-41.

Fogelson, Robert M. "White On Black: A Critique of the McCone Commission Report on the Los Angeles Riots," *Political Science Quarterly* 82 (September 1967):337-367.

Gans, Herbert J. "The Ghetto Rebellions and Urban Class Conflict," Academy of Political Science. *Proceedings* 29 (July 1968):42-51. Revised excerpt from his testimony before the National Commission on Civil Disorders.

Geschwender, James A. "Civil Rights Protest and Riots: A Disappearing Distinction," *Social Science Quarterly* 49 (December 1968):474-484. Analyzes characteristics of the disorders, rioters, tactics, and lootings.

Gilbert, Ben W. *Ten Blocks from the White House: Anatomy of the Washington Riots of 1968.* New York: Praeger, 1968. Based on the collaborative findings of staff members of the *Washington Post.* Statistical appendices.

Good, Paul. "Bossism, Racism and Dr. King," *Nation* 203 (September 19, 1966):237-242. Chicago during the summer of 1966.

Goodman, George W., Jr. "Watts, U.S.A.: A Post Mortem," *Crisis* 72 (October 1965):487-492+.

Grimshaw, Allen D. "Factors Contributing to Colour Violence in the United States and Great Britain," *Race* 3 (May 1962):3-19.

Grimshaw, Allen D. "Police Agencies and the Prevention of Racial Violence," *Journal of Law, Criminology and Police Science* 54 (March 1963):110.

Grimshaw, Allen D., ed. *Racial Violence in the United States.* Chicago: Aldine, 1969. Traces the pattern of racial disorder from slave insurrections to current urban riots.

Hahn, Harlan. "Ghetto Sentiments on Violence," *Science and Society* 33 (Spring 1969): 197-208. Complements Campbell and Schuman's research incorporated in section one of the *Supplemental Studies for the National Advisory Commission on Civil Disorders.*

"Harlem Diary," *Ramparts* 3 (October 1964):14-28. A special report on the Harlem riots of 1964, largely in the form of a taped record by Lez Edmond, who was present throughout the period.

Hayden, Tom. *Rebellion in Newark: Official Violence and Ghetto Response.* New York: Random, 1967.

Hersey, John. *The Algiers Motel Incident.* New York: Knopf, 1968. Author attempts to deal with the confusion surrounding the killing of three Negroes during the Detroit race riots of 1967. Reviews differ as to importance of this study.

Hoffman, Gene. "Let the Rage Uncoil," *Liberation* 12 (March 1967):7-10. The Watts' self-help center, Operation Bootstrap.

Isenberg, Irwin, ed. *The City in Crisis.* New York: H. W. Wilson, 1968.

Janowitz, Morris. *Social Control of Escalated Riots.* Chicago: University of Chicago Press, 1968. Thesis: in addition to economic and social reforms, the stemming of Negro violence in the United States requires social control of law enforcement agencies and mass media within a realistic framework of political and moral commitments.

Jeffries, Vincent, and H. Edward Ransford. "Interracial Social Contact and Middle-Class White Reactions to the Watts Riot," *Social Problems* 16 (Winter 1969):312-324.

Johnson, Lyndon B. "Law and Order in America: The President's Address to the Nation on Civil Disorders," *Weekly Compilation of Presidential Documents* 3 (July 31, 1967): 1055-1059.

Kerber, Linda K. "Abolitionists and Amalgamators: The New York City Race Riots of 1834," *New York History* 48 (January 1967):28-39.

Kerner Report. *See* U.S. National Commission on Civil Disorders.

Knopf, Terry Ann. "Sniping, a New Plan of Violence?" *Trans-action* 6 (July-August 1969):22-29. Reply with rejoinder by J. R. Corse and L. H. Masotti. *ibid.,* September 1969. Violence as black protest; the role of the press.

Knopf, Terry Ann. *Youth Patrols: An Experiment in Community Participation.* Waltham, Mass.: The Lemberg Center for the Study of Violence, Brandeis University, 1969. The structure, function, and effectiveness of youth patrols, organized to help contain ghetto community violence.

Komorowski, Conrad. "The Detroit Ghetto Uprisings," *Political Affairs* 46 (September 1967):12-24.

Lachman, Sheldon J., and Thomas F. Waters. "Psychosocial Profile of Riot Arrestees," *Psychological Report* 24 (February 1969):171-181. One hundred male Negroes involved in the Detoit riot of July 1967 were studied.

Lang, Kurt, and Gladys Engel Lang. "Racial Disturbances as Collective Protest," *American Behavioral Scientist* 11 (March-April 1968):11-13.

Larner, Jeremy. "Initiation for Whitey: Notes on Poverty and Riot," *Dissent* 14 (December 1967):692-700.

Lee, Alfred McClung, and Norman D. Humphrey. *Race Riot.* 1943. New York: Octagon, 1968. Reprinted with a new introductory essay by Alfred McClung Lee. A chronology of the Detroit riot of 1943 and its aftermath from which one can draw disturbing parallels to contemporary events and society's stagnant attitudes and unwillingness to initiate real change.

Lieberson, Stanley, and Arnold R. Silverman. "The Precipitants and Underlying Conditions of Race Riots," *American Sociological Review* 30 (December 1965):887-898. Analysis of 76 race riots which occurred in the United States between 1913 and 1963.

Light, Richard J., and Robert L. Green. "Report Analysis: National Advisory Commission on Civil Disorders," *Harvard Educational Review* 38 (Fall 1968):756-771.

Lincoln, James H. *The Anatomy of a Riot: A Detroit Judge's Report.* New York: McGraw-Hill, 1968. The viewpoint of a probate judge of Wayne County (which includes Detroit). Emphasis on juvenile participants.

Locke, Herbert. *The Detroit Riot of 1967.* Detroit: Wayne State University Press, 1969. And the political and social repercussions following the riot, followed by suggestions for alleviating the crises in other American communities.

McCone Commission Report. *See* California. Governor's Commission on the Los Angeles Riot.

McCord, William, and John Howard. "Negro Opinions in Three Riot Cities," *American Behavioral Scientist* 11 (March 1968):24-27. Houston, Watts, and Oakland. Views on speed of integration, police, housing, use of violence, and other aspects.

McMillan, George. "Racial Violence and Law Enforcement," *New South* 15 (November 1960):4-32.

McWilliams, Carey. "Watts: The Forgotten Slum," *Nation* 201 (August 30, 1965):89-90.

Masotti, Louis H., and Don R. Bowen, eds. *Riots and Rebellion: Civil Violence in the Urban Community.* Beverly Hills, Calif.: Sage Publications, 1968. Notable bibliography.

Masotti, Louis H., and Jerome R. Corsi. *Shoot-Out in Cleveland: Black Militants and the Police, July 23, 1968.* New York: Praeger, 1969. A report submitted to the National

Commission on the Causes and Prevention of Violence, May 16, 1969. Includes an epilog which describes the trial and conviction of the militant leader, Fred Evans.

Masotti, Louis H., et al. *A Time to Burn? An Evaluation of the Present Crisis in Race Relations.* Chicago: Rand McNally, 1969. A sharp reminder to white America of the immediate need to grant equality to all Americans—by a group of authors connected with the Civil Violence Research Center of Cleveland.

Mattick, Hans W. "The Form and Content of Recent Riots," *University of Chicago Law Review* 35 (Summer 1968):660-685.

Meyer, Philip. *A Survey of Attitudes of Detroit Negroes after the Riot of 1967.* Detroit, Michigan: Detroit Urban League, 1969.

Miller, Alexander. "Crisis without Violence." Anti-Defamation League, 1964. Pamphlet. Account of how New Rochelle, N.Y., avoided violence despite a crisis situation in race relations.

Miller, E. Eugene. "The Woman Participant in Washington's Riots," *Federal Probation* 33 (June 1969):30-34. Study of background and nature of violations of female participants, predominantly Negro.

Mincieli, Michael. "New York City: Why Not Riot?" *New City* 6 (May 1968):9-14. Weighs potential gains and losses of rioting to the ghetto.

Morris, Richard T., and Vincent Jeffries. "Violence Next Door," *Social Forces* 46 (March 1968):352-358. A preliminary study of white reactions to the 1965 Watts riots.

Nieburg, H. L. "The Threat of Violence and Social Change," *American Political Science Review* 56 (December 1962):865-873.

Oberschall, Anthony. "The Los Angeles Riot of August, 1965," *Social Problems* 15 (Winter 1968):322-341. A sociological explanation for the causes and course of the riot.

O'Dell, J. H. "The July Rebellions and the 'Military State,'" *Freedomways* 7 (Fall 1967):288-301. Probes social and economic reasons for ghetto unrest.

Paletz, David L., and Robert Dunn. "Press Coverage of Civil Disorders: A Case Study of Winston-Salem, 1967," *Public Opinion Quarterly* 33 (Fall 1969):328-345. Reports the unbalanced perspective, with Afro-American opinion lacking.

"Profile of an Urban Rioter," *Employment Service Review* 5 (March-April 1968):38-40. Based on interviews of 500 Negroes jailed in connection with the July 1967 riot.

Pynchon, Thomas. "A Journey into the Mind of Watts," *New York Times Magazine,* June 11, 1966, pp. 34-35+.

Rainwater, Lee. "Open Letter on White Justice and the Riots," *Trans-action* 4 (September 1967):22-32. A diagnosis of riots in Negro ghettos. Illustrations.

Ransford, H. Edward. "Isolation, Powerlessness, and Violence: A Study of Attitudes and Participation in the Watts Riot," *American Journal of Sociology* 73 (March 1968): 581-591. Analysis of cumulative effects of three independent variables: isolation, powerlessness, and dissatisfaction.

Ritchie, Barbara, ed. *The Riot Report: A Shortened Version of the Report of the National Advisory Commission on Civil Disorders.* New York: Viking, 1969. An effective shortened version of the Kerner Report, maintaining for the white lay reader, the impact of the Commission's findings. Includes a historical summary of blacks in the United States.

Roshco, Bernard. "The Negro Press Views the Riots," *Interplay* 1 (February 1968):9-11.

Rudwick, Elliott M., and August Meier. "Negro Retaliatory Violence in the Twentieth Century," *New Politics* 5 (Winter 1966):41-51.

Rudwick, Elliott M. *Race Riot at East St. Louis, July 2, 1917.* Carbondale: Southern Illinois University Press, 1964. An historical case study with strong contemporaneous interest.

Rustin, Bayard. "The Watts Manifesto and the McCone Report," *Commentary* 41 (March 1966):29-35.

Sandburg, Carl. *The Chicago Race Riots, July 1919.* 1919. New York: Harcourt, Brace & World, 1969. First appeared in the Chicago Daily News, thereafter published by Harcourt. This reissue includes a preface by Ralph McGill and an introductory note by Walter Lippmann.

Sauter, Van Gordon, and Burleigh Hines. *Nightmare in Detroit: A Rebellion and Its Victims.*

Chicago: Regnery, 1968. Profiles of the 43 casualties of the 1967 disorder for the purpose of arousing the national moral consciousness. Their conclusions deserve careful reading.

Sayre, Nora. "Conversations in Watts," *New Statesman* 75 (February 2, 1968):137-138.

Scoble, Harry M. "The McCone Commission and Social Science," *Phylon* 29 (Summer 1968):167-181.

Sears, David O., and John B. McConahay. "Participation in the Los Angeles Riot," *Social Problems* 17 (Summer 1969):3-20.

Sears, David O., and T. M. Tomlinson. "Riot Ideology in Los Angeles: A Study of Negro Attitudes," *Social Science Quarterly* 49 (December 1968):485-503.

Shapiro, Fred C., and James W. Sullivan. *Race Riots New York 1964.* New York: Crowell, 1964. Authors were staff reporters for the *New York Herald-Tribune.*

Sherman, Jimmie. "From the Ashes: A Personal Reaction to the Revolt of Watts," *Antioch Review* 27 (Fall 1967):285-293.

Sitkoff, Harvard. "The Detroit Race Riot of 1943," *Michigan History* 53 (Fall 1969):183-194.

Spear, Allan. "The Changing Nature of Racial Violence," *New Politics* 5 (Spring 1966):115-122.

"Symposium on Watts 1965," *Law in Transition Quarterly* 3 (Summer 1966):174-196. Contents: "Arrests and Trials," "Analysis and Statistics," and "Attitudes of Negroes toward the Los Angeles Riots."

Tomlinson, T. M. "Development of a Riot Ideology among Urban Negroes," *American Behavioral Scientist* 11 (March 1968):27-31.

Tumin, Melvin M. "Some Social Consequences of Research on Racial Relations," *American Sociologist* 3 (May 1968):117-124. Cites usefulness of social science research as a means of forestalling violence and racial tensions. Warns against pressures for action by militant anti-intellectual facets of the black community.

U.S. Commission on Civil Rights. California Advisory Committee. *An Analysis of the McCone Commission Report.* n.p., 1966.

U. S. Congress. Senate. Committe on the Judiciary. *Gaps in International Security Laws: Hearings Pt. 5, May 2-10, 1967.* Washington: U. S. Govt. Print. Off., 1967. (90th Congress, 1st Session). Testimony about militant civil rights groups and black nationalist organizations in Cleveland.

U. S. Department of Labor. Manpower Administration. *The Detroit Riot: A Profile of 500 Prisoners.* Washington, 1968.

U.S. National Advisory Commission on Civil Disorders. *Report of the National Advisory Commission on Civil Disorders.* Washington: U.S. Govt. Print. Off., 1968. Widely known as the Kerner Report.

U.S. National Advisory Commission on Civil Disorders. *Supplemental Studies,* 1968. Washington: U.S. Govt. Print. Off., 1968. Three studies conducted independently of the Commission by research groups from Michigan, Johns Hopkins, and Columbia University provide information on racial attitudes and riot participation. Statistics and notes on the methodology of the research are included.

Urban America, Inc., and the Urban Coalition. *One Year Later: An Assessment of the Nation's Response to the Crisis Described by the National Commission on Civil Disorders.* New York: Praeger, 1969. Describes the worsening of U.S. race relations. Forewords, written by John W. Gardner and Terry Sanford, stress the urgency of effective action.

Urban Violence. Charles V. Daley, ed. Chicago: University of Chicago Center for Policy Study, 1969.

"The Violence," *Nation* 205 (August 14, 1967):101-107. Racial disorders in Harlem, Detroit, Los Angeles, and Newark viewed by local white reporters.

Waskow, Arthur L. *From Race Riot to Sit In, 1919 and the 1960's.* Garden City, N.Y.: Doubleday, 1966. The story of two periods of racial clashes in the United States. The author explores the possibility that violent conflict can be replaced by nonviolent means.

"What Happened to the Kerner Report," *Social Education* 33 (January 1969):24-27 +. Members of the Commission on Civil Disorders comment on changes and programs which have been effected since the report was filed.

Wheeler, Harvey. "Moral Equivalent to Riots," *Saturday Review* 51 (May 11, 1968):19-22. Reply and rejoinder *ibid.,* (June 15, 1968):19-20.

Wilson, James Q. "Black and White Tragedy," *Encounter* 29 (October 1967):63-68.

Witcover, Jules. "Rochester Braces for Another July," *Reporter* 33 (July 15, 1965):33-35.

Young, Michael. "The Liberal Approach: Its Weaknesses and Its Strengths—A Comment on the U.S. Riot Commission Report," *Daedalus* 97 (Fall 1968):1379-1389.

13   Economic Status and Problems

General

A. Philip Randolph Institute. *A "Freedom Budget" for All Americans.* New York, 1966.

Aldridge, Dan. "Politics in Command of Economics: Black Economic Development," *Monthly Review* 21 (November 1969):14–27. Revision of a speech given at the National Black Economic Development Conference, April 1969 by an activist in the Detroit Black Liberation movement.

Allen, Irving L. "Selecting an Economic Probability Sample of Negro Households in a City," *Journal of Negro Education* 38 (Winter 1969):4–13.

Allen, Robert L. *Black Awakening in Capitalist America.* Garden City, N. Y.: Doubleday, 1969. A staff writer of the *Guardian* offers a sharp critique of the white business establishment and the "bourgeois black establishment."

American Assembly. *Black Economic Development: Report of the 35th American Assembly Arden House.* New York: Harriman, 1969. Prospects for black businessmen and incentives for business development in the ghetto.

Batchelder, Alan B. "Decline in the Relative Income of Negro Men," *Quarterly Journal of Economics* 78 (November 1964):525–548. See also Rashi Fein. *ibid.,* 80 (May 1966):336 updating this information.

Batchelder, A. B. "Economic Forces Serving the Ends of the Negro Protest," *Annals of the American Academy of Political and Social Science* 357 (January 1965):80–88.

Becker, Gary S. *The Economics of Discrimination.* Chicago: University of Chicago Press, 1957. An interesting study of the economic consequences of discrimination. The author's purpose is "to develop a theory of non-pecuniary motivation and to apply it quantitatively to discrimination in the market place."

Blalock, H. M. "Economic Discrimination and Negro Increase," *American Sociological Review* 21 (October 1956):584–588.

Bloch, Herman D. *The Circle of Discrimination: An Economic and Social Study of the Black Man in New York.* New York: New York University Press, 1969. A comprehensive historical survey covering the period 1625–1965, and an epilogue citing cases of current prejudice through 1968.

Brimmer, Andrew F. "The Black Revolution and the Economic Future of Negroes in the United States," *American Scholar* 38 (Autumn 1969):629–643.

Brimmer, Andrew F. "Economic Progress in Black and White," *Interracial Review* 39 (February 1966):26–30.

Brown, Robert, and Franklin M. Fisher. "Negro-White Savings Differentials and the Modigliani-Brumberg Hypothesis," *Review of Economics and Statistics* 40 (February 1958):79–81.

California. Division of Fair Employment Practices. *Negroes and Mexican Americans in South and East Los Angeles: Changes between 1960 and 1965 in Population, Employment, Income, and Family Status.* San Francisco, 1966.

Conroy, E. J. "What the Insurance Companies Are Doing in the Ghetto," *Business Lawyer* 25 (September 1969):27 +.

Cowles, Arthur W. "Businessmen and Negro Leaders Weigh Their Current Concerns," *Conference Board Record* 5 (July 1968):20-22.

Denison, Edward F. *The Sources of Economic Growth in the United States and the Alternative Before Us.* Washington: Committee on Economic Development, 1962. Has relevance for participation of the Negro.

Drake, St. Clair. "The Social and Economic Status of the Negro in the United States," *Daedalus* 94 (Fall 1965):771-814.

Edgeworth, Arthur B., Jr. "Civil Rights Plus Three Years: Banks and the Anti-Discrimination Law," *Bankers Monthly* (Boston) 150 (Summer 1967):23-30.

Erskine, Hazel. "The Polls: Negro (Domestic) Finances," *Public Opinion Quarterly* 33 (Summer 1969):272-282.

Farmer, James. "Providing Mobility for America's Immobile Population," in Conference on the Education and Training of Racial Minorities, 1967, *Proceedings.* Madison: University of Wisconsin, Center for Studies in Vocational and Technical Education, 1968, pp. 95-105. Increased economic mobility for the lower economic class Negro through job training, education, and new apprenticeship techniques.

Fein, Rashi. "An Economic and Social Profile of the Negro American," *Daedalus* 94 (Fall 1965):815-846.

Fein, Rashi. "Relative Income of Negro Men: Some Recent Data," *Quarterly Journal of Economics* 80 (May 1966):336. Updates the information presented earlier by A. B. Batchelder.

Foley, Eugene P. *The Achieving Ghetto.* Washington: National Press, 1968. Economic development of the urban Negro ghetto. Describes a ghetto Marshall plan.

Franklin, Raymond S. "A Framework for the Analysis of Interurban Negro-White Economic Differentials," *Industrial and Labor Relations Review* 21 (April 1968):367-374. Study concludes that Negro-White income and occupational status differentials are dependent upon the degree of "convergence" among the sources of discrimination, e.g., employees, employers, and consumers, to hinder occupational mobility. Maintains that an attack on discrimination, to be effective, must first change the de facto occupational status of the Negro.

Frazier, E. Franklin. "The Status of the Negro in the American Social Order," *Journal of Negro Education* 4 (July 1935):293-307. On the hypothesis that the Negro's status has been bound up with his role in the economic system, the author concludes, "In the urban environment he is showing signs of understanding the struggle for power between the proletariat and the owning classes, and is beginning to cooperate with white workers in this struggle which offers the only hope of his complete emancipation." A fascinating presentation of the thinking of the 1930's.

Ginzberg, Eli, ed. *Business Leadership and the Negro Crisis.* New York: McGraw-Hill, 1968. Contributions of experts assessing the needs of the Negro in the areas of housing, education, and business, and the potential role of private enterprise.

Ginzberg, Eli, and Dale L. Hiestand. *Mobility in the Negro Community: Guidelines for Research on Social and Economic Progress.* Washington: U.S. Govt. Print. Off., 1968.

Ginzberg, Eli. *The Negro Potential.* New York: Columbia University Press, 1956. A publication of Columbia's Conservation of Human Resources Project. Premises are that, "It is never sensible or right for a nation to waste valuable human resources through failure to develop or utilize them," and that "the best hope for the Negro's speedy and complete integration into American society lies in . . . a strong and virile economy."

Ginzberg, Eli. "Segregation and Manpower Waste," *Phylon* 21 (Winter 1960):311-316.

Grindstaff, Carl F. "Negro Urbanization and Relative Deprivation in the Deep South," *Social Problems* 15 (Winter 1968):342-352. Thesis: as the Southern Negro becomes more urban, the discrepancy between him and the white population in terms of education, occupation, and income increases.

Guscott, Kenneth I. "NAACP Views Conditions," *Industry* 28 (July 1963):12-13, 29.

Haddad, William F., and G. Douglas Pugh, eds. *Black Economic Development.* Englewood Cliffs, N.J.: Prentice-Hall, 1969. Twelve essays by experts, black and white, describing the potential efficacy of "green power" and the building of a black managerial class.

Haynes, Marion. "A Century of Change: Negroes in the U.S. Economy, 1860-1960," *Monthly Labor Review* 85 (December 1962):1359-1365.

Henderson, G. "The Negro Recipient of Old-Age Assistance: Results of Discrimination," *Social Casework* 46 (April 1965):208-214.

Henderson, Vivian W. "Economic Dimensions in Race Relations," in Jitsuichi Masuoka and Preston Valien, eds., *Race Relations: Problems and Theory.* Chapel Hill: University of North Carolina Press, 1961.

Henderson, Vivian W. "The Economic Imbalance: An Enquiry into the Economic Status of Negroes in the United States, 1935-1960, with Implications for Negro Education," *Quarterly Review of Higher Education among Negroes* 28 (January 1960):84-98.

Henderson, Vivian W. *The Economic Status of Negroes: In the Nation and in the South.* Atlanta: Southern Regional Council, 1963. Thorough and revelatory.

Henderson, W., and L. Ledebur. "Government Incentives and Black Economic Development," *Review of Social Economy* 27 (September 1969):202-221.

Hill, Herbert. "Recent Effects of Racial Conflict on Southern Industrial Development," *Phylon* 20 (Winter 1959):319-326.

Holland, Jerome H. *Black Opportunity.* New York: Weybright & Talley, 1969. Analyzes place of the young black people in the economic mainstream; the limitations and hurdles still outstanding. Author appointed U.S. Ambassador to Sweden in January 1970.

Hughes, Emmet John. "The Negro's New Economic Life," *Fortune* 54 (September 1956):126-131 +.

Javits, Jacob. "A 'Marshall Plan' for Americans," *Interracial Review* 39 (July 1966):133-134 +.

Kain, John F., ed. *Race and Poverty: The Economics of Discrimination.* Englewood Cliffs, N.J.: Prentice-Hall, 1969. The editor traces the economics of discrimination from the post-bellum period to the present. The collection includes previously published, important pieces by experts and scholars, both black and white.

Kalvans, Irena. "Economic Brief on Conditions of Negroes in the United States and in Detroit," *Michigan Manpower Quarterly Review* 4 (Winter 1968):12-15.

Kessler, Matthew A. "Economic Status of Nonwhite Workers, 1955-1962," *Monthly Labor Review* 86 (July 1963):780-788.

Kosa, J., and Nunn, C. Z. "Race, Deprivation and Attitude toward Communism," *Phylon* 25 (Winter 1964):337-346.

Krueger, A. O. "The Economics of Discrimination," *Journal of Political Economy* 71 (October 1963):481-486. Economic effects of discrimination, how the majority profit from discrimination against the minority, with minority unable to retaliate.

Lane, R. E. "The Fear of Equality," *American Political Science Review* 53 (March 1959):33-51. On resistance to economic, or income, equality, not only of Negroes specifically, but of all groups.

Lang, Gladys Engel. "Minority Groups and Economic Status in New York State," in Aaron Antonovsky and Lewis L. Lorwin, eds., *Discrimination and Low Incomes.* New York: New School for Social Research, 1959.

Lipset, Seymour M., and Reinhard Bendix. *Social Mobility in Industrial Society.* Berkeley: University of California Press, 1959. Emphasizing that it is the rate of economic expansion which is most significant in determining the extent of social mobility in a society, the authors point out the factors inhibiting the Negro from sharing the opportunities presented by such expansion.

Lumer, Hyman. "The Economics of Rebellion," *Political Affairs* 46 (September 1967):1-11.

Miller, Helen Hill. "Business Citizenship in the Deep South," *Business Horizons* 5 (Spring 1962):61-66.

Miller, Helen Hill. "Private Business and Education in the South," *Harvard Business Review* 38 (July-August 1960):75-88.

Miller, Herman Phillip. *Income of the American People.* New York: Wiley, 1955. Prepared for Social Science Research Council in cooperation with U.S. Department of Commerce, Bureau of Census.

Muller, Andre L. "Economic Growth and Minorities," *American Journal of Economics and Sociology* 26 (July 1967):225–230. Evaluates the contention that the Negro has not gained in economic status.

National Urban League. *Economic and Social Status of the Negro in the U.S.* Washington, 1961.

Needham, Maurice d'Arlan. *Negro Orleanian: Status and Stake in a City's Economy and Housing.* New Orleans: Tulane Publications, 1962.

Newman, Dorothy. *The Negroes in the United States: Their Economic and Social Situation.* Washington: U.S. Govt. Print. Off., 1966. Bibliography.

Nicholls, William H. "The South as a Developing Area," *Journal of Politics* 26 (February 1964):22–40.

Percy, Charles H. *Building the New America.* New York: American Management Association, 1968. Discusses the proposed Community Self-Determination Act as an instrument for accelerating economic growth of the ghetto.

Perlo, Victor. "Trends in the Economic Status of the Negro People," *Science and Society* 16 (Spring 1952):115–150. Continuing trend since war, despite great Negro gains in economic and social status, has been for living costs of Negroes to rise more rapidly than those of whites, and for living standards of Negroes in cities to be cut very sharply.

Ratchford, R. U. "The Reorganization of the Southern Economy," in Jessie P. Guzman, ed., *The New South and Higher Education.* Tuskegee: Tuskegee Institute, 1954.

Ring, H. H., et al. *Negroes in the United States: Their Employment and Economic Status.* Washington: U.S. Bureau of Labor Statistics, 1953. (Bulletin no. 1119)

Robcock, Stefan H. "The Negro in the Industrial Development of the South," *Phylon* 14 (Fall 1953):319–325.

Rose, Alvin W. "The Changing Economic Background of American Race Relations," *Southwestern Social Science Quarterly* 31 (December 1950):159–173.

Rustin, Bayard. "The Lessons of the Long Hot Summer," *Commentary* 44 (October 1967):39–45. An appeal for government attention and budget allocation to the social, economic, and educational needs of Negroes. Attention to the proposed Freedom Budget proposed by A. Philip Randolph.

Schultz, Theodore W. "Investment in Human Capital," *American Economic Review* 51 (March 1961):1–17. Presidential address before American Economic Association, December 1960. Education of Negroes and other disadvantaged groups must be considered as investment. Cost of welfare and human deterioration are too great to be borne by society.

Siegel, Paul M. "On the Cost of Being a Negro," *Sociological Inquiry* 35 (Winter 1965):41–57.

Singer, Herman. "Not All Black," *Dissent* 11 (Spring 1964):157–159. Relation between movement for civil rights and opportunity to share in affluence.

Sterner, Richard. *The Negro's Share.* New York: Harper, 1943. Still a useful study of Negro income, consumption, housing, and public assistance, it is one of a series of investigations concerning the Negro instituted and financed by the Carnegie Corporation. Contains a mass of statistical data on occupational and employment trends, family composition and incomes, expenditures and consumption, housing conditions, both rural and urban, as well as discussion of Negro's economic position in American society.

Sullivan, Leon H. *Build, Brother, Build.* Philadelphia: Macrae, 1969. Achievement of a black minister. A list of Opportunities Industrialization Center programs (Philadelphia) as of January 1969 is appended.

Tobin, James. "On Improving the Economic Status of the Negro," *Daedálus* 94 (Fall 1965):878–898. "By far the most powerful factor determining the economic status of Negroes is the over-all state of the U.S. economy. A vigorously expanding economy with a steadily tight labor market will rapidly raise the position of the Negro."

Tucker, Francis. "White-Nonwhite Age Differences and the Accurate Assessment of the Cost of Being Negro," *Social Forces* 47 (March 1969):343–345.

U.S. Bureau of the Census. *Income Distribution in the United States,* by Herman P. Miller. Washington: U.S. Govt. Print. Off., 1966.

U.S. Bureau of the Census. *Recent Trends in Social and Economic Conditions of Negroes in the United States,* prepared by Herman P. Miller and Dorothy K. Newman. Washington: U.S. Govt. Print. Off., 1968.

U.S. Bureau of the Census. *Social and Economic Conditions of Negroes in the United States.* Washington: U.S. Govt. Print. Off., 1967. (Bureau of Labor Statistics Report no. 332)

U.S. Bureau of the Census. *Trends in the Income of Families and Persons in the United States, 1947-1960,* by Herman P. Miller. Washington: U.S. Department of Commerce, Bureau of the Census, 1963.

U.S. Bureau of the Census. *Trends in Social and Economic Conditions in Metropolitan Areas.* Washington: U.S. Govt. Print. Off., 1969. (Current Population Report P-23, no. 27). Population changes and distribution and median family income of white and Negro population in the United States. 212 standard metropolitan statistical areas, 1960-1968. Where possible, data are presented for whites and Negroes separately.

U.S. Commission on Civil Rights. *Hearing Held in Montgomery, Alabama, April 27-May 2, 1968.* Washington: U.S. Govt. Print. Off., 1969. Maps.

U.S. Department of Labor. *The Economic Situation of Negroes in the United States.* 1960. Rev. ed. Washington: U.S. Govt. Print. Off., 1962. Many Negroes felt that this bulletin (S-3), issued during the closing weeks of the 1960 presidential campaign with a foreword by Secretary of Labor James P. Mitchell, was unrealistically optimistic about Negro gains and that its chief purpose was to attract Negro votes for the Republican ticket rather than to present the true facts of the Negroes' economic situation.

U.S. Department of Labor. *The Negroes in the United States: Their Economic and Social Situation.* Washington: U.S. Govt. Print. Off., 1966. (Bulletin no. 1511). Bibliography.

U.S. Departments of Labor and Commerce. *Recent Trends in Social and Economic Conditions of Negroes in the United States.* Washington: U.S. Govt. Print. Off., 1968. (Current Population Reports, Series P-23, no. 26; BLS Report no. 347)

U.S. National Advisory Commission on Civil Disorders. *Report.* Washington: U.S. Govt. Print. Off., 1968. Includes important data on White-Negro income differentials.

Walter, Ingo, and John F. Kramer, Jr. "Human Resources and Economic Growth in a Negro Municipality," *University of Missouri Business and Government Review* 9 (July-August 1968):5-17.

Weaver, Robert C. "Challenges to Democracy." Paper given at a symposium in Chicago and published in *The Negro as an American,* Santa Barbara, Calif.: Center for the Study of Democratic Institutions, 1963. Author emphasizes economic aspects of Negro problem, and stresses importance of involvement of middle-class Negroes with total Negro community.

"What Business Can Do for the Negro," *Nation's Business* 55 (October 1967):67-70. An interview with Kenneth B. Clark.

Wright, Nathan, Jr. "The Economics of Race," *American Journal of Economics and Sociology* 26 (January 1967):1-12.

The Poor

Bagdikian, Ben H. *In the Midst of Plenty: The Poor in America.* Boston: Beacon, 1964. Deals with America's "forgotten poor" in urban and rural slums and with the Negro problem as part of problem of the poor in general.

Batchelder, Alan. "Poverty: The Special Case of the Negro," *American Economic Review* 55 (May 1965):530-540. Bibliography.

Boskin, Michael. "The Negative Income Tax and the Supply of Work Effort," *National Tax Journal* 20 (December 1967):353-367.

Bremmer, Robert H. *From the Depths: The Discovery of Poverty in the United States.* New York: New York University Press, 1964.

Broadfield, George W. "A Different Drum," *Nation* 201 (September 20, 1965):161-165. 100th anniversary issue. Author designed and directed the country's first Domestic Peace Corps (1962-1964).

Bryant, M. Darrol. *To Whom It May Concern: Poverty, Humanity, Community.* Philadelphia: Fortress Press, 1969. The author's response as a participant in the Poor People's Campaign, Resurrection City, and National Solidarity Day.

"Camping-in for a Dream," *Economist* 227 (May 25, 1968):37-38. The Poor People's March.

Carl, Earl L. "The Shortage of Negro Lawyers: Pluralistic Legal Education and Legal Services for the Poor," *Journal of Legal Education* 20 (1967):21-32.

Clark, Kenneth, and Jeanette Hopkins. *A Relevant War against Poverty.* New York: Harper & Row, 1968.

Coles, Robert, and Harry Huge. "In Jamie Whitten's Back Yard," *New South* 24 (Spring 1969):42-47.

Coles, Robert, and Maria Piers. *Wages of Neglect.* Chicago: Quadrangle, 1969. A study of the Child Development Group of Mississippi, the Boston North Point Project and other projects for reaching deprived children.

Crow, John E. *Discrimination, Poverty, and the Negro: Arizona in the National Context.* Tucson: University of Arizona Press, 1968.

David, Martin. "Incomes and Dependency in the Coming Decades," *American Journal of Economics and Sociology* 3 (July 1964):249-267. A study by the Survey Research Center at the University of Michigan finds 29 percent of all families in the U.S. are "poor," and 10.4 million families need additional income for an adequate standard of living. Of these 1.4 million are nonwhite families.

Davies, Vernon. "Fertility versus Welfare: The Negro American Dilemma," *Phylon* 27 (Fall 1966):226-232.

Dunbar, Anthony. *The Will to Survive: A Study of a Mississippi Plantation Community Based on the Words of Its Citizens.* Atlanta: Published by the Southern Regional Council and the Mississippi Council on Human Relations, 1969. Negro tenant farmers in the Delta.

Duncan, Otis Dudley. "Inheritance of Poverty or Inheritance of Race?" in Daniel P. Moynihan, ed., *On Understanding Poverty.* New York: Basic Books, 1969, pp. 85-110. Contends that the disproportionate number of the Negro poor stems not from the "legacy of poverty but from the legacy of race."

Dunne, George H., ed. *Poverty in Plenty.* New York: Kenedy, for Georgetown University, 1964. Symposium marking the 175th anniversary of the University.

Fager, Charles E. *Uncertain Resurrection: The Poor People's Washington Campaign.* Grand Rapids, Mich.: Eerdmans, 1969.

Gallaway, Lowell E. "The Negro and Poverty," *Journal of Business* 40 (January 1967): 27-35. Evaluates the contributory factors to Negro poverty.

Ginzberg, Eli. "Poverty and the Negro," in *The Disadvantaged Poor: Education and Employment.* Washington: Chamber of Commerce of the United States, Task Force on Economic Growth and Opportunity, 1966, pp. 207-228. Outlines twelve key determinants of Negro poverty and proposes policy changes to counteract them.

Harrington, Michael. *The Other America: Poverty in the United States.* New York: Macmillan, 1962. Because of the disproportionately large number of Negroes who belong to the impoverished class, Negro poverty is considered throughout. Chapter 4, "If You're Black, Stay Back," is specifically concerned with the Negro.

Harrington, Michael. "The Will to Abolish Poverty," *Saturday Review* 51 (July 27, 1968): 10-12+. Resurrection City.

Hauser, Philip M. "Demographic and Social Factors in the Poverty of the Negro," in *The Disadvantaged Poor: Education and Employment.* Washington: Chamber of Commerce of the United States, Task Force on Economic Growth and Opportunity, 1966, pp. 229-261. The demographic background of the Negro in the United States; a comparison of the acculturation process of the Negro with that of other white immigrant groups.

Henderson, George. "Beyond Poverty of Income," *Journal of Negro Education* 36 (Winter 1967):42-50. Summary of author's unpublished doctoral dissertation. Emphasizes the role of education in preparing lower-class students to compete in a social arena where success symbols dominate.

Herzog, Elizabeth. *About the Poor: Some Facts and Some Fictions.* Washington: U.S. Govt. Print. Off., 1967. (U. S. Health, Education, and Welfare. Children's Bureau Publication no. 451)

Hunt, Linda. "Nixon's Guaranteed Annual Poverty," *Ramparts* 8 (December 1969):64–70.

Hunter, Charlayne A. "On the Case in Resurrection City," *Trans-action* 5 (October 1968):47–55. Retrospective appraisal by a participant-observer in the Poor People's campaign.

Jackson, Jesse L. "Resurrection City: The Dream, the Accomplishments," *Ebony* 23 (October 1968):65–66 + .

James, W. "Black Poverty," *Personnel Administrator* 13 (January–February 1968):36–39. The dilemma of the poor Negro: public and private efforts to alleviate the condition through training for better employment prospects.

Jeffers, Camille. *Living Poor: A Participant Observer Study of Priorities and Choices.* Ann Arbor, Mich.: Ann Arbor Publishers, 1967. A report of the Child Rearing Study of low-income families in the District of Columbia.

Kosa, John, Aaron Antonovsky, and Irving Kenneth Zola, eds. *Poverty and Health: A Sociological Analysis.* Cambridge, Mass.: Harvard University Press, 1969. A joint venture of 13 scholars, this book is a systematic and exhaustive study of one of the crucial problems of present day American society.

La Barre, Maurine. "Strengths of the Self-Supporting Poor," *Social Casework* 49 (October 1968):459–466. Results of a Durham, North Carolina project involving mostly Negro families.

Lampman, Robert J. *The Low Income Population and Economic Growth.* Washington: U.S. Govt. Print. Off., 1959.

Lampman, Robert J. "Recent Thought on Egalitarianism," *Quarterly Journal of Economics* 71 (May 1957):234–266.

Miller, Herman Phillip. *Rich Man, Poor Man.* New York: Crowell, 1964. Author, an economic statistician with long experience at Bureau of the Census, analyzes characteristics of the poor, Negro-White income differential over time, and relative economic advantage of education for Negroes and whites. Tables and statistics with commentary intelligible to general reader.

Moynihan, Daniel P. *Maximum Feasible Misunderstanding: Community Action in the War on Poverty.* New York: Free Press, 1969.

Myrdal, Gunnar. *Challenge to Affluence.* New York: Pantheon, 1964. Addressing himself to problems of poverty and the rate of economic growth in the United States, the author foresees that the proletariat of the unemployed, the uneducated, and the migrant, of whom Negroes form a large proportion, will increase in number and become a permanent class unless economic growth rate rises sharply.

National Workshop on the Urban Poor. *Manpower and Consumer Potentials, 1968: Proceedings, March 26–27, 1968.* Washington: Chamber of Commerce of the United States, 1968. Emphasis on the Negro ghetto.

North, George E., and O. Lee Buchanan. "Maternal Attitudes in a Poverty Era," *Journal of Negro Education* 37 (Fall 1968):418–425. Study of parents with nursery and kindergarten children in an impoverished area of Phoenix, Arizona.

Orshansky, M. "Aged Negro and His Income," *Social Security Bulletin* 27 (February 1964): 3–13.

Orshansky, Mollie. "Children of the Poor," *Social Science Research Council Bulletin,* July 1963.

Orshansky, M. "Counting the Poor: Another Look at the Poverty Profile," *Social Security Bulletin* 28 (January 1965):3–29.

Ross, Arthur M., and Herbert Hill, eds. *Employment, Race and Poverty.* New York: Harcourt, Brace & World, 1967. Jacket subtitle: "A critical study of the disadvantaged status of Negro workers from 1865 to 1965." Broad, authoritative coverage of subject in 20 papers. The third volume of research and conferences on "Unemployment and the

American Economy," Institute of Industrial Relations, University of California,
Berkeley. Essays discuss and assess the Negro's position in the labor market; the role of
government, management, and labor; legal responses to employment discrimination;
social effects of unemployment; programs for guidance and training.

Sexton, Patricia Cayo. *Spanish Harlem: Anatomy of Poverty*. New York: Harper, 1965. The
author argues for organizing the poor to organize themselves and to use their political
power to effect social change.

Southern Regional Council. *A City Slum: Poor People and Problems*. Atlanta, 1967.

Southern Regional Council. *Hungry Children*. Atlanta, 1967. A report of six physicians on
the health and living conditions of Negro children in rural Mississippi.

Street, David, and John C. Leggett. "Economic Deprivation and Extremism: A Study of
Unemployed Negroes," *American Journal of Sociology* 67 (July 1961):53-57.

Sturdivant, Frederick D., and Walter T. Wilheim. "Poverty, Minorities, and Consumer
Exploitation," *Social Science Quarterly* 49 (December 1968):643-650. Examines the
question: Are higher consumer prices paid by the poor because of economic or minority
group status? Findings suggest both. Negroes, Mexicans, and Anglo-whites were tested
in study.

Thurow, Lester C. *Poverty and Discrimination*. Washington: Brookings Institution, 1969.
Important critical bibliographical essays by chapter.

Ulmer, Al. *Cooperatives and Poor People in the South*. Atlanta: Southern Regional Council,
1969. An appraisal of nine operating cooperatives.

U.S. Congress. Joint Committee on the Economic Report. *Characteristics of the Low-Income
Population and Related Federal Programs*. Washington: U.S. Govt. Print. Off., 1955.

U.S. Congress. Senate. Committee on Labor and Public Welfare. *Hearings . . . Examining the
War on Poverty (S1545); Parts 5-7*. Washington: U.S. Govt. Print. Off., 1967. (90th
Congress, 1st Session). The interacting forces of poverty and racial discrimination. The
operations of antipoverty agencies as they have, or have not, enhanced the Negro's
economic and social position.

U.S. National Advisory Commission on Rural Poverty. "The Negro Population of the
South," in *Rural Poverty in the United States*. Washington: U.S. Govt. Print. Off., 1968,
pp. 13-39.

Valentine, Charles A. *Culture and Poverty: Critique and Counter-Proposals*. Chicago: University of Chicago Press, 1968.

Whitehead, John S. *Ida's Family: Adaptations to Poverty in a Suburban Ghetto*. Yellow
Springs, Ohio: Antioch College, 1969. Describes a low-income black family in a
Washington, D.C. ghetto. Prepared for the National Institute of Mental Health.

The Negro as Consumer

Alexis, Marcus. "Pathways to the Negro Market," *Journal of Negro Education* 28 (Spring
1959):114-128.

Barnes, Nickolas L. *Some Potentialities and Limitations of the Negro Market in Chicago*.
Chicago: T & T, 1953.

Bauer, Raymond, Scott M. Cunningham, and Lawrence H. Wortzel. "The Marketing
Dilemma of Negroes," *Journal of Marketing* 29 (July 1965):1-6.

Black, L. E. "Negro Market: Growing, Changing, Challenging," *Sales Management* 91 (October 4, 1963):7.

"Black is Beautiful, but Maybe Not Profitable . . .," *Media/Scope* 13 (August 1969):31-37 + .

Braguglia, Marilyn Hunter, and Mary Lou Rosencranz. "A Comparison of Clothing Attitudes and Ownership of Negro and White Women of Low Socio-Economic Status,"
Journal of Consumer Affairs 2 (Winter 1968):182-187.

Bullock, Henry Allen. "Consumer Motivations in Black and White—Part I," *Harvard Business Review* 33 (May-June 1961):89-104; "Part II," *ibid.*, 33 (July-August
1961):110-124. Two thorough and thoughtful articles.

Caplovitz, David. "The Merchant and the Low-Income [Negro] Consumer," *Jewish Social Studies* 27 (January 1965):45–52. A paper delivered at the Conference of Negro-Jewish Relations in the United States, 1964.

Cook, Marvin K. "Negro Cosmetics," *Drug and Cosmetics Industry* 103 (December 1968):40–44 +. Describes products and the consumer market for them.

Danzig, Fred. "Negro Marketer Gets Bigger Role as Awareness of Specialized Field Grows," *Advertising Age* 33 (September 10, 1962):96, 98.

Gibson, D. Parker. *The $30 Billion Negro.* New York: Macmillan, 1969. The Negro in the market place, and guidelines for effective business practice to capture this market.

"Guide to Marketing for—:The Negro Market," *Printers' Ink* 265 (October 31, 1958):137–138. These reports appear periodically in issues of *Printers' Ink.* They include bibliographies on Negro marketing information and useful surveys.

"Heavy Buying by Negro Households Is Shown by WWRL," *Advertising Age* 34 (August 26, 1963):242.

Holte, C. L. "Negro Market: To Profit from It, Recognize It and Service Its Needs," *Printers' Ink* 263 (April 4, 1958):29–32.

"Is There Really a Negro Market?" *Marketing Insights* 2 (January 29, 1968):14–17.

Kaplowitz, E. "Short Measure of Negro Cosmetics," *Drug and Cosmetic Industry* 105 (July 1969):39 +.

Korenvaes, P. "Negro Market," *Dun's Review and Modern Industry* 82 (November 1963):61–62.

Lancaster, Emmer Martin. *A Guide to Negro Marketing Information.* Washington: U.S. Department of Commerce, Business and Defense Services Administration, 1966.

"Market Basics," *Sponsor* 15 (October 9, 1961):16–21. Selection of articles dealing with Negro market and radio.

"Marketing to the Negro Consumer: Special Report," *Sales Management* 84 (March 4, 1960):5.

"Negro Boycott Could Have Serious, Lasting Effect on Sales, Study Shows," *Advertising Age* 34 (September 30, 1963):110.

"Negro Brand Preferences: They Are Different," *Sponsor* 21 (July 1967):38–41.

"Negro Impact on Market," *Broadcasting* 64 (June 17, 1963):96.

"Negro Market: Buying Power Changes Market Place," *Printers' Ink* 284 (August 30, 1963):9.

"The Negro Market: 23 Million Consumers Make a $30 Billion Market Segment," *Marketing Insights* 2 (January 29, 1969):9–12.

"The Negro Market—Two Viewpoints," *Media/Scope* 11 (November 1967):70–72 +. "A Misnomer," by W. Leonard Evans and "A Communications Phenomenon," by H. Naylor Fitzhugh.

"Negro Market Data: Still Inadequate, but Starting to Flow," *Sponsor* 13 (September 26, 1959):12–13.

"Negro Marketing Basics," *Sponsor* 14 (September 26, 1960):17–28. Includes tables.

"Negro-Owned Outlet Due for St. Louis," *Broadcasting* 24 (June 23, 1969):44.

Petrof, John V. "Reaching the Negro Market: A Segregated vs. a General Newspaper," *Journal of Advertising Research* 8 (June 1968):40–43.

Petrof, John V. "Readership Study of the Influence of Printed Commercial Messages on Negro Readers in Atlanta, Georgia," *Phylon* 28 (Winter 1967):399–407. Implications for the future of Negro newspapers are also discussed.

Ponder, Henry. "An Example of the Alternative Cost Doctrine Applied to Racial Discrimination," *Journal of Negro Education* 35 (Winter 1966):42–47. Study of a six-week Negro economic boycott of the Petersburg, Va. central business district in 1964.

Sawyer, Broadus E. "An Examination of Race as a Factor in Negro-White Consumption Patterns," *Review of Economics and Statistics* 44 (May 1962):217–220.

Sommers, Montrose S., and Gladys D. Bruce. "Blacks, Whites, and Products: Relative Deprivation and Reference Group Behavior," *Social Science Quarterly* 49 (December 1968):631–642. Reasons offered for differences in Negro-White consumption patterns and aspirations.

"Soul Market in Black and White," *Sales Management* 102 (June 1, 1969):36–38 +.

Southern Regional Council. "Negro Buying Power." Atlanta, 1960. Mimeographed.

Stafford, James, Keith K. Cox, and James B. Higginbotham. "Some Consumption Pattern Differences between Urban Whites and Negroes," *Social Science Quarterly* 49 (December 1968):619-630.

Sturdivant, Frederick D. "Better Deal for Ghetto Shoppers," *Harvard Business Review* 46 (March-April 1968):130-139. A program for retailing based on the concept of investment guarantees and credits to those who build branch stores in ghetto areas.

Sturdivant, Frederick D., and Walter T. Wilhelm. "Poverty, Minorities, and Consumer Exploitation," *Social Science Quarterly* 49 (December 1968):643-650. Examines the question: are higher consumer prices paid by the poor because of economic or minority group status? Findings suggest both. Negroes, Mexicans, and Anglo-whites were tested in study.

"$2 Billion Negro Furnishing Market Seen by *Ebony*," *Advertising Age* 34 (March 25, 1963):88.

U.S. Department of Labor. Bureau of Labor Statistics. *The Negro in the West: The Negro Consumer.* San Francisco: U.S. Department of Labor, 1967?

"Ways of Reaching the Negro Market Are Changing, AMA Told," *Advertising Age* 40 (May 26, 1969):98.

"Why an Ethnic Appeal is Working," *Printers' Ink* 279 (June 1, 1962):54-55. In radio.

The Negro as Entrepreneur

Abrams, Elliott. "Black Capitalism and Black Banks," *New Leader* 52 (March 17, 1969):14-16.

America, Richard F., Jr. "What Do You People Want?" *Harvard Business Review* 47 (March-April 1969):103-112. The author outlines a proposal for transferring to black ownership and operation a portion of the United States' largest corporations.

"Black Builders Are Moving in on Rehab Opportunity," *American Builder* 101 (December 1968):62-64.

"Black Capitalism," *Economist* 229 (December 14, 1968):39.

"Black Contractors Sharpen Their Pencils," *Engineering News-Record* 183 (July 3, 1969):48. Results of black power in the construction industry as viewed by a trade journalist.

"Black Expo: Trade Fair in Chicago," *Ebony* 25 (December 1969):106-108 + .

"Black-Owned Firm Announces First Titles, Direct Marketing," *Publishers' Weekly* 196 (December 29, 1969):41-42. A Chicago black-owned and operated publishing firm.

Blocker, J. Lester. "Under-Employed Human Resources—Problem or Opportunity," *Personnel Administrator* 14 (September-October 1969):8-11. Black executive potential.

Bloom, Gordon F. *Black Capitalism and Black Supermarkets.* Cambridge, Mass.: Alfred P. Sloan School of Management, Massachusetts Institute of Technology, 1969.

Bluestone, Barry. "Black Capitalism: The Path to Black Liberation?" *Review of Radical Political Economics* 1 (May 1969):36-55.

Bogie, William P. "Negro Bankers Look Ahead," *Banking* 61 (December 1968):33 + .

Buckley, William F., Jr. "On Black Capitalism," *National Review* 21 (March 25, 1969): 298-299.

"Building Up Minority Contractors," *Manpower* 1 (October 1969):23-25.

The Census of Negro-Owned Businesses. Philadelphia: Drexel Institute of Technology, 1964. Includes every Negro business in Philadelphia, no matter how small.

Cervantes, Alfonso J. "To Prevent a Chain of Super-Watts," *Harvard Business Review* 45 (September-October 1967):55-65. An appeal for greater business initiative and support for ghetto enterprises.

Clark, E. "Multi Racial Bank Proves Its Worth," *Burroughs Clearing House* 53 (May 1969):23-24 + .

Conrad, Richard, and Haym Jaffe. "Careers in Little Business for Negro Americans: Caveat Venditor," *Vocational Guidance Quarterly* 16 (December 1967):125-129. Bibliography.

Cotton, Stephen. "Black Power—Capitalist Slow Down," *New Republic* 161 (September 27,

1969):15-16. Outlines the vagueness and slow pace of Nixon's program to improve the ghetto economy, specifically from the Office of Minority Business Enterprise.

Cross, Theodore L. *Black Capitalism: Strategy for Business in the Ghetto.* New York: Atheneum, 1969. A critical assessment of government and private economic "seed" programs. Argument for locally financed black enterprises is supported by illustrative methods and a descriptive list of black enterprises.

Dammann, George H. "Negro Companies Striving to Gain Identity in Own Market," *National Underwriter* (Life Ed.) 72 (August 10, 1968):1+.

Davis, Milton O. "Green Money, Black Business," *New City* 6 (December 1968):10-13. Need for white financial community to infuse risk capital and private credit to build a viable economic base in the ghetto.

"Dialogue: Corporate Aid vs. Community Control," *New Generation* 50 (Spring 1968):22-23.

Ebright, J. N. "Watts Manufacturing Company: The Prototype of the Ghetto Company," *Business Lawyer* 25 (September 1969):107+.

Farmer, Richard N. "Black Businessmen in Indiana," *Indiana Business Review* 43 (November-December 1968):11-16.

Fitzhugh, H. Naylor, ed. *Problems and Opportunities in the Field of Business.* Washington: U.S. Department of Commerce, 1962.

Foley, Eugene P. "The Negro Businessman: In Search of a Tradition," *Daedalus* 95 (Winter 1966):107-144. An examination of why Negro business has not developed in America, with suggestions of steps that are most needed to encourage future development. Tables.

Frazier, E. Franklin. "Some Aspects of Negro Business," *Opportunity* 2 (October 1924):293-297.

Garrity, John T. "Red Ink for Ghetto Industries," *Harvard Business Review* 46 (May-June 1968):4-16+. Discusses the economic realities and the options to be balanced against emotional appeals in implementing employment opportunities in the ghetto.

Glazer, Nathan. "The Missing Bootstrap," *Saturday Review* 52 (August 23, 1969):19-21+.

Goodwin, Carl R. "Public Relations Volunteers Help New Negro Company; How a Cleveland Counseling Firm Serves an Infant Black Enterprise on a Deferred Payment Basis," *Public Relations Journal* 25 (February 1969):26.

Harris, Abram L. *The Negro as Capitalist.* Philadelphia: American Academy of Political and Social Science, 1936. Still useful for reference.

Henderson, Carter. "Helping Negro Business Prosper," *Nation's Business* 56 (August 1968):50-55. Includes a discussion of the Interracial Council for Business Opportunity.

Hodge, J. L., et al., comps. "Bibliography of Minority-Group Business Leaders," *Business Education World* 49 (January 1969):22-24.

Hunter, Charlayne. "The New Black Businessmen," *Saturday Review* 52 (August 23, 1969):27-29+.

Javitts, Jacob K. "Big Business and the Ghetto," *New Generation* 50 (Spring 1968):2-6. Suggests training programs for entrepreneurs and managers.

Jones, Thomas B. *How the Negro Can Start His Own Business.* New York: Pilot Books, 1968.

Kentucky Commission on Human Rights. *Black Business in Louisville.* Louisville, Kentucky, 1968. Survey indicating the dearth of black entrepreneurial enterprises.

Kinzer, Robert H., and Edward Sagarin. *The Negro in American Business.* New York: Greenberg, 1950. Examines the dilemma of separation or integration for Negro business. Statistics are out of date, but still useful as background. Authors advocate joint development of "the separate and the integrated philosophies of business."

Kurland, Norman G., and Norman A. Bailey. "The Crawfordville Story," *Columbia Forum* 2 (Fall 1968):28-32. A Georgia textile enterprise owned and managed by previously unemployed Negroes.

Levine, Charles H. "The Dilemma of the Black Businessman: A New Approach?" *Indiana Business Review* 44 (March-April 1969):12-13+.

Levitan, Sar. A., and Robert Taggart. "Developing Business in the Ghetto," *Conference Board Record* 6 (July 1969):13-21.

Levitan, Sar A., and Robert Taggart. "Entrepreneurship—Another Option toward Equal Opportunity," *Poverty and Human Resources Abstract* 4, no. 2 (1969):15-22. Includes a discussion of the proposed Community Self-Determination bill and the role of the Small Business Administration.

Lipset, Seymour M., and Reinhard Bendix. *Social Mobility in Industrial Society.* Berkeley: University of California Press, 1960. Emphasizing that it is the rate of economic expansion which is most significant in determining extent of social mobility, the authors point out factors inhibiting Negroes from sharing economic opportunities of expansion.

McKersie, Robert B. "Vitalize Black Enterprise; With the Emphasis on Jobs, the Condition of Negro-Owned Business—Crucial for the Ghettos' Economic Health—Has Been Neglected," *Harvard Business Review* 46 (September–October 1968):88–99.

McPeak, William. "A Plea for Cooperatives," *Interracial Review* 36 (November 1963): 215–217. As a means of relieving economic disabilities, Negroes should establish credit cooperatives, housing cooperatives, marketing cooperatives.

"Negro-Owned and Managed Plant Fills Big Ghetto Need—Jobs," *Modern Manufacturing* 1 (September 1968):80–81. Progress Aerospace Enterprises, Philadelphia.

"Negroes and Business Ownership," *Banking* 61 (September 1968):57.

"An Open Letter to the President on Minority Enterprise: A Ripon Paper," *Ripon Forum* 5 (July 1969):7–9. Specific ideas to encourage black capitalism.

Patterson, William L. "Mr. A. D. Fuller and Negro Unity," *Political Affairs* 43 (February 1964):57–59. Remarks on speech by Negro millionaire before the National Association of Manufacturers.

Petrof, John V. "Customer Strategy for Negro Retailers," *Journal of Retailing* 43 (Fall 1967):30–38.

Petrof, John V. "Negro Entrepreneurship: Myth or Reality?" *Marquette Business Review* 13 (Spring 1969):34–37.

Pierce, J. A. *Negro Business and Business Education.* New York: Harper, 1947. Still useful as general study, both for its examination, in part I, of the characteristics and structure of Negro business, and for its recommendations, in part II, for preparing Negroes for greater participation in business.

"Project Own Gets Going," *Banking* 61 (February 1969):26. Small Business Association's project to foster Negro-owned business.

Puth, Robert C. "Supreme Life: The History of a Negro Life Insurance Company, 1919–1962," *Business History Review* 43 (Spring 1969):1–20.

"Putting Blacks in the Black," *Nation's Business* 56 (December 1968):58–60+.

Rein, Martin. "Social Stability and Black Capitalism," *Trans-action* 6 (June 1969):4+.

Rendon, Armando. "Portland Blacks Get Their Company Thing Together," *Civil Rights Digest* (1969):15–25.

Samuels, Howard J. "Black Capitalism in the Ghetto," *Employment Service Review* 5 (October–November 1968):6–8. Attention to the role of the Small Business Administration.

Samuels, Howard. "How to Even the Odds," *Saturday Review* 52 (August 23, 1969):22–26.

Sherwood, Hugh C. "Franchising: Big Business Cashes in on the American Dream," *Business Management* 34 (August 1968):26–34. Opportunities for Negroes in franchised enterprises.

Sturdivant, Frederick D. "The Limits of Black Capitalism," *Harvard Business Review* 47 (January–February 1969):122–128. Critical of the proposed Congressional legislation to create community-owned development corporations in disadvantaged areas.

"Symposium on Black Capitalism," *Bankers Monthly* 152 (Spring 1969):10–46.

"Training for Black Bankers," *Banking* 61 (March 1969):36–37.

U.S. Congress. Senate. Committee on Small Business. *Economic Development Opportunity: Hearings before the Select Committee on Small Business on the Role of the Federal Government in the Development of Small Business Enterprises in the Urban Ghetto.* Washington: U.S. Govt. Print. Off., 1968. (90th Congress, 2d Session). Bibliographical footnotes.

White, Wilford L. "The Negro Entrepreneur," *Occupational Outlook Quarterly* 10 (February 1966):19–22.

White, Wilford L. "They Mind Their Own Business: University Small Business Guidance Center," *American Education* 4 (March 1968):8–11. Describes the 19 business guidance centers begun in 1964 as a division of Howard University's Department of Business Administration. Object: to serve Negro businessmen from low-income areas.

Whitney, C. A. "Black Banks Are Good Business," *Bankers Magazine* 152 (Spring
    1969):20–24.
Young, Harding B., and James M. Hund. "Negro Entrepreneurship in Southern Economic
    Development," in Melvin L. Greenhut and W. Tate Whitman, eds., *Essays in Southern
    Economic Development.* Chapel Hill: University of North Carolina Press, 1964.
Young, Harding B. "The Negro's Participation in American Business," *Journal of Negro
    Education* 32 (Fall 1963):390–401.

14 Employment

Historical Background

Bloch, Howard D. "Labor and the Negro, 1866-1910," *Journal of Negro History* 50 (July 1965):163-184.

Bradford, S. Sydney. "The Negro Ironworker in Ante-Bellum Virginia," *Journal of Southern History* 25 (May 1959):194-206.

Fosner, Philip S., ed. "Knights of Labor," (with text of letters) *Journal of Negro History* 53 (January 1968):70-77.

Ginzberg, Eli., and Hyman Berman. *The American Worker in the Twentieth Century: A History Through Biographies.* New York: Free Press, 1963. An attempt to portray American labor history through the words of the workers themselves. Includes some life histories of Negro workers, especially from the years since 1941.

Gutman, Herbert G., ed. "Black Coal Miners and the Greenback Labor Party in Redeemer, Alabama: 1878-1879," *Labor History* 10 (Summer 1969):506-535. Letters written by black and white coal miners to the *Pittsburgh National Labor Tribune* in the period following the Reconstruction.

Mandel, Bernard. "Samuel Gompers and the Negro Workers, 1886-1914," *Journal of Negro History* 49 (January 1955):234-260.

Marcus, Irvin M. "The Southern Negro and the Knights of Labor," *Negro History Bulletin* 30 (March 1967):5-7.

Marshall, Ray. *The Negro Worker.* New York: Random, 1967. History of the Negro worker, the Negro and the unions, economic conditions, and public policy. Bibliography.

Meier, August, and Elliott Rudwick. "The Rise of Segregation in the Federal Bureaucracy, 1900-1930," *Phylon* 28 (Summer 1967):178-184.

Porter, Kenneth O. "Negro Labor in the Western Cattle Industry, 1866-1900," *Labor History* 10 (Summer 1969):346-374.

Rogers, William Warren. "Negro Knights of Labor in Arkansas: A Case Study of the 'Miscellaneous' Strike," *Labor History* 10 (Summer 1969):498-505. Details of a wage dispute in 1896.

Ross, Arthur M., and Herbert Hill, eds. *Employment, Race and Poverty.* New York: Harcourt, Brace & World, 1967. Jacket subtitle: "A critical study of the disadvantaged status of Negro workers from 1865 to 1965." Broad, authoritative coverage of subject in 20 papers. The third volume of research and conferences on "Unemployment and the American Economy," Institute of Industrial Relations, University of California, Berkeley. Essays discuss and assess the Negro's position in the labor market; the role of government, management, and labor; legal responses to employment discrimination; social effects of unemployment; programs for guidance and training.

Tuttle, William M., Jr. "Labor Conflict and Racial Violence: The Black Workers in Chicago, 1894-1919," *Labor History* 10 (Summer 1969):408-432.

Wagstaff, Thomas. "Call Your Old Master—'Master': Southern Political Leaders and Negro Labor during Presidential Reconstruction," *Labor History* 10 (Summer 1969):323-345.

Walker, Joseph E. "A Comparison of Negro and White Labor in a Charcoal Iron Industry," *Labor History* 10 (Summer 1969):487-497. In Berks County, Pennsylvania, 1805-1853. Includes tabular presentation.

Walker, Joseph E. "Negro Labor in the Charcoal Iron Industry of Southeastern Pennsylvania," *Pennsylvania Magazine of History and Biography* 93 (October 1969):466-486.

Walters, Raymond. "Section 7a and the Black Worker," *Labor History* 10 (Summer 1969): 459-474. Section of the National Industrial Recovery Act. The Negro and New Deal legislation.

Worthman, Paul B. "Black Workers and Labor Unions in Birmingham, Alabama, 1897-1904," *Labor History* 10 (Summer 1969):375-407.

The Law, the Courts, and Regulatory Action

Aaron, Benjamin. "The Labor-Management Reporting and Disclosure Act of 1959," *Harvard Law Review* 73 (March 1960):858-907.

Bamberger, Michael A., and Nathan Levin. "The Right to Equal Treatment: Administrative Enforcement of Antidiscrimination Legislation," *Harvard Law Review* 74 (January 1961):526-589.

Barone, Sam. "The Impact of Recent Developments in Civil Rights on Employers and Unions," *Labor Law Journal* 17 (July 1966):413-440. Argues the inadequacy of current legislation to ensure equal employment opportunity. Cases cited to substantiate.

Becker, William. "After FEPC—What?" *Journal of Intergroup Relations* 3 (Fall 1962): 337-343. Discrimination in apprenticeship programs and its effect.

Berger, Morroe. *Equality by Statute: Legal Controls over Group Discrimination.* New York: Columbia University Press, 1952. A study based on the New York State law against discrimination.

Birnbaum, O. "Equal Employment Opportunity and Executive Order 10925," *University of Kansas Law Review* 11 (October 1962):17-34.

Blumrosen, Alfred W. "Duty of Fair Recruitment Under the Civil Rights Act of 1964," *Rutgers Law Review* 22 (Spring 1968):465-508.

Bullock, Paul. *Merit Employment: Non-Discrimination in Industry.* Los Angeles: Institute of Industrial Relations, UCLA, 1960. A brief history of fair employment regulations, with a description of various federal and local programs.

Bureau of National Affairs, Washington D. C. *The Civil Rights Act of 1964: Text, Analysis, Legislative History: What it means to Employers, Businessmen, Unions, Employees, Minority Groups.* Washington, 1964.

Christopher, Maurine. "Television," *Nation* 207 (August 5, 1968):93-94. Federal Communications Commission's policy on discrimination against blacks in radio and television employment and programming.

"The Controversy Over the 'Equal Opportunity' Provisions of the Civil Rights Bill," *Congressional Digest* 43 (March 1964):67-96.

Cox, Archibald. "The Duty of Fair Representation," *Villanova Law Review* 2 (January 1957):151-177. Admonitions addressed to labor unions.

"Discrimination in Employment and in Housing: Private Enforcement Provisions of the Civil Rights Act of 1964 and 1968," *Harvard Law Review* 82 (February 1969):834-863.

"Discrimination in the Hiring and Assignment of Teachers in Public School Systems," *Michigan Law Review* 64 (February 1966):692-702.

"Discrimination in Union Membership: Denial of Due Process under Federal Collective Bargaining Legislation," *Rutgers Law Review* 12 (Summer 1958):543-556.

Donahue, Charles. "Equal Employment Opportunity," *Federal Bar Journal* 24 (Winter 1964):76-86. The Author, Solicitor, Department of Labor, discusses inequities in hiring practices and discriminative practices within certain unions.

Ellis, Greeley H., Jr. "The Constitutional Right to Membership in a Labor Union—Fifth and Fourteenth Amendments," *Journal of Public Law* 8 (Fall 1959):580-595.

"Employment Discrimination: State FEPC Laws and the Impact of Title VII of the Civil Rights Act of 1964," *Western Reserve Law Review* 16 (May 1965):608.

"Equal Employment Opportunity in the United States: The Civil Rights Act of 1964," *International Labour Review* 90 (October 1964):377-379.

Garfinkel, Herbert, and Michael D. Cahn. "Racial-Religious Designations, Preferential Hiring and Fair Employment Practices Commissions," *Labor Law Journal* 20 (June 1969):357-372.

Ginsburg, Gilbert J. "Non-discrimination in Employment: Executive Order 10925," *Military Law Review* 1961 (October 1961):141.

Good, Earle Williamson. "Minimum Wage Law Bar to Jobless Negro Teens," *Barron's*, January 27, 1969, pp. 28-29.

Gould, William B. "The Emerging Law Against Racial Discrimination in Employment," *Northwestern University Law Review* 64 (July-August 1969):359-386.

Gould, William B. "Employment Security, Seniority and Race: The Role of Title VII of the Civil Rights Act of 1964," *Howard Law Journal* 13 (Winter 1967):1-50. Proposal for action to be taken by the Equal Employment Opportunities Commission to improve seniority conditions for Negro employees.

Gould, William B. "Seniority and the Black Worker: Reflections on *Quarles* and Its Implications," *Texas Law Review* 47 (June 1969):1039-1074.

Groves, H. E. "States as 'Fair' Employers," *Howard Law Journal* 7 (Winter 1961):1-16.

Gutman, D., ed. "Discrimination in Employment and Housing: A Symposium," *New York Law Forum* 6 (January 1960):1+.

Hartman, Paul. *Comparative Analysis of State Fair Employment Practices Laws.* New York: Anti-Defamation League, 1962.

Hill, Herbert, et al. "Twenty Years of State Fair Employment Practice Commissions: A Critical Analysis with Recommendations," *Buffalo Law Review* 14 (Fall 1964):22-78.

Jenkins, Timothy Lionel. "Study of Federal Effort to End Job Bias: A History, a Status Report, and a Prognosis," *Howard Law Journal* 14 (Summer 1968):259-329.

King, Robertson L. "Protecting Rights of Minority Employees," *Labor Law Journal* 11 (February 1960):143-154.

Kovarsky, Irving. "The Negro and Fair Employment," *Kentucky Law Journal* 56 (Summer 1967-1968):757-829. Historical survey of employment practices traced through major legal decisions.

Kovarsky, Irving. "Some Social and Legal Aspects of Testing under the Civil Rights Act," *Labor Law Journal* 20 (June 1969):346-356.

Levitan, S. A. *Youth Employment Act.* Kalamazoo, Mich.: Upjohn Institute for Employment Research, 1963.

Lunden, Leon E. *Antidiscrimination Provisions in Major Contracts, 1961.* Washington: U.S. Department of Labor, Bureau of Labor Statistics, 1962. (Bulletin no. 1336)

Maloney, W. H., Jr. "Racial and Religious Discrimination in Employment and the Role of the NLRB," *Maryland Law Review* 21 (Summer 1961):219-232.

Morgan, Chester A. "An Analysis of State FEPC Legislation," *Labor Law Journal* 8 (July 1957):478.

"NAACP Wants Legal Labor Guidelines," *Engineering News-Record* 182 (May 22, 1969):170.

"A 'New' Weapon to Combat Racial Discrimination in Employment: The Civil Rights Act of 1866: *Dobbins v. Local 212, International Brotherhood of Electrical Workers,*" *Maryland Law Review* 29 (Spring 1969):158-176.

Norgren, Paul H., and Samuel Hill, with the assistance of F. Ray Marshall. *Toward Fair Employment.* New York: Columbia University Press, 1964. An important work which includes a survey of racial discrimination arising either from management or union practices, and an examination and assessment of all FEP laws and executive orders. The authors also advance proposals for what they consider the most effective legislation, together with suggestions for improving the administration of laws and regulations.

Rabkin, Sol. "Enforcement of Laws against Discrimination in Employment," *Buffalo Law Review* 14 (Fall 1964):100-113.

"Racial Discrimination and the Duty of Fair Representation," *Columbia Law Review* 65
   (February 1965):273–287. Racial discrimination is subject to the remedies of the Na-
   tional Labor Relations Act.
"Racial Discrimination in Employment under the Civil Rights Act of 1866," *University of
   Chicago Law Review* 36 (Spring 1969):615–641.
"Racial Discrimination in Union Membership," *University of Miami Law Review* 13 (Spring
   1959):364–369.
"Racial Employment Picketing: Availability and Extent of Injunctive Relief," *Minnesota
   Law Review* 51 (November 1966):92–114.
"Remedies Available to a Victim of Employment Discrimination," *Ohio State Law Journal*
   29 (Spring 1968):456+. Ohio fair employment practices law and federal compliance
   regulations.
Ruchames, Louis. *Race, Jobs, and Politics: The Story of FEPC.* New York: Columbia
   University Press, 1953.
Screiber, Harry N. "The Thirteenth Amendment and Freedom of Choice in Personal Service
   Occupations: A Reappraisal," *Cornell Law Quarterly* 49 (Spring 1964):508–514.
Shirk, E. M. "Cases are People: An Interpretation of the Pennsylvania Fair Employment
   Practice Law," *Dickinson Law Review* 62 (June 1958):289–305.
Shostak, Arthur. "Appeals from Discrimination in Federal Employment: A Case Study,"
   Social Forces 42 (December 1963):174–178. Study of appeals records in 27 cases,
   1952–1962, in a Northeastern federal manufacturing center. Most of the cases involved
   the failure of Negroes to secure promotion; only one was decided in appellant's favor.
Sovern, Michael I. *Legal Restraints on Racial Discrimination in Employment.* New York:
   Twentieth Century Fund, 1966. Bibliography.
Spitz, H. "Tailoring the Techniques to Eliminate and Prevent Employment Discrimination,"
   Buffalo Law Review 14 (Fall 1964):79–99.
"Title VI of the Civil Rights Act of 1964—Implementation and Impact," *George Washington
   Law Review* 36 (May 1968):824–1015. Text of Title VI. See especially pp. 1007–1015.
"Title VII, Seniority Discrimination and the Incumbent Negro," *Harvard Law Review* 80
   (April 1967):1260–1283.
"Toward Equal Opportunity in Employment," *Buffalo Law Review* 14 (Fall 1964):1+.
   Entire issue devoted to reports of a conference held at the University of Buffalo Law
   School.
Tower, John. "FEPC—Some Practical Considerations," *Federal Bar Journal* 24 (Winter
   1964):87–92. The author, U.S. Senator from Texas, attacks general proposition that
   discrimination is illegal and maintains that FEPC has been given arbitrary power to
   "ram . . . racial quotas" down the throats of employers.
U.S. Commission on Civil Rights. *Equal Employment Opportunities Under the Federal Law.*
   Washington: U.S. Govt. Print. Off., 1969. (CCR publication no. 17)
U.S. Congress. House. *Equal Employment Opportunity: Hearings before the Special Subcommittee on Labor of the Committee on Education and Labor, October 23, 1961–January 24,
   1962.* Washington: U.S. Govt. Print Off., 1962. (87th Congress, 1st and 2d Sessions)
U.S. Congress. House. *Equal Opportunity in Apprenticeship Programs: Hearings before the
   Special Subcommittee on Labor of the Committee on Education and Labor, August 21–23,
   1961.* Washington: U.S. Govt. Print. Off., 1961. (87th Congress, 1st Session)
U.S. Congress. Senate. *Equal Employment Opportunities Enforcement Act. Report Together
   with Minority, Individual and Supplemental Views from the Committee on Labor and Public
   Welfare to Accompany S 3465.* Washington, 1968. (90th Congress, 2d Session, Senate
   Report 1111). Corrected print.
U.S. Equal Employment Opportunity Commission. *First Annual Report.* Washington: U.S.
   Govt. Print. Off., 1967. Report of fiscal year, 1966. Also issued as House Document no.
   86 of the 90th Congress, 1st Session.
U.S. Equal Employment Opportunity Commission. *Second Annual Report.* Washington: U.S.
   Govt. Print. Off., 1968. Covers fiscal year 1967. Also issued as House Document no. 326
   of the 90th Congress, 2d Session.
U.S. Equal Employment Opportunity Commission. *Hearings before the . . . Commission on*

Discrimination in White Collar Employment, January 15-18, 1968. Washington: U.S. Govt. Print. Off., 1968.

Weiss, L. "Federal Remedies for Racial Discrimination by Labor Unions," *Georgetown Law Journal* 50 (Spring 1962):457-477.

Winter, Ralph K., Jr. "Improving the Economic Status of Negroes through Laws against Discrimination: A Reply to Professor Sovern," *University of Chicago Law Review* 34 (Summer 1967):817-855. A reply to Sovern's views expressed in *Legal Restraints on Racial Discrimination in Employment.*

Woll, J. Albert. "Labor Looks at Equal Rights in Employment," *Federal Bar Journal* 24 (Winter 1964):98 + . The author, general counsel for the AFL-CIO, maintains that Titles VI and VII of the Civil Rights Bill are reasonable and provide ample opportunity for voluntary compliance.

Patterns and Conditions

Abts, Henry W. "A Positive Policy," *Employment Service Review* 4 (March-April 1967):10-11 + . Managerial attitude toward the Negro.

Aiken, Michael, Louis A. Ferman, and Harold L. Sheppard. "Race and Unemployment," in *Economic Failure, Alienation, and Extremism.* Ann Arbor: University of Michigan Press, 1968, pp. 130-151. A study of 45 Negro workers who were displaced by the closing of the Packard plant.

Aiken, Michael, and Louis A. Ferman. "Social and Political Reactions of Older Negroes to Unemployment," *Phylon* 27 (Winter 1966):333-346.

Apprenticeship Training in New York Openings in 1963. New York: Workers Defense League, 1963.

Babow, Irving, and Edward Howden. *A Civil Rights Inventory of San Francisco: Part I, Employment.* San Francisco: Council for Civic Unity, 1958.

Bancroft, Gertude. *The American Labor Force: Its Growth and Changing Composition.* New York: Wiley, 1958. Statistics and description of trends and patterns since 1890. Data on white and nonwhite components of labor force considered in this changing context. Volume in Census Monograph Series, prepared for Social Science Research Council in cooperation with U.S. Department of Commerce.

Baron, Harold. "Negro Unemployment: A Case Study," *New University Thought* 3 (September-October 1963):279-282.

Barrett, Richard S. "Gray Areas in Black and White Testing," *Harvard Business Review* 46 (January-February 1968):92-95.

Becker, Gary S. "Discrimination and the Occupational Progress of Negroes: A Comment," *Review of Economics and Statistics* 44 (May 1962):214-215.

Bienstock, Herbert. "The Employment Outlook: What the Statistics Show," *New Generation* 50 (Winter 1968):2-6. The Negro's non-job position is shown to be about twice the white unemployment rate.

Blalock, H. M., Jr. "Occupational Discrimination: Some Theoretical Propositions," *Social Problems* 9 (Winter 1962):240-247.

Bloch, Herman D. "Employment Status of the New York Negro in Retrospect," *Phylon* 20 (December 1959):327-344.

Blocker, J. Lester. "Under-Employed Human Resources—Problem or Opportunity," *Personnel Administration* 14 (May 1969):8-11. A plea for consideration of qualified Negroes for executive positions.

Blood, Robert O. *Northern Breakthrough.* Belmont, Calif.: Wadsworth, 1968. Employment outlook in the twin cities.

Bloom, Robert, and John R. Berry. "Determinants of Work Attitudes among Negroes," *Journal of Applied Psychology* 51 (June 1967):291-294.

Blum, Albert A. "Securing Skills Needed for Success: Community Job Training for Negroes," *Management of Personnel Quarterly* 5 (Fall 1966):30-35.

Blumrosen, Alfred W. "Job Seniority and Discrimination," *Monthly Labor Review* 92 (March 1969):52-53. Excerpted from "Discrimination in the Union and on the Job," in Industrial Relations Research Association, *Proceedings*. Madison, Wis.: 1969.

Buckley, Louis F. "Discriminatory Aspects of The Labor Market of the 60's," *Review of Social Economy* 19 (March 1961):25-42.

Buckley, Louis F. "Nonwhite Employment in the United States," *Interracial Review* 36 (February 1963):32-33.

Burck, Gilbert. "New Business for Business: Reclaiming Human Resources," *Fortune* 77 (January 1968):158-161 +. Productive use of hard-core unemployed, mostly Negro, by selected companies nationwide.

"Business, Labor, and Jobs in the Ghetto: A Staff Survey," *Issues in Industrial Society* 1 (1969):3-18. Focuses on apprenticeship programs devised by business, labor, and other organizations. Discussion also includes small firm enterprises in the ghetto and unions in Watts.

Campbell, Joel T., and Leon H. Belcher. "Changes in Nonwhite Employment, 1960-1966," *Phylon* 28 (Winter 1967):325-337. Compares and evaluates changes in Negro employment for the two periods 1960-1963 and 1963-1966.

Chalmers, W. Ellison, and Nathaniel W. Dorsey. "Research on Negro Job Status," *Journal of Intergroup Relations* 3 (Fall 1962):344-359.

"Changing Status of Negro Woman Workers," *Monthly Labor Review* 87 (June 1964): 671-673.

"Chicago Negroes Push for Jobs," *Engineering News-Record* 183 (August 14, 1969):11. Article is illustrative of Negro employment as viewed by a business-oriented trade journalist.

Cohen, Albert K., and Harold M. Hodges. "Characteristics of the Lower-Blue-Collar Class," *Social Problems* 10 (Spring 1963):303-334.

Daniel, W. G. "The Relative Employment and Income of American Negroes," *Journal of Negro Education,* 32 (Fall 1963):349-357.

Decker, Paul M. "A Study of Job Opportunities in the State of Florida for Negro College Graduates," *Journal of Negro Education* 29 (Winter 1960):93-95.

Dewey, Donald. *Four Studies of Negro Employment in the Upper South.* Washington: National Planning Association, 1953.

Dewey, Donald. "Negro Employment in Southern Industry," *Journal of Political Economy* 60 (August 1952):279-293.

Dewey, Donald. "Southern Poverty and the Racial Division of Labor," *New South* 17 (May 1962):3-5, 11-13. Penetrating and thorough studies of Negro employment in the South.

Doeringer, Peter B. "Discriminatory Promotion Systems," *Monthly Labor Review* 90 (March 1967):27-28.

Doeringer, Peter B. "Labor Market Report from the Boston Ghetto," *Monthly Labor Review* 92 (March 1969):55-56. Excerpted from paper "Ghetto Labor Markets and Manpower Programs," in the Industrial Relations Research Association, *Proceedings*. Madison, Wis., 1969.

Duncan, Otis D., and Beverly Duncan. *The Negro Population of Chicago: A Study of Residential Succession.* Chicago: University of Chicago Press, 1957. Occupational patterns also examined.

Eatherly, Billy J. "The Occupational Progress of Mississippi Negroes 1940-1960," *Mississippi Quarterly* 21 (Winter 1967-1968):49-62. Progress measured against that of Mississippi whites, using a quantitative index.

Eckstein, Otto. *Education, Employment, and Negro Equality.* Washington: U.S. Department of Labor, Manpower Administration, 1968.

"Employment Discrimination," *Race Relations Law Reporter* 5 (Summer 1960):569-592.

Erskine, Hazel. "The Polls: Negro Employment," *Public Opinion Quarterly* 32 (Spring 1968):132-135. Tabulations on: job discrimination, Negro competence, willingness to work, occupational prejudice, the government in fair employment, and politics in Negro employment. Covers the period 1935 to date.

Ferman, Louis A., Joyce L. Kornbluh, and J. A. Miller, eds. *Negroes and Jobs: A Book of Readings.* Ann Arbor: University of Michigan Press, 1968. Carefully selected articles which provide an understanding of the social, psychological, and institutional deterrants to the Negro's rise in the labor mart. Chapter bibliographies.

Florida Council on Human Relations. "Negro Employment in Miami," *New South* 17 (May 1962):6-10.

Formby, John P. "Extent of Wage and Salary Discrimination against Non-White Labor," *Southern Economic Journal* 35 (October 1968):140-150.

Gallaher, Art, Jr. *The Negro and Employment Opportunities in the South—Houston.* Atlanta: Southern Regional Council, 1961.

Gibbs, Jack P. "Occupational Differentiation of Negroes and Whites in the United States," *Social Forces* 44 (December 1965):159-165.

Ginzberg, Eli, et al. *The Middle-Class Negro in the White Man's World.* New York: Columbia University Press, 1967.

Ginzberg, Eli, and Hyman Berman. "The Negro's Problem is the White's," *New York Times Magazine,* February 9, 1964, pp. 14+.

Glenn, Norval D. "Changes in the American Occupational Structure and Occupational Gains of Negroes during the 1940's," *Social Forces* 41 (December 1962):188-195.

Glenn, Norval D. "Some Changes in the Relative Status of American Non-whites, 1940-1960," *Phylon* 24 (Summer 1963):109-122. Relative changes in occupation, employment, income, and educational status.

Glenn, Norval D. "White Gains from Negro Subordination," *Social Problems* 14 (Fall 1966):159-178.

Goeke, Joseph R., and Caroline S. Weymar. "Barriers to Hiring the Blacks," *Harvard Business Review* 47 (September-October 1969):144-149+.

Gottlieb, David, and Jay Campbell, Jr. "Winners and Losers in the Race for the Good Life: A Comparison of Blacks and Whites," *Social Science Quarterly* 49 (December 1968):593-602. How race affects occupational aspiration and achievement.

Gould, William B. "Labor Arbitration of Grievances Involving Racial Discrimination," *University of Pennsylvania Law Review* 118 (November 1969):40-68.

Gourlay, Jack G. *The Negro Salaried Worker.* New York: American Management Association, 1965.

Greenwald, William, and Robert E. Weintraub. "Money Benefits of Education by Sex and Race in New York State, 1956," *Journal of Educational Sociology* 34 (March 1961):312-319.

Hare, Nathan. "Recent Trends in the Occupational Mobility of Negroes, 1930-1960: An Intracohort Analysis," *Social Forces* 44 (December 1965):166-173.

Harper, R. M. "Racial Contrasts in Income," *Alabama Lawyer* 21 (July 1960):257-260.

Hawley, Langston T. *Negro Employment in the Birmingham Metropolitan Area.* Washington: National Planning Association, 1954.

Hentoff, Nat. "Race Prejudice in Jazz," *Harper's* 218 (June 1959):72-77.

Hiestand, Dale L. *Economic Growth and Employment Opportunities for Minorities.* New York: Columbia University Press, 1964. Introduction by Eli Ginzberg. The author finds the labor demand factor more important for the Negro than supply. Opportunities for Negro workers tend to open up chiefly to replace white workers with better opportunities, that is, in declining occupational areas with little long-run significance. Bibliography.

Hiestand, Dale L. *White Collar Employment Opportunities for Minorities in New York City.* Washington: Equal Employment Opportunities Commission, 1967. Employment patterns and statistics for Negroes and Puerto Ricans.

Hill, Herbert. "Employment, Manpower Training and the Black Worker," *Journal of Negro Education* 38 (Summer 1969):204-217.

Hill, Herbert. "Patterns of Employment Discrimination," *Crisis* 69 (March 1962):137-147.

Hill, Herbert. "Racial Discrimination in the Nation's Apprenticeship Training Program," *Phylon* 23 (Fall 1962):215-224.

Hill, Norman. "Which Jobs for Blacks," *New Generation* 50 (Winter 1968):7-10.

Hodge, Claire C. "The Negro Job Situation: Has It Improved?" *Monthly Labor Review* 92 (January 1969):20–28. Despite recent occupational gains, the Negro today is shown to hold a larger share of lower occupational jobs than the white worker. Statistical tables and charts.

Hope, John, II. "Central Role of Intergroup Agencies in the Labor Market: Changing Research and Personnel Requirements," *Journal of Intergroup Relations* 2 (Spring 1961):132–144.

Hope, John, II. "The Employment of Negroes in the United States by Major Occupation and Industry," *Journal of Negro Education* 22 (Summer 1953):307–321. Period 1940–1950.

Hope, John, II, and E. Shelton. "The Negro in the Federal Government," *Journal of Negro Education* 32 (Fall 1963):367–374.

Huson, Carolyn F., and Michael E. Schlitz. *College, Color, and Employment: Racial Differentials in Postgraduate Employment among 1964 Graduates of Louisiana Colleges.* Chicago: National Opinion Research Center, 1966.

Jones, Major J. *The Negro and Employment Opportunities in the South—Chattanooga.* Atlanta: Southern Regional Council, 1962.

Kain, John F. *Coping with Ghetto Unemployment.* Cambridge, Mass.: Program on Regional and Urban Economics, Harvard University, 1968.

Kain, John F. "Housing Segregation, Negro Employment, and Metropolitan Decentralization," *Quarterly Journal of Economics* 82 (May 1968):175–197. See also related article by J. D. Monney *ibid.,* 83 (May 1969):299–311. Also issued as an offprint, Cambridge, Mass. by the Joint Center for Urban Studies, Harvard University and Massachusetts Institute of Technology, 1967.

Kelleher, James F. "Selling Jobs to the Ghetto," *Public Relations Journal* 24 (September 1968):18–21. The meaning of the pledge of jobs for the hard-core unemployed under the National Alliance of Businessmen.

Kidder, Alice Handsaker. "Paths from Poverty to Employment: Job Search among Negroes," *Labor Law Journal* 19 (August 1968):482–488. Discrimination in job search.

Killingsworth, Charles C. *Jobs and Income for Negroes.* Washington: National Manpower Policy Task Force, 1968. References appended. Also published in Irwin Katz and Patricia Gurin, eds., *Race and the Social Sciences.* New York: Basic Books, 1969, pp. 194–273.

Killingsworth, Charles C. "Negro Unemployment: Causes and Cures," *Centennial Review* 10 (Spring 1966):131–146.

King, Carl B., and Howard W. Risher, Jr. *The Negro in the Petroleum Industry.* Philadelphia: University of Pennsylvania, Wharton School of Finance and Commerce. Distributed by University of Pennsylvania Press, 1969.

Klein, Lawrence R. "Racial Patterns of Income and Employment, U.S.A.," *Social and Economic Administration* 1 (January 1967):32–42.

Kovarsky, Irving. "Testing and the Civil Rights Act," *Harvard Law Journal* 15 (Winter 1969):227–249.

Koziara, Edward C., and Karen S. Koziara. *The Negro in the Hotel Industry.* Philadelphia: University of Pennsylvania, Wharton School of Finance and Commerce. Distributed by University of Pennsylvania Press, 1968. Bibliography.

Krislov, Samuel. *The Negro in Federal Employment: The Quest for Equal Opportunity.* Minneapolis: University of Minnesota Press, 1967. Survey based on interviews in federal departments and agencies.

Kuebler, Jeanne. "Negro Jobs and Education," *Educational Research Reports, January 23, 1963.*

Lang, Gladys Engel. "Discrimination in the Hiring Hall," in Aaron Antonovsky and Lewis L. Lorwin, eds., *Discrimination and Low Income.* New York: New School for Social Research, 1959.

Levine, Martin J. "The Private Sector and Negro Employment Problems: Marked Progress Is in Sight towards a Change in Attitude by the Business Community," *M[ichigan] S[tate] U[niversity] Business Topics* 17 (Winter 1969):63–70.

Lieberson, Stanley, and Glen V. Fuguitt. "Negro-White Occupational Differences in the

Absence of Discrimination," *American Journal of Sociology* 73 (September 1967): 188–200.

Longstreth, Thacher. "Rewarding Efforts of a Private Agency—OIC," *Labor Law Journal* 19 (August 1968):472–474. Opportunities Industrialization Center, Philadelphia.

Lurie, Melvin, and Elton Rayack. "Employment Opportunities for Negro Families in 'Satellite' Cities," *Southern Economic Journal* 36 (October 1969):191–195.

Lurie, Melvin, and Elton Rayack. "Racial Differences in Migration and Job Search: A Case Study," *Southern Economic Journal* 33 (July 1966):81–95. Based on a study of the Middletown, Conn. labor market. Concludes that informal method of job search works to perpetuate existing patterns of Negro employment. Proposals are advanced for governmental action to alter this and other existing discriminatory practices. See reply by D. M. Stevens in April 1967 issue.

Luthans, Fred. "Training for Qualification: The Negro Worker's Dilemma," *Training and Development Journal* 22 (October 1968):3–7. Assesses way in which business executives view Negro workers and their qualifications for promotion.

McFarlane, Alexander N. "Leaping the Ghetto Gap," *Conference Board Record* 6 (March 1969):26–28.

Maddox, James G., et al. *The Advancing South; Manpower Prospects and Problems.* New York: Twentieth Century Fund, 1967. Assesses changes in the economy of the South and its effect upon Negro employment. Attention to economic implications of racial discrimination.

Malim, T. H. "Black Hiring: Industry's Two Faces," *Iron Age* 204 (July 24, 1969):43–44.

Marcus, Stanley. "Who Is Responsible? A Businessman Looks at Civil Rights," *Business Horizons* 11 (June 1968):23–28. Neiman Marcus president discusses black employment potential.

Marshall, F. Roy, and Vernon M. Briggs, Jr. *The Negro and Apprenticeship.* Baltimore: Johns Hopkins Press, 1967. Purpose: to identify and recommend methods to improve Negro opportunities in skilled crafts. Reports discrimination in unions and industry.

Meinen, K. L. "Closing the Job Gap," *Employment Service Review* 5 (January–February 1968):6–7. Contends that although job opportunities for Negroes are improving, the pace of progress is decreasing.

Meyer, Burton I. "Racial Discrimination on the Jobsite: Competing Theories and Competing Forums," *UCLA Law Review* 12 (May 1965):1186–1206.

Mihlon, Lawrence F. "Industrial Discrimination—The Skeleton in Everyone's Closet," *Factory* 70 (April 1962):80–87.

Miller, Herman P. "The Job Gap," *New York Times Magazine,* May 8, 1966, pp. 30–31 +. "At peak prosperity the unemployment rate for Negroes now is still higher than that for whites in any of the past three recessions."

Mooney, Joseph D. "Housing Segregation, Negro Employment and Metropolitan Decentralization: An Alternative Perspective," *Quarterly Journal of Economics* 83 (May 1969):299–311. Study based on examination of twenty-five standard metropolitan statistical areas. See also J. Kain's article, *ibid.,* May 1968.

Morgan, Gordon D. "Representation of Negroes and Whites as Employees in the Federal Prison System," *Phylon* 23 (Winter 1962):372–378.

Morrow, Joseph J. "American Negroes—A Wasted Resource," *Harvard Business Review* 35 (January–February 1957):65–74. An examination of the opportunities, problems, advantages, and disadvantages of accelerated hiring of Negroes by business.

Moynihan, Daniel Patrick. "Employment, Income, and the Ordeal of the Negro Family," *Daedalus* 94 (Fall 1965):745–770.

National Citizens' Committee for Community Relations. *Putting the Hard-Core Unemployed into Jobs.* Washington: U.S. Govt. Print. Off., 1968.

National Industrial Conference Board. *Company Experience with Negro Employment.* 2 vols. New York, 1966. (Studies in Personnel Policy no. 201). Summary report of approach of 47 major companies to Negro employment; also 45 case studies. Bibliography.

"Negro Apprentices Nearly Doubled in 18 Months," *Training and Development Journal* 23 (January 1969):18–19.

"Negro Employment Problem," *Dun's Review and Modern Industry* 82 (August 1963): 59–60+.

"The Negro in [School] Administration," *Overview* 2 (June 1961):35–37.

The Negro Wage-Earner and Apprenticeship Training Programs. New York: NAACP, 1960.

"Negroes in Apprenticeship: New York State," *Monthly Labor Review* 83 (September 1960):952–957.

New York City Commission on Human Rights. "Ethnic Survey of Municipal Employees." March 19, 1964. Mimeographed

New York State Commission against Discrimination. *Apprentices, Skilled Craftsmen and the Negro: An Analysis*. 1960.

New York State Commission against Discrimination. *The Banking Industry: Verified Complaints and Informal Investigations*. 1958.

New York State Commission against Discrimination. *Employment in the Hotel Industry*. 1958.

New York State Commission against Discrimination. *The Employment of Negroes as Driver Salesmen in the Baking Industry*. 1960.

New York State Commission against Discrimination. *Nonwhite Unemployment in the U.S. 1947–1958*. 1958.

New York State Commission against Discrimination. *Railroad Employment in New York and New Jersey*. 1958.

New York State Department of Labor. *Jobs, 1960–1970: The Changing Pattern*. Albany, 1960.

Nicol, Helen, with Merci L. Drake. *Negro Women Workers in 1960*. Washington: U.S. Govt. Print. Off., 1964. Prepared for the Women's Bureau, Department of Labor.

Norgren, Paul H., et al. *Employing the Negro in American Industry: A Study of Management Practices*. New York: Industrial Relations Counselors, 1959. A study of 44 firms. Negro employment treated within the framework of industrial relations issues, and the realization of success within this framework.

Northrup, Herbert R. *Intra-Plant Mobility of Negroes: Some Industry Differences*. Philadelphia: Wharton School of Finance and Commerce, University of Pennsylvania, 1968? Prepared for joint meeting of the American Economic Association and the Industrial Relations Research Association.

Northrup, Herbert, and Richard Rowan, eds. *The Negro and Employment Opportunity*. Ann Arbor: University of Michigan, Bureau of Industrial Relations, 1965.

Northrup, Herbert R. *The Negro in the Aerospace Industry*. Philadelphia: University of Pennsylvania, Wharton School of Finance and Commerce. Distributed by University of Pennsylvania Press, 1968.

Northrup, Herbert R. *The Negro in the Automobile Industry*. Philadelphia: University of Pennsylvania, Wharton School of Finance and Commerce. Distributed by University of Pennsylvania Press, 1968.

Northrup, Herbert R., with Alan Batchelder. *The Negro in the Rubber Tire Industry*. Philadelphia: University of Pennsylvania, Wharton School of Finance and Commerce. Distributed by University of Pennsylvania Press, 1969.

Northrup, Herbert R. "Racial Policies of American Industry," *Monthly Labor Review* 90 (July 1967):41–43.

Osburn, Donald D. *Negro Employment in St. Louis, 1966*. Carbondale, Ill.: Southern Illinois University, 1968.

Osburn, Donald D. *Negro Employment in the Textile Industries of North and South Carolina*. Washington: Equal Employment Opportunity Commission, 1966. Bibliography.

Patten, Thomas H., Jr., and Gerald E. Clark, Jr. "Literacy Training and Job Placement of Hard-Core Unemployed Negroes in Detroit," *Journal of Human Resources* 3 (Winter 1968):25–46. Evaluates the training in terms of job placement and social adjustment.

Petshek, Kirk R. "Barriers to Employability of Negroes in White Collar Jobs," in Gerald G. Somers, ed., *The Development and Use of Manpower*. Madison, Wis.: Industrial Relations Research Association, 1968, pp. 105–111. From the *Proceedings of the Industrial Relations Research Association*. Madison, Wis., 1967.

Price, Dan O. "Occupational Changes among Whites and Non-Whites, with Projections for 1970," *Social Science Quarterly* 49 (December 1968):563-572.

Puryear, Mahlon T. "No Time for 'Tragic Ironies,' " *Interracial Review* 36 (February 1963):34-35. Negroes, employment, and technological change.

Quay, William Howard, Jr., with Marjorie C. Denison. *The Negro in the Chemical Industry*. Philadelphia: University of Pennsylvania, Wharton School of Finance and Commerce. Distributed by University of Pennsylvania Press, 1969.

Rayack, Elton. "Discrimination and the Occupational Progress of Negroes," *Review of Economics and Statistics* 43 (May 1961):209-214.

Roberts, Gene, Jr. "Waste of Manpower—Race and Employment in a Southern State," *South Atlantic Quarterly* 61 (Spring 1962):141-150.

Rowan, Richard L. *The Negro in the Steel Industry*. Philadelphia: University of Pennsylvania, Wharton School of Finance and Commerce. Distributed by the University of Pennsylvania Press, 1968.

Ruda, E., and L. E. Abright. "Racial Differences on Selection Instruments Related to Subsequent Job Performance," *Personnel Psychology* 21 (Spring 1968):31-41. Certain personnel tests found irrelevant for Negro applicants.

Rutledge, Aaron L., and Gertrude Zemon Gass. *Nineteen Negro Men: Personality and Manpower Retraining*. San Francisco: Jossey-Bass, 1967. A case study of retraining for practical nursing, with recommendations for wider applications in industry and social services.

Ryan, William F. "Race and Jobs: Uncle Sam's Betrayal," *Progressive* 32 (May 1968):25-28. The author draws from his experience as a New York Democrat in the House of Representatives.

Schwartz, M. "Why They Don't Want to Work," *Personnel Administration* 27 (March 1964):6-10. Study of work motivation of Negroes.

Seidenberg, Jacob. *Negroes in the Work Group*. Ithaca: New York State School of Industrial and Labor Relations, Cornell University, 1950.

Shaeffer, Ruth G. "Big Brother to the Disadvantaged: How a Small Company Handles the Large Problem of Employing 'Unemployables,' " *Conference Board Record* 6 (March 1969):10-15.

Sheppard, Harold L., and Herbert E. Striner. *Civil Rights, Employment, and the Social Status of American Negros*. Kalamazoo, Mich.: Upjohn Institute for Employment Research, 1966. Based on a report prepared for the U.S. Commission on Civil Rights.

Silberman, Charles E. "The Businessman and the Negro," *Fortune* 68 (September 1963): 97-99+. The author, from a survey of a number of representative firms, demonstrates that most of them have done very little to open up job opportunities for Negroes.

Sorkin, Alan L. "Education, Migration and Negro Unemployment," *Social Forces* 47 (March 1969):265-274. Covers Negro employment for the period 1930-1966.

Steele, H. Ellsworth. "Jobs for Negroes: Some North-South Plant Studies," *Social Forces* 32 (December 1953):152-162.

Stevens, David W. "Reply," (to Lurie and Rayack, "Racial Differences in Migration and Job Search . . .,") *Southern Economic Journal* 33 (April 1967):574-577.

Street, James H. *The New Revolution in the Cotton Economy*. Chapel Hill: University of North Carolina Press, 1957. And how it affects labor force.

Strutt, Joseph W. *Survey of Non-White Employees in State Government*. Harrisburg, Penna.: Human Relations Commission, March 1963.

Sullivan, Leon H. "New Trends in the Development of Self-Help in the Inner City," *American Philosophical Society Proceedings* 112 (December 9, 1968):358-361. Manpower training program initiated in 1964 by the Philadelphia Negro community.

Survey of Ohio College and University Placement Offices with Regard to Job Placement of Minority Students. Columbus: Ohio Civil Rights Commission, 1962.

Taeuber, Alma F., Karl E. Taeuber, and Glen G. Cain. "Occupational Assimilation and the Competitive Process: A Reanalysis," *American Journal of Sociology* 72 (November 1966):273-289.

Taylor, David P. "Discrimination and Occupational Wage Differences in the Market for

Unskilled Labor," *Industrial and Labor Relations Review* 21 (April 1968):375–390. Based on a survey in the environs of Chicago.

"Tensions in the Labor Markets," *First National City Bank,* July 1968, pp. 77–81.

Thurow, Lester. "The Determinants of the Occupational Distribution of Negroes," in Conference on the Education and Training of Racial Minorities, 1967, *Proceedings.* Madison: University of Wisconsin, Center for Studies in Vocational and Technical Education, 1968, pp. 187–211. Discussion of the paper follows.

Training of Negroes in the Skilled Trades. Hartford: Connecticut Commission on Civil Rights, 1954. Limited vocational education facilities available to Negroes.

Trooboff, Benjamin M. "Employment Opportunities for Negroes in the Health Related Occupations," *Journal of Negro Education* 38 (Winter 1969):22–31.

Turner, Ralph H. "Occupational Patterns of Inequality," *American Journal of Sociology* 59 (March 1954):437–447.

Turner, Ralph H. "Relative Position of the Negro Male in the Labor Force of Large American Cities," *American Sociological Review* 16 (August 1951):524–529.

U.S. Civil Service Commission. *Study of Minority Group Employment in the Federal Government, 1967.* Washington: U.S. Govt. Print. Off., 1968, pp. 1–151. Tabular presentation concerning the Negro—by category and by geographical area.

U.S. Congress. Joint Economic Committee. *Employment and Manpower Problems in the Cities: Implications of the Report of the National Advisory Commission on Civil Disorders: Hearings, May 28–June 6, 1968.* Washington: U.S. Govt. Print. Off., 1968. (90th Congress, 2d Session)

U.S. Congress. Joint Economic Committee. *Employment and Manpower Problems in the Cities: Implications of the Report of the National Advisory Commission on Civil Disorders. Report, Together with Supplementary Views.* Washington: U.S. Govt. Print. Off., 1968. (90th Congress, 2d Session, Senate Report no. 1568)

U.S. Council of Economic Advisors. *The High Cost of Racial Discrimination in Employment.* Statement presented to the Joint Economic Committee of Congress in September 1962; released by the Southern Regional Council, Atlanta, October 15, 1962.

U.S. Department of Labor. *Negro Women . . . in the Population and the Labor Force.* Washington: Women's Bureau, Wages and Labor Standards Administration, 1967.

U.S. Department of Labor. *Negro Women Workers in 1960.* Washington: U.S. Govt. Print. Off., 1963. (Women's Bureau Bulletin no. 287)

U.S. Department of Labor. Bureau of Labor Statistics. *The Negro in the West: The Negro Worker.* San Francisco, 1967?

U.S. Department of Labor. Manpower Administration. *Finding Jobs for Negroes: A Kit of Ideas for Management.* Washington, 1968.

U.S. Department of Labor. Office of Manpower, Automation, and Training. *Characteristics of 6,000 White and Nonwhite Persons Enrolled in Manpower Development and Training Act Training.* Washington, 1963.

Viorst, J. "Negroes in Science," *Science News Letter* 87 (April 3, 1965):218–219.

Wachtel, Dawn. *The Negro and Discrimination in Employment.* Ann Arbor: Institute of Labor and Industrial Relations, University of Michigan, 1965. Bibliography.

Watson, James H., and G. J. Finley. "Business Support of Education for the Disadvantaged," *Conference Board Record* 5 (May 1968):57–64.

Weaver, Robert C. *Negro Labor: A National Problem.* New York: Harcourt, Brace, 1946. Study of Negro employment opportunities through World War II. Best and most comprehensive work on this subject up to date of publication.

Welch, Finis. "Labor-Market Discrimination: An Interpretation of Income Differences in the Rural South," *Journal of Political Economy* 75 (June 1967):225–240.

Wellman, David. "Jobs-for-Negroes That Flopped," *Business Management* 34 (June 1968):37–44.

Wetzel, James R., and Susan S. Holland. "Poverty Areas of Our Major Cities: The Employment Situation of Negro and White Workers in Metropolitan Areas," *Monthly Labor Review* 89 (October 1966):1105–1110.

Willhelm, Sidney M., and Edwin H. Powell. "Who Needs the Negro?" *Trans-action* 1 (September-October 1964):3-6. Subtitled "From the economics of exploitation to the economics of uselessness." The issue today is "a search for human rights in a world of machines that makes so many human beings utterly dispensable."

Wilson, C. E. "Automation and the Negro: Will We Survive?" *Liberator* 5 (July 1965):8-11. Study of the consequences of automation on the economic life of black workers.

Young, Whitney M., Jr. "The Split-Level Challenge," *Saturday Review* 52 (August 23, 1969):16-18. Inequalities in employment and business opportunities.

See also The Poor.

Employment of Youth

Amos, W. E., and Jane Perry. "Negro Youth and Employment Opportunities," *Journal of Negro Education* 32 (Fall 1963):358-366.

Antonovsky, Aaron, and Melvin J. Lerner. "Negro and White Youth in Elmira," in Aaron Antonovsky and Lewis L. Lorwin, eds., *Discrimination and Low Incomes.* New York: New School for Social Research, 1959.

Bergmann, Barbara R., and David E. Kaun. "Negro and Youth Unemployment," in *Structural Unemployment in the United States.* Washington: U.S. Department of Commerce, 1967, pp. 77-104.

Buckley, Louis F. "Youth Employment Problems," *Interracial Review* 36 (September 1963):174-175.

Good, Earle Williamson. "Minimum Wage Law Bar to Jobless Negro Teens," *Barron's* 49 (January 27, 1969):28-29.

Gurin, Gerald. *Inner-City Negro Youth in a Job Training Project: A Study of Factors Related to Attrition and Job Success.* Ann Arbor: Institute for Social Research, University of Michigan, 1968.

Harrington, Michael. "The New Lost Generation: Jobless Youth," *New York Times Magazine,* May 24, 1964, pp. 13+.

Harwood, Edwin. "Youth Unemployment—A Tale of Two Ghettos," *Public Interest* no. 17 (Fall 1969):78-87. The neighborhood youth corps, especially as related to Negro youths.

Keig, Norman G. "Occupational Aspirations and Labor Force Experience of Negro Youth: A Case Study," *Business and Economic Dimensions* 3 (May 1967):1-5. Selected Negro high school graduates interviewed in 1964 and again in 1966 to determine the impact of the Civil Rights Act on their lives and ambitions.

Michael, Donald. *The Next Generation.* New York: Random, 1965. The author concludes that without long-term, extensive effort to eliminate the sources of low capability, a "Negro menial, unskilled, worker society" will be perpetuated. Report prepared for President's Committee on Juvenile Delinquency and Youth Crime.

Paradis, Adrian A. *Job Opportunities for Young Negroes.* New York: McKay, 1969.

Piker, Jeffry. *Entry into the Labor Force: A Survey of Literature on the Experience of Negro and White Youths.* Ann Arbor: Institute of Labor and Industrial Relations, University of Michigan and Wayne State University, 1968.

Rogers, Charles H., and Benjamin Harris. "Generic Bases of Negro Teen-Age Unemployment: A Preliminary Investigation." Washington: U.S. Department of Labor, Manpower Administration, 1967. Mimeographed.

Russell, R. D. "Experiences of Negro High School Girls with Domestic Placement Agencies," *Journal of Negro Education* 31 (Spring 1962):172-176.

Tucci, Michael A. "Predicted vs. Actual Job Performance of Disadvantaged Negro Youth," *Vocational Guidance Quarterly* 16 (September 1967):45-47.

U.S. Commission on Civil Rights. Michigan State Advisory Committee. *Employment Problems of Non-White Youths.* Washington, 1966. Bibliography.

"Youth and Employment: Scope and Solution," *American Federationist* 75 (June 1968):1-8.
    Jobless plight of many young Negroes, and ways to mitigage it.

See also Education—Elementary and Secondary—Guidance and Occupational Choice.

The Negro and the Labor Movement

"Anti-Discrimination Action in the United States," *International Labour Review* 98 (September 1968):275-276. AFL-CIO building and construction trades pledge affirmative action against discrimination by their local unions.

Bain, M. "Organized Labor and the Negro Worker," *National Review* 14 (June 4, 1963):455.

Battle, Robert, III, and Horace Sheffield. "Trade Union Leadership Council—Experiment in Community Action," *New University Thought* 3 (September-October 1963):34-41. Civil rights and unions in Detroit.

Bell, Daniel. "Reflections on the Negro and Labor," *New Leader* 46 (January 21, 1963): 18-20.

Bell, Daniel, and Seymour M. Lipset, eds. "Trade Unions and Minority Problems," *Journal of Social Issues* 9 (January 1953):2-62. Entire issue.

Black, Tim. "Chicago Negro Labor and Civil Rights," *Freedomways* 6 (Fall 1966):309-314. The author is president of the Chicago chapter of the Negro American Labor Council.

Bloch, Herman D. "Craft Unions, A Link in the Circle of Negro Discrimination," *Phylon* 18 (Winter 1957):361-372.

Bloch, Herman D. "Craft Unions and the Negro in Historical Perspective," *Journal of Negro History* 43 (January 1958):10-33.

Bloch, Herman D. "Negroes and Organized Labor," *Journal of Human Relations* 10 (Summer 1962):357-374.

Boggs, James. "The American Revolution: Pages from a Negro Worker's Notebook," *Monthly Review* 15 (July-August 1963):13-93.

Brooks, Thomas R. "DRUMbeats in Detroit," *Dissent* (January-February 1970):16-25. Dodge Revolutionary Union Movement, the founding group of the League of Revolutionary Black Workers. Note also the sequel article on the rise of black contingents within unions in subsequent issue.

Brooks, Tom. "Negro Militants, Jewish Liberals, and the Unions," *Commentary* 32 (September 1961):209-216.

Brooks, Tom. "The Negro's Place at Labor's Table," *Reporter* 27 (December 6, 1962):38-39.

Carey, James B. "Race Hate: Newest Union-Busting Weapon," *Progressive* 22 (January 1958):16-18.

"The Civil Rights Act of 1964—Racial Discrimination by Labor Unions," *St. John's Law Review* 41 (July, 1966):58-81.

Denby, Charles. "Black Caucuses in the Unions," *New Politics* 7 (Summer 1968):10-17.

Deutermann, William V. "Steelworkers Debate Black Representation," *Monthly Labor Review* 91 (November 1968):16-17.

Doyle, William, et al. "Negroes and the Labor Movement: Record of the 'Left Wing' Unions," *New Politics* 2 (Fall 1962):142-151.

Fleischman, Harry. "Is Labor Color Blind?" *Progressive* 23 (November 1959):24-28.

Fleischman, Harry, and James Rorty. *We Open the Gates: Labor's Fight for Equality.* New York: National Labor Service, 1958.

Gould, William B. "Black Power in the Unions: The Impact upon Collective Bargaining Relationships," *Yale Law Journal* 79 (November 1969):46-84.

Gould, William B. "Racial Equality in Jobs and Unions, Collective Bargaining, and the Burger Court," *Mighigan Law Review* 68 (December 1969):237-258.

Greer, Scott. *Last Man In: Racial Access to Union Power.* Glencoe, Ill.: Free Press, 1959.

Greer, Scott. "The Place of the Negro in the American Labor Movement," *American Review* 1 (Winter 1961):98-109.

Grob, Gerald N. "Organized Labor and the Negro Worker, 1865-1900," *Labor History* 1 (Spring 1960):164-176.

Henle, Peter. "Some Reflections on Organized Labor and the New Militants," *Monthly Labor Review* 92 (July 1969):20-25. Independent black union organizations. Bibliography.

Hennessy, Thomas A. "Black Power—Rebuff in Pittsburgh," *New Republic* 161 (September 27, 1969):18-19. Reports white response to the Black Construction Coalition's move to protest discriminatory hiring practices of the local construction craft unions.

Hill, Herbert. "Black Protest and the Struggle for Union Democracy," *Issues in Industrial Society* 1 (1969):19-29+.

Hill, Herbert. "The ILGWU—Fact and Fiction," *New Politics* 2 (Winter 1963):7-27.

Hill, Herbert. "No End of Pledges," *Commonweal* 87 (March 15, 1968):709-712. Continued discrimination in the building and construction trades.

Hill, Herbert. "Organized Labor and the Negro Earner: Ritual and Reality," *New Politics* 1 (Winter 1962):8-19.

Hill, Herbert. "Racism within Organized Labor: A Report of Five Years of the AFL-CIO, 1955-1960," *Journal of Negro Education* 30 (Spring 1961):109-118.

Hope, John, II. "Equality of Employment Opportunity: A Process Analysis of Union Initiative," *Phylon* 18 (Summer 1957):140-154.

Hope, John, II. *Equality of Opportunity: A Union Approach to Fair Employment.* Washington: Public Affairs, 1956.

Hope, John, II. "The Self-Survey of the Packing House Union," *Journal of Social Issues* 9 (January 1953):28-36.

Jacobs, Paul. *The State of the Unions.* New York: Atheneum, 1963. Inside look at American labor, view of its leaders and members, their problems, scandals, and future. See particularly chapter, "The Negro Worker Asserts His Rights," pp. 174 ff.

Jacobson, Julius, ed. *The Negro and the American Labor Movement.* Garden City, N.Y.: Doubleday, 1968. Essays which reveal the past and present practices of the labor movement as it relates to the Negro. Reflects labor's basic conservatism.

Johnson, Oakley C. "Marxism and the Negro Freedom Struggle," *Journal of Human Relations* 13 (Autumn 1965):21-39. Expectations and failures of efforts to join working class and Negro causes.

Kahn, Stephen D. "Racial Discrimination in Unions," *Temple Law Quarterly* 38 (Spring 1965):311-341.

Kahn, Tom. *The Economics of Equality.* New York: League for Industrial Democracy, 1964. Thesis: the uniting of the Negro and the labor movements is the key to the future of America as a nation.

Kornhauser, William. "Ideology and Interests," *Journal of Social Issues* 9 (Winter 1953): 49-60. Of the trade unions.

Kornhauser, William. "The Negro Union Official," *American Journal of Sociology* 57 (March 1952):443-452.

Litwack, Leon. *The American Labor Movement.* New York: Prentice-Hall, 1962.

Marshall, Ray. "Labor Unions and Equal Opportunity: Collective Bargaining and Minority Employment," in Lafayette G . Harter, Jr., and John Keltner, eds., *Labor in America.* Corvallis: Oregon State University Press, 1967, pp. 49-82. Concerns the patterns of Negro employment as they have influenced collective bargaining.

Marshall, Ray. *The Negro and Organized Labor* New York, Wiley, 1965.

Marshall, Ray. "Union Structure and Public Policy: The Control of Union Racial Practices," *Political Science Quarterly* 78 (September 1963):444-458.

Marshall, Ray. "Unions and the Negro Community," *Industrial Labor Relations Review* 17 (January 1964):179-202.

Masse, Benjamin L. "Trade Unions Grapple with Race Prejudice," *America* 120 (June 21, 1969):701.

Mitchell, George S., and Horace R. Cayton. *Black Workers and the New Unions.* Chapel Hill: University of North Carolina Press, 1939. Good on impact of the CIO.

"The Negro and the American Labor Movement: Some Selected Chapters," *Labor History*

10 (Summer 1969):entire issue. A selective contents analysis is provided in this bibliography.

Olson, James S. "Organized Black Leadership and Industrial Unionism: The Racial Response, 1936-1945," *Labor History* 10 (Summer 1969):475-486.

Plastrik, Stanley. "Confrontation in Pittsburgh," *Dissent* (January-February 1970):25-31. The Black Construction Coalition and white union response.

Poinsett, Alex. "Crusade against the Craft Unions: Blacks Continue Attack on Blatant Racism in High Paying Building Trades," *Ebony* 25 (December 1969):33-38.

Randolph, A. Philip. "The Unfinished Revolution," *Progressive* 26 (December 1962):20-25. Persuasive plea for job retraining as answer to automation. Includes short summary of Negro and labor union relations since 1830's.

Raskin, A. H. "Civil Rights: The Law and the Unions," *Reporter* 31 (September 10, 1964):23-28.

Read, F. T. "Minority Rights and the Union Shop," *Minnesota Law Review* 49 (December 1964):227.

Rich, J. C. "The NAACP versus Labor," *New Leader* 45 (November 26, 1962):20-21.

Rony, Vera. "Labor Drives to Close the South's Open Shop," *The Reporter* 33 (November 18, 1965):31-34.

Rowan, Richard L. "Discrimination and Apprentice Regulation in the Building Trades," *Journal of Business* 40 (October 1967):435-447. Violations related to federal regulation, "Title 29," and to experiences in Philadelphia unions.

Rustin, Bayard. "Labor-Negro Coalition—A New Beginning," *American Federationist* 75 (May 1968):1-5. Author was a planner for the march of the Memphis sanitation workers. Article reflects the emotional impact of Dr. King's death.

Segal, Robert M. "Unions and Discrimination," *Trial* 4 (February-March 1968):34-36.

Taft, Philip. *Organized Labor in American History*. New York: Harper, 1964. Chapter 50, "Organized Labor and the Negro," although brief, is good historical resumé. Bibliographies to each chapter and an index.

Tyler, Gus. "The Truth About the ILGWU," *New Politics* 2 (Fall 1962):6-17.

"Union Program for Eliminating Discrimination," *Monthly Labor Review* 86 (January 1963):58-59.

Winston, Henry. "Forge Negro-Labor Unity," *Political Affairs* 46 (February 1967):1-10.

Zuckerman, George D. "Sheet Metal Worker's Case: A Case History of Discrimination in the Building Trades," *Labor Law Journal* 20 (July 1969):416-427.

Efforts to Integrate

Bird, C. "More Room at the Top: Company Experience in Employing Negroes in High Jobs," *Management Review* 52 (March 1963):4-16.

Blasky, Harold F. "Equal Employment in the Construction Industry," *William and Mary Law Review* 10 (Fall 1968):3-17.

Bloch, Herman D. "Recogition of Discrimination—A Solution," *Journal of Social Psychology* 48 (November 1958):291-295.

Bowman, Garda W. "Employment by Merit Alone," *Office Executive* 36 (May 1961):14-15, 37.

Bowman, Garda W. "What Helps or Harms Promotability," *Harvard Business Review* 42 (January-February 1964):6-8+. A survey of executive thinking concerning management opportunities.

Brecher, Ruth, and Edward Brecher. "The Military's Limited War against Segregation," *Harper's* 227 (September 1963):79-82, 90-92. Army and air force bases are becoming islands of decency and progress in turbulent areas of South.

Brimmer, Andrew F. "Patterns of Minority Employment in Banking," *Bankers Magazine* 152 (Spring 1969):25-33.

"Broad Study Urged on Blacks in the News and J- Careers," *Editor and Publisher* 102 (September 20, 1969):17.

Browne, V. J. "Racial Desegregation in the Public Service, with Particular Reference to the U.S. Government," *Journal of Negro Education* 23 (Summer 1954):242-248.

Bullock, Paul. "Combating Discrimination in Employment," *California Management Review* 3 (Summer 1961):18-32.

Calvet, Ivis J. "Operation Achievement," *Interracial Review* 36 (September 1963):170-172. Progress in New York in obtaining jobs for Negroes.

Cassell, Frank H. "Positive Action on Unemployment," *Integrated Education* 1 (June 1963):36.

Christopher, Maurice. "CORE Seeks More Integrated Ads," *Advertising Age* 34 (September 9, 1963):128.

Cleghorn, Reese. "The Mill: A Giant Step for the Southern Negro," *New York Times Magazine,* November 9, 1969, pp. 34-35 +. Employment in textile mills in the South seen as a vehicle for black upward economic mobility.

Cox, T. "Counselor's Views on Changing Management Policies," *Public Relations Journal* 19 (November 1963):8-9. How public relations organizations can meet problem of job discrimination.

Douglass, Joseph H. "Intergroup Relations in the Federal Service," *Journal of Intergroup Relations* 2 (Winter 1960-1961):37-48.

Dworkin, Martin S. "The New Negro on Screen," *Progressive* 24 (October 1960):39-41; 24 (November 1960):33-36; 24 (December 1960):34-36. Three short articles discussing effect of Negro demands for "equality in imagery," and the realistic use of Negro actors.

"Equal Employment Opportunity: Probing and Problems," *Monthly Labor Review* 90 (October 1967):III-IV.

Farmer, James. "Employment Opportunity and the Negro," *Economic and Business Bulletin* (Temple University) 20 (September 1967):17-27.

Ferman, Louis A. *The Negro and Equal Employment Opportunities: A Review of Management Experiences in Twenty Companies.* New York: Praeger, 1968.

Field, E. L. "Minority Hiring by National Companies," *Business Lawyer* 25 (September 1969):125 +.

"First Two Negro Trucking Salesmen," *Fleet-Owner* 64 (June 1969):198-199. Article is illustrative of Negro employment as treated in a business-oriented trade journal.

Fleming, Harold C. "Equal Job Opportunity: Slogan or Reality?" *Personnel Administration* 26 (March 1963):25-28.

Four Years on the Job in Michigan. Lansing: Michigan F.E.P.C., 1960.

Garvey, Ernest [pseud.] "Black Houses, Black Jobs," *Commonweal* 88 (June 7, 1968): 355-357. A discussion of HR 16266, a bill to increase federally aided housing construction with black labor.

Gould, John. "NOW: Massachusetts Plan for Equal Employment Opportunity," *Industry* (Mass.) 29 (December 1963):10-11, 34.

Habbe, Stephen. *Company Experience with Negro Employment.* 2 vols. New York: National Industrial Conference Board, 1966.

Haynes, Ulric, Jr. "Equal Job Opportunity: The Credibility Gap," *Harvard Business Review* 46 (May-June 1968):113-120. The gap between business claims and actuality in the number of Negroes in white collar jobs.

"Hiring of Non-White Employees," *Public Utilities* 82 (October 10, 1968):80 +.

Homan, H. L., and R. A. Enion. "What Are Some Industrial Relations Approaches to Integration?" *Personnel Administration* 26 (November 1963):55-57.

Hope, John, II. "Efforts to Eliminate Racial Discrimination in Industry—With Particular Reference to the South," *Journal of Negro Education* 23 (Summer 1954):262-272.

Hope, John, II. "Equal Employment Opportunity: Changing Problems, Changing Techniques," *Journal of Intergroup Relations* 4 (Winter 1962-1963):29-36.

Hope, John, II. "Industrial Integration of Negroes: The Upgrading Process," *Human Organization* 11 (Winter 1952):5-14. Case studies of three Southern plants of the International

Harvester Company, where an active nondiscrimination policy demonstrated possibility of moving toward color-blindness in upgrading workers on basis of efficiency.

"How to Hire Minorities," *Chemical Week* 105 (September 20, 1969):40.

Hunton, Harold. "Implementing 'Affirmative Action' with Air Force Contractors," *Interracial Review* 36 (February 1963):36-38.

"Industry Acts to Bar Apprenticeship Bias," *Engineering News-Record,* October 3, 1963.

James, J. H. "Guidelines for Initiating Fair Employment Practices," *Personnel* 40 (May 1963):53-59.

"Joint Stand Rejects Racial Quotas for Plumbing Apprentices," *Air Conditioning, Heating, and Refrigeration News,* August 26, 1963.

Katz, Irwin, Judith Goldston, and Lawrence Benjamin. "Behavior and Productivity in Bi-Racial Work Groups," *Human Relations* 11 (May 1958):123-141.

Killens, John Oliver. "Hollywood in Black and White," *Nation* 201 (Semptember 20, 1965):157-160. 100th anniversary issue.

Kirkpatrick, James J., et al. *Testing and Fair Employment: Fairness and Validity of Personnel Tests for Different Ethnic Groups.* New York: New York University Press, 1968. Includes comparative data for white and Negro applicants in work situations. Bibliography.

Kopp, R. W. "Management's Concern with Recent Civil Rights Legislation," *Labor Law Journal* 16 (February 1965):67.

London, Jack, and Richard Hammett. "Impact of Company Policy upon Discrimination," *Sociology and Sociological Research* 39 (1954):88-91. A study of two industrial plants in the Midwest. Both professed a policy of nondiscrimination, but effective results were achieved only in the plant (automotive) where management and union took positive action.

Lunden, Leon E. "Antidiscrimination Provisions in Major Contracts," *Monthly Labor Review* 85 (June 1962):643-651.

McManus, G. J. "How Industry Views Integration," *Iron Age* 193 (February 27, 1964): 44-45.

The Management of Racial Integration in Business. New York: McGraw-Hill, 1964. A "Special Report to Management" prepared by a research team in Harvard Graduate School of Business Administration. On the basis of field interviews and case studies, the group suggests techniques for personnel managers and makes projections for the future. Useful appendices list Negro newspapers, Negro radio stations, and predominantly Negro colleges and universities. Bibliography.

Marshall F. Ray, and Vernon Briggs. *Equal Apprenticeship Opportunities: The Nature of the Issue and the New York Experience.* Ann Arbor: Institute of Labor and Industrial Relations, University of Michigan and Wayne State University, 1968. Suggests ways to enlarge Negro opportunities in the Workers Defense League apprenticeship program and similar projects.

"Mechanical Contractors Association of America Directors OK Construction Industry Joint Committee Standard on Apprenticeship," *Air Conditioning, Heating, and Refrigeration News,* November 25, 1963.

"Merit for Hire: How On-the-Job Integration Has Worked Out in Leading Companies," *Supervisory Management* 3 (May 1958):8-14.

"Minority Manpower in Publishing," *Publishers Weekly,* February 3, 1969, pp. 34-36.

"Minority Worker Hiring and Referral in San Francisco," *Monthly Labor Review* 81 (October 1958):1131-1136.

Mitchell, James P. "The Intimate State of Man," *New South* 15 (February 1960):9-13. Integration and problems of the human potential.

Morris, R. B. "Adopting a Human Relations Policy," *Public Management* 45 (September 1963):198-200. Glencoe, Illinois, develops formula for equal opportunity and nondiscrimination.

Moss, James Allen. "Negro Teachers in Predominantly White Colleges," Journal of Negro Education 27 (Fall 1958):451-462.

Moss, James Allen. "The Utilization of Negro Teachers in the Colleges of New York State," *Phylon* 21 (Spring 1960):63-70.

Mulford, R. H. "The Integrated Work Force: Where Are We Now?" *Management Review* 55 (November 1966):4-13.

"NAACP Demands Hit Snag," *Broadcasting* 32 (August 5, 1963):42-44. State Employees Union turns down request for adding a Negro to each crew.

"NAACP Sticks to Hollywood Deadline: No Set Quota for Negroes on Production Crews," *Broadcasting* 32 (September 16, 1963):84.

"New Challanges from Every Side," *Broadcasting* 77 (September 8, 1969):25-28. Negroes in broadcasting.

"Negro Employment: Should You Be Involved?" *Savings and Loan News* 89 (August 1968):28-36.

"Negro Employment in Banks," *Banking* 61 (October 1968):24-25.

Nichols, Lee. *Breakthrough on the Color Front.* New York: Random, 1954. A detailed study of the desegregation of the armed forces.

"One Company's Answer to Negro Job Problem," *Business Management* 25 (February 1964):42-45. Pitney-Bowes, Inc., Stamford, Connecticut.

Patten, Thomas H., Jr. "The Industrial Integration of the Negro," *Phylon* 24 (Winter 1963):334-352.

Peabody, Malcolm E., Jr. "Government-Industry Unite for Civil Rights Program," *Industry* (Mass.) 288 (August 1963):10-12, 32.

Pearson, Leonard E. "Equal Opportunity, Equal Justice," *Christian Century* 75 (July 9, 1958):806-807. Job Opportunity Program of Indianapolis, Ind., Society of Friends.

Perry, John. "Business—Next Target for Integration," *Harvard Business Review* 41 (March-April 1963):104-115. An important article suggesting practical methods of integration and outlining aspects of the problem as they apply both to Negroes and to managers.

"Pittsburgh Now a Symbol of Mounting Negro Protest," *Engineering News-Record* 183 (September 4, 1969):14-15. A view of the force of black power in the construction industry as revealed in a trade journal.

"Plan for Equal Opportunity at Lockheed," *Monthly Labor Review* 84 (July 1961):748-749.

Purcell, Theodore V. "Break Down Your Employment Barriers," *Harvard Business Review* 46 (July-August 1968):65-76. Describes some imaginative approaches of some companies toward elimination of unequal employment opportunities against Negroes and other minorities.

"Race Demonstrations Open Union Doors," *Engineering News-Record,* January 2, 1964. In the New York City building trades.

"Readying for Rights Law," *Chemical Week* 94 (February 22, 1964):77. Preparation on hiring practices.

Rico, Leonard. "Urban Job Discrimination: Abuses and Redress," *Quarterly Review of Economics and Business* 6 (Winter 1966):7-24. Efforts of Philadelphia Commission on Human Relations to overcome racial job discrimination.

Robinson, Jackie. "The Racial Crisis," *Sales Management* 91 (August 16, 1963):33-37. Reprinted in entirety in *Negro Digest,* November 1963, under title "Race and Big Business."

Sawyer, David A. "Fair Employment in the Nation's Capital: A Study of Progress and Dilemma," *Journal of Intergroup Relations* 4 (Winter 1962-1963):37-54.

Shostak, A. B. "Human Problems in Improving Industrial Race Relations," *Personnel Administration* 26 (March 1963):28-31.

Speroff, B. "Problems and Approaches in Integrating Minority Group Work Forces," *Journal of Social Psychology* 37 (May 1953):271-273.

Stuart, Irving R. "Intergroup Relations and Acceptance of Puerto Ricans and Negroes in an Immigrant's Industry," *Journal of Social Psychology* 56 (February 1962):89-96.

"Study Finds Anti-Bias Laws Ignored," *Engineering News-Record,* August 8, 1963.

"Text of Plumbing Industry's Policy Statement Rejecting Racial Quota System," *Air Conditioning, Heating, and Refrigeration News,* September 9, 1963.

"URW Pushes Civil Rights; Beset by Bias Charges," *Chemical Week* 93 (September 14, 1963):121.

U.S. Commission on Civil Rights. *For All the People, By All the People: A Report on Equal Opportunity in State and Local Government.* Washington: U.S. Govt. Print. Off., 1969. Occupational recruitment patterns and obstacles to Negro employment in seven metropolitan areas. Includes a discussion of the merit system vis-à-vis the minority worker and federal requirements for equal employment opportunity. Statistical supporting data.

U.S. Commission on Civil Rights. *Hearings, May 4-6, 1967.* Washington, 1967. Chiefly concerned with issues of housing and employment opportunities for Negroes and other minority groups in the San Francisco-Oakland Bay area. Tables, maps.

U.S. Commission on Civil Rights. *Report.* Washington: U.S. Govt. Print. Off., 1959- Annual. In 1961 only, issued in five parts. See entry following.

U.S. Commission on Civil Rights. *Report, 1961: Employment.* Washington: U.S. Govt. Print. Off., 1961.

U.S. Equal Opportunities Commission. *Annual Report* [Fiscal year 1967-   ]. Washington: U.S. Govt. Print. Off., 1968-   .

"Urban League Hits New York Agencies on Racial Discrimination in Employment," *Advertising Age* 34 (April 22, 1963):1, 96.

Via, Emory F. "Discrimination, Integration, and Job Equality," *Monthly Labor Review* 91 (March 1968):82-89. Employment desegregation in the South; the ambivalent role of unions.

Weiner, Harold M. "Negro Picketing for Employment Equality," *Howard Law Journal* 13 (Spring 1967):271-302.

Weintraub, Robert. "Employment Integration and Racial Wage Differences in a Southern Plant," *Industrial and Labor Relations Review* 12 (January 1959):214-226.

Wheeler, J. H. "Impact of Race Relations on Industrial Relations in the South," *Labor Law Journal* 15 (July 1964):474.

Wood, David G. "How Businessmen Can Fight 'Big Government'—and Win," *Harper's* 227 (November 1963):77-81. Suggestions by a steel man that business step in and make plans to provide jobs, particularly for Negroes, and take initiative in obtaining rights for Negroes.

Wortman, M. S., Jr., and F. Luthans. "How Many Contracts Ban Discrimination in Employment?" *Personnel* 41 (January 1964):75-79.

The Negro in the Professions

Albee, George W. "A Conference on Recruitment of Black and Other Minority Groups and Faculty," *American Psychologist* 24 (August 1969):720-723.

Applewhite, Harold L. "The Shortage of Negro Dentists," *New York Journal of Dentistry* 38 (October 1968):363-365+.

Association of American Law Schools. *Opportunities for Negroes in Law.* Wilberforce, Ohio: Central State University Press, 1967.

Back, Kurt W., and Ida Harper Simpson. "The Dilemma of the Negro Professional," *Journal of Social Issues* 20 (April 1964):60-70. Data collected from students at Howard Medical School to find out what kind of students sought protection by functioning in a Negro environment.

Barnard, J. "How Fares the Negro Nurse? Better, but . . . " *RN* 31 (November 1968):34-40.

Bock, E. Wilbur. "Farmer's Daughter Effect: The Case of the Negro Female Professionals," *Phylon* 30 (Spring 1969):17-26. Comparison by race of professional women in the labor force.

Bowers, John Z., Lee Cogan, and E. Lovell Becker. "Negroes for Medicine," *Journal of the American Medical Association* 202 (October 16, 1967):213-214. Report of a conference convened by the Macy Foundation in cooperation with the National Medical Fellowships Inc., June 25-28, 1967.

Calnek, Maynard. "Racial Factors in the Countertransference: The Black Therapist and the Black Client," *American Journal of Orthopsychiatry* 40 (January 1970):39-46. References appended.

Carl, E. L., and K. R. Callahan. "Negroes and the Law," *Journal of Legal Education* 17 (1964-1965):250-271. On the great need to increase the number of Negro lawyers. Strong motivation, satisfactory qualifications, and likelihood of professional opportunity have in the past militated against attraction of Negro students to the law.

Carl, Earl L. "The Shortage of Negro Lawyers: Pluralistic Legal Education and Legal Services for the Poor," *Journal of Legal Education* 20 (1967):21-32.

Carter, Luther J. "Negroes Demand and Get Voice in Medical School Plans," *Science* 160 (April 19, 1968):290-292.

Cobb, W. Montague. "Not to the Swift: Progress and Prospects of the Negro in Science and the Professions," *Journal of Negro Education* 27 (Spring 1958):120-126.

Cogan, Lee. *Negroes for Medicine.* Baltimore: Johns Hopkins Press, 1968. Explores ways by which the percentage of Negro physicians to total population can be redressed.

"Confirmations," *U.S. Department of State Bulletin* 62 (March 16, 1970):363. The appointment of Dr. Jerome H. Holland as U.S. Ambassador to Sweden.

"Confirmations," *U.S. Department of State Bulletin* 61 (July 28, 1969):80. The appointment of Dr. Samuel Z. Westerfield as U.S. Ambassador to the Republic of Liberia.

"Confirmations," *U.S. Department of State Bulletin* 61 (October 27, 1969):364. The appointment of Dr. Clinton Everett Knox as U.S. Ambassador to the Republic of Haiti.

Connes, Keith. "Can a Black Man Fly?" *Flying* 85 (July 1969):53-57. Outlines discrimination in aviation.

Conyers, James E. "Negro Doctorates in Sociology: A Social Portrait," *Phylon* 29 (Fall 1968):209-223.

Cunningham, George E. "Reasons for Belated Education: A Study of the Plight of Older Negro Teachers," *Journal of Negro Education* 27 (Spring 1958):195-200.

Daniel, Walter C. "Negroes as Teaching Assistants in Some Publicly-Supported Universities," *Journal of Negro Education* 31 (Spring 1962):202-204.

Edwards, G. Franklin. "The Occupational Mobility of Negro Professional Workers," in E. W. Burgess and D. J. Bogue, eds., *Contributions to Urban Sociology.* Chicago: University of Chicago Press, 1964, pp. 443-458.

Fichter, Joseph H. "Career Expectations of Negro Women Graduates," *Monthly Labor Review* 90 (November 1967):36-42.

Gellhorn, Walter. "Presidential Address," *Proceedings of the Association of American Law Schools* 29 (1964):33-44. The shortage of Negro lawyers cited as a major problem for American law schools.

Grossett, William T. "Bar Must Encourage More Negro Lawyers," *Trial* 4 (April-May 1968):22-24.

Harris, Edward E. *Some Social Effects of Race Relations.* New York: American Press, 1967. Five essays emphasize the place of Negroes in the academic marketplace.

Harrison, Lincoln J. "The Status of the Negro CPA in the United States," *Journal of Negro Education* 31 (Fall 1962):503-506.

Haynes, M. Alfred. "Distribution of Black Physicians in the United States, 1967," *Journal of the American Medical Association* 210 (October 6, 1969):93-95.

Haynes M. Alfred, and Victor H. Dates. "Educational Opportunities in the Health Professions for Negroes in the State of Maryland," *Journal of Medical Education* 43 (October 1968):1075-1082

Haynes, M. Alfred. "Problems Facing the Negro in Medicine Today," *Journal of the American Medical Association* 209 (August 18, 1969):1067-1069. Both as student and practitioner.

Henry, Joseph L. "The Negro Health Professional: How Can Kentucky Help?" *Journal of the National Medical Association* 61 (July 1969):327-332. Recruitment programs, improved educational preparation, and, most important, the elimination of bigotry. The author is Dean of Howard University College of Dentistry.

Howard, David H. "An Exploratory Study of Attitudes of Negro Professionals toward Competition with Whites," *Social Forces* 45 (September 1966):20–27. Based on 100 responses of Negro teachers, dentists, lawyers, and physicians.

Hutchins, Edwin B., Judith B. Reitman, and Dorothy Klaub. "Minorities, Manpower, and Medicine," *Journal of Medical Education* 42 (September 1967):809–821. Considerable data on Negro medical students.

Johnson, Edward E. "The Role of the Negro in American Psychology," *Bulletin of the Southern University and A & M College* 55 (June 1969):37–43.

Kalb, W. J. "Vital Need: More Black Managers," *Iron Age* 202 (October 17, 1968):63–66.

Kiehl, Robert. "Negro Engineers and Students Report on their Profession," *Journal of Negro Education* 27 (Spring 1958):189–194.

Kuiken, J. D., and Russell Eisenman. "Negro in the Field of Medicine," *Educational Forum* 30 (May 1966):475–481. A discussion of the barriers to the Negro in medical education due to institutionalized discrimination.

Mitchell, Bert N. "The Black Minority in the CPA Profession," *Journal of Accountancy* 128 (October 1969):41–48.

Morris, J. P. "The Denial of Staff Positions to Negro Physicians: A Violation of the Sherman Act," *Journal of the National Medical Association* 52 (May 1960):211–215.

Morris, R. G., Jr. "The Problems in Securing Hospital Staff Appointments for Negro Physicians in Chicago," *Journal of the National Medical Association* 52 (May 1960): 194–197.

Mueller, Marti. "AMA Moves to End Discrimination," *Science* 160 (June 28, 1968):1434. Statistics on the practical effect of discrimination against Negro physicians.

"Negro Dental Power," *Journal of the American Dental Association* 76 (January 1968):23–24. Replies *ibid.,* (February 1968):233–234.

"Negro Members of the Alabama Bar," *Alabama Law Review* 21, no. 2 (1969):306–332.

Nelson, Bryce. "Black Psychologists' Association Makes Proposals to APA," *Science* 162 (October 11, 1968):243.

New Opportunities for Negroes in Medicine. Chicago: National Medical Fellowships, 1962.

"New York University Steps Up Recruitment of Negro Nurse Students," *American Journal of Nursing* 68 (June 1968):1314–1315.

Nyren, Karl. "Black Decision-Makers," *Library Journal* 94 (June 1, 1969):2203–2206. Finds few black administrators in library administration. Responses *ibid.,* (September 1, 1969):2845–2846.

Pierce, Chester M. "Manpower: The Need for Negro Psychiatrists," *Journal of the National Medical Association* 60 (January 1968):30–33.

Ravitz, M. J. "Integration of Nurses: A Latent Function of Hospital Discrimination," *Phylon* 16 (Fall 1955):295–301.

Reed, Eugene T. "I Am a Controversial Dentist," *Interracial Review* 35 (April 1962): 100–101. Professional problems of a New York Negro Catholic dentist seeking admission to the New York State Dental Society.

Reitzes, Dietrich C., and H. Reitzes. "Factors Which Block or Facilitate Integration in the Field of Medicine," *Interracial Review,* September 1960.

Reitzes, Dietrich C. *Negroes and Medicine.* Cambridge, Mass.: Harvard University Press, 1958. Part I is a study of medical education for Negro students, with emphasis on factors limiting their entry into the profession.

Rose, Harold M. "An Appraisal of the Negro Educator's Situation in the Academic Marketplace," *Journal of Negro Education* 35 (Winter 1966):18–26.

Scott, Hugh J. "The Black Administrator and the Black Community," *Integrated Education* 7 (July–August 1969):52–56.

Shanahan, T. J. "Negroes in Nursing Education: A Report on Catholic Schools," *Hospital Progress* 42: (July 1961):100–102.

"The Shock of Black Recognition: Awakenings to the American Dream," *Esquire* 710 (May 1969):138–141. Reflections of six successful black men in a white world.

Staupers, Mabel Keaton. *No Time for Prejudice: A Story of the Integration of Negroes in Nursing in the United States.* New York: Macmillan, 1961.

"Supreme Court Justice Thurgood Marshall," *Negro History Bulletin* 30 (October 1967):4-5. First Negro Supreme Court Justice. Includes portrait.

Tate, Barbara L. "Negro Admissions, Enrollments and Graduations, 1963," *Nursing Outlook* 13 (February 1965):61-63.

Thorpe, Earl E. *Negro Historians in the United States.* Baton Rouge, La.: Fraternal Press, 1958.

Trayes, Edward J. "The Negro in Journalism: Surveys Show Low Ratios," *Journalism Quarterly* 46 (Spring 1969):5-8.

Ubben, Gerald C., and Larry W. Hughes. "Preparation Programs for Top Level Negro Public School Administrators," *Journal of Negro Education* 38 (Spring 1969):169-172.

"What It's Like to Be a Negro in Management," *Business Management* 29 (April 1966):60-70, 72-74+.

Wispi, Lauren, et al. "The Negro Psychologist in America," *American Psychologist* 24 (February 1969):142-150. Survey of origin, education, training, and population distribution of Negro professionals in the field; also a commentary on discriminatory practices.

The Negro in the Armed Forces

"The American Negro in World Wars I and II," *Journal of Negro Education* 12 (Summer 1943):entire issue.

Billington, Monroe. "Freedom to Serve: The President's Committee on Equality of Treatment and Opportunity in the Armed Forces, 1949-1950," *Journal of Negro History* 51 (October 1966):262-274.

Blassingame, John W. "Recruitment of Colored Troops in Kentucky, Maryland and Missouri, 1863-1865," *Historian* 29 (August 1967):533-545.

Blassingame, John W. "Union Army as an Educational Institution for Negroes, 1862-1865," *Journal of Negro Education* 34 (Spring 1965):152-159.

Bogart, Leo, ed. *Social Research and the Desegregation of the U.S. Army: Two Original 1951 Field Reports.* Chicago: Markham, 1969. Two troop opinion surveys, one of Negro troops in Korea, the other in continental United States, which were the basis of Project Clear, from which stemmed the official desegregation of the Army.

Brittain, Victoria. "GIs' Fight for Peace," *New Statesman* 77 (May 9, 1969):643-644.

Burchard, Peter. *One Gallant Rush.* New York: St. Martin's, 1965. Biography of Robert Gould Shaw and his black regiment in the Union Army.

Cornish, Dudley T. *The Sable Arm: Negro Troops in the Union Army, 1861-1865.* New York: Longmans, Green, 1956.

Dalfiume, Richard M. *Desegregation of the U.S. Armed Forces: Fighting on Two Fronts, 1939-1953.* Columbia: University of Missouri Press, 1969. Extensive bibliography of primary and secondary sources.

Dalfiume, Richard M. "The Fahy Committee and Desegregation of the Armed Forces," *Historian* 31 (November 1968):1-20.

Dalfiume, Richard M. "Military Segregation and the 1940 Presidential Election," *Phylon* 30 (Spring 1969):42-55.

Dwyer, Robert J. "The Negro in the U.S. Army," *Sociology and Social Research* 38 (November 1953):103-112. Wherever the pattern of segregation has broken down, there has been a marked absence of friction or tension, and in many cases changes in the Negro's relations with the civilian community have followed.

"Equality in the Selective Service System: The Racial Composition of Draft Boards," *Iowa Law Review* 54 (December 1968):521-533. An analysis of federal policy.

Evans, James C., and David A. Lane, Jr. "Integration in the Armed Services," *Annals of the American Academy of Political and Social Science* 304 (March 1956):78-85.

Feldman, J. Arnold. "The 1960 Audit of Negro Veterans and Servicemen," *Journal of Intergroup Relations* 2 (Winter 1960-1961):79-81.

Fendrich, James, and Michael Pearson. "Black Veterans Return," *Trans-action* 7 (March 1970):32-37.

Grove, Gene. "The Army and the Negro," *New York Times Magazine,* July 24, 1966, pp. 4-5, 49-51.

Higginson, Thomas Wentworth. *Army Life in a Black Regiment.* 1870. Edited by John Hope Franklin. Boston: Beacon, 1962. Impressions of a commander of the first black regiment in the Civil War.

Integration in the Armed Services: A Progress Report. Washington, 1955. Prepared for the Office of the Assistant Secretary of Defense for Manpower and Personnel.

Johnson, Jesse J. *Ebony Brass: An Autobiography of Negro Frustration and Aspiration.* New York: William-Frederick Press, 1967. Based on personal experiences of Negro officers in the armed forces.

Katz, William Loren. "Six New Medal of Honor Men," *Journal of Negro History* 53 (January 1968):77-81.

Langley, Harold D. "The Negro in the Navy and Merchant Marine, 1798-1860," *Journal of Negro History* 52 (October 1967):273-286. Drawn from diaries, journals, and memoirs.

Leckie, William H. *Buffalo Soldiers: A Narrative of the Negro Cavalry in the West.* Norman: University of Oklahoma Press, 1967. Bibliography of published and unpublished sources.

Lee, Irvin H. *Negro Medal of Honor Men.* 1967. 3d ed. rev. and enl. New York: Dodd, Mead, 1969.

Lee, Ulysses. *The Employment of Negro Troops: United States Army in World War II; Special Studies.* Washington: U.S. Govt. Print. Off., 1966. Official account of the participation of Negro troops in World War II.

McConnell, Roland C. *Negro Troops of Antebellum Louisiana: A History of the Battalion of Free Men of Color.* Baton Rouge: Louisiana State University Press, 1968.

McKissick, Floyd B., and Whitney M. Young, Jr. "The Negro and the Army: Two Views," *New Generation* 48 (Fall 1966):10-15. Parallel articles debate the McNamara draft plan and the effect upon the number of Negro inductees.

McPherson, James M. *The Negro's Civil War: How American Negroes Felt and Acted during the War for the Union.* New York: Pantheon, 1965. See especially chapters 10-17.

Marshall, Thurgood. *Report on Korea.* NAACP, 1951. The author, who went to Korea to investigate alleged injustice in court martials, found that Jim Crow policies still existed in army.

Marshall, Thurgood. "Summary Justice—The Negro GI in Korea," *Crisis* 58 (May 1951):297-304, 350-355.

Morris, Steven. "How Blacks Upset the Marine Corps: 'New Breed' Leathernecks Are Tackling Racist Vestiges," *Ebony* 25 (December 1969):55-62.

Moskos, Charles C., Jr. "Racial Integration in the Armed Forces," *American Journal of Sociology* 72 (September 1966):132-148. Also appears in *Army* 16 (August 1966):50-54.

"Negro Cadets Set Record—87 Enter Academies," *Air Force Times* 30 (August 13, 1969):10.

"Negro Progress in Armed Forces," *Armed Forces Journal* 105 (August 10, 1968):2.

Newton, I. E. "The Negro and the National Guard," *Phylon* 23 (Spring 1962):18-28.

"Paradox of a Black Soldier," *Ebony* 23 (August 1968):142-143.

Paszek, Lawrence J. "Negroes and the Air Force, 1939-1949, *Military Affairs* 31 (Spring 1967):1-9.

Reddick, L. D. "The Negro Policy of the American Army since World War II," *Journal of Negro History* 38 (April 1953):194-215. The Army has gone a considerable way toward abandoning Jim Crow policy, but practices have not yet caught up with policy.

Resor, Stanley R. "Meeting the Challenge of a Changing World," *Army* 18 (November 1968):19-22.

Silvera, John D., ed. *The Negro in World War II.* New York: Arno Press, 1968.

Smith, Philip R., Jr. "The Negro's Army Heritage," *Army Digest* 23 (July 1968):13-21.

Stern, Sol. "When the Black G.I. Comes Back from Vietnam," *New York Times Magazine,* March 24, 1968, pp. 27 +.

Stillman, Richard J. *Integration of the Negro in the U.S. Armed Forces.* New York: Praeger, 1968.

Stillman, Richard J. "Negroes in the U.S. Armed Forces," *Phylon* 30 (Summer 1969):139-159.

"Systematic Exclusion of Negroes from Selective Service Boards: Some Proposals for Reform," *Michigan Law Review* 67 (February 1969):756-811.

"These Truly are the Brave; History of U.S. Black Soldier," *Ebony* 23 (August 1968):164-170.

Thompson, E. N. "Negro Soldiers on the Frontier: A Fort Davis Case Study," *Journal of the West* 7 (April 1968):217-235.

U.S. Dept. of Defense. *Integration and the Negro Officer in the Armed Forces of the United States of America.* Washington 1962. Historical notes on the Negro officer in the United States through the Korean War, together with a sample listing of officer personnel and assignments.

Young, Whitney M., Jr. "When the Negroes In Vietnam Come Home," *Harper's* 234 (June 1967):63-69. The impact of complete integration in the services on Negro and white soldiers and its civilian effects.

Zelnik, Melvin. "The Census and Selective Service," *Eugenics Quarterly* 15 (September 1968):173-176. Compares Census and Selective Service data for 1940, 1950, and 1960 re: Negro males.

15 Housing

The Law, the Courts, and Regulatory Action

Abrams, Charles. "The Housing Order & Its Limits," *Commentary* 35 (January 1963):10-14.

Aurbach, Herbert A., John R. Coleman, and Bernard Mausner. "Restrictive and Protective Viewpoints of Fair Housing Legislation: A Comparative Study of Attitudes," *Social Problems* 8 (Fall 1960):118-125.

Avins, Alfred, ed. *Open Occupancy vs. Forced Housing Under the 14th Amendment: A Symposium on Anti-Discrimination Legislation, Freedom of Choice, and Property Rights in Housing.* New York: Bookmailer, 1963. Included are pieces by lawyers, social scientists, real estate dealers from several areas of the country. While a wide range of opinions is covered, the volume is weighted on the side of "freedom of choice."

Bartell, Jeffrey B., Charles A. Buss, and Edward R. Stege, Jr. "Mediation of Civil Rights Disputes: Open Housing in Milwaukee," *Wisconsin Law Review* (1968):1127-1191. A comprehensive analysis of the mediatory process between the black community and the white power structure.

Bittker, B. I. "The Case of the Checker-board Ordinance: An Experiment in Race Relations," *Yale Law Journal* 71 (July 1962):1387-1423.

Blumrosen, A. B. "Antidiscrimination Laws in Action in New Jersey: A Law-Sociology Study," *Rutgers Law Review* 19 (Winter 1965):189+.

Boles, Alan. "Black Homeowning," *New Republic* 161 (December 12, 1969):7-9. Legal efforts of the Contract Buyers League to deter exploitation of black homebuyers.

Branscomb, A. W. "Analysis of Attempts to Prohibit Racial Discrimination in the Sale and Rental of Publicly Assisted Private Housing," *George Washington Law Review* 28 (April 1960):758-778.

"Civil Rights: Discrimination in Private Housing," *Marquette Law Review* 46 (Fall 1962):237-241.

Colley, N. S., and M. L. McGhee. "The California and Washington Fair Housing Cases," *Law in Transition* 22 (Summer 1962):79-92.

"Constitutional Law—Owner of Private Subdivision May Refuse to Sell to Negroes," *Vanderbilt Law Review* 21 (March 1968):271-277. Legal implications of a housing discrimination case.

"Constitutional Law—State Action: Significant Involvement in Ostensibly Private Discriminations, *Mulkey v. Reitman*," *Michigan Law Review* 65 (February 1967):777-785. Legal survey of California housing decisions leading to this one.

"Development of Open Occupancy Laws: A Survey of Legislation against Discrimination in Housing," *Milwaukee Bar Association Gavel* 24 (September 1963):13-20.

"Discrimination in Employment and in Housing: Private Enforcement Provisions of the Civil Rights Act of 1964 and 1968," *Harvard Law Review* 82 (February 1969):834-863.

Eisenberg, Lawrence D. "Uncle Tom's Multi-Cabin Subdivision—Constitutional Restrictions on Racial Discrimination by Developers," *Cornell Law Review* 53 (January 1968):314-324.

"The Federal Fair Housing Requirements: Title VIII of the 1968 Civil Rights Act," *Duke Law Journal* 1969 (August 1969):733-771.

Fisher, Margaret, and Frances Levenson. *Federal, State and Local Action Affecting Race and Housing.* National Association of Intergroup Relations Officials, September 1962.

Frey, D. S. " 'Freedom of Residence' in Illinois," *Chicago Bar Record* 41 (October 1959):9-21.

Ginger, A. F. "Little Democracy—Housing for America's Minorities in 1960," *Lawyers Guild Review* 20 (Spring 1960):6-17.

Goldblatt, Harold, and Florence Cromien. "The Effective Social Reach of the Fair Housing Practices Law of the City of New York," *Social Problems* 9 (Spring 1962):365-370.

Gutman, D., ed. "Discrimination in Employment and Housing: A Symposium," *New York Law Forum* 6 (January 1960):entire issue.

Hager, Don J. "Housing Discrimination, Social Conflict, and the Law," *Social Problems* 8 (Summer 1960):80-87.

Hellerstein, W. E. "Benign Quota, Equal Protection, and 'The Rule in Shelley's Case,' " *Rutgers Law Review* 17 (Spring 1963):531-561. On restrictive covenants.

Henkin, Louis. *"Shelley v. Kraemer,* Notes for a Revised Opinion," *University of Pennsylvania Law Review* 110 (February 1962):473-505. On restrictive covenants and the constitutionality of state action in private cases.

"Integration in Housing," *Lawyers Guild Review* 18 (Spring 1958):entire issue.

"Is There a Civil Right to Housing Accommodations?" *Notre Dame Lawyer* 33 (May 1958): 463-488.

Kaplan, M. "Discrimination in California Housing: The Need for Additional Legislation," *California Law Review* 50 (October 1962):635-649.

Kozol, L. H. "The Massachusetts Fair Housing Practices Law," *Massachusetts Law Quarterly* 47 (September 1962):295-305.

"Law and the Demise of the Urban Ghetto," *Catholic Lawyer* 15 (Winter 1969):39-55; (Spring 1969):143-157.

Lehman, W. W. "Discrimination in F.H.A. Home Financing," *Chicago Bar Record* 40 (May 1959):375-379.

Lehman, W. W. "Must I Sell My House to a Negro?" *Chicago Bar Record* 42 (March 1961):283-288.

McEntire, Davis. "Government and Racial Discrimination in Housing," *Journal of Social Issues* 13 (Fall 1957):60-67.

McGraw, B. T. "The Housing Act of 1954 and Implications for Minorities," *Phylon* 16 (Spring 1955):171-182.

Mayhew, Leon H. *Law and Equal Opportunity; A Study of the Massachusetts Commission against Discrimination.* Cambridge, Mass.: Harvard University Press, 1968. The impact of the state's antidiscrimination law seen through actual complaints and their settlement.

Miller, Loren. "Government's Role in Housing Equality," *Journal of Intergroup Relations* 1 (Winter 1959-1960):56-61.

Miller, Loren. "The Law and Discrimination in Housing," *Lawyers Guild Review* 20 (Winter 1960):123-136.

Miller, Loren. "Supreme Court Covenant Decision—An Analysis," *Crisis* 55 (September 1948):265-266.

Morris, Arval A., and L. A. Powe, Jr. "Constitutional and Statutory Rights to Open Housing," *Washington Law Review* 44 (October 1968):1-84. Available means of redress against racial discrimination in housing.

Nesbitt, George B. "Federal Concerns and Responsibilities with Relocation," *Phylon* 19 (Spring 1958):75-76.

"New Jersey Housing Anti-Bias Law: Applicability to Non-State-Aided Developments," *Rutgers Law Review* 12 (Summer 1958):557-581.

"The 'New' Thirteenth Amendment: A Preliminary Analysis," *Harvard Law Review* 82 (April

1969):1294-1321. The scope of the amendment reexamined in the light of the *Jones v. Alfred H. Mayer Co.* case.

New York State Commission against Discrimination. *Legislation on Discrimination in Housing: Federal, State and City.* Albany, 1956.

"New York's Anti-Bias Statute of 1961 as It Affects Cooperative Apartments," *New York University Intramural Law Review* 18 (May 1963):269.

Prather, William. "Open Housing: The Statutes and the Court Decisions," *Legal Bulletin of the U.S. Savings and Loan League* 34 (September 1968):221-233.

Rabkin, Sol. *A Landmark Decision on Segregation in Housing:* Jones v. Meyer. New York: Anti-Defamation League of B'nai B'rith, 1969. History and importance of the case. The opinions of the court are appended.

"Racial Discrimination by State Lessee as State Action," *Iowa Law Review* 47 (Spring 1962):718.

"Racial Discrimination in Housing," *University of Pennsylvania Law Review* 107 (February 1959):515-550.

"Racial Restriction in Leaseholds," *University of Florida Law Review* 11 (Fall 1958):344-351.

"Racially Restrictive Covenants in Deeds," *Georgia Bar Journal* 25 (November 1962): 232-238.

Rice, Roger L. "Residential Segregation by Law, 1910-1917," *Journal of Southern History* 34 (May 1968):179-199.

Roberts, Richard J. "Fair Housing Laws: A Tool for Racial Equality," *Social Order* 12 (January 1962):20-34.

Roseman, D.M. "May Operative Builders of F.H.A. Housing Be Barred from Discriminating against Purchasers on Basis of Race?" *Boston Bar Journal* 3 (December 1959):21-24.

Rosenblum, Michael S. "Constitutional Law—Equal Protection—Constitutional Amendment Prohibiting State Fair Housing Laws Is State Action Denying Equal Protection of the Laws," *Villanova Law Review* 13 (Fall 1967):199-205.

Saks, J. H., and Sol Rabkin. "Racial and Religious Discrimination in Housing: A Report of Legal Progress," *Iowa Law Review* 45 (Spring 1960):488-524.

Semer, Milton, and Martin Sloane. "Equal Housing Opportunities and Individual Property Rights," *Federal Bar Journal* 24 (Winter 1964):47-75. Authors, legal counsel for Housing and Home Finance Agency, defend constitutionality of nondiscrimination orders in housing as preserving freedom of choice, and discuss "equal protection of law" clause, restrictive covenants, federal and state fair housing acts.

Sparkman, John. "Civil Rights and Property Rights," *Federal Bar Journal* 24 (Winter 1964):31-46. Author, U.S. Senator from Alabama, attacks overemphasis on civil rights at expense of "natural" rights, *i.e.,* free choice of associates, free control of property and conduct of business. Special targets: Title II, Title VI of Civil Rights Bill of 1964, and 1962 executive order on integration in federal housing.

"State Statute Prohibiting Discrimination in Private Sale of Publicly Assisted Housing Denies Equal Protection of the Laws," *Harvard Law Review* 75 (June 1962):1647-1649.

"Title VI of the Civil Rights Act of 1964—Implementation and Impact," *George Washington Law Review* 36 (May 1968):824-1015. Text of Title VI and commentary.

U.S. Housing and Home Finance Agency. *State Statutes and Local Ordinances and Resolutions Prohibiting Discrimination in Housing and Urban Renewal Operations.* Washington: U.S. Govt. Print Off., 1962.

Van Alstyne, W. W. "Discrimination in State University Housing Programs—Policy and Constitutional Considerations," *Stanford Law Review* 13 (December 1960):60-79.

Van Alstyne, W. W. "The O'Meara Case and Constitutional Requirements of State Anti-Discrimination Housing Laws," *Howard Law Journal* 8 (Spring 1962):158-168.

"Voluntary Segregation Held Not Illegal Discrimination," *Ohio State Law Journal* 24 (Spring 1963):412-416.

Vose, Clement E. *Caucasians Only—The Supreme Court, the NAACP, and the Restrictive Covenant Cases.* Berkeley: University of California Press, 1959.

Vose, Clement E. "NAACP Strategy in the Covenant Cases," *Western Reserve Law Review* 6 (Winter 1955):101-145.

Patterns and Conditions

Abrams, Charles. "Discrimination and the Struggle for Shelter," *New York Law Forum* 6 (January 1960):3-12. The author, President of the National Committee against Discrimination in Housing, argues for a program to create decent environments, with emphasis on vacant land utilization rather than large-scale housing developments, on rental housing in small units, and on a mortgage loan program.

Abrams, Charles. *Forbidden Neighbors.* New York: Harper, 1955. A thorough analysis of corporate practices that determine housing choice.

Abrams, Charles. "The Housing Problem and the Negro," *Daedalus* 95 (Winter 1966):64-76. The author emphasizes the factors which reinforce the ghettoization of the Negroes, and reminds the reader that "the poverty of people and the poverty of cities are parts of the same problem."

Anderson, Martin. *The Federal Bulldozer: A Critical Analysis of Urban Renewal: 1949-1962.* Cambridge, Mass.: Massachusetts Institute of Technology Press, 1964. Including the impact on the Negro of urban development.

Aukofer, Frank A. *City With a Chance.* Milwaukee, Wis.: Bruce, 1968. A journalist's concise appraisal of the Milwaukee civil rights protests in 1967 led, for the most part, by Father James Groppi and the Youth Council of the NAACP.

Ball, William B. "Housing and the Negro," *America* 119 (July 6, 1968):11-13.

Banfield, Edward C., and Morton Grodzins. *Government and Housing in Metropolitan Areas.* New York: McGraw-Hill, 1958. A volume in ACTION's Series on Housing and Community Development, this work considers not only government housing operations in metropolitan areas, but population trends in cities, with implications for political parties and metropolitan reorganization.

Barth, Ernest A. T., and Sue March. "A Research Note on the Subject of Minority Housing," *Journal of Intergroup Relations* 3 (Fall 1962):314-319.

Bauer, Catherine. "Social Questions in Housing and Community Planning," *Journal of Social Issues* 7 (Winter 1951):1-34. The author points out the class character of residential housing in Western countries regardless of race.

Bell, Wendell. "Comment on Cowgill's 'Trends in Residential Segregation of Nonwhites,' " *American Sociological Review* 22 (April 1957):221-222.

Bickers, J. T. "The Real Estate Broker," *Phylon* 19 (Summer 1958):87-88.

Blayton, J. B. "Secondary Mortgage Operations," *Phylon* 19 (Summer 1958):86.

Boichel, Margery R., et al. "Exposure, Experience and Attitudes: Realtors and Open Occupancy," *Phylon* 30 (Winter 1969):325-337. Based on a study of the Greater Pittsburgh Board of Realtors.

Bradshaw, Barbara Robinson, and Edward L. Holmgren. "Open Occupancy and Open Minds: A Study of Realtors," *Interracial Review* 39 (April 1966):92-95.

Commission on Race and Housing. *Where Shall We Live?* Berkeley: University of California Press, 1958. Report of a three-year study on discrimination and segregation in housing. Includes a bibliography of published and unpublished studies of various areas in the nation.

Cowgill, Donald D. "Segregation Scores for Metropolitan Areas," *American Sociological Review* 27 (June 1962):400-402. A numerical index for 21 metropolitan areas showing degree of residential segregation.

Cowgill, Donald D. "Trends on Residential Segregation of Non-Whites in American Cities, 1940-1950," *American Sociological Review* 21 (February 1956):43-47. See also commentary by Wendell Bell, *ibid.,* 22 (April 1957):221-222.

Dorson, Norman. "Discrimination," in *Frontiers of Civil Liberties.* New York: Pantheon 1968, pp. 377-392.

Duncan, Beverly, and Philip M. Hauser. *Housing a Metropolis: Chicago.* Glencoe, Ill.: Free Press, 1961. A cooperative research program by the Chicago Community Inventory of the University of Chicago and the governmental agencies of the City of Chicago. A general work, with one chapter on "White-nonwhite Differentials in Housing." Also treats of demolition and new construction, characteristics of lower-income families and housing, and the family cycle.

DeFriese, Gordon H., and W. Scott Ford, Jr. "Open Occupancy—What the Whites Say: What They Do," *Trans-action* 5 (April 1968):53-56.

Duncan, John B., and Albert Mindlin. "Municipal Fair Housing Legislation: Community Beliefs and Facts," *Phylon* 25 (Fall 1964):217-237.

Duncan, Otis Dudley, and Stanley Lieberson. "Ethnic Segregation and Assimilation," *American Journal of Sociology* 64 (January 1959):364-374. A study of residential patterns in Chicago 1930-1950, showing a positive relationship between assimilation and length of residence, along with a remarkably stable pattern of differential segregation and spatial separation of ethnic colonies.

Duncan, Otis Dudley, and Beverly Duncan. "A Methodological Analysis of Segregation Indexes," *American Sociological Review* 20 (April 1955):210-217.

Duncan, Otis Dudley, et al. *Metropolis and Region.* Baltimore: Johns Hopkins Press, 1960.

Duncan, Otis Dudley, and Beverly Duncan. *The Negro Population of Chicago: A Study of Residential Succession.* Chicago: University of Chicago Press, 1957.

Duncan, Otis Dudley, and Beverly Duncan. "Residential Distribution and Occupational Stratification," *American Journal of Sociology* 60 (March 1955):493-503.

Egan, John J. "Why Are We Rebuilding Our Cities?" *Interracial Review* 35 (November 1962):244-246.

Erskine, Hazel. "Polls: Negro Housing," *Public Opinion Quarterly* 31 (Fall 1967):482-498. Tabular summary, 1963 to date, with additional background figures.

"Fair Housing: Next Steps," *Social Action* 33 (May 1967):5-35.

Farley, Reynolds, and Karl E. Taeuber. "Population Trends and Residential Segregation Since 1960: Special Censuses for 13 Cities Reveal Increasing Concentration of Highly Segregated Negroes," *Science* 159 (March 1, 1968):953-956.

Feingold, Eugene, and Robert J. Harris. "Obstacles to Fair Housing," *American Federationist* 74 (June 1967):5-8.

Foote, N. N., et al. *Housing Choices and Housing Constraints.* New York: McGraw-Hill, 1960. Factors, including personal decisions, that determine choice.

Friedrichs, Robert W. "Christians and Residential Exclusion: An Empirical Study of a Northern Dilemma," *Journal of Social Issues* 15 (October 1959):14-23.

Gans, Herbert J. "The Failure of Urban Renewal," *Commentary* 39 (April 1965):29-37.

Glazer, Nathan, and Davis McEntire, eds. *Studies in Housing and Minority Groups.* Berkeley: University of California Press, 1960. Independent studies of Negro housing in Atlanta, Birmingham, San Antonio, Houston, New Orleans, Dade County (Miami area), and Detroit.

Greeley, Andrew M., and Robert D. Crain. "Housecleaning in the Negro Community?" *Interracial Review* 35 (November 1962):247-249.

Greer, Frank. "Financing Programs of the National Mortgage Association," *Phylon* 19 (Spring 1958):77-81.

Grier, Eunice S. "Factors Hindering Integration in American Urban Areas," *Journal of Intergroup Relations* 2 (Fall 1961):293-301.

Grier, Eunice S., and George Grier. *In Search of Housing: A Study of Experiences of Negro Professional and Technical Personnel in New York State.* New York State Commission against Discrimination, 1958. In upstate New York cities.

Grier, Eunice, and George Grier. "Obstacles to Desegregation in America's Urban Areas," *Race* 6 (July 1964):3-17.

Grier, George W., and Eunice Grier. *Equality and Beyond: Housing Segregation and the Goals of the Great Society.* Chicago: Quandrangle, 1966.

Grier, George W. "Negro Ghettos and Federal Housing Policy," *Law and Contemporary Problems* 32 (Summer 1967):550-560. Also appears in R. O. Everett and J. D. Johnston, *Housing.* Dobbs Ferry, N.Y., 1968, pp. 366-376.

Grodzins, Morton. "Metropolitan Segregation," *Scientific American* 197 (October 1957):24, 33-41.

Gurin, David. "The Winter Revolution," *The Second Coming* 1 (January 1965):12-15. On the Harlem rent strike.

Hahn, Harlan. "Northern Referenda on Fair Housing: The Response of White Voters," *Western Political Quarterly* 21 (September 1968):483-495.

Hartman, Chester W. *Low-Income Housing in the Boston Area: Needs and Proposals.* Prepared by Housing Advisory Research Committee, Massachusetts Committee on Discrimination in Housing, July 1964.

Helper, Rose. *Racial Policies and Practices of Real Estate Brokers.* Minneapolis: University of Minnesota Press, 1969. Discrimination in housing in the Chicago area; brokers' practices.

Hendon, William S. "Discrimination against Negro Homeowners in Property Tax Assessment," *American Journal of Economics and Sociology* 27 (April 1968):125-132.

Hill, Herbert. "Demographic Change and Racial Ghettos: The Crisis of American Cities," *Journal of Urban Law* 44 (Winter 1966):231-285. Contents: Negro population characteristics; housing and the pattern of the segregated slums; public housing programs; governmental power and housing segregation.

Holmes, Bob. "A Study in Subtlety: Riverside Renewal," *Interracial Review* 36 (June 1963): 118-120. Urban renewal and Negroes in Riverside, California.

"Housing and Minorities," *Phylon* 19 (Summer 1958):8-124. Entire issue, covering such topics as urban renewal, slum clearance, relocation, community participation, public and private financing.

"Income and Ability to Pay for Housing of Nonwhite Families in New York State," New York State Temporary Housing and Rent Commission, August, 1955.

Isaacs, Reginald R. "Are Urban Neighborhoods Possible?" *Journal of Housing* 5 (July 1948):177-180.

Isaacs, Reginald R. "The 'Neighborhood Unit' As an Instrument for Segregation," *Journal of Housing* 5 (August 1948):215-219.

Jackson, Hubert M. "Public Housing and Minority Groups," *Phylon* 19 (Spring 1958):21-30.

Johnson, Reginald A. *Racial Bias and Housing.* New York: National Urban League, 1963.

Jones, Malcolm. "The Workable Program of a Southern Metropolis, Atlanta, Georgia," *Phylon* 19 (Spring 1958):60-63.

Kain, John F. "Housing Segregation, Negro Employment, and Metroplitan Decentralization," *Quarterly Journal of Economics* 82 (May 1968):175-197. Also issued as an offprint, Cambridge, Mass. by the Joint Center for Urban Studies, Harvard University and Massachusetts Institute of Technology.

Kain, John F. *Theories of Residential Location and Realities of Race.* Cambridge, Mass.: Program on Regional and Urban Economics, Harvard University, 1969. Analyzes the effects of Negro segregation on housing markets and broad patterns of urban development.

Kelley, Joseph B. "Racial Integration Policies of the New York City Housing Authority, 1958-1961," *Social Service Review* 38 (June 1964):153-162.

Keyes, Walter E. "Federal Agencies in Urban Redevelopment," *Phylon* 19 (Summer 1958):90-91.

Kistin, Helen. *Housing Discrimination in Massachusetts.* Prepared by Housing Advisory Research Committee, Massachusetts Committee on Discrimination in Housing, May 1964.

Kopkind, Andrew. "Civil Rights and Housing," *New Statesman* 72 (September 16, 1966):380-381.

Lansing, John B., Charles Wade Clifton, and James N. Morgan. *New Homes and Poor People: A Study of Chains of Moves.* Ann Arbor: Institute of Social Research, 1969. The effect of new housing construction on the poor and especially on black families.

Lee, Alfred McClung. "The Impact of Segregated Housing on Public Schools," *School and Society* 88 (May 7, 1960):241-243.

Lieberson, Stanley. "The Impact of Residential Segregation on Ethnic Assimilation," *Social Forces* 40 (October 1961):52-57.

Linn, Karl. "'White Solutions' Won't Work in Black Neighborhoods: Proposals," *Landscape Architecture* 59 (October 1968):23-25.

Lipsky, Michael. "Rent Strikes: Poor Man's Weapon," *Trans-action* 6 (February 1969): 10-15. The Harlem rent strikes of 1963 and 1964 organized by Jesse Gray.

McEntire, Davis. *Residence and Race: Final and Comprehensive Report to the Commission on Race and Housing by the Director.* Berkeley: University of California Press, 1960. Statistical tables based on 1950 census, and therefore do not show gains as revealed in 1960 census. Contains especially valuable material on growth of New York Negro sections, and expresses strong belief in efficacy of law to effect change. Good bibliography.

McGhee, M. L., and A. F. Ginger. "The House That I Live In: A Study of Housing for Minorities," *Cornell Law Quarterly* 46 (Winter 1961):194–257.

McGraw, B. T. "Potentials for Equal Opportunity in Housing and Community Development," *Journal of Intergroup Relations* 3 (Spring 1962):126–137.

McGraw, B. T. "Urban Renewal in the Interest of All People," *Phylon* 19 (Spring 1958):45–55.

McGrew, John M. "How 'Open' Are Multiple-Dwelling Units?" *Journal of Social Psychology* 72 (August 1967):223–226.

McKee, James B. "Changing Patterns of Race and Housing: A Toledo Study," *Social Forces* 41 (March 1963):253–260.

Madden, J. Patrick. "Poverty by Color and Residence—Projections to 1975 and 1980," *American Journal of Agricultural Economics* 50 (December 1968):1399–1412.

Maslen, Sidney. "Relocation in the Southeastern Region during the Process of Urban Renewal," *Phylon* 19 (Spring 1958):70–71.

Massachusetts Committee on Discrimination in Housing. *Housing Discrimination in Massachusetts,* 1964.

Mercer, N. A. "Discrimination in Rental Housing: A Study of Resistance of Landlords to Non-White Tenants," *Phylon* 23 (Spring 1962):47–54.

Meyerson, Martin, Barbara Terrett, and William Wheaton. *Housing, People, and Cities.* New York: McGraw-Hill, 1962. On housing and community development.

Meyerson, Martin, and Edward C. Banfield. *Politics, Planning, and the Public Interest.* Glencoe, Ill.: Free Press, 1955. An analysis of how decisions were reached on sites for low-rent public housing in Chicago after passage of federal public housing act of 1949, of how Negro groups react on public issues, and of the impossibility of separating housing from racial and political problems.

Midwestern Minority Housing Markets. Special Report by Advance Mortgage Corporation, Chicago, December 1, 1962.

Miller, Alexander F. "Levittown, U.S.A.," *Phylon* 19 (Spring 1958):108–112.

Miller, Mike, and Carl Werthman. "Public Housing: Tenants and Troubles," *Dissent* 8 (Summer 1961):282–288.

Murray, Thomas F. "Problems and Techniques in Financing Ghetto Housing," *Bankers Monthly* 152 (Spring 1969):34–40.

Nash, William. *The Impact of Public Programs on the Housing Shortage in the Boston Area.* Prepared by Housing Advisory Research Committee, Massachusetts Committee on Discrimination in Housing, April 1963.

National Committee against Discrimination in Housing. *How the Federal Government Builds Ghettos.* New York, 1967.

Needham, Maurice d'Arlan. *Negro Orleanian: Status and Stake in a City's Economy and Housing.* New Orleans: Tulane Publications, 1962.

Nesbitt, George B. "Urban Renewal in Perspective," *Phylon* 19 (Spring 1958):64–68.

Northwood, Lawrence K. "The Threat and Potential of Urban Renewal: A 'Workable Program' for Better Race Relations," *Journal of Intergroup Relations* 2 (Spring 1961):101–114.

Novasky, Victor S. "The Benevolent Housing Quota," *Howard Law Journal* 6 (January 1960):30–68.

Page, Alfred N. "Race and Property Values," *Appraisal Journal* 36 (July 1968):334–341.

Papageorge, George T. "Relocation: An Essential of Urban Renewal," *Phylon* 19 (Spring 1958):69–70.

Rainwater, Lee. "The Lessons of Pruitt-Igoe," *Public Interest* no. 8 (Summer 1967):116–126. Sociological factors of a public high-rise housing development for some 2,000 Negro households.

Rapkin, Chester. "Price Discrimination against Negroes in the Rental Housing Market," in California. University Graduate School of Business Administration. *Essays in Urban Land Economics.* Berkeley, 1966, pp. 333–345.

Ravitz, Mel J. "Effects of Urban Renewal on Community Racial Patterns," *Journal of Social Issues* 13 (October 1957):38-49. Detroit.

Raymond, George M., Malcolm D. Rivkin, and Herbert J. Gans. "Urban Renewal," *Commentary* 40 (July 1965):72-80. Mr. Raymond and Mr. Rivkin present their criticisms of Mr. Gans's article in *Commentary,* April 1965, and Mr. Gans replies.

Richey, Elinor. "Splitsville, U.S.A.: An Ironic Tale of Urban Renewal and Racial Segregation," *Reporter* 28 (May 23, 1963):35-38.

Rivers, Marie D. "Upward Mobile Trends in Negro Housing in Selected Cities of Indiana from 1950 through the 60's," *Interracial Review* 39 (January 1966):3-13; (February 1966):35-38+.

Rothman, Jack. "The Ghetto Makers," *Nation* 193 (October 7, 1961):222-225.

Sager, Lawrence Gene. "Tight Little Islands: Exclusionary Zoning, Equal Protection and the Indigent," *Stanford Law Review* 21 (April 1969):767-800.

Schietinger, E. Frederick. "Racial Succession and Changing Property Values in Residential Chicago," in E. W. Burgess and D. J. Bogue, eds., *Contributions to Urban Sociology.* Chicago: University of Chicago Press, 1964, pp. 86-99.

Schnore, Leo F., and Philip C. Evenson. "Segregation in Southern Cities," *American Journal of Sociology* 72 (July 1966):58-67. Examines 1960 levels of residential segregation in 76 Southern cities.

Schwartz, Raymond J. "The Federal Housing Authority and Urban Planning," *Phylon* 19 (Spring 1958):89-90.

Scott, Barbara W. *The Status of Housing of Negroes in Pittsburgh.* Pittsburgh Commission on Human Relations, May 1962.

Smith, Ralph L. "Racial Discrimination in Metropolitan Housing," *New Leader,* February 16, 1959.

Smolensky, Eugene, Selwyn Becker, and Harvey Molotch. "The Prisoner's Dilemma and Ghetto Expansion," *Land Economics* 44 (November 1968):419-430.

Southern Regional Council. *Neighborhood Stabilization.* Atlanta, 1966.

Sternlieb, George. *The Tenement Landlord.* New Brunswick, N. J.: Rutgers University Press, 1969. Functioning of the housing market in a black slum in Newark, New Jersey.

Sutton, R. O. "Conventional Mortgage Financing," *Phylon* 19 (Spring 1958):84-86.

Taeuber, Karl E. "The Effect of Income Redistribution on Racial Residential Segregation," *Urban Affairs Quarterly* 4 (September 1968):5-14. In the Cleveland area. Based on a report prepared for the U. S. Commission on Civil Rights.

Taeuber, Karl E. "Negro Population and Housing: Demographic Aspects of a Social Accounting Scheme," in Irwin Katz and Patricia Gurin, eds., *Race and the Social Sciences.* New York: Basic Books, 1969, pp. 145-193. Bibliographical notes.

Taeuber, Karl E., and Alma F. Taeuber. *Negroes in Cities; Residential Segregation and Neighborhood Change.* Chicago: Aldine, 1965. Analysis and comparison of racial migration in 10 urban neighborhoods. Based on doctoral research of each author; scientific, exhaustive investigation.

Taeuber, Karl E. "Problem of Residential Segregation," *Academy of Political Science Proceedings* 29 (July 1968):101-110.

Taeuber, Karl E. "Residential Segregation," *Scientific American* 213 (August 1965):12-19. The author finds that the principal cause of Negro segregation in urban ghettos is discrimination, and that there is "no basis for anticipating major changes . . . until patterns of housing discrimination can be altered." An important study based on calculation of the segregation indices for 207 American cities.

Thompson, Robert A. "The Social Dynamics in Demographic Trends and the Housing of Minority Groups," *Phylon* 19 (Spring 1958):31-43.

Tilly, Charles, Wagner D. Jackson, and Barry Kay. *Race and Residence in Wilmington, Delaware.* New York: Bureau of Publications, Teachers College, Columbia University, 1965.

United Community Services of Metropolitan Boston. *Black and White in Boston: A Report Based on the Community Research Project.* Boston, 1968. Immigration, population, and housing patterns of black and white families.

U.S. Commission on Civil Rights. *Civil Rights U. S. A.: Housing in Washington, D. C., 1962.* Washington, 1962.

U.S. Commission on Civil Rights. *Hearings, May 4-6, 1967.* Washington, 1967. Chiefly concerned with issues of housing and employment opportunities for Negroes and other minority groups in the San Francisco-Oakland Bay area. Tables, maps.

U.S. Commission on Civil Rights. *Report.* Washington: U.S. Govt. Print. Off., 1959- . Annual. In 1961 only, issued in five parts. See entry following.

U.S. Commission on Civil Rights. *Report 1961: Housing.* Washington: U.S. Govt. Print. Off., 1961.

U.S. Commission on Civil Rights. Massachusetts Advisory Committee. *Discrimination in Housing in the Boston Metropolitan Area.* Boston, 1963.

U.S. Commission on Civil Rights. Massachusetts Advisory Committee. *Report on Massachusetts: Housing Discrimination in the Springfield-Holyoke-Chicopee Metropolitan Area.* Washington: U. S. Govt. Print. Off., 1966.

U.S. Housing and Home Finance Agency. *Our Nonwhite Population and Its Housing: Changes between 1950 and 1960.* Washington, May 1963. Statistics on population, income, education, employment, household composition, and housing.

"Urban Revival: Goals and Standards," *Annals of the American Academy of Political and Social Science* 352 (March 1964):1-151. Entire issue, with the majority of articles having some relevance for problem of Negro housing.

Vax, John J. "Home Financing Assistance by Voluntary Home Mortgage Credit Program," *Phylon* 19 (Spring 1958):81-82.

Von Eckardt, Wolf. "Black Neck in the White Noose," *New Republic* 149 (October 19, 1963):14-17. "The vast majority of displaced poor Negroes are worse off after urban renewal than they were before."

Warner, A. E., and Milton S. Goldberg. "Governments and Housing: Accessibility of Minority Groups to Living Space," *Land Economics* 37 (November 1961):369-373.

Watts, Lewis J., et al. *The Middle-Income Negro Family Faces Urban Renewal.* Waltham, Mass.: Brandeis University, for the Department of Commerce and Development, Commonwealth of Massachusetts, 1964. A study of families in the Washington Park section of Boston during the rehabilitation of the neighborhood.

Wedge, E. Bruce. "The Concept 'Urban Renewal,' " *Phylon* 19 (Spring 1958):55-60.

Whitson, Edmund R., and Paul A. Brinker. "The Housing of Negroes in Oklahoma," *Phylon* 19 (Spring 1958):106-108.

Young, Whitney M., Jr. "Participation of Citizens," *Phylon* 19 (Spring 1958):96. In decisions on urban renewal.

Efforts to Integrate

Abrahamson, Julia. *A Neighborhood Finds Itself.* New York: Harper, 1959. The Hyde Park-Kenwood urban renewal effort in Chicago and its repercussions.

Abrams, Charles. *Equal Opportunity in Housing.* National Committee against Discrimination in Housing, April 1963. Survey of effects of federal housing program.

Adams, Frankie V. "The Community-Wide Stake of Citizens in Urban Renewal," *Phylon* 19 (Spring 1958):92-96.

Alfred, Stephen J., and Charles R. Marcoux. "Impact of a Community Association on Integrated Suburban Housing Patterns," *Cleveland State Law Review* 19 (January 1970):90-99.

Bacon, Margaret H. "The White Noose of the Suburbs," *Progressive* 24 (October 1960): 37-38. An account of the attempt of the Friends Suburban Housing Agency to establish integrated residential areas in suburban Philadelphia.

Balk, Alfred. "A Builder Who Makes Integration Pay," *Harper's* 231 (July 1965):94-99. On Morris Milgram.

"Benign Quotas: A Plan for Integrated Private Housing," *Yale Law Journal* 70 (November 1960):126-134.

Berry, John M. "Open Housing," *Editorial Research Reports* August 16, 1967, pp. 599-616. Contents: approaches to housing bias; racial segregation in American cities; resistance to open housing enforcement.

Bressler, Marvin. " 'The Myers' Case: An Instance of Successful Invasion," *Social Problems* 8 (Fall 1960):126-142.

Caplan, Eleanor, and Eleanor P. Wolf. "Factors Affecting Racial Change in Two Middle Income Housing Areas," *Phylon* 21 (Fall 1960):225-233.

Clark, Dennis. "Comeback Parish," *Interracial Review* 35 (November 1962):250-254.

Clark, Dennis. "Strategy in Suburbia," *Interracial Review* 35 (July 1962):160, 164-167. Utilization of committees of conscience to challenge housing segregation.

Clark, Henry. *The Church and Residential Desegregation: A Case Study of an Open Housing Covenant Campaign.* New Haven, Conn.: College and University Press, 1965.

Clarke, Douglas V. "Banks, Negro Church Join Forces to Ease Racial Tensions," *Banking* 61 (February 1969):34. Newburgh, New York housing project.

Cohen, Oscar. "The Benign Quota in Housing: The Case For and Against," *Anti-Defamation League Bulletin* 16 (January 1959):3, 7.

Connecticut Commission on Civil Rights. *Private Interracial Neighborhoods in Connecticut.* 1957.

Connecticut Commission on Civil Rights. *Racial Integration in Public Housing Projects in Connecticut.* 1955.

Deutsch, Martin, and Mary Evans Collins. *Interracial Housing: A Psychological Evaluation of a Social Experiment.* Minneapolis: University of Minnesota Press, 1951. The authors conclude that public policy can change social attitudes under certain favorable circumstances.

Dodson, Dan W. "Can Intergroup Quotas Be Benign?" *Journal of Intergroup Relations* 1 (Fall 1960):12-17. An evaluation of means of achieving racial balance, with suggestions of alternatives to quotas.

Ekola, Giles C. "Interracial Residence Sponsorship: A Proposal," *Christian Century* 85 (February 14, 1968):200-201.

Fauman, S. Joseph. "Housing Discrimination, Changing Neighborhoods, and Public Schools," *Journal of Social Issues* 13 (October 1957):21-30.

Fishman, Joshua A. "Some Social and Psychological Determinants of Intergroup Relations in Changing Neighborhoods: An Introduction to the Bridgeview Study," *Social Forces* 40 (October 1961):42-51. Study of New Jersey suburb, and its experience of integration. Contains a summary of recent writings on intergroup relations in changing neighborhoods.

Greenfield, Robert W. "Factors Associated with Attitudes toward Desegregation in a Florida Residential Suburb," *Social Forces* 40 (October 1961):31-42.

Grier, Eunice S., and George Grier. *Buyers of Interracial Housing: A Study of the Market for Concord Park.* Philadelphia: University of Pennsylvania Institute for Urban Studies, January 1957. A study of an early middle-class project.

Grier, Eunice S., and George Grier. "Market Characteristics in Interracial Housing," *Journal of Social Issues* 13 (Fall 1957):50-67. Authors analyze Negroes and whites who seek mixed housing.

Grier, Eunice S. "Research Needs in the Field of Housing and Race," *Journal of Intergroup Relations* 1 (Summer 1960):21-31. Twelve leading intergroup practitioners in field of housing suggest research projects for study.

Heifeta, Robert. "The Public Sector, Residential Desegregation and the Schools: A Case Study from Buffalo, New York," *Urban Review* (February 1968):30-34.

Hepburn, Richard. "White Suburbia—Token Integration Northern Style," *Interracial Review* 35 (July 1962):169-170.

Horne, Frank S. "Interracial Housing in the United States," *Phylon* 19 (Spring 1958):13-20.

Hunt, Chester L. "Negro-White Perception of Interracial Housing," *Journal of Social Issues* 15 (October 1959):24-29.

Hunt, Chester L. "Private Integrated Housing in a Moderate Size Northern City," *Social Problems* 7 (Winter 1959-1960):195-209.

Hunt, Chester L. "A Research Report on Integrated Housing in a Small Northern City," *Journal of Intergroup Relations* 3 (Winter 1961-1962):65-79. Study of Kalamazoo, Michigan, disclosed strong market for mixed housing.

Johnson, Philip A. *Call Me Neighbor, Call Me Friend: The Case History of the Integration of a Neighborhood on Chicago's South Side.* Garden City, N. Y.: Doubleday, 1965. The account by a Lutheran minister of a neighborhood's progress from panic over the entrance of one Negro family to peaceful integration.

Kerckhoff, Richard K. "A Study of Racially Changing Neighbors," *Merrill-Palmer Quarterly* 3 (Fall 1957):15-49.

Killingsworth, Mark R. "Desegregating Public Housing," *New Leader* 51 (October 7, 1968):13-14.

Krasner, Barbara. "Open Housing and the Black Community," *Renewal* 7 (March 1967): 16-18. Fair housing in Philadelphia.

Ladd, W. M. "The Effect of Integration on Property Values," *American Economic Review* 52 (September 1962):801-808.

Langendorf, Richard. "Residential Desegregation Potential," *Journal of the American Institute of Planners* 35 (March 1969):90-95.

Laurenti, Luigi. *Property Values and Race: Studies in Seven Cities.* Special Research Report to the Commission on Race and Housing, Berkeley: University of California Press, 1960. Detailed study of price trends in 20 well defined neighborhoods where nonwhite entry occurred in all-white areas. The author found nonwhite entry most often associated with price improvement or stability. He detected no single or uniform pattern of nonwhite influence on property values.

Leacock, Eleanor, Martin Deutsch, and Joshua A. Fishman. "The Bridgeview Study: A Preliminary Report," *Journal of Social Issues* 15 (October 1959):30-37. Study of a New Jersey suburb of New York to determine reasons for the ultimate failure, after initial success, of efforts to integrate the community.

Lees, Hannah, "Making Our Cities Fit to Live In," *Reporter* 16 (February 21, 1957):30-34. Chiefly concerned with Philadelphia projects and progress. The success of Morris Milgram in building for open occupancy receives special note.

Marcus, Matityahu. "Racial Composition and Home Price Changes: A Case Study," *Journal of the American Institute of Planners* 34 (September 1968):334-338. A study of Plainfield, New Jersey disproves the hypothesis that integration of a suburban community will adversely affect property values.

Mayer, Albert J. "Race and Private Housing: A Social Problem and a Challenge to Understanding Human Behavior," *Journal of Social Issues* 13 (October 1957):3-6. A brief article pointing out that the "invasion-succession" sequence of changing neighborhoods is susceptible to scientific investigation.

Meer, Bernard, and Edward Freedman. "Impact of Negro Neighbors on White Home Owners," *Social Forces* 45 (September 1966):11-19. Tests the hypothesis that equal-status contact between Negroes and whites in a predominantly white high socio-economic residential area leads to reduced prejudice.

Milgram, Morris. "Commercial Development of Integrated Housing," *Journal of Intergroup Relations* 1 (Summer 1960):55-60. Description by the president of Modern Community Developers of several integrated projects.

Nesbitt, George B. "Dispersion of Nonwhite Residence in Washington, D. C.," *Land Economics* 32 (August 1956):201-212.

Nesbitt, George B. "Misconceptions in the Movement for Civil Rights in Housing," *Journal of Intergroup Relations* 2 (Winter 1960-1961):61-67.

Nesbitt, George B., and Marian P. Yankauer. "The Potential for Equalizing Housing Opportunity in the Nation's Capital," *Journal of Intergroup Relations* 4 (Winter 1962-1963): 73-97.

Northwood, L. K., and Ernest A. T. Barth. *Urban Desegregation: Negro Pioneers and Their White Neighbors.* Seattle: University of Washington Press, 1965. Analysis based on interviews of Negro families and their neighbors in formerly "all white" areas of Seattle. Bibliography.

Northwood, Lawrence K., and Louise H. Klein. "The Benign Quota, an Unresolved Issue of Attitudes of Agency Personnel," *Phylon* 25 (Summer 1964):111. On the effectiveness of social agency campaigns in advance of Negro entry.

Palmore, Erdman. "Integration and Property Values in Washington, D. C.," *Phylon* 27 (Spring 1966):15-19.

Palmore, Erdman, and John Howe. "Residential Integration and Property Values," *Social Problems* 10 (Summer 1962):52-55.

Rames, Jose. "How Not to Pass Open Occupancy," *New University Thought* 3 (December 1963-January 1964):16-21.

Rapkin, Chester, and William G. Grigsby. *The Demand for Housing in Racially Mixed Areas: A Study of the Nature of Neighborhood Change.* Berkeley: University of California Press, 1960. Factors influencing white and nonwhite demand for housing in several racially mixed areas in Philadelphia.

Rapkin, Chester. *Market Experience and Occupancy Patterns in Interracial Housing Developments.* Philadelphia: Institute for Urban Studies, University of Pennsylvania, 1957.

Richey, Elinor. "Kenwood Foils the Block-busters," *Harper's* 227 (August 1963):42-47. Action to preserve Kenwood area in Chicago as fully integrated single-home area.

Rose, Arnold M. "Inconsistencies in Attitudes toward Negro Housing," *Social Problems* 8 (Spring 1961):286-292.

Rose, Arnold M., F. J. Atelsek, and L. R. McDonald. "Neighborhood Reactions to Isolated Negro Residents: An Alternative to Invasion and Succession," *American Sociological Review* 18 (October 1953):497-507.

Rosen, Ellsworth E., with Arnold Nicholson. "When a Negro Moves Next Door," *Saturday Evening Post* 231 (April 4, 1959):32-33 + . Account of a Baltimore neighborhood where Negroes have been welcomed and white residents have remained.

Rosen, Harry, and David Rosen. *But Not Next Door.* New York: Avon, 1963.

Rosenthal, Bernard G., Donald Miller, and Frank Teryenyi. "The Measurement of Social Interaction among Negro and White Children in a Housing Community," *Journal of Social Psychology* 71 (February 1967):27-37.

Roshco, Bernard. "The Integration Problem and Public Housing," *New Leader* 43 (July 4-11, 1960):10-13.

Rossi, Peter H., and Robert A. Dentler. *The Politics of Urban Renewal: The Chicago Findings.* New York: Free Press, 1961. Study of Hyde Park-Kenwood Community. Planning objectives: that Negroes in the area were to be of the same socio-economic level as whites, and that there should be a fixed balance between races.

Rubin, Morton. "The Function of Social Research for a Fair Housing Practice Committee," *Journal of Intergroup Relations* 2 (Fall 1961):325-331.

Rubin, Morton. "The Negro Wish to Move: The Boston Case," *Journal of Social Issues* 15 (October 1959):4-13.

Rutledge, Edward. "Housing Bias in the College Community," *Journal of Intergroup Relations* 1 (Fall 1960):30-39.

Schermer, George, and Arthur J. Levin. *Housing Guide to Equal Opportunity: Affirmative Practices for Integrated Housing.* Washington: Potomac Institute, 1968.

Schiltz, Michael E. "Interracial Housing," *Social Order* 11 (June 1961):276-279. Review of books in Race and Housing Studies, stressing failure of construction industry to build for lower-middle-income groups.

Shaffer, Helen B. "Interracial Housing," *Editorial Research Reports,* (February 6, 1963):87-104.

Smith, Bulkeley, Jr. "The Differential Residential Segregation of Working-class Negroes in New Haven," *American Sociological Review* 24 (August 1959):529-533.

Smith, Bulkeley, Jr. "The Reshuffling Phenomenon: A Pattern of Residence of Unsegregated Negroes," *American Sociological Review* 24 (February 1959):77-79.

Snowden, George W. "Some Problems in the Relocation of Minority Families in the Nation's Capital," *Phylon* 19 (Spring 1958):73-74.

Southern Regional Council. *Neighborhoods: Where Human Relations Begin.* Atlanta, 1967. Evaluation of three interracial neighborhoods.

Spiegel, Hans B. C. "Tenants' Intergroup Attitudes in a Public Housing Project with Declining White Population," *Phylon* 21 (Spring 1960):30-39.

Stetler, Henry G. *Racial Integration in Private Residential Neighborhoods in Connecticut.* Hartford: Connecticut Commission on Civil Rights, 1957.

Stetler, Henry G. *Racial Integration in Public Housing Projects in Connecticut.* Hartford: Connecticut Commission on Civil Rights, 1955.

A Study of the Resources, Capabilities for Rehabilitation, and Preferences of Families Living or Owning Property in the Lippitt Hill Rehabilitation Area and Their Attitudes toward Their Neighborhood and Its Rehabilitation. Providence Redevelopment Agency, 1962. Study made by Urban League of Rhode Island.

Sudman, Seymour, Norman M. Bradburn, and Galen Gockel. "The Extent and Characteristics of Racially Integrated Housing in the United States," *Journal of Business* 42 (January 1969):50-92. Tables; references.

Sussman, Marvin B. "The Role of Neighborhood Associations in Private Housing for Racial Minorities," *Journal of Social Issues* 13 (October 1957):31-37.

Tillman, James A., Jr. "Fair Housing: A Conceptual and Analytic Frame of Reference," *Journal of Intergroup Relations* 1 (Fall 1960):18-29.

Tillman, James A., Jr. "Morningtown, U.S.A.—A Composite Case History of Neighborhood Change," *Journal of Intergroup Relations* 2 (Spring 1961):156-166.

Tillman, James A., Jr. "The Quest for Identity and Status: Facets of the Desegregation Process in the Upper Midwest," *Phylon* 22 (Winter 1961):329-339. Residential patterns and restrictions, and collective resistance to fair housing in non-Southern communities. Describes the Greater Minneapolis Fair Housing Program in detail.

U.S. Commission on Civil Rights. Georgia State Advisory Committee. *Toward Equal Opportunity in Housing in Atlanta, Georgia.* Washington: U.S. Govt. Print. Off., 1968.

Weaver, Robert C. *Dilemmas of Urban America.* Cambridge, Mass.: Harvard University Press, 1965. On the difficulties of urban renewal, the racial problems in urban planning, and the roles of government versus private enterprise.

Weaver, Robert C. "The Effects of Anti-Discrimination Legislation Upon the FHA- and VA-Insured Housing Market in New York State," *Land Economics* 31 (November 1955):303-313.

Weaver, Robert C. "Integration in Public and Private Housing," *Annals of the American Academy of Political and Social Science* 304 (March 1956):86-97.

Weisbord, Marvin. "Homes Without Hate," *Progressive* 25 (January 1961):28-32. On Morris Milgram and his Modern Community Developers, Inc., established to develop open occupancy housing.

Wertz, R. C. "Power of Positive Action: Rockville, Maryland, Moves Quickly to Prevent Violence When Negro Family Moves into Suburb," *National Civic Review* 52 (November 1963):540.

Wolf, Eleanor P. "The Invasion-Succession Sequence as a Self-Fulfilling Prophecy," *Journal of Social Issues* 13 (October 1957):7-20. As seen in a Detroit suburb.

Wolf, Eleanor P. "Racial Transition in a Middle-Class Area," *Journal of Intergroup Relations* 1 (Summer 1960):75-81. Findings of a study of Russel Woods, near Detroit.

Works, E. "Residence in Integrated and Segregated Housing and Improvements in Self-Concepts of Negroes," *Sociology and Social Research* 46 (April 1962):294-301.

Wyant, William K. "Holding Action," *New Leader* 40 (July 8, 1957):16-19. Example of benevolent quotas aiding the stability of a racially mixed situation.

Yankauer, Marian P., and M. B. Sunderhauf. "Housing: Equal Opportunity to Choose Where One Shall Live," *Journal of Negro Education* 32 (Fall 1963):402-414.

16　Education

Historical Background

Avins, Alfred. "Federal Aid to Education Policies, 1865-1888: Some Reflected Light on School Segregation and the Fourteenth Amendment," *Alabama Law Review* 21 (Fall 1968):61-118.

Armstrong, Warren B. "Union Chaplains and the Education of the Freedmen," *Journal of Negro History* 52 (April 1967):104-115.

Beam, Lura. *He Called Them by the Lightning: A Teachers Odyssey on the Negro South, 1908-1919.* Indianapolis: Bobbs-Merrill, 1967. Recollections of a Northern educator in the South. Significant as a chronicle of the time and as good historical background for understanding the present.

Bernstein, Barton J. "Case Law in *Plessy v. Ferguson,*" *Journal of Negro History* 47 (July 1962):192-198.

Bernstein, Barton J. "*Plessy v. Ferguson*: Conservative Sociological Jurisprudence," *Journal of Negro History* 48 (July 1963):196-205.

Bond, Horace Mann. *Negro Education in Alabama; A Study in Cotton and Steel.* New York: Atheneum, 1969. Published in 1939 as a thesis submitted to the University of Chicago under the title: Social and Economic Influences on the Public Education of Negroes in Alabama, 1865-1930.

Bond, Horace Mann. *The Education of the Negro in the American Social Order.* 1934. New York: Octagon, 1966. 1966 edition with new preface and a new chapter, "A 1965 Retrospective of Negro Education."

Boskin, Joseph. "The Origins of American Slavery: Education as an Index of Early Differentiation," *Journal of Negro Education* 35 (Spring 1966):125-133.

Brickman, William W. "Segregation: Past and Present," *School and Society* 88 (May 7, 1960):219-220.

Bullock, Henry Allen. *A History of Negro Education in the South: From 1619 to the Present.* Cambridge, Mass.: Harvard University Press, 1967.

Clement, Rufus E. "The Historical Development of Higher Education for Negro Americans," *Journal of Negro Education* 35 (Summer 1966):299-305.

Clift, Virgil A. "The History of Racial Segregation in American Education," *School and Society* 88 (May 7, 1960):220-229.

Fen, Sing-Nan. "Notes on the Education of Negroes at Norfolk and Portsmouth, Virginia during the Civil War," *Phylon* 28 (Summer 1967):197-201.

Fen, Sing-Nan. "Notes on the Education of Negroes in North Carolina during the Civil War," *Journal of Negro Education* 36 (Winter 1967):24-31.

Gordon, Vivian Verdell. "A Short History of Storer College, Harpers Ferry, West Virginia," *Journal of Negro Education* 30 (Fall 1961):445-449.

Graham, Edward K. "The Hampton Institute Strike of 1927: A Case Study in Student Protest," *American Scholar* 38 (Autumn 1969):668-681.

Greer, Colin. "Inmigrants, Negroes, and the Public Schools," *Urban Review* 3: (January 1969):9-12. A summary of the Negro in the New York public schools, 1890-1960.

Harlan, Louis R. *Separate and Unequal: Public School Campaigns and Racism in the Southern Seaboard States, 1901-1915.* Chapel Hill: University of North Carolina Press, 1958. Reissued with a new preface by the author. New York: Atheneum, 1968. A study of the first significant effort by native Southerners to improve schools according to Northern standards and of how this widened the gap between Negro and white education.

Holmes, Eugene C. "Alain L. Locke and the Adult Education Movement," *Journal of Negro Education* 34 (Winter 1965):5-10.

Kelly, Alfred H. "The Congressional Controversy over School Segregation, 1867-1875," *American Historical Review* 64 (April 1959):537-563.

Mabee, Carleton. "A Negro Boycott to Integrate Boston Schools," *New England Quarterly* 41 (September 1968):341-361. Campaign led by William C. Nell, John T. Hilton, and other Negro Garrisonians.

Meier, August, and Elliott M. Rudwick. "Early Boycotts of Segregated Schools: The Alton, Illinois Case, 1897-1908," *Journal of Negro Education* 36 (Fall 1967):394-402.

Meier, August, and Elliott M. Rudwick. "Early Boycotts of Segregated Schools: The Case of Springfield, Ohio, 1922-1923," *American Quarterly* 20 (Winter 1968):744-758.

Meier, August, and Elliott M. Rudwick. "Early Boycotts of Segregated Schools: The East Orange, New Jersey Experience, 1899-1906," *History of Education Quarterly* 7 (Spring 1967):22-35.

Miller, H. "John Dewey on Urban Education: An Extrapolation," *Record* 69 (May 1968):771-783. The Negro within Dewey's educational philosophy.

North, Arthur A. "The Plessy Doctrine: Rise and Demise," *Thought* 35 (Fall 1960):138. Constitutional history of segregation cases up to the date of writing.

Palmer, R. Roderick. "Colonial Statutes and Present-Day Obstacles Restricting Negro Education," *Journal of Negro Education* 26 (Fall 1957):525-529.

Payne, Joseph Arthur, Jr. "The Role of the Association of Colleges and Secondary Schools for Negroes from 1934-1954," *Journal of Negro Education* 27 (Fall 1958):532-536.

Robbins, Gerald. "William F. Allen: Classical Scholar among the Slaves," *History of Education Quarterly* 5 (December 1965):211-223.

Roucek, Joseph S. "Milestones in the History of Education of the Negro in the United States," *International Review of Education* 10, no. 2 (1964):162-178.

Toppin, Edgar A. "Walter White and the Atlanta NAACP's Fight for Equal Schools, 1916-1917," *History of Education Quarterly* 7 (Spring 1967):3-21.

Vaughn, William P. "Separate and Unequal: The Civil Rights Act of 1875 and Defeat of the School Integration Clause," *Southwestern Social Science Quarterly* 48 (September 1967):146-154. Charles Sumner's abortive attempt to incorporate a school desegregation clause in the 1875 act signed by President Grant.

Weinberg, Meyer. *Race and Place; A Legal History of the Neighborhood School.* Washington: U.S. Office of Education, 1967. Bibliography.

Weinberg, Meyer. "A Yearning for Learning: Blacks and Jews through History," *Integrated Education* 7 (May-June 1969):20-29.

West, Earle H. "Peabody Education Fund and Negro Education, 1867-1880," *History of Education Quarterly* 6 (Summer 1966):3-21. The Freedmen's Bureau.

White, Arthur O. "The Black Movement against Jim Crow Education in Buffalo, New York, 1800-1900," *Phylon* 30 (Winter 1969):375-393.

Wilkerson, Doxey A. "The Ghetto School Struggle in Historical Perspective," *Science and Society* 33 (Spring 1969):130-149. Viewed within the total framework of the Negro's relation to American society.

Ziegler, Benjamin Munn, ed. *Desegregation and the Supreme Court.* Boston: Heath, 1958. Historical aspects of desegregation and their relation to the Supreme Court.

The Law, the Courts, and Regulatory Action

Armstrong, Robert G. "A Reply to Herbert Wechsler's Holmes Lecture 'Toward Neutral Principles of Constitutional Law,' " *Phylon* 21 (Fall 1960):211-224.

Avins, Alfred. "De Facto and De Jure School Segregation: Some Reflected Light on the Fourteenth Amendment from the Civil Rights Act of 1875," *Mississippi Law Journal* 38 (March 1967):179-247. Author supports creation of schools for each segment of community to allow parents freedom of choice in educational environments. See also rejoinder by Walter E. Dellinger.

Avins, Alfred. "Toward Freedom of Choice in Education," *Journal of Urban Law* 45 (Fall 1967):23-112. Legal opinions of issues of educational imbalance in northern states.

Berger, Morroe. "Desegregation, Law, and Social Science," *Commentary* 23 (May 1957):471-477. The author seeks to assess how far the Supreme Court was influenced by the findings of social science and what the role of the social sciences can and should be in jurisprudence.

Bickel, Alexander M. "The Decade of School Desegregation: Progress and Prospects," *Columbia Law Review* 64 (February 1964):193-222. On the assumption that the "establishment phase, characterized by permissive tokenism," is over, the author considers what enforcement policies and legal action should be pursued to obtain complete Southern compliance and resolution of the problem of Northern de facto school segregation. See also rebuttal by John Kaplan which follows.

Bickel, Alexander M. *The Least Dangerous Branch.* Indianapolis, Ind.: Bobbs-Merrill, 1962. Namely, the judicial branch. Arguing that the basis of all law is consensual, the author finds this especially true of judge-made constitutional law.

Bickel, Alexander M. "The Original Understanding and the Segregation Decision," *Harvard Law Review* 69 (November 1955):1-34. The author concludes that the Court was able to reach the decision it did "because the record of history, properly understood, left the way open to, in fact invited, a decision based on the moral and material state of the nation in 1954, not 1866."

Black, C. L., Jr. "Lawfulness of the Segregation Decisions," *Yale Law Journal* 69 (January 1960):421.

Blaustein, Albert P. *Civil Rights U.S.A.: Public Schools, Cities in the North and West, 1963: Camden and Environs.* Washington, 1963. Staff report submitted to the U.S. Commission on Civil Rights.

Blaustein, Albert P., and Clarence Clyde Ferguson, Jr. *Desegregation and the Law: The Meaning and Effect of the School Segregation Cases.* New Brunswick, N.J.: Rutgers University Press, 1957; 2d ed. rev. New York: Vintage, 1962. Revision consists of addition of chapter "The Aftermath 1957-1961." A comprehensive examination of the whole legal issue, the book contains texts of the Supreme Court opinions of 1954 and 1955, bibliographical notes to each chapter, a table of cases, and an index.

Bluford, Lucile H. "The Lloyd Gaines Story," *Journal of Educational Sociology* 32 (February 1959):242-246. Gaines and the University of Missouri Law School: a 1938 Supreme Court case.

Bolner, James. *Civil Rights in the Political Process: An Analysis of the Massachusetts Racial Imbalance Law of 1965.* Amherst: University of Massachusetts, Bureau of Government Research, 1967.

Bolner, James. "The Supreme Court and Racially Imbalanced Public Schools in 1967," *Journal of Negro Education* 38 (Spring 1969):125-134.

Borinski, Ernst. "A Legal and Sociological Analysis of the Segregation Decision of May 17, 1954," *University of Pittsburgh Law Review* 15 (Summer 1954):622-627.

Briggs, David C., ed. "Private Schools Must Integrate?" *Southwestern Law Journal* 16 (July 1962):284-319.

Bromberg, Lee Core. "Constitutional Law—Public School Desegregation . . .," *Harvard Civil Rights-Civil Liberties Law Review* 3 (Fall 1967):167-182. Suit against the Macon County, Alabama Board of Education.

Buck, Richard T., Richard A. Nelson, and David M. Truitt. "Public School Segregation:

Does the Fourteenth Amendment Require Affirmative Integration?" *Chicago-Kent Law Review* 38 (October 1961):169-184.

Cahn, Edmond. "Jurisprudence," *New York University Law Review* 30 (January 1955): 150-159. Commenting on "the meaning of the victory," the author believes that the 1954 decision spared the nation a genuine constitutional crisis, that only the institution of judicial review could abolish "separate but equal" without both protracted delay and great conflict.

Carter, Robert L. "The Law and Racial Equality in Education," *Journal of Negro Education* 37 (Summer 1968):204-211.

Carter, Robert L., and Thurgood Marshall. "The Meaning and Significance of the Supreme Court Decree on Implementation," *Journal of Negro Education* 24 (Summer 1955):397-404.

Carter, Robert L. "The Warren Court and Desegregation," *Michigan Law Review* 67 (December 1968):237-248.

"Civil Rights—Desegregation—Freedom of Choice Plans Are Not To Be Used When More Effective Means for Desegregation Are Available," *Vanderbilt Law Review* 21 (November 1968):1093-1099.

Clark, Kenneth B. "Desegregation: An Appraisal of the Evidence," *Journal of Social Issues* 9 (October 1953):2-76. Entire issue. The author, professor of psychology, College of the City of New York, prepared this material as part of the evidence presented to the Supreme Court in the case of *Brown v. Board of Education.* Topics covered: I. The Background: The Role of Social Scientists; II. The Question Posed and the Strategy for the Reply; III. Findings; IV. Some Implications for a Theory of Social Change. An impressive piece of work.

Clark, Kenneth B. "The Desegregation Cases: Criticism of the Social Scientist's Role," *Villanova Law Review* 5 (Winter 1959-1960):224+.

"Constitutionality of De Facto School Segregation," *North Dakota Law Review* 41 (March 1965):346+.

"Controversy in Congress over Federal 'School Desegregation Guidelines'; Pro & Con," *Congressional Digest* 48 (February 1969):34-64.

Cook, Eugene, and William I. Potter. "The School Segregation Cases: Opposing the Opinion of the Supreme Court," and Stumberg, G. W., "Supporting the Opinion of the Supreme Court," *American Bar Association Journal* 42 (April 1956):313-315.

"The Courts, HEW, and Southern School Desegregation," *Yale Law Journal* 77 (December 1967):321-365. The efficacy of Titles IV and VI of the Civil Rights Act of 1964 in the courts to effect Southern desegregation.

Daffner, Gerald Nathan. "The Effect of Pupil Placement Laws upon Southern Education," *Albany Law Review* 23 (May 1959):376-385.

"Declaration of Constitutional Principles," *Congressional Record* 102 (March 12, 1956):4459. Formulated by the Congressional delegations from the Southern states, this statement came to be known as the "Southern Manifesto."

"De Facto Segregation—A Study in State Action," *Northwestern University Law Review* 57 (January-February 1963):722-737.

Dellinger, Walter E. "School Segregation and Professor Avins' History: A Defense of *Brown v. Board of Education,*" *Mississippi Law Journal* 38 (March 1967):248-253. Rejoinder to Alfred Avins's article, which supports a narrow interpretation of the Fourteenth Amendment.

Dent, Tom. "New Law Against Tokenism," *New South* 8 (January 1963):10-15.

"Desegregation of Public Schools: An Affirmative Duty to Eliminate Racial Segregation Root and Branch," *Syracuse Law Review* 20 (Fall 1968):53+.

Detweiler, John S. "The Negro Teacher and the Fourteenth Amendment," *Journal of Negro Education* 36 (Fall 1967):403-409. Emphasizes the legal implementation.

Deutsch, E. P. "Views from Many Bridges on School Segregation and Integration," *American Bar Association Journal* 51 (March 1965):233-238.

"Dillard Case, Desegregation and the Doctrine of Non-Integration: A Review," *Virginia Law Review* 49 (March 1963):367-385. The Dillard case arose out of the division of

Charlottesville, Va., into six school districts. The schools in each were not officially segregated, but one district was all Negro. Negroes who applied for transfers were denied.

Drinan, Robert F. "Racially Balanced Schools: Psychological and Legal Aspects," *Catholic Lawyer* 11 (Winter 1965):16-20. Author was, at time of writing, Dean of Boston College Law School and chairman of the Advisory Committee for Massachusetts to the U.S. Commission on Civil Rights.

Ducharme, Gerald D., and Eugene H. Eickholt. "Brown and Bussing," *Journal of Urban Law* 44 (Summer 1967):635-652.

Dunn, James R. "Title VI, the Guidelines and School Desegregation in the South," *Virginia Law Review* 53 (January 1967):42-88. Description of the act, its implementation, and its subsequent judicial support.

Dure, Leon. "Virginia's New Freedoms," *Georgia Review* 18 (Winter 1961). Author was an early supporter of "freedom of choice" school laws, under which school scholarships are offered to all pupils, who are then free to choose whether to go to public or private schools. His thesis: "our virtuous American governments have been destroying the freedom of assembly" since 1954.

Eastland, James O. "The Supreme Court's 'Modern Scientific Authorities' in the Segregation Cases," *Congressional Record* 101 (May 26, 1955):7119-7122. Speech before the U.S. Senate by the Senator from Mississippi.

"Effects of Segregation and the Consequences of Desegregation: A Social Science Statement," *Minnesota Law Review* 37 (May 1953):427-439.

"Equality of Educational Opportunity: Are Compensatory Programs Constitutionally Required?" *Southern California Law Review* 42 (Fall 1968):146+.

Ethridge, Samuel B. "Court Decisions: Impact on Staff Balance," *Educational Leadership* 26 (December 1968):235-239.

Fairman, Charles. "The Attack on the Segregation Cases," *Harvard Law Review* 70 (November 1956):83-94.

Faubus, Orval. "Address," *Mississippi Law Journal* 30 (October 1959):520-540.

"Federal Courts and Integration of Southern Schools: Troubled Status of the Pupil Placement Acts," *Columbia Law Review* 62 (December 1962):1448-1473. Concludes by predicting "the impending obsolescence of the pupil placement acts."

Fiss, Owen M. "Racial Imbalance in the Public Schools: The Constitutional Concepts," *Harvard Law Review* 78 (January 1965):564-617. Thorough survey of all remedial measures already undertaken or proposed, and the responsibility of the courts to require reform.

Forkosch, Morris D. "The Desegregation Opinion Revisited: Legal or Sociological?" *Vanderbilt Law Review* 21 (December 1967):47-76.

Franklin, Mitchell. "The Constitution, the Supreme Court and Integration," *Lawyers Guild Review* 18 (Winter 1958):153-155.

Freilich, William B. "De Facto Segregation—The Elusive Spectre of *Brown,*" *Villanova Law Review* 9 (Winter 1964):283-294.

Freund, Paul A. "Storm over the American Supreme Court," *Modern Law Review* 21 (July 1958):345-358.

Gaillard, Samuel Palmer. "Origin of the Races and Their Development for Peace (Separate but Equal)," *Alabama Lawyer* 20 (April 1959):115-128.

Garsand, Marcel, Jr. "Public School Integration: A Call for Legislative Action," *Loyola Law Review* 9, no. 2 (1958-1959):208-218.

Gates, Robbins L. *The Making of Massive Resistance: Virginia's Politics of Public School Desegregation, 1954-1956.* Chapel Hill: University of North Carolina Press, 1962. An examination of all the political ramifications of the resistance to the 1954 Supreme Court decision. Bibliography.

Gillmor, George W., and Alan L. Gosule. "Duty to Integrate Public Schools? Some Judicial Responses and a Statute," *Boston University Law Review* 46 (Winter 1966):45-82.

Gegan, B. E. "De Jure Integration in Education," *Catholic Lawyer* 11 (Winter 1965):4-15.

Gill, Robert L. "The Negro in the Supreme Court, 1962," *Quarterly Review of Higher*

Education among Negroes 31 (July 1963):77–96. Chiefly concerned with the Meredith case in Mississippi, but other school and public accommodations cases included.

Givens, Richard A. "The Impartial Constitutional Principles Supporting *Brown v. Board of Education,*" *Howard Law Journal* 6 (June 1960):179–185.

Gordon, Milton M. "The Girard College Case: Desegregation and a Municipal Trust," *Annals of the American Academy of Political and Social Science* 304 (March 1956):53–61.

Gordon, Milton M. "The Girard College Case: Resolution and Social Significance," *Social Problems* 7 (Summer 1959):15–27. Girard College in Philadelphia is a 118-year-old privately endowed boarding school for "poor, white male orphans." It was the subject of litigation from 1954 to 1958, when Negroes twice carried unsuccessfully to the Supreme Court their fight to integrate it. New action is being prepared by NAACP under Civil Rights Act of 1964.

Greenberg, Jack. "Social Scientists Take the Stand: A Review and Appraisal of Their Testimony in Litigation," *Michigan Law Review* 54 (May 1956):953–970.

Gregor, A. James. "Law, Social Science, and School Segregation: An Assessment," *Western Reserve Law Review* 14 (September 1963):621–636.

Guzman, Jessie P. "Twenty Years of Court Decisions Affecting Higher Education in the South: 1938–1958," *Journal of Educational Sociology* 32 (February 1959):247–253.

Hamilton, Charles V. "The Constitutional Status of the 'Colored Youth' Provision in State Charters for Private Negro Colleges," *Journal of Negro Education* 28 (Fall 1959):467–471.

Harrington, Ronald G. "Should Congress Define Racial Imbalance?" *Hastings Law Journal* 17 (March 1966):625–635.

Hartman, Paul. "United States Supreme Court and Desegregation," *Modern Law Review* 23 (July 1960):353–372.

Heyman, Ira Michael. "The Chief Justice, Racial Segregation, and the Friendly Critics," *California Law Review* 49 (March 1961):104–125.

Horowitz, Harold W. "Unseparate But Equal—The Emerging Fourteenth Amendment Issue in Public School Education," *U.C.L.A. Law Review* 13 (August 1966):1147–1172. Legal review of the "equal protection" aspect of this amendment interpreted as meaning that the right "to achieve to the full extent of [one's] capacities" implies compensatory school programs.

Hyman, Jacob D., and Wade J. Newhouse, Jr. "Desegregation of the Schools: The Present Legal Situation," *Buffalo Law Review* 14 (Winter 1964):208–231.

"Implementation of the Segregation Decision," *Northwestern University Law Review* 49 (September-October 1954):557–566.

Irving, Florence B. "Segregation Legislation by Southern States," *New South* 12 (February 1957):3–8. To circumvent 1954 Supreme Court decision.

Jager, Melvin F. "Injunction—School Boards May Have an Affirmative Duty to End De Facto Segregation," *University of Illinois Law Forum* 1961 (Winter 1961):741–745.

Jansen, Donald Orville. "Private and State Actions in School Segregation," *Loyola Law Review* 11, no. 1 (1961–1962):92–99. Author suspects that such devices as support of private schools by public funds will not long be permitted.

Jenkins, Thomas Miller. "Judicial Discretion in Desegregation: The Hawkins Case," *Howard Law Journal* 4 (June 1958):193–202. Concerning Negro student who attempted to enter University of Florida Law School.

Johnson, Charles S. "Some Significant Social and Educational Implications of the U.S. Supreme Court's Decision," *Journal of Negro Education* 23 (Summer 1954):368–369.

Kaplan, John. "Comment," *Columbia Law Review* 64 (February 1964):223–229. On article by A. M. Bickel, "The Decade of School Desegregation." Author takes issue with Bickel's position that political opposition to a judicial doctrine is legitimate and proper safety valve, on grounds that it seems to legitimize delay.

Kaplan, John. "Segregation Litigation and the Schools," *Northwestern University Law Review* 58 (March-April 1963):121–170.

Kaplan, John. "Segregation Litigation and the Schools—Part II: The General Northern Problem," *Northwestern University Law Review* 58 (May-June 1963):157–214.

Kaplan, John. "Segregation Litigation and the Schools—Part III: The Gary Litigation," *Northwestern University Law Review* 59 (May–June 1964):121–170.

Kelly, Alfred H. "Brown v. Board of Education," in John A. Garraty, ed., *Quarrels That Have Shaped the Constitution.* New York: Harper, 1964. Author took part in NAACP strategy conferences on these cases, and his analysis reflects his first-hand involvement.

Laney, Lynn M. "State Segregation Laws and Judicial Courage," *Arizona Law Review* 1 (Spring 1959):102–104.

Leflar, Robert A., and Wylie H. Davis. "Public School Segregation," *Harvard Law Review* 67 (January 1954):377–392.

Leverett, E. Freeman. "School Segregation Cases," *Georgia Bar Journal* 23 (August 1960): 9–23.

Lewis, Ovid C. "Parry and Riposte to Gregor's 'The Law, Social Science, and School Segregation: An Assessment,'" *Western Reserve Law Review* 14 (September 1963): 637–682.

Logan, Rayford W. "The United States Supreme Court and the Segregation Issue," *Annals of the American Academy of Political and Social Science* 304 (March 1956):10–16.

McCarrick, Earlean M. "Desegregation and the Judiciary: The Role of the Federal District Court in Educational Desegregation in Louisiana," *Journal of Public Law* 16 (1967):107–127.

McKay, Robert B. " 'With All Deliberate Speed': Legislative Reaction and Judicial Development, 1956–1957," *Virginia Law Review* 43 (December 1957):1205–1245.

McWhinney, Edward. "An End to Racial Discrimination in the United States?" *Canadian Bar Review* 32 (May 1954):545–566. Author foresees wide ramifications of 1954 Supreme Court decision in many other areas than education.

Maryland Commission on Interracial Problems and Relations and the Baltimore Commission on Human Relations. *Desegregation in the Baltimore City Schools.* July 1955.

Maslow, Will. "De Facto Public School Segregation," *Villanova Law Review* 6 (Spring 1961):353–376.

"Massachusetts Racial Imbalance Act," *Harvard Journal on Legislation* 5 (November 1967):83–119.

Meador, Daniel J. "The Constitution and the Assignment of Pupils to Public Schools," *Virginia Law Review* 45 (May 1959):517–571.

Milbourn, Don L. "De Facto Segregation and the Neighborhood School," *Wayne Law Review* 9 (Spring 1963):514–523.

Miller, Arthur S. *Racial Discrimination and Private Education: A Legal Analysis.* Chapel Hill: University of North Carolina Press, 1957.

"Mr. Putnam's Letter to U.S. Attorney General Rogers," *Alabama Lawyer* 20 (July 1959): 276–284.

Morse, Oliver. "Policy and the Fourteenth Amendment: A New Semantics," *Fordham Law Review* 27 (Summer 1958):187–200.

Morsell, John A. "Schools, Courts, and the Negro's Future," *Harvard Educational Review* 30 (Summer 1960):179–194.

Murphy, J. W. "Can Public Schools Be 'Private'? " *Alabama Law Review* 7 (Fall 1954):48–73.

Murphy, Walter F. "Desegregation in Public Education—A Generation of Future Litigation," *Maryland Law Review* 15 (Summer 1955):221–243.

Nabrit, James M., Jr. "Legal Inventions and the Desegregation Process," *Annals of the American Academy of Political and Social Science* 304 (March 1956):35–43. Formerly dean of the Law School, the author was president of Howard University, 1960–1967.

Ogburn, William F., and Charles M. Grigg. "Factors Related to the Virginia Vote on Segregation," *Social Forces* 34 (May 1956):301–308.

Ohio Civil Rights Commission. *Legal Trends in De Facto Segregation: The Meaning to Ohio's Public Schools.* Columbus: Civil Rights Commission, 1962.

Palmer, Ben W. "Resolving a Dilemma: Congress Should Implement Integration," *American Bar Association Journal* 45 (January 1959):39–42.

Palmer, Charles L. "The Fourteenth Amendment: Some Reflections on Segregation in Schools," *American Bar Association Journal* 49 (July 1963):645-651.

Papale, A. E. "Judicial Enforcement of Desegregation: Its Problems and Limitations," *Northwestern University Law Review* 52 (July-August 1957):301-319. The author, dean of the Law School of Loyola University in New Orleans, concludes that if Southern political leaders would stop leading their constituents to believe that segregation can be preserved, peaceful integration would not be too far off.

Partee, Carter. "Secession—A Century Later," *Interracial Review* 36 (January 1963):7-9. Legal steps taken to circumvent compliance with 1954 Supreme Court decision.

Peltason, J. W. *Fifty-Eight Lonely Men: Southern Federal Judges and School Desegregation.* New York: Harcourt, Brace, 1962.

Pollak, Louis H. "Racial Discrimination and Judicial Integrity: A Reply to Professor Wechsler," *University of Pennsylvania Law Review* 108 (November 1959):1-34.

Pollak, Louis H. "Ten Years after the Decision," *Federal Bar Journal* 24 (Winter 1964):123+.

"Presumption of Unconstitutionality Applied to Pupil Placement Plan," *Columbia Law Review* 63 (March 1963):546-553.

Puryear, Paul L. "Equity Power and the School Desegregation Cases: The Law of Circumvention and Implementation," *Harvard Educational Review* 33 (Fall 1963):421-438. The author, at Tuskegee Institute, examines the nature and current status of the major legal defenses against desegregation and discusses issues of judicial interpretation which remain unsolved. Tables on progress of desegregation by state and school district.

Racial Balance in the Public Schools: The Current Status of Federal and New York Law. Albany: New York State Bar Association, October 20, 1964.

Record, Wilson. "Human Rights, Law, and Education," *Journal of Negro Education* 29 (Fall 1960):453-457.

"Report of Commission on Public Education," *Race Relations Law Reporter* 1 (February 1956):241-247. Report of the "Gray Commission" to the Governor of Virginia recommending legislation to circumvent the 1954 and 1955 decisions of the Supreme Court.

Rogers, William P. "Desegregation in the Schools: The Citizen's Responsibility," *Cornell Law Quarterly* 45 (Spring 1960):488-513.

Rogers, William P. "The Problem of School Segregation: A Serious Challenge to American Citizens," *American Bar Association Journal* 45 (January 1959):23-26.

Rogers, William P. "U.S. Policy on Desegregation," *New South* 13 (October 1958):3-7. Speech to American Bar Association by the then Attorney General.

Schlesinger, Gary A. "The Law, the Mob, and Desegregation," *California Law Review* 47 (March 1959):126-143. Includes examination of possible legal remedies against school officials, individuals, and state officials.

"School Closing Plans," *Race Relations Law Reporter* 3 (August 1958):807-840.

Schutter, Claude W. "Segregation Cases," *South Dakota Law Review* 6 (Spring 1961):31-53.

Sedler, R. A. "School Segregation in the North and West: Legal Aspects," *St. Louis University Law Journal* 7 (Spring 1963):228+.

"Segregation," *Southern California Law Review* 36, no. 3 (1963):493-496. In the case of *Jackson v. Pasadena City School District,* the Court, while acknowledging the school board's right of discretion, equated abuse of discretion with the establishment of segregation.

Selkow, Samuel. "Hawkins, the United States Supreme Court and Justice," *Journal of Negro Education* 31 (Winter 1962):97-101. Attempt of a Negro student to enter University of Florida Law School.

Spicer, George W. "Supreme Court and Racial Discrimination," *Vanderbilt Law Review* 11 (June 1958):821-852.

Spurlock, Clark. *Education and the Supreme Court.* Urbana: University of Illinois Press, 1955. Detailed discussions of constitutional issues involved, not only in *Brown v. Board of Education,* but in other school cases that appeared before the Court.

"State Statute Authorizing Grants in Aid to Private Segregated Schools after a Partial

Closing of Public Schools under 'Local Option' Plan Held Unconstitutional," *Fordham Law Review* 30 (Fall 1962):510-518.

Stennis, John C. "Multiplying Evils of Bad Law," *Mississippi Law Journal* 29 (October 1958):430-443.

Sutherland, Arthur E. "Alabama's Placement Law's Test Will Be Application," *New South* 14 (January 1959):6-7.

Tansill, Charles Callan. "How Long Will Southern Legislatures Continue to Acquiesce in the Alleged Decision of the Supreme Court on May 17, 1954?" *Alabama Lawyer* 23 (October 1962):364-384.

Taylor, William L. "Actions in Equity by the U.S. to Enforce School Desegregation," *George Washington Law Review* 29 (March 1961):539-554.

"Title VI of the Civil Rights Act of 1964—Implementation and Impact," *George Washington Law Review* 36 (May 1968):824-1015. Text of Title VI. See especially pp. 887-967.

"Unconstitutional Racial Classification and De Facto Segregation," *Michigan Law Review* 63 (March 1965):913-923.

U.S. Commission on Civil Rights. *Equal Protection of the Laws in Higher Education.* Washington: U.S. Govt. Print. Off., 1961. Study of the impact of various forms of federal subsidy and assistance on racial discrimination in public higher education.

U.S. Commission on Civil Rights. *Federal Rights under School Desegregation Law.* Washington, 1966. (CCR Clearinghouse Pub. no. 6) Question-answer format. Appendix contains revised statement of plans under Title VI of the Civil Rights Act of 1964.

U.S. Commission on Civil Rights. *Hearing Held in Boston, Massachusetts, October 4-5, 1966.* Washington: U.S. Govt. Print. Off., 1967.

U.S. Commission on Civil Rights. *Hearing Held in Rochester, New York, September 16-17, 1966.* Washington: U.S. Govt. Print. Off., 1967. Tables, maps.

Van den Haag, Ernest. "Social Science Testimony in the Segregation Cases: A Reply to Professor Kenneth Clark," *Villanova Law Review* 6 (Fall 1960):69-79.

Walker, James. "Constitutionality of Adventitious Segregation in the Public Schools," *University of Illinois Law Forum* 1967 (Fall 1967):680-689. Legal approaches to defining and resolving de facto segregation.

Waring, Thomas R. "The Southern Case against Desegregation," *Harper's* 212 (January 1956):39-45. Author is editor of Charleston, S.C., *News and Courier.*

Wechsler, Herbert. "Toward Neutral Principles of Constitutional Law," *Harvard Law Review* 73 (November 1959):1-35. The author, professor at Columbia Law School, singles out three crucial instances in which the Supreme Court has found race discrimination incompatible with the Constitution—the white primary, the restrictive covenant, and segregated public schools. He contends none of them is based "on neutral principles" and therefore doubts that they are supportable.

Wilson, Paul E. *"Brown v. Board of Education* Revisited," *Kansas Law Review* 12 (May 1964):507-524.

Winter, William F. "Mississippi's Legislative Approach to the School Segregation Problem," *Mississippi Law Journal* 26 (March 1955):165-172.

Wright, J. S. "Public School Desegregation: Legal Remedies for De Facto Segregation," *New York University Law Review* 40 (April 1965):285-309.

Elementary and Secondary Education

Patterns and Conditions

GENERAL

Alsop, Joseph. "Ghetto Education," *New Republic* 157 (November 18, 1967):18-23.

Alsop, Joseph. "No More Nonsense about Ghetto Education!" *New Republic* 157 (July 22, 1967):18-23.

Applefield, Lawrence. "Racial Imbalance in the Public Schools," *Portia Law Journal* 2 (Fall 1966):163-169.

Arnez, Nancy Levi. "A Study of Attitudes of Negro Teachers and Pupils toward Their School," *Journal of Negro Education* 32 (Summer 1963):289-293.

Ashmore, Harry S. *The Negro and the Schools*. Chapel Hill: University of North Carolina Press, 1954. Summary of the work of 45 scholars on the condition of Negro schools in 1954 on eve of the Supreme Court decision.

Baldwin, James. "A Talk to Teachers," *Saturday Review* 46 (December 21, 1963):42-44.

Bibbly, Cyril. *Race, Prejudice, and Education*. New York: Praeger, 1961.

Bowles, Frank. "Two School Systems within One Society," in C. E. Beeby, ed., *Qualitative Aspects of Educational Planning*. Paris: UNESCO, International Institute for Educational Planning, 1969, pp. 220-231.

Boykin, Leander L. "An Experiment in Reducing the Number of Over-Age Pupils in Elementary School," *Journal of Negro Education* 29 (Winter 1960):30-36.

Brameld, Theodore. "Educational Costs in Discrimination and National Welfare," in Robert MacIver, ed., *Discrimination and National Welfare: A Series of Addresses and Discussions*. New York: Institute for Religious and Social Studies, 1949. Cited in 1954 decision: *Brown v. Board of Education*.

Brickman, William W., and Stanley Lehrer, eds. *The Countdown on Segregated Education*. New York: Society for the Advancement of Education, 1960.

Brickman, William W. "The NEA and School Racial Segregation," *School and Society* 87 (September 26, 1959):356-358.

Brickman, William W. "Speaking Up against Segregation," *School and Society* 86 (November 22, 1958):420.

Brookover, William B., and Sigmund Nosow. *A Sociological Analysis of Vocational Education in the United States*. Washington: U.S. Govt. Print. Off., 1963.

Bullock, Henry Allen. "The Prediction of Drop-Out Behavior among Urban Negro Boys." Washington: Educational Research Information Center, 1967. Mimeographed. Final report of a project undertaken for the U.S. Office of Education.

Cazden, Courtney. "Subcultural Differences in Child Language: An Interdisciplinary Review," *Merrill Palmer Quarterly* 12 (July 1966):185-219.

Clift, Virgil A., Archibald W. Anderson, and H. Gordon Hullfish. *Negro Education in America: Its Adequacy, Problems and Needs*. New York: Harper, 1962. Authors from different fields present wide range of points of view.

Coombs, Philip. "The Search for Facts," *Annals of the American Academy of Political and Social Science* 304 (March 1956):26-34. Segregation in schools.

Cozart, L. S. "Education in a Scientific Age—Problems and Responsibilities," *Journal of Negro Education* 28 (Spring 1959):173-184. Report on conference of Association of Colleges and Secondary Schools.

Cronin, Joseph M. "Negroes in Catholic Schools," *Commonweal* 85 (October 7, 1966):13-16.

Dentler, Robert A., Bernard Mackler, and Mary E. Warshauer, eds. *The Urban R's: Race Relations as the Problem in Urban Education*. New York: Praeger, 1967. Essays explore ways by which schools and the urban community can formulate a meaningful educational program. Special emphasis on the Negro.

"Displaced Teachers," *Commonweal* 82 (September 3, 1965):613.

Dorson, Norman. "Discrimination," in *Frontiers of Civil Liberties*. New York: Pantheon Books, 1968, pp. 333-376.

Dwyer, Robert J. "A Report on Patterns of Interaction in Segregated Schools," *Journal of Educational Sociology* 31 (March 1958):253-256.

Dye, Thomas R. "Urban School Segregation: A Comparative Analysis," *Urban Affairs Quarterly* 4 (December 1968):141-165.

Edwards, Esther P. "The Children of Migratory Agricultural Workers in the Public Elementary Schools of the United States: Needs and Proposals in the Area of Curriculum," *Harvard Educational Review* 30 (Winter 1960):12-52.

Ferguson, Harold A., and Richard L. Plaut. "Talent—To Develop or Lose," *Educational Record* 35 (April 1954):137-140.

Friedenberg, Edgar Z. "An Ideology of School Withdrawal," *Commentary* 35 (June 1963):492-500.

Garfinkel, Herbert. "Social Science Evidence and the School Segregation Cases," *Journal of Politics* 21 (February 1959):37-59.

Geschwender, James A. "Negro Education: The False Faith," *Phylon* 29 (Winter 1968):371-379. Contends that increased education for Negroes has not significantly reduced racial inequalities. Supports equal opportunity legislation.

Ginzberg, Eli, ed. *The Nation's Children:* Vol. II. *Development and Education.* New York: Columbia University Press, 1960.

Green, Maxine. "People Are Beautiful," *Record* 69 (October 1967):83-88. The role of education in channelling the black student toward constructive positive goals.

Green, Robert L., ed. *Racial Crisis in American Education.* Chicago: Follett, 1970.

Hentoff, Nat. *Our Children Are Dying.* New York: Viking, 1966.

Holland, Florence N. "A Comment on the Segregated Learning Situation as an Insulating Device for the Negro Child," *Psychiatry* 27 (August 1964):301-303.

Hurst, Charles G., and Wallace L. Jones. "Generating Spontaneous Speech in the Underprivileged Child," *Journal of Negro Education* 36 (Fall 1967):362-367. Results of Negro children in a Head Start type program at Howard University.

Kollin, Gilbert. "Reading and Rioting," *Reconstructionist* 34 (February 14, 1969):20-24. Towards the improvement of urban Negro education.

Kopkind, Andrew. "How School Segregation Failed," *New Statesman* 76 (October 18, 1968):483-484.

Kvaraceus, William C., John S. Gibson, and Thomas J. Curtin, eds. *Poverty, Education and Race Relations: Studies and Proposals.* Boston: Allyn and Bacon, 1967. Annotated bibliography appended.

Lee, Frank F. "A Comparative Analysis of Colored Grade School Children: Negroes in the United States and West Indians in Britain," *Journal of Educational Sociology* 34 (November 1960):127-136.

Levine, Daniel U., and Robert J. Havighurst. "Negro Population Growth and Enrollment in the Public Schools: A Case Study and Its Implications," *Education and Urban Society* 1 (November 1968):21-46. References.

Levine, Daniel U. "The Segregated Society: What Must Be Done," *Phi Delta Kappan* 50 (January 1969):264-269. Strong arguments for educational leadership toward an integrated society.

Lieberman, Myron. "Civil Rights and the N.E.A.," *School and Society* 85 (May 11, 1957): 166-169. On the weak record of the N.E.A. in the area of civil rights.

Lincoln, C. Eric. "The Relevance of Education for Black Americans," *Journal of Negro Education* 38 (Summer 1969):218-223.

McDill, Mary Sexton, Arthur L. Stinchcombe, and Dollie Walker. "Segregation and Educational Disadvantage: Estimates of the Influence of Different Segregating Factors," *Sociology of Education* 41 (Summer 1968):239-246.

McGill, Ralph. "It Was the Best of Times; It Was the Worst of Times," in American Association of School Administrators, *Official Report.* 1968, pp. 41-51.

Martin, Thomas. "An Anti-Poem: *Plessy vs. Ferguson:* Theme and Variations," *Commonweal* 89 (February 7, 1969):592-593.

Meyer, Agnes E. "Race and the Schools," *Atlantic* 201 (January 1958):29-34.

Michigan-Ohio Regional Educational Laboratory. *Racism and Education: A Review of Selected Literature Related to Segregation, Discrimination, and Other Aspects of Racism in Education.* Detroit, 1969.

Miller, S. M. "Dropouts: A Political Problem," *Integrated Education* 1 (August 1963):32-40.

Monro, John U. "Escape from the Dark Cave," *Nation* 209 (October 27, 1969):434-439. Insights into the dichotomy of American social structure as regards the black man; the constructive force of black power, and the critical task of education.

Morse, H. T. "White House Meeting on Schools," *Integrated Education* 1 (October- November 1963):13-14.

"Negro Education in the United States," *Harvard Educational Review* 30 (Summer 1960): entire issue. Articles listed separately.

Noble, Jeanne L. "Negro Women Today and Their Education," *Journal of Negro Education* 26 (Winter 1957):15-21.

Obsatz, Michael. "Reaching and Teaching the Ghetto Child," *Main Currents in Modern Thought* 24 (March-April 1968):102-104.

Passow, A. Harry, Miriam Goldberg, and Abraham J. Tannenbaum, eds. *Education of the Disadvantaged: A Book of Readings.* New York: Holt, Rinehart & Winston, 1967. Articles focus on both theoretical and practical aspects of school problems with emphasis on racial and ethnic groups, including the Negro.

Patterson, Fred D. "Negro Youth on Democracy's Edge," in *Reference Papers on Children and Youth, Golden Anniversary White House Conference on Children and Youth.* New York: Columbia University Press, 1960.

Pettigrew, Thomas F. "The Negro and Education: Problems and Proposals," in Irwin Katz and Patricia Gurin, eds., *Race and the Social Sciences.* New York: Basic Books, 1969, pp. 49-112. Extensive bibliographical notes.

Pettigrew, Thomas F. "Social Evaluation Theory: Convergences and Applications," in David Levine, ed., *Nebraska Symposium on Motivation, 1967.* Lincoln: University of Nebraska Press, 1967, pp. 241-311. Postscript by Irwin Katz. Bibliography.

Sager, Lawrence Gene. "Tight Little Islands: Exclusionary Zoning, Equal Protection and the Indigent," *Stanford Law Review* 21 (April 1969):767-800.

Schrag, Peter. *Voices in the Classroom.* Boston: Beacon, 1965. The author studies various school systems throughout the country and discusses both big city and rural Southern situations that compound the educational disabilities of Negro children.

Schreiber, Daniel, ed. *The School Dropout.* Washington: National Education Association, 1964. A symposium in which the problem of the Negro dropout is a recurring topic.

Sexton, Patricia Cayo. *Education and Income: Inequalities in our Public Schools.* New York: Viking, 1961.

Slaughter, Charles H. "Cognitive Style: Some Implications for Curriculum and Instructional Practices Among Negro Children," *Journal of Negro Education* 38 (Spring 1969):105-111. References appended.

Sledd, James. "Bi-Dialectalism: The Linguistics of White Supremacy," *English Journal* 58 (December 1969):1307-1315+. Scores the righteousness of the linguistic censor and his efforts to force linguistic change upon minority groups. Urges efforts to educate minority children, dialectical differences will then be of no consequence.

Stodolsky, Susan S., and Gerald Lesser. "Learning Patterns in the Disadvantaged," *Harvard Educational Review* 37 (Fall 1967):546-593. The article appears in adapted form in *Equal Educational Opportunity.* Cambridge, Mass.: Harvard University Press, 1969, pp. 126-138.

Stoll, Clarice S., and James McPartland. *Inferiority, Efficacy, and Race.* Baltimore: Center for the Study of Social Organization of Schools, Johns Hopkins University, 1969. Study of differences between Negro and White, and among Negro students from segregated and desegregated classes in the North.

"Textbooks, Civil Rights, and the Education of the American Negro," *Publishers' Weekly* 187 (May 10, 1965):26-32. Report of conference sponsored by American Textbook Publishers Institute and National Urban League.

Thompson, Charles H. "Some Unfinished Business for the 1960's," *Journal of Negro Education* 29 (Winter 1960):1-6.

Trubowitz, Sidney. *A Handbook for Teaching in the Ghetto School.* Chicago: Quadrangle, 1968. Bibliography.

Tyack, David. "Catholic Power, Black Power, and the Schools," *Educational Forum* 32 (November 1967):27-29.

U.S. Commission on Civil Rights. *Racial Isolation in the Public Schools: A Report.* 2 vols. Washington: U.S. Govt. Print. Off., 1967. Volume 2 contains appendices.

U.S. Commission on Civil Rights. *Report.* Washington: U.S. Govt. Print. Off., 1959-   . Annual. In 1961 only, issued in five parts. See entry following.

U.S. Commission on Civil Rights. *Report 1961: Education.* Washington: U.S. Govt. Print. Off., 1961.

U.S. Commission on Civil Rights. *Third Annual Conference on Problems of Schools in Transition from the Educators' Viewpoint.* Washington, 1961.

Vieira, Norman. "Racial Imbalance, Black Separatism, and Permissible Classification by Race," *Michigan Law Review* 67 (June 1969):1553-1626.

Vosk, Jeannette S. "Study of Negro Children with Learning Difficulties at the Outset of Their School Careers," *American Journal of Orthopsychiatry* 36 (January 1966):32-40.

Weaver, S. Joseph, and Ann Weaver. "Psycholinguistic Abilities of Culturally Deprived Negro Children," *American Journal of Mental Deficiency* 72 (September 1967):190-197. Bibliography.

Weber, George H., and Annabelle B. Motz. "School as Perceived by the Dropout," *Journal of Negro Education* 37 (Spring 1968):127-134. Based on interviews of 16 disadvantaged Negro boys.

West, Earle H. "Summary of Research during 1963 Related to the Negro and Negro Education," *Journal of Negro Education* 34 (Winter 1965):30-38. Member of Howard University Department of Education finds that for the most part "we are engaged in refining our understanding of the status quo." The time has come for new directions and new thinking.

Willie, Charles V. "Education, Deprivation and Alienation," *Journal of Negro Education* 34 (Summer 1965):209-219.

Wilson, Alan B. "Social Class and Educational Opportunity," in *Equal Educational Opportunity.* Cambridge, Mass.: Harvard University Press, 1969, pp. 80-87. Originally appeared in the *Harvard Educational Review,* Winter 1968.

"With All Deliberate Speed," *Trans-action* 6 (July-August 1969):3. Commentary on Beth VanFossen's study of school segregation in *Social Forces* 47 (September 1968):39-45.

Yoshino, I. Roger. "Children, Teachers, and Ethnic Discrimination," *Journal of Educational Sociology* 34 (May 1961):391-397.

NORTH

American Jewish Committee. Philadelphia Chapter. *Equal Educational Opportunities and the Philadelphia Public Schools.* Philadelphia, 1963.

Bell, Odessa Khaton. "School Segregation in Gary," *Integrated Education* 1 (October-November 1963):31-35.

Blake, Elias, Jr. "Color Prejudice and the Education of Low-Income Negroes in the North and West," *Journal of Negro Education* 34 (Summer 1965):288-299. Bibliography.

Bolner, James. *Civil Rights in the Political Process: An Analysis of the Massachusetts Racial Imbalance Law of 1965.* Amherst: University of Massachusetts, Bureau of Government Research, 1967.

Bolner, James. "Defining Racial Imbalance in Public Educational Institutions," *Journal of Negro Education* 37 (Spring 1968):114-126. Variation in definition applied by such states as New York, New Jersey, Massachusetts, and California discussed. Exceptional footnotes provide references for further study.

Browne, Rose Butler, and James English. *Love My Children: An Autobiography.* New York: Meredith, 1969. A sensitive recounting of upbringing in a Northern ghetto coupled with specific proposals for teaching young disadvantaged Negro children.

Bullock, Paul, and Robert Singleton. "Some Problems of Minority-Group Education in the Los Angeles Public Schools," *Journal of Negro Education* 32 (Spring 1963):137-145.

Carter, Thomas P., and Nathaniel Hickerson. "A California Citizens' Committee Studies Its Schools and De Facto Segregation," *Journal of Negro Education* 37 (Spring 1968):98-105.

Chandler, Christopher. "Diverse but Equal," *New City* 6 (June 1968):13-17. Presses for meaningful school integration to dispel racial stereotypes and social inequities. Conditions at Marshall High School in a poor black section of Chicago are described as an unacceptable alternative.

Chesler, Mark, Simon Wittes, and Norma Radin. "What Happens When Northern Schools Desegregate," *American Education* 4 (June 1968):2-4.

Citizens Commission of the Berkeley Unified School District. *De Facto Segregation in Berkeley Public Schools.* Berkeley, Calif., 1963.

Clark, Kenneth B. "Segregated Schools in New York City," *Journal of Educational Sociology* 36 (Feburary 1963):245-250.

Clark, Leroy D., and W. Haywood Burns. "The Realpolitik of Racial Segregation in Northern Public Schools: Some Pragmatic Approaches," *Howard Law Journal* 14 (Summer 1968):217-240.

Coles, Robert. "Northern Children under Desegregation," *Psychiatry* 31 (February 1968):1-15. Negro children bussed to a white school. The effect of experience of both Negro and white children is examined.

Colum, J. L. "Black and White: Desegregation Dispute in Mt. Vernon," *Columbia Journal of Law and Social Problems* 5 (August 1969):112 +.

Conant, James B. *Slums and Schools.* New York: McGraw-Hill, 1961. The first two chapters, "City Slums and Negro Education," and "Schools and Jobs in the Big Cities," recommend provision of educational experiences to fit future employment, the continuation of responsibility by guidance officers for post-high-school careers of youth, and improvement of slum area schools in order to counteract unfavorable socio-economic factors of the environment.

Cowgill, Donald O. "Segregation Scores for Metropolitan Areas," *American Sociological Review* 27 (June 1962):400-402.

Damerell, Reginald G. *Triumph in a White Suburb; The Dramatic Story of Teaneck, N.J., the First Town in the Nation to Vote for Integrated Schools.* With an introduction by Robert J. Havighurst and Neil V. Sullivan. New York: Morrow, 1968. A carefully drawn popular account of the racial and religious currents in the city.

Decker, Sunny. *An Empty Spoon.* New York: Harper & Row, 1969. Insight into a ghetto high school in Philadelphia.

Decter, Midge. "The Negro and the New York Schools," *Commentary* 38 (September 1964):25-43.

Dodson, Dan W. "Public Education in New York City in the Decade Ahead," *Journal of Educational Sociology* 34 (February 1961):274-287.

Dunnegan, Marjorie Lord. "Vocational Education at Dunbar," *Integrated Education* 1 (June 1963):29-35. Dunbar is in Chicago.

Fauman, S. Joseph. "Housing Discrimination, Changing Neighborhoods, and Public Schools," *Journal of Social Issues* 13 (Winter 1957):21-30. Primarily a set of hypotheses contending that school quality is a key factor in causing moves from interracial middle-class neighborhoods, and that school administrators must act on the belief that standards can be maintained.

Fischer, John H. "*De Facto* Issue: Notes on the Broader Context," *Teachers College Record* 65 (March 1964):490-495.

Fuchs, Estelle. *Pickets at the Gates.* New York: Free Press, 1966. Two case studies on civil rights for teachers-in-training. Second study concerned with 1965 school boycott in New York against de facto segregation. Bibliography.

Goldblatt, Harold, and Cyril Tyson. *Some Self-Perceptions and Teacher Evaluations of Puerto Rican, Negro, and White Pupils in 4th, 5th and 6th Grades.* New York: Commission on Human Rights, October 1962.

Golightly, Cornelius L. "De Facto Segregation in Milwaukee Schools," *Integrated Education* 1 (December 1963-January 1964):27-31.

Green, Mary Frances, and Orletta Ryan. *The Schoolchildren Growing Up in the Slums.* New York: Pantheon, 1965. Two sensitive teachers report and transcribe their experiences in two Harlem public elementary schools.

Haskins, Jim. *Diary of a Harlem Schoolteacher.* New York: Grove, 1970. A stark portrayal of the environment and educational program at P.S. 92, by a black teacher.

Havighurst, Robert J. *The Public Schools of Chicago: A Survey.* Chicago: Board of Education, 1964.

Heifetz, Robert. "The Public Sector, Residential Desegregation and the Schools: A Case Study from Buffalo, New York," *Urban Review* 2 (February 1968):30-34.

Herndon, James. *The Way It Spozed to Be.* New York: Simon & Schuster, 1968. Experience of a teacher in a "deprived" Negro junior high school in California.

Heyman, Ira Michael. *Civil Rights U.S.A., Public Schools, Cities in the North and West, 1963: Oakland.* Staff Report submitted to the United States Commission on Civil Rights, Washington, 1963.

Hill, Beatrice M., and Nelson S. Burke. "Some Disadvantaged Youths Look at Their Schools," *Journal of Negro Education* 37 (Spring 1968):135-139. Opinions of 15 Negro youths enrolled in the neighborhood youth corps program in 1966 in California.

Howe, Harold. "Education's Most Crucial Issue," *Urban Review* 1 (June 1966):1-6. Text of an address delivered at Teachers College, Columbia University questioning the progress of school desegregation in the North.

Inger, Morton, and Robert T. Stout. "School Desegregation: The Need to Govern," *Urban Review* 3 (November 1968):35-38.

Isaacs, Charles S. "A J.H.S. 271 Teacher Tells It Like He Sees It," *New York Times Magazine,* November 24, 1968, pp. 52-53 +. A black militant teacher in the Ocean Hill-Brownsville experiment.

Jones, Frederick, and June Shagaloff. "NAACP on New York Situation," *Integrated Education* 2 (February-March 1964):33-36.

Kohl, Herbert. *36 Children.* New York: New American Library, 1967. Cumulative, perceptive portrait of a sixth grade class in a Harlem school.

Kozol, Jonathan. *Death At An Early Age: The Destruction of the Hearts and Minds of Negro Children in the Boston Public Schools.* Boston: Houghton Mifflin, 1967.

Kozol, Jonathan. "Halls of Darkness: In the Ghetto Schools," *Harvard Educational Review* 37 (Summer 1967):379-407. Excerpts from *Death at an Early Age* with discussion, 37 (Summer 1967):644-646; 38 (Fall 1967):341-343.

Larson, Richard, and James Olson, eds. *I Have a Kind of Fear: Confessions from the Writings of White Teachers and Black Students in City Schools.* Chicago: Quadrangle, 1969. The text is complemented with excellent photographs.

"Like It Is: Pressures in a Ghetto School," *Theory in Practice* 7 (February 1968):17-22.

Maslow, Will, and Richard Cohen. *School Segregation, Northern Style.* New York: Public Affairs Committee, 1961.

Mayer, Martin. "The Good Slum Schools," *Harper's* 222 (April 1961):46-52. Such projects as New York City's "Higher Horizons" and programs in Detroit, Philadelphia, Kansas City, and Tucson demonstrate value of utilizing special teaching methods.

Meckler, Zane. "De Facto Segregation in California," *California Teachers Association Journal,* January 1963.

Miller, S. M., Carolyn Comings, and Betty Saleem. *The School Dropout Problem: Syracuse.* Syracuse, N.Y.: Syracuse University Youth Development Center, 1963.

Poinsett, Alex. "School Segregation up North," *Ebony* 17 (June 1962):89-90.

Public School Segregation: City of Chicago 1963-1964 and 1964-1965. Chicago Urban League, May 12, 1965.

Reller, Theodore L. *Problems of Public Education in the San Francisco Bay Area.* Berkeley, Calif.: Institute of Governmental Studies, 1963.

Richan, Willard C. *Racial Isolation in the Cleveland Public Schools.* Cleveland: Case Western Reserve University, 1967. Report of a study for the U.S. Commission on Civil Rights.

Robison, Joseph B. "De Facto Segregation in the Northern Public Schools: Its Anatomy and Treatment," *Journal of Jewish Communal Service* 39 (Fall 1962):98-106.

Roeser, Veronica A. "De Facto School Segregation and the Law: Focus San Diego," *San Diego Law Review* 5 (January 1968):57-82.

Rogers, David. *110 Livingston Street: Politics and Bureaucracy in the New York City Schools.* New York: Random, 1968. A case study of the city's failure to create a viable integrated educational program.

Schwartz, Robert, Thomas Pettigrew, and Marshall Smith. "Fake Panaceas for Ghetto Education," *New Republic* 157 (September 23, 1967):16-19.

Singer, Harry, and Irving G. Hendrick. "Total School Integration: An Experiment in Social Reconstruction," *Phi Delta Kappan* 49 (November 1967):143-147. Pasadena's attempt to eliminate de facto segregation.

Stetler, Henry G. *Comparative Study of Negro and White Dropouts in Selected Connecticut High Schools.* Hartford: State of Connecticut Commission on Civil Rights, 1959.

Teele, James E., and Clara Mayo. "School Racial Integration: Tumult and Shame," *Journal of Social Issues* 25 (January 1969):137-156. Focus on Operation Exodus, Boston. References appended.

Tree, Chris. "Storefront Schools," *Urban Review* 2(February 1968):16-18+.

Twachtman, Walter A., Jr. "De Facto Segregation—The Northern Problem," *Connecticut Bar Journal* 40 (September 1966):493-504.

U.S. Commission on Civil Rights. *Civil Rights U.S.A.—Public Schools North and West 1962.* Washington, 1962.

U.S. Commission on Civil Rights. *Process of Change: The Story of School Desegregation in Syracuse, New York.* Washington: U.S. Govt. Print. Off., 1968. Map.

U.S. Commission on Civil Rights. Massachusetts Advisory Committee. *Racial Imbalance in the Boston Public Schools.* Washington, 1965.

Warshauer, Mary Ellen. "Glen Cove, New York—The Evolution of a Desegregation Plan," *Urban Review* 2 (February 1968):25-34. According to the Board of Education statistics in 1965, the school population was 65.9 percent Negro.

Weinberg, Carl. "Education Level and Perceptions of Los Angeles Negroes of Educational Conditions in a Riot Area," *Journal of Negro Education* 36 (Fall 1967):377-384.

Wilkerson, Doxey A. "School Integration, Compensatory Education and the Civil Rights Movement in the North," *Journal of Negro Education* 34 (Summer 1965):300-309.

Wolff, Max. "Segregation in the Schools of Gary, Indiana," *Journal of Educational Sociology* 36 (February 1963):251-261.

SOUTH

Anderson, C. Arnold. "Inequalities in Schooling in the South," *American Journal of Sociology* 60 (May 1955):547-561.

Anderson, Margaret. *The Children of the South.* New York: Farrar, Straus & Giroux, 1966.

Brady, Tom P. "A Review of 'Black Monday.' " Winona, Miss.: Association of Citizens' Councils of Mississippi, n.d. "Black Monday" is May 17, 1954, Supreme Court decision day. Author is Circuit Judge, 14th Judicial District, former chairman of the States' Rights Democratic Party in 1948.

Brown, Aaron, ed. *Ladders to Improvement.* New York: Phelps-Stokes Fund, 1960. Report of five year study conducted in Alabama, Georgia, Mississippi, and North Carolina seeking ways to improve the quality of instruction in secondary schools.

Cahn, Edgar S., and Jean Camper Cahn. "The New Sovereign Immunity," *Harvard Law Review* 81 (March 1968):929-991. Child Development Group of Mississippi.

Caliver, Ambrose. "Segregation in American Education: An Overview," *Annals of the American Academy of Political and Social Science* 304 (March 1956):17-25. Author suggests Southern whites deliberately instituted policy of segregation in order to condition Negroes to inferior status.

Campbell, Ernest Q. "Negroes, Education, and the Southern States," *Social Forces* 47 (March 1969):253-265.

Campbell, Ernest Q., with the assistance of Charles E. Bowerman and Daniel O. Price. *When a City Closes Its Schools.* Chapel Hill: University of North Carolina Press, 1960. In September 1958 Norfolk, Virginia, "acted out the ritual of resistance" by closing the public junior and senior high schools rather than to desegregate. In the author's words, "Norfolk learned the hard way that public schools are a necessity if a city is to remain a city."

Carmichael, Omer, and Weldon James. *The Louisville Story.* New York: Simon & Schuster, 1957. Account by the Superintendent of Schools and a staff writer on the Louisville *Courier-Journal* of compliance procedures adopted in that city.

Chesler, Mark A., and Phyllis Segal. *Characteristics of Negro Students Attending Previously All-White Schools in the Deep South.* Ann Arbor: Center for Research on Utilization of Scientific Knowledge, Institute for Social Research, University of Michigan, 1967. Bibliography.

Comer, James P., Martin Harrow, and Samuel H. Johnson. "Summer Study—Skills Program: A Case for Structure," *Journal of Negro Education* 38 (Winter 1969):38-45. Data on a compensatory educational program for predominantly Southern Negro students, ages 14-16, for the period 1964-1966.

DeMott, Benjamin. "Encounter in Mississippi: Tougaloo Summer Enrichment Program," *Saturday Review* 51 (January 20, 1968):51-53+.

Georgia Conference on Educational Opportunities. "Georgia's Education: Separate and Unequal," *New South* 15 (December 1960):9-11.

Goodman, Mary Ellen. "The Future of Private Schools," *New South* 16 (April 1961):3-6.

Greenberg, Polly. *The Devil Has Slippery Shoes: A Biased Biography of the Child Development Group of Mississippi.* London: Macmillan, 1969. Combines an account of the educational program with the intricate political struggle for survival of the project.

Greene, James E. "A Comparison of Certain Characteristics of White and Negro Teachers in a Large Southeastern School System," *Journal of Social Psychology* 58 (December 1962):383-391.

Greene, James E. "A Comparison of the 'School Morale' of White and Negro Students in a Large Southeastern School System," *Journal of Negro Education* 31 (Spring 1962):132-138.

Greene, James E. "Disciplinary Status of White and Negro High School Students in a Large Southeastern School System," *Journal of Negro Education* 31 (Winter 1962):25-29.

Griswold, Nat. "Arkansans Organize for Public Schools," *New South* 14 (June 1959):3-7. By the Executive Director of Arkansas Council on Human Relations.

Harris, Edward E. "Prejudice and Other Social Factors in School Segregation," *Journal of Negro Education* 37 (Fall 1968):440-443.

Hart, Norris. "You Must Go Home Again," *Center Magazine* 2 (July 1969):15-20. Comments on the conditions in a Texas black community by a black educator working with the disadvantaged child.

Howe, Florence. "Mississippi's Freedom Schools: The Politics of Education," *Harvard Educational Review* 35 (Spring 1965):141-160.

Howell, Elva J. "Student Activities in Twenty-Five High Schools in Alabama, 1955-56," *Journal of Negro Education* 27 (Winter 1958):90-93. Negro schools and extracurricular activities.

Johnson, Guy B. "A Southern Sociologist Views Segregation," *School and Society* 86 (January 18, 1958):45.

Kilpatrick, James Jackson. *The Southern Case for School Segregation.* New York: Crowell, 1962. Presented as a case at law, with sections on the evidence, the law, and the prayer of the petitioner. Author's position is that the "Negro says he's the white man's equal; *show me";* and "He has no right—no legal right, no moral right—to intrude upon the private institutions of his neighbors."

Klausler, Alfred P. "The Shame and the Glory," *Christian Century* 79 (August 15, 1962):977-979. Prince Edward County, Virginia.

McIntyre, William R. "School Integration: Fifth Year," *Editorial Research Reports,* August 27, 1958, pp. 655-672. Discussion of the role of the Supreme Court, of the sources of resistance, and particularly of the struggle to resist compliance in Virginia.

Maclachlan, John M. "Population Factors Affecting Education in the South," *Journal of Public Law* 3 (Spring 1954):108-121.

Matthews, Donald R., and James W. Prothro. "Stateways versus Folkways: Critical Factors in Southern Reactions to *Brown v. Board of Education,"* in Gottfried Dietze, ed., *Essays on the American Constitution.* Englewood Cliffs, N.J.: Prentice-Hall, 1964, pp. 139-156.

Miller, Carroll L. "Educational Opportunities and the Negro Child in the South," *Harvard Educational Review* 30 (Summer 1960):195-208.

Miller, Helen Hill. "Private Business and Education in the South," *Harvard Business Review* 38 (July–August 1960):75–88.

Muse, Benjamin. *Virginia's Massive Resistance.* Bloomington: Indiana University Press, 1961.

National Education Association. Commission on Professional Rights and Responsibilities. *Wilcox County, Alabama: A Study of Social, Economic, and Educational Bankruptcy.* Washington, 1967.

Noland, James R., Jerry Robinson, Jr., and Edward Martin. "How It Was in Houston, Texas," *Integrated Education* 7 (May–June 1969):38–43. Traces questionable progress in a metropolitan school district with a 30% Negro enrollment (1963) to date.

Orfield, Gary. *The Reconstruction of Southern Education: The Schools and the 1964 Civil Rights Act.* New York: Wiley, 1969. Bibliography.

Orfield, Gary. "The Court, The Schools, and the Southern Strategy," *Saturday Review* 52 (December 20, 1969):62 + .

Patrick, T. L. "Segregation and the Future of Public Education in the South," *School and Society* 89 (April 8, 1961):175–177.

Pettigrew, Thomas F. "Continuing Barriers to Desegregated Education in the South," *Sociology of Education* 38 (Winter 1965):99–111. Three factors discussed: social structural facets, white resistance, and the lack of Negro insistance upon change.

Pettigrew, Thomas F. "De Facto Segregation, Southern Style," *Integrated Education* 1 (October–November 1963):15–18.

Pierce, T. M., et al. *White and Negro Schools in the South.* Englewood, N.J.: Prentice-Hall, 1955. Still useful for comparative data.

Powledge, Fred. "Black Man, Go South," *Esquire,* August 1965. A comparison of race relations, especially in school segregation, between Atlanta, Ga., and New York City.

Price, Daniel O. "Educational Differentials between Negroes and Whites in the South." Paper presented at the meeting of the Population Association of America, April 27–29, 1967, in Cincinnati. Abstracted in *Population Index* 33 (July–September 1967):307–308.

Reif, Janet. *Crisis in Norfolk.* Richmond: Virginia Council on Human Relations, 1960. The closing of public schools to prevent integration.

Rich, John Martin. "Social Pressures and School Segregation in a Southern Town," *Journal of Negro Education* 29 (Winter 1960):91–92.

Smith, Bob. *They Closed Their Schools: Prince Edward County, Virginia, 1951–1964.* Chapel Hill: University of North Carolina Press, 1965. The author, an associate editor of the Norfolk *Virginian-Pilot,* concludes with a description of "The Crippled Generation."

Smith, Ralph Lee. "The South's Pupil Placement Laws: Newest Weapon against Integration," *Commentary* 30 (October 1960):326–329.

Smith, Robert C. "Breakthrough in Norfolk: After Five Months without Public Schools," *Commentary* 27 (March 1959):185–193.

Southern Schools: Progress and Problems. Nashville, Tenn.: Benson Printing Co., 1959. Prepared by staff members and associates of the Southern Education Reporting Service.

Swanson, Ernst W., and John A. Griffin, eds. *Public Education in the South Today and Tomorrow.* Chapel Hill: University of North Carolina Press, 1955. Presents comparative data on white and Negro schools, including extensive data on expenditures, costs of desegregation.

Thompson, Lorin A. "Virginia Education Crisis and Its Economic Aspects," *New South* 14 (February 1959):3–8.

Vander Zanden, James W. "Foundations of the Second Reconstruction," *School and Society* 88 (May 7, 1960):229–231.

Vander Zanden, James W. *Race Relations in Transition: The Segregationist Crisis in the South.* New York: Random, 1965.

Walker, LeRoy T. "Performance Level of Negro Teachers of Physical Education in North Carolina," *Journal of Negro Education* 28 (Winter 1959):76–80.

Wasserman, Miriam. "The Loud, Proud, Black Kids," *Progressive* 32 (April 1968):35–38. The Tougaloo Summer Enrichment Program, a summer resident tutorial project conducted in Mississippi.

Watters, Pat. "Mississippi: Children and Politics," *Dissent* 14 (May-June 1967):293-310. Traces history of the Child Development Group of Mississippi, a Head Start program which began in the summer of 1955.

Wilkerson, Doxey A. "Conscious and Impersonal Forces in Recent Trends toward Negro-White School Equality in Virginia," *Journal of Educational Sociology* 32 (April 1959):402-408.

Desegregation and Equal Opportunity

GENERAL

Aber, Elaine M. "A Reverse Pattern of Integration," *Journal of Educational Sociology* 32 (February 1959):283-289.

Alexander, Theron, Judith Stoyle, and Charles Kirk. "The Language of Children in the 'Inner City,'" *Journal of Psychology* 68 (March 1968):215-221. Vocabulary deficiencies in Negro children attending a Head Start center in an urban ghetto.

Amos, R. T. "The Dominant Attitudes of Negro Teachers toward Integration in Education," *Journal of Educational Psychology* 41 (December 1955):470-476.

Anastasi, Anne. "Psychological Research and Educational Desegregation," *Thought* 35 (Fall 1960):421-429.

Anderson, Margaret. "After Integration—Higher Horizons," *New York Times Magazine,* April 21, 1963, pp. 10+.

Armstrong, C. P., and A. James Gregor. "Integrated Schools and Negro Character Development: Some Considerations of the Possible Effects," *Psychiatry* 27 (February 1964):69-72.

Baratz, John C., and Roger W. Shuy. *Teaching Black Children to Read.* Washington: Center for Applied Linguistics, 1969.

Beck, Armin, Eliezer Krumbein, and F. D. Erickson. "Strategies for Change: Conditions for School Desegregation," *Phi Delta Kappan* 50 (January 1969):280-283. Probes aspects of personnel recruitment and training and curriculum revision.

Bickel, Alexander M. "Desegregation: Where Do We Go from Here?" *New Republic* 162 (February 7, 1970):20-22. First response by Leon E. Panetta, Director of the Office for Civil Rights, HEW until February 1970 when he tendered his resignation, *ibid.,* (February 28, 1970):29-30. For additional responses, see subsequent issues.

Boucher, Bertrand P., and Hugh C. Brooks. "School Integration and Its Relation to the Distribution of Negroes in U.S. Cities," *Educational Forum* 24 (January 1960):185-190.

Bowles, Samuel. "Towards Equality of Educational Opportunity?" in *Equal Educational Opportunity.* Cambridge, Mass.: Harvard University Press, 1969, pp. 115-125. Originally appeared in the *Harvard Educational Review,* Winter 1968.

Clark, Kenneth B. "Alternative Public School Systems," in *Equal Educational Opportunity.* Cambridge, Mass.: Harvard University Press, 1969, pp. 173-186. Originally appeared in the *Harvard Educational Review,* Winter 1968.

Bradley, Gladyce H. "Teacher Education and Desegregation," *Journal of Negro Education* 26 (Spring 1957):200-203.

Brain, George B., ed. *School Superintendents' Conference on the Practical Problems of Public School Desegregation.* Bureau of Publications, Baltimore City Public Schools, 1964.

Brown, Ronald, and Geraldine Reed. "The Constitutionality of One-Way Racial Bussing," *Harvard Civil Rights-Civil Liberties Law Review* 5, no. 2 (April 1970):488-500.

Carmack, William R., and Theodore Freedman. *Factors Affecting School Desegregation.* New York: Anti-Defamation League, 1962.

Carter, Barbara. "Integrating the Negro Teacher Out of a Job," *Reporter* 33 (August 12, 1965):31-33.

Clark, Dennis. "Color and Catholic Classrooms," *Integrated Education* 1 (June 1963):9-15.

Clark, Kenneth B. "Clash of Cultures in the Classroom," *Integrated Education* 1 (August 1963):7-14. American use of education as an instrument for socio-economic mobility.

Clark, Kenneth B. "Desegregation: An Evaluation of Social Science Predictions," *Teachers College Record* 62 (October 1960):1-17. In addition to his own article, Professor Clark served as general editor of a special section in this issue on "Segregation: Six-Year Perspective." Other articles listed separately.

Clark, Kenneth B. "The Most Valuable Hidden Resource," *College Board Review* no. 29 (1956):23-26.

Clift, Virgil A. "Does the Dewey Philosophy Have Implications for Desegregating the Schools?" *Journal of Negro Education* 29 (Spring 1960):145-154.

Cohen, David K. "Defining Racial Equality in Education," *U.C.L.A. Law Review* 16 (February 1969):255-280.

Cohen, David K. "Policy for the Public Schools: Compensation and Integration," in *Equal Educational Opportunity*. Cambridge, Mass.: Harvard University Press, 1969, pp. 91-114. Originally appeared in the *Harvard Educational Review,* Winter 1968.

Coleman, James S. "The Concept of Equality of Educational Opportunity," in *Equal Educational Opportunity*. Cambridge, Mass.: Harvard University Press, 1969, pp. 9-24. Originally appeared in the *Harvard Educational Review,* Winter 1968.

Coleman, James S., et al. *Equality of Educational Opportunity*. Washington: U.S. Govt. Print. Off., 1966. Report to Congress and the President on inequalities for Negroes and other racial and ethnic minorities in education. Bound in two parts; part two has title page: "Supplemental Appendix" and comprises a summary report, supplemental appendix, and correlation tables.

Coleman, James S. "Toward Open Schools," *Public Interest* no. 9 (Fall 1967):20-27. Some implications of the Coleman Report regarding redress of unequal educational resources and opportunities for achievement, and its public reception.

Coles, Robert. *The Desegregation of Public Schools*. New York: Anti-Defamation League, 1963.

Coons, John E., William Clune, and Stephen Sugarman. *Private Wealth and Public Education*. Foreword by James S. Coleman. Cambridge, Mass.: Harvard University Press, 1970. An analysis and description of the discrimination by wealth inherent in existing state systems of school finance. The authors suggest "power equalizing"—the manipulation of state and local taxes following judicial intervention.

Cooper, Dan. "School Desegregation and the Office of Education Guidelines," *Duquesne University Law Review* 6 (Summer 1968):373-382.

Cottle, Thomas J. "Revolt and Repair: A Comparative Study of Two University Tutorial Movements," *Sociological Quarterly* 8 (Winter 1967):21-36. Tutoring lower-class Negro youths.

Crane, Robert L., et al. *The Politics of School Desegregation: Comparative Case Studies of Community Structure and Policy-Making*. Chicago: Aldine, 1968. An inquiry into the political and social processes in eight Northern and seven Southern cities used to achieve racial integration of their public schools.

Daniel, Walter C. "New Perspectives on School Desegregation," *Journal of Negro Education* 28 (Fall 1959):480-483.

"The Desegregation Decision—One Year Afterward," *Journal of Negro Education* 24 (Summer 1955):161-404. Entire issue. State by state survey of action taken—or not taken.

Dewing, Rolland. "The National Education Association and Desegregation," *Phylon* 30 (Summer 1969):109-124.

Dewing, Rolland. "Teacher Organizations and Desegregation," *Phi Delta Kappan* 49 (January 1968):257-260.

Dodson, Dan W. "Schools Administration, Control, and Public Policy concerning Integration," *Journal of Negro Education* 34 (Summer 1965):249-257.

Dodson, Dan. "The Schools and the Civil Rights Revolution," *Integrated Education* 3 (August-November 1965):20-29.

Dyer, Henry S. "School Factors and Equal Educational Opportunity," in *Equal Educational Opportunity*. Cambridge, Mass.: Harvard University Press, 1969, pp. 41-59. Originally appeared in the *Harvard Educational Review,* Winter 1968.

"Education and Civil Rights in 1965," *Journal of Negro Education* 34 (Summer 1965): 197-379. Entire issue. Discussions of scope of issues involved, administrative, community, and psychological aspects of the problems, and methods for equalizing educational opportunities.

Equal Educational Opportunity. Cambridge, Mass.: Harvard University Press, 1969. Analytics for essays examining the concept are provided under the appropriate sections herein. The volume includes a brief summary of the Coleman report.

Fischer, John H. "Race and Reconciliation: The Role of the Schools," *Daedalus* 95 (Winter 1966):24-44. Proceeding from the 1954 decision that "separate schools are inherently unequal," the author examines various plans for urban school integration, including compensatory and remedial programs.

Fischer, John H. "School Parks for Equal Opportunities," *Journal of Negro Education* 37 (Summer 1968):301-309.

Fischer, Louis, and Donald G. Lahr. "Social Policy and Education: Integration and Segregation in Education," *Review of Educational Research* 37 (February 1967):34-39.

Forbes, Jack D. "Segregation and Integration: The Multi-Ethnic or Uni-Ethnic School," *Phylon* 30 (Spring 1969):34-41.

"Ghetto Education," *Center Magazine* 1 (November 1968):45-60. An evaluation of integrated education by Robert F. Kennedy, Kenneth B. Clark, Oscar Lewis, and others.

Giles, H. Harry. *The Integrated Classroom.* New York: Basic Books, 1959.

Gray, Susan W., and Rupert A. Klaus. "An Experimental Preschool Program for Culturally Deprived Children," *Child Development* 36 (December 1965):887-898. Negro children with parents in an annual income bracket below $3,000 annually.

Green, Gordon G. "Negro Dialect, the Last Barrier to Integration," *Journal of Negro Education* 32 (Winter 1963):81-83.

Greenberg, Jack. "The Tortoise Can Beat the Hare," *Saturday Review* 51 (February 17, 1968):57-59+.

Groff, Patrick J. "The NEA and School Desegregation," *Journal of Negro Education* 29 (Spring 1960):181-186.

Groff, Patrick J. "Teacher Organizations and School Desegregation," *School and Society* 90 (December 15, 1962):441-443.

Grossack, Martin M. "Psychological Considerations Essential to Effective Educational Integration," *Journal of Negro Education* 34 (Summer 1965):278-287.

Hager, Don J. "Social and Psychological Factors in Integration," *Journal of Educational Sociology* 31 (October 1957):57-63. A study of variations in response to integration which emphasizes the need for preparation.

Hall, Morrill, M., and Harold W. Gentry. "Isolation of Negro Students in Integrated Public Schools," *Journal of Negro Education* 38 (Spring 1969):156-161.

Halpern, Ray. "Tactics for Integration," *Saturday Review* 51 (December 1968):47-49+. Desegregation in Berkeley, California.

Haubrich, Vernon. "The Culturally Different: New Context for Teacher Education," *Journal of Teacher Education* 14 (June 1963):163-167.

Havighurst, Robert J. "The Bearing of Integration on Educational Problems," *American Journal of Orthopsychiatry* 34 (March 1964):217-218.

Hickerson, Nathaniel. "Physical Integration Alone Is Not Enough," *Journal of Negro Education* 35 (Spring 1966):110-116. An appeal for integrated faculty with special training in the education of minority groups, special programs in compensatory education, and a revised curriculum to include the Negro's contribution to man's culture.

Hudgins, H. G., Jr. "Desegregation: Where Schools Stand with the Courts as the New Year Begins," *American School Board Journal* 156 (January 1969):21-25+.

Humphrey, Hubert H., ed. *Integration vs. Segregation: The Crisis in our Schools as Viewed by 17 Outstanding Commentators.* New York: Crowell, 1964. Useful collection of material covering history of litigation on school segregation as well as selections on complexities of enforcement under varying circumstances and in various regions. Published as textbook under title *School Desegregation: Documents and Commentaries.*

"Integration: A Tool for the Achievement of the Goal of Quality Education," *Howard Law Journal* 14 (Summer 1968):372-384.

Johnson, Carroll F., and Michael D. Usdan, eds. *Equality of Educational Opportunity in the Large Cities of America: The Relationship between Decentralization and Racial Integration.* New York: Teachers College, Columbia University, 1968. Proceedings of an institute on problems of school desegregation under the 1964 Civil Rights Act.

Johnson, Norman J., Robert Wyer, and Neil Gilbert. "Quality Education and Integration: An Exploratory Study," *Phylon* 28 (Fall 1967):221-229.

Juvigny, Pierre. *Towards Equality of Education: The Fight against Discrimination.* Paris: UNESCO, 1962. Short book on international movement against discrimination in education on the basis of race, sex, religion, and origins.

Kenealy, William J. "Desegregation," *Social Order* 12 (June 1962):249-256. In a debate with William F. Buckley, Jr., editor of *National Review,* Father Kenealy advocates use of federal power to combat segregation.

Keppel, Francis H. "Segregation and the Schools," *National Education Association Proceedings* 102 (1964):36-40.

Killian, Lewis M., and Charles M. Grigg. "Community Resistance to and Acceptance of Desegregation," *Journal of Negro Education* 34 (Summer 1965):268-277.

Kirp, David L. "The Poor, the Schools, and Equal Protection," in *Equal Educational Opportunity.* Cambridge, Mass.: Harvard University Press, 1969, pp. 139-172. Originally appeared in the *Harvard Educational Review,* Fall 1968.

Klopf, Gordon J., and Israel A. Laster. *Integrating the Urban School.* New York: Teachers College, Columbia University, 1963. An introduction to problems of de facto segregation. Selective bibliography.

Kupferer, Harriet J. "An Evaluation of the Integration Potential of a Physical Education Program," *Journal of Educational Sociology* 28 (September 1954):89-96.

Lessler, Ken, and Ronald E. Fox. "An Evaluation of a Head Start Program in a Low Population Area," *Journal of Negro Education* 38 (Winter 1969):46-54. Based on a sampling of 10 white and 10 Negro children, randomly selected. Bibliography.

Levine, Daniel U. "Integration-Compensatory Education Controversy," *Educational Forum* 32 (March 1968):323-332.

Levine, Daniel U. "Issues in the Provision of Equal Opportunity," *Journal of Negro Education* 37 (Winter 1968):4-14. Considers arguments for homogeneous and heterogeneous groupings.

Levine, Naomi, and Will Maslow. "An Integration Program," *Integrated Education* 2 (February-March, 1964):37-40.

Lieberman, Hal R. "Teachers and the Fourteenth Amendment—The Role of the Faculty in the Desegregation Process," *North Carolina Law Review* 46 (February 1968):313-365.

Lieberman, Martin. "Civil Rights Fiasco in Public Education: Desegregation since 1964," *Phi Delta Kappan* 47 (May 1966):482-486. Also printed in *Teachers College Record* 68 (November 1966):120-126.

Lieberman, Myron. "Equality of Educational Opportunity," *Harvard Educational Review* 29 (Summer 1959):167-183.

Lightfoote-Wilson, Thomasyne. "Institutional Access: The Road to National Integration," *Journal of Human Relations* 16 (Third Quarter 1968):343-353. Scores the simplistic solutions to racial unrest. Emphasizes the role of educational institutions in improving race relations.

Lovell, John T., and John C. Walden. "Quiet Revolution in Alabama: Faculty Desegregation," *Phi Delta Kappan* 49 (June 1968):607-608.

McGavern, John, and Douglas K. Stafford. "TN: A Modest Proposal for Educators," *Journal of Negro Education* 31 (Fall 1962):511-514. The token Negro in educational institutions.

Mack, Raymond W., ed. *Our Children's Burden: Studies of Desegregation in Nine American Communities.* New York: Random, 1968. A study of desegregation in communities in both North and South.

McPartland, James. *The Segregated Student in Desegregated Schools: Sources of Influence on Negro Secondary Students.* Baltimore: Johns Hopkins University, 1968.

Mahan, Thomas W. "The Bussing of Students for Equal Opportunities," *Journal of Negro Education* 37 (Summer 1968):291-300. Bibliography.

Marcus, Robert, Edward Bispo, and Irving Katuna. "Social Change and Curriculum Innovation," *Journal of Negro Education* 36 (Spring 1967):121-128. The basis of the Franklin Plan for achievement of racially balanced schools and an integrated curriculum.

Mays, N. "Behavioral Expectations of Negro and White Teachers on Recently Desegregated Public School Faculties," *Journal of Negro Education* 32 (Summer 1963):218-226.

Miller, Harry L. *Education for the Disadvantaged: Current Issues and Research.* New York: Free Press, 1967. Special attention is called to the sections "Teaching the Teacher," and "The Status of Northern School Desegregation."

Mitchell, John N., and Robert H. Finch. "School Desegregation Policy, 1969," *Current History* 57 (November 1969):303-305. Excerpts from a joint statement on the policies of the Nixon administration in pursuance of school desegregation.

Moore, William P. "Why Difficult Schools," *Integrated Education* 1 (June 1963):37-42. Difficult schools and a proposal for change.

Morland, J. Kenneth. *Token Desegregation and Beyond.* New York: Anti-Defamation League, 1963.

Morsell, John A. "Racial Segregation and Integration in Public Education," *Journal of Negro Education* 38 (Summer 1969):276-284.

Moynihan, Daniel F. "Sources of Resistance to the Coleman Report," in *Equal Educational Opportunity.* Cambridge, Mass.: Harvard University Press, 1969, pp. 25-38. Originally appeared in the *Harvard Educational Review,* Winter 1968.

Muse, Benjamin. *Ten Years of Prelude: The Story of Integration Since the Supreme Court's 1954 Decision.* New York: Viking, 1964. Because of its accuracy, its comprehensiveness, and its thorough documentation, this is a work that should be of lasting value.

Nabrit, James M., Jr. "Desegregation and Reason," *Phylon* 17 (Fall 1956):286-290.

"The Negro Teacher in Desegregated Schools," *New York University Law Review* 42 (November 1967):916-927.

Newton, Eunice Shaed. "The Culturally Deprived Child in Our Verbal Schools," *Journal of Negro Education* 31 (Spring 1962):184-187. Lack of language fluency a serious bar to the Negro child's educational progress.

Newton, Eunice Shaed. "Verbal Destitution: The Pivotal Barrier to Learning," *Journal of Negro Education* 29 (Fall 1960):497-499.

Pettigrew, Thomas F. "Desegregation and Its Chances for Success: Northern and Southern Views," *Social Forces* 35 (May 1957):339-344.

Pettigrew, Thomas F. "Race and Equal Educational Opportunity," in *Equal Educational Opportunity.* Cambridge, Mass.: Harvard University Press, 1969, pp. 69-79. Originally appeared in the *Harvard Educational Review,* Winter 1968.

Pettigrew, Thomas F. "Racially Separate or Together?" *Journal of Social Issues* 25 (January 1969):43-69. Also appears in *Integrated Education* 7 (January-February 1969):36-56. References appended.

Pettigrew, Thomas F. "School Desegregation: Expanding Educational Opportunities to All Americans," in Edward Landy and Arthur M. Kroll, eds., *Guidance in American Education III: Needs and Influencing Forces.* Cambridge, Mass.: Harvard University Press, 1966, pp. 49-61.

Pettigrew, Thomas F. "School Integration in Current Perspective," *Urban Review* 3 (January 1969):4-8.

"Problems and Responsibilities of Desegregation: A Symposium," *Notre Dame Lawyer* 34, no. 5 (1959):607+. Topics discussed: the roles of public officials, the legal profession, the churches, and educators; toward a national education policy; the problems and responsibilities of the Negro community with regard to integration.

"Racial Integration: Roads to Understanding," *Educational Leadership* 26 (November 1968):entire issue.

"Racial Integration and Academic Freedom," *New York University Law Review* 34 (May 1959):725-752.

Reid, Ira De A. "Integration Reconsidered," *Harvard Educational Review* (Spring 1957):85-91. Racial integration in education put into the wider context of goals and community.

Robinson, William H. "Integration's Delay and Frustration Tolerance," *Journal of Negro Education* 28 (Fall 1959):472-476.

Rogers, David. "Obstacles to School Desegregation in New York City: A Benchmark Case," in Marilyn Gittell, ed., *Educating an Urban Population.* Beverly Hills, Calif.: Sage, 1967, pp. 155-184.

Rogers, William P. "Desegregation in the Schools," *Cornell Law Quarterly* 45 (Spring 1960):488.

Rooney, Isabel W. "Integration of Parochial Schools in New York," *Interracial Review* 37 (February 1964).

Rosenthal, Jonas O. "Negro Teachers' Attitudes toward Desegregation," *Journal of Negro Education* 26 (Winter 1957):63-71. Many fear resultant loss of jobs.

Rosner, Joseph. "When White Children Are in the Minority," *Journal of Educational Sociology* 28 (October 1954):69-72.

"School Bussing and Parental Anxiety," *School and Society* 97 (January 1969):5-6.

Schrag, Peter. "Why Our Schools Have Failed," *Commentary* 45 (March 1968):31-40. Reviews the concept of "equality of educational opportunity" vis-à-vis the ghetto child.

Schwab, Joseph J. "Integration and Disintegration of Education," in Roald F. Campbell, Lucy Ann Marx, and Raphael O. Nystrand, eds., *Education and Urban Renaissance.* New York: Wiley, 1969, pp. 37-43. Also reprinted in *School and Society* 96 (December 7, 1968):463-466.

Shaffer, Helen B. "School Desegregation: 1954-1964," *Editorial Research Reports,* April 29, 1964, pp. 301-320.

Southern Regional Council. *The Federal Retreat in School Desegregation.* Atlanta, 1969.

Spruill, Albert W. "The Negro Teacher in the Process of Desegregation of Schools," *Journal of Negro Education* 29 (Winter 1960):80-84.

Stember, Charles Herbert. "Evaluating Effects of the Integrated Classroom," *Urban Review* 2 (June 1968):3-4+.

Stephan, A. Stephen. "Integration and Sparse Negro Populations," *School and Society* 81 (April 30, 1955):133-135. Sparsely populated communities especially suitable for early desegregation, particularly since they are heavily burdened by school costs.

Strauss, Susan. "The Effect of Negro Integration on the Self-Concept of Negro and Puerto-Rican Children," *Graduate Research in Education and Related Disciplines* 3 (April 1967):63-76. Comparisons of children of low socioeconomic background in a paired and in a non-paired school. References appended.

Teele, James E., Ellen Jackson, and Clara Mayo. "Family Experiences in Operation Exodus: The Bussing of Negro Children," *Community Mental Health Journal Monograph* 3 (1967):1-32. Study of the first year of a cooperative program to transport Negro children from substandard racially-imbalanced schools to predominantly white schools in the larger metropolitan area.

Thompson, Charles H. "Desegregation Pushed Off Dead Center," *Journal of Negro Education* 29 (Spring 1960):107-111.

Thompson, Charles H. "Race and Equality of Educational Opportunity: Defining the Problem," *Journal of Negro Education* 37 (Summer 1968):191-203.

Thompson, Daniel C. "Social Class Factors in Public School Education as Related to Desegregation," *American Journal of Orthopsychiatry* 26 (July 1956):449-452.

Toepfer, Conrad F. "Integration . . . A Curricular Concern," *Educational Leadership* 26 (December 1968):285-288.

Trachtenberg, S. J. "We Must Not Drag on the Chain," *Catholic Educational Review* 66 (September 1968):361-375.

Tumin, Melvin M., et al. "Education, Prejudice and Discrimination: A Study in Readiness for Desegregation," *American Sociological Review* 23 (February 1958):41-49.

Turman, James A., and Wayne H. Holtzman. "Attitudes of White and Negro Teachers toward Non-Segregation in the Classroom," *Journal of Social Psychology* 42 (August 1955):61–70.

Tyson, Cyril. " 'Open Enrollment': An Assessment," *Journal of Educational Sociology* 35 (October 1961):93–96.

U.S. Commission on Civil Rights. *Process of Change: The Story of School Desegregation in Syracuse, New York.* Washington: U.S. Govt. Print. Off., 1968. (CCR Clearinghouse Publication no. 12).

U.S. Commission on Civil Rights. *Schools Can Be Desegregated.* Washington, 1967. (CCR Clearinghouse Publication no. 8).

U.S. Congress. House. *Integration in Public Education Programs: Hearings before the Subcommittee on Integration in Federally Assisted Education of the Committee on Education and Labor, March 1, 1962-June 15, 1962.* Washington: U.S. Govt. Print. Off., 1962. (87th Congress, 2d Session)

Vander Zanden, James W. "Turbulence Accompanying School Desegregation," *Journal of Educational Sociology* 32 (October 1958):68–75.

"The Wall of Racial Separation: The Role of Private and Parochial Schools in Racial Integration," *New York University Law Review* 43 (May 1968):514–540. Posits that, in urban areas, public schools may become increasingly non-white, and parochial and private schools may become 90 percent white within two to three decades.

Weinberg, Meyer. *Desegregation Research: An Appraisal.* Bloomington, Ind.: Phi Delta Kappa, 1968.

Weinberg, Meyer. *Integrated Education: A Reader.* Beverly Hills, Calif.: Glencoe Press, 1968. Essays on problems and new developments in racial integration. Bibliography and useful chronology of events.

West, Earle H. "Progress toward Equality of Opportunity in Elementary and Secondary Education," *Journal of Negro Education* 37 (Summer 1968):212–219. A summary appraisal of the gains and losses.

Wey, Herbert W. "Desegregation and Integration," *Phi Delta Kappan* 47 (May 1966): 508–515.

Wey, Herbert. *Planning and Preparation for Successful School Desegregation: A Guidebook.* Bloomington, Ind.: Phi Delta Kappa, 1965.

Williams, Robin, Jr., Burton R. Fisher, and Irving L. Janis. "Educational Desegregation as a Context for Basic Social Science Research," *American Sociological Review* 21 (October 1956):577–583.

Williams, Robin M., Jr., and Margaret W. Ryan, eds. *Schools in Transition: Community Experiences in Desegregation.* Chapel Hill: University of North Carolina Press, 1954.

Wise, Arthur E. *Rich Schools, Poor Schools: The Promise of Equal Educational Opportunity.* Chicago: University of Chicago Press, 1969.

"With All Deliberate Speed," *Phi Delta Kappan* 45 (May 1964):361–425. Entire issue on tenth anniversary of 1954 Supreme Court decision.

Wolff, Max. "The Issues in Integration," *Journal of Educational Sociology* 36 (February 1963):241–244.

Wolff, Max. "A Plan for Desegregation," *Integrated Education* 2 (February–March 1964):43–47.

NORTH

Baron, Harold. "Samuel Shepard and the Banneker Project," *Integrated Education* 1 (April 1963):25–27. Shepard is director of the Banneker Elementary School District in St. Louis, where 95 percent of the school children are Negro. Purpose of the project: to bring the achievement of the culturally deprived Negro children up to national standards.

Bensfield, James A. "Progress Report: Boston School Committee Suit," *Inequality in Education* no. 2 (February 1970):3 + . Suit claiming that Boston's school committee election system contravenes the Fourteenth and Fifteenth Amendments.

Boston. Superintendent of Schools. *The Boston Blueprint for Equal Educational Opportunity.* Boston, 1966. Report of a study for the U.S. Commission on Civil Rights.

Coles, Robert. "Bussing in Boston," *New Republic* 153 (October 2, 1965):12-15.

Crockett, Harry J., Jr. "A Study of Some Factors Affecting the Decision of Negro High School Students to Enroll in Previously All-White High Schools, St. Louis, 1955," *Social Forces* 35 (May 1957):351-356.

Dentler, Robert A. "Barriers to Northern School Desegregation," *Daedalus* 95 (Winter 1966):45-63. While school desegregation in smaller cities can be accomplished relatively easily, in the very largest Northern cities racial imbalance will continue to be an intractable problem.

Donavan, James B. "We Are the Leaders," *Integrated Education* 2 (February-March 1964):29-33.

Gibel, Inge Lederer. "How *Not* to Integrate the Schools," *Harper's* 227 (November 1963):57-60. White wife of a Negro, with two children in New York schools. "Their increasingly orthodox slogans are blinding some civil-rights leaders to the real needs of most Negro—and white—children."

Glazer, Nathan. "Is Integration Possible in New York Schools?" *Commentary* 30 (September 1960):185-193.

Glazer, Nathan. "School Integration Policies in Northern Cities," *Journal of the American Institute of Planners* 30 (August 1964):178-188.

Gross, Calvin E. "Progress toward Integration," *Integrated Education* 2 (February-March 1964):12-21. By head of New York City public schools.

Hickey, Philip J. *Replies to 136 Statements, Accusations, and Criticisms of Desegregation Policies and Practices of the St. Louis Board of Education and School Administration.* St. Louis, 1963.

Landry, Lawrence. "The Chicago School Boycott," *New University Thought* 3 (December 1963-January 1964):21-29.

Lasch, Robert. "Surprise in St. Louis," *Progressive* 21 (January 1957):14-16.

Lurie, Ellen. "School Integration in New York City," *Integrated Education* 2 (February-March 1964):3-11.

Massachusetts. Board of Education. *Because It Is Right—Educationally: Report of the Advisory Committee on Racial Imbalance and Education.* Boston, April 1965. In March 1964 the State Board of Education and Dr. Owen Kiernan, State Commissioner of Education, appointed an advisory committee to determine whether racial imbalance existed in the public schools, whether, if so, it was educationally harmful, and what steps should be taken to eliminate it. With affirmative findings in the first two cases, the committee made recommendations for remedial action.

New York (State). Department of Education. *Desegregating the Schools of New York City.* Albany, May 1964. Report of the state advisory committee (Allen Report).

New York City Commission on Human Rights. *Study of the Effect of the 1964-1970 School Building Program on Segregation in New York City's Public Schools.* New York, 1964.

Proceedings of the Invitational Conference on Northern School Desegregation: Progress and Problems, April 29, 1962. New York: Graduate School of Education, Yeshiva University, 1962.

A Proposal for Integrating Philadelphia Public Schools. Philadelphia: Urban League, 1964.

Raubinger, Frederick M. "The New Jersey Doctrine," *Integrated Education* 1 (August 1963):14-17. Extracts from statement by New Jersey State Commissioner of Education on integration.

Ravitz, Mel. "Unequal School Progress in Detroit," *Integrated Education* 1 (June 1963):3-9.

Record, Wilson. "Racial Integration in California Schools," *Journal of Negro Education* 27 (Winter 1958):17-23.

Record, Wilson. "Racial Diversity in California Public Schools," *Journal of Negro Education* 29 (Winter 1960):15-25.

Report to the Board of Education of Chicago by the Advisory Panel on Integration of the Public Schools. Chicago: Board of Education, March 31, 1964.

Schickel, Richard. "P.S. 165," *Commentary* 27 (January 1964):43-51. On a New York elementary school, a program of cultural enrichment, and the relations between Negroes and the white middle class.

Schools for Hartford. Cambridge: Center for Field Studies, Harvard Graduate School of Education, 1965. The proposal of a "metropolitan plan" for Hartford, Conn., which recommends that surrounding suburban communities assume part of the burden of educating children from the city's poverty areas.

Sexton, Patricia Cayo. "Comments on Three Cities," *Integrated Education* 1 (August 1963):27-32. New York, Chicago, Detroit, and their schools.

Shagaloff, June. "A Review of Public School Desegregation in the North and West," *Journal of Educational Sociology* 36 (February 1963):292-294.

Solomon, Benjamin. "Integration and the Educators," *Integrated Education* 1 (August 1963):18-26. Tactics, strategies, and goals of Northern and Western school integration movements.

Sullivan, Neil V. "Compensation and Integration: The Berkeley Experience," in *Equal Education Opportunity.* Cambridge, Mass.: Harvard University Press, 1969, pp. 220-227. Originally appeared in the *Harvard Educational Review,* Winter 1968.

Sullivan, Neil, and Evelyn S. Stewart. *Now Is the Time: Integration in the Berkeley Schools.* Bloomington: Indiana University Press, 1970.

Tillman, James A., Jr. *Segregation and the Minneapolis Public Schools: An Overview with Recommendations for its Arrest and Reversal.* Minneapolis: Greater Minneapolis Interfaith Fair Housing Program, 1962.

Tillman, James A., Jr. "Minneapolis: Chronology of Success," *Integrated Education* 1 (August 1963):41-44. Problem of de facto segregation.

Turner, Francis A. "Integration in the New York City Schools," *Journal of Human Relations* 7 (Summer 1959):491-503.

Vespa, Marcia Lane. "Chicago's Regional School Plans," *Integrated Education* 1 (October-November 1963):24-31.

Vincent, William S., and Maurice A. Lohman. *Meeting the Needs of New York City's Schools.* New York: Public Education Association, United Federation of Teachers, and United Parents Association, 1965.

Walker, Gerald. "Englewood and the Northern Dilemma," *Nation* 197 (July 6, 1963):7-10.

Wennerberg, C. H. *Desegregation of the Berkeley Public Schools: Its Feasibility and Implementation.* Berkeley, Calif.: Berkeley Unified School District, 1964.

Wolff, Max. "Racial Imbalance in Plainfield Public Schools," *Journal of Educational Sociology* 36 (February 1963):275-286.

Wolff, Max, ed. "Toward Integration of Northern Schools," *Journal of Educational Sociology* 36 (February 1963):1-296. Entire issue.

SOUTH

Abraham, Henry J. "School Desegregation in the South," *Current History* 41 (August 1961):94-96.

Bates, Daisy. *The Long Shadow of Little Rock.* New York: McKay, 1962. The author was engaged in every stage of the effort to enroll the Negro children in the high school.

Billington, Monroe. "Public School Integration in Missouri, 1954-1964," *Journal of Negro Education* 35 (Summer 1966):252-262.

Blossom, Virgil T. *It Has Happened Here.* New York: Harper, 1959. This is the personal account by Little Rock superintendent of schools of the sequence of events from early preparations for compliance down to the climax in the fall of 1957.

Brazziel, William F., and Margaret Gordon. "Replications of Some Aspects of the Higher Horizons Program in a Southern Junior High School," *Journal of Negro Education* 32 (Spring 1963):107-113.

Brown, Richard W. "Freedom of Choice in the South: A Constitutional Perspective," *Louisiana Law Review* 28 (April 1968):455-468. Interpretations of Southern school desegregation stemming from *United States v. Jefferson County Board of Education* and *Brown v. Board of Education* decisions.

Chesler, Mark A. *In Their Own Words*. Atlanta: Southern Regional Council, 1967. Abstracted conversations of 20 Negro teenagers concerning school desegregation in
Alabama.

Clark, Kenneth B. "Observations on Little Rock," *New South* 13 (June 1958):3-8.

Cohen, D. K. "Jurists and Educators on Urban Schools: The Wright Decision and the
Passow Report," *Record* 70 (December 1968):233-246. Deals with Washington, D.C.
schools. Commentary pp. 246-250 by Robert L. Carter, former General Counsel of
NAACP.

Coles, Robert. "Southern Children under Desegregation," *American Journal of Psychiatry*
120 (October 1962):332-344.

Cooke, Paul. "Desegregated Education in the Middle-South Region: Problems and Issues,"
Journal of Negro Education 30 (Winter 1961):75-79.

Cramer, M. Richard. "Factors Related to Willingness to Experience Desegregation among
Students in Segregated Schools," *Social Science Quarterly* 49 (December 1968):684-696.
A Southern sampling.

Cramer, M. Richard. "School Desegregation and New Industry: The Southern Community
Leaders' Viewpoint," *Social Forces* 41 (May 1963):384-389.

"Deep South Now Facing School Desegregation," *New South* 16 (May 1961):4-8.

Demerath, Nick J. "Desegregation, Education, and the South's Future," *Phylon* 18 (Spring
1957):43-49.

"Desegregation—Or No Public Schools," *New South* 14 (March 1959):3-6.

Dewing, Rolland. "Desegregation of State NEA Affiliates in the South," *Journal of Negro
Education* 38 (Fall 1969):395-403.

Doddy, Hurley H., and G. Franklin Edwards. "Apprehensions of Negro Teachers Concerning Desegregation in South Carolina," *Journal of Negro Education* 24 (Winter
1955):26-43.

Donahue, John W. "Biracial Public School Education in the South," *Thought* 35 (Fall
1960):393-420. Historical and philosophical background of biracial education.

Dunne, George H. "Footnote on Gradualism," *Interracial Review* 35 (December 1962):273.

Eight Years of Desegregation in the Baltimore Public Schools: Fact and Law. Baltimore:
Baltimore Neighborhoods, Inc., 1963.

Gandy, Willard E. "Implications of Integration for Southern Teachers," *Journal of Negro
Education* 31 (Spring 1962):191-197.

Goodall, Merrill R. "Southern Politics and School Integration," *Journal of Educational
Sociology* 32 (October 1958):62-67.

Griffin, John Howard, and Theodore Freedman. *Mansfield, Texas: A Report of the Crisis
Situation Resulting from Efforts to Desegregate the School System*. New York: Anti-Defamation League, 1957.

Hansen, Carl F. *Danger in Washington: The Story of My Twenty Years in the Public Schools
in the Nation's Capital*. West Nyack, N.Y.: Parker, 1968. Outlines the de jure segregation
prior to 1954. Describes the subsequent white exodus from the schools, his programs, and
philosophy for biracial education.

Holden, Anna, et al. *Clinton, Tennessee: A Tentative Description and Analysis of the School
Desegregation Crisis*. New York: Anti-Defamation League, n. d.

Horton, Aimée. "Highlander Folk School: Pioneer of Integration in the South," *Teachers
College Record* 68 (December 1966):242-250. Narrates the history of the school and its
contribution toward promoting desegregation in the South.

Hronek, Mary Linda. "A Catholic High School Integrates," *Interracial Review* 36 (December
1963):238-241. A day-to-day account of the desegregation of a school in New Orleans.

"Integration by Tracking To Be Tried in Mississippi," *Inequality in Education* (Harvard
Center for Law and Education) 1 (October 10, 1969):9-11. A pilot school desegregation
plan provisionally approved for a Mississippi County using aptitude tests to determine
school assignment.

Johnson, R. O. "Desegregation of Public Education in Georgia—One Year Afterward,"
Journal of Negro Education 24 (Summer 1955):228-247.

Kentucky Council on Human Relations. "Kentucky Is Successfully Integrating Its Teachers," *New South* 12 (April 1957):7–12.

Kentucky. Department of Education. Report. "Kentucky Desegregation Proceeds At All Levels," *New South* 14 (February 1959):9–10.

Knoll, Erwin. "Washington: Showcase of Integration: A Progress Report," *Commentary* 27 (March 1959):194–202.

Knoll, Erwin. "The Truth about Desegregation in the Washington, D.C., Public Schools," *Journal of Negro Education* 28 (Spring 1959):92–113.

Korey, William, and Charlotte Lubin. "Arlington—Another Little Rock: School Integration Fight on Washington's Doorstep," *Commentary* 26 (September 1958):201–209.

McCauley, Patrick, and Edward D. Ball, eds. *Southern Schools: Progress and Problems.* Nashville, Tenn.: Southern Education Reporting Service, 1959.

Miller, Arthur S. *Racial Discrimination and Private Education.* Chapel Hill: University of North Carolina Press, 1957. The author believes success in integrating private education might ease Southern doubts about public facilities.

"New Orleans Experience Is New Lesson for South: An Analysis of New Orleans Crisis," *New South* 16 (March 1961):3–8. Strife over desegregation of both public and parochial schools.

Osborne, Irene, and Richard K. Bennett. "Eliminating Educational Segregation in the Nation's Capital, 1951–1955," *Annals of the American Academy of Political and Social Science* 304 (March 1956):98–108.

Parmenter, Tom. "Guidelines, Deadlines, & Between the Lines: Nixon's July 3 Declaration," *Inequality in Education* 1 (October 10, 1969):13–19. Text and analysis of the administration's statement on Southern school desegregation.

Powledge, Fred. "The Summer Institutes," *New South* 18 (April 1963):11–12. Integration of federally sponsored summer institutes in South.

Record, Wilson, and Jane Cassels Record, eds. *Little Rock, U.S.A.: Materials for Analysis.* San Francisco: Chandler, 1960.

"Report: Desegregation of Southern Parochial Schools," *Interracial Review* 36 (November 1963):218–219. Prepared by the Southern Regional Council.

Sarratt, Reed. *The Ordeal of Desegregation: The First Decade.* New York: Harper & Row, 1966. A documentary account of the accelerated struggle for desegregation and equal education in the decade following 1954. Data drawn from the files of the Southern Education Reporting Service.

"School Desegregation Is Entering New Phase: Analysis of Houston and New Orleans," *New South* 15 (October 1960):3–7.

Schuler, Edgar A., and Robert L. Green. "A Southern Educator and School Integration: An Interview," *Phylon* 28 (Spring 1967):28–40. The Prince Edward Country, Virginia school controversy.

Shoemaker, Don, ed. *With All Deliberate Speed.* New York: Harper, 1959. Collection of essays about the progress—or lack of progress—in public school desegregation in South, prepared by Southern Education Reporting Service. Bibliography.

Southern Regional Council. *Lawlessness and Disorder: Fourteen Years of Failure in Southern School Desegregation.* Atlanta, 1968.

Southern Regional Council. *School Desegregation 1966: The Slow Undoing.* Atlanta, 1966. A progress review and a critical look at the U.S. Office of Education guidelines and enforcement procedures.

Stallings, Frank H. *Desegregation and Academic Achievement.* Atlanta, 1960.

Stinchcombe, Arthur L., Mary Sexton McDill, and Dollie R. Walker. "Demography of Organizations," *American Journal of Sociology* 74 (November 1968):221–229. Outlines in demographic terms why Baltimore schools have failed to achieve their goal of desegregation.

Stinchcombe, Arthur L., Mary McDill, and Dollie R. Walker. "Is There a Racial Tipping Point in Changing Schools?" *Journal of Social Issues* 25 (January 1969):127–136. Analysis drawn from Baltimore City Public Schools.

Sullivan, Neil V., with Thomas LaSalle and Carol Lynn Yellin. *Bound for Freedom: An Educator's Adventures in Prince Edward County, Virginia.* Boston: Little, Brown, 1965. Account of the author's experience in setting up the Free Schools in that county, and of who did, and who did not, help in the task.

Tumin, Melvin M. "Imaginary vs. Real Children: Some Southern Views on Desegregation'" *School and Society* 86 (October 11, 1958):357-360.

U.S. Commission on Civil Rights. *Civil Rights U.S.A.—Public Schools Southern States, 1962.* Washington, 1962.

U.S. Commission on Civil Rights. *Southern School Desegregation, 1966-67.* Washington, 1967. Bibliographical footnotes.

U.S. Commission on Civil Rights. *Survey of School Desegregation in the Southern and Border States, 1965-1966; A Report.* Washington: U.S. Govt. Print. Off., 1966. Bibliographical footnotes.

Vander Zanden, James W. "The Impact of Little Rock," *Journal of Educational Sociology* 35 (April 1962):381-384.

"Vanishing Black Principals and Teachers in the South," *School and Society* 97 (September 1969):470-472. Legislation requiring desegregation frequently causes school closing and the "displacement" of Negro personnel.

Wall, Marvin. "Events in Southern Education since 1954," *Harvard Educational Review* 30 (Summer 1960):209-215. Good tables of statistics.

Wilkerson, Doxey A. "The Negro School Movement in Virginia: From 'Equalization' to 'Integration,'" *Journal of Negro Education* 29 (Winter 1960):17-29.

William, Robert L., and Fred Venditti. "Effect of Academic Desegregation on Southern White Students' Expressed Satisfaction with School," *Journal of Negro Education* 38 (Fall 1969):338-341. Study conducted to test the validity of the segregationist argument that desegregation imposes an academic penalty on white students.

Community Control

Berube, Maurice R., and Marilyn Gittell, eds. *Confrontation at Ocean Hill-Brownsville: The New York School Strikes of 1968.* New York: Praeger, 1969.

"Black Leaders Speak Out on Black Education," *Today's Education* 58 (October 1969): 25-32.

"Black Power 1968," *Phi Delta Kappan* 49 (April 1968):447-452. Four papers about black activism and community control in education.

Cohen, David K. "Price of Community Control," *Commentary* 48 (July 1969):23-32. Discussion, *ibid.,* (September 1969):4-10; (November 1969):12-18.

Cohen, S. Alan. "Local Control and the Cultural Deprivation Fallacy," *Phi Delta Kappan* 50 (January 1969):255-259. A reading specialist argues that local control can improve student achievement in ghetto schools.

Featherstone, Joseph. "Wiping Out the Demonstration Schools," *New Republic* 162 (January 10, 1970):10-11. The single black member of the New York City Interim Board of Education dissents in the decision to remove I.S.201 and Ocean Hill-Brownsville schools from community control.

Gittell, Marilyn. "Community Control of Education," *American Academy of Political Science Proceedings* 29 (July 1968):60-71.

Gold, Stephen F. "School-Community Relations in Urban Ghettos," *Record* 69 (November 1967):144-150.

Hentoff, Nat. "Overturning the School System at I.S. 201," *Motive* 27 (January 1967):17+.

Lauter, Paul. "The Short, Happy Life of the Adams-Morgan Community School Project," *Harvard Educational Review* 38 (Spring 1968):235-262.

Levine, Richard H. "They Made a Better School: Community School in Providence," *American Education* 5 (November 1969):8-10.

Poinsett, Alex. "Battle to Control Black Schools," *Ebony* 24 (May 1969):44-46+.

Rempson, Joel L. "For an Elected Local School Board," *Urban Review* (November

1966):2-15. Analyzes the potential contributions of the Negro community toward quality segregated education. Illustrations.

Solomon, Victor. "An Independent Board of Education for Harlem," *Urban Affairs Quarterly* 4 (September 1968):39-43.

Willie, Charles V. "New Perspectives in School-Community Relationships," *Journal of Negro Education* 37 (Summer 1968):220-226.

Young, Whitney M., Jr. "Minorities and Community Control of the Schools," *Journal of Negro Education* 38 (Summer 1969):285-290.

Aspiration and Achievement

Ames, Louise B., and Frances L. Ilg. "Search for Children Showing Academic Promise in a Predominantly Negro School," *Journal of Genetic Psychology* 110 (June 1967):217-231. 1964-1965 study of an elementary school in New Haven, Connecticut.

Arnez, Nancy L., and Clara Anthony. "Working with Disadvantaged Negro Youth in Urban Schools," *School and Society* 96 (March 30, 1968):202-204.

Ashbury, Charles A. "Some Selected Problems Involved in Assessing the Intelligence and Achievement of Disadvantaged Groups: With Emphasis on the Negro," *Quarterly Review of Higher Education among Negroes* 36 (July 1968):133-144.

Benson, Arthur L. "Problems of Evaluating Test Scores of White and Negro Teachers," *Proceedings of the Fifty-ninth Annual Meeting.* Southern Association of Colleges and Secondary Schools, 1954.

Boldon, Wiley S. "Tasks for the Negro Teacher in Improving Academic Achievement of Negro Pupils in the South," *Journal of Negro Education* 32 (Spring 1963):173-178.

Bond, Horace Mann. "Talents and Toilets," *Journal of Negro Education* 28 (Winter 1959):3-14. Relation of "talent" to percentage of toilets in census areas, and its relation to educational opportunity.

Boney, J. Don. "Predicting the Academic Achievement of Secondary School Negro Students," *Personnel and Guidance Journal* 44 (March 1966):700-703. Report of a study of aptitude and mental ability measures to predict grades.

Bowles, Samuel, and Henry M. Levin. "The Determinants of Scholastic Achievement—An Appraisal of Some Recent Evidence," *Journal of Human Resources* 3 (Winter 1968):1+.

Brazziel, William F., and Mary Terrell. "An Experiment in the Development of Readiness in a Culturally Disadvantaged Group of First Grade Children," *Journal of Negro Education* 31 (Winter 1962):4-7.

Clift, Virgil A. "Factors Relating to the Education of Culturally Deprived Negro Youth," *Educational Theory* 14 (April 1964):76-82.

Cohen, S. Alan. "Local Control and the Cultural Deprivation Fallacy," *Phi Delta Kappan* 50 (January 1969):255-259. A reading specialist argues that local control can improve student achievement in ghetto schools.

Cramer, M. Richard, Ernest A. Campbell, and Charles E. Bowerman. *Social Factors in Educational Achievement and Aspirations among Negro Adolescents.* Vol. I: *Demographic Study.* Vol. II: *Survey Study.* Chapel Hill: Institute for Research in Social Science Monographs, University of North Carolina, 1966. Data drawn from counties in the eleven Confederate states. Footnotes and bibliography are lacking.

Davis, Allison. "The Educability of the Children of the Poor," *Phi Delta Kappan* 50 (October 1968):128-130. An assessment of previous studies of disadvantaged Negro children. Excerpt from the author's, *The Unfinished Journey: Issues in American Education.* New York: John Day, 1968.

Davis, Allison, "The Future Education of Children from Low Socio-Economic Groups," in Stanley Elam, ed., *New Dimensions for Educational Progress.* Bloomington, Ind.: Phi Delta Kappa, 1962, pp. 27-43.

De Charms, Richard, and Virginia Carpenter. "Measuring Motivation in Culturally Disadvantaged School Children," *Journal of Experimental Education* 37 (Fall 1968):31-41. Report and analysis of preliminary research. Bibliography.

Desegregation and Academic Achievement. Atlanta: Southern Regional Council, 1960.

Deutsch, Martin. "Minority Group and Class Status as Related to Social and Personality Factors in Scholastic Achievement," in Martin M. Grossack, ed., *Mental Health and Segregation.* New York: Springer, 1963.

Elkind, David, and Jo A. Deblinger. "Perceptual Training and Reading Achievement in Disadvantaged Children," *Child Development* 40 (March 1969):11-19. Negro second grade inner-city children were subjects of the study.

Freyberg, Joan T. "The Effect of Participation in an Elementary School Buddy System on the Self Concept, School Attitudes and Behaviors, and Achievement of Fifth Grade Negro Children," *Graduate Research in Education and Related Disciplines* 3 (April 1967):3-29. Subjects were Negro children from the central Harlem neighborhood. Bibliography.

Gist, Noel P., and William S. Bennett, Jr. "Aspirations of Negro and White Students," *Social Forces* 42 (October 1963):40-48.

Green, Robert L., and Louis J. Hoffman. "A Case Study of the Effects of Educational Deprivation on Southern Rural Negro Children," *Journal of Negro Education* 34 (Summer 1965):327-341. Effects both on academic achievement and measured intelligence of the Negro children of Prince Edward County, Va., of closing of public schools.

Green, Robert Lee, and William W. Farquhar. "Negro Academic Motivation and Scholastic Achievement," *Journal of Educational Psychology* 56 (October 1965):241-243.

Guggenheim, Fred. "Self-Esteem and Achievement Expectations for White and Negro Children," *Journal of Projective Techniques and Personality Assessment* 33 February 1969):63-71. References appended.

Hansen, Carl F. "The Scholastic Performance of Negro and White Pupils in the Integrated Public Schools of the District of Columbia," *Harvard Educational Review* 30 (Summer 1960):216-236.

Harrison, E. C. "Working at Improving the Motivational and Achievement Levels of the Deprived," *Journal of Negro Education* 32 (Summer 1963):301-307.

Herson, Phyliss F. "An Assessment of Changes in Achievement Motivation among Upward Bound Participants at the University of Maryland," *Journal of Negro Education* 37 (Fall 1968):383-391. Twenty-five of the thirty research subjects were Negro.

Hess, R. D. "Maternal Behavior and the Development of Reading Readiness in Urban Negro Children," *Claremont Reading Conference Yearbook* 32 (1968):83-99. Bibliography.

Hobart, Charles W. "Underachievement among Minority Group Students: An Analysis and a Proposal," *Phylon* 24 (Summer 1963):184-196. Advocates special enrichment programs.

Hurley, Philip S. "Fordham's Tutorial Program: 'Before They Drop Out!'" *Interracial Review* 36 (November 1963):222-223.

Joseph, Ellis A. "Selected Aspects of the Internality of the Negro in Education," *Education* 88 (November 1967):149-152. Relation of scholastic achievement to self-esteem. Bibliography.

Katz, Irwin. "Academic Motivation and Equal Opportunity," in *Equal Educational Opportunity.* Cambridge, Mass.; Harvard University Press, 1969, pp. 60-68. Originally appeared in the *Harvard Educational Review,* Winter 1968.

Katz, Irwin. "The Effects of Desegregation on the Performance of Negroes," in Joan I. Roberts, ed., *School Children in the Urban Slums.* New York: Free Press, 1967, pp. 261-292. Bibliography.

Katz, Irwin, Thomas Henchy, and Harvey Allen. "Effects of Race of Tester, Approval-Disapproval, and Need on Negro Children's Learning," *Journal of Personality and Social Psychology* 8 (January 1968):38-42.

Katz, Irwin. "Factors Influencing Negro Performance in the Desegregated School," in Martin Deutsch, Irwin Katz, and Arthur R. Jensen, eds., *Social Class, Race, and Psychological Development.* New York: Holt, Rinehart & Winston, 1968, pp. 254-289.

Katz, Irwin. "The Socialization of Academic Motivation in Minority Group Children," in David Levine, ed., *Nebraska Symposium on Motivation, 1967.* Lincoln: University of

Nebraska Press, 1967, pp. 133-191. Considers motivational factors underlying racial differences as applied to scholastic achievement. Bibliography.

Kornberg, Leonard. "Slum Children and New Teachers," *Journal of Negro Education* 32 (Winter 1963):74-80.

Labov, William, and Clarence Robins. "A Note on the Relation of Reading Failure to Peer Group Status in Urban Ghettos," *Record* 70 (February 1969):395-405. Suggests specific knowledge of Negro street culture is requisite for teachers to effectively motivate learning in certain ghetto children.

Mackler, Bernard. "The '600' Schools: Dilemmas, Problems, and Solutions," *Urban Review,* June 1966, pp. 8-15. The author questions the number of Negroes and Puerto Ricans in these special New York schools for socially maladjusted and emotionally disturbed children. Rebuttals by Albert Budwich and David N. Shapiro, and a rejoinder by the author appear, ibid., November 1966, pp. 28-30.

Mitchell, Lonnie E. "Aspiration Levels of Negro Delinquent, Dependent, and Public School Boys," *Journal of Negro Education* 26 (Winter 1957):80-85.

"Motivation and Academic Achievement of Negro Americans," *Journal of Social Issues* 25 (Summer 1969):1-147. Entire issue. Correlates of academic achievement, the effects of desegregation on motivation and achievement, and of expanding opportunity. Edited by Edgar G. Epps. Contributors include: Irwin Katz, Patricia Gurin, and James McPartland.

Nelson, John C. "Interests of Disadvantaged and Advantaged Negro and White First Graders," *Journal of Negro Education* 37 (Spring 1968):168-173.

Newton, Eunice Shaed, and E. H. West. "The Progress of the Negro in Elementary and Secondary Education," *Journal of Negro Education* 32 (Fall 1963):465-484.

Otto, Wayne. "Inhibitory Potential Related to the Reading Achievement of Negro Children," *Psychology in the Schools* 3 (April 1966):161-163.

Riessman, Frank. *The Culturally Deprived Child and His Education.* New York: Harper, 1962. Chapters 4 and 11 are particularly concerned with Negro children, although their problems are considered throughout.

Robins, Lee N., Robin S. Jones, and George E. Murphy. "School Milieu and School Problems of Negro Boys," *Social Problems* 13 (Spring 1966):428-436. A systematic investigation of which social characteristics of Negro boys relate to adequate school performance.

Rousseve, Ronald. "Teachers of Culturally Disadvantaged American Youth," *Journal of Negro Education* 32 (Spring 1963):114-121.

Ryckman, David B. "A Comparison of Information Processing Abilities of Middle and Lower Class Negro Kindergarten Boys," *Exceptional Children* 33 (April 1967):545-552.

St. John, Nancy. "The Effect of Segregation on the Aspirations of Negro Youth," *Harvard Educational Review* 36 (Summer 1966):284-294. In a medium-sized New England city.

Sand, Mary E. "To Show the Way," *New South* 17 (November-December 1962):11-12. Program for closing cultural gap between Negro and white children.

Scales, Eldridge E. "A Study of College Student Retention and Withdrawal," *Journal of Negro Education* 29 (Fall 1960):438-444.

Sigel, Irving E., and Cereta Perry. "Psycholinguistic Diversity among 'Culturally Deprived' Children," *American Journal of Orthopsychiatry* 38 (January 1968):122-126. Questions the validity of the term "culturally deprived" as applied to a Negro homogeneous group. Implications for education are discussed.

Solomon, Daniel, Kevin Houlihan, and Robert J. Parelius. "Intellectual Achievement Responsibility in Negro and White Children," *Psychological Reports* 24 (April 1969): 479-483.

Stallings, Frank H. *Racial Differences in Academic Achievement.* Atlanta: Southern Regional Council, 1960.

Stallings, Frank H. "A Study of the Immediate Effects of Integration on Scholastic Achievement in the Louisville Public Schools," *Journal of Negro Education* 28 (Fall 1959): 439-444.

Weiner, Max, and Walter Murray. "Another Look at the Culturally Deprived and the Levels of Aspirations," *Journal of Educational Sociology* 36 (March 1963):319-321.

Wells, Twyla Teresa. "The Effects of Discrimination upon Motivation and Achievement of Black Children in Urban Ghetto Schools," *American Behavioral Scientist* 12 (March–April 1969):26-33.

Wilcox, Preston R. "Teacher Attitudes and Student Achievement," *Teachers College Record* 68 (February 1967):371-379. A social worker's suggestions to middle-class teachers of lower-class Negroes.

Wilcox, Roger. "Music Ability among Negro Grade School Pupils: Or, I Got Rhythm?" *Perceptual and Motor Skills* 29 (February 1969):167-168.

Wolfe, Deborah Partridge. "Curriculum Adaptations for the Culturally Deprived," *Journal of Negro Education* 31 (Spring 1962):139-151.

Zito, Robert J., and Jack I. Bardon. "Achievement Motivation among Negro Adolescents in Regular and Special Education Programs," *American Journal of Mental Deficiency* 74 (July 1969):20-26. Objective goal setting of 150 Negro adolescents measured using thematic apperception visuals, the WRAT, and other designed tasks.

See also Intelligence.

Guidance and Occupational Choice

Amos, William E. "A Study of the Occupational Awareness of a Selected Group of 9th Grade Negro Students," *Journal of Negro Education* 29 (Fall 1960):500-503. Students are in acute need of realistic knowledge of what occupational opportunities and requirements they will confront.

Antonovsky, Aaron, and Melvin J. Lerner. "Occupational Aspirations of Lower-Class Negro and White Youth," *Social Problems* 7 (Fall 1959):132-138.

Antonovsky, Aaron. "Looking Ahead at Life: A Study of the Occupational Aspirations of New York City Tenth Graders." New York State Commission against Discrimination, 1960. Mimeographed.

Arnez, Nancy L. "A Thoughtful Look at Placement Policies in a New Era," *Journal of Negro Education* 35 (Winter 1966):48-54. Teacher integration in biracial schools in Southern and border states.

Blalock, H. M., Jr. "Education Achievement and Job Opportunities: A Vicious Circle," *Journal of Negro Education* 27 (Fall 1958):544-548.

Boykin, Leander L., and William F. Brazziel, Jr. "Occupational Interests of 1741 Teacher Education Students as Revealed on the Lee-Thorpe Inventory," *Journal of Negro Education* 28 (Winter 1959):42-48.

Brazziel, William F., Jr. "Meeting the Psychological Crises of Negro Youth through a Coordinated Guidance Service," *Journal of Negro Education* 27 (Winter 1958):79-83.

Briggs, William A., and Dean L. Hummel. *Counseling Minority Group Youth: Developing the Experience of Equality through Education.* Columbus: Ohio Civil Rights Commission, 1962.

"Broadcasting Courses for Negroes Planned," *Broadcasting* 75 (August 19, 1968):44. A proposal of the University of Detroit.

"Business, Labor, and Jobs in the Ghetto: A Staff Survey," *Issues in Industrial Society* 1 (1969):3-18. Focuses on apprenticeship programs devised by business, labor, and other organizations. Discussion also includes small firm enterprises in the ghetto and unions in Watts.

Coleman, A. Lee. "Occupational, Educational and Residence Plans of Negro High-School Seniors in Lexington and Fayette County, Kentucky," *Journal of Negro Education* 29 (Winter 1960):73-79.

Ekberg, Dennis, and Claude Ury. " 'Education for What?'—A Report on an M.D.T.A. Program," *Journal of Negro Education* 37 (Winter 1968):15-22. Evaluation of a Management Development Training Act program involving Negroes from the ghetto of West Oakland, California.

Freedman, Marcia K. "Part-Time Work Experience and Early School-Leavers," *American Journal of Orthopsychiatry* 33 (April 1963):509-514.

Ginzberg, Eli. "Strategies for Self Development," in Conference on the Education and Training of Racial Minorities, 1967, *Proceedings*. Madison: University of Wisconsin, Center for Studies in Vocational and Technical Education, 1967, pp. 55-61. Occupational aspiration and drive.

Grier, Eunice S. *In Search of a Future: A Pilot Study of Career-Seeking Experiences of Selected High-School Graduates in Washington, D.C.* Washington: The Washington Center for Metropolitan Studies, 1963.

Guba, E. G., P. W. Jackson, and C. E. Bidwell. "Occupational Choice and the Teaching Career," *Educational Research Bulletin* 38 (January 14, 1959):1-12, 27-28.

Holloway, Robert G., and Joel V. Berreman. "The Educational and Occupational Aspirations and Plans of Negro and White Male Elementary School Students," *Pacific Sociological Review* 2 (Fall 1959):56-60. While educational aspirations may be similar, occupational hopes and plans reflect the subculture of the Negro in that he anticipates more limited opportunity.

Ingerman, Sidney, and George Strauss. "Preparing Underprivileged Negro Youths for Jobs," *Poverty and Human Resources Abstracts* 2 (July-August 1967):5-16. An overview, with bibliographical footnotes.

Jordan, Marion. "How to Rescue the Mediocre: NEED Gives Pittsburgh Some New Options," *Conference Board Record* 6 (March 1969):21-25. Negro Educational Emergency Drive. A plan to provide post high school training for Negro students. Financed by the Pittsburgh business community.

Keig, Norman G. "The Occupational Aspirations and Labor Force Experience of Negro Youth," *American Journal of Economics and Sociology* 28 (April 1969):113-130.

Kuvlesky, William P., and George W. Ohlendorf. "A Rural-Urban Comparison of the Occupational Status Orientations of Negro Boys," *Rural Sociology* 33 (June 1968): 141-152. Data based on study of a group of Texas high school youths.

Landes, Ruth. "Cultural Factors in Counselling," *Journal of General Education* 15 (April 1963):55-67.

Levenson, Bernard, and Mary McDill. "Vocational Graduates in Auto Mechanics: A Follow-Up Study of Negro and White Youth," *Phylon* 27 (Winter 1967):347-357. Data shows earnings about 50 percent lower for Negroes in Baltimore, Maryland area.

McGlotten, Robert M., and Doris Gibson Hardesty. "Outreach: Skills for Minority Youth," *American Federationist* 76 (April 1969):13-18. Apprenticeship training program.

Mose, Ashriel I. *A Study of the Nature of Guidance and Counseling Services among Negro High Schools in South Carolina.* Orangeburg, S.C.: School of Education, South Carolina State College, 1962.

Ostlund, Leonard A. "Occupational Choice Patterns of Negro College Women," Journal of Negro Education 26 (Winter 1957):86-91.

Pelosi, John William. *A Study of the Effects of Examiner's Race, Sex, and Style on Test Responses of Negro Examinees.* Springfield, Va.: Clearinghouse for Federal Scientific and Technical Information, 1968.

Phillips, Waldo B. "Counseling Negro Pupils: An Educational Dilemma," *Journal of Negro Education* 29 (Fall 1960):504-507.

Plaut, Richard L. "Increasing the Quantity and Quality of Negro Enrollment in College," *Harvard Educational Review* 30 (Summer 1960):270-279. Project by National Scholarship Services and Fund for Negro Students.

Record, Wilson. "Counseling and Communication," *Journal of Negro Education* 30 (Fall 1961):450-454.

Rousseve, R. J. "Counselor Education and the Culturally Isolated: An Alliance for Mutual Benefit," *Journal of Negro Education* 34 (Fall 1965): 395-403. Emphasizes the responsibility of counselors to understand and adapt to the experiences and needs of the Negro student.

Rousseve, Ronald, "Updating Guidance and Personnel Practices," *Journal of Negro Education* 31 (Spring 1962):182-187.

Russell, James W. "Counseling Negro Students," *Journal of Negro Education* 28 (Winter 1959):74-75.

Sadofsky, Stanley. *A Study of the Meaning, Experience and Effects of the Neighborhood Youth Corps on Negro Youth Seeking Work.* New York: Graduate School of Social Work, New York University, 1968.

Shulman, Lee S. "Negro-White Differences in Employability, Self-Concept, and Related Measures among Adolescents Classified as Mentally Handicapped," *Journal of Negro Education* 37 (Summer 1968):227-240.

Sprey, Jetse. "Sex Differences in Occupational Choice Patterns among Negro Adolescents," *Social Problems* 10 (Summer 1962):11-23.

Strong, Edward K., Jr. "Are Medical Specialist Interest Scales Applicable to Negroes?" *Journal of Applied Psychology* 39 (February 1955):62-64. On degree of vocation represented by stated preference by Negroes for medical profession.

Trueblood, Dennis L. "The Role of the Counselor in the Guidance of Negro Students," *Harvard Educational Review* 30 (Summer 1960):252-269.

Vontress, Clemmont E. "Counseling Negro Students for College," *Journal of Negro Education* 37 (Winter 1968):37-44. Includes possible sources of scholarship aid.

Washington, Kenneth S. "What Counselors Must Know about Black Power," *Personnel and Guidance Journal* 47 (November 1968):204-208.

Wellman, David. "The Wrong Way to Find Jobs for Negroes," *Trans-action* 5 (April 1968):9-18. A case history of a federal program, TIDE, designed to facilitate employment search for lower-class youths in Oakland, California.

Wrightstone, J. Wayne. "Demonstration Guidance Project in New York City," *Harvard Educational Review* 30 (Summer 1960):237-251. Report of a project which identified and tried to stimulate able but culturally deprived students.

Zito, Robert J., and Jack I. Bardon. "Negro Adolescents' Success and Failure Imagery Concerning Work and School," *Vocational Guidance Quarterly* 16 (March 1968):181-184.

Higher Education

Patterns and Conditions

Allman, Reva White. "An Evaluation of the Goals of Higher Education by 294 College Seniors of Alabama," *Journal of Negro Education* 29 (Spring 1960):198-203.

American Association of University Professors. "Council Resolution of October 27, 1962, on Recent Events at the University of Mississippi and on Racial Discrimination in Higher Education," *School and Society* 91 (January 26, 1963):45.

Aptheker, Bettina. "Aspects of the Crisis in Higher Education," *Political Affairs* 46 (October 1967):9-18.

Aptheker, Herbert. "The Negro College Student in the 1920's—Years of Preparation and Protest: An Introduction," *Science and Society* 33 (Spring 1969):150-167.

Astin, Alexander W. "Folklore of Selectivity," *Saturday Review* 51 (December 20, 1969): 57-58+. Open college admissions policies and the black student.

Barrett, Russell. *Integration at Ole Miss.* Chicago: Quadrangle, 1965. The author, professor of political science at the University of Mississippi, covers much the same material as James Silver in *The Closed Society.*

Barros, Francis. "Equal Opportunity in Higher Education," *Journal of Negro Education* 37 (Summer 1968):310-315. Includes the role of the Federal government.

Bayton, James A., et al. "Reflections and Suggestions for Further Study Concerning the Higher Education of Negroes," *Journal of Negro Education* 36 (Summer 1967):286-294.

Berger, Leslie. "University Programs for Urban Black and Puerto Rican Youth," *Educational Record* 49 (Fall 1968):382-388. SEEK program.

Billingsley, Andrew. "Black Students in a Graduate School of Social Welfare," *Social Work Education Reporter* 17 (June 1969):38-44+.

Bindman, Aaron M. "Pre-College Preparation of Negro College Students," *Journal of Negro Education* 35 (Fall 1966):313-321. Research sampling and analysis of Negro male undergraduates at a large mid-western university.

Bittle, William E. "The Desegregated All-White Institution . . . The University of Oklahoma," *Journal of Educational Sociology* 32 (February 1959):275-282.

Blumenfeld, Warren S. "College Preferences of Able Negro Students: A Comparison of Those Naming Predominantly Negro Institutions and Those Naming Predominantly White Institutions," *College and University* 43 (Spring 1968):330-341.

Boykin, Leander L. "The Adjustment of 2,078 Negro Students," *Journal of Negro Education* 26 (Winter 1957):75-79. To college.

Bradley, Nolen E. "The Negro Undergraduate Student: Factors Relative to Performance in Predominantly White State Colleges and Universities in Tennessee," *Journal of Negro Education* 36 (Winter 1967):15-23.

Brazeal, B. R. "Some Problems in the Desegregation of Higher Education in the 'Hard Core' States," *Journal of Negro Education* 27 (Summer 1958):352-372.

Breed, Warren. *Beaumont, Texas: College Desegregation without Popular Support.* New York: Anti-Defamation League, 1957.

Bressler, Marvin. "White Colleges and Negro Higher Education," *Journal of Negro Education* 36 (Summer 1967):258-265.

Buck, Joyce F. "The Effects of Negro and White Dialectal Variations Upon Attitudes of College Students," *Speech Monographs* 35 (June 1968):181-186.

Cikins, Warren I. "Graduate Education, Public Service, and the Negro," *Public Administration Review* 26 (September 1966):183-191. Programs to enable Negroes to pursue graduate studies to prepare them for professional government service.

Clark, Kenneth B. "Higher Education for Negroes: Challenges and Prospects," *Journal of Negro Education* 36 (Summer 1967):196-215. With discussion following.

Cleary, Robert E. "Gubernatorial Leadership and State Policy on Desegregation in Public Higher Education," *Phylon* 27 (Summer 1966):165-170. Also published under a similar title in the *Journal of Negro Education* 35 (Fall 1966):439-444.

Clift, Virgil A. "Higher Education of Minority Groups in the United States," *Journal of Negro Education* 38 (Summer 1969):291-302. With emphasis on the Negro.

Cohen, Arthur M. "The Process of Desegregation: A Case Study," *Journal of Negro Education* 35 (Fall 1966):445-451. Miami—Dade Junior College.

Cooke, Paul. "Desegregated Higher Education in the District of Columbia," *Journal of Negro Education* 27 (Summer 1958):342-351.

Cuninggim, Merrimon. "Integration in Professional Education: The Story of Perkins, Southern Methodist University," *Annals of the American Academy of Political and Social Science* 304 (March 1956):109-115.

"Desegregation in Higher Education," *Interracial Review* 36 (May 1963):104-108. List of formerly all-white colleges and universities now desegregated.

Dummett, Clifton O. "The Negro in Dental Education: A Review of Important Occurrences," *Phylon* 20 (Winter 1959):439-454.

Dyer, Henry S. "Toward More Effective Recruitment and Selection of Negroes for College," *Journal of Negro Education* 36 (Summer 1967):216-229.

Elam, Lloyd C. "Problems of the Predominantly Negro Medical School," *Journal of the American Medical Association* 209 (August 18, 1969):1070-1072.

Elliott, Paul R. "Enrollment of Black Students in Professional and Graduate Study: A Program to Increase Enrollment at the University of Florida," *Journal of the American Medical Association* 209 (August 18, 1969):1073-1076.

Engs, Robert F., and John B. Williams. "Integration by Evasion," *Nation* 209 (November 17, 1969):537-540. Black students in a white university.

Falls, Arthur G. "The Search for Negro Medical Students," *Integrated Education* 1 (June 1963):15-19.

Fen, Sing-Nan. "Liberal Education for Negroes: As Viewed in the General Context of American Higher Education," *Journal of Negro Education* 30 (Winter 1961):17-24.

Fichter, Joseph H. "Career Preparation and Expectations of Negro College Seniors," *Journal of Negro Education* 35 (Fall 1966):322-335.

Fields, Carl A. "Princeton University's Response to Today's Negro Student," *National Association of Women Deans and Counselors Journal* 32 (Winter 1969):67-74.

Fleming, G. J. "Desegregation in Higher Education in Maryland," *Journal of Negro Education* 27 (Summer 1958):275-283.

Foreman, Paul B. "Race Confronts Universities: A Preface for Policy," *Journal of General Education* 20 (July 1968):81-97.

Francis, Gloria M. "A Minority of One," *Nursing Outlook* 15 (June 1967):36-38. Comments on racial integration in a school of nursing.

Frazier, E. Franklin. "Post High-School Education of Negroes in New York State," in David S. Kerkowitz, ed., *A Report to the Temporary Commission on the Need for a State University.* Albany: Williams Press, 1948, pp. 159-174.

Froe, Otis D. "A Comparative Study of a Population of 'Disadvantaged' College Freshmen," *Journal of Negro Education* 37 (Fall 1968):372-382. A profile comparison of students at Morgan State College, predominantly Negro, with that of freshmen in selected predominantly white institutions throughout the United States.

Gandy, Samuel L. "Desegregation of Higher Education in Louisiana," *Journal of Negro Education* 27 (Summer 1958):269-274.

Gellhorn, E. "Law Schools and the Negro," *Duke Law Journal* no. 6 (December 1968): 1069-1100.

"Georgia Abandons Laws of Massive Resistance," *New South* 16 (February 1961):3-6. A report on the desegregation of the University of Georgia.

Gessell, John M. "Test at Sewanee," *Christian Century* 79 (May 16, 1962):626-627. University of the South and integration.

Gittell, Marilyn. "A Pilot Study of Negro Middle-Class Attitudes toward Higher Education in New York," *Journal of Negro Education* 34 (Fall 1965):385-394. An information program and closer identification of Negroes with community colleges considered necessary to spur interest in higher education.

Godwin, Winfred L. "A Determined Effort to Improve Higher Education," *Monthly Labor Review* 91 (March 1968):44-48.

Green, Robert L. "Black Quest for Higher Education: An Admissions Dilemma," *Personnel and Guidance Journal* 47 (May 1969):905-911.

Guzman, Jessie P., ed. *The New South and Higher Education.* Montgomery, Ala.: Paragon, 1954. Prepared by the Department of Records and Research of Tuskegee Institute.

Hannah, John A. "Civil Rights and the Public Universities: The Chairman of the U.S. Commission on Civil Rights Pleads for Equality of Educational Opportunity," *Journal of Higher Education* 37 (February 1966):61-67.

Harris, Nelson H. "Desegregation in North Carolina Institutions of Higher Learning," *Journal of Negro Education* 27 (Summer 1958):295-299.

Henry, J. L. "The Problems Facing Negroes in Dental Education," *Journal of the American College of Dentistry* 36 (October 1969):233-243.

Henry, Oliver. "A Negro Student on Campus Turmoil," *Dissent* 16 (July-August 1969):297-300. Also appears in *Connection,* March 11, 1969.

"Higher Education Desegregation Slowly Gaining Ground in South: Report on 17 States and District of Columbia," *New South* 16 (February 1961):8-12.

"The Higher Education of Negro Americans: Prospects and Programs," *Journal of Negro Education* 36 (Summer 1967):entire issue. Conference papers. Analytics provided in this bibliography.

"Integration of Higher Education in the South," *Columbia Law Review* 69 (January 1969):112-128.

Jaffe, Abram J., Walter Adams, and Sandra G. Meyers. *Negro Higher Education in the 1960's.* New York: Praeger, 1968. Research questionnaire with critical analysis of students' status and problems, and educational policies drawn from a broad sampling of predominantly Negro Southern colleges.

Jenkins, Iredell. "Segregation and the Professor," *Yale Review* 46 (Winter 1957):311-320. Views of university professor in the South.

Johnson, Guy B. "Progress in the Desegregation of Higher Education," *Journal of Educational Sociology* 32 (February 1959):254-259.

Johnson, Guy B. "Racial Integration in Southern Higher Education," *Social Forces* 34 (May 1956):309-312.

Johnson, Roosevelt. "Black Administrators and Higher Education," *Black Scholar* 1 (November 1969):66-76.

Jones, Douglas L. "The Sweatt Case and the Development of Legal Education for Negroes in Texas," *Texas Law Review* 47 (March 1969):677-693.

Jordan, Lawrence V. "Desegregation of Higher Education in West Virginia," *Journal of Negro Education* 27 (Summer 1958):332-341.

Kelly, Ernece B. "Black Community and White College," *Integrated Education* 6 (November-December 1968):30-37.

Kirk, W. Astor, and John Q. Taylor King. "Desegregation of Higher Education in Texas," *Journal of Negro Education* 27 (Summer 1958):318-323.

Long, Herman H. "The Status of Desegregated Higher Education in Tennessee," *Journal of Negro Education* 27 (Summer 1958):311-317.

Lord, Walter. *The Past That Would Not Die.* New York: Harper, 1965. Account of Mississippi's defiance of federal authority as triggered by the 1962 Meredith case at the University of Mississippi.

McLinden, James E., and Joseph M. Doyle. "Negro Students and Faculty on Catholic College Campuses," *National Catholic Education Bulletin* 62 (February 1966):1-49. Survey of 239 Catholic institutions of higher education, from junior college on up.

Martin, William H. "Desegregation in Higher Education," *Teachers College Record* 62 (October 1960):36-47.

Mays, Benjamin E. "Centennial Commencement Address (Higher Education and the American Negro)," *Journal of Religious Thought* 24, no. 2 (1967-1968):4-12.

Meredith, James. *Three Years in Mississippi.* Bloomington: University of Indiana Press, 1966. Landmark breaching of state's educational color barrier.

Miller, Albert H. "Problems of the Minority Student on the Campus," *Liberal Education* 55 (March 1969):18-23.

Moon, F. D. "Higher Education and Desegregation in Oklahoma," *Journal of Negro Education* 27 (Summer 1958):300-310.

Muir, Donald E., and C. Donald McGlamery. "Evolution of Desegregation Attitudes of Southern University Students," *Phylon* 29 (Summer 1968):105-117.

National Association of State Universities and Land-Grant Colleges, and the Southern Education Foundation. *State Universities and Black Americans.* Atlanta: Southern Education Foundation, 1969. Survey pointing up the disproportionate ratio of white to Negro students in the nation's major state universities.

"Negro Enrollments This Year on the Nation's Campuses," *Chronicle of Higher Education,* April 21, 1969, pp. 3-4. Tabular presentation of a federal survey of Negro undergraduate enrollments and total enrollment.

Nelson, Bryce. "Michigan: Ruckus over Race Has Relevance to Other Universities," *Science* 156 (June 2, 1967):1209-1212. The racial composition of Negro students and Negro faculty is scrutinized. Replies *ibid.,* 157 (August 4, 1967):190; 158 (October 13, 1967): 205-206.

Nelson, J. Robert. "Vanderbilt's Time of Testing," *Christian Century* 77 (August 10, 1960): 921-925. Former Dean comments on dismissal of James Lawson.

Oppenheimer, Martin. "Institutions of Higher Learning and the 1960 Sit-Ins: Some Clues for Social Action," *Journal of Negro Education* 32 (Summer 1963):286-288.

Parrish, Charles H. "Desegregated Higher Education in Kentucky," *Journal of Negro Education* 27 (Summer 1958):260-268.

Parsons, Howard L. "Integration and the Professor," *Journal of Negro Education* 27 (Fall 1958):439-450.

Picott, J. Rupert. "Desegregation of Higher Education in Virginia," *Journal of Negro Education* 27 (Summer 1958):324-331.

Pittman, Joseph A. "A Study of the Academic Achievement of 415 College Students in

Relation to Remedial Courses Taken," *Journal of Negro Education* 29 (Fall 1960):426–437.

Plaut, Richard L. "Prospects for the Entrance and Scholastic Advancement of Negroes in Higher Educational Institutions," *Journal of Negro Education* 36 (Summer 1967):230–237.

Redding, Louis L. "Desegregation of Higher Education in Delaware," *Journal of Negro Education* 27 (Summer 1958):253–259.

Reedy, Sidney J. "Higher Education and Desegregation in Missouri," *Journal of Negro Education* 27 (Summer 1958):284–294.

Reid, Robert D. "Curricular Changes in Colleges and Universities for Negroes," *Journal of Higher Education* 38 (March 1967):153–160. Analysis and interpretation of a questionnaire survey.

Robinson, William H. "Desegregation in Higher Education in the South," *School and Society* 88 (May 7, 1960):234–239.

Rose, Arthur M. "Graduate Training for the Culturally Deprived," *Sociology of Education* 39 (Spring 1966):201–208. A discussion of the limitations in student perspective, personality, recruitment, and scholarship.

Rosenbaum, J. B. "The Integration of 'Ole Miss,' " *Bulletin of the Philadelphia Association of Psychoanalysis* 13 (March 1963):25–27.

Rossman, Michael. "Blacks at Mainstream U.," *Commonweal* 89 (October 4, 1968):15–17. Problem of desegregation.

Samuels, Gertrude. "There are 300 Negroes at the University of Alabama," *New York Times Magazine,* May 14, 1967, pp. 32–33 +. A measure of progress since 1963.

Silard, John. "Federal Aid to Segregated Universities and Colleges: Suggestions for a Remedial Program," *Journal of Intergroup Relations* 2 (Spring 1961):115–123. Federal aid should be withheld from institutions practicing segregation.

Smith, Stanley H. "Academic Freedom in Higher Education in the Deep South," *Journal of Educational Sociology* 32 (February 1959):297–308.

Sorkin, Alan L. "A Comparison of Quality Characteristics in Negro and White Public Colleges and Universities in the South," *Journal of Negro Education* 38 (Spring 1969):112–119.

Stephan, A. Stephen. "Desegregation of Higher Education in Arkansas," *Journal of Negro Education* 27 (Summer 1958):243–252.

Stembridge, Barbara Penn. "A Student's Appraisal of the Adequacy of Higher Education for Black Americans," *Journal of Negro Education* 37 (Summer 1968):316–322. Includes proposals for elimination of the inadequacies, and advocates the establishment of universal community college education.

Trillin, Calvin. *An Education in Georgia: The Integration of Charlayne Hunter and Hamilton Holmes.* New York: Viking, 1963. Recounts the day-to-day experiences of first two Negro students to attend the University of Georgia, and the coldness, hostility, and only occasional understanding they encountered.

U.S. Commission on Civil Rights. *Equal Protection of the Laws in Public Higher Education, 1960.* Washington, 1961.

Valien, Preston. "Improving Programs in Graduate Education for Negroes," *Journal of Negro Education* 36 (Summer 1967):238–248.

Walker, George W., Jr., and David W. Hazel. "Integration in the Junior College," *Journal of Negro Education* 29 (Spring 1960):204–206.

Wiggins, Sam P. "Dilemmas in Desegregation in Higher Education," *Journal of Negro Education* 35 (Fall 1966):430–438.

Wright, Stephen J. "The Promise of Equality," *Saturday Review* 51 (July 20, 1968):45–46 +.

Negro Colleges and Universities

Allen, LeRoy B. "The Possibilities of Integration for Public Colleges Founded by Negroes," *Journal of Negro Education* 35 (Fall 1966):452-458.

Badger, Henry G. "Colleges That Did Not Survive," *Journal of Negro Education* 35 (Fall 1966):306-312.

Bakelman, W. Robert, and Louis A. D'Amico. "Changes in Faculty Salaries and Basic Student Charges in Negro Colleges: 1960-61 and 1961-62," *Journal of Negro Education* 31 (Fall 1962):507-510.

Brazziel, William F. "Curriculum Choice in the Negro College," *Journal of Negro Education* 29 (Spring 1960):207-209.

Brazziel, William F. "Federal Aid and the Negro Colleges," *Teachers College Record* 68 (January 1967):300-306. A discussion of the implications of Title III of the Higher Education Act of 1965.

Brazziel, William F. "Some Dynamics of Curriculum Choice in the Negro Colleges," *Journal of Negro Education* 33 (Fall 1961):436-439.

Brown, Aaron. "Graduate and Professional Education in Negro Institutions," *Journal of Negro Education* 27 (Summer 1958):233-242.

Bryant, Lawrence C. "Graduate Training in Negro Colleges," *Journal of Negro Education* 30 (Winter 1961):69-71.

Buszek, Beatrice R. "Differential Treatment of Test Scores," *College and University* 43 (Spring 1968):294-307. At predominantly Negro colleges. Bibiliography.

"C A A and Negro Colleges," *Art Journal* 28 (Winter 1968-1969):228. College Art Association considers problems of art departments and programs in Negro colleges.

Clark, Kenneth B., and Lawrence Plotkin. *The Negro Student at Integrated Colleges.* New York: National Scholarship Service and Fund for Negro Students, 1964. Based on the analysis of college records of 1,278 Negro students.

Coles, Anna B. "The Howard University School of Nursing in Historical Perspective," *Journal of the National Medical Association* 61 (March 1969):105-118.

DeCosta, Frank A. "The Tax-Supported College for Negroes," *Journal of Educational Sociology* 32 (February 1959):260-266.

"Desegregation and the Negro College," *Journal of Negro Education* 27 (Summer 1958):209-435. Entire issue.

Directory of Predominantly Negro Colleges and Universities in the United States of America, Four Year Institutions Only. Washington: U.S. Govt. Print. Off., 1969.

Doddy, Hurley H. "The Progress of the Negro in Higher Education, 1950-1960," *Journal of Negro Education* 32 (Fall 1963):485-492.

Doddy, Hurley H. "The Status of the Negro Public College: A Statistical Summary," *Journal of Negro Education* 31 (Summer 1962):370-385.

Eells, Walter Crosby. "The Higher Education of Negroes in the United States," *Journal of Negro Education* 24 (Fall 1955):426-434.

Fichter, Joseph H. *Graduates of Predominantly Negro Colleges, Class of 1964.* Prepared for the National Institute of Health, the U.S. Dept. of Labor, and the National Science Foundation, Washington: U.S. Govt. Print. Off., 1967. Based on extensive, self-evaluative research questionnaires. Sections include: childhood experiences, talented Negro women, segregated colleges, prospects for employment, and further graduate study. Text supplemented by clear tabular summaries.

Foster, Luther H., and Charles E. Prothro. "Minimum Income Necessary to Maintain a Small College Effectively," *Journal of Negro Education* 29 (Summer 1960):345-355.

Friedman, Neil, ed. "Learning in Black Colleges," *Wilson Library Bulletin* 44 (September 1969):49-74. Three essays by teachers, one by a student, reflect personal experiences in Negro higher education.

Friedman, Neil. "The Miles College Freshman Social Science Program: Educational Innovation in a Negro College," *Journal of Negro Education* 38 (Fall 1969):361-369.

Goldman, Freda H., ed. *Educational Imperative: The Negro in the Changing South.* Chicago: Center for Study of Liberal Education for Adults, 1963. Papers presented at a twelve-day institute on "The Negro College in the Changing South," held at Fisk University, Nashville, Tenn., June 9-21, 1962.

Grant, George C. "An Approach to Democratizing a Phase of College Education," *Journal of Negro Education* 27 (Fall 1958):463-475. Curriculum reconsiderations at Morgan State College.

Gurin, Patricia, and Daniel Katz. *Motivation and Aspiration in the Negro College.* Ann Arbor: Institute for Social Research, University of Michigan, 1966.

Gurin, Patricia. "Social Class Constraints on the Occupational Aspirations of Students Attending Some Predominantly Negro Colleges," *Journal of Negro Education* 35 (Fall 1966):336-350. Bibliography.

Gurin, Patricia, and Edgar Epps. "Some Characteristics of Students from Poverty Backgrounds attending Predominantly Negro Colleges in the Deep South," *Social Forces* 45 (September 1966):27-40.

Hare, Nathan. "Black Students and Negro Colleges: The Legacy of Paternalism," *Saturday Review* 51 (July 20, 1968):44-45 + .

Harrington, Eugene M. "Negro Law Schools: The Liberals Dilemma," *Commonweal* 88 (April 12, 1968):94-95.

Harris, Edward E. "Some Comparisions among Negro-White College Students: Social Ambition and Estimated Social Mobility," *Journal of Negro Education* 35 (Fall 1968):351-368.

Havice, Doris Webster. "Learning the Black Student: A White Teacher in a Black College," *Soundings* 52 (Summer 1969):154-161.

Henderson, Thomas H. "The Role of the Negro College in Retrospect and Prospect," *Journal of Negro Education* 27 (Spring 1958):136-140.

Henderson, Vivian W. "Role of Predominantly Negro Institutions," *Journal of Negro Education* 36 (Summer 1967):266-273.

Hope, John, II. "The Negro College, Student Protest and the Future," *Journal of Negro Education* 30 (Fall 1961):368-376.

Jackson, Jacqueline J. "Exploration of Attitudes toward Faculty Desegregation at Negro Colleges," *Phylon* 28 (Winter 1967):338-352.

Jencks, Christopher, and David Riesman. "The American Negro College," *Harvard Educational Review* 37 (Winter 1967):3-60. Its role and possibilities for change. Discussion *ibid.,* 37 (Spring 1967):267-269; (Summer 1967):451-468; (Fall 1967):646-647. Authors' rejoinder, ibid., 38 (Spring 1968):343-347. Also appears in the authors' *The Academic Revolution.* Garden City, N.Y.: Doubleday, 1969, pp. 406-479.

Josey, E. J. "The Future of the Black College Library," *Library Journal* 94 (September 15, 1969):3019-3022.

Kopkind, Andrew. "Black Backlash [Negro Colleges]," *New Statesman* 73 (May 26, 1967):708.

Kuritz, Hyman. "Integration on Negro College Campuses," *Phylon* 28 (Summer 1967):121-130.

Lehfeldt, Martin C. "A Very Mixed Bag: White Teachers at Black Colleges," *Soundings* 52 (Summer 1969):128-153.

Le Melle, Tilden J., and Wilbert J. Le Melle. *The Black College: A Strategy for Achieving Relevancy.* New York: Praeger, 1969.

Logan, Rayford. *Howard University: The First Hundred Years, 1867-1967.* New York: New York University Press, 1969. Includes biographical sketches of prominent alumni.

Lowe, Gilbert A. "Howard University Students and the Community Service Project," *Journal of Negro Education* 36 (Fall 1967):368-376.

McGrath, Earl J. *The Predominantly Negro Colleges and Universities in Transition.* New York: Bureau of Publications, Teachers College, Columbia University, 1965.

Manley, Albert E. "The Role of the Negro College in Retrospect and Prospect," *Journal of Negro Education* 27 (Spring 1958):132-135.

Meeth, L. Richard. "The Report on Predominantly Negro Colleges One Year Later," *Journal of Negro Education* 35 (Summer 1966):204-209. An addendum to Earl J. McGrath's, *The Predominantly Negro Colleges and Universities in Transition.*

Miller, Carroll L. "Issues and Problems in the Higher Education of Negro Americans," *Journal of Negro Education* 35 (Fall 1966):485-493. Attention to the student, the faculty, policies, and experimental programs of predominantly Negro colleges.

Miller, K. C. "Take Them Where You Find Them," *Journal of Negro Education* 26 (Fall 1957):530-531. Role of Negro colleges.

Mitchell, James J. "Negro Higher Education—Years of Crisis," *Quarterly Review of Higher Education for Negroes* 30 (January 1962):18-21. Problems faced by Negro institutions in years of increasing integration.

Morris, Eddie W. "Admissions in Predominantly Negro Colleges: A View from the Inside," *College and University* 44 (Winter 1969):130-144.

Mortimer, Kingsley E. "The Melanoblasts of Fate: Aspects and Attitudes at the 'Black Harvard,' " *Journal of the National Medical Association* 60 (September 1968):357-365. Comments by a visiting Australian teaching physician to Howard University Medical College students and faculty.

Munro, John U. "Escape from the Dark Cave," *Nation* 209 (October 27, 1969):434-439. Author is Director of Freshmen Students at Miles College in Birmingham, Alabama.

"The Negro Private and Church-Related College," *Journal of Negro Education* 29 (Summer 1960):211-407. Entire issue.

"The Negro Public College," *Journal of Negro Education* 31 (Summer 1962):215-428. Entire issue.

"Outlook for Graduates from Segregated Schools," *Negro History Bulletin* 18 (February 1955):117+. Negroes represent ten percent of the population but less than one percent of interracial colleges.

Patterson, Fred D. "Colleges for Negro Youth and the Future," *Journal of Negro Education* 27 (Spring 1958):107-114.

Patterson, Frederick D. "Cooperation among Predominantly Negro Colleges and Universities," *Journal of Negro Education* 35 (Fall 1966):477-484.

Patterson, Fred D. "Foundation Policies in Regard to Negro Institutions of Higher Learning," *Journal of Educational Sociology* 32 (February 1959):290-296.

Pettigrew, Thomas F. "Social Psychological View of the Predominantly Negro College," *Journal of Negro Education* 36 (Summer 1967):274-285.

Rand, E. W. "The Cost of Board, Room and Student Fees in a Selected Group of Negro Publicly Supported Colleges," *Journal of Negro Education* 26 (Spring 1957):207-212.

Reddick, L. D. "Critical Review: The Politics of Desegregation," *Journal of Negro Education* 31 (Summer 1962):414-420. Integration of Negro public colleges.

Roth, Robert M. "The Adjustment of Negro College Students at Hampton Institute," *Journal of Negro Education* 30 (Winter 1961):72-74.

Roth, Robert M. "A Self-Selection Process by Northern Negroes Existing in a Southern Negro College," *Journal of Negro Education* 28 (Spring 1959):185-186.

Sawyer, Broadus E. "The Baccalaureate Origins of the Faculties of the Twenty-One Selected Colleges," *Journal of Negro Education* 31 (Winter 1962):83-87.

Sekora, John. "Murder Relentless and Impassive: The American Academic Community and the Negro College," *Soundings* 51 (Fall 1968):237-271. With a reply by Vincent Harding, *ibid.,* 51 (Winter 1968):465-472.

Sekora, John. "On Negro Colleges: A Reply to Jencks and Riesman," *Antioch Review* 28 (Spring 1968):5-26. See also replies in *Harvard Educational Review* 37 (Summer 1967):451-468.

Shockley, Ann Allen. "Negro Librarians in Predominantly Negro Colleges," *College and Research Libraries* 28 (November 1967):423-426. Backgrounds and professional attitudes.

Stephens, Ernest. "The Black University in America Today: A Student's Viewpoint," *Freedomways* 7 (Spring 1967):131-138. The author was a graduate student at Tuskegee Institute at the time of writing.

Stevenson, Janet. "Ignorant Armies," *Atlantic* 224 (October 1969):57-63. Academic problems and frustrations at a predominantly black Southern college.

Taylor, Andress, and John Sekora. "A Woodrow Wilson Teaching Internship Program,"

Improving College and University Teaching 16 (Autumn 1968):260-264. A case study of the program at St. Augustine College, a small Episcopal Negro institution.

Terrell, Robert L. "Black Awareness versus Negro Traditions: Atlanta University Center," *New South* 24 (Winter 1969):29-40.

Thompson, Charles H. "The Negro College: In Retrospect and in Prospect," *Journal of Negro Education* 27 (Spring 1958):127-131.

Thompson, Charles H. "The Prospect of Negro Higher Education," *Journal of Educational Sociology* 32 (February 1959):309-316.

Thompson, Charles H. "The Southern Association and Negro College Membership," *Journal of Negro Education* 27 (Winter 1958):1-3.

Thompson, Charles H. "The Southern Association and the Predominantly Negro High School and College," *Journal of Negro Education* 31 (Spring 1962):105-107.

Trent, William J., Jr. "Private Negro Colleges Since the Gaines Decision," *Journal of Educational Sociology* 32 (February 1959):267-274.

Trent, William J., Jr. "Solvency of the Private Colleges," *Journal of Negro Education* 27 (Spring 1958):145-150.

Trent, William J., Jr. "The United Negro College Fund's African Scholarship Program," *Journal of Negro Education* 31 (Spring 1962):205-209.

"Upgrading Negro Colleges in the South," *School and Society* 97 (October 1969):350-351. Carnegie grants to the Southern Regional Council designed to strengthen programs in Southern Negro institutions.

Van Wright, Aaron, Jr. "Negro Land-Grant Institutions," *Improving College and University Teaching* 15 (Autumn 1967):254-259. Bibliography.

Weaver, Robert C. "The Private Negro Colleges and Universities—An Appraisal," *Journal of Negro Education* 29 (Spring 1960):113-120.

Willie, Charles V. "Researchers to Work! Education of Negroes in Predominantly White Colleges," *Integrated Education* 7 (September 1969):32-38.

Wright, Stephen J. "The Negro College in America," *Harvard Educational Review* 30 (Summer 1960):280-297.

Black Studies

Banks, James A. "Relevant Social Studies for Black Pupils," *Social Education* 33 (January 1969):66-69. Arguments for revamping curriculum to enhance the Negro's self image and to mitigate urban racial tensions.

Baren, D. "Do You Dare: Negro Literature and the Disadvantaged Student," *Phi Delta Kappan* 50 (May 1969):520-524.

"Bibliography on Afro-American History and Culture," *Social Education* 33 (April 1969):447-461. Designed as a resource guide for teachers. Arrangement is under broad headings. Short descriptive annotations are provided.

Black Consciousness and Higher Education. Cambridge, Mass.: Church Society for College Work, 1968. Report of conference convened in Atlanta in 1968. Participants included Vincent Harding whose "Uses of the Afro-American Past" is reprinted in the appendix.

Black Studies: Myths & Realities. New York: A. Philip Randolph Educational Institute, 1969.

Blassingame, John W. "Black Studies: An Intellectual Crisis," *American Scholar* 38 (Autumn 1969):548-561.

Bunzel, John H. "Black Studies at San Francisco State," *Public Interest* no. 13 (Fall 1968):22-38.

Clark, Kenneth B. "A Charade of Power: Students at White Colleges," *Antioch Review* 29 (Summer 1969):145-148. See also views of Stephen Lythcott.

Cudjoe, Selwyn R. "Needed: A Black Studies Consortium," *Liberator* 9 (September 1969):14-15.

Dunbar, Ernest. "The Black Studies Thing," *New York Times Magazine,* April 6, 1969, pp. 25-27+. The Afro-American studies program at Cornell.

Easum, Donald B. "The Call for Black Studies," *Africa Report* 14 (May-June 1969):16-22.

Fischer, Roger A. "Ghetto and Gown: The Birth of Black Studies," *Current History* 57 (November 1969):290-294.

Genovese, Eugene D. "Black Studies: Trouble Ahead," *Atlantic* 223 (June 1969):37-41. Outlines framework for legitimate and constructive programs in higher education.

Harding, Vincent. "Black Brain Drain," *Columbia Forum* 11 (Winter 1968):38-39. Resources for adequate Afro-American study programs, and the "drain of competence from such departments in Negro colleges."

Hare, Nathan, "What Should be the Role of Afro-American Education in the Undergraduate Curriculum?" *Liberal Education* 55 (March 1969):42-50.

Harvard University. Faculty of Arts and Sciences. *Report of the Faculty Committee on African and Afro-American Studies.* Cambridge, Mass.: Harvard University Press, 1969. The Rosovsky Report.

Hatch, John. "Black Studies: The Real Issue," *Nation* 208 (June 16, 1969):755-758.

Hayes, Jane Banfield. "ASA Meeting Disrupted by Racial Crisis: Black Militants Challenge the Association and Question the Moral Bases of African Studies," *Africa Report* 14 (December 1969):16-17. This, and several articles following it in the journal, discusses the challenge of the black caucus group to the Association and the possible channels for radical scholarship in African studies in the United States.

Henshel, Anne-Marie, and Richard L. Henshel. "Black Studies Programs: Promise and Pitfalls," *Journal of Negro Education* 38 (Fall 1969):423-429.

Katz, William Loren. "Black History in Secondary Schools," *Journal of Negro Education* 38 (Fall 1969):430-434.

Kilson, Martin. "Black Studies Movement: A Plea for Perspective," *Crisis* 76 (October 1969):327-332.

Lerner, Abba P. "Black Studies: The Universities in Moral Crisis," *Humanist* 29 (May-June 1969):9-10+.

Lythcott, Stephen. "The Case for Black Studies," *Antioch Review* 29 (Summer 1969): 149-154. See also Kenneth Clark's views.

Neyland, Leedell W. "Why Negro History in the Junior and Senior High Schools?" *Social Studies* 58 (December 1967):315-321. Bibliography.

Pickens, William G. "Teaching Negro Culture in High Schools—Is It Worthwhile?" *Journal of Negro Education* 34 (Spring 1966):106-113.

Robinson, Armstead L, Craig C. Foster, and Donald H. Ogilvie. *Black Studies in the University: A Symposium.* New Haven: Yale University Press, 1969. Political and intellectual issues discussed by Harold Cruse, Martin Kilson, McGeorge Bundy, and others.

Rosovsky, Henry. "Black Studies at Harvard: Personal Reflections Concerning Recent Events," *American Scholar* 38 (Autumn 1969):562-572.

17 Public Accommodations

American Library Association. *Access to Public Libraries.* Chicago, 1963.

"Arts and Entertainment for Southern Negroes," *New South* 17 (September 1962):10-14. What types of entertainment are available to Negroes: statistics and examples.

Avins, Alfred. "Racial Segregation in Public Accommodations: Some Reflected Light on the Fourteenth Amendment from the Civil Rights Act of 1875," *Western Reserve Law Review* 18 (May 1967):1251-1283.

Avins, Alfred. "Social Equality and the Fourteenth Amendment: The Original Understanding," *Houston Law Review* 4 (Spring 1967):640-656. Examines Congressional discussion concerning the Fourteenth Amendment to determine if the amendment can be used to enjoin social discrimination in private and public accommodation.

Avins, Alfred. "Toward Freedom of Choice in Places of Public and Private Accommodation," *Nebraska Law Review* 48 (November 1968):21-90.

Avins, Alfred. "What Is a Place of 'Public' Accommodation?" *Marquette Law Review* 52 (Summer 1968):1-74.

Babow, Irving. "Discrimination in Places of Public Accommodation: Findings of the San Francisco Civil Rights Inventory," *Journal of Intergroup Relations* 2 (Fall 1961):332-341.

Babow, Irving. "Restrictive Practices in Public Accommodations in a Northern Community," *Phylon* 24 (Spring 1963):5-12.

"Biracial Conventions Pose Added Problems for South," *New South* 15 (September 1960):3-10. State by state review of convention facilities available to groups including Negroes, a report prepared by the Southern Regional Council.

Caldwell, Wallace F. "State Public Accommodations Laws, Fundamental Liberties, and Enforcement Programs," *Washington Law Review* 40 (October 1965):841-872.

Carl, E. L. "Reflections on the 'Sit-ins,'" *Cornell Law Quarterly* 46 (Spring 1961):444-457.

Chasteen, Edgar. "Public Accommodations: Social Movements in Conflict," *Phylon* 30 (Fall 1969):233-250. An analysis of a plan to equate public accommodations for Negroes and whites in a large midwestern city.

"Civil Rights—Civil Rights Act of 1964—Amusement Park Is 'Place of Entertainment' as Defined in Subsection 201 (b) (3) of the Act," *Wayne Law Review* 15 (Spring 1969):861+.

"Civil Rights—Public Accommodations—Recreational Facility Held Not a Covered Establishment under 1964 Act," *New York University Law Review* 43 (December 1968): 1219-1226. Legislative history and implications.

"The Common-Law and Constitutional Status of Anti-Discrimination Boycotts," *Yale Law Journal* 66 (January 1957):397-412.

"Conviction for Disturbing the Peace in Lunch-Counter Sit-in Held to Violate Due Process for Lack of Evidence," *Vanderbilt Law Review* 15 (October 1962):1325-1329.

Davis, Morris, Robert Seibert, and Warren Breed. "Interracial Seating Patterns on New Orleans Public Transit," *Social Problems* 13 (Winter 1966):298-306. Attempts to assess the degree of actual integration.

De Jarmon, Le Marquis. "Public Accommodations," *University of Illinois Law Forum* 1968 (Summer 1968):189-200.

DeLacy, G. L. " 'Segregation Cases' Supreme Court," *Nebraska Law Review* 38 (June 1959):1017-1038.

Dixon, R. G., Jr. "Civil Rights in Air Transportation and Government Initiative," *Virginia Law Review* 49 (March 1963):205-231.

Dixon, R. G., Jr. "Civil Rights in Transportation and the I.C.C.," *George Washington Law Review* 31 (October 1962):198-241.

Drinan, Robert F. "Will Public Accommodations Be Desegregated in 1963?" *Interracial Review* 36 (October 1963):188-190.

Ervin, R. W., and B. R. Jacob. " 'Sit-in' Demonstrations: Are They Punishable in Florida?" *University of Miami Law Review* 15 (Winter 1960):123-137.

Feagans, Janet. "Atlanta Theatre Segregation: A Case of Prolonged Avoidance," *Journal of Human Relations* 13 (Winter 1965):208-218.

Ferguson, Clarence Clyde, Jr. "Civil Rights Legislation, 1964: A Study of Constitutional Resources," *Federal Bar Journal* 24 (Winter 1964):102. The author deals in detail with constitutional issues of the public accommodations section.

Graves, J. W. "Arkansas Separate Coach Law of 1891," *Journal of the West* 7 (October 1968):531-541.

Gremley, William H. "A Survey of Eating Places," *Journal of Intergroup Relations* 1 (Autumn 1960):53-58.

"Innkeeper's 'Right' to Discriminate," *University of Florida Law Review* 15 (Summer 1962):109-128.

Jones, Charles. "Outcome Up to Conscience and to Sense of Fair Play," *New South* 15 (March 1960):14. By a student sit-in.

Karst, K. L., and W. W. Van Alstyne. "Comment: Sit-ins and State Action—Mr. Justice Douglas, Concurring," *Stanford Law Review* 14 (July 1962):762-776.

Kenealy, William. "The Legality of the Sit-Ins," in Matthew Ahmann, ed., *The New Negro*. Notre Dame, Ind.: Fides Press, 1962. The author, former dean of Boston College Law School, argues that the Supreme Court should reverse convictions of Louisiana sit-ins.

Knoxville Area Human Relations Council. *A Chronology of Negotiations Leading to Lunch Counter Desegregation in Knoxville, Tennessee.* Knoxville, Tenn., n.d.

"Lunch Counter Demonstrations: State Action and the Fourteenth Amendment," *Virginia Law Review* 47 (January 1961):105-121.

McKay, Robert B. "Segregation and Public Recreation," *Virginia Law Review* 40 (October 1954):697-717.

McKinney, Theophilus E., Jr. "United States Transportation Segregation, 1865-1954," *Quarterly Review of Higher Education among Negroes* 22 (July 1954):101-149.

Meier, August, and Elliott Rudwick. "The Boycott Movement against Jim Crow Streetcars in the South, 1900-1906," *Journal of American History* 55 (March 1969):756-775.

Meier, August, and Elliott M. Rudwick. "Negro Protest at the Chicago World's Fair, 1933-1934," *Journal of the Illinois State Historical Society* 59 (1966):161-171.

Morland, Kenneth. *Lunch-Counter Desegregation in Corpus Christi, Galveston, and San Antonio, Texas.* Atlanta: Southern Regional Council, May 1960.

Navasky, Victor S. "The Freedom Rides Revisited," *Atlantic* 222 (July 1968):44-46.

Pollitt, David H. "Dime Store Demonstrations: Events and Legal Problems of the First Sixty Days," *Duke Law Journal* 1960 (Summer 1960):315 +.

Quick, Harry T. "Public Accommodations: A Justification of Title II of the Civil Rights Act of 1964," *Western Reserve Law Review* 16 (May 1965):660-710.

"Racial Discrimination by Restaurant Serving Interstate Travelers," *Virginia Law Review* 46 (January 1960):123-131.

"Racial Integration of Public Libraries," *School and Society* 91 (November 16, 1963): 345-347.

"Racial Segregation of Spectator Seating in Courtroom," *Michigan Law Review* (Fall 1962):503-506.

Rice, Charles E. "Federal Public Accommodations Law: A Dissent," *Mercer Law Review* 17 (Spring 1966):338-346.

Rudman, W. G. "Sitting-in on the Omnibus—The 1961 Segregation Cases," *Law in Transition* 22 (Winter 1963):206-221.

Rudwick, Elliott M. "Oscar De Priest and the Jim Crow Restaurant in the U.S. House of Representatives," *Journal of Negro Education* 35 (Winter 1966):77-82. In the 1930's.

Schwelb, F. E. "The Sit-in Demonstration: Criminal Trespass or Constitutional Right?" *New York University Law Review* 36 (April 1961):779-809.

Sherwood, Devon F. "Constitutional Law—Private Persons Succeeding City as Trustee of Park under Racially Discriminatory Device Held Subject to Fourteenth Amendment: *Evans v. Newton,*" *Missouri Law Review* 32 (Winter 1967):147-154.

"Sit-ins and the Civil Rights Act," *Tennessee Law Review* 32 (Winter 1965):183.

"State Anti-Discrimination Act and Interstate Commerce," *University of Cincinnati Law Review* 32 (Summer 1963):313-323.

"Survey of Waiting Rooms in 21 Southern Cities," *New South* 14 (September 1959):11-12.

"Theories of State Action as Applied to the 'Sit-in' Cases," *Arkansas Law Review* 17 (Summer 1963):147-162.

"Threat of Mob Violence as Justification for Restraint on Exercise of Right to Travel in Interstate Commerce," *Michigan Law Review* 60 (April 1962):802-805.

"*United States v. Northwest Louisiana Restaurant Club*—The Spurious Club and Public Accommodations Laws," *Northwestern University Law Review* 62 (May-June 1967): 244-253. Discussion of public organizations operating as "private clubs" and suggested standards for latter label.

Van Alstyne, W. W. "Civil Rights: A New Public Accommodations Law for Ohio," *Ohio State Law Journal* (Fall 1961):683-690.

Verst, Edward C. "State Anti-Discrimination Acts and Interstate Commerce," *University of Cincinnati Law Review* 32 (Summer 1963):313-323.

Von Eschen, Donald, Jerome Kirk, and Maurice Pinard. "The Conditions of Direct Action in a Democratic Society," *Western Political Quarterly* 22 (June 1969):309-325. A study of a Maryland drive for equal public accommodations, 1960-1964.

Wright, M. A. "Sit-in Movement: Progress Report and Prognosis," *Wayne Law Review* 9 (Spring 1963):445-457.

See also The Freedom Revolution—Civil Rights; The Freedom Revolution—Protest: Theory and Practice. . .

18   Politics and Suffrage

Historical Background

Allswang, John M. "The Chicago Negro Voter and the Democratic Consensus: A Case Study, 1918-1936," *Journal of the Illinois State Historical Society* 60 (Summer 1967):145-175. Traces pattern of the Negro vote in five ghetto areas to a decisive Democratic majority by 1936.

Bryant, Lawrence C., ed. *Negro Legislators in South Carolina, 1865-1894: Preliminary Report.* Orangeburg, S. C.: School of Graduate Studies, South Carolina State College, 1966.

Buni, Andrew. *The Negro in Virginia Politics, 1902-1965.* Charlottesville: University Press of Virginia, 1967. Traces the challenge and response of the race issue in the politics of this state. Bibliography.

Callcott, Margaret Law. *The Negro in Maryland Politics, 1870-1912.* Baltimore: Johns Hopkins Press, 1969.

Chafe, William H. "The Negro and Populism: A Kansas Case Study," *Journal of Southern History* 34 (August 1968):402-419.

Cheek, William F. "A Negro Runs for Congress: John Mercer Langston and the Virginia Campaign of 1888," *Journal of Negro History* 52 (January 1967):14-34.

Coulter, E. Merton. "Aaron Alpeonia Bradley, Georgia Negro Politician during Reconstruction Times," *Georgia Historical Quarterly* 51 (March 1967):15-41; (June 1967): 154-174; (September 1967):264-306.

Coulter, E. Merton. "Tunis G. Campbell, Negro Reconstructionist in Georgia," *Georgia Historical Quarterly* 51 (December 1967):401-424; (March 1968):16-52. Based on research in newspapers and state records.

Cox, La Wanda, and John H. Cox. "Negro Suffrage and Republican Politics: The Problem of Motivation in Reconstruction Historiography," *Journal of Southern History* 33 (August 1967):303-330.

Dyer, Brainerd. "One Hundred Years of Negro Suffrage," *Pacific Historical Review* 37 (February 1968):1-20.

Dykstra, Robert R., and Harlan Hahn. "Northern Voters and Negro Suffrage: The Case of Iowa, 1868," *Public Opinion Quarterly* 32 (Summer 1968):202-215.

Fischel, Leslie H. "The Negro in Northern Politics, 1870-1900," *Mississippi Valley Historical Review* 42 (December 1955):466-489.

Gatewood, Willard B. "William D. Crum: A Negro in Politics," *Journal of Negro History* 53 (October 1968):301-320. His role in the Negro's struggle to retain influence in the Republican party in South Carolina at the turn of the century.

Gosnell, Harold F. *Negro Politicians: The Rise of Negro Politics in Chicago.* 1935. Chicago: University of Chicago Press, 1967. Reissue of a 1935 study of Negroes in Chicago politics with a new introduction by James Q. Wilson.

Grantham, Dewey W., Jr. "The South and the Reconstruction of American Politics," *Jour-

nal of American History 53 (Summer 1966):227-246. The effect of the Negro's political activation.

Graves, John William. "Negro Disfranchisement in Arkansas," *Arkansas Historical Quarterly* 26 (Autumn 1967):199-225. The late nineteenth century.

Gutman, Herbert G. "Peter H. Clark: Pioneer Negro Socialist, 1877," *Journal of Negro Education* 34 (Fall 1965):413-418.

Harrell, James A. "Negro Leadership in the Election Year 1936," *Journal of Southern History* 34 (November 1968): 546-564.

Hiller, Amy M. "The Disfranchisement of Delaware Negroes in the Late Nineteenth Century," *Delaware History* 13 (October 1968):124-153.

Key, V. O., Jr. *Southern Politics in State and Nation.* New York: Knopf, 1949. A classic study which underlines the historical and contemporary importance of the Negro in Southern politics. While all the data are from the period before 1949, the comprehensiveness of the analysis of the one-party system and of a Southern unity based on the maintenance of white supremacy and the willingness to subordinate all other issues makes this an indispensable work for the understanding of present developments.

Negro Protest Pamphlets: A Compendium. New York: Arno Press, 1969. (The American Negro, His History and Literature)

Osofsky, Gilbert. "Progressivism & the Negro: New York, 1900-1915," *American Quarterly* 16 (Summer 1964):153-168.

Pease, Jane., and William H. Pease. "Black Power—The Debate in 1840," *Phylon* 29 (Spring 1968):19-26. All-black conventions of free Negroes in New York and other Northern cities in an attempt to acquire full suffrage and civil equality—considered then by most whites as inverse racism.

Ruchames, Louis. "William Lloyd Garrison and the Negro Franchise," *Journal of Negro History* 50 (January 1965):37-49.

Saunders, Robert. "Southern Populists and the Negro, 1893-1905," *Journal of Negro History* 54 (July 1969):240-261.

Scheiner, Seth M. "President Theodore Roosevelt and the Negro, 1901-1908," *Journal of Negro History* 47 (July 1962):169-182.

Sherman, Richard. "The Harding Administration and the Negro: An Opportunity Lost," *Journal of Negro History* 49 (July 1964): 151-168.

Sherman, Richard B. "Republicans and Negroes: The Lessons of Normalcy," *Phylon* 27 (Spring 1966):63-79. The party's relationship to the Negro and the South during the post-World War I decade.

Thornbrough, Emma Lou. "The Brownsville Episode and the Negro Vote," *Mississippi Valley Historical Review* 44 (December 1957):469-483.

Urofsky, Melvin I. "Blanche K. Bruce: United States Senator, 1875-1881," *Journal of Mississippi History* 29 (May 1967):118-141. A Negro senator from Mississippi. Material is drawn in part from the Senator's papers and the *Congressional Record.*

Wolgemuth, Kathleen L. "Woodrow Wilson and Federal Segregation," *Journal of Negro History* 44 (April 1959):158-173.

Wolgemuth, Kathleen L. "Woodrow Wilson's Appointment Policy and the Negro," *Journal of Southern History* 24 (November 1958):457-471.

Woodward, C. Vann. "The Political Legacy of Reconstruction," *Journal of Negro Education* 26 (Summer 1957):231-240.

The Law, the Courts, and Regulatory Action

Aikin, Charles, ed. *The Negro Votes.* San Francisco: Chandler, 1962. A compilation of leading cases dealing with Negro voting rights, including cases involving the "grandfather clause," the white primary, and the use of the gerrymander.

"Alteration of Municipality's Boundary to Exclude Almost All Negro Voters Presents No Justiciable Issue," *Virginia Law Review* 46 (January 1960):132-134.

Amerine, Larry F. "Civil Rights—Voting Rights Act of 1965. . .," *Texas Law Review* 44 (July 1966):1411–1416. Potential effect of the act on voter registration.

"Attorney-General Authorized to Seek Injunctive Relief against Interference with Right to Vote: The Civil Rights Act of 1957," *Harvard Law Review* 71 (January 1958):573–575.

Avins, Alfred. "Fourteenth Amendment and Jury Discrimination: The Original Understanding," *Federal Bar Journal* 27 (Summer 1967):257–290.

Bernd, Joseph L., and Lynwood M. Holland. "Recent Restrictions upon Negro Suffrage: The Case of Georgia," *Journal of Politics* 21 (August 1959):487–513.

Bernhard, B. I. "The Federal Fact-Finding Experience—A Guide to Negro Enfranchisement," *Law and Contemporary Problems* 27 (Summer 1962):468–480.

Beth L. P. "The White Primary and the Judicial Function in the United States," *Political Quarterly* 29 (October–December 1958):366–377.

Bickel, Alexander M. "Voting Rights Bill Is Tough," *New Republic* 152 (April 3, 1965):16–18.

Blackford, Staige. "The Twenty-Fourth Amendment," *New South* 19 (February 1964):13–15.

Bonfield, A. E. "The Right to Vote and Judicial Enforcement of Section Two of the Fourteenth Amendment," *Cornell Law Quarterly* 46 (Fall 1960):108–137.

Claude, Richard. "Constitutional Voting Rights and Early U.S. Supreme Court Doctrine," *Journal of Negro History* 51 (April 1966):114–124.

The Congress, the Court and Jury Selection: A Critique of Titles I and II of the Civil Rights Bill of 1966—and State Juries," *Virginia Law Review* 52 (October 1966):1069–1156. Impact on Negroes serving on Southern juries.

"Congressional Authority to Restrict the Use of Literacy Tests," *California Law Review* 50 (May 1962):265–282.

"The Constitutionality of an Alabama Statute Re-defining Municipal Boundaries Is Not a 'Political Question' If It Effects a Deprivation of a Negro's Right to Vote," *Temple Law Quarterly* 34 (Spring 1961):326–331.

"Controversy Over the Federal Voting Rights Act: Pro & Con," *Congressional Digest* 48 (November 1969):257–288. Entire issue devoted to the origin and contents of the present law, voting tests by state, the proposal of the Nixon administration, and action of the 91st Congress to date.

De Grazia, Alfred. "A New Way toward Equal Suffrage," *New York University Law Review* 34 (April 1959):716–724.

Ervin, Sam J. "Political Rights as Abridged by Pending Legislative Proposals," *Federal Bar Journal* 24 (Winter 1964):4–17. U.S. Senator from North Carolina denounces provision for federal protection of voter registration in Civil Rights Act of 1964 as unconstitutional. He also considers Title VI unconstitutional, and the Court's protection of demonstrators guilty of "civil disobedience" indefensible.

"Exclusion of Negro Voters by Alteration of Municipality's Boundary Held Unconstitutional," *Ohio State Law Journal* 22 (Winter 1961):213–219.

Franklin, John Hope. "'Legal' Disfranchisement of the Negro," *Journal of Negro Education* 26 (Summer 1957):241–248. A review of the period around the turn of the century.

Geeslin, Gary L. "Peremptory Challenge—Systematic Exclusion of Prospective Jurors on the Basis of Race," *Mississippi Law Journal* 39 (December 1967):157–165.

Gill, Robert L. "Shaping the Negro Revolution through Court Decisions, 1964–1966," *Journal of Human Relations* 15 (Fourth Quarter 1967):423–442. Reviews decisions involving miscegenation, disenfranchisement, exclusion of Negroes from jury service, and the Civil Rights Act of 1964.

Hamilton, Charles V. "Southern Judges and Negro Voting Rights: The Judicial Approach to the Solution of Controversial Social Problems," *Wisconsin Law Review* 1965 (Winter 1965):72–102.

Havens, Charles W., III. "Federal Legislation to Safeguard Voting Rights: The Civil Rights Act of 1960," *Virginia Law Review* 46 (June 1960):945–975.

Heyman, Ira M. "Federal Remedies for Voteless Negroes," *California Law Review* 48 (May 1960):190–215.

Horsky, C. A. "The Supreme Court, Congress, and the Right to Vote," *Ohio State Law Journal* 20 (Summer 1959):549–556.

Katzenbach, Nicholas de B. "The Protection of 'Political Rights,'" *Federal Bar Journal* 24 (Winter 1964):18–30. Pointing to Congressional tardiness in implementing the Fifteenth Amendment, the author urges passage of civil rights bill in order to prevent continuation of traditional evasions of Negro right to register.

Kroll, Ellen, and Howard N. McCue. "Constitutional Law—Representative Government and Equal Protection—Invidious Discrimination of a Multi-Member Districting Scheme (*Chavez v. Whitcomb*)," *Harvard Civil Rights-Civil Liberties Law Review* 5 (January 1970):160+.

Kyle, Keith. "Desegregation and the Negro Right to Vote," *Commentary* 24 (July 1957):15–19.

McCarty, L. Thorne, and Russell B. Stevenson. "Voting Rights Act of 1965: An Evaluation," *Harvard Civil Rights Law Review* 3 (Spring 1968):357–411.

McIntyre, William R. "Right to Vote," *Editorial Research Reports,* March 19, 1958, pp. 201–219. An examination of the prospects for effective implementation of the Civil Rights Bill of 1957.

McKay, Robert B. *Reapportionment: The Law and Politics of Equal Representation.* New York: Twentieth Century Fund, 1965.

Marshall, Thurgood. "The Rise and Collapse of the 'White Democratic Primary,'" *Journal of Negro Education* 26 (Summer 1957):249–254. The author, former United States Solicitor General and for many years special counsel of the NAACP Legal Fund, in 1944 argued the Texas Primary case before the Supreme Court of which he is now an Associate Justice.

Norris, Harold. "Official Disobedience and Civil Disorder," *Journal of Urban Law* 46 (1969):249–268. Emphasizes the efforts of the U.S. Commission on Civil Rights to contravene "official" obstacles to Negro rights, especially as regards suffrage.

"Power of a State to Alter or Destroy the Corporate Boundaries of a City, Extensive Though It Is, Is Met and Overcome by the 15th Amendment to the Federal Constitution," *University of Pittsburgh Law Review* 22 (June 1961):773–776.

"The Right to Vote," *New Republic* 162 (January 3, 1970):8–9. Attacks the Administration's bill which would delete Section V of the 1965 Civil Rights Act in projected renewal of the Act in August 1970.

Sager, Lawrence Gene. "Tight Little Islands: Exclusionary Zoning, Equal Protection and the Indigent," *Stanford Law Review* 21 (April 1969):767–800. The poll tax issue.

Spicer, George W. "The Federal Judiciary and Political Change in the South," *Journal of Politics* 26 (February 1964):154–176.

"State Statute Altering Municipal Boundaries with Effect of Excluding Negro Voters Held Invalid," *Villanova Law Review* 6 (Spring 1961):411–415.

Strong, Donald S. *Negroes, Ballots, and Judges: National Voting Rights Legislation in the Federal Courts.* University: University of Alabama Press, 1968. A succinct critical appraisal of Southern legislative and juridical opposition to Negro Voting rights stemming from the Civil Rights Acts of 1957, 1960, and 1964.

Taper, Bernard. *Gomillion versus Lightfoot: The Tuskegee Gerrymander Case.* New York: McGraw-Hill, 1962. At issue in the Tuskegee case was whether districting was a political or a constitutional question. The Supreme Court held it to be constitutional. The decision had relevance for subsequent decisions on reapportionment of districts for Congressional elections.

Tucker, S. W. "Racial Discrimination in Jury Selection in Virginia," *Virginia Law Review* 52 (May 1966):736–750. Establishes fact of discrimination, examines current selection procedure, and suggests improvements.

"Tuskegee Case and the Political Question Dilemma," *Georgia Bar Journal* 23 (May 1961):545–548.

Tuttle, Elbert P. "Equality and the Vote," *New York University Law Review* 41 (April 1966):245–266.

"Unconstrued State Registration Statute Basis for Court Abstention Where Federal Jurisdiction Invoked under Civil Rights Acts," *Rutgers Law Review* 14 (Fall 1959):185-192.

U.S. Congress. House. Committee on the Judiciary. *Abolition of Poll Tax in Federal
Elections: Hearings before Subcommittee No. 5 of the Committee on the Judiciary,
March 12-May 14, 1962.* Washington: U.S. Govt. Print. Off., 1962. (87th Congress, 2d
Session)

U.S. Congress. House. Committee on the Judiciary. *Leading Court Decisions Pertinent to the
Proposed Voting Rights Act of 1965.* Washington: U.S. Govt. Print. Off., 1965. (89th
Congress, 1st Session)

U.S. Congress. House. Committee on the Judiciary. *Voting Rights: Hearings . . . , February 9
and 16, 1960.* Washington: U.S. Govt. Print. Off., 1960. (86th Congress, 1st Session)

U.S. Congress. House. Committee on the Judiciary. *Voting Rights: Hearings before Subcom-
mittee No. 5 on HR 5400 and Other Proposals to Enforce the 15th Amendment to the
Constitution of the United States, Held March 18-April 1, 1965.* Washington: U.S. Govt.
Print. Off., 1965. (89th Congress, 1st Session).

U.S. Congress. Senate. *Preservation of Evidence in Federal Elections: Hearings before the
Subcommittee on Privileges and Elections of the Committee on Rules and Administration,
July 13, 1961.* Washington: U.S. Govt. Print. Off., 1961. (87th Congress, 1st Session)

U.S. Congress. Senate. Committee on the Judiciary. *Literacy Tests and Voter Requirements in
Federal and State Elections: Hearings before the Subcommittee on Constitutional Rights of
the Committee on the Judiciary, March 27-April 12, 1962.* Washington: U.S. Govt. Print.
Off., 1962. (87th Congress, 2d Session)

U.S. Congress. Senate. Committee on the Judiciary. *Poll Tax and Enfranchisement of District
of Columbia: Hearings before the Subcommittee on Constitutional Amendments of the Committee on the Judiciary, August 17 and 27, 1959.* Washington: U.S. Govt. Print. Off., 1959.
(86th Congress, 1st Session)

U.S. Laws. Statutes. *Civil Rights Acts of 1957, 1960, 1964, 1968, and Voting Rights Act of
1965.* Washington: U.S. Congress. House of Representatives, 1969. (91st Congress, 1st
Session). A committee print. Text of the laws.

U.S. President (Johnson). *. . . Right to Vote.* Washington: U.S. Govt. Print. Off., 1965. (89th
Congress, 1st Session. H. Document no. 117)

Weaver, Robert C., and Hortense W. Gabel. "Some Legislative Consequences of Negro
Disfranchisement," *Journal of Negro Education* 26 (Summer 1957):225-261. Analysis of
Southern Congressmen and their effectiveness as impediments to liberal legislation.

Werdegar, Kathryn Mickle. "The Constitutionality of Federal Legislation to Abolish
Literacy Tests," *George Washington Law Review* 30 (April 1962):723-743.

Patterns and Conditions

General

Aikin, Charles, ed. *The Negro Votes.* San Francisco: Chandler, 1962.

Bailey, Harry A., Jr., ed. *Negro Politics in America.* Columbus, Ohio: Charles E. Merrill,
1967. Twenty-seven essays. Includes text of Civil Rights Act of 1964.

Banfield, Edward C., and James Q. Wilson. *City Politics.* Cambridge, Mass.: Harvard
University Press and MIT Press, 1963. While authors consider the role of the Negro
throughout, chapter 20 specifically analyzes "the anomaly of the Negro's numerical
strength and political weakness," with the result that much of the Negro's civic action
takes place in the courts or in the streets.

"Blacks and the Antiwar Movement," *Liberation* 12 (November 1967):29-31.

Bond, Julian. "The Negro in Politics," *Motive* 28 (May 1968):16-20.

Brogan, Dennis W. *Politics in America.* New York: Harper, 1954. See especially chapter 3,
"Race and Politics."

Brooks, Maxwell R. *The Negro Press Re-examined: Political Content of Leading Negro Newspapers.* Boston: Christopher, 1959.

Campbell, Angus. "Civil Rights and the Vote for President," *Psychology Today* 1 (January 1968):26-31 +. Tabular presentation.

"The Case for an Independent Black Political Party," *International Socialist Review* 29 (January-February 1968):39-55.

Clayton, Edward T. *The Negro Politician: His Success and Failure.* Chicago: Johnson, 1964.

Clubok, Alfred B., John M. Degrove, and Charles D. Farris. "The Manipulated Negro Vote: Some Pre-Conditions and Consequences," *Journal of Politics* 26 (February 1964): 112-129.

Commission on American Citizenship of the Catholic University of America. *The American Negro.* Washington: Catholic University Press, 1962.

Conway, M. Margaret. "The White Backlash Re-examined: Wallace and the 1964 Primaries," *Social Science Quarterly* 49 (December 1968):710-719.

Cornwell, Elmer E. "Bosses, Machines, and Ethnic Groups," *Annals of the American Academy of Political and Social Science* 353 (May 1964):27-39.

Dorson, Norman. "Discrimination," in *Frontiers of Civil Liberties.* New York: Pantheon 1968, pp. 317-332.

Douglas, Paul H. "Trends and Developments: The 1960 Voting Rights Bill: The Struggle, the Final Results and the Reason," *Journal of Intergroup Relations* 1 (Summer 1960):82-86.

Gillette, William. *The Right to Vote: Politics and the Passage of the Fifteenth Amendment.* Baltimore: Johns Hopkins Press, 1965. Bibliography.

Gosnell, Harold F., and R. E. Martin. "The Negro as Voter and Office Holder," *Journal of Negro Education* 32 (Fall 1963):415-425.

Halloway, Harry. "Negro Political Strategy: Coalition or Independent Power Politics?" *Social Science Quarterly* 49 (December 1968):534-547. Considers the alternatives of conservative or liberal coalition or an independent sally and concludes that the last mentioned is the most perilous but is also the most potentially rewarding to a Negro power bloc.

Hamilton, Charles V. "Race, Morality and Political Solutions," *Phylon* 20 (September 1959):242-247.

Hatcher, Richard G. "The Black Role in Urban Politics," *Current History* 57 (November 1969):287-289 +.

Hero, Alfred O., Jr. "American Negroes and U.S. Foreign Policy, 1937-1967," *Journal of Conflict Resolution* 13 (June 1969):220-251.

Kornberg, Allan, Elliot L. Tepper, and George L. Watson. "National Elections and Comparative Positions of Negroes and Whites on Policy," *South Atlantic Quarterly* 67 (Summer 1968):405-418.

Kramer, John, and Ingo Walter. "Politics in an All-Negro City," *Urban Affairs Quarterly* 4 (September 1968):65-87.

Lane, Robert E. *Political Life.* Glencoe, Ill.: Free Press, 1959. Includes analysis of Negro politics as form of ethnic behavior.

Levitt, Morris. "Negro Student Rebellion against Parental Political Beliefs," *Social Forces* 45 (March 1967):438-440.

Lipsky, Roma. "Electioneering among the Minorities," *Commentary* 31 (May 1961): 428-432.

Lubell, Samuel. *The Future of American Politics.* New York: Harper, 1952. Two chapters on the Negro: 5, "Civil Rights Melting Pot," deals with problems of Negro migrants to Northern cities, the Negro slums as seedbeds of violence and protest, and possible balance of political power; 6, "The Conservative Revolution," focuses on the South, the hardening of white supremacism, and the expansion of the Negro franchise.

Lubell, Samuel. "The Negro and the Democratic Coalition," *Commentary* 38 (August 1964):19-27. Contends that Negroes will continue to pull Democrat levers, but that Democrats must "unify the nation racially."

Marshall, Kenneth E. "Goals of the Black Community," in Robert H. Connery and Demetrios Caraley, eds., *Governing the City: Changes and Options for New York.* New York: Academy of Political Science, Columbia University, 1969, pp. 193-205.

Marvick, Dwaine. "The Political Socialization of the American Negro," *Annals of the American Academy of Political and Social Science* 361 (September 1965):112-127.

Matthews, Donald R. "Political Science Research on Race Relations," in Irwin Katz and Patricia Gurin, eds., *Race and the Social Sciences.* New York: Basic Books, 1969, pp. 113-144. Extensive bibliographical notes.

Moon, Henry Lee. "The Negro Vote in the Presidental Election of 1956," *Journal of Negro Education* 26 (Summer 1957):219-230.

Orum, Anthony M. "A Reappraisal of the Social and Political Participation of Negroes," *American Journal of Sociology* 72 (July 1966):32-46.

Patterson, Jack E. "Black Power, Municipal Style," *Commonweal* 90 (August 8, 1969): 477-478. Fayette, Mississippi.

Piven, Frances Fox, and Richard A. Cloward. "Dissensus Politics: Negroes and the Democratic Coalition," *New Republic* 158 (April 20, 1968):20-24.

Randolph, A. Philip. "The Negro's Stake in the Elections," *American Federationist* 75 (October 1968):24-25.

Roady, Elston E. *The Negro's Role in American Society.* Tallahassee: Florida State University, 1958. Extension of Negro participation in politics now demands greater efforts by Negro citizens themselves.

Segal, David R., and Richard Schaffner. "Status, Party and Negro Americans," *Phylon* 29 (Fall 1968):224-230.

Sindler, Allen P. "Negroes, Ethnic Groups and American Politics," *Current History* 55 (October 1968):207-212+. A comparison of the Negro's problem to earlier patterns of ethnic adjustment, noting the belatedness of the Negro's attempts to advance his status as a significant hurdle.

"Socialism and the Negro Movement," *Monthly Review,* September 1963.

Thomas, Jay. "Negro-White Unity and the Communists," *Political Affairs* 46 (May 1967):49-54.

U.S. Commission on Civil Rights. *Hearings . . . held in Jackson, Mississippi, February 16-20, 1965.* Washington: U.S. Govt. Print. Off., 1965.

U.S. Commission on Civil Rights. *Report.* Washington: U.S. Govt. Print. Off., 1959-   . Annual. In 1961 only, issued in five parts. See entry following.

U.S. Commission on Civil Rights. *Report 1961: Voting.* Washington: U.S. Govt. Print. Off., 1962.

U.S. Commission on Civil Rights. *Voting: Hearings . . . Montgomery, Ala., December 8, 1958-January 9, 1959; New Orleans, September 27, 1960-May 6, 1961.* Washington: U.S. Govt. Print. Off., 1961.

Vander, Harry J. *The Political and Economic Progress of the American Negro 1940-1963.* Dubuque, Iowa: W.C. Brown, 1968.

Van Zanten, John W. "Communist Theory and the Negro Question," *Review of Politics* 29 (October 1967):435-456.

Von Eschen, Donald, Jerome Kirk, and Maurice Pinard. "The Conditions of Direct Action in a Democratic Society," *Western Political Quarterly* 22 (June 1969):309-325.

Walton, Hanes, Jr. "Blacks and Conservative Political Movements," *Quarterly Review of Higher Education among Negroes* 39 (October 1969):177-190.

Walton, Hanes. *The Negro in Third-Party Politics.* Philadelphia: Dorrance, 1969.

Walton, Hanes, Jr. "The Political Leadership of Martin Luther King," *Quarterly Review of Higher Education among Negroes* 36 (July 1968):163-171. A bibliography is appended.

Wilson, James Q. *The Amateur Democrat.* Chicago: University of Chicago Press, 1962. See especially chapter 9 for a discussion of reform-Negro relations.

Wilson, James Q. "The Negro in Politics," *Daedalus* 94 (Fall 1965):949-973. To the author, the possibility of an "effective radical political strategy seems remote"; Negro alliances with labor or white liberals will continue to be *ad hoc;* Negro politics, *qua* politics, will achieve limited objectives.

Wilson, James Q. *Negro Politics: The Search for Leadership.* Glencoe, Ill.: Free Press, 1960. A valuable study of contemporary Negro politics in Northern cities, this volume is an examination of Negro public life at leadership level, with the main emphasis on Chicago.

The author comments on the greater aggressiveness of Negroes in New York than in Chicago, and on the fact that New York Negroes in public office are apt to take stronger stands on race issues.

Wilson, James Q., and Edward C. Banfield. "Public-Regardingness as a Value Premise in Voting," *American Political Science Review* 58 (December 1964):876-887.

Worsnop, Richard L. "Protection of Voting Rights," *Editorial Research Reports,* April 18, 1962, pp. 277-296.

North

Banfield, Edward C. *Political Influence.* Glencoe, Ill.: Free Press, 1961. Drawing on six case studies of Chicago politics, the author analyzes the way influence works in a large American city, pointing out that in Chicago Negro political leadership is more apt to operate through the machine than in New York, with consequent greater indifference to issues.

Banfield, Edward C., and Martha Derthick, eds. "A Report on the Politics of Boston." Cambridge, Mass.: Joint Center for Urban Studies, 1960. Mimeographed. The role of the Negro is considered throughout the study, and is also the subject of a special chapter by Ralph Otwell.

Baron, Harold M., et al. "Black Powerlessness in Chicago," *Trans-action* 5 (November 1968):27-33. A study of the exclusion of the black community in political decision-making.

Becker, John F., and Eugene E. Heaton, Jr. "Election of Senator Edward W. Brooke," *Public Opinion Quarterly* 31 (Fall 1967):346-358.

Daley, Mary Dowling. "Mayor Stokes' West Side Story," *Commonweal* 91 (November 28, 1969):270-271. A brief analysis of the campaign and Cleveland's voting pattern in the election of the incumbent.

Glantz, Oscar. "The Negro Voter in Northern Industrial Cities," *Western Political Quarterly* 13 (December 1960):999-1010.

Glantz, Oscar. "Recent Negro Ballots in Philadelphia," *Journal of Negro Education* 28 (Fall 1959):430-438. Includes presidential elections of 1944-1956. Author foresees Negroes exercising balance of power in the future. In November 1965, reform Republican Arlen Specter, with Negro support, became first Republican elected District Attorney in Philadelphia since 1953.

Gray, Kenneth. "A Report on City Politics in Cincinnati." Cambridge, Mass.: Joint Center for Urban Studies, 1959. Mimeographed. An examination of the circumstances under which PR was abandoned, which took the form of a struggle between two coalitions, each of which had its Negro bosses or leaders.

Greenstone, David. "A Report on the Politics of Detroit." Cambridge, Mass.: Joint Center for Urban Studies, 1961. Mimeographed.

Hadden, Jeffrey K., Louis H. Masotti, and Victor Thiessen. "The Making of Negro Mayors, 1967," *Trans-action* 5 (January-February 1968):21-30. An examination of the implications of Negro mayors in Gary, Indiana and Cleveland, Ohio viewed against the mayoralty campaign of Louise Day Hicks, a symbol of white backlash in Boston.

Leggett, John C. "Working-Class Consciousness, Race, and Political Choice," *American Journal of Sociology* 69 (September 1963):171-176. Among 375 Detroit blue-collar workers, race was found to be the decisive factor in political choice.

Miller, Loren. "The Negro Voter in the Far West," *Journal of Negro Education* 26 (Summer 1957):262-272.

Morrison, Allan. "Negro Political Progress in New England," *Ebony* 18 (October 1963): 25-28+. Chiefly on Edward W. Brooke, then Attorney General of Massachusetts.

O'Hare, Leo. "The Senator from Massachusetts," *Political Affairs* 46 (January 1967):15-23. Political ramifications of Edward Brooke's election.

Patterson, Beeman C. "Political Action of Negroes in Los Angeles: A Case Study in the Attainment of Councilmanic Representation," *Phylon* 30 (Summer 1969):170-183.

Ranney, Austin. *Illinois Politics*. New York: New York University Press, 1960. A short, well-executed analysis of contemporary politics in Illinois. Treatment of Negro participation is brief, limited to statistical data and comments on leadership.

Sigel, Roberta S. "Race and Religion as Factors in the Kennedy Victory in Detroit, 1960," *Journal of Negro Education* 31 (Fall 1962):436-447.

Straetz, Ralph A. *PR Politics in Cincinnati*. New York: New York University Press, 1958. For the effect of proportional representation on Negro politics in that city, see especially chapter 8.

Weinberg, Kenneth G. *Black Victory: Carl Stokes and the Winning of Cleveland*. Chicago: Quadrangle, 1968. A political biography of the first black man elected mayor of a major U.S. city.

Wilson, James Q. "The Flamboyant Mr. Powell," *Commentary* 41 (January 1966):31-35.

Wilson, James Q. "How the Northern Negro Uses His Vote," *Reporter* 22 (March 31, 1960):20-22.

Wilson, James Q. "Two Negro Politicians: An Interpretation," *Midwest Journal of Political Science* 4 (November 1960):346-369. Congressmen Adam Clayton Powell and William L. Dawson.

Young, Richard. "The Impact of Protest Leadership on Negro Politicians in San Francisco," *Western Political Quarterly* 22 (March 1969):94-111.

South

Bacote, C. A. "The Negro in Atlanta Politics," *Phylon* 16 (Winter 1955):333-350.

Bacote, C. A. "The Negro Voter in Georgia Politics Today," *Journal of Negro Education* 26 (Summer 1957):307-318.

Bond, Julian. *Black Candidates: Southern Campaign Experiences*. Atlanta: Southern Regional Council, 1969.

Brazeal, Brailsford R. "A Blackbelt County: Total Disfranchisement," in Margaret Price, *The Negro and the Ballot in the South*. Atlanta: Southern Regional Council, 1959. A pessimistic in-depth report on one rural county in the Deep South by the Dean of Morehouse College. Whites control all power, and though there are 60 percent Negro inhabitants in the county, there is no prospect today for equal Negro civil rights in any area.

Brittain, Joseph M. "Some Reflections on Negro Suffrage in Alabama—Past and Present," *Journal of Negro History* 47 (April 1962):127-138.

Bullock, Henry Allen. "Expansion of Negro Suffrage in Texas," *Journal of Negro Education* 26 (Summer 1957):369-377.

Buni, Andrew. *The Negro in Virginia Politics, 1902-1965*. Charlottesville: University of Virginia Press, 1967. Traces the challenge and response the race issue in the politics of this state. Bibliography.

Carleton, W. G., and H. D. Price. "America's Newest Voter: A Florida Case Study," *Antioch Review* 14 (Winter 1954):441-457.

Carter, Barbara. "The Fifteenth Amendment Comes to Mississippi," *Reporter* 28 (January 17, 1963):20-24.

Chatfield, Jack. "Challenging White Rule: Mississippi's Robert Clark," *New Leader* 52 (March 17, 1969):17-19.

Cothran, Tilman C., and William M. Phillips, Jr. "Expansion of Negro Suffrage in Arkansas," *Journal of Negro Education* 26 (Summer 1957):287-296.

Daniel, Johnnie. "Negro Political Behavior and Community Political and Socioeconomic Structural Factors," *Social Forces* 47 (March 1969):274-280. Alabama communities are subjects of this study. Author finds substantial changes since the Voting Rights Act of 1965.

"Desegregation Resistance Slows Negro Registration," *New South* 14 (October 1959):3-5.

Diamond, M. Jerome. "The Impact of the Negro Vote in Contemporary Tennessee Politics," *Tennessee Law Review* 34 (Spring 1967):435-481.

Dowd, Douglas F. "The Campaign in Fayette County," *Monthly Review* 15 (April 1964): 675-679. Tennessee vote drive.

Eggler, Bruce W. "A Long Way To Go in Mississippi," *New Republic* 160 (June 28, 1969): 19-21.

Farris, Charles D. "The Re-Enfranchisement of Negroes in Florida," *Journal of Negro History* 39 (October 1954):259-283. The author suggests that among reasons for defeat of white primary was the conviction among whites that political apathy among Negroes and an absence of vigorous Negro leadership would inhibit any great increase in registration.

Fenton, John H., and Kenneth N. Vines. "Negro Registration in Louisiana," *American Political Science Review* 51 (September 1957):704-713. How Catholic culture creates a permissive climate for Negro registration and weakens white segregationists' effectiveness.

Fenton, John H. "The Negro Voter in Louisiana," *Journal of Negro Education* 26 (Summer 1957):319-328.

Fleming, G. James. *An All-Negro Ticket in Baltimore.* New York: Holt, 1960. A case study in local politics issued by the Eagleton Institute of Politics. In 1958 congressional and state elections in the 4th district in Baltimore, an all-Negro coalition (bipartisan) ticket challenged the Democratic machine for seven seats in the state legislature—and lost.

Gauntlett, John, and John B. McConaughy. "Some Observations on the Influence of the Income Factor on Urban Negro Voting in South Carolina," *Journal of Negro Education* 31 (Winter 1962):78-82.

Gauntlett, John, and John B. McConaughy. "Survey of Urban Negro Voting Behavior in South Carolina," *South Carolina Law Quarterly* 13 (Spring 1962):365.

Gomillion, Charles G. "Civic Democracy and the Problems of Registration and Voting of Negroes in the South," *Lawyers Guild Review* 18 (Winter 1958):149-151. It was in the name of Professor Gomillion of Tuskegee Institute that litigation was entered against the gerrymandering of Tuskegee municipal boundaries to exclude Negro voters (see earlier, Bernard Taper, *Gomillion versus Lightfoot*). In November, 1964, he was elected to the Macon County Board of Education, one of the first three Negroes ever to obtain elective office in that county.

Gomillion, Charles G. "The Negro Voter in Alabama," *Journal of Negro Education* 26 (Summer 1957):281-286.

Guyot, Lawrence, and Mike Thelwell. "The Politics of Necessity and Survival in Mississippi," *Freedomways* 6 (Spring 1966):120-132.

Halberstam, David. " 'Good Jelly's' Last Stand," *Reporter* 24 (January 19, 1961):40-41. "Good Jelly" Jones, a Negro restaurant owner and bootlegger, runs a one-precinct machine in Nashville.

Holloway, Harry. "The Negro and the Vote: The Case of Texas," *Journal of Politics* 23 (August 1961):526-556. Negro voters often manipulated by landowners and white conservatives.

Holloway, Harry. *The Politics of the Southern Negro: From Exclusion to Big City Organization.* New York: Random, 1969. Bibliography.

Holloway, Harry. "The Texas Negro as a Voter," *Phylon* 24 (Summer 1963):135-145.

Hunter, Floyd. *Community Power Structures.* Chapel Hill: University of North Carolina Press, 1953. Useful for observations on Negro politics in the South and on the class status of the Negro leaders.

Ippolito, Dennis S. "Political Orientations among Negroes and Whites," *Social Science Quarterly* 49 (December 1968):548-562. Based on research in Petersburg and Norfolk, Virginia in 1967.

Jennings, M. Kent, and L. Harmon Zeigler. "A Moderate's Victory in a Southern Congressional District," *Political Opinion Quarterly* 28 (Winter 1964):595-603. In a district with 33.3 percent Negro population, Negroes support moderate Democrat.

Jewell, Malcolm. "State Legislatures in Southern Politics," *Journal of Politics* 26 (February 1964):177-196.

Jones, Lewis, and Stanley Smith. *Voting Rights and Economic Pressure*. New York: Anti-Defamation League, 1958. Prepared at Tuskegee in cooperation with the National Council of Churches. Reports on Mansfield, Tex., Clinton, Tenn., Sturgis, Ky., and Tallahassee, Fla.

Jones, Lewis W. "Struggle in the Vote at Tuskegee," in Jitsuichi Masuoka and Preston Valien, eds., *Race Relations: Problems and Theory*. Chapel Hill: University of North Carolina Press, 1961.

Keech, William R. *The Impact of Negro Voting: The Role of the Vote in the Quest for Equality*. Chicago: Rand McNally, 1968. Analyzes the impact and limitations of the Negro electorate in Durham, North Carolina and Tuskegee, Alabama. Bibliography.

Kesselman, Louis C. "Negro Voting in a Border Community: Louisville, Kentucky," *Journal of Negro Education* 26 (Summer 1957):273-280.

Ladd, Everett Carel, Jr. *Negro Political Leadership in the South*. Ithaca, N.Y.: Cornell University Press, 1966. A carefully researched study of urban political activity and patterns of leadership. Bibliography.

Lewinson, Paul. *Race, Class, and Party: A History of Negro Suffrage and White Politics in the South*. 1932 New York: Grosset & Dunlap, 1965. Reissued with a new foreword, "Postscript, 1964," which reviews briefly Negro suffrage gains of the past thirty years and speculates concerning the future political alignments of both Negro and white Southerners. Bibliography.

Lewis, Earl M. "The Negro Voter in Mississippi," *Journal of Negro Education* 26 (Summer 1957):329-350.

Lichtman, Allan. "The Federal Assault against Voting Discrimination in the Deep South, 1957-1967," *Journal of Negro History* 54 (October 1969):346-367.

Long, Margaret. "Black Power in the Black Belt," *Progressive* 30 (October 1966):20-24.

Lyon, John W. "Mississippi Ballot Box," *Saturday Review* 52 (May 17, 1969):20-21. Effectiveness of the Voting Rights Act of 1965 to date. Prognosis for the future.

McCain, James T. "The Negro Voter in South Carolina," *Journal of Negro Education* 26 (Summer 1957):359-366.

McGuinn, Henry J., and Tinsley Lee Spraggins. "Negro Politics in Virginia," *Journal of Negro Education* 26 (Summer 1957):378-389.

Madron, Thomas W. "Some Notes on the Negro as a Voter in a Small Southern City," *Public Opinion Quarterly* 30 (Summer 1966):279-284. Based on economic, occupational, and other statistics of Jackson, Tennessee.

Matthews, Donald R., and James W. Prothro. *Negroes and New Southern Politics*. New York: Harcourt, Brace & World, 1966. Research study and analysis of contemporary Southern Negro participation in politics. Also provides additional insights of economic, educational, and sociological aspects.

Middleton, Russell. "The Civil Rights Issue and Presidential Voting among Southern Negroes and Whites," *Social Forces* 40 (March 1962):209-215. Analysis of the 1960 election.

Minnis, Jack. "The Mississippi Freedom Democratic Party: A New Declaration of Independence," *Freedomways* 5 (Spring 1965).

"The Mississippi Freedom Vote," *New South* 18 (December 1963):10-13.

Mitchell, George S. "The Extension of Citizenship," in Jessie P. Guzman, ed., *The New South and Higher Education*. Tuskegee: Tuskegee Institute, 1954.

Moon, Henry Lee. "The Southern Scene," *Phylon* 16 (Winter 1955):351-358. Gains in the franchise since the banning of the white primary.

"The Negro Voter in the South," *Journal of Negro Education* 26 (Summer 1957):213-431. Entire issue.

"Negro Voter Registration Remains Constant in South," *New South* 14 (January 1959):8-9.

Newton, I. G. "Expansion of Negro Suffrage in North Carolina," *Journal of Negro Education* 26 (Summer 1957):351-358.

Ogden, Frederick D. *The Poll Tax in the South*. University: University of Alabama Press, 1958.

Price, Hugh D. *The Negro and Southern Politics: A Chapter of Florida History.* New York: New York University Press, 1957. A detailed study of the actual voting behavior of Negro voters in Florida, including Negro registration, the Negro Political League, the Negro as candidate, and campaign tactics.

Price, Margaret. *The Negro Voter in the South.* Atlanta: Southern Regional Council, 1957. A report on Negro registration, political consciousness, political organization, and leadership. Also included are data on Negro voting performance in 10 Southern states as of 1956. Brief but useful. Also appears in *New South* 12 (September 1957):1-55.

Roady, Elston E. "The Expansion of Negro Suffrage in Florida," *Journal of Negro Education* 26 (Summer 1957):297-306.

Ross, David F. "Black Power—Alabama: First Steps," *New Republic* 161 (September 27, 1969):14-15. Attempts of Greene County blacks to assert political leverage; white judicial opposition.

Seasholes, Bradbury, and Frederic W. Cleaveland. "Negro Political Participation in Two Piedmont Crescent Cities," in F. Stuart Chapin and Shirley F. Weiss, eds., *Urban Growth Dynamics.* New York: Wiley, 1962.

Smith, Stanley H. "A Case Study on Socio-Political Change," *Phylon* 29 (Winter 1968):380-387. The force of the Negro vote in the rural social structure of the South.

Southern Regional Council. *Black Elected Officials in the Southern States.* Atlanta, 1969. Roster of black elected officials after the Fall 1968 general elections.

Southern Regional Council. *The Effects of Federal Examiners and Organized Registration Campaigns on Negro Voter Registration.* Atlanta, 1966.

Southern Regional Council. Voter Education Project. *Voter Registration in the South, Summer, 1968.* Atlanta, 1968. White and Negro adult population and registered voters by county. In part, a tabular presentation.

Southwide Conference of Black Elected Officials. *Proceedings, 1968.* Atlanta: Southern Regional Council, 1969. Conference held in Atlanta, Ga., December 11-14, 1968.

Steinberg, C. "The Southern Negro's Right to Vote," *American Federationist* 69 (July 1962):1-6.

Stroud, Virgil C. "Voter Registration in North Carolina," *Journal of Negro Education* 30 (Spring 1961):153-155.

Taper, Bernard. "A Break With Tradition," *New Yorker*, June 24, 1965, pp. 58+. Changes that have occurred in Tuskegee and in Macon County since most of the obstacles to Negro registration have been removed in that voting district.

Travis, Fred. "The Evicted," *Progressive* 25 (February 1961):10-13. An account of pressure by landlords to prevent Negroes of Fayette and Haywood counties in Tennessee from voting.

U.S. Commission on Civil Rights. *Political Participation: A Study of the Participation by Negroes in the Electoral and Political Processes in 10 Southern States since Passage of the Voting Rights Act of 1965.* Washington: U.S. Govt. Print. Off., 1968. Includes statistical data, maps, and bibliographical footnotes.

U.S. Commission on Civil Rights. *Voting in Mississippi.* Washington: U.S. Govt. Print. Off., 1965. Bibliographical footnotes.

Valien, Preston. "Expansion of Negro Suffrage in Tennessee," *Journal of Negro Education* 26 (Summer 1957):362-368.

Vines, Kenneth N. "A Louisiana Parish: Wholesale Purge," in Margaret Price, *The Negro and the Ballot in the South.* Atlanta: Southern Regional Council, 1959.

Walker, Jack. "Negro Voting in Atlanta: 1953-1961," *Phylon* 24 (Winter 1963):379-387.

Watters, Pat, and Reese Cleghorn. *Climbing Jacob's Ladder: The Arrival of Negroes in Southern Politics.* New York: Harcourt, Brace & World, 1967.

Zinn, Howard. "Registration in Alabama," *New Republic* 149 (October 26, 1963):11-12.

19   The Freedom Revolution

Civil Rights

Alfange, Dean, Jr. "'Under Color of Law': *Classic* and *Screws* Revisited," *Cornell Law Quarterly* 47 (Spring 1962):395-428. The problem of state officers who, in the course of their duties but in violation of state law, deprive others of federal rights.

American Jewish Congress. Commission on Law and Social Action. *Assault Upon Freedom of Association.* New York, 1957. A study of the Southern attack on the NAACP.

American Jewish Congress. Commission on Law and Social Action. *The Civil Rights and Civil Liberties Decisions of the U.S. Supreme Court: A Summary and Analysis.* New York. Annual.

Anderson, John Weir. *Eisenhower, Brownell and the Congress: The Tangled Origin of the Civil Rights Bill of 1956-57.* University: University of Alabama Press, 1964. A detailed account of all stages leading up to passage of the Civil Rights Bill of 1957, especially of Brownell's achievement of inclusion of the right of the Justice Department to bring suit on behalf of Negroes denied voting rights.

"Anti-Discrimination Commissions," *Race Relations Law Reporter* 3 (October 1958): 1085-1108.

Aptheker, Herbert. *Soul of the Republic: The Negro Today.* New York: Marzani and Munsell, 1964. After attacking racist mythology, the author examines the data on which the 1963 reports of the U.S. Commission on Civil Rights were based.

Avins, Alfred. "Weapons against Discrimination in Public Office," *Syracuse Law Review* 14 (Fall 1962):24-41.

Barnett, Richard, and Joseph Garai. *Where the States Stand on Civil Rights.* New York: Sterling, 1962.

Bartley, Numan V. "Looking Back at Little Rock," *Arkansas Historical Quarterly* 25 (Summer 1966):101-116.

Berger, Morroe. *Equality by Statute: The Revolution in Civil Rights.* 1952. Rev. ed. Garden City, N.Y.: Doubleday, 1967. Deals with governmental role in eliminating discrimination and the force of the Supreme Court decrees. Notable bibliography of historical and current works.

Berman, Daniel M. *A Bill Becomes a Law: Congress Enacts Civil Rights Legislation.* 1962. 2d ed. New York: Macmillan, 1966.

Berman, Daniel M. "The Racial Issue and Mr. Justice Black," *American University Law Review* 16 (June 1967):386-402.

Bickel, Alexander M. "Belated Civil Rights Legislation of 1968," *New Republic* 158 (March 30, 1968):11-12.

Bickel, Alexander M. "Civil Rights: The Kennedy Record," *New Republic* 147 (December 15, 1962):11-16.

Bickel, Alexander M. "The Civil Rights Act of 1964," *Commentary* 38 (August 1964):33-39. A survey of the genesis and final form of the 1964 Act. Anticipating substantial compliance, the author considers Act soundly constitutional, while pointing out certain questions for judicial definition.

Bickel, Alexander M. *Politics and the Warren Court.* New York: Harper, 1965.

Bloch, Charles P. "Civil Rights—or Civil Wrongs?" *Georgia Bar Journal* 22 (November 1959):127–139.

Bloch, Charles P. *States Rights: The Law of the Land.* Atlanta: Harrison, 1958. A Southern view of the legal aspects of the Negro problem.

Bonfield, Arthur Earl. "State Civil Rights Statutes: Some Proposals," *Iowa Law Review* 49 (Summer 1964):1067–1129.

Borinski, Ernst. "The Litigation Curve and the Litigation Filibuster in Civil Rights Cases: A Study of Conflict between Legally Commanded and Socio-Culturally Accepted Changes in the Negro-White Caste Order in the Southern Community," *Social Forces* 37 (December 1958):142–147.

Carter, Elmer. "Policies and Practices of Discrimination Commissions," *Annals of the American Academy of Political and Social Science* 304 (March 1956):62–77.

Carter, Robert L., et al. *Equality.* New York: Pantheon, 1965. The views of four legal authorities on the issue of quotas and preferential treatment for Negroes as a means of achieving racial equality.

"A Chronology of Principal Cases on Segregation, 1878–1959," *New South* 14 (October 1959):8–13. Listed according to type (school, housing, transportation, etc.), together with legal references.

"Civil Disobedience and the Law: A Symposium," *American Criminal Law Quarterly* 3 (Fall 1964):11 + . Contributors include J. W. Riehm, M L. Ernst, H. Brownell.

"Civil Rights Act of 1964," *Harvard Law Review* 78 (January 1965):684–696.

The Civil Rights Act of 1964: Operations Manual. Washington: Bureau of National Affairs, 1964. Text, analysis, legal history.

"Civil Rights Bill: Pro and Con," *Milwaukee Bar Association Gavel* 25 (June 1964):8–15.

Countryman, Vern, ed. *Discrimination and the Law.* Chicago: University of Chicago Press, 1965. What the due processes of the law have achieved in four areas: employment, education, public accommodation, and housing. Discussions of specific cases and general principles in relation to constitutional law against race discrimination.

Cox, Archibald, Mark De Wolfe Howe, and J. R. Wiggins. *Civil Rights, the Constitution, and the Courts.* Cambridge, Mass.: Harvard University Press, 1967.

"Custom as Law within the Meaning of the Equal Protection Clause—An Approach to Problems of Racial Discrimination," *Rutgers Law Review* 17 (Spring 1963):563–578.

Dennis, James L. "State Involvement in Private Discrimination under the Fourteenth Amendment," *Louisiana Law Review* 21 (February 1961):433–448.

Dodson, William P. "Constitutional Law—Private Racial Discrimination," *Mississippi Law Journal* 40 (May 1969):452–458.

Dorsen, Norman. "The American Law on Racial Discrimination," *Public Law* 1968 (Winter 1968):304–324. General survey from a British viewpoint.

Dulles, Foster Rhea. *The Civil Rights Commission: 1957–1965.* East Lansing: Michigan State University Press, 1968. Bibliographical notes.

"Equal Protection and the Race Problem," *West Virginia Law Review* 62 (February 1960): 171–178.

Ervin, R. W. "Freedom of Assembly and Racial Demonstrations," *Cleveland and Marshall Law Review* 10 (January 1961):88 + .

"The Federal Executive and Civil Rights," *New South* 16 (March 1961):11–14. Summary of report submitted to President Kennedy by the Southern Regional Council.

Ferguson, Clarence Clyde, Jr. "Civil Rights Legislation, 1964: A Study of Constitutional Resources," *Federal Bar Journal* 24 (Winter 1964):102 + . The ultimate test of the Civil Rights Bill is not its strength or weakness but "the completeness of the constitutional response to the present social crisis in America."

Fleming, Harold C. "The Federal Executive and Civil Rights," *Daedalus* 94 (Fall 1965): 921–948.

Franklin, Mitchell. "Relation of 5th, 9th and 14th Amendments to the Third Constitution," *Howard Law Journal* 4 (June 1958):170-192.

Freund, Paul A. "Civil Rights and the Limits of Law," in *On Law and Justice*. Cambridge, Mass.: Harvard University Press, 1968, pp. 38-50.

Freund, Paul A. "The Civil Rights Movement and the Frontiers of Law," in *Daedalus, The Negro American*. Edited by Talcott Parsons and Kenneth Clark. Cambridge, Mass.: Houghton Mifflin, 1966, pp. 363-370.

Friedman, Leon, ed. *The Civil Rights Reader: Basic Documents of the Civil Rights Movement*. New York: Walker, 1967. From the 1947 Report of the President's Commission on Civil Rights to President Johnson's message to Congress on the Civil Rights Bill of 1966.

Friedman, Leon, ed. *Southern Justice*. New York: Pantheon, 1965. Reports of the practices of local police, sheriffs, prosecuting attorneys, trial courts, and juries in the South, as well as of the Federal courts and the F.B.I., all of which demonstrate that the law is made to work against individuals who seek its protection.

Gill, Robert L. "The Role of Five Negro Lawyers in the Civil Rights Struggle," *Quarterly Review of Higher Education among Negroes* 31 (April 1963):31-58. Description of general professional position of Negro lawyers and a brief resumé of cases in which they were involved.

Greenberg, Jack,. *Race Relations and American Law*. New York: Columbia University Press, 1959. The author is special counsel of NAACP Legal and Educational Fund. After chapters on the capacity of law to affect race relations and on leading legal issues (i.e., equal protection of law and due process), he analyzes the basic law dealing with race relations in institutional fields, education, employment, travel, armed forces, etc. Full bibliographical data in appendices.

Greenberg, Jack. "The Supreme Court, Civil Rights and Civil Dissonance," *Yale Law Journal* 77 (June 1968):1520-1544. Illustrates the social consciousness of the Court by reviewing its civil rights decisions.

Griffith, William C. "Racial Discrimination and the Role of the State," *Michigan Law Review* 59 (May 1961):1054-1077.

Griswold, Erwin N. "The Problem of Civil Rights—Its Legal Aspects," in *Law and Lawyers in the United States: The Common Law Under Stress*. Cambridge, Mass.: Harvard University Press, 1964, pp. 104-150.

Hackney, Hugh E. "Racial Discrimination and the Civil Rights Act of 1866," *Southwestern Law Journal* 23 (May 1969):373-383.

Handlin, Oscar. *Fire-Bell in the Night: The Crisis in Civil Rights*. Boston: Atlantic-Little, Brown, 1964. Assessing, after ten years, the consequences of the 1954 Court decision, the author believes that concentration on segregation as the evil and integration as the good has obscured the real issue, the complex problem of achieving equality under present urban and technological circumstances.

Hannah, J. A. "Civil Rights—A National Challenge," *South Dakota Law Review* 6 (Spring 1961):1+.

Harris, Robert J. *The Quest for Equality: The Constitution, Congress and the Supreme Court*. Baton Rouge: Lousiiana State University Press, 1960. A history of judicial interpretations of the Fourteenth Amendment. Last two chapters, "The Court Returns to the Constitution," and "The Judicial Burial of Jim Crow," cover period of public school and other segregation cases.

Henderson, George. "Legal Aspirations and Successes in the American Negro Revolution," *Journal of Human Relations* 13 (Winter 1965):185-195.

Henderson, Thelton. "The Law and Civil Rights: The Justice Department in the South," *New University Thought* 3 (February 1964):36-45.

Hirsch, Herbert, and Lewis Donohew. "A Note on Negro-White Differences in Attitudes toward the Supreme Court," *Social Science Quarterly* 49 (December 1968):557-562. Negro attitude toward the Court significantly more positive than that of whites.

Hopkins, L. L., and J. V. Hopkins. "How Some States Combat Bigotry," *Progressive* 22 (February 1958):33-35. State commissions on civil rights.

Howard, A. E. Dick. "Mr. Justice Black: The Negro Protest Movement and the Rule of Law," *Virginia Law Review* 53 (June 1967):1030-1090.

Howe, Mark DeWolfe. "Religion and Race in Public Relations," *Buffalo Law Review* 8 (Winter 1959):242+.

"J. Edgar Hoover and the F.B.I.," *Progressive* 24 (February 1960):24-30. An attack on erratic enforcement of civil rights by F.B.I.

Kalven, Harry, Jr. *The Negro and the First Amendment.* Columbus: Ohio State University Press, 1965. Lectures originally given at Ohio State Law Forum, April 7-9, 1964.

Kaplan, John. "Equal Justice in an Unequal World: Equality for the Negro—The Problem of Special Treatment," *Northwestern University Law Review* 61 (July-August 1966): 363-410.

Katz, Lawrence A. "Proposed Uniform State Civil Rights Act: An Analysis with Recommendations," *Boston College Industrial and Commercial Law Review* 7 (Spring 1966): 666-695.

King, Donald B., and Charles W. Quick, eds. *Legal Aspects of the Civil Rights Movement.* Detroit, Wayne State University Press, 1965. Bibliography.

Kinoy, Arthur. "Constitutional Right of Negro Freedom," *Rutgers Law Review* 21 (Spring 1967):387-441.

Konvitz, Milton R., and Theodore Leskes. *A Century of Civil Rights: With a Study of State Law against Discrimination.* New York: Columbia University Press, 1961. Legislation and judicial decisions on the federal level from the Civil War to the present, and the history of state laws and decisions with reference to public accommodations, employment, education, housing, etc.

Konvitz, Milton R., ed. "Freedom from Race Discrimination," in *Bill of Rights Reader: Leading Constitutional Cases.* 3d ed., rev. and enl. Ithaca, N.Y.: Cornell University Press, 1965, pp. 775-852. Cases cover spectrum of segregation in areas of zoning, suffrage, education, public accommodation, and employment.

Kovarsky, Irving. "Testing and the Civil Rights Act," *Howard Law Journal* 15 (Winter 1969): 227-249. And related legislation. Its effect upon Negro employment.

Kunstler, William M. *Deep in My Heart.* New York: Morrow, 1966. A white advocate in many civil rights cases writes with total commitment to the cause.

Leskes, Theodore. "The Federal Executive and Civil Rights," *Journal of Intergroup Relations* 3 (Spring 1962):171-178.

Leskes, Theodore. "State Segregation Laws," *Journal of Intergroup Relations* 2 (Summer 1961):243-251.

Losos, J. "Impact of the 14th Amendment upon Private Law," *St. Louis University Law Journal* 6 (Spring 1961):368+.

Lusky, Louis. "Justice with a Southern Accent: Do Our Federal Courts Need Emancipating?" *Harper's* 228 (March 1964):69-70+.

Lytle, Clifford M. "History of the Civil Rights Bill of 1964," *Journal of Negro History* 51 (October 1966):275-296.

McCloskey, R. G. "Deeds without Doctrines: Civil Rights in the 1960 Term of the Supreme Court," *American Political Science Review* 56 (March 1962):71-89. Deals with all civil rights issues as well as with Negro rights.

McKay, Robert B. "The Repression of Civil Rights as an Aftermath of the School Segregation Decision," *Howard Law Journal* 4 (January 1958):9+.

Mann, D. S. "Not for Lucre or Malice: The Southern Negro's Right to Out-of-State Counsel," *Northwestern University Law Review* 64 (May-June 1969):143-187.

Marshall, Burke. *Federalism and Civil Rights.* New York: Columbia University Press, 1964. A penetrating, deeply informed examination by the former Assistant Attorney General of efforts of the federal government to secure full civil rights and equality of opportunities for Negroes, together with an appraisal of problems likely to be caused by Southern maladministration of justice.

Marshall, Thurgood. "Law and the Quest for Equality," *Washington University Law Quarterly* 1967 (Winter 1967):1-9. The law and race relations.

Miller, Loren. *The Petitioners: The Story of the Supreme Court of the United States and the Negro.* New York: Pantheon, 1966. Judge Miller analyzes the reversal of the Court's position from the time of its declaring the 1875 Civil Rights Act unconstitutional to its decision affirming the constitutionality of 1964 Civil Rights Act.

Moore, John Hammond. "Jim Crow in Georgia," *South Atlantic Quarterly* 66 (Autumn 1967):554–565. Segregation and the legal status of the Negro.

Moreton, Alfred E. "Power of State Legislature to Exclude Negroes from Municipal Corporations," *Mississippi Law Journal* 31 (March 1960):173–175.

Morse, Oliver. "Civil Rights Removal: 'The Letter Killeth, but the Spirit Giveth Life,' " *Howard Law Journal* 11 (Winter 1965):149–186. Civil rights in historical perspective.

Murphy, Walter F. "The Southern Counterattacks: The Anti-NAACP Laws," *Western Political Quarterly* 12 (June 1959):371–390.

"Negro Defendants and Southern Lawyers: Review in Federal *Habeas Corpus* of Systematic Exclusion of Negroes from Juries," *Yale Law Journal* 72 (January 1963):559–573.

Nelson, Gaylord. "The Civil Rights Bill: Pro and Con: The Conservative Compromise," *Milwaukee Bar Association Gavel* 25 (June 1964):8–15. On the Civil Rights Act of 1964.

Nelson, Jack. "Law Enforcement: The Poor Want It Too," *New South* 23 (Summer 1968): 47–49. Deplores failure of government enforcement of laws designed to remedy discrimination against blacks in housing, education, and employment.

"Notre Dame Conference on Civil Rights," *Notre Dame Lawyer* 35 (May 1960):328–367.

"Notre Dame Conference on Congressional Civil Rights Legislation—A Report," *Notre Dame Lawyer* 38 (June 1963):430–446.

"Permissive Area of State Anti-Discrimination Acts," *Duquesne University Law Review* 1 (Spring 1963):231–238.

Pollak, Louis H. "Ten Years after the Decision," *Federal Bar Journal* 24 (Winter 1964): 123 +. The author traces the major types of civil rights action covered by Supreme Court decisions and speculates that the Court may, in the future, begin to "probe the constitutional dimensions" of economic discrimination.

Pollitt, Daniel H. "The President's Powers in Areas of Race Relations: An Exploration," *North Carolina Law Review* 39 (April 1961):238–281.

Rabkin, Sol. "Administrative Rulings on Civil Rights," *Journal of Intergroup Relations* 2 (Winter 1960–1961):82–84.

Revolution in Civil Rights. 4th ed. Washington: Congressional Quarterly Service, 1968. Legislative history, current developments, political and governmental aspects, the Black Power movement.

"The Right to Equal Treatment: Administrative Enforcement of Anti-Discrimination Legislation," *Harvard Law Review* 74 (January 1961):526–589.

Robison, Joseph B. "Protection of Associations from Compulsory Disclosure of Membership," *Columbia Law Review* 58 (May 1958):614–649.

Robison, Joseph B. "The Supreme Court and Civil Rights in the 1959-1960 Term," *Journal of Intergroup Relations* 1 (Fall 1960):64–70.

St. Antoine, T. J. "Color Blindness but Not Myopia: A New Look at State Action, Equal Protection, and 'Private' Racial Discrimination," *Michigan Law Review* 59 (May 1961):993–1016. The question of when private action is state action hinges on "whether a private activity was so invested with the public interest, and so subject to the control of powerful private forces, that effective impairment of Fourteenth Amendment rights could result."

Sengstock, Frank S., and Mary C. Sengstock. "Discrimination: A Constitutional Dilemma," *William and Mary Law Review* 9 (Fall 1967):59–125.

Shapiro, Harry H. "Limitations in Prosecuting Civil Rights Violations," *Cornell Law Quarterly* 46 (Summer 1961):532–554.

Shuman, Howard E. "Senate Rules and the Civil Rights Bill," *American Political Science Review* 51 (December 1957):955–975. Survey and analysis of role of the filibuster in retarding Civil Rights Bill of 1957.

Silard, John, and Harold Galloway. *State Executive Authority to Promote Civil Rights.*

Washington: Potomac Institute, 1963. Study of civil rights measures promulgated by executive branch of state governments.

Silk, Kenneth R. "Application of Exhaustion of State Remedies to Anti-NAACP Legislation," *Southern California Law Review* 33 (Fall 1959):82-87.

"State Universities and the Discriminatory Fraternity: A Constitutional Analysis," *UCLA Law Review* 8 (January 1961):169+.

Strauss, Frances. *Where Did the Justice Go?* Boston: Gambit, 1970. The Giles-Johnson case in Maryland: three Negro youths convicted of rape in 1961 were sentenced to death and subsequently, after six years in prison, acquitted.

"Symposium on Civil Rights," *Federal Bar Journal* 24 (Winter 1964):1+. Three main areas explored: political rights, property rights, employment rights.

Thompson, Daniel C. "The Role of the Federal Courts in the Changing Status of Negroes since World War II," *Journal of Negro Education* 30 (Spring 1961):94-101.

Tussman, Joseph, ed. *The Supreme Court on Racial Discrimination.* New York: Oxford University Press, 1963. The full texts of significant Supreme Court decisions in the following areas: segregation in education, segregation while traveling and dining, race and freedom of speech, discrimination and livelihood, restrictive covenants, discrimination and the jury, voting. Extremely useful.

Ulmer, S. S. "Supreme Court Behavior in Racial Exclusion Cases: 1935-1960," *American Political Science Review* 56 (June 1962):325-330. Chiefly Negro exclusion from state jury systems.

U.S. Commission on Civil Rights. *The 50 States Report.* Washington: U.S. Govt. Print. Off., 1961. Cites the "condonation of or connivance in private violence" on the part of Southern police officers.

U.S. Commission on Civil Rights. *Law Enforcement: A Report on Equal Protection in the South.* Washington: U.S. Govt. Print. Off., 1965. Three main sections consider denials of constitutional rights, remedies, and a conclusion, with recommendations for criminal remedies, civil remedies, and excutive action. In a separate statement Erwin N. Griswold, then Dean of the Harvard Law School, points out that the need for federal action is caused by the South's flagrant flouting of justice, and that the Negro has taken to protest in the streets because he knows any appeal to the courts and to officers of the law would be fruitless. A damning indictment of a whole society.

U.S. Commission on Civil Rights. *Report.* Washington: U.S. Govt. Print. Off., 1959-   . Annual. In 1961 only, issued in five parts.

U.S. Commission on Civil Rights. *The Voting Rights Act . . . The First Months.* Washington: U.S. Govt. Print. Off., 1965. Bibliographical footnotes.

U.S. Congress. House. "Civil Rights," *Hearings before Subcommittee No. 5 of the Committee on the Judiciary, February 4-26, 1957.* Washington, 1957. (85th Congress, 1st Session)

U.S. Congress. House. "Civil Rights," *Hearings before the Committee on Rules, June 20-27, 1956, and May 2-17, 1957.* Washington, 1956, 1957. (84th Congress, 2d Session, and 85th Congress, 1st Session)

U.S. Congress. House. "Civil Rights," *Hearings before the Committee on the Judiciary, July 13-27, 1955.* Washington, 1955. (84th Congress, 1st Session)

U.S. Congress. Senate. "Civil Rights Act of 1960," *Hearings before the Committee on the Judiciary, March 28-29, 1960.* Washington, 1960. (86th Congress, 2d Session)

U.S. Congress. Senate. "Civil Rights Proposals," *Hearings before the Committee on the Judiciary, April 24, July 13, 1956.* Washington, 1956. (84th Congress, 2d Session)

U.S. Laws. Statutes. *Civil Rights Acts of 1957, 1960, 1964, 1968, and Voting Rights Act of 1965.* Washington: U.S. Congress. House of Representatives, 1969. (91st Congress, 1st Session). A committee print. Text of the laws.

Van Alstyne, W. W., and K. L. Karst. "State Action," *Stanford Law Review* 14 (December 1961):3+. Examination of the relation between state action and the national interest in racial equality in all areas.

Van Der Slik, Jack R. "Constituency Characteristics and Roll Call Voting on Negro Rights in the 88th Congress," *Social Science Quarterly* 49 (December 1968):720-731.

Vines, K. N. "Southern State Supreme Courts and Race Relations," *Western Political Quarterly* 18 (March 1965):5-18.

Williams, Franklin H. "California's New Civil Rights Tool," *Christian Century* 77 (June 15, 1960):720-721. Constitutional rights section in State Justice Department.

Wilson, R. B. "Massive Insistence or Massive Resistance? The Judicial Administration of the Civil Rights Revolution," *George Washington Law Review* 33 (April 1965):827 + .

Wollett, Donald H. "Race Relations," *Louisiana Law Review* 21 (December 1960):85-108. A survey of action on interracial relations taken by Louisiana legislature during 1960, namely, 35 acts and 4 resolutions for constitutional amendments covering everything from cohabitation to public welfare.

Woodward, C. Vann. "The Great Civil Rights Debate," *Commentary* 24 (October 1957): 283-291. Civil Rights Act of 1957.

Protest: Theory and Practice through 1965

Abrams, Charles. "Civil Rights in 1956," *Commentary* 22 (August 1956):101-109. A survey by the then chairman (1955-1959) of the New York State Commission against Discrimination.

Ahmann, Mathew, ed. *The New Negro: A Symposium.* Notre Dame, Ind.: Fides Press, 1962.

Amaker, Norman C. "The 1950's: Racial Equality and the Law," *Current History* 57 (November 1969):275-280.

Aptheker, Herbert. *Toward Negro Freedom.* New York: New Century, 1956.

Baldwin, James. "The Dangerous Road before Martin Luther King," *Harper's* 222 (February 1961):33-42. Baldwin doubts that Dr. King's role in the Negro movement of protest will continue to be of as great importance as in the past.

Baldwin, James. *The Fire Next Time.* New York: Dial, 1963. Powerful jeremiad, apocalyptic warning, and call to repentance, this volume consists of a "Letter to My Nephew on the One Hundredth Anniversary of the Emancipation," and "Letter from a Region of My Mind," including an examination of the Black Muslims.

Belfrage, Sally. *Freedom Summer.* New York: Viking, 1965. The author's experience as a SNCC worker with the summer project in Greenwood, Mississippi.

Bell, Daniel. "Plea for a 'New Phase in Negro Leadership,' " *New York Times Magazine,* May 31, 1964, p. 11 + .

Bennett, Lerone, Jr. *Confrontation: Black and White.* Chicago: Johnson, 1965. An account of the steadily growing intensity of the Negro-White confrontation, both during America's past and in the Freedom Revolution.

Bennett, Lerone, Jr. *The Negro Mood.* Chicago: Johnson, 1964. Five essays by the senior editor of *Ebony* which examine the "mood" of the Negro revolt both on the streets and in the mind. The author's analysis of the black establishment and its responses to the world of white power is especially penetrating.

Bennett, Lerone, Jr. "What Sit-Downs Mean to America," *Ebony* 15 (June 1960):35-38 + .

Blackwood, George D. "Civil Rights and Direct Action in the Urban North," *Public Policy* 14 (1965):292-320.

Booker, Simeon. *Black Man's America.* Englewood Cliffs, N.J.: Prentice-Hall, 1964. The author is a newspaperman of wide experience whose account of observed facts is lively and interesting.

Braden, Anne. "The Southern Freedom Movement in Perspective," *Monthly Review* 17 (July-August 1965):entire issue.

Brink, William, and Louis Harris. *The Negro Revolution in America.* New York: Simon & Schuster, 1964. Based on surveys made by *Newsweek* in 1963 for special reports in that magazine on July 29, 1963, and October 21, 1963. Expanded to book form, the present volume analyzes the two surveys, the first of the Negro's opinions and attitudes, and the second of what whites think of Negroes. For later coverage, see the authors' *Black and White: A Study of U.S. Racial Attitudes Today.* 1967; Rev. ed. 1969.

Burns, W. Haywood. *The Voices of Negro Protest in America.* New York: Oxford University Press, 1963. The nature of and relationship among legal-judicial, nonviolent, and radical-separatist forms of Negro protest in the United States.

Bushnell, Paul E. "Passive Insistence—Its Principles and Procedures, Its Promise and Peril," *Chapel and College,* Fall 1960, pp. 4-12.

Carawan, Guy, and Candie Carawan. *We Shall Overcome! Songs of the Southern Freedom Movement.* New York: Oak, 1963.

Carter, Hodding, III. "The Young Negro Is a New Negro," *New York Times Magazine,* May 1, 1960, p. 11+. On the militancy of the new generation of Negroes.

Clark, Kenneth B. "The Civil Rights Movement: Momentum and Organization," *Daedalus* 95 (Winter 1966):239-267.

Clark, Kenneth B. *The Negro Protest.* Boston: Beacon, 1963. Conversations conducted by Dr. Clark with James Baldwin, Malcolm X, and Martin Luther King on Boston's WGBH-TV station for National Educational Television.

Clarke, Jacquelyne. *These Rights They Seek: A Comparison of Goals and Techniques of Local Civil Rights Organizations.* Washington: Public Affairs Press, 1962. A study of three civil rights groups in Alabama.

Clayton, Edward T., ed. *The SCLC Story.* Atlanta: Southern Christian Leadership Conference, 1964. Historical and descriptive story told in words and pictures.

Coles, Robert. "Children and Racial Demonstrations," *American Scholar* 34 (Winter 1964-1965):78-92.

Constable, John. "Negro Student Protests Challenge N [orth] C [arolina] Leaders," *New South* 15 (March 1960):3-10.

Cook, Samuel DuBois. "Revolution and Responsibility," *New South* 19 (February 1964): 8-12. On the responsibility of the Negro revolution to follow a nonviolent, nonracist course.

Cothran, Tilman C. "Potential and Responsibility for National, World Leadership," *New South* 15 (June 1960):3-8.

Daniel, Bradford, ed. *Black, White, and Gray: Twenty-one Points of View on the Race Question.* New York: Sheed & Ward, 1964. Views of a wide range of figures from Orval Faubus to Roy Wilkins.

Danzig, David. "The Meaning of Negro Strategy," *Commentary* 37 (February 1964):41-46. Remarking on the emergence in a number of cities of organized Negro communities which represent and negotiate Negro interests, the author sees rights of individuals coming to rest on the status of the group, with the possibility that group self-interest and Negro solidarity may contribute to reshaping goals.

The Day They Changed Their Minds. New York: NAACP, 1960. Account of how demonstrations developed in 1960.

Delavan, V., et al. "Why They Sat In," *Social Progress* 51 (February 1961):3-46. Entire issue.

"The Demonstrations in the South," *New University Thought* 1 (Spring 1960):21-27. A catalogue of places and dates.

DeVree, Charlotte. "The Young Negro Rebels," *Harper's* 222 (October 1961):133-138.

Dienstfrey, Ted. "A Conference on the Sit-Ins," *Commentary* 29 (June 1960):524-528.

"Direct Action in the South," *New South* 18 (October-November 1963):1-32. Entire issue covers such topics as sit-ins, freedom riders, the ballot, civil disobedience, and events in Albany, Ga., and Birmingham, Ala.

Doddy, Hurley. "The 'Sit-In' Demonstration and the Dilemma of the Negro College President," *Journal of Negro Education* 30 (Winter 1961):1-3.

Dorman, Michael. *We Shall Overcome: A Reporter's Eyewitness Account of the Year of Racial Strife and Triumph.* New York: Delacorte, 1964. A Scripps-Howard reporter writes of 1962-1963.

Doss, George A., Jr. "Homegrown Movement in Macon," *New South* 18 (April 1963):3-10.

Dunbar, Leslie W. "Reflections on the Latest Reform of the South," *Phylon* 22 (Fall 1961):249-257. Sit-ins as a social movement.

Dunbar, Leslie W. *A Republic of Equals.* Ann Arbor: University of Michigan Press, 1966. An overview of the effect of the black revolt on American political institutions.

Dykeman, Wilma, and James Stokely. " 'Sit Down Chillun, Sit Down! ' " *Progressive* 24 (June 1960):8-13. The authors assert that the "deeper meaning of the 'sit-in' demonstrations is to show that segregation cannot be maintained in the South short of continuous coercion."

Ehle, John. *The Free Men.* New York: Harper, 1965. Account of attempts to integrate Chapel Hill, N.C., in 1963 and 1964, which vividly reveals the strains within the community and the failures of leadership.

Evers, Mrs. Medgar, with William Peters. *For Us the Living.* Garden City, N.Y.: Doubleday, 1969. A biography of her husband; also some interesting autobiographical aspects.

Farmer, James. *Freedom—When?* New York: Random, 1966. About the role of CORE in the civil rights movement.

Farmer, James. " 'I Will Keep My Soul,' " *Progressive* 25 (November 1961):21-22. On the first Freedom Ride.

Feagans, Janet. "Voting, Violence and Walkout in McComb, Mississippi," *New South* 16 (October 1961):3-4+. On the SNCC voter registration drive in McComb County.

Fey, Harold E. "Revolution without Hatred," *Christian Century* 80 (September 11, 1963): 1094-1095. March on Washington.

Fields, Uriah J. *The Montgomery Story: The Unhappy Effects of the Montgomery Bus Boycott.* New York: Exposition Press, 1959. According to the minister of the Bell Street Baptist Church, the bus boycott in Montgomery, Ala., did more harm than good. The people were betrayed by their leaders Martin Luther King and R. D. Abernathy, who got more than his share of funds raised to repair bombed-out churches.

Fischer, John. "A Small Band of Practical Heroes," *Harper's* 227 (October 1963):16+. Account of the work of SNCC in Mississippi, especially in voter registration.

Fischer, John. "What the Negro Needs Most: A First Class Citizens' Council," *Harper's* 225 (July 1962):12+.

Fleming, Harold C. "The Changing South and Sit-Ins," *Journal of Intergroup Relations* 2 (Winter 1960-1961):56-60.

"For Jobs and Freedom: Three Views of the Washington March," *Midwest Quarterly* 5 (Winter 1964):99-116.

Forman, James. *Sammy Younge, Jr.: The First Black Student to Die in the Black Liberation Movement.* New York: Grove, 1968.

[Freedom Rides] *New South* 17 (July-August 1961):1-18.

Friedman, Murray. "The White Liberal Retreat," *Atlantic* 211 (January 1963):42-46. The diminution of the role of the white liberal, whether because of his recoiling from increased Negro militancy or because of aggressive Negro assumption of leadership.

Fuller, H. W. "Rise of the Negro Militant," *Nation* 197 (September 14, 1963):138-140.

Garfinkel, Herbert. *When Negroes March: The March on Washington Movement in the Organizational Politics for FEPC.* Glencoe, Ill.: Free Press, 1959.

Goodman, Paul. "The Children of Birmingham," *Commentary* 36 (September 1963): 242-244.

Graham, Frank. "Students 'Standing Up' for the American Dream," *New South* 15 (July-August 1960):7-8.

Hansberry, Lorraine. *The Movement: Documentary of a Struggle for Equality.* New York: Simon & Schuster, 1964.

Hardwick, Elizabeth. "Selma, Alabama: The Charms of Goodness," *New York Review of Books,* April 22, 1965. The author describes the "moral justice of the civil rights movement, the responsible program of the leaders, the tragic murderous rage of the white people."

Hare, Nathan. "Integrated Southern Town: How a Small Southern Town Made Integration Work," *Phylon* 22 (Summer 1961):180-187.

Hare, Nathan. "Rebels Without a Name," *Phylon* 23 (Fall 1962):271-277. On the terms "colored" and "Negro."

Hayes, Charles L. "The Sit-In Demonstrations—In Retrospect," *Interracial Review* 35 (June 1962):147-148.

Hedgeman, Anna Arnold. *The Trumpet Sounds: A Memoir of Negro Leadership.* New York: Holt, Rinehart, 1964. Fascinating account of the early—and recent— years of the civil rights movement. The author deals chiefly with experiences of segregation in the North.

Hentoff, Nat. *The New Equality.* New York: Viking, 1964. Rev. with new material, Compass, 1965. Firm, factual, sober of tone and objectively detached in manner, the author's program calls for a revolutionary reordering of society in the areas of unemployment, education, and housing.

Hernton, Calvin C. *White Papers for White Americans.* Garden City, N. Y.: Doubleday, 1966. Four essays and a short piece about the 1963 Negro march in Washington.

Hines, Ralph H., and James E. Pierce. "Negro Leadership after the Social Crisis: An Analysis of Leadership Changes in Montgomery, Alabama," *Phylon* 26 (Spring 1965):162-172.

Holt, Len. *An Act of Conscience.* Boston: Beacon, 1965. Account of Danville, Virginia's, "Summer of Protest."

Holt, Len. *The Summer That Didn't End.* New York: Morrow, 1965. How the summer project continued to operate in Mississippi.

Hughes, Langston. *Fight for Freedom: The Story of the NAACP.* New York: Norton, 1962.

Huie, William Bradford. *Three Lives for Mississippi.* New York: Trident, 1965. About the murder of the civil rights workers, Michael Schwerner, James Chaney, and Andy Goodman.

Ianiello, Lynne, ed. *Milestones Along the March: Twelve Historic Civil Rights Documents from World War II to Selma.* New York: Praeger, 1965. Record of statutes and federal pronouncements from the Fair Employment Practices Commission, 1941 to "We Shall Overcome" address by President Johnson to Congress, March 15, 1965.

Isaacs, Harold R. "Integration and the Negro Mood," *Commentary* 34 (December 1962):487-497.

James, Beauregard. *The Road to Birmingham.* New York: Book Awards, 1964.

Johnson, Haynes. *Dusk at the Mountain: The Negro, the Nation, and the Capital: A Report on Problems and Progress.* Garden City, N.Y.: Doubleday, 1963. Developed from a series of prizewinning articles on the Negro by a Washington, D.C. newspaperman.

Jones, Charles. "SNCC: Non-violence and Revolution," *New University Thought* 3 (September-October 1963):8-19.

Jones, Hubert E. "STOP—A Method of Protest," *Industry* (Massachusetts) 28 (July 1963):14+.

Kahn, Tom. "The 'New Negro' and the New Moderation," *New Politics* 1 (Fall 1961):61-76.

Kahn, Tom. "Problems of the Negro Movement: A Special Report," *Dissent* 11 (Winter 1964):108-138.Thorough review of the civil rights movement as of date, and of the problem it faces in developing new tactics and fresh approaches.

Kempton, Murray. "A. Philip Randolph," *New Republic* 149 (July 6, 1963):15-17.

Killens, John Oliver. *Black Man's Burden.* New York: Trident, 1966. The burden is the prejudiced white man.

King, Marion. "Reflection on the Death of a Child," *New South* 18 (February 1963):9-10. Mrs. Slater King, of Albany, Ga., on the loss of a child through miscarriage resulting from police treatment during a racial incident.

King, Martin Luther, Jr. "The Burning Truth in the South," *Progressive* 24 (May 1960):8-10. Sit-ins as a "demand for respect," combining direct action with nonviolence.

King, Martin Luther, Jr. "The Current Crisis in Race Relations," *New South* 13 (March 1958):8-12.

King, Martin Luther, Jr. "Facing the Challenge of a New Age," *Phylon* 18 (Spring 1957):25-34.

King, Martin Luther, Jr. "Let Justice Roll Down," *Nation* 200 (March 15, 1965):269-273.

King, Martin Luther, Jr. "Letter from Birmingham Jail," *Christian Century* 80 (June 12, 1963):767-773. Dr. King's widely published answer to 8 Alabama clergymen who called for an end of Negro demonstrations. He directly challenged the churchmen to act by Christian principles.

King, Martin Luther, Jr. "Love, Law and Civil Disobedience," *New South* 16 (December 1961):3-11.

King, Martin Luther, Jr. "The Luminous Promise," *Progressive* 26 (December 1962): 34-37. Reflections on the 100th anniversary of the Emancipation Proclamation.

King, Martin Luther, Jr. *Strength to Love.* New York: Harper, 1963.

King, Martin Luther, Jr. *Stride toward Freedom: The Montgomery Story.* New York: Harper, 1958. The impressive account of the Montgomery bus boycott, which catapulted Dr. King into leadership of Negro protest.

King, Martin Luther, Jr. "The Time for Freedom Has Come," *New York Times Magazine,* September 10, 1961, p. 25 + .

King, Martin Luther, Jr. *Why We Can't Wait.* New York: Harper, 1964. This work is among the most vigorous and cogent statements of Dr. King's philosophy of nonviolence. He stresses the important gains Negroes have made by nonviolent demonstrations, the most significant being their new sense of dignity and of power.

Kotler, Neil. "SNCC Strikes the Landlords: A Report from Washington, D.C.," *Dissent* 11 (Summer 1964):328-332.

Ladd, Everett C., Jr. "Agony of the Negro Leader," *Nation* 198 (September 7, 1964):88-91. "Negro leadership in the United States has been, and remains, issue leadership, and the one issue that matters is race advancement." See also author's *Negro Political Leadership in the South.*

Lees, Hannah. "The Not-Buying Power of Philadelphia's Negroes," *Reporter* 24 (May 11, 1961):33-35. A description of the "selective patronage program" organized and run by 400 ministers.

Lincoln, C. Eric. "Anxiety, Fear, and Integration," *Phylon* 21 (Fall 1960):278-285. Develops theme that "Ours is an era characterized by fear and tension, loneliness and anxiety," and compares events in Birmingham, Ala., and Budapest at time of Hungarian revolt.

Lincoln, C. Eric. "The Strategy of a Sit-In," *Reporter* 24 (January 5, 1961):20-23.

Link, Eugene P. "The Civil Rights Activities of Three Great Negro Physicians—1840-1940," *Journal of Negro History* 52 (July 1967):169-184. John S. Rock, Dan H. Williams, Louis Tompkins Wright.

Lissovoy, Peter de. "Freedom Wars in Georgia," *Dissent* 11 (Summer 1964):296-302. Author is a full-time worker (white) in the freedom movement out of Albany, Ga.

Lomax, Louis E. *The Negro Revolt.* New York: Harper, 1962. An important statement concerning the background, the forces, and the events that have shaped the Negro revolt.

Lomax, Louis E. "The Unpredictable Negro," *New Leader* 44 (June 5, 1961):3-4.

Long, Herman H. "The Challenge to Negro Leadership," *Journal of Intergroup Relations* 1 (Spring 1960):75-79.

Long, Herman H. "Marginal Man and New Negro Identity," *New South* 17 (April 1962): 6-12. On the need for a new Negro leadership that will understand how to use Negro power in new tasks.

Long, Margaret. "March on Washington," *New South* 18 (September 1963):3-17.

Lubell, Samuel. *White and Black: Test of a Nation.* New York: Harper, 1964. As always astute and hardheaded, Lubell proceeds from the contention that "A totally unrealistic, nightmarish concept has been built up by both Negroes and Whites about what can be accomplished through desegregation." He discusses residential mobility, education, crime, job restrictions, political action.

Lynd, Staughton. "Freedom Riders to the Polls," *Nation* 195 (July 28, 1962):29-32.

Lynd, Staughton, and Roberta Yancy. "Southern Negro Students: The College and the Movement," *Dissent* 11 (Winter 1964):39-45. The paternalism and restrictive regulations of most Negro colleges are contrasted with the stimulation and liberation of spirit and responsibility generated by "the movement."

Mabee, Carleton. "Evolution of Non-violence: Two Decades of Sit-ins," *Nation* 193 (August 12, 1961):78–81.

Mabee, Carleton. "Freedom Schools, North and South," *Reporter* 31 (September 10, 1964):30–32.

Mabee, Carleton. "Prepared for Arrest," *Christian Century* 78 (January 11, 1961):52–53. Howard University students demonstrate.

McCord, Charles. "The Anatomy of a Registration Drive: A Success Story from New Orleans," *Interracial Review* 35 (May 1962):122–125.

McCord, William. *Mississippi: The Long Hot Summer.* New York: Norton, 1965. Probably the best treatment of the summer project, particularly in its realistic appraisal of future prospects.

McCoy, Donald R., and Richard T. Ruetten. "The Civil Rights Movement, 1940–1954." *Midwest Quarterly* 11 (October 1969):11–34.

McDermott, John. "Wade-In Witness at Rainbow Beach," *Interracial Review* 35 (June 1962):146–147. In Chicago.

Margolis, Joseph. "The American Negro and the Issue of Segregation," *American Scholar* 28 (Winter 1958–1959):73–79.

Mayer, Milton. "The Last Time I Saw Selma," *Progressive* 29 (May 1965):18–21.

Mayfield, Julian. "Challenge to Negro Leadership: The Case of Robert Williams," *Commentary* 31 (April 1961):297–305.

Meier, August. "Boycotts of Segregated Street Cars, 1894–1909—A Research Note," *Phylon* 18 (Fall 1957):296–297.

Meier, August, and Elliott Rudwick. "The First Freedom Ride," *Phylon* 30 (Fall 1969): 213–222. The Journey of Reconciliation in 1947 at the invitation of CORE as the prototype for the movement in the early 1960's.

Meier, August, and Elliott M. Rudwick. *From Plantation to Ghetto: An Interpretative History of American Negroes.* New York: Hill & Wang, 1966. A notable final chapter on the civil rights revolution. Bibliography.

Meier, August, and Elliott Rudwick. "How CORE Began," *Social Science Quarterly* 49 (March 1969):789–799. Its origins, ideology, purposes, and change. Discusses the "sit-in" as an instrument of social change.

Meier, August. "Negro Protest Movements and Organizations," *Journal of Negro Education* 32 (Fall 1963):437–450.

Meier, August. "New Currents in the Civil Rights Movement," *New Politics* 2 (Summer 1963):7–32.

Meier, August. "The Successful Sit-Ins in a Border City: A Study in Social Causation," *Journal of Intergroup Relations* 2 (Summer 1961):230–237.

Mendelsohn, Jack. *The Martyrs: Sixteen Who Gave Their Lives for Racial Justice.* New York: Harper & Row, 1966.

Millard, Thomas L. "The Negro and Social Protest," *Journal of Negro Education* 32 (Winter 1963):92–98.

Miller, Loren. "Freedom Now—But What Then?" *Nation* 196 (June 29, 1963):539–542.

Miller, Robert William. *Nonviolence.* New York: Association Press, 1964. Background and ideology of the nonviolent Negro movement.

Mississippi Black Paper: Statements and Notarized Affidavits. New York: Random, 1965. Collection of affidavits assembled as evidence for a suit against Sheriff Rainey and other state officials.

"The Negro Movement: Where Shall It Go Now?" *Dissent* 11 (Summer 1964):279–295. Jobs and political action stressed as objectives, acts of social dislocation considered useful only when directed to specific ends.

Nelson, William Stuart. "Do We Dare to Break the Law?" *Interracial Review* 35 (June 1962):150–151.

Newfield, Jack. "The Question of SNCC," *Nation* 201 (July 19, 1965):38–40. Description and prognosis, with discussion of SNCC prospects in urban centers.

Norris, Marjorie M. "Early Instance of Nonviolence: The Louisville Demonstrations of 1870–1871," *Journal of Southern History* 32 (November 1966):487–504.

O'Dell, J. H. "Climbin' Jacob's Ladder: The Life and Times of the Freedom Movement," *Freedomways* 9 (Winter 1969):7-23.

Oppenheimer, Martin. "Current Negro Protest Activities and the Concept of Social Movement," *Phylon* 24 (Summer 1963):154-159.

Oppenheimer, Martin. "Southern Student Sit-ins: Intra-group Relations and Community Conflict," *Phylon* 27 (Spring 1966):20-26.

Peck, James. *Cracking the Color Line: Non-Violent Direct Action Methods of Eliminating Racial Discrimination.* New York: CORE, 1960.

Peck, James. *Freedom Ride.* New York: Simon & Schuster, 1962. By the editor of CORE-lator, who participated in the ride from Washington to New Orleans.

Petrof, John V. "The Effect of Student Boycotts upon the Purchasing Habits of Negro Families in Atlanta, Georgia," *Phylon* 24 (Fall 1963):266-270.

Phillips, W. M., Jr. "The Boycott: A Negro Community in Conflict," *Phylon* 22 (Spring 1961):24-30.

Price, Margaret. *"Toward a Solution of the Sit-In Controversy."* Atlanta: Southern Regional Council, 1960. Mimeographed. Analysis of methods used to solve sit-in problems in several cities.

Proudfoot, Merrill. *Diary of a Sit-In.* Chapel Hill: University of North Carolina Press, 1962.

Record, Wilson. "Intellectuals in Social and Racial Movements," *Phylon* 15 (Fall 1954): 231-242. Negro intellectuals have a specific, obvious, and constant grievance, whereas white intellectuals are only occasionally involved with concrete, well-defined grievances. Whites can choose whether to become involved, Negroes cannot.

Reed, Roy. "The Deacons, Too, Ride by Night," *New York Times Magazine,* August 15, 1965, pp. 10-11 +. On the Deacons for Defense and Justice, organized in Jonesboro, La., in 1964.

"The Revolt of Negro Youth," *Ebony* 15 (May 1960):36 +. The Negro student movement as a new force in the civil rights struggle.

Rodell, Fred. "Our Languid Liberals," *Progressive* 21 (March 1957):5-7. Democratic party and the Negro.

Rostow, Eugene. "The Freedom Riders and the Future," *Reporter* 24 (June 22, 1961):18-21.

Rovere, Richard. "Negro Crisis, Letter from the American Kitchen," *Encounter* 31 (August 1963):3-7.

Rowan, Carl T. "Are Negroes Ready for Equality?" *Saturday Evening Post* 233 (October 22, 1960):21 +.

Rustin, Bayard. "From Protest to Politics: The Future of the Civil Rights Movement," *Commentary* 39 (February 1965):25-31.

St. James, Warren D. *The National Association for the Advancement of Colored People: A Case Study in Pressure Groups.* New York: Exposition Press, 1958. Most useful portions are the addenda: NAACP constitutions, bibliography, and summary of cases.

Saunders, Doris E. *The Day They Marched.* Chicago: Johnson, 1963. March on Washington, briefly described, with illustrations.

Searles, Ruth, and J. Allen Williams, Jr. "Negro College Students' Participation in Sit-Ins," *Social Forces* 40 (March 1962):215-220.

Sibley, Mulford Q., ed. *The Quiet Battle: Writings on the Theory and Practice of Non-violent Resistance.* Garden City, N.Y.: Doubleday, 1963.

Silberman, Charles E. *Crisis in Black and White.* New York: Random, 1964. The problem of acting with justice toward the Negro is "the greatest moral imperative of our time," and "the question. . . is no longer what to do, but whether there is still time in which to do it."

Simpson, George E. "Recent Political Developments in Race Relations," *Phylon* 19 (Summer 1958):208-221. As a result of the growing impact of Negro protest action in areas of housing, education, public accommodations.

"Sit-In, Other Techniques Are Likely to Continue," *New South* 16 (June 1961):3-5.

Sit-Ins, the Students Report. New York: CORE, 1960.

Sitton, Claude. "When a Southern Negro Goes to Court," *New York Times Magazine,* January 7, 1962, p. 10 +.

Smith, Charles U. "The Sit-Ins and the New Negro Student," *Journal of Intergroup Relations* 2 (Summer 1961):223-229. Account of civil rights movements at Florida Agriculture and Mechanical University, Tallahassee, by chairman of the Department of Sociology.

Smith, Charles U., and Lewis M. Killian. *Tallahassee, Florida: The Tallahassee Bus Protest.* New York: Anti-Defamation League, 1958.

Smith, Howard K. "Luxury We Cannot Afford," *New South* 12 (October 1957):6-9. That is, another Little Rock. CBS broadcast of September 29, 1957.

Smith, Lillian. "The Winner Names the Age," *Progressive* 21 (August 1957):6-10. Need for individual commitment and Negro revolution.

Sobel, Lester A., ed. *Civil Rights, 1960-66.* New York: Facts on File, 1967. A capsule summary, chronologically arranged.

Southern Regional Council, and the American Jewish Committee. *The Continuing Crisis.* Atlanta: Southern Regional Council, 1966.

Sullivan, Terry. "What Is It Like to be a Freedom Rider?" *Interracial Review* 35 (June 1962):143-145.

Sutherland, Elizabeth, ed. *Letters from Mississippi.* New York: McGraw-Hill, 1965. By white "visitors" to Mississippi in 1964 summer project.

Thompson, Daniel C. *The Case for Integration.* Atlanta: Southern Regional Council, 1961.

Thompson, Daniel C. "The Rise of the Negro Protest," *Journal of Human Relations* 14 (First Quarter 1966):56-73. An historical synopsis.

Thompson, Era Bell, and Herbert Nipson. *White on Black.* Chicago: Johnson, 1963. Twenty-two pieces from *Ebony* by a variety of white figures, from Bishop Oxnam to Mike Jacobs.

Thurman, Howard. *Disciplines of the Spirit.* New York: Harper, 1963. Technique of nonviolence in the revolutionary struggle of the Negro.

Toby, Jackson. "Bombing in Nashville: A Jewish Center and the Desegregation Struggle," *Commentary* 25 (May 1958):385-389.

Turner, John B., and Whitney M. Young, Jr. "Who Has the Revolution or Thoughts on the Second Reconstruction," *Daedalus* 94 (Fall 1965):1148-1163.

Valien, Preston. "The Montgomery Bus Protest as a Social Movement," in Jitsuichi Masuoka and Preston Valien, eds., *Race Relations: Problems and Theory.* Chapel Hill: University of North Carolina Press, 1961.

Vander Zanden, James W. "The Non-Violent Movement against Segregation," *American Journal of Sociology* 68 (March 1963):544-550.

Vanderburgh, Charles. "A Draftee's Diary from the Mississippi Front," *Harper's* 228 (February 1964):37-45.

Vose, Clement E. "Litigation as a Form of Pressure Group Politics," *Annals of the American Academy of Political and Social Science* 319 (September 1958):20-31.

Wakefield, Dan. *Revolt in the South.* New York: Grove—Evergreen, 1960.

Walker, Wyatt Tee. "Albany, Failure or First Step," *New South* 18 (June 1963):3-8.

Walter, Norman W. "The Walking City: A History of the Montgomery Boycott," *Negro History Bulletin* 20 (October-November 1956); (February-April 1957). The continued story of the Montgomery bus boycott.

Warren, Robert Penn. *Who Speaks for the Negro?* New York: Random, 1965. Based on interviews with Negroes of every social status and from many regions of the country, most effective in its refraction of images and impressions as they presented themselves to the novelist's eye and ear.

"Washington March Is 'Played By Ear,'" *Editor and Publisher* 96 (August 24, 1963):11. Press coverage for March on Washington.

Watts, Marzette. "Sit-ins and Pickets: The Students Move in Montgomery," *New University Thought* 1 (Spring 1960):16-20.

Weaver, Robert C. "The NAACP Today," *Journal of Negro Education* 29 (Fall 1960): 421-425.

Westfeldt, Wallace. *Settling a Sit-In.* Nashville, Tenn.: Nashville Community Relations Conference, 1960.

Westin, Alan F., ed. *Freedom Now! The Civil Rights Struggle in America.* New York: Basic Books, 1964. An anthology of 51 brief articles on "The moral dimension of the civil

rights struggle." The volume constitutes a sustained dialogue on the management and
methods of the civil rights struggle.

White, Lewis W. "A Current Lament," *New South* 18 (May 1963):12-13. Reflections of a
Negro teacher in Birmingham on the need for more forceful and realistic leadership.

White House Conference. *To Secure These Rights.* Washington: U.S. Govt. Print. Off., 1947.
Report of President's Committee on Civil Rights.

Wilkins, Roy. "Freedom Tactics for 18,000,000," *New South* 19 (February 1964):3-7.

Wilson, C. E. "The Pilgrimage: A Reappraisal of August 28," *Liberator* 3 (October
1963):4-7.

Wright, Marion A. "The Right to Protest," *New South* 17 (February 1962):6-13.

Young, Whitney M., Jr. *To Be Equal.* New York: McGraw-Hill, 1964. A stern, factual
presentation of why Negroes demand, in simple justice, the opportunity "to be equal,"
and a persuasive argument for a special program for the Negro on the grounds that he
has the right to equality of opportunity, and that as things now stand, that equality is not
available to him.

Zietlow, Carl P. "Race, Students, and Non-Violence," *Religious Education* 59 (January-
February 1964):116-120.

Zinn, Howard. *Albany: A Study in National Responsibility.* Atlanta: Southern Regional
Council, 1962. Report based on the Albany crises of December 1961 and the following
summer.

Zinn, Howard. "The Battle-Scarred Youngsters," *Nation* 197 (October 5, 1963):193-197.

Zinn, Howard. "The Double Job in Civil Rights," *New Politics* 3 (Winter 1964):29-34.
Discussion of strategies to be pursued: civil rights and the more general social revolution.

Zinn, Howard. "A Fate Worse Than Integration," *Harper's* 219 (August 1959):53-56.

Zinn, Howard. *SNCC: The New Abolitionists.* Boston: Beacon, 1964. Through accounts of
the many protest campaigns SNCC has engaged in, the author illustrates the spirit of
revolution in this youth organization.

Protest: Theory and Practice since 1965

Alexander, Raymond Pace. "Civil Rights, the Negro Protest and the War on Poverty:
Efforts to Cure America's Social Ills," *New York State Bar Journal* 41 (February
1969):90-99.

*Argument: The History-Making Decision That Spurred the Civil Rights Revolution in the
United States.* New York: Chelsea House, 1969. With an important introduction by
Kenneth B. Clark, the substance of which appears in an article entitled, "Fifteen Years
of Deliberate Speed," in *Saturday Review* 52 (December 20, 1969):59-61 +.

Asinof, Eliot. "Dick Gregory Is Not So Funny Now," *New York Times Magazine,* March 17,
1968, pp. 36-37 +. The comedian as militant civil rights spokesman.

Aukofer, Frank A. *City with a Chance.* Milwaukee, Wis.: Bruce, 1968. A journalist's concise
appraisal of the Milwaukee civil rights protests in 1967 led, for the most part, by Father
James Groppi and the Youth Council of the NAACP.

Baldwin, James. "White Racism or World Community," *Religious Education* 64 (September
October 1969):342-346. Also published in *Ecumenical Review* 20 (October 1968):
371-376. An appeal to the Christian conscience.

Bass, Jack. "Strike at Charleston," *New South* 24 (Summer 1969):35-44.

Bosmajian, Haig A., and Hamida Bosmajian, eds. *The Rhetoric of the Civil Rights Movement.*
New York: Random, 1969.

Brink, William, and Louis Harris. *Black and White: A Study of U.S. Racial Attitudes Today.*
New York: Simon & Schuster, 1967. An opinion sampling of whites, Negroes, and Negro
leaders concerning the racial conflict since 1963. Comparisons with a 1963 survey published under the title *The Negro Revolution in America* indicate the change in the Negro
movement and the force of the black power concept.

Carson, Josephine. *Silent Voices: The Southern Negro Woman Today.* New York: Delacorte,

1969. Records of a white author who traveled through the South with a group of Negro women involved in the civil rights struggle.

Carter, Wilmoth. *The New Negro of the South.* New York: Exposition Press, 1967. The civil rights movement and the nature of Negro leadership.

Chatfield, Jack. "Port Gibson, Mississippi: A Profile of the Future?" *New South* 24 (Summer 1969):45-55.

Clark, Kenneth B. "The Present Dilemma of the Negro," *Journal of Negro History* 53 (January 1968):1-11.

Clarke, James W., and John W. Soule. "How Southern Children Felt about King's Death," *Trans-action* 5 (October 1968):34-40. Reactions of white and Negro children, and the effect upon them of parental attitudes. Tables.

Coles, Robert. "Civil Rights Is Also a State of Mind," *New York Times Magazine,* May 7, 1967, pp. 32-33+.

Dabbs, James McBride. *Civil Rights in Recent Southern Fiction.* Atlanta: Southern Regional Council, 1969.

Danzig, David. "The Racial Explosion in American Society," *New University Thought* 5 (1966-1967):30-45. An historical review of the civil rights movement.

Dye, Thomas R. "Inequality and Civil-Rights Policy in the States," *Journal of Politics* 31 (November 1969):1080-1097.

Geschwender, James A. "Civil Rights Protest and Riots: A Disappearing Distinction," *Social Science Quarterly* 49 (December 1968):474-484. Analyzes characteristics of the disorders, rioters, tactics, and lootings.

Good, Paul. "A Tale of Two Cities," *Nation* 203 (November 21, 1966):534-538. Compares newspaper with other accounts of the role of SNCC in racial disturbances in Philadelphia and Atlanta.

Gordon, David M. "Communities of Despair and the Civil Rights Movement," *Harvard Review* 4 (Summer 1966):49-68. The future of the American Negro's civil rights movement.

Greene, Maxine. "You White Folks Ain't Ready . . . ," *Record* 70 (January 1969):361-371.

Hall, Robert L. "SNCC's Call to Northern Black Students," *Harvard Journal of Negro Affairs* 2, no.1 (1968):35-39. A review of the New England Regional Black Student Conference, March 3-5, 1967.

Handlin, Oscar. "The Goals of Integration," *Daedalus* 95 (Winter 1966):268-286. An examination and critique of long-term goals of the Negro freedom movement.

Harkey, Ira B. *The Smell of Burning Crosses: An Autobiography of a Mississippi Newspaperman.* Jacksonville, Ill.: Harris-Wolfe, 1967.

Harris, Sheldon. "San Fernando's Black Revolt," *Commonweal* 89 (January 31, 1969): 549-552.

Hilton, Bruce. *The Delta Ministry.* New York: Macmillan, 1969.

Hofstetter, G. Richard. "Political Disengagement and the Death of Martin Luther King," *Public Opinion Quarterly* 33 (Summer 1969):174-179.

"How Can We Get the Black People to Cool It?" *Esquire* 70 (July 1968):49-53+. Interview with James Baldwin illustrating the dichotomy between white and black society.

Howell, Leon. *Freedom City: The Substance of Things Hoped For.* Richmond: John Knox, 1969. Mississippi.

Humphrey, Hubert H. *Beyond Civil Rights: A New Day of Equality.* New York: Random, 1968.

Jackson, J. H. *Unholy Shadows and Freedom's Holy Light.* Nashville, Tenn.: Townsend Press, 1967. Progress and goals ahead of the civil rights struggle. Bibliography.

Jackson, Maurice. "The Civil Rights Movement and Social Change," *American Behavioral Scientist* 12 (March-April 1969):8-17. References.

Kaplan, John. "Equal Justice in an Unequal World: Equality for the Negro—The Problem of Special Treatment," *Northwestern University Law Review* 61 (July-August 1966): 363-410. A discussion of the practical and moral problems stemming from special treatment for the Negro in employment, housing, and public education.

Kelman, Herbert C. "The Relevance of Nonviolent Action," in *A Time to Speak*. San Francisco: Jossey-Bass, 1968, pp. 231–260.

Kenyatta, C. 37X "The Changing Role of the Militants," *Harvard Review* 4, no. 3 (1968):45–48.

King, Martin Luther, Jr. "The Future of Integration," *Humanist* 28 (March–April 1968):2–6. Abridgement of his address in Buffalo, New York.

King, Martin Luther, Jr. "The Role of the Behavioral Scientist in the Civil Rights Movement," *Journal of Social Issues* 24 (January 1968):1–12. Also appears in *American Psychologist* 23 (March 1968):180–186. Negro leadership in labor and political action and the psychological and ideological changes in Negroes as areas for examination by the social scientist.

King, Martin Luther, Jr. *The Trumpet of Conscience.* New York: Harper & Row, 1968. Succinct statements of author's convictions. 1967 Massey Lectures delivered over Canadian Broadcasting Corporation. Includes views on nonviolence, race relations, and Vietnam.

King, Martin Luther, Jr. *Where Do We Go from Here: Chaos or Community?* New York: Harper, 1967. Author's reassessment of the conflicts existing in the civil rights movement and a pragmatic approach to courses of action. Includes his reasoned rejection of the Black Power movement.

Konvitz, Milton R. "Civil Rights," in *Expanding Liberties: Freedom's Gains in Postwar America.* New York: Viking, 1966, pp. 245–340.

Kristol, Irving. "It's Not a Bad Crisis to Live In," *New York Times Magazine,* January 22, 1967, pp. 50–51+.

Lawson, J. M., Jr. "From a Lunch Counter Stool," *Motive* 26 (February 1966):41–43. Assesses Christian nonviolence.

Levy, Charles J. *Voluntary Servitude: Whites in the Negro Movement.* New York: Appleton-Century-Crofts, 1968. Observations based on author's four-year experience as a white faculty member of a Southern predominantly Negro college and as a civil rights activist.

Lincoln, C. Eric. *Sounds of the Struggle: Persons and Perspectives in Civil Rights.* New York: Morrow, 1967. Collection of articles, for the most part, previously published in journals.

Lipsky, Michael. "Rent Strikes: Poor Man's Weapon," *Trans-action* 6 (February 1969): 10–15. The Harlem rent strikes of 1963 and 1964 organized by Jesse Gray.

Logue, Cal M. "Ralph McGill: Convictions of a Southern Editor," *Journalism Quarterly* 45 (Winter 1968):647–652.

Love, Sam. "Mississippi College Students Challenge the Courthouse Gang," *New South* 24 (Spring 1969): 17–21.

McCord, John H., ed. *With All Deliberate Speed: Civil Rights Theory and Reality.* Urbana: University of Illinois Press, 1969. A comprehensive survey of civil rights legislation in the United States and the continued discrimination in the areas of public accommodations, employment, housing, and education. Documented sources.

McKissick, Floyd. *Three-Fifths of a Man.* New York: Macmillan, 1969. A history of the black man's struggle for equality.

Mackler, Bernard. "Civil Rights Movement: From Reflection to Heartbreak; Black Power," *Teachers College Record* 68 (October 1966):42–48. "An expression of personal outrage" at the recent history of the civil rights movement.

Mahadewan, T.W. "A Search for Meaning: An Indian Approach to the Negro Revolution," *Gandhi Marg* 42 (1967):128–132. The strengths of nonviolence.

Marx, Gary T. "Religion: Opiate or Inspiration of Civil Rights Militancy among Negroes?" *American Sociological Review* 32 (February 1967):64–72. The implications of religion as a vehicle for protest.

Meier, August. "The Dilemmas of Negro Protest Strategy," *New South* 21 (Spring 1966): 1–18. The politics of civil rights organizations in the South.

Meyer, Philip. "Aftermath of Martyrdom: Negro Militancy and Martin Luther King," *Public Opinion Quarterly* 33 (Summer 1969):160–173.

Murphy, Raymond J., and Howard Elinson, eds. *Problems and Prospects of the Negro Move-*

ment. Belmont, Calif.: Wadsworth, 1966. A compendium of articles reflecting major and sometimes conflicting forces in the Negro movement. Annotated bibliography.

Muse, Benjamin. *The American Negro Revolution: From Nonviolence to Black Power, 1963-1967.* Bloomington: Indiana University Press, 1968. Account by a former Virginia state senator of the concerted drive for civil rights from the nonviolent demonstrations in 1963 to the militancy of attitude in 1967.

Newfield, Jack. "SSOC: Bridging the Gap between Bureaucracy and Anarchy," *Motive* 26 (March 1966):13-15. Southern Student Organizing Committee.

Nolan, David. "The 'Movement' Finally Arrives," *Nation* 208 (May 26, 1969):654-656. Hospital strike and black student rebellion in Beaufort County, South Carolina. For a related view of the area, see Bynum Shaw's article in *Esquire,* June 1968.

O'Dell, J. H. "Charleston's Legacy to the Poor People's Campaign," *Freedomways* 9 (Summer 1969):197-211. The Charleston hospital workers' strike and its ramifications.

"Operation Breadbasket: SCLC," *Steel Labor* 34 (March 1969):12. Economic goals and accomplishments of the Southern Christian Leadership Conference.

Orbell, John M. "Protest Participation among Southern Negro College Students," *American Political Science Review* 61 (June 1967):446-456.

Pinard, Maurice, Jerome Kirk, and Donald von Eschen. "Processes of Recruitment in the Sit-In Movement," *Public Opinion Quarterly* 33 (Fall 1969):355-369.

Rathburn, John W. "Martin Luther King: The Theology of Social Action," *American Quarterly* 20 (Spring 1968):38-53.

Reagin, Ewell. "A Study of the Southern Christian Leadership Conference," *Review of Religious Research* 9 (Winter 1968):88-96.

Roberts, Adam. "Martin Luther King and Non-Violent Resistance," *World Today* 24 (June 1968):226-236.

Rustin, Bayard. "The Total Vision of A. Philip Randolph," *New Leader* 52 (April 14, 1969):15-17. A tribute to Randolph's visionary perception and his steadfast adherence to it.

Saunders, Albert C. "Civil Rights: The Current Scene in Washington," *Social Progress* 57 (March-April 1967):5-10. Need for legislation in four areas of civil rights.

Scott, Joseph W. "Social Class Factors Underlying the Civil Rights Movement," *Phylon* 27 (Summer 1966):132-144.

Scroth, Raymond A. "Self Doubt and Black Pride," *America* 116 (April 1, 1967):502-505. FIGHT, the Rochester black political group, vs. Eastman Kodak Corporation.

Sharma, Mohan Lal. "Martin Luther King: Modern America's Greatest Theologian of Social Action," *Journal of Negro History* 53 (July 1968):257-263.

Shaskolsky, Leon. "Negro Protest Movement—Revolt or Reform?" *Phylon* 29 (Summer 1968):156-166. From the protest demonstrations seeking civil rights, the author describes the transformation of the movement into one demanding economic, political, and social equality.

Slaiman, Donald. *Civil Rights in the Urban Crisis.* Washington: U.S. Department of Labor, Manpower Administration, 1968.

Smith, Donald Hugh. "Civil Rights: A Problem in Communication," *Phylon* 27 (Winter 1966):379-387.

Stanfield, J. Edwin. *In Memphis: A Tragedy Averted.* Atlanta: Southern Regional Council, 1968.

Stanfield, J. Edwin. *In Memphis: Mirror to America?* Atlanta: Southern Regional Council, 1968.

Stanfield, J. Edwin. *In Memphis: More Than a Garbage Strike.* Atlanta: Southern Regional Council, 1968.

Sterling, Dorothy. *Tear Down the Walls! A History of the American Civil Rights Movement.* Garden City, N.Y.: Doubleday, 1968.

Strong, Augusta. "Negro Women in Freedom's Battles," *Freedomways* 7 (Fall 1967): 302-315.

Sullivan, William C. "Communism and the American Negro," *Religion in Life* 37 (Winter 1968):591-601. Assistant Director of the Federal Bureau of Investigation seeks to dispel charges that the Comunist party in the United States has a stronghold within Negro ranks or the civil rights movement.

Surace, Samuel J., and Melvin Seeman. "Some Correlates of Civil Rights Activism," *Social Forces* 46 (December 1967):197-207.

Taylor, William L. "Update Civil Rights," *Phi Delta Kappan* 50 (October 1968):80-84. Under the aegis of educational leadership. "A pessimistic report—and a hopeful prescription."

U.S. Commission on Civil Rights. *Hearing Held in Cleveland, Ohio, April 1-7, 1966.* Washington, U.S. Govt. Print. Off., 1966. Concerns the denials of equal legal protection in housing, education, employment, health, and police-community relations in Cleveland. Maps.

Walker, Alice. "Civil Rights Movement: What Good Was It," *American Scholar* 36 (Autumn 1967):550-554.

Watters, Pat. "Enforcing Civil Rights Laws," *Current* 102 (December 1968):33-42.

Watters, Pat, and Edwin Stanfield. *In Memphis: One Year Later.* Atlanta: Southern Regional Council, 1969.

Watters, Pat. "To Fulfill These Rights," *New South* 21 (Summer 1966):26-46. Commentary on, and excerpts from the Advisory Council's recommendations to the White House Conference, June 1-2, 1966.

Weiss, Samuel A. "Dilemmas of Negro Militancy," *Midwest Quarterly* 9 (Autumn 1967): 97-107. A commentary on James Farmer's *Freedom—When?* Exposes the dichotomy of philosophy of separatism and integration.

Wheeler, John H. "Civil Rights Groups—Their Impact Upon the War on Poverty," *Law and Contemporary Problems* 31 (Winter 1966):152-158.

"Where Is the Negro Movement Today," *Dissent* 15 (November-December 1968):491-504. Conversation with Bayard Rustin, Tom Kahn, Paul Feldman, and Irving Howe.

White House Conference. *"To Fulfill These Rights," June 1-2, 1966.* Washington: U.S. Govt. Print. Off., 1966.

Wilson, Warner. "The Rank Order of Discrimination and Its Relevance to Civil Rights Priorities," *Proceedings of the American Psychological Association* 4, Pt. 1 (1969):307-308.

Woodward, C. Vann. "What Happened to the Civil Rights Movement," *Harper's* 234 (January 1967):29-37.

Zangrando, Robert L. "From Civil Rights to Black Liberation: The Unsettled 1960's," *Current History* 57 (November 1969):281-286 + .

See also Urban Problems—Race Violence and Riots.

Response and Resistance

Alexander, Charles C. *The Ku Klux Klan in the Southwest.* Lexington: University of Kentucky Press, 1965. The author contends that the "distinctive quality of the Klan . . . lay not so much in racism and nativism as in moral authoritarianism," a thesis hardly borne out by facts he himself brings forth.

American Friends Service Committee of the Society of American Friends, Southern Office. *Intimidation, Reprisal, and Violence in the South's Racial Crisis.* Atlanta: Southern Regional Council, 1959. 530 cases between January 1, 1955, and January 1, 1959.

Ashmore, Harry S. *The Other Side of Jordan.* New York: Norton, 1960.

Bachrach, Arthur J., and Gordon W. Blackwell, eds. "Human Problems in the Changing South," *Journal of Social Issues* 10 (January 1954):1-43. Entire issue.

Bartley, Numan V. *The Rise of Massive Resistance: Race and Politics in the South during the 1950's.* Baton Rouge: Louisiana State University Press, 1969.

Beach, Waldo. "The Changing Mind of the South," *Christianity and Crisis* 22 (July 9, 1962):119-122.

Bernard, Raymond. "Calm Voices in the South," *Social Order* 8 (February 1958):74-84.

Summaries of works on segregation and integration in the South as evidence that Southern writers are speaking out.

Boyle, Sarah Patton. *The Desegregated Heart.* New York: Morrow, 1962. Account by a Southern woman of what it means actively to work for desegregation in the South.

Boyle, Sarah Patton. *For Human Beings Only: A Primer of Human Understanding.* New York: Seabury, 1964.

Cahill, Edward. "The Changing South: Revolution or Reconciliation," *Phylon* 19 (Summer 1958):199-207.

Caldwell, Erskine. "The Deep South's Other Venerable Tradition," *New York Times Magazine,* July 11, 1965, pp. 10-11 + . Extent to which cruelty and violence are indigenous characteristics of the Deep South.

Canzoneri, Robert. *"I Do So Politely": A Voice From the South.* Boston: Houghton Mifflin, 1965. A Mississippian, cousin of Ross Barnett, attacks the closed society.

Carter, Hodding. *First Person Plural.* Garden City, N.Y.: Doubleday, 1963. Author, editor-publisher of the *Delta Democrat-Times,* Greenville, Miss., is saddened by the path the South has taken.

Carter, Hodding. *So the Heffners Left McComb.* Garden City, N.Y.: Doubleday, 1965.

Carter, Hodding. *The South Strikes Back.* Garden City, N.Y.: Doubleday, 1959. Through the White Citizens' Councils.

Carter, Hodding. *Southern Legacy.* Baton Rouge: Louisiana State University Press, 1950.

Cave, Clarence L. "A Creative Response to Racism," *Social Progress* 57 (March-April 1967):26-32. Proposed remedies for civil rights inequities.

Chalmers, David M. *Hooded Americanism: The First Century of the Ku Klux Klan, 1865 to the Present.* Garden City, N.Y.: Doubleday, 1965.

Cook, James Graham. *The Segregationists.* New York: Appleton, 1962. Impressionistic interviews with a variety of Southern segregationists, white and Negro, and descriptions of various organizations combating integration.

Cook, Samuel DuBois. "Political Movements and Organizations," *Journal of Politics* 26 (February 1964):130-153. The 1950's and the organization of support for the status quo.

Cramer, M. Richard. "School Desegregation and New Industry: The Southern Community Leaders' Viewpoint," *Social Forces* 41 (May 1963):384-389.

Dabbs, James McBride. "The Myth, the Movement, and the American Dream," *New South* 18 (December 1963):3-9. Presidential address to Southern Regional Council.

Dabbs, James McBride. *The Southern Heritage.* New York: Knopf, 1958. The author examines the roots of segregation in the past and the present, the fears and the economic and political reasons for the persistence of white supremacy.

Dabbs, James McBride. "To Define Our Love," *New South* 17 (November-December 1962):3-9. Presidential address to Southern Regional Council.

Dabbs, James McBride. *Who Speaks for the South?* New York: Funk & Wagnalls, 1964. The author's purpose: to discover and explain the "Southern type." While the Negro does not enter the story prominently until toward the end, Mr. Dabbs calls on the white South to recognize and accept the Negro in his new role.

Daniels, Frank. "Speak Out Strongly," *New South* 13 (January 1958):3-10. The vice-president of the Charlottesville, Virginia, Council on Human Relations speaks out at Sweet Briar College against economic discrimination, irrational fear, and hysterical notions about miscegenation and intermarriage.

Danzig, David. "Rightists, Racists, and Separatists: A White Bloc in the Making?" *Commentary* 38 (August 1964):28-32.

Deutsch, Martin, and Kay Steele. "Attitude Dissonances among Southville's Influentials," *Journal of Social Issues* 15 (October 1959):44-52. A secondary study based on the Southville investigations (see Johann Galtung), the "influentials" being upper- and middle-class individuals, spokesmen for the community and leaders in organizing private schools. Some cracks in the segregationists' armor are perceived.

Dugger, Ronnie. "Filibusters and Majority Rule," *Progressive* 21 (August 1957):21-22. In Texas, liberals use filibuster to aid Negro.

Dunbar, Leslie W. "The Changing Mind of the South: The Exposed Nerve," *Journal of Politics* 26 (February 1964):3-21.

Dykeman, Wilma, and James Stokely. "The Klan Tries a Comeback: In the Wake of Desegregation," *Commentary* 29 (January 1960):45-51.

Dykeman, Wilma, and James Stokely. "McCarthyism Under the Magnolias," *Progressive* 23 (July 1959):6-10.

Dykeman, Wilma, and James Stokely. *Neither Black Nor White.* New York: Rinehart, 1957. Account of trip taken after 1954 through the South by two former Southerners.

Dykeman, Wilma, and James Stokely. *Seeds of Southern Change: The Life of Will Alexander.* Foreword by Alexander Heard. Chicago: University of Chicago Press, 1962. The career and influence of a white champion of the Negro cause in the South from 1915 to 1954.

Dykeman, Wilma. "Two Faces of the South," *Current History* 35 (November 1958):257-261.

East, P. D. *The Magnolia Jungle.* New York: Simon & Schuster, 1960. A well-written autobiographical sketch by a Mississippi newspaper editor who, aroused by the injustices around him, became an ardent anti-segregationist and critic of Southern bigotry.

Eddy, Mrs. George A. "Alexandria, Va., Council on Human Relations Seeks Improved Race Relations," *New South* 16 (June 1961):6-12.

Ernst, Harry W. "West Virginia Press Sets Good Example," *New South* 13 (September 1958):3-8. Responsibility of mass media in freeing American psyche from prejudice, and what some editors have already done.

Faulkner, William. "American Segregation and the World Crisis," in *Three Views of the Segregation Decisions.* Atlanta: Southern Regional Council, 1956.

Fleming, Harold C. "Resistance Movements and Racial Desegregation," *Annals of the American Academy of Political and Social Science* 304 (March 1956):44-52.

Fleming, Harold C. "The South and Segregation: Where Do We Stand?" *Progressive* 22 (February 1958):12-14.

Fowler, Grady. "Southern White Citizens and the Supreme Court," *Phylon* 18 (Spring 1957):59-68.

Galtung, Johann. "A Model for Studying Images of Participants in a Conflict: Southville," *Journal of Social Issues* 15 (October 1959):38-43. Study of a typical Southern community which actively resisted 1954 Supreme Court decision, designed to determine what kinds of images each of three groups (segregationists, integrationists, Negroes) has of the other groups.

Gilbert, Arthur. "Violence and Intimidation in the South," *Social Order* 10 (December 1960):450-456. Relationship between prejudice against Negroes and anti-Semitism.

Glenn, Norval D. "The Role of White Resistance and Facilitation in the Negro Struggle for Equality," *Phylon* 26 (Spring 1965):105-116.

Good, Paul. "Birmingham Two Years Later," *The Reporter* 33 (December 2, 1965):21-27.

Good, Paul. "Klan Town, U.S.A.," *Nation* 200 (February 1, 1965):110-112. On Bogalusa, Louisiana.

Goodwyn, Larry. "Anarchy in St. Augustine," *Harper's* 230 (January 1965):74-81.

Guzman, Jessie P., ed. *Race Relations in the South—1963.* Tuskegee, Ala.: Tuskegee Institute, March 12, 1964. A report covering legal action on the federal, state, and local levels in the areas of education, employment, recreation, registration and voting, transportation, public accommodations. Provides data on compliance and noncompliance, on voluntary group action, and on violence.

Hayden, Tom. "The Power of Dixiecrats," *New University Thought* 3 (December 1963-January 1964):6-16.

Hays, Brooks. *A Southern Moderate Speaks.* Chapel Hill: University of North Carolina Press, 1959. By a moderate Arkansas Congressman who was defeated by an extreme segregationist in the wake of Little Rock.

Heard, Eliza (pseud.). "In the Name of Southern Womanhood," *New South* 17 (November-December 1962):16-18. By a white woman ashamed of what has been done in her name.

Heer, David M. "The Sentiment of White Supremacy: An Ecological Study," *American Journal of Sociology* 64 (May 1959):592-598.

Heller, Ben I. "My Brother's Brother," *New South* 15 (July-August 1960):9-11.

Hill, Haywood N. "This I Believe," *New South* 16 (April 1961):7-10. White Southerner who feels that he must live by his conviction and conscience (Christian and scientific) rather than by his preferences and prejudices.

"A Hundred Years Later," *New South* (July-August 1962):entire issue. Articles by James McBride Dabbs, Frank P. Graham, Paul Green, Benjamin E. Mays, James Stokely, Marion A. Wright.

Hyman, Herbert H., and P. B. Sheatsley. "Attitudes toward Desegregation," *Scientific American* 195 (December 1956):35-39. Attitudes of white Southerners, and degree to which change has taken place.

Jennings, M. Kent. *Community Influentials: The Elites of Atlanta.* New York: Free Press, 1964. A study seeking to discover patterns of political influence in what is regarded as a progressive Southern community.

Jewell, Malcolm. "State Legislatures in Southern Politics," *Journal of Politics* 26 (February 1964):177-196.

Johnson, Haynes. "Money and Mississippi," *Progressive* 29 (May 1965):21-23. Economic interests and the impact of U.S. Civil Rights Commission hearings as instruments of change.

Johnson, Manning. *Color, Communism and Common Sense.* New York: Alliance, 1958. With a foreword by Archibald B. Roosevelt. A representative example of right-wing extremist, states-rights indictments of the "communist" inspiration of the Negro drive to obtain the franchise.

Jones, Lewis W. *Cold Rebellion: The South's Oligarchy in Revolt.* London: MacGibbon & Kee, 1962. On Southern rebels who participate in the federal government "while ruling their domain as an oligarchy—irresponsible to federal authority and contemptuous of federal law."

Jones, W. B. "I Speak for the White Race," *Alabama Lawyer* 18 (April 1957):201-203.

Killian, Lewis M., and Charles M. Grigg. "The Bi-Racial Committee as a Response to Racial Tensions in Southern Cities," *Phylon* 23 (Winter 1962):379-382.

Killian, Lewis M. "Consensus in the Changing South," *Phylon* 18 (Summer 1957):107-117.

Kilpatrick, James Jackson. *The Sovereign States: Notes of a Citizen of Virginia.* Chicago: Regnery, 1957. A Southern view by the editor of the Richmond *News Leader.*

Laue, James H. "The Movement, Negro Challenge to the Myth," *New South* 18 (July-August 1963):9-17. The myth being that of a benevolent South.

Lerche, Charles O., Jr. *The Uncertain South: Its Changing Patterns of Politics in Foreign Policy.* Chicago: Quadrangle, 1964. See especially chapters 5, 7, and 8 for exposition of ways in which political demagogues have exploited poor whites' hatred of Negroes as growing urbanization has exacerbated racial animosities and heightened competition for jobs.

Levy, Charles J. "Deterrents to Militancy," *Race* 5 (January 1964):20-29. Study of segregationist militant in Virginia.

Long, Margaret. "A Southern Teen-Ager Speaks His Mind," *New York Times Magazine,* November 10, 1963, p. 15 +. Extreme white-supremacist attitude of a young student.

Long, N. E. "Local Leadership and the Crisis in Race Relations," *Public Management* 46 (January 1964):2-6.

Lustig, Norman I. "The Relationships between Demographic Characteristics and Pro-Integration Vote of White Precincts in a Metropolitan Southern Community," *Social Forces* 40 (March 1962):205-208.

McGill, Ralph. *The South and the Southerner.* Boston: Little, Brown, 1963. Closes with plea for compliance with Supreme Court decisions.

McIntyre, William R. "Spread of Terrorism and Hatemongering," *Editorial Research Reports,* December 3, 1958, pp. 893-911.

McLean, George A. "Mississippi: The Crisis in Review," *South Atlantic Quarterly* 65 (Spring 1966):279-288.

McMillan, George. *Racial Violence and Law Enforcement.* Atlanta: Southern Regional

Council, November 1960. Pamphlet on violence in Chattanooga, Montgomery, and Little Rock.

Malev, William S. "The Jew of the South in Conflict on Segregation," *Conservative Judaism* 13 (Fall 1958):33–46. Strategy considerations for Jewish community.

Manderson, Marge. "A Solid South . . . Or Else," *New South* 15 (April 1960):3–11. The aims of Southern segregationists.

Margolis, Joseph. "The Role of the Segregationist," *New South* 13 (February 1958):7–11. He plays many roles, among them the military hero, the knightly crusader, the martyr, but he always casts the Negro in the same role.

Marion, John H. "Behind Dixie's Gentler Standpatters," *Christian Century* 79 (October 24, 1962):1288–1290. Southern gentry at bay.

Martin, John Bartlow. *The Deep South Says "Never."* New York: Ballantine, 1957.

Matthews, Donald R., and James W. Prothro. "Southern Racial Attitudes: Conflict, Awareness, and Political Change," *Annals of the American Academy of Political and Social Science* 344 (November 1962):108–121.

Mayer, Milton. "Deep in the Heart," *Progressive* 21 (July 1957):12–14. Story of confrontation with White Citizens' Council in Texas.

"Mississippi," *New South* 17 (October 1962):3 + . Entire issue.

"Mississippi Eyewitness," *Ramparts.* Special issue, 1964. On the three civil rights workers, Andrew Goodman, James Chaney, and Michael Schwerner, and how they were murdered.

Morgan, Charles, Jr. *A Time to Speak.* New York: Harper, 1964. The author indicts all the good, respectable white citizens of Birmingham, Alabama, who bear, he says, the responsibility for the acts of violent men, and in particular for the bombing of Negro children in church.

Morgan, Charles, Jr. "Who is Guilty in Birmingham," *Christian Century* 80 (October 2, 1963):1195–1196. Local lawyer's speech at Young Men's Business Club after bombing church Sunday School.

Morsell, John A. "Legal Opposition to Desegregation: Its Significance for Intergroup Agencies in the Years Ahead," *Journal of Intergroup Relations* 1 (Winter 1959–1960):68–75.

Muse, Benjamin. *Virginia's Massive Resistance.* Bloomington: Indiana University Press, 1961. State legislative and executive action to preserve segregated schools.

Newby, I. A. *Challenge to the Court: Social Scientists and the Defense of Segregation, 1954–1966.* 1967. 2d ed. Baton Rouge: Louisiana State University Press, 1969. Explores the recent literature of scientific racism. Includes essays of rebuttal by A. James Gregor, R. T. Osborne, and others.

Nolen, Claude. *The Negro's Image in the South: The Anatomy of White Supremacy.* Lexington: University of Kentucky Press, 1967.

Norris, Hoke, ed. *We Dissent.* New York: St. Martin's, 1962. Articles by white Protestant Southerners designed "to give voice to the opposition in the South" and to restore a balance in the nation's one-sided view of the South.

Opotowsky, Stan. "Silence in the South," *Progressive* 21 (August 1957):10–12. No word from the moderates.

Pannell, William E. *My Friend, the Enemy.* Waco: Word Books, 1968. Angry, open expression of a Negro looking at unchristian responses of white society.

Parenti, Michael. "White Anxiety and the Negro Revolt," *New Politics* 3 (Winter 1964): 35–39.

Perlmutter, Nathan. "Bombing in Miami: Anti-Semitism and the Segregationists," *Commentary* 25 (June 1958):498–503.

Peters, William. *The Southern Temper.* Garden City, N.Y.: Doubleday, 1959. A study of the "second South"—the people who are either indifferent to integration or who are actively trying to bring it about.

Pittman, R. Carter. "Equality versus Liberty: The Eternal Conflict," *American Bar Association Journal* 46 (August 1960):873–880. Georgia lawyer considers "equality" as a Marxist "tool."

Piven, Frances Fox, and Richard A. Cloward. "The Case Against Urban Desegregation," *Social Work* 12 (January 1967):12–21. Say the authors: "Although efforts at integration have produced significant gains in some areas, they have worked against the interests of the urban Negro poor in housing and education."

Polk, William Tarnahill. *Southern Accent: From Uncle Remus to Oak Ridge.* New York: Morrow, 1953. A Southerner's attempt to describe the modern South, compounded of the "surviving South" and the industrialized South, and its dilemma as between the ideal of equality and the ideal of excellence.

Powledge, Fred. *Black Power, White Resistance: Notes on the New Civil War.* Cleveland: World, 1967. Views of race relations in both North and South by a white Southern reporter.

Prothro, Edwin Terry. "Social Psychology of the South, Challenge without Response," *Journal of Social Issues* 10 (January 1954):36–43.

Quint, Howard H. *Profile in Black and White: A Frank Portrait of South Carolina.* Washington: Public Affairs Press, 1959. White Southerners were permitted, by the year's delay in implementation order for 1954 decision, to gather their forces to fight integration.

Randel, William Peirce. *The Ku Klux Klan: A Century of Infamy.* Philadelphia: Chilton, 1965.

Ransome, Coleman B., Jr. "Political Leadership in the Governor's Office," *Journal of Politics* 26 (February 1964):197–220. In the Southern states.

Record, Jane Cassels. "The Red-Tagging of Negro Protest," *American Scholar* 26 (Summer 1957):325–333.

Rice, Arnold S. *The Ku Klux Klan in American Politics.* Washington: Public Affairs Press, 1962.

Rose, Arnold M. "The Course of the South: Descent into Barbarism?" *Commentary* 27 (June 1959):495–499.

Ross, Jack C., and Raymond Wheeler. "Structural Sources of Threat to Negro Membership in Militant Voluntary Associations in a Southern City," *Social Forces* 45 (June 1967): 583–586.

Rubin, Louis D., Jr., and James Jackson Kilpatrick. *The Lasting South.* Chicago: Regnery, 1957.

Samet, Elaine R. "Quiet Revolution in Miami," *Progressive* 29 (April 1965):34–37.

Secrest, A. M. "Moderation Is Key to South's Dilemma," *New South* 15 (February 1960):3–8.

Shaffer, Helen B. "Changing South," *Editorial Research Reports,* June 10, 1959, pp. 423–440. Economic and population changes and the South's resistance.

Shaffer, Helen B. "Violence and Non-Violence in American Race Relations," *Editorial Research Reports,* March 25, 1960, pp. 221–238.

Sherrill, Robert. "Portrait of a 'Southern Liberal' in Trouble," *New York Times Magazine,* November 7, 1965, pp. 46–47+. On Senator John Sparkman of Alabama, his "liberal" record in Congress, and what his chances would be were then Governor George C. Wallace to contest his reelection to the Senate.

Silver, James W. *Mississippi: The Closed Society.* 1964. New enl. ed. New York: Harcourt, Brace, 1966. Includes a new section entitled "Revolution Begins in the Closed Society."

Simkins, Francis Butler. *The Everlasting South.* Baton Rouge: Louisiana State University Press, 1963. Five essays on the position of Southern states.

Sisson, John P. "A Southern City Changes Gracefully: Pensacola Pattern," *Interracial Review* 36 (May 1963):98–100. The moral being that if local leaders take realistic steps toward granting Negro demands, there will be no crisis.

Smith, Frank E. *Congressman from Mississippi.* New York: Pantheon, 1964. Autobiography of a "moderate" Congressman defeated after 12 years by a fanatical white-supremacist. He rather disingenuously justifies his own earlier failure to speak out on the grounds that "as a condition of holding my office, I made obeisance to the Southern way of life."

Smith, Frank E. *Look Away from Dixie.* Baton Rouge: Louisiana State University Press, 1965. Describes the corrosive effect of racism on Southern life.

Smith, Frank E. "Valor's Second Prize: Southern Racism and Internationalism," *South Atlantic Quarterly* 64 (Summer 1965):296-303.

Smith, Lillian. *Killers of the Dream.* New York: Norton, 1949. Author shows, with great insight, the costs to both white and Negro Southerners of the pattern of segregation, deprivation, guilt and fear, especially in the stultification of white lives.

Smith, Lillian. "The South's Moment of Truth," *Progressive* 24 (September 1960):32-35.

Smith, Lillian. "Words That Chain Us and Words That Set Us Free," *New South* 17 (March 1962):3-12. Semantic journey in the South.

"South Increases Propaganda," *New South* 14 (May 1959):3-7. The propaganda campaign being waged by white supremacists.

"Southern Bombings," *New South* 18 (May 1963):8-11. Tabulation of bombings from January 1, 1956, to June 1, 1963.

Southern Regional Council and American Jewish Committee. *The Continuing Crisis: An Assessment of New Racial Tensions in the South.* Atlanta: Southern Regional Council, 1966. Includes an extensive section on acts of raw intimidation and violence against Negroes for a six months period preceding February 1966.

"The Southern Regional Council, 1944-1964," *New South* 19 (January 1964):1-22. Review of twenty years' work.

"Southerners Look at Desegregation," *Antioch Review* 14 (Winter 1954):387-557. Entire issue.

Spearman, Walter, and Sylvan Myer. *Racial Crisis and the Press.* Atlanta: Southern Regional Council, 1960. Analysis of treatment of racial news by the press.

Starrs, James E. "Southern Juvenile Courts: A Study of Irony, Civil Rights, and Judicial Practice," *Crime and Delinquency* 13 (April 1967):289-306. Discusses the juvenile court as an instrument of segregation.

Three Views of the Segregation Decisions. Atlanta: Southern Regional Council, 1956.

Tindall, George B. "The Benighted South: Origins of a Modern Myth," *Virginia Quarterly* 40 (Spring 1964):281-294.

Tucker, Shirley. *Mississippi from Within.* New York: Arco, 1965. An analysis of 5,000 issues of 20 Mississippi newspapers between July 2, 1964, and May 1965, to show local response to Civil Rights Act of 1964.

Tyre, Nedra. "The Diligent Knitters of Southern Sanity," *New South* 17 (February 1962): 3-5+, How Southerners of good will can become "knitters" of accord.

Vander Zanden, James W. "Accommodation to Undesired Change: The Case of the South," *Journal of Negro Education* 31 (Winter 1962):30-35.

Vander Zanden, James W. "Desegregation and Social Strains in the South," *Journal of Social Issues* 15 (October 1959):53-60.

Vander Zanden, James W. "The Klan Revival," *American Journal of Sociology* 65 (March 1960):456-462.

Vander Zanden, James W. "Turmoil in the South," *Journal of Negro Education* 29 (Fall 1960):445-452.

Vander Zanden, James W. "Voting on Segregationist Referenda," *Public Opinion Quarterly* 25 (Spring 1961):92-105. Analysis of voting in 15 Southern communities: points to lack of simple evidence of correlation of class and attitudes, and presents evidence contradictory to the usual hypothesis that there is an inverse relation between socioeconomic class and affirmation of segregationism.

Vandiver, Frank E., ed. *The Idea of the South: Pursuit of a Central Theme.* Chicago: University of Chicago Press, 1964. In his own essay, "The Southerner as Extremist," the editor explains the South's reaction to the 1954 Supreme Court decision as "defensive." Northerners can help by not openly provoking Southern resentments and "defenses."

Vanfossen, Beth E. "Variables Related to Resistance to Desegregation in the South," *Social Forces* 47 (September 1968):39-44. Basic economic and social factors related to the percentage of black students in schools with white pupils. See also commentary in *Transaction* 6 (July-August 1969):3.

Waring, Thomas R. "The Southern Case against Desegregation," *Harper's* 212 (January 1956):39-45.

Warner, Bob. "The Southern Press: Violence and the News," *Editor and Publisher* 94 (June 24, 1961):25.

Warner, Bob. "The Southern Story: Omens in Alabama: Editors Resentful of Northern Attention," *Editor and Publisher* 94 (June 17, 1961):24.

Warren, Robert Penn. *Segregation: The Inner Conflict in the South.* New York: Random, 1956. The conflict is brilliantly presented through conversations with both Negroes and whites.

Weeks, O. Douglas. "The South in National Politics," *Journal of Politics* 26 (February 1964):221-240.

Weltner, Charles Longstreet. *Southerner.* Philadelphia: Lippincott, 1966. An encouraging commentary of a white racial liberal congressman from the fifth Georgia district.

"White Americans and Civil Rights," *Political Affairs* 43 (May 1964):1-6.

Witherspoon, Joseph P. *Administrative Implementation of Civil Rights.* Austin: University of Texas, 1966. The response at various governmental levels to the needs of Negroes and other minority groups.

Woodward, C. Vann. "The South and the Law of the Land: The Present Resistance and Its Prospects," *Commentary* 26 (November 1958):369-374.

Woodward, C. Vann. "The South in Perspective," *Progressive* 26 (December 1962):12-17.

Woofter, Thomas J. *Southern Race Progress: The Wavering Color Line.* Washington: Public Affairs Press, 1957. Substantively a plea for good will and cooperation.

Workman, William D. *The Case for the South.* New York: Devin-Adair, 1960. A white Southerner presents his case for "separate but equal" based on the "unique character" of the South.

Wright, Marion A. "Integration and Public Morals," *New South* 12 (November 1957):7-14. On author's retirement as president of Southern Regional Council.

Wynes, Charles E. *Forgotten Voices: Dissenting Southerners in an Age of Conformity.* Baton Rouge: Louisiana State University Press, 1967.

Zinn, Howard. *The Southern Mystique.* New York: Knopf, 1964. After presenting the lineaments of the white Southerner, with every trait of prejudice, violence, racial intolerance, the author reminds the reader these traits are also present in the North, that they are not instinctive and unchangeable. Not only can they be changed; they have been changing.

The Role of the Churches

General

Abbott, Walter M. "The Bible Abused," *Interracial Review* 36 (February 1963):26-27 +. By white Catholics who resisted school desegregation.

Ahmann, Mathew, and Margaret Roach, eds. *The Church and the Urban Crisis.* Techny, Ill.: Divine Word Publications, 1967. Addresses and background papers of the National Catholic Conference for Interracial Justice, August 1967. Contributors include: Robert F. Kennedy, Meyer Weinberg, Vivian Henderson.

Ahmann, Mathew, ed. *Race: Challenge to Religion.* Chicago: Regnery, 1963. Essays deriving from a meeting of the National Conference on Religion and Race.

Alexander, W. W. *Racial Segregation in the American Protestant Church.* New York: Friendship, 1946.

American Friends Service Committee of the Society of American Friends. *Race and Conscience in America.* Norman: University of Oklahoma Press, 1959.

Ball, William B. "New Frontiers of Catholic Community Action," *Interracial Review* 35 (February 1962):49-51.

Barbour, Russell, B. *Black and White Together: Plain Talk for White Christians.* Philadelphia: United Church Press, 1967. Bibliography.

Barry, James T., and James J. Vanecko. "White Priest, Black Ghetto," *New City* 6 (July 1968):14–18. Need for the whole Church to understand and support the priest as a link to the ghetto community. The work of the inner city clergy needs to be considered as part of the metropolitan Church.

Bell, John L. "The Presbyterian Church and the Negro in North Carolina," *North Carolina Historical Review* 40 (January 1963):15–36. A study of how racial segregation was established in the Presbyterian churches in North Carolina.

Bernard, Raymond. "Some Anthropological Implications of the Racial Admission Policy of the U.S. Sisterhoods," *American Catholic Sociological Review* 19 (June 1958):124–135.

Berrigan, Philip. *No More Strangers.* New York: Macmillan, 1965. A Jesuit priest presents arguments for the Christian obligation to commit oneself to the struggle for racial justice.

"Black Life in Church and Society," *Social Progress* 60 (September–October 1969):3–47. Entire issue.

Boyd, Malcolm. "Black Voice, White Voice," *Christianity and Crisis* 27 (October 16, 1967):236–239.

Boyd, Malcolm, ed. *On the Battle Lines.* New York: Morehouse-Barlow, 1964. Challenge to Christians by 27 clergymen.

Brown, Aubrey N., Jr. "Presbyterians, U.S.: En Route to Broader Concerns," *Christian Century* 80 (December 18, 1963):1577–1580.

Campbell, Will D. *Race and Renewal of the Church.* Philadelphia: Westminster, 1962. The author, director of the Committee of Southern Churchmen, charges that the church "has waited too long to carry out its mandate, and to a large part of the world, what we Christians do from here on out really does not matter very much."

"The Church's Teaching on Race," *America* 115 (December 3, 1966):730–731.

Clark, Henry. "Churchmen and Residential Segregation," *Review of Religious Research* 5 (Spring 1964):157–164.

Cogley, John. "The Clergy Heeds a New Call," *New York Times Magazine,* May 2, 1965, pp. 42–43 +. On the Selma, Alabama march and its role in the growing involvement of church leaders in the civil rights movement.

Communism, Christianity and Race Relations. Valparaiso, Ind.: Lutheran Human Relations Association of America, 1960. Report of twelfth annual Valparaiso University Institute on Human Relations.

Congar, Yves M. J. *The Catholic Church and the Race Question.* Paris: UNESCO, 1953.

Creger, Ralph, with Erwin McDonald. *A Look Down the Lonesome Road.* Garden City, N.Y.: Doubleday, 1964. A fundamentalist Baptist attempts to offer a "Christian solution" to the moral problem of integration.

Crook, Roger H. *No South or North.* St. Louis, Mo.: Bethany, 1959. A Southern white Christian who favors integration raises and answers various arguments used to justify segregation and relates the question of race relations to the demands of Christian faith.

Culver, Dwight W. *Negro Segregation in the Methodist Church.* New Haven: Yale University Press, 1953.

"Discrimination and the Christian Conscience," *Journal of Negro Education* 28 (Winter 1959):66–69. Position of Catholic bishops in the United States.

Egan, John J. "Compassion and Community Life," *Interracial Review* 35 (March 1962): 66–69.

Fey, Harold E. "Churches Meet Racial Crisis," *Christian Century* 80 (December 18, 1963):1572–1573. Statement of General Assembly of National Council of Churches on civil rights.

Fey, Harold E. "Disciples on Civil Rights," *Christian Century* 80 (October 30, 1963): 1326–1327. Disciples of Christ Convention.

Fey, Harold E. "N.C.C. Acts on Racial Crisis," *Christian Century* 80 (June 19, 1963): 1602–1604. Action taken by General Board of National Council of Churches.

Fey, Harold E. "Reconciliation in Rochester," *Christian Century* 80 (September 18, 1963): 1125–1127. World Council of Churches meets and discusses racial issues.

Fichter, Joseph H. "American Religion and the Negro," *Daedalus* 94 (Fall 1965):1085–1106.

The author finds that "this test of America's religious ideology has resulted . . . in the deliberate moral impact of religious leaders on the extra-church institutions of the American culture."

Fichter, Joseph. "Negro Spirituals and Catholicism," *Interracial Review* 35 (September 1962):200–203. "In inquiring thoroughly into the spirituals, we find that both in form and content they can stand comparison with the Hebrew psalms." They have not been put "sufficiently to Catholic use."

Fish, John H. "A New Role for the Church in the Urban Ghetto," *Lutheran Quarterly* 19 (November 1967):385–396.

Fitzpatrick, Joseph P. "The Dynamics of Change," *Interracial Review* 35 (January 1962):7–9. The parish and social change.

Foley, Albert S. *God's Men of Color.* New York: Farrar, Straus, 1955. Negro priests in the Catholic Church.

Fry, John K. "United Presbyterians: Prophecy vs. Tradition," *Christian Century* 80 (October 9, 1963):1235–1237. Some notes on new tendencies, including those in race relations.

Gallagher, Buell. *Color and Conscience: The Irrepressible Conflict.* New York: Harper, 1946. Race relations in terms of the moral dilemma between the "color caste" system and ethical notions of Christianity, brotherhood, and justice.

Gasnick, Roy M. "Franciscan Pledge to Interracial Justice," *Social Order* 12 (April 1962):173–177. Action for Interracial Understanding, the interracial movement founded by the Third Order of St. Francis.

Gillard, John T. *The Catholic Church and the Negro.* Baltimore: St. Joseph's Society Press, 1929.

Gillespie, G. T. *A Christian View on Segregation.* Greenwood, Miss.: Association of Citizens' Councils of Mississippi, n.d.

Gleason, Robert W. "Immortality of Segregation," *Thought* 35 (Autumn 1960):138. Chairman of Departments of Theology and Religious Education, Fordham University, considers the theological aspects of segregation.

Greeley, Andrew M. "White Parish—Refuge or Resource," *Interracial Review* 35 (July 1962):168–169.

Hadden, Jeffrey K. *The Gathering Storm in the Churches.* Garden City, N.Y.: Doubleday, 1969. Role of the clergy in the civil rights struggle.

Harte, Thomas J. *Catholic Organizations Promoting Negro-White Race Relations in the United States.* Washington: Catholic University Press, 1947. An extensive survey of organizations, objectives, and activities of five types of voluntary Catholic groups for promoting better race relations.

Haseldon, Kyle. *Mandate for White Christians.* Richmond: John Knox Press, 1966.

Haselden, Kyle. "Religion and Race," *Christian Century* 80 (January 30, 1963):133–135.

Holden, Anna. "A Call to Catholics," *Interracial Review* 35 (June 1962):140–143. To participate in nonviolent direct action movement.

Holmes, Thomas J., with Gainer E. Bryan, Jr. *Ashes for Breakfast: A Diary of Racism in an American Church.* Valley Forge, Penna.: Judson Press, 1969. Author is a Southern Baptist minister.

Hood, Robert E. *The Placement and Deployment of Negro Clergy in the Episcopal Church.* Atlanta: Episcopal Society for Cultural and Racial Unity, 1967.

Horchler, Richard. "The Layman's Role in the Changing Community," *Interracial Review* 35 (January 1962):12–13.

Howlett, Duncan. *No Greater Love: The James Reeb Story.* New York: Harper & Row, 1966.

Huckaby, Phillip. "The Black Identity Crisis," *Theology Today* 24 (January 1968):498–506. Discusses ways in which the Church can assist the Negro in gaining equal status in a pluralist society.

Hunt, Lawrence E. "A Lutheran in Black America: The View from Here," *Lutheran Quarterly* 20 (May 1968):111–120.

Hunton, George K. *All of Which I Saw, Part of Which I Was: The Autobiography of George K. Hunton as Told to Gary MacEóin.* Garden City, N.Y.: Doubleday, 1967. Describes the development of the Catholic Interracial Council and its contributions toward racial justice.

Hurley, Denis E. "Second Vatican and Racism," *Interracial Review* 36 (December 1963):11.

Hurley, Phillip S. "Role of the Churches in Integration," *Journal of Intergroup Relations* 1 (Summer 1960):41-46.

Jones, Howard O. *Shall We Overcome? A Challenge to Negro and White Christians.* Westwood, N.J.: F. H. Revell, 1966. The Negro Church.

Kean, Charles D. "District of Columbia," *Christian Century* 80 (May 29, 1963):725-726. Christians and Negroes in the capital.

Kean, Charles D. "For Law and Integration," *Christian Century* 75 (November 5, 1958): 1262-1263. Integration and the Protestant Episcopal Church.

Kelsey, George D. *Racism and the Christian Understanding of Man.* New York: Scribners, 1965.

Kenealy, William J. "Racism Desecrates Liberty, Perverts Justice and Love," *Social Order* 13 (May 1963):5-20. By professor of law, Loyola University, Chicago.

Kitagawa, Daisuke. *The Pastor and the Race Issue.* New York: Seabury, 1965.

Kitagawa, Daisuke. *Race Relations and Christian Mission.* New York: Friendship, 1964.

Kramer, Alfred S. "Patterns of Racial Inclusion among the Churches of Three Protestant Denominations," *Phylon* 16 (Summer 1955):283-294.

Kruuse, Elsa. "The Churches Act on Integration," *National Council Outlook* 7 (March 1957):6-8.

La Farge, John. "American Catholics and the Negro, 1962," *Social Order* 12 (April 1962): 153-161.

La Farge, John. *The Catholic Viewpoint on Race Relations.* Garden City, N.Y.: Doubleday, 1956; 2d ed., Garden City, N.Y.: Hanover, 1960.

La Farge, John. "Direct Action," *Interracial Review* 36 (September 1963):159+. Admonitions addressed to Catholic employers of labor.

La Farge, John. "Pope John on Racism," *Interracial Review* 36 (June 1963):110-111+.

La Farge, John. *The Race Question and the Negro.* New York: Longmans, Green, 1943.

Lee, J. Oscar. "The Churches and Race Relations—A Survey," *Christianity and Crisis* 17 (February 4, 1957):4-7.

Liu, William T. "The Community Reference System, Religiosity, and Race Attitudes," *Social Forces* 39 (May 1961):324-328.

McManus, Eugene P. *Studies in Race Relations.* Baltimore: Josephite, 1961. Emphasis is on Christian principles rather than on sociological approaches to the problem.

McPeak, William. "Social Problems are Human Problems," *Interracial Review* 35 (November 1962):253-254.

Maston, T. B. *Segregation and Desegregation: A Christian Approach.* New York: Macmillan, 1959. Chiefly concerned with school desegregation.

Mather, P. Boyd. "Religion and Race: Local Efforts," *Christian Century* 80 (March 27, 1963):412-414. Strategy of National Conference on Religion and Race.

Mather, P. Boyd. "Search for Sufficiency," *Christian Century* 80 (September 18, 1963): 1139-1140. Methodist Church and its "Central" (Negro) jurisdiction.

Mays, Benjamin E. *Seeking To Be Christian in Race Relations.* New York: Friendship, 1957.

Mehan, Joseph. "Catholic Perspectives on Interracialism," *Interracial Review* 35 (October 1962):222-223.

Meyer, Sylvan. "They Share a Mission," *Christian Century* 79 (August 22, 1962):1103-1105. Church and press.

Miller, Robert M. *American Protestantism and Social Issues.* Chapel Hill: University of North Carolina Press, 1958.

Miller, William Robert. *Nonviolence: A Christian Interpretation.* New York: Association Press, 1965.

Mitchell, Henry H. "Toward the 'New' Integration," *Christian Century* 85 (June 12, 1968):780-782. Need for the white church to make additional efforts to relate to the black church.

Moellering, Ralph L. *Christian Conscience and Negro Emancipation.* Philadelphia: Fortress, 1965. The struggle for racial equality is examined within a historical and theological framework.

National Catholic Conference for Interracial Justice. "Statement and Resolutions adopted by Council Delegates in Convention, November 17, 1963, at Washington, D.C.," *Interracial Review* 37 (January 1964):1+.

National Conference on Religion and Race. *Religion's Role in Racial Crisis: A Report . . . and Recommendations for Action.* New York, 1963?

"New Trends in Race Relations: The Negro's Quest for Identity," *Social Progress* 57 (March–April 1967):3–47. Entire issue. Articles on the white church and search for black power and a creative response to racism.

Nichols, Lee, and Louis Cassels. "The Churches Repent," *Harper's* 211 (October 1955): 53–57.

Niebuhr, Reinhold. "The Crisis in American Protestantism," *Christian Century* 80 (December 4, 1963):1498–1501. Protestant churches must take a stand on issues of justice.

Northwood, Lawrence K. "Ecological and Attitudinal Factors in Church Desegregation," *Social Problems* 6 (Fall 1958):150–163.

O'Connor, John J. "Catholic Interracial Movement," *Social Order* 10 (September 1960): 290–295.

O'Neill, Joseph E., ed. *A Catholic Case Against Segregation.* New York: Macmillan, 1961.

Osborne, William. "The Church and the Negro: A Crisis in Leadership," *Cross Currents* 15 (September 1965):129–150.

Parker, James H. "The Interaction of Negroes and Whites in an Integrated Church Setting," *Social Forces* 46 (March 1968):359–366. Data collected about the first church at the American Baptist Convention to adopt a policy of racial integration.

"Pastoral Statement on Race Relations and Poverty," *Catholic Mind* 65 (February 1967): 59–62. Statement of U.S. Bishops.

Pettigrew, Thomas F. "The Myth of the Moderates," *Christian Century* 78 (May 24, 1961): 649–651.

Pettigrew, Thomas F. "Our Caste-Ridden Protestant Campuses," *Christianity and Crisis* 21 (May 29, 1961):88–91.

Pettigrew, Thomas F. "Wherein the Church Has Failed in Race," *Religious Education* 59 (January–February 1964):64–73.

Pohlhaus, J. Francis. "Catholic Involvement in Civil Rights Legislation," *Interracial Review* 36 (October 1963):192–195. Report by a NAACP leader.

Pope, Liston. *The Kingdom Beyond Caste.* New York: Friendship, 1957. A work of scholarship and conviction which examines racial prejudice in general and the forms it may take, particularly in the churches.

Posey, Walter B. "The Protestant Episcopal Church: An American Adaptation," *Journal of Southern History* 25 (February 1959):3–30.

Ramsey, Paul. *Christian Ethics and the Sit-In.* New York: Association Press, 1961.

Reimers, David M. "The Race Problem and Presbyterian Union," *Church History* 31 (June 1962):203–215. Bibliography.

Reimers, David M. *White Protestantism and the Negro.* New York: Oxford University Press, 1965. After an historical retrospect of white Protestantism's relation to the Negro, the author deals with the emergence of changing attitudes and with recent attempts to implement Christian commitments to end segregation.

Reuter, George S., Jr., August M. Hintz, and Helen H. Reuter. *One Blood.* New York: Exposition Press, 1964. On the Christian approach to civil rights.

Rose, Stephen C. "Student Interracial Ministry: A Break in the Wall," *Christian Century* 79 (March 14, 1962):327–328.

Sabourin, Clemonce. "The Lutheran Church Needs to Apply Word and Sacrament to the Problem of Changing the Racist Mind," *Lutheran Forum* 3 (April 1969):9–12.

Schneider, William J., ed. *The Jon Daniels Story: With His Letters and Papers.* New York: Seabury, 1968.

Schulze, Andrew. *Fire From the Throne: Race Relations in The Church.* St. Louis, Mo.: Concordia, 1968. A Christian theological view of white man's relation to the Negro.

Senn, Milton. "Race, Religion and Suburbia," *Journal of Intergroup Relations* 3 (Spring 1962):159-170.

Senser, Robert. *Primer on Interracial Justice.* Baltimore: Helicon, 1962. The Roman Catholic position.

"Statement of the National Conference of Catholic Bishops on the National Race Crisis," *The Pope Speaks* 13, no. 2 (1968):175-178.

Stotts, Herbert E., and Paul Deats. *Methodism and Society: Guidelines for Strategy.* Nashville, Tenn.: Abingdon, 1962. The last of a four-volume survey prepared for the Methodist Board of Social and Economic Relations.

Tanenbaum, Marc H. "The American Negro: Myths and Realities," *Religious Education* 59 (January-February 1964):33-36. Christian purpose should be that of "discovering a relationship between white man and Negro."

Thomas, Neil. "White Church and Black Business," *Commonweal* 90 (August 22, 1969): 503-504. The Black Affairs Council of the Unitarian-Universalist Association.

Thurman, Howard. *The Luminous Darkness: A Personal Interpretation of the Anatomy of Segregation and the Ground of Hope.* New York: Harper & Row, 1965.

Tilson, Everett. *Segregation and the Bible.* Nashville, Tenn.: Abingdon, 1958.

Trout, Nelson. "Meeting the Challenge of Urban Unrest," *Lutheran Quarterly* 20 (May 1968):136-143. Utilizing human resources of good will. One of a series of symposium articles on Lutherans in America.

United Church Board for Homeland Ministries. "Are 'Sanctions' Sub-Christian?" *Social Action* 30 (May 1964):12-16. End of moral and financial support of work that involves segregation.

"U.S. Bishops on Racial Harmony: Joint Pastoral," *Interracial Review* 36 (October 1963): 182-183. Issued August 1963.

Urban Crisis: A Symposium on the Racial Problem in the Inner City. Edited by David McKenna. Grand Rapids, Mich.: Zondervan, 1969. Papers presented at a seminar held at Spring Arbor College in January 1968.

Visser 't Hooft, W. A. *The Ecumenical Movement and the Racial Problem.* Paris: UNESCO, 1954.

Vorspan, Albert. "The Negro Victory—And the Jewish Failure," *American Judaism* 13 (Fall 1963): 7, 50-52 + .

Vorspan, Albert. "Segregation and Social Justice," *American Judaism* 7 (January 1958): 10-11.

Whitman, Frederick L. "Subdimensions of Religiosity and Race Prejudice," *Review of Religious Research* 3 (Spring 1962):166-174.

Wilmore, Gayraud S., Jr. "The New Negro and the Church," *Christian Century* 80 (February 6, 1963):168-171.

Wilson, Robert L., and James H. Davis. *The Church in a Racially Changing Community.* Nashville, Tenn.: Abingdon, 1966.

Wimberly, Fred. "My People and the Church," *Lutheran Quarterly* 20 (May 1968): 125-127. A Negro seminarian speaks to the American Lutheran Church on its role in race relations.

Wogaman, Philip. "Focus on Central Jurisdiction," *Christian Century* 80 (October 23, 1963):1296-1298. Methodist Negro section.

Wood, James R., and Mayer N. Zald. "Aspects of Racial Integration in the Methodist Church: Sources of Resistance to Organizational Policy," *Social Forces* 45 (December 1966):255-265.

Young, Andrew J. "Demonstrations: A Twentieth Century Christian Witness," *Social Action* 30 (May 1964):5-12.

North

"Cardinal McIntyre: A Ramparts Special Report," *Ramparts* 3 (November 1964):35-44.
  Three articles on the effect of Cardinal McIntyre's refusal to support racial equality in
  his southern California jurisdiction.
Cobb, Charles E. "Cincinnati Story: A Case Study of the Sixth General Synod of the Use of
  Moral Suasion and Economic Power of the Church," *Social Action* 34 (September
  1967):40-46. Case of Synod's success in removing job discrimination against a Negro
  hotel employee.
Ehle, John. *Shepherd of the Streets: The Story of the Reverend James A. Gusweller and His
  Crusade on the New York West Side.* New York: Sloane, 1960.
Fish, John. *The Edge of the Ghetto: A Study of Church Involvement in Community Organi-
  zation.* Chicago: Church Federation of Greater Chicago, 1966. Also issued in New York
  by Seabury Press.
Fry, John R. *Fire and Blackstone.* Philadelphia: Lippincott, 1969. The Blackstone Rangers.
Hadden, Jeffrey K. "Clergy Response to Urban Violence," *Dialog* 8 (Winter 1969):40-47.
  Attitudes of the clergymen of Grand Rapids to that city's riots in the summer of 1967;
  interpreted findings.
Herberg, Will. *Protestant, Catholic, Jew.* Garden City, N.Y.: Doubleday, 1955. Includes
  consideration of the Negro problem in Protestant churches in the city.
Jones, Madison. "On the Neighborhood Level," *Interracial Review* 35 (January 1962):22-23.
  Negroes and Catholics.
Lally, Francis J. "Needed—A People's Program," *Interracial Review* 35 (January 1962):2-3.
Loescher, F. S. "Racism in Northern City Churches," *Christian Century* 73 (February 8,
  1956):174-176.
Millea, Thomas V. *Ghetto Fever.* Milwaukee, Wis.: Bruce, 1968. Incisive look by a white
  priest into injustices of a Chicago west-side community, Lawndale, presented with his
  ecumenical "slum theology."
Mulholland, Joseph A. "The Community and Crime," *Interracial Review* 35 (January
  1962):18-19. Negroes and Catholics.
"Open or Closed Cities?" *Christian Century* 78 (May 10, 1961):579-580. Inaugurates controversy on role of the churches in Chicago segregation, continued by "Woodlawn—Open
  or Closed," *ibid.,* (May 31, 1961):685-688, and editorial rejoinder, *ibid.,* (June 7,
  1961):711.
Peerman, Dean. "Death Down a Dark Street," *Christian Century* 80 (February 6, 1963):
  166-167. Louis Cordell Marsh, a Christian youth worker, killed by a New York gang: an
  article written by a former classmate at Yale Divinity School.
Schiltz, Michael E. "Catholics and the Chicago Riots," *Commonweal* 85 (November 11,
  1966):159-163. Replies and rejoinder, *ibid.,* 85 (December 16, 1966):321-324.
Schuyler, Joseph B. "Apostolic Opportunity," *Interracial Review* 35 (January 1962):20-21.
Schuyler, Joseph B. *Northern Parish: A Sociological and Pastoral Study.* Chicago: Loyola
  University Press, 1960. Survey of a Bronx parish showed majority favoring racial
  equality.
Simms, David McD. "Ethnic Tensions in the 'Inner-City' Church," *Journal of Negro Edu-
  cation* 31 (Fall 1962):448-454.
Spike, Robert W. *The Freedom Revolution and the Churches.* New York: Association Press,
  1965. A manual of recommendations for community action, especially in the North, by
  the director of the Commission on Religion and Race, National Council of Churches of
  Christ in the U.S.A.
Stringfellow, William. *My People Is the Enemy: An Autobiographical Polemic.* New York:
  Holt, 1964. A passionate indictment of the Christian response to racial crisis by a young
  white lawyer and Episcopal layman, who lived and worked among Harlem poor.
Stringfellow, William. "Race, Religion and Revenge," *Christian Century* 79 (February 14,
  1962):192-194. In Harlem.
Thurman, Howard. *Footprints of a Dream: The Story of the Church for the Fellowship of All*

People. New York: Harper, 1959. A description of the various activities of this "interracial, intercultural, interdenominational" church (35 percent Negro) in San Francisco.

South

Bailey, Kenneth K. *Southern White Protestantism in the Twentieth Century.* New York: Harper, 1964.

Barnwell, William H. *In Richard's World: The Battle of Charleston.* Boston: Houghton Mifflin, 1968. Reflective diary of a theological student who worked within the Charleston Negro youth community in 1966.

Bouton, Ellen Naylor, and Thomas F. Pettigrew. "When a Priest Made a Pilgrimage," *Christian Century* 80 (March 20, 1963):863-865.

Brown, Robert R. *Bigger Than Little Rock.* Greenwich, Conn.: Seabury, 1958. Episcopal Bishop in Little Rock since 1955 discusses dilemma of clergymen who favor compliance with Supreme Court ruling, and concludes that the clergy must become involved in the political controversy.

Campbell, Ernest Q., and Thomas F. Pettigrew. *Christians in Racial Crisis: A Study of Little Rock's Ministry, Including Statements on Desegregation and Race Relations by the Leading Religious Denominations of the United States.* Washington: Public Affairs Press, 1959.

Carr, Warren. "Notes from an Irrelevant Clergyman," *Christian Century* 80 (July 10, 1963):879-881. In Durham, N.C., laymen are ready to take moral stand on civil rights before the churches are.

Cartwright, Colbert S. "Band Together for Genuine Unity," *New South* 16 (January 1961):6-10. Little Rock pastor at Fourth Conference on Community Unity.

Cartwright, Colbert S. "The Southern Minister and the Race Question," *New South* 13 (February 1958):3-6.

Catchings, L. Maynard, "Interracial Activities in Southern Churches," *Phylon* 13 (March 1952):54-56.

"'Christian Guide' to Race Attitudes," *New South* 13 (May 1958):3-7. A strong statement by the Gainesville-Hall County Ministerial Association in Georgia.

"A Church Looks at Civil Rights in North Carolina," *New South* 18 (April 1963):13-15. Statement of Committee on Human Relations of North Carolina Council of Churches.

Collie, Robert. "A 'Silent Minister' Speaks Up," *New York Times Magazine,* May 24, 1964, p. 12+. Pastor in small Louisiana town answers charge that Southern clergy have failed their duty on segregation—a defense and rationalization.

Cox, Harvey. "Letter from Williamston," *Christian Century* 80 (December 4, 1963): 1516-1518. North Carolina and protest.

Daniels, Jonathan, and Judith Upham. "Report from Selma," *Episcopal Theological School Journal* 10 (May 1965):2-8. An account written in April 1965 of experiences in Alabama by the young seminarian who was murdered in Hayneville, Alabama in August 1965.

Evans, John B. "Alabama," *Christian Century* 80 (February 6, 1963):188-190. Clergymen and Governor Wallace.

Fichter, Joseph H. "The Catholic South and Race," *Religious Education* 59 (January-February 1964):30-33.

Fichter, Joseph H., and George L. Maddox. "Religion in the South, Old and New," in John McKinney and Edgar Thompson, eds., *The South in Continuity and Change.* Durham, N.C.: Duke University Press, 1965.

Forshey, Gerald. "Divided Flocks in Jackson," *Christian Century* 80 (November 27, 1963):1469-1471. Church segregation in Jackson, Mississippi.

"The Full Catholic Teaching in Racial Justice," *Interracial Review* 35 (October 1962): 224-225. Syllabus prepared by the Diocesan Department of Education, Charleston, South Carolina.

Geier, Woodrow A. "Tennessee," *Christian Century* 80 (December 4, 1963):1526-1527. Survey of integration in Southern Baptist churches.

Harbutt, Charles. "The Church and Integration," *Jubilee* 6 (February 1959):6-15. Survey of Catholics' response to South's most pressing problem.

Hill, Samuel S., Jr. "Southern Protestantism and Racial Integration," *Religion in Life* 33 (Summer 1964):421-429.

Hill, Samuel S., Jr. "The South's Cultural Protestantism," *Christian Century* 79 (September 12, 1962):1094-1096.

Johnson, Benton. "Ascetic Protestantism and Political Preference in the Deep South," *American Journal of Sociology* 69 (January 1964):359-366. Tie between Republicans and Fundamentalists.

McGill, Ralph. "The Agony of the Southern Minister," *New York Times Magazine,* September 27, 1959, p. 16+.

McMillan, George. "Silent White Ministers of the South," *New York Times Magazine,* April 5, 1964, p. 22+.

McNeill, Robert. *God Wills Us Free: The Ordeal of a Southern Minister.* New York: Hill & Wang, 1965. White clergyman was dismissed from his pulpit because of his stand on segregation.

"Ministers' Statement of Conviction on Race," *New South* 12 (April 1957):3-6. By ministers' association of Richmond, Virginia.

"A Missionary Presence in Mississippi 1964," *Social Action* 31 (November 1964):1-48. Background information on the role of the NCC and the Mississippi Summer Project.

"The Other Mississippi," *New South* 18 (March 1963):entire issue. Including statements by groups of the state's ministers.

Schomer, Howard. "Race and Religion in Albany [Georgia]," *Christian Century* 79 (September 26, 1962):1155-1156.

Sellers, James. *The South and Christian Ethics.* New York: Association Press, 1962. Viewing segregation theologically as a "regional variety of the inevitable fall of man," the author analyzes racial problems in terms of Southern traditions.

Seymour, Robert. "Interracial Ministry in North Carolina," *Christian Century* 80 (January 23, 1963):109-111.

Shriver, Donald W., Jr., ed. *The Unsilent South.* Richmond, Va.: John Knox Press, 1965. Sermons delivered by eighteen Presbyterian ministers and one layman in the South, all speaking out on the interracial crisis. Prefatory notes to each detail circumstances of delivery and what later happened to these men who preached equality of all men.

Smith, Lauren A. "Saints in the Basement," *Christian Century* 75 (September 17, 1958): 1050-1052. Negroes and clergymen in Arkansas.

Smythe, Lewis S. C., ed. *Southern Churches and Race Relations: Report of the Third Interracial Consultation.* Lexington, Ky.: College of the Bible, 1961.

Southard, Samuel. "Are Southern Churches Silent?" *Christian Century* 80 (November 20, 1963):1429-1432.

Thomas, Mary S. "The Ordeal of Koinonia Farm," *Progressive* 21 (January 1957):23-25. Account of a Georgia religious and interracial camp and community, and the attacks on it.

Ungar, Andre. "To Birmingham, and Back," *Conservative Judaism* 18 (Fall 1963):1-17. Trip to South by 19 rabbis.

Warnock, Henry Y. "Southern Methodists, the Negro, and Unification: The First Phase," *Journal of Negro History* 52 (October 1967):287-304. Background information of the merger of the Northern and Southern Methodists in 1939 and early aftermath.

Young, Merrill Orne. "For Church's Sake," *Christian Century* 78 (November 1, 1961): 1300-1301. Episcopal pilgrimage in Mississippi.

20   Black Nationalism and Black Power

Background

Ash, William. "Marxism and the Negro Revolt," *Monthly Review* 18 (May 1966):19-30.

"Baldwin: Gray Flannel Muslim?" *Christian Century* 80 (June 12, 1963):791. An examination of the extent to which Baldwin inclines toward repudiation of the white world.

Barbour, Floyd B., ed. *The Black Power Revolt: A Collection of Essays.* Boston: Porter Sargent, 1968. Traces the concept of black power from the eighteenth century to the present. Bibliography.

Bell, Howard H. "Negro Nationalism: A Factor in Emigration Projects, 1858-1861," *Journal of Negro History* 47 (January 1962):42-53.

Bittle, William E., and Gilbert Geis. *The Longest Way Home: Chief C. Sam's Back-to-Africa Movement.* Detroit: Wayne State University Press, 1964.

"Black America," *Social Science Quarterly* 49 (December 1968):entire issue. Articles cited individually under appropriate sections.

Blake, J. Herman. "Black Nationalism," *Annals of the American Academy of Political and Social Science* 382 (March 1969):15-25.

Boggs, James. *The American Revolution.* New York: Monthly Review Press, 1964. The author, a Negro radical, starts with premise that the American power elite is evil, that the Negro has nothing to hope for from the CIO-AFL or the NAACP, and that the Negro revolt must proceed by means of economic and political power.

Boggs, Grace, and James Boggs. "The City Is the Black Man's Land," *Monthly Review* 17 (April 1966):35-46.

Brink, William, and Louis Harris. *Black and White: A Study of U.S. Racial Attitudes Today.* New York: Simon & Schuster, 1967. An opinion sampling of whites, Negroes, and Negro leaders concerning the racial conflict since 1963. Comparisons made with a 1963 survey published under the title *The Negro Revolution in America,* indicate the directed change in the Negro movement and the force of the black power concept.

Chachas, John. *Americans, Save America: The Solution to America's Racial Dilemma; Separate and Equal Negro States.* New York: Pageant, 1966.

Cronon, E. D. *Black Moses.* Madison: University of Wisconsin Press, 1955. Biography of Marcus Garvey and the best study of Garvey's Universal Negro Improvement Association, founded in 1918, which appealed to Negro ethnocentrism, and roused considerable enthusiasm for his plan to lead American Negroes back to Africa.

Danzig, David. "In Defense of Black Power," *Commentary* 42 (September 1966):41-46.

Delany, M. R., and Robert Campbell. *Search for a Place: Black Separatism and Africa, 1860.* 1861. Introduction by Howard H. Bell. Ann Arbor: University of Michigan Press, 1969. A Negro abolitionist who, having rejected the panaceas offered to his race prior to the Civil War, outlines a program of emigration.

DuBois, W. E. B. *The Souls of Black Folk: Essays and Sketches.* Chicago: McClurg, 1903. Desire for a militant Negro movement. Frequently reprinted.

Epps, Archie. "A Negro Separatist Movement of the 19th Century," *Harvard Review* 4 (Summer–Fall 1966):69–87.

Fanon, Frantz. *Black Skin, White Masks.* Translated by Charles Lam Markmann. New York: Grove, 1967.

Fanon, Frantz. *The Wretched of the Earth.* New York: Grove, 1963. Also published in English under the title *The Damned.*

Feldman, Paul. "How the Cry for Black Power Began," *Dissent* 13 (September–October 1966):472–477.

Garvey, Marcus. *Philosophy and Opinions of Marcus Garvey.* Edited by Amy Jacques-Garvey, 1923. Reissued with a lengthy preface by Hollis R. Lynch. New York: Atheneum, 1969. Also reissued as 2d ed. with an introduction by E. U. Essien-Udom. London: Frank Cass, 1968.

Gregor, A. James. "Black Nationalism," *Science and Society* 27 (Fall 1963):415–432.

"Integrated or Separate: Which Road to Progress?" *New Generation* 49 (Fall 1967):1–28. Entire issue. Focuses on areas of education, housing, and political action.

Isaacs, Harold R. "DuBois and Africa," *Race* 2 (November 1960):3–23.

Killian, Lewis M. *The Impossible Revolution? Black Power and the American Dream.* New York: Random, 1968. Traces evolution of black protests of the 1950's to black power revolts of the 1960's. Cogent analysis of the growing dichotomy between the races with severe warnings of greater violence as white Americans resist making economic and social commitments necessary to create an integrated, viable society.

Langley, Jabez Ayodele. "Garveyism and African Nationalism," *Race* 11 (October 1969): 157–172.

Lincoln, C. Eric, ed. *Is Anybody Listening to Black America?* New York: Seabury, 1968. Quotations excerpted to present a spectrum of Negro opinion and the white response. Selections run the gamut from strong racist sentiments to sensitive appraisals of injustice to the black man.

Lincoln, C. Eric. *My Face Is Black.* Boston, Beacon, 1964. The author's thesis is that the pauperized Southern Negro masses and the Northern black ghetto masses are being pushed into acceptance of being black, the "mood ebony" which fosters black chauvinism. The book constitutes a sequel to *The Black Muslims in America.*

Marine, Gene, and Adam Hochschild. "Color Black Gloomy," *Ramparts* 5 (December 1966):39–43. Disillusionment expressed at the "myth" of the Negro revolution.

Mason, Philip. "The Revolt against Western Values," *Daedalus* (Spring 1967):328–352.

Morsell, John A. "Black Nationalism," *Journal of Intergroup Relations* 3 (Winter 1961–1962): 5–11. Black Nationalism as a response to inner tensions and frustrations.

Mphahlele, Ezekiel. *The African Image.* New York: Praeger, 1962. Includes a discussion of the black nationalists in the United States.

Muse, Benjamin. *The American Negro Revolution: From Nonviolence to Black Power, 1963–1967.* Bloomington: Indiana University Press, 1968. Account by a former Virginia state senator of the concerted efforts for civil rights from the non-violent demonstrations in 1963 to the militancy of attitude in 1967.

Obatala, J. K. "Exodus: Black Zionism," *Liberator* 9 (October 1969):14–17.

Pease, Jane H., and William H. Pease. "Black Power—The Debate in 1840," *Phylon* 29 (Spring 1968):19–26. All-black conventions of free Negroes in New York and other cities in an attempt to acquire full suffrage and civil equality—considered then by most whites as inverse racism.

Rawick, George. "The Historical Roots of Black Liberation," *Radical America* 2 (July–August 1968):1–13.

Record, Wilson. "Extremist Movements among American Negroes," *Phylon* 17 (Spring 1956):17–23. Historically, Negro extremist movements have been basically urban movements, arising in moments of distress and crisis in Negro life, feeding on the disorganization of migrants.

Record, Wilson. "The Negro Intellectual and Negro Nationalism," *Social Forces* 32 (October 1954):10–18. The Negro intellectual, even though he may view African nationalist aspirations with sympathy, does not believe solution of Negro problems in America lies in separation from American society.

Redkey, Edwin S. "Bishop Turner's African Dream," *Journal of American History* 54 (September 1967):271-290. The spokesman for black nationalism in the period between Reconstruction and World War I.

Redkey, Edwin S. *Black Exodus: Black Nationalists and the Back-to-Africa Movements, 1890-1910.* New Haven: Yale University Press, 1969.

Roucek, Joseph S. "The Rise of Black Power in the United States," *Contemporary Review* 212 (January 1968):31-39.

Snellings, Rolland. "The New Afro-American Writer," *Liberator* 3 (October 1963):10-11. Concerned with growing militancy of young Negro writers, and their interest in black nationalism.

Staudenraus, P. J. *The African Colonization Movement, 1816-1865.* New York: Columbia University Press, 1961.

Sternsher, Bernard, ed. *The Negro in Depression and War: Prelude to Revolution, 1930-1945.* Chicago: Quadrangle, 1969. Historical literature on black America for the period. Bibliography.

Thomas, Tony. "Which Way for Black Liberation?" *Young Socialist* 12 (December 1969):4-7.

Thorne, Richard. "Integration or Black Nationalism: Which Route Will Negroes Choose?" *Negro Digest* 12 (August 1963):36-47. A young California intellectual thinks black nationalism the only honorable road to follow.

Tinker, Irene. "Nationalism in a Plural Society: The Case of the American Negro," *Western Political Quarterly* 19 (March 1966):112-122.

Weisbord, Robert G. "Africa, Africans and the Afro-American: Images and Identities in Transition," *Race* 10 (January 1969):305-321.

Weisbord, Robert G. "The Back-to-Africa Idea," *History Today* 18 (January 1968):30-37. Discusses proposals of whites, and prominent Negroes such as Turner, Delaney, and Garvey for immigration to Africa from America.

Worthy, William. "An All Black Party," *Liberator,* October 1963. Urging support of the all-black Negro Freedom Now party as the only effective instrument of Negro political power.

Young, Harrison. "The Ivy League Negro: Black Nationalist?" *Harvard Crimson,* September 21, 1964. Attitudes of both American and African Negro students.

Zolberg, Aristide, and Verz Zolberg. "The Americanization of Franz Fanon," *Public Interest* 3 (Fall 1967):49-63.

Theory

Aberback, Joel D., and Jack L. Walker. *The Meanings of Black Power: An Empirical Assessment.* Washington: American Political Science Association, 1968.

Aronowitz, Stanley. "White Radicals and Black Revolt," *Liberation* 12 (August 1967):11-13.

Barndt, Joseph R. *Why Black Power.* New York: Friendship, 1968.

Baskin, Darryl. "Black Separatism," *Journal of Higher Education* 40 (December 1969): 731-734.

"The Battle for Black Liberation," *Political Affairs* 47 (February 1968):1-97. Entire issue.

Becker, William H. "Black Power in Christological Perspective," *Religion in Life* 38 (Autumn 1969):404-414. "Christ the rebel" is perhaps a more appropriate model for black power today than is "Christ the sufferer."

"Black Power: A Discussion," *Partisan Review* 35 (Spring 1968):195-232. Responses to Martin Duberman's article on black power (in the previous issue) by Robert Coles, Paul Feldman, Charles Hamilton, Tom Kahn, William M. Kelley, Norman Mailer, and others.

Boggs, James. "Black Power," *Liberator* 7 (April 1967):4-7; *ibid.,* (May 1967):8-10.

Borgese, Elizabeth Mann. "The Other Hill," *Center Magazine* 1 (July 1968):2-11. Proposals for the right of self-management.

Breitman, George. "In Defense of Black Power," *International Socialist Review* 28 (January-February 1967):4-16.

Brimmer, Andrew F. "Negroes in an Integrated Society," *Public Relations Journal* 24 (July 1968):19. An approach to the black power issue which differs from that of the Black Nationalists.

Browne, Robert S. "The Case for Black Separatism," *Ramparts* 6 (December 1967):46-51. The author is a member of the advisory committee of the Newark Black Power Conference, held July 1967.

Burgess, Parke G. "Rhetoric of Black Power: A Moral Demand?" *Quarterly Journal of Speech* 54 (April 1968):122-133.

Carmichael, Stokely, and Charles V. Hamilton. *Black Power: The Politics of Liberation in America.* New York: Random, 1967. Discussion of the development and goals of black power. Bibliography.

Carmichael, Stokely. "Toward Black Liberation," *Massachusetts Review* 7 (Autumn 1966):639-651.

"The Case for an Independent Black Political Party," *International Socialist Review* 29 (January-February 1968):39-55.

Clark, Kenneth B. "Thoughts on Black Power," *Dissent* 15 (March-April 1968):98, 192-193.

Cleage, Albert B., Jr. *The Black Messiah.* New York: Sheed & Ward, 1968. Black power and theology.

Cleage, Albert B. "Black Power—An Advocate Defines It," *Public Relations Journal* 24 (July 1968):16-18. Author was a founder of both the Freedom Now party and the Black Christian Nationalist movement.

Cleaver, Eldridge. "Education and Revolution," *Black Scholar* 1 (November 1969):44-53.

Cleaver, Eldridge. "The Land Question," *Ramparts* 6 (May 1968):51-53. Black power as a "projection of sovereignty."

Cleaver, Eldridge. *Post Prison Writings and Speeches.* Edited by Robert Scheer. New York: Random, 1969. The mind of the black revolution and the legitimacy of violence.

Cleaver, Eldridge. "Three Notes from Exile," *Ramparts* 8 (September 1969):29-35.

Comer, James P. "The Social Power of the Negro," *Scientific American* 216 (April 1967):21-27. The necessity of the Negro to attain political and economic control to secure status as other imigrant groups have done.

Cook, Samuel DuBois. "The Tragic Myth of Black Power," *New South* 21 (Summer 1966):58-64.

Cruse, Harold. *Rebellion or Revolution?* New York: Morrow, 1968.

Cruse, Harold W. "Revolutionary Nationalism and the Afro-American," *Studies on the Left* 2, no. 3 (1962):12-25. Discussion by Robert Greenleaf, Harold W. Cruse, and Clark H. Foreman, *ibid.,* 3, no. 1 (1962):1-8.

Day Noel A. "The Case for All-Black Schools," in *Equal Educational Opportunity.* Cambridge, Mass.: Harvard University Press, 1969, pp. 205-212. An expansion of an article which originally appeared in the *Harvard Educational Review,* Winter 1968.

Dionne, Roger. "Radicalism and Black Liberation," *New Politics* (Summer 1968):90-93.

Draper, Theodore. *Black Nationalism in America.* New York: Viking, 1970.

Dratch, Howard. "The Emergence of Black Power," *International Socialist Journal* nos. 26-27 (July 1968):321-365.

Duberman, Martin. "Black Power in America," *Partisan Review* 35 (Winter 1967):34-48. An analysis of the slogan and the phenomenon which generated it. See also responses, "Black Power: A Discussion," *ibid.,* 35 (Spring 1968):195-232.

Fager, Charles E. *White Reflections on Black Power.* Grand Rapids, Mich.: Eerdmans, 1967. Bibliography.

Feldman, Paul. "The Pathos of Black Power," *Dissent* 14 (January-February 1967):69-79.

Ferry, W. H. "Black Colonies: A Modest Proposal," *Center Magazine* 1 (January 1968):74-76.

Ferry, W. H. "Farewell to Integration," *Center Magazine* 1 (March 1968):35-40. Sees current racial progress as a myth. Also appears in *Liberator* 8 (January 1968):4-11.

Franklin, Raymond S. "The Political Economy of Black Power," *Social Problems* 16 (Winter 1969):286-301. An ideology challenging basic premises of American capitalism and the nation's political underpinnings.

Frazier, Arthur, and Virgil Roberts. "A Discourse on Black Nationalism," *American Behavioral Scientist* 12 (March-April 1969):50-56.

Gayle, Addison, "Black Power: Existential Politics," *Liberator* 9 (January 1969):4-7.

Gershman, Carl. "Black Nationalism and Conservative Politics," *Dissent* (January-February 1970):10-12.

Gill, Robert Lewis, and Roberta Louise Gill. "International Implications of Black Power as Viewed by Their Advocates," *Quarterly Review of Higher Education among Negroes* 37 (October 1969):158-176. Bibliography included.

Good, Paul. "A White Look at Black Power," *Nation* 203 (August 8, 1966):112-116.

Gordon, Edmund W. "Relevance or Revolt," *Perspectives in Education* 3 (Fall 1969):10-16.

Gregg, Richard B., A. Jackson McCormack, and Douglas J. Pedersen. "The Rhetoric of Black Power: A Street-Level Interpretation," *Quarterly Journal of Speech* 55 (April 1969):151-160.

Hamilton, Charles V. "Race and Education: A Search for Legitimacy," in *Equal Educational Opportunity*. Cambridge, Mass.: Harvard University Press, 1969, pp. 187-202. Originally appeared in the *Harvard Educational Review,* Fall 1968. Proposals for new directions in education for the black community.

Harris, Paul. "Black Power Advocacy: Criminal Anarchy or Free Speech," *California Law Review* 56 (May 1968):702-755.

Huckaby, Phillip. "The Black Identity Crisis," *Theology Today* 24 (January 1968):498-506. Black power represents a logical way for Negroes to regain identity—a necessary prerequisite for true integration.

Innis, Roy, and Norman Hill. "Black Self—Determination: A Debate," *New Generation* 51 (Summer 1969):18-26.

Jackson, James E. "National Pride—Not Nationalism," *Political Affairs* 46 (May 1967):43-48.

Jacobs, Harold. "SNCC and Black Power," *International Socialist Journal* no. 22 (August 1967):647-656.

Jencks, Christopher, and Milton Kotler. "Government of the Black, by the Black, and for the Black," *Ramparts* 5 (July 1966):51-54.

Kaminsky, Marc. "Radical Affirmatives," *American Scholar* 36 (Autumn 1967):621-630. In part a discussion of Malcolm X's autobiography.

Kilson, Martin. "Black Power: Anatomy of a Paradox," *Harvard Journal of Negro Affairs* 2, no. 1 (1968):30-34.

Kilson, Martin. "Negro Militancy," *Saturday Review* 52 (August 16, 1969):28-31.

Kilson, Martin. "The New Black Intellectuals," *Dissent* 16 (July-August 1969):304-310.

Kirschenmann, Frederick. "The Danger and Necessity of Black Separatism," *The Lutheran Quarterly* 21 (November 1969):352-357.

Leeds, Olly. "The Separatists' Fantasy," *Liberator* 9 (February 1969):4-7. See also reply of Casey Mann, et al. *ibid.,* April 1969.

Lester, Julius. *Look Out, Whitey! Black Power's Gon' Get Your Mama!* New York: Dial, 1968. Author, a leader of SNCC, offers an intensely personal explication of the Black Power movement.

Lester, Julius. *Revolutionary Notes.* New York: Baron, 1969. A collection of essays originally written for the *Guardian* during the last two years.

Lester, Julius. *Search for a New Land.* New York: Dial, 1969.

Lightfoot, Claude M. *Ghetto Rebellion to Black Liberation.* New York: International Publishers, 1968. The goals of black power and ghetto revolt by an Afro-American exponent of communism.

Lightfoot, Claude. "The Right of Black America To Create a Nation," *Political Affairs* 47 (November 1968):1-11.

Lincoln, Eric. "Black Revolution in Cultural Perspective," *Union Seminary Quarterly Review* 23 (Spring 1968):219–247. Includes replies by Don W. Watts, Malcolm Boyd, and Nathan Wright, Jr.

McKissick, Floyd. "Black Power," *Interracial Review* 39 (July 1966):127–128. An interpretation by the director of CORE.

Mann, Casey, et al. "The Separatists' Fantasy: A Reply," *Liberator* 9 (April 1969):4–9. See also O. Leed's article, *ibid.,* February 1969.

Marion, John H. "Is Black Power Being Oversold?" *Social Progress* 57 (March—April 1967):21–25. Meaning of "black power" must be clarified, then supported by whites.

Marx, Gary T. "The White Negro and the Negro White," *Phylon* 28 (Summer 1967): 168–177. Contrasts the "black bourgeoisie" and the white "beats."

Mayer, Milton. "By Power Possessed," *Massachusetts Review* 8 (Spring 1967):371–375. A reply to S. Carmichael's article on black power, *ibid.,* 7 (Autumn 1966):639–651.

"The Meaning and Measure of Black Power," *Negro Digest* 16 (November 1966):20–37.

Mills, Nicolaus C. "Black Power," *Yale Review* 57 (Spring 1968):346–357. The psychology of black power.

Morrison, Derrick. "The Rise of Black Power," *Young Socialist* 10 (October–November 1966):12–19.

Moss, James A. "The Negro Church and Black Power," *Journal of Human Relations* 19 (First Quarter 1968):119–128.

Moynihan, Daniel P. "The New Racialism," *Atlantic* 222 (August 1968):35–40.

Nelson, Truman. *The Right of Revolution.* Boston: Beacon, 1968. Views the inevitability of a revolutionary attempt given an increasingly unenlightened white response to oppressive conditions and governance.

Piderhughes, Charles A. "Understanding Black Power: Processes and Proposals," *American Journal of Psychiatry* 125 (May 1969):1552–1557.

Piven, Frances Fox, and Richard A. Cloward. "What Chance for Black Power?" *New Republic* 158 (March 30, 1968):19–23.

Poussaint, Alvin F., and Joyce Ladner. "Black Power: A Failure for Racial Integration within the Civil Rights Movement," *Archives of General Psychiatry* 18 (April 1968): 385–391.

Poussaint, Alvin F. "A Psychiatrist Looks at Black Power," *Ebony* 24 (March 1969): 142–144+.

Proctor, Roscoe. "Notes on 'Black Power' Concept," *Political Affairs* 46 (March 1967):36–51.

Quinlivan, Frank J. "Black Power: Reflections of an Outsider," *America* 119 (November 2, 1968):413–414.

Relyea, Harold C. "'Black Power': The Genesis and the Future of a Revolution," *Journal of Human Relations* 16 (Fourth Quarter 1968):502–513.

Relyea, Harold C. "The Theology of Black Power," *Religion in Life* 38 (Autumn 1969): 415–420.

Ricks, Timothy. "Black Revolution: A Matter of Definition," *American Behavioral Scientist* 12 (March–April 1969):21–26. Extensive references.

Riesman, David. "Some Reservations about Black Power," *Trans-action* 5 (November 1967):20–22.

Rustin, Bayard. "The Failure of Black Separatism," *Harper's* 240 (January 1970):25–34.

Rustin, Bayard. "Towards Integration as a Goal," *American Federationist* 76 (January 1969):5–7. The author's presentation of a dialogue with Prof. Robert Browne on separation versus integration.

Schuchter, Arnold. *White Power/Black Freedom: Planning the Future of Urban America.* Boston: Beacon, 1968. Argument for the necessity of black power. Offers specific challenging proposals to government and industry. Extensive bibliography.

Scott, Robert L., and Wayne Brockriede. *The Rhetoric of Black Power.* New York: Harper & Row, 1969. The concept as viewed critically by Martin Luther King, Hubert Humphrey, Stokely Carmichael, and Charles V. Hamilton. Well documented.

Sherrill, Robert. "Birth of a (Black) Nation," *Esquire* 71 (January 1969):70-76+. Demands of the Republic of New Africa, a plan for black autonomy in the contiguous states of Louisiana, Mississippi, Georgia, Alabama, and South Carolina. Reaction of white officials.

Smith, Bob. "The Case against Blackthink," *Virginia Quarterly Review* 44 (Winter 1968):43-50. Contends that political expediency and ideological hyperconsciousness have obscured the goals of a truly free society where race does not matter.

[Symposium] *Ramparts* 64 (November 1967):99-102. On the program of the "Black Caucus" stemming from the Chicago National Conference for New Politics in August-September 1967.

Tretton, Rudie. "Black Power and Education," *School and Society* 96 (November 23, 1968):428-430. The necessary educational response.

Tucker Sterling. *Black Reflections on White Power.* Grand Rapids, Mich.: Eerdmans, 1969. Author is Director of Field Services for the National Urban League. See also Fager counterpart.

Wagstaff, Thomas, comp. *Black Power: The Radical Response to White America.* Beverly Hills, Calif.: Glenco, 1969.

Washington, Kenneth S. "What Counselors Must Know about Black Power," *Personnel and Guidance Journal* 47 (November 1968):204-208.

Worthy, William. "The American Negro Is Dead: International Support for Black Power," *Esquire* 68 (November 1967):126-133.

Wright, Nathan, Jr. *Black Power and Urban Unrest: Creative Possibilities.* New York: Hawthorne, 1967. Constructive exposition of black power in political, economic, social, and religious terms.

Young, Whitney M., Jr. *Beyond Racism: Building an Open Society.* New York: McGraw-Hill, 1969. Essential requirements of black people for "an open society" or new equilibrium of national power.

Practice

General

Allen, Gary. "Black Power," *American Opinion* 10 (January 1967):1-14. Commentary on the Berkeley Black Power Conference.

Altschuler, Alan. *Community Control: The Black Demand for Participation in Large American Cities.* New York: Pegasus, 1970.

Aronson, James. "The New Politics of Black Power," *Monthly Review* 19 (October 1967): 11-21. The National Convention for New Politics, Chicago, August 29-September 4, 1967.

"The Black Manifesto," *New York Review of Books* 13 (July 10, 1969):32-33. Text.

"Black Power 1968," *Phi Delta Kappan* 49 (April 1968):447-452. Four papers about black activism and community control in education.

"Black Priority," *Saturday Review* 52 (November 15, 1969):90.

"The Black Revolution," *Ebony* 24 (August 1969):entire issue.

Brubacker, John S. "Anatomy of Black Power," *Record* 70 (May 1969):729-737. Black power in education.

Cass, James. "Can the University Survive the Black Challenge? *Saturday Review* 52 (June 21, 1969):68-71+.

Conant, Ralph W. "Black Power: Rhetoric and Reality," *Urban Affairs Quarterly* 4 (September 1968):15-25.

De Berry, Clyde E., Joseph Fashing, and Calvin Harris. "Black Power and Black Population: A Dilemma," *Journal of Negro Education* 38 (Winter 1969):14-21. Based on survey in Eugene, Oregon.

Donadio, Stephen. "Black Power at Columbia," *Commentary* 46 (September 1968):67–76. Implications of the racial aspect of the confrontation for future protests.

Dowey, Edward A., Jr. "'The Black Manifesto': Revolution, Reparation, Separation," *Theology Today* 26 (October 1969):288–293. The issues of "The Black Manifesto."

Downes, Bryan T., and Stephen W. Burks. *The Black Protest Movement and Urban Violence.* Washington: American Political Science Association, 1968.

Durley, Gerald L. "A Center for Black Students on University Campuses," *Journal of Higher Education* 40 (June 1969):473–476.

Edwards, Harry. *The Revolt of the Black Athlete.* New York: Free Press, 1969. Traces inequities for the black man in athletics as background for the 1968 Olympic boycott which author directed. Bibliography.

Eisen, Jonathan. "Black Culture at Oberlin," *Commonweal* 87 (March 8, 1968):676–677.

Ellis, William W. *White Ethics and Black Power: The Emergence of the West Side Organization.* Chicago: Aldine, 1969. A study of a black independent community organization in Chicago; a case analysis of the achievement and use of power in a black community.

Goodman, Walter. "When Black Power Runs the New Left," *New York Times Magazine,* September 24, 1967, pp. 28–29+. The Chicago New Politics Convention.

Graham, Hugh D. "The Storm over Black Power," *Virginia Quarterly Review* 43 (Autumn 1967):545–565.

Guns on Campus: Student Protest at Cornell. Chicago: Urban Research, 1969.

Hamilton, Charles V. "Black Rebels Are Not Pranksters: They Are Raising Vital Issues," *New York Times Magazine,* May 4, 1969, pp. 138+. Demands of black students on college campuses.

Hammerquist, Don. "A First Reaction to the New Politics Convention," *Political Affairs* 46 (December 1967):60–64.

Hampden-Turner, Charles. "Black Power: A Blueprint for Psycho-Social Development?" in Richard S. Rosenbloom and Robin Marris, eds., *Social Innovation in the City: New Enterprises for Community Development.* Cambridge, Mass.: Harvard University Press, 1969, pp. 63–95. Bibliography.

Hennessy, Thomas A. "Black Power—Rebuff in Pittsburgh," *New Republic* 161 (September 27, 1969):18–19. Reports white response to the Black Construction Coalition's move to protest discriminatory hiring practices of the local construction craft unions.

Jenkins, Thomas H. "A Positive Agenda for Social Power," *Harvard Journal of Negro Affairs* 2, no. 1 (1968):16–29. Declines to use the term, "Black Power," instead considers the need for the Negro to "share in the possession and exercise of social power—as individual participants in strategic places . . . "

Johnson, William R., Jr. "A Black Prayer and Litany," *Theology Today* 26 (October 1969):262–265. Satirical use of liturgical forms to voice black outrage.

Knopf, Terry Ann. "Sniping, a New Plan of Violence?" *Trans-action* 6 (July–August 1969):22–29. Reply with rejoinder by J. R. Corse and L. H. Masotti, *ibid.,* September 1969. Violence as black protest; the role of the press.

Ladner, Joyce. "What 'Black Power' Means to Negroes in Mississippi," *Trans-action* 5 (November 1967):7–15.

Lawrence, Earl. "Black Power and New Politics," *Political Affairs* 46 (December 1967): 48–59. The New Politics Convention and the "Black Caucus" program.

Lecky, Robert S., and H. Elliott Wright, eds. *Black Manifesto: Religion, Facism and Reparations.* New York: Sheed & Ward, 1969. Pressure to obtain reparations from churches and synagogues is appraised by James Forman, Harvey Cox, Dick Gregory, and others. Includes a chronology of the movement and the text of the manifesto.

Levine, Daniel U. "Black Power: Implications for the Urban Educator," *Education and Urban Society* 1 (February 1969):139–159.

Lewis, W. Arthur. "Black Power and the American University," *Africa Report* 14 (May–June 1969):23–25.

Lucas, C. Payne. "Black Pride: Black Action," *Vital Speeches* 35 (June 1, 1969):505–508.

McEvoy, James, and Abraham Miller. *Black Power and Student Rebellion.* Belmont, Calif.: Wadsworth, 1969.

Mack, Raymond W. "The Negro Opposition to Black Extremism," *Saturday Review* 51 (May 4, 1968):52-55. An attitude survey.

Mathews, John, and Ernest Holsendolph. "When Black Students Take Over a Campus," *Nation* 158 (April 13, 1968):10. The Harvard University student revolt.

"Negroes Escalate Job Demands," *Engineering News-Record* 183 (September 25, 1969): 15-16. Illustrative of black power potential in employment as viewed by a trade journalist.

Nelson, Bryce. "Brandeis: How a Liberal University Reacts to A Black Take-Over," *Science* 163 (March 28, 1969):1431-1434.

Nicolaus, Martin. "S. F. State: History Takes a Leap," *New Left Review* no. 54 (March-April 1969):21-31.

"Operation Shakedown: How They're Putting the Squeeze on Business," *Nation's Business* 56 (September 1968):37-41. Reports unscrupulous pressure on white businesses by some Negro groups.

"Pittsburgh Now a Symbol of Mounting Negro Protest," *Engineering News-Record* 183 (September 4, 1969):14-15. A view of the force of black power in the construction industry as revealed in a trade journal.

Rosenthal, Jamie. "With A 'New Thrust' toward Blackness, the Urban League Prepares To Turn Itself Around," *City* 3 (February 1969):12-14.

Rosenthal, Michael, Pamela Ritterman, and Bob Sherman. "Blacks at Brandeis," *Commonweal* 89 (March 14, 1969):727-730. A confrontation with militant liberals.

Schrag, Peter. "New Black Myths," *Harper's* 238 (May 1969):37-42.

Scott, Benjamin. *The Coming of the Black Man.* Boston: Beacon, 1969. An appeal for the commitment of black community talent and an interpretation of black power by an activist leader in the Boston ghetto.

"Segregated Professional Association?" *Social Service Review* 41 (December 1967):435. The creation of the Association of Black Social Workers.

Shaffer, Helen B. "Negro Power Struggle," *Editorial Research Reports,* February 21, 1968, pp. 123-140. The changing tenor of the Negro protest; currents and conflicts in power drive; future of the black movement.

Skolnick, Jerome H., ed. "Black Militancy," in *The Politics of Protest.* New York: Simon & Schuster, 1969, pp. 125-175.

Skolnick, Jerome H. "Black Separatism," *Chicago Today* 5 (Summer 1968):17-21.

Steinberg, David. "Black Power Roots on Black Campuses," *Commonweal* 88 (April 19, 1968):127-129.

Stenfors, Brian D., and John J. Woodmansee. "A Scale of Black Power Sentiment," *Psychological Reports* 22 (June 1968):802.

Stern, Sol. "America's Black Guerillas," *Ramparts* 6 (September 1967):24-27.

Thelwell, Michael, and Nathan Hare. "Two Black Radicals Report on Their Campus Struggles," *Ramparts* 8 (July 1969):47-59.

Turbee, Florence. "Black Revolutionary Language," *Liberator* 9 (November 1969):8-10.

U.S. Congress. Senate. Committee on the Judiciary. *Gaps in International Security Laws: Hearings Pt. 5, May 2-10, 1967.* Washington: U.S. Govt. Print. Off., 1967. (90th Congress, 1st Session). Testimony about militant civil rights groups and black nationalist organizations in Cleveland.

Wallenstein, Steve, and George Fisher, with Jacob Brackman. *Backfire: Ordeal at Cornell.* New York: Chelsea House, 1970.

Washington, Kenneth S. "Black Power—Action or Reaction," *American Behavioral Scientist* 12 (March-April 1969):47-49.

Wills, Garry. *The Second Civil War: Arming for Armageddon.* Cleveland: World, 1968. A concise analysis of the present cataclysmic course of black and white communities.

Wilson, James A. "White Power and Black Supremacy," *Pittsburgh Business Review* 37 (August 1967):12-14.

Black Muslims

Berger, Morroe. "The Black Muslims," *Horizon* 6 (January 1964):48–65. A number of slaves brought to America were genuine "black Moslems." Professor Berger's article is based on accounts of these groups preserved by nineteenth-century amateur ethnologists.

Breitman, George. *The Last Year of Malcolm X*. New York: Merit Publishers, 1967. Bibliography.

Brotz, Howard. *The Black Jews of Harlem: Negro Nationalism and the Dilemmas of Negro Leadership*. New York: Free Press, 1964. While the first half of this book deals with the "Ethiopian" Jews of Harlem, the second half deals with the problem of Negro leadership, the total Negro situation in America, and the role that Negro nationalism may play in its alleviation.

Brown, L. P. "Black Muslims and the Police," *Journal of Criminal Law, Criminology and Police Science* 56 (March 1965):119–126.

Burns, W. Haywood. "Black Muslims in America: A Reinterpretation," *Race* 5 (July 1963):26–37.

Clarke, John Henrik, ed. *Malcolm X: The Man and His Time*. New York: Macmillan, 1969. Festschrift. Critical appraisals of the black leader and some of his own speeches. Complements his autobiography.

Cleage, Albert, and George Breitman. "Myths about Malcolm X," *International Socialist Review* 28 (July–August 1967):43–51.

"Constitutional Law—Black Muslimism Is a Religion within the Meaning of the First Amendment," *Georgia Bar Journal* 24 (May 1962):519.

"Discretion of Director of Corrections Not Abused in Refusing to Grant Black Muslim Prisoners Rights Afforded Other Religious Groups," *UCLA Law Review* 9 (March 1962):501.

Essien-Udom, E. U. *Black Nationalism: A Search for an Identity in America*. Chicago: University of Chicago Press, 1962. Valuable assessment by an African of the Muslim movement and the nature of its appeal to lower-class urban Negroes.

Hatchett, John F. "The Moslem Influence among American Negroes." *Journal of Human Relations* 10 (Summer 1962):375–382.

Hentoff, Nat. "Elijah in the Wilderness," *Reporter* 23 (August 4, 1960):37–40.

Hernton, Calvin C. "White Liberals and Black Muslims," *Negro Digest* 12 (October 1963):3–9. The failure of the one gave birth to the other.

Kaminsky, Marc. "Radical Affirmatives," *American Scholar* 36 (Autumn 1967):621–630. In part, a discussion of Malcolm X's autobiography.

Kaplan, Howard M. "Black Muslims and the Negro American's Quest for Communion," *British Journal of Sociology* 20 (June 1969):164–176.

Kirman, J. M. "Challenge of the Black Muslims," *Social Education* 27 (November 1963):365–368.

Krosney, Herbert. "America's Black Supremacists," *Nation* 192 (May 6, 1961):390–392.

Landry, Lawrence. "Black Muslims and Sit-ins," *New University Thought* 2 (Winter 1962):3–7.

Laue, James E. "A Contemporary Revitalization Movement in American Race Relations: The 'Black Muslims,'" *Social Forces* 42 (March 1964):315–323.

Lincoln, C. Eric. "The Black Muslims," *Progressive* 26 (December 1962):43.

Lincoln, C. Eric. *The Black Muslims in America*. Boston: Beacon, 1961. A full-scale case study of the Black Muslim movement. As a Negro the author was able to attend Muslim meetings and he had many interviews with Muhammad and many other Muslim leaders. His analysis of both the sociological and psychological context of the movement is penetrating and thorough. Bibliography.

Lincoln, C. Eric. "Extremist Attitudes in the Black Muslim Movement," *New South* 18 (January 1963):3–10.

Little, Malcom. *The Autobiography of Malcolm X*. New York: Grove, 1965. The life story and spiritual evolution of an extraordinary man—from rootless hipster to fiercely racist Black Muslim leader who, by the time of his assassination in 1965, had adopted a world view of Islam and was moving towards a position of understanding and toleration for all men. One of the most powerful, influential books of the 1960's.

Little, Malcolm. *Malcolm X Speaks.* Edited by George Breitman. New York: Merit Publishers, 1965. Speeches and statements made during the last eight months of his life, edited and published by a group of Trotzkyists.

Little, Malcolm. *Speeches of Malcolm X at Harvard.* Edited by Archie Epps. New York: Morrow, 1968.

Lomax, Louis E. *When the Word Is Given: A Report on Elijah Muhammad, Malcolm X, and the Black Muslim World.* Cleveland: World, 1963. The history and growing power of the Black Muslim movement and its leaders.

Makdisi, Nadim. "The Moslems of America," *Christian Century* 76 (August 26, 1959): 969-971.

Malcolm X *see* Little, Malcolm.

Muhammad, Elijah. *Message to the Black Man in America.* Chicago: Muhammad's Mosque No. 2, 1965.

Muhammad, Elijah. *The Supreme Wisdom: The Solution to the So-called Negroes' Problem.* 2d ed. Chicago: University of Islam, 1957. The leader's exposition of the basic doctrines of Black Muslimism. See also his column, "Mr. Muhammad Speaks," in the *Pittsburgh Courier.*

"The Right to Practice Black Muslim Tenets in State Prisons," *Harvard Law Review* 75 (February 1962):837 + .

Samuels, Gertrude. "Feud within the Black Muslims," *New York Times Magazine,* March 22, 1964, p. 17 + . Between Malcolm X and Elijah Muhammad.

Samuels, Gertrude. "Two Ways: Black Muslim and NAACP," *New York Times Magazine,* May 12, 1963, pp. 26-27 + .

Shack, William A. "Black Muslims: A Nativistic Religious Movement among Negro Americans," *Race* 3 (November 1961):57-67.

Sherwin, Mark. *The Extremists.* New York: St. Martin's, 1963. Black Muslims.

Southwick, Albert B. "Malcolm X: Charismatic Demagogue," *Christian Century* 80 (June 5, 1963):740-741.

Spellman, A. B. "Black Nationalism and Radical Unity," *The Second Coming* 1 (January 1965):10-12. On the appeal of Malcolm X to Harlem masses who are indifferent to the orthodox Negro leadership.

Spellman, A. B. "Interview with Malcolm X," *Monthly Review,* May 1964.

Tyler, Lawrence L. "The Protestant Ethic among the Black Muslims," *Phylon* 27 (Spring 1966):5-14.

Warren, Robert Penn. "Malcolm X: Mission and Meaning," *Yale Review* 56 (Winter 1967):161-171.

Black Panthers

Anthony, Earl. *Picking Up the Guns: The Story of the Black Panthers.* New York: Dial, 1970. Narrative by an original organization member.

Baruch, Ruth-Marion, and Pirkle Jones. *The Vanguard: A Photographic Essay on the Black Panthers.* With an introduction by William Worthy. Boston: Beacon, 1970.

"The Black Panther Party: Toward Liberation of the Colony," *New Left Review* no. 56 (July-August 1969):40-43. Resolution passed by the SDS national council meeting on March 30, 1967.

"The Black Panther Ten-Point Program," *North American Review* (new series) 5 (July-August 1968):16-17.

"Black Panthers: The Afro-Americans' Challenge," *Tricontinental* (January-February 1969):96-111. Interview with two young party leaders: George Murray and John Major Ford.

Buckley, William F., Jr. "In Re Bobby Seale," *National Review* 21 (December 2, 1969): 1234-1235.

Buckley, William F., Jr. "Total Confrontation," *National Review* 21 (November 18, 1969):1157–1158.

Chandler, Christopher. "Black Panther Killings in Chicago," *New Republic* 162 (January 10, 1970):21–24.

Cleaver, Eldridge. "Revolution in the White Mother Country & National Liberation in the Black Colony," *North American Review* (new series) 5 (July–August 1968):13–15. Discussion of the alliance of the Black Panther party and the Peace and Freedom party.

Cleaver, Eldridge. "Tears for the Pigs," *Humanist* 29 (March–April 1969):5, 8–10.

Cover, Robert. "A Year of Harassment," *Nation* 210 (February 2, 1970):110–113.

Francis, Theodore O. *The Black Panthers.* New York: Praeger, 1969.

Harris, Michael. "Black Panthers: The Cornered Cats," *Nation* 207 (July 8, 1968):15–18.

Haughey, John C. "Those Black Panthers," *America* 122 (January 17, 1970):43–44. The origins and goals of the organization.

Keveli, Hamaji Udumu. "Black Panthers vs. the Police," *Liberator* 9 (February 1969):9–11.

Marine, Gene. *The Black Panthers.* New York: New American Library, 1969.

Marine, Gene. "The Persecution and Assassination of the Black Panthers as Performed by the Oakland Police under the Direction of Chief Charles R. Gain, Mayor John Reading, et al.," *Ramparts* 6 (June 29, 1968):37–47.

"Marked for Extinction," *Nation* 209 (December 22, 1969):684.

"A New Breed of Blacks," *Economist* 228 (August 31, 1968):22–23. Black Panthers.

Newton, Huey P. "The Black Panthers," *Ebony* 24 (August 1969):106–108.

Rogers, R. "Black Guns on Campus: Black Panthers and US," *Nation* 208 (May 5, 1969):558–560.

Sayre, Nora. "Black Panthers," *Progressive* 33 (July 1969):20–23.

Sayre, Nora. "The Black Panthers Are Coming: America on the Eve of Race Revolution," *New Statesman* 77 (May 2, 1969):613–616.

Seale, Bobby. "A Rap from Bobby Seale," *University Review* (February 1970):13.

Steel, Ronald. "Letter from Oakland: The Panthers," *New York Review of Books* 13 (September 11, 1969):14–23. Activities and analysis of the Black Panther party; response of police and Federal Bureau of Investigation.

Stern, Sol. "The Call of the Black Panthers," *New York Times Magazine,* August 6, 1967, pp. 10–11+.

Swados, Harry. "Old Con, Black Panther, Brilliant Writer and Quintessential American: E. Cleaver," *New York Times Magazine,* September 7, 1969, pp. 38–39+.

Swain, Lawrence. "Eldridge Cleaver," *North American Review* (new series) 5 (July–August, 1968):18–21. Cleaver's political message and the April 6, 1968 confrontation between the Oakland Panthers and the local police.

Response and Resistance

Abernathy, Ralph David. "Black Preacher Looks at the Black Manifesto," *Christian Century* 86 (August 13, 1969):1064–1065.

"Black Manifesto Demand from U.S. Catholics," *Catholic Mind* 67 (June 1969):4–6. Text taken from the mimeographed release of James Forman addressed to Cardinal Cooke of New York.

Bolner, James. "Toward a Theory of Racial Reparations," *Phylon* 29 (Spring 1968):41–47. Discussion of the theory and possible objections to a program of reparations to the Negro minority who have been humiliated or injured.

Booker, Simeon. "What Blacks Can Expect from Nixon," *Ebony* 24 (January 1969):27–30+.

Campbell, Ernest T. "The Case for Reparations," *Theology Today* 26 (October 1969):266–283. Response of Riverside Church to Forman's confrontation.

Cochrane, Eric. "The Church and Black Power," *New City* 6 (May 1968):17–22. Sees black power as a necessary instrument to force the Catholic church to face racism as both sinful and heretical.

Cone, James H. *Black Theology and Black Power*. New York: Seabury, 1969.

Davis, J. "The Position of the Catholic Church in the Black Community," *Homiletic and Pastoral Review* 69 (June 1969):699–707. Black Catholic Clergy Caucus.

Gannon, Thomas M. "What the Black Community Wants," *America* 121 (December 6, 1969):558–562. In response to questioning, three black leaders recommend to a Jesuit group an apostolic program for racial justice.

Geyer, Alan. "May Day in Manhattan," *Christian Century* 86 (May 14, 1969):671–672. James Forman's "Black Manifesto" to the National Council of Churches, demanding "reparations" from religious institutions.

Goetz, Ronald. "Black Manifesto: The Great White Hope," *Christian Century* 86 (June 18, 1969):832–833. Discussion: *ibid.*, (August 6, 1969):1046–1047.

Harding, Vincent. "Black Power and the American Christ," *Christian Century* 84 (January 4, 1967):10–13. Subtitled "Behind the theology of 'blackness' is the deep ambivalence of American Negroes to the white man's genteel, oh-so-white Jesus."

Harding, Vincent. "The Religion of Black Power," in Donald R. Cutler, ed., *The Religious Situation: 1968*. Boston: Beacon, 1968, pp. 3–38.

Harrington, Michael, and Arnold Kaufman. "Black Reparations: Two Views," *Dissent* 16 (July–August 1969):317–320.

Haselden, Kyle, and Whitney M. Young, Jr. "Should There Be 'Compensation' for Negroes?" *New York Times Magazine*, October 6, 1963, p. 43 +. Mr. Young, Executive Secretary of the Urban League. Dr. Haselden, Managing Editor of *Christian Century*.

Haughey, John C. "Black Catholicism," *America* 120 (March 22, 1969):325–327. Subhead: "Black ecclesiastical power is not incompatible with the structure or doctrine of the Catholic Church. How can its demands be met and made a part of the American Church?"

Hough, Joseph C., Jr. *Black Power and White Protestants: A Christian Response to the New Negro Pluralism*. New York: Oxford University Press, 1968.

Howe, Irving. "Nixon's Dream—and Black Reality," *Dissent* 16 (March–April 1969): 101–107.

Hughes, Graham. "Reparations for Blacks?" *New York University Law Review* 43 (December 1968):1063–1074. Author considers possibilities of tax and other economic concessions to redress past and present economic standards of the Negro. If economic improvement is not achieved soon, he sees justification in political, militant black separatism.

Kempton, Murray. "The Black Manifesto," *New York Review of Books* 13 (July 10, 1969): 31–32. Background material and evaluation.

McGraw, Jim. "Unity, Ecumenicity and Black Power," *Renewal* 9 (January 1969):4. Black Caucus activity in Protestantism and Roman Catholicism.

Margolis, Richard J. "The Two Nations at Wesleyan University," *New York Times Magazine,* January 18, 1970, pp. 9 +. Blacks and whites as students and administrators; problems of assimilation.

Merton, Thomas. *Faith and Violence*. Notre Dame, Ind.: University of Notre Dame Press, 1968. Christian teaching and Christian practice. See especially section 3 entitled "From Non-Violence to Black Power," pp. 121–188.

Mitchell, Henry H. "Black Power and the Christian Church," *Foundations* 11 (April–June 1968):99–109.

Mulder, John M. "The Church as a Financial Institution, or Forgive Us Our Debts," *Theology Today* 26 (October 1969):294–298. In context of James Forman's challenge, author examines current and possible uses of church's immense wealth.

"N.A.A.C.P. Executive Urges Churches to Reject Demands for Reparations," *Christian Century* 86 (November 5, 1969):1413.

National Committee of Black Churchmen. "Black Theology," *Christian Century* 86 (October 15, 1969):1310. A statement of the National Committee prepared by the (Sub)-Committee on Theological Prospectus. See also P. N. William's explanatory article, *ibid.*, pp. 1311–1312.

Niebuhr, Reinhold. "The Negro Minority and Its Fate in a Self-Righteous Nation," *Social Action* 35 (October 1968):53–64.

Offer, Henry J. "Black Power, A Great Saving Grace," *American Ecclesiastical Review* 159 (September 1968):193-201. Posits that black power, if received by white society with enlightened consideration, could benefit all America. A plea for the voice of conscience to respond.

"Office for Black Catholics: Formation of National Office for Black Catholics," *America* 121 (November 29, 1969):516.

"Racist Church? Black Clergy Conference," *Commonweal* 88 (May 10, 1968):222.

Reuther, Rosemary. "Black Theology and Black Church," *America* 120 (June 14, 1969): 684-687. Poses the question: Is black theology a subterfuge for racial propaganda, or is it a sensitive Christian concern?

Schuchter, Arnold. *Reparations: The Black Manifesto and Its Challenge to White Churches.* Philadelphia: Lippincott, 1970.

Serrin, William. "Cleage's Alternative," *Reporter* 38 (May 30, 1968):20-30.

Sleeper, C. Freeman. *Black Power and Christian Responsibility: Some Biblical Foundations for Social Ethics.* Nashville, Tenn.: Abingdon, 1969. Analysis of ethical tradition in the Bible as related to the issue considered. Argues that it is imperative that the white community reflect and respond to the question, "What is a responsible use of white power to enable blacks to achieve an effective share in the total assets of society?" Notable bibliography.

Stackhouse, Max L. "Reparations: A Call to Repentance?" *The Lutheran Quarterly* 21 (November 1969):358-380. Ethical questions raised by James Forman's "Black Manifesto."

"Symposium on Black Power," *Lutheran Quarterly* 20, (May 1968):152-160. Position paper written by the parish council of a Chicago Lutheran Church; responses.

Vorspan, Albert. "How James Forman Lost His Cool but Saved Religion in 1969," *Christian Century* 86 (August 6, 1969):1042.

Washington, Joseph R., Jr. *Black and White Power Subreption.* Boston: Beacon, 1969.

Wildavsky, Aaron. "The Empty-Head Blues: Black Rebellion and White Reaction," *Public Interest* no. 11 (Spring 1968):3-16. The dilemma of the white liberal facing Negro's deprivations. Practical proposals for response.

"Will the Black Manifesto Help Blacks?" *Christian Century* 86 (May 21, 1969):701.

Williams, Preston N. "The Atlanta Document: An Interpretation," *Christian Century* 86 (October 15, 1968):1311-1312. Black theology defined by the co-chairman of the National Committee of Black Churchmen.

Wilmore, Gayraud S., Jr. *The Church's Response to the Black Manifesto.* New York: United Presbyterian Church U.S.A., 1969. Response to the National Black Economic Development Conference confrontation by the General Assembly of the Presbyterian Church.

21   A Guide to Further Research

The preceding bibliography is necessarily selective of the wealth of materials relating to the black American published since 1954. It is intended to span several areas of social change. To facilitate more extensive research, including that in unpublished materials, and to enable the student to keep abreast of current developments, this chapter attempts to serve as a guide to indexes, abstracts, bibliographies, serials, checklists, and other tools covering a broader time span. Of the specific titles mentioned below, some are cited above in the body of the text, but are not as fully analyzed as would be required for comprehensive research on a single aspect of a topic. For the convenience of the user, the frequency, duration or suspension, imprint, and variation in title or relation to previous serials are indicated whenever possible.

1   General Background

The mass of information in the daily press is made accessible through the indexes of two national newspapers. The *New York Times Index* (1913–   ), now semi-monthly with annual cumulations, provides a detailed contents analysis of its late city edition, and, by its citations, serves concurrently as a reference to other files. For historical research, an earlier index of the *New York Times* covers the period beginning 1851. The *Subject Index to the Christian Science Monitor* (January 1960–   ) Boston, a monthly with annual cumulations, is also useful.

The *Monthly Catalog of United States Government Publications,* with its subject index and annual cumulations, is the major key to materials available from the Government Printing Office or other issuing departments, as well as indication of those to be found in depository collections. Drawn from this and from publication lists of individual agencies is a *Selective List of Government Publications about the American Negro,* prepared by the Prince George's County Memorial Library (Oxon Hill, Md., 1969). For a current overview of Congressional activity and the efforts of individual legislators on matters relating to the Negro, the *Congressional Quarterly Almanac* and the *Congres-*

297

sional Weekly Reports are particularly useful. Congressional debates, voting records, and presidential messages to that body relating to measures affecting the Negro can be traced through the indexes of the *Congressional Record.*

A number of state and municipal commissions against discrimination conduct investigations, issue reports, make recommendations for action, and perform other functions in the area of minority community relations. Among these are the New York State Commission against Discrimination, Michigan Fair Employment Practices Commission, Human Relations Commission of Illinois, Ohio Civil Rights Commission, Pennsylvania Human Relations Commission, Massachusetts Commission against Discrimination, California Fair Employment Practices Commission, and Connecticut Commission on Civil Rights. Some of their publications are listed in the *Monthly Checklist of State Publications* (1910-   ) issued by the Library of Congress. Inquiries to gubernatorial or mayoral offices will elicit information on local agencies. *Race Relations Law Survey* (May 1969-   ) is a bi-monthly replacement of *Race Relations Law Reporter* (February 1956-Fall 1967), both published by Vanderbilt University School of Law. Summaries of court decisions, legislative acts, executive orders, and administrative agency regulations on all levels of government pertaining to several areas or disciplines are found therein. Citations are made to published sources whenever available. Representing an opposing view are the Governor's Commission on Constitutional Government, Atlanta, Ga., and the State Sovereignty Commissions of Mississippi and Louisiana.

The *Index to Periodical Articles by and about Negroes,* compiled by the staffs of the Hallie Q. Brown Library of Ohio Central State College and the Schomburg Collection of the New York Public Library, analyzes many Negro periodicals not indexed elsewhere. It is a quarterly subject index published 1960-1965 under the variant title *Index to Selected Periodicals* and 1950-1959 as *Index to Selected Negro Periodicals,* for which there is a decennial cumulation. A *Guide to Negro Periodical Literature* covered the period 1941-1946.

Other interdisciplinary journals not presently covered by the above service merit attention. *Afro-American Studies* (April 1970-   ) is published in New York with the editorial advice of Andrew Billingsly, Julian Bond, Hylan Lewis, Alvin F. Pouissant, and others. *Black Scholar* (November 1969-   ) San Francisco, is committed to black studies and research by the black intellectual community. The *Journal of Afro-American Affairs* (May 1970-   ) continues the former *Harvard Journal of Negro Affairs* (1964-1968) as a semiannual publication of the Afro-American Center of Harvard University and Radcliffe College with the expectation of moving to a quarterly format in 1971. *Black Dialogue: A Black Magazine for Black People* is a quarterly (1965-   ) initiated by students at San Francisco State College, with editorial offices now in New York. *Soulbook,* formerly subtitled *The Quarterly Journal of Revolutionary Afro-America,* now subtitled *The Revolutionary Journal of the Black World* (1967-   ), is a mimeographed collation covering aspects of the social sciences and humanities. See also the notes on chapter 5.

Monroe N. Works's *Bibliography of the Negro in Africa and America* (1928. Reprinted New York: Octagon, 1965) is an indispensable compilation of references to the Negro for the earlier period. S. H. Kessler lists 93 bibliographies dealing with many phases of Negro life in "American Negro Literature, A Bibliographic Guide," *Bulletin of Bibliography* 21 (September 1955):181-185. Dorothy B. Porter's *Working Bibliography on the Negro in the United States* (Ann Arbor, Mich.: University Microfilms, 1969), focusing on the twentieth century, is essentially limited to monograph references. Lorraine Hildebrand and Richard S. Aiken have prepared an extensive *Bibliography of Afro-American Print and Nonprint Resources in Libraries of Pierce County, Washington* (Tacoma Community College Library, 1969?). The Washington State Library has compiled *The Negro in the State of Washington, 1788-1967: A Bibliography of Published Works and of Unpublished Source Materials on the Life and Achievements of the Negro in the Evergreen State* (Olympia, Wash., 1968). The New Jersey Library Association is responsible for *New Jersey and the Negro: A Bibliography, 1715-1966* (Trenton, 1969). Rutgers University Library has prepared *The Negro and New Jersey: A Checklist of Books, Pamphlets, Official Publications, Broadsides, and Dissertations, 1754-1964, in the Rutgers University* (New Brunswick, 1965). Dorothy R. Homer and Ann M. Swarthout are compilers of *Books about the Negro: An Annotated Bibliography* (New York: Praeger, 1966). The New York Public Library is responsible for quinquennial editions of *The Negro in the United States: A List of Significant Books* (9th ed., 1965), an annotated sampling of some 300 titles. For an excellent overview of contemporary writing, see Louis Filler's "Negro Materials of the 1960s," *Choice* 5 (April 1968):161-170; also available as an offprint.

The Negro in Print (May 1965-   ) is a bibliographical survey in serial form of the Negro Bibliographic and Research Center, Washington, selectively annotating current publications about the Negro and occasionally other minority groups. *The Negro in the United States: A Research Guide* (Bloomington: Indiana University Press, 1965) by Edwin K. Welsch is a brief, useful guide which has been supplemented, in a sense, by a series of individual lists on various facets of Negro life and experience collectively entitled *Focus: Black America* (1969), prepared under the aegis of the Indiana University Libraries. *A Bibliography of Doctoral Research on the Negro, 1933-1966* (Ann Arbor, Mich.: University Microfilms, 1969) is a classified compilation by Earle H. West; an author index includes references to page and volume of *Dissertation Abstracts*. For dissertations since 1966, consult the subject indexes of the abstract volumes. Among the bibliographies of relevant paperbacks are: *The American Negro in Paperback: A Selected List . . .* by Joseph E. Penn et al. (Washington: National Education Association, 1967); *Red, White, and Black: Minorities in America* (Briarcliff Manor, N.Y.: Combined Paperback Exhibit, 1969), a list of books prepared for display at the American Library Association Conference in Atlantic City in June 1969; and *1150 Black Studies* (Holbrook, Mass.: A & A Paperback Distributors, 1969), a classified short-title list on American Negro history, social institutions, and culture.

Of the many special libraries possessing unique collections, the Schomburg Collection of the New York Public Library is the most renowned. Its *Dictionary Catalog ... of Literature and History,* 9 vols. and a 2 vol. *Supplement* (Boston: G. K. Hall, 1962, 1967) reproduce the card file of bound monographs and periodicals on the experience of peoples of African descent, past and present. It is international in scope and language. The collectors have also amassed vertical file data, records, music, and objets d'art for which use is restricted to the premises. Also noteworthy is the published *Catalogue of the Heartman Negro Collection, Texas Southern University Library* (Houston, 1956?) comprising over 15,000 items dating from 1600–1955. The American Negro Project at Princeton University assays to build a broad collection of monographs, serials, and ephemera arranged in over 500 subject classifications. Description of the contents of other collections can be found in Lee Ash's *Subject Collections* (3d ed. New York: Bowker, 1967) and through the detailed subject index of Anthony T. Kruzas' *Directory of Special Libraries and Information Centers* (2d ed. Detroit: Gale Research, 1968).

The National Union Catalog of Manuscripts, 1959–   (Washington: U.S. Library of Congress, 1961–   ) with its periodic cumulative subject indexes is an invaluable guide. Also noteworthy is John McDonough's "Manuscript Resources for the Study of Negro Life and History," *Quarterly Journal of the Library of Congress* 26 (July 1969):126–148.

2   History

There are three historical Negro periodicals, each addressed to a different audience. The *Journal of Negro History* (1916–   ) is a quarterly containing essays, often reprints of short historical documents, and book reviews. There is a cumulative subject, author, and documents index for 1916–1968 to which annual supplements will be added. The *Negro History Bulletin* (1937–   ) is a monthly emphasizing shorter articles, also with book reviews. Both are published in Washington by the Association for the Study of Negro Life and History. *Negro Heritage* (1961–   ) is a monthly in loose-leaf format now published in Reston, Virginia. It is cumulatively indexed through 1968.

The American Jewish Committee has prepared *Negro History and Literature: A Selected Annotated Bibliography* (New York: Anti-Defamation League of B'nai B'rith, 1968). Capital University Library has issued *Black Culture* (Columbus, Ohio, 1969), a resource guide in black history encompassing books, pamphlets, periodicals, and audio-visual materials. The Conference on the Negro in America, Princeton University was responsible for an excellent bibliographical essay entitled *The Negro in America* (Lincoln University: Lincoln University, Penna., 1966). Edwin A. Salk has edited *A Layman's Guide to Negro History* (New York: McGraw-Hill, 1967). William L. Katz has compiled a well-annotated *Teacher's Guide to American Negro History* (Chicago: Quadrangle, 1968). The National Council of the Churches of Christ in the

U.S.A. has issued the *Negro Heritage Resource Guide: A Bibliography of the Negro in Contemporary America* (New York, 1967). Earl Spangler is compiler of *Bibliography of Negro History, Selected and Annotated Entries: General and Minnesota* (Minneapolis: Ross and Haines, 1963); approximately two thirds of the references are to Minnesota. "The Availability of Negro Source Material in Philadelphia," *Negro History Bulletin* 32 (March 1968):17, is complemented by an illustrated exhibition catalog of the Library Company of Philadelphia and the Historical Society of Pennsylvania, *Negro History: 1533–1903* (1969) and a bibliography of the Free Library of Philadelphia, *To Be Black in America* (1970).

For the ante-bellum period, Henry J. Carman and Arthur W. Thompson's *Guide to the Principal Sources for American Civilization, 1800–1900, in the City of New York: Printed Materials* (New York: Columbia University Press, 1962) provides a selective bibliography and list of sources, both general and as they apply to particular states, giving library location. Greatest emphasis is accorded works published in the nineteenth century. A companion volume on manuscripts (1960) contains unpublished sources and considerable material on slavery. Dwight L. Dumond's *Bibliography of Antislavery in America* (Ann Arbor: University of Michigan Press, 1961) includes works published up to the Civil War. The May issues of the *Journal of Southern History* review "Southern History in Periodicals," a component section of which deals with the Negro and slavery. For further research on the role of the churches in American Negro history, see "The Christianization and Emancipation of the Negro: Colonial Period to the Civil War," a bibliographical essay of primarily nineteenth-century publications with selected documents appended in *Source Book and Bibliographical Guide for American Church History* by Peter G. Mode (1920. Reprinted, Boston: J. S. Canner, 1964), and the chapter, "The Anti-Slavery Crusade," in Nelson R. Burr's *A Critical Bibliography of Religion in America.* Vol. IV: *Religion in American Life* (Princeton, N.J.: Princeton University Press, 1961). Many articles on abolition with regional emphasis can be found in state and independent historical society publications.

Available in microcard form is *A Collection of Anti-Slavery Propaganda in the Oberlin College Library* (Louisville, Ky.: Lost Cause Press, 1968). It consists largely of American anti-slavery propaganda published before 1863, with the addition of some pro-slavery documents. The *Classified Catalogue of the Negro Collection of the Hampton Institute,* Collis P. Huntington Library (Hampton, Va., 1940) is important for its material on slavery and Reconstruction. James D. Graham has published "Negro Protest in America, 1900–1955: A Bibliographical Guide," *South Atlantic Quarterly* 67 (Winter 1968):94–107.

3   Demography

The monthly publications list of the U.S. Bureau of the Census is the most complete and current source for pertinent government demographic reports and statistics. Summaries of these figures are in the annual *Statistical Abstract of the United States.* One can expect to find more detailed analytical data drawn from the current decennial census in forthcoming Census publications.

4 Definition and Description

Franklin Frazier wrote that "the Negro church has left its imprint upon practically every aspect of Negro life." Burr's bibliography of religion (q.v.) contains two extensive essays indispensable to a thorough understanding of the historical aspects. They are entitled "The Negro Church" and "Negro Religious Literature."

Newspapers and periodicals constitute a unique contemporaneous record of the social institutions of a group and their relations to the society at large. The section "Negro Publications" in N. W. Ayer and Son's annual *Directory of Newspapers and Periodicals* provides a lengthy list essentially of newspapers. Complementing it is an alphabetical list of newspapers and periodicals of Negro interest in the United States and Canada in the *Standard Periodical Directory* (New York: Oxbridge, 1970). The U.S. Library of Congress has prepared *Negro Newspapers on Microfilm: A Select List* (Washington, 1953). Under the direction of August Meier, Bell & Howell has acquired a significant microfilm list of leading newspapers of the black community, both historical and current. *Crisis: A Record of the Darker Races* (1910-   ) is the official monthly organ of the National Association for the Advancement of Colored People. Reprint volumes 1-50 for the period 1910-1960 have been published by Arno Press in an authorized edition. Negro Universities Press has reprinted *Crisis* volumes for the period 1910-1940 as well as several other Negro periodicals and anti-slavery tracts. Four popular general magazines issued by Johnson Publishing Co. regularly found on metropolitan newsstands are: *Ebony* (1945-   ) and *Tan* (1950-   ), both monthlies; *Jet* (1951-   ), a weekly; and *Negro Digest* (1952-   ), a monthly review. *Essence* (May 1970-   ) New York, a new monthly magazine for black women published by the Hollingsworth Group features food, fashion, and entertainment columns in addition to articles on heritage and folklore and a regular news section.

5 Biography

Since *Who's Who in Colored America* ceased publication in 1950, there has been no equally comprehensive biographical source. The *Negro Handbook* (q.v.) contains biographical sketches of men and women of "contemporary significance." A dictionary of notable American women, forthcoming from Harvard University Press, includes a few score well-researched biographies of

Negro women, for the most part of the nineteenth century. Louis Kaplan's *Bibliography of American Autobiographies* registers a number of references under the entry "Negro," divided by period. Juanita B. Fuller's thesis, *An Annotated Bibliography of Biographies and Autobiographies,* available only on microcard from the Association of College and Research Libraries, has limited usefulness. Reprints of slave narratives, many with critical introductions, are being issued in increasing numbers.

6   Folklore and Literature

Folklore and literature present a particularly vivid picture of black experience and aspiration. Charles Haywood's *Bibliography of North American Folklore and Folksong* (2d ed. New York: Dover, 1961) contains many references to material on the beliefs, customs, legends, and speech of the Negro as it has been transcribed into folklore. There is a short essay on Negro folklore in *Literary History of the United States: Bibliography,* edited by Robert E. Spiller et al. (3d ed. New York: Macmillan, 1963) with particular attention given to publications in the first decade of this century.

For a critical examination of early literature, Dorothy Porter's "Early American Negro Writing: A Bibliographical Study," *Papers of the Bibliographical Society of America* 39 (January 1945):192-268, is recommended; also "The American Negro in American Literature: A Selected Bibliography of Critical Materials," by John S. Lash in *Journal of Negro Education* 15 (Fall 1946):722-730. With emphasis on the twentieth century, Abraham Chapman has compiled a useful handbook, *The Negro in American Literature and A Bibliography of Literature by and about Negro Americans* (Oshkosh: Wisconsin Council of Teachers of English, Wisconsin State University, 1966). An introductory essay is followed by an extensive classified bibliography with brief annotations. *Afro-American Writers* by Darwin Turner (New York: Appleton-Century-Crofts, 1970) is a recent volume in the Goldentree Bibliographies in Language and Literature. Focusing on the literature and critical studies of black writers in the United States, it enumerates recent scholarship with emphasis on the twentieth century. Within the section on American twentieth-century literature of the *MLA International Bibliography* (1921-   ), citations are made to significant articles about individual black writers and by genre. It is especially useful for publications outside the United States which are otherwise not easily found. Addressed primarily to teachers and introductory students, *Negro Literature for High School Students* by Barbara Dodds (National Council of Teachers of English: Champaign, Ill., 1968) includes an historical survey of individual writers with biographical notes and an extensive bibliography.

Amistad (April 1970-   ) is a black-oriented literary periodical issued by Random House with the avowed purpose of giving broader public attention to outstanding fiction and nonfiction pieces on black subjects written by both black and white authors. Indiana State University, School of Education issues *Negro American Literature Forum* (1967-   ), a quarterly with critical book reviews. *A Century of Fiction by American Negroes, 1853-1952* by Maxwell Whiteman (Philadelphia: Maurice Jacobs, 1955) is a descriptive register which attempts not only to list all fiction by Negroes during this period, but corrects mistaken attributions to Negroes of several books. A sampling of bibliographies of individual writers follows:

Fischer, Russell G. "James Baldwin: A Bibliography, 1947-1962," *Bulletin of Bibliography* 24 (January-April 1965):127-130.

Kindt, Kathleen A. "James Baldwin: A Checklist, 1947-1962," *Bulletin of Bibliography* 24 (January-April 1965):123-127. Works by, biographical and critical.

Standley, Fred J. "James Baldwin: A Checklist, 1963-1967," *Bulletin of Bibliography* 25 (May-August 1968):135-137+.

Kaiser, Ernest. "A Selected Bibliography of the Published Writings of W. E. B. DuBois," *Freedomways* 5 (Winter 1965):207-213.

Dickinson, Donald C. *A Biobibliography of Langston Hughes, 1902-1967.* Hamden, Conn.: Archon Books, 1967.

Fabre, Michel, and Edward Margolis. "Richard Wright (1908-1960): A Bibliography," *Bulletin of Bibliography* 24 (January-April 1965):131-133+. Updates a 1953 bibliography of the author by M. D. Sprague published in the same periodical.

So much poetry is of a fugitive nature that it is often difficult to record its existence. For an intensive study of the contemporary period one must search individual issues of such journals as *Black Dialogue, Black Theatre, Freedomways* (q.q.v.), and the *Journal of Black Poetry* (1967-   ), a quarterly emanating from San Francisco. To identify earlier verse there is Arthur A. Schomburg's *Bibliographical Checklist of American Negro Poetry* (New York: Heartman, 1916) and Dorothy B. Porter's *North American Poets: A Bibliographical Checklist of Their Writings, 1760-1944* (1945. Reprinted Philadelphia: Burt Franklin, 1963).

7   Theater, Dance, and the Arts

Black Theatre (1969?-   ) is a bi-monthly featuring one-act plays, essays on theater, and short poems. It is published by the New Lafayette Theatre, New York. Oda Jurges has compiled a "Selected Bibliography: Black Plays, Books and Articles Related to Black Theatre Published from 1/1960 to 2/1968," *Drama Review* 12 (Summer 1968):176-180. One of the series of *Focus: Black America* (q.v.) entitled *Fine Arts and the Black American* ... is helpful in identifying black artists and their special fields; it also provides additional references. With the impetus of C. Eric Lincoln and the financial assistance of the Twentieth-Century Fund, a Black Academy of Arts and Letters was formed in 1969. Designed to foster and affirm excellence of black people in the performing and plastic arts, in writing, and in scholarship, it seeks to encourage recognition of their achievement by both blacks and whites.

8   The Negro in Literature and the Arts

"The Negro in American Drama," by Hilda Josephine Lawson, *Bulletin of Bibliography* 17 (January 1940):7-8+ and sections of the bibliographies of John S. Lash and Abraham Chapman (q.q.v.) give guidance and dimension to the subject of the treatment of the Negro in American drama. References to material selected from the Schomburg Collection was compiled by J. B. Hutson in "Harlem, A Cultural History," *Metropolitan Museum Bulletin* 27 (January 1969):280-288.

9   Music

It is impossible to separate completely much sophisticated Negro folklore and literature from music and minstrelsy as a performing art; spirituals, work songs, and the blues are an integral part of both. Reference is therefore made again to Haywood, calling particular attention to the section on folksongs. The bibliography cites monographs, periodicals, records, and sheet music arrangements, both in collection and as individual titles. Sections in Spiller and in Burr (q.q.v.) on Negro spirituals are worthy of attention. A good checklist of English language monographs, *Black Music,* has been prepared by Richard Colvig for the Oakland Public Library (Oakland, Calif., 1969). The literature of jazz is represented as well as biographies of black musicians. "Black Music," *Choice* 6 (November 1969):1169-1179, is an annotated bibliography of English language monographs on Afro-American music, with a section specifically related to music indigenous to the United States; it is especially important for older works. In this chapter I have refrained from including a large number of references on jazz not because they are unimportant to an understanding of black heritage and culture, but because information about jazz is more readily available than material covering other facets of black music, and because of the exceptional bibliographies listed below. Alan F. Merriam's *A Bibliography of Jazz* (Philadelphia: American Folklore Society, 1954) is an author listing of over 3,000 items with a subject index and a comprehensive list of periodicals devoted to jazz. Robert George Reisner in *The Literature of Jazz* (2d ed. rev. and enl. New York: New York Public Library, 1959) analyzes monographs and serial articles. *Ethnomusicology and Folk Music: An International Bibliography of Dissertations and Theses,* compiled by Frank Gillis and Alan P.

Merriam (Middletown, Conn.: Wesleyan University Press, 1966), provides references to Negro folk music and jazz. The Institute of Jazz Studies, New York, serves as a clearing house to coordinate the studies of jazz authors and musicians with those of social science specialists in American civilization. The North Texas State University, which has acquired extensive records, tapes, discographies, and books relating to Duke Ellington, is illustrative of the special library collections in this field. The music division of the Library of Congress reports a collection of more than 6,000 Negro spirituals drawn from over one hundred sources.

10   Intergroup Relations

The Journal of Human Relations (1953-   ) is a quarterly publication of Central State College, Wilberforce, Ohio, pledged to social integration; the journal is analyzed in *Index to Periodical Articles by and about Negroes. Community* (1943-   ) is a monthly newsletter of Friendship House, Chicago, concerned with programs on interracial affairs. The National Association of Intergroup Relations Officials, New York, is co-sponsor with the Council on Social Work Education of *Intergroup Relations Agencies* (1969), a directory of private and university intergroup and human relations agencies and social action units of religious organizations.

The classic reference in this area is Edgar T. and Alma M. Thompson's *Race and Region: A Descriptive Bibliography* (Chapel Hill: University of North Carolina Press, 1949), drawn from the resources of Duke University, the University of North Carolina, and North Carolina College, Durham. It is especially concerned with relations between whites and Negroes in the United States. Although not strictly analagous for research purposes, Melvin M. Tumin and Robert Rotberg's *Segregation and Desegregation: A Digest of Recent Research* (New York: Anti-Defamation League of B'nai B'rith, 1956) and the *Supplement, 1956-1959* (1960) provide a retrospective look at the decade of the 1950s. Thereafter, see *Research Annual on Intergroup Relations* by Melvin M. Tumin, the 1966 volume (New York: Praeger, 1967), published prior to 1965 by the Committee on Desegregation and Integration in cooperation with the Anti-Defamation League of B'nai B'rith. Jean D. Grambs prepared *Intergroup Education: Methods and Materials* (New York: Praeger, 1968). Annie L. McPheeter's *Negro Progress in Atlanta, Georgia, 1950-1960: A Selected Bibliography* (Atlanta Public Library, 1964) is a regional resource guide. The San Fernando Valley State College has issued *Black Brown Bibliography* (Northridge, Calif., 1969), an annotated subject guide to significant materials on racial minorities in its college collection. It includes reprints but gives no indication of original publication dates. Emphasis is on the period 1950-1967.

11   Rural Problems

Publications of the Southern Regional Council are reliable sources of additional information. See also pertinent serial titles related to civil rights in the note to chapter 19.

12   Urban Problems

Renewal (1961-   ), issued monthly by the Chicago City Missionary Society, is concerned largely with inequities of the black minorities in an urban environment. The Council of Planning Librarians has published *The Role of Urban Planning in the Residential Integration of Middle-Class Negroes and Whites* (1968), a thesis abstract and bibliography by Lewis Bolan. Urban problems are the inevitable outgrowth of joblessness, substandard schools, and congested slum neighborhoods. Separate notes below on employment, housing, and education cover these areas of special concern.

13   Economic Status

The *Statistical Abstract of the United States* is a source of data on annual income and purchasing power. See also the note to chapter 14.

14   Employment

Employment and Earnings provides employment characteristics and data on a monthly basis, comparing white with Negro and other races. Quarterly averages of employment status can be found in the *Monthly Labor Review;* both are prepared by the U.S. Department of Labor, Bureau of Labor Statistics.

Only a sampling of citations related to black employment are given in chapter 14. For further references to articles in business and trade journals, see the monthly issues of *Business Periodicals Index.* The *Negro American Labor Council Newsletter,* New York, presents monthly another viewpoint. Encompassing monographs are Paul H. Norgren's bibliography, *Racial Discrimination in Employment* (Princeton, N.J.: Princeton University Press, 1962) and *Equal Employment Opportunity: Selected References* by Dorothy Poehlman (Washington: U.S. Department of Transportation, Federal Aviation Administration, 1968). James A. Gross' "Historians and the Literature of the Negro Worker," *Labor History* 10 (Summer 1969):536-546, is a critical guide.

15   Housing

Trends in Housing (1956-   ) is a monthly publication of the National Committee against Discrimination in Housing, New York, which furnishes current information on anti-discrimination housing laws and ordinances throughout the nation. Stephen D. Messner has edited *Minority Groups and Housing: A Selected Bibliography* (Storrs, Conn.: Center for Real Estate and Urban Economic Studies, University of Connecticut, 1968).

16   Education

The Journal of Negro Education (1932-   ), published quarterly by Howard University, includes, in addition to the principal articles cited in chapter 16, shorter papers and critical book reviews. The summer yearbook issue is devoted to various aspects of a single topic chosen for its particularly current concern. It is indexed annually with a cumulation for the years 1932-1962. *Integrated Education* (1963-   ), Chicago, is a semi-monthly containing special articles, a state-by-state report on integration in education, and a current bibliography as regular features. *Southern Education Report* (1965-   ), formerly *Southern Education News,* is issued monthly by the Southern Regional Council. Subject analysis of these journals can be found in the *Index to Periodical Articles by and about Negroes. Inequality in Education* (1969-   ) is the bulletin of the Center for Law and Education, Harvard University. It reports on research, litigation, legislation, and other items of reform; frequency varies.

The following bibliographies supplement the chapter references. S. M. Miller, Betty Saleem, and Harrington Bryce are compilers of *School Dropouts: A Commentary and Annotated Bibliography* (Syracuse, N.Y.: Syracuse University Youth Development Center, 1963); Meyer Weinberg of *School Integration: A Comprehensive Classified Bibliography of 3,100 References* (Chicago: Integrated Education Associates, 1967), and by the same author, "De Facto School Segregation: A Select Bibliography," *Law and Society Review* 2 (November 1967):151-165. Franklin Parker has assembled "Public School Desegregation: A Partial Bibliography of 113 Doctoral Dissertations," *Negro History Bulletin* 26 (April 1963):288+. For more up-to-date coverage, see the reference to dissertations in the note to chapter 1.

The *CLA Journal* is a scholarly quarterly publication of the College Language Association, Morgan State College, Baltimore, devoted to language and literature relating to the Afro-American; it is serviced by the *Index to Periodical Articles by and about Negroes. The Quarterly Review of Higher Education among Negroes* (1933-   ) from Johnson C. Smith University, Charlotte, N.C., treats educational topics at all levels. Student scholarships in dentistry for Negroes are listed in the February and September issues of the *Journal of the American Dental Association.*

18   Politics and Suffrage

The *Black Politician* (1969-   ) is a quarterly journal of political thought published by the Center on Urban and Minority Affairs, Los Angeles, California, focusing on the political issues affecting the black politician and his constituency. For current political activity use the newspaper indexes (see note to chapter 1), and for the parallel time period or topic, report and commentary in the black press is recommended. It is expected that the statistical tabulations from the 1970 decennial census will enable the political scientist to refine his measurements of voting patterns by geographic areas and racial or ethnic groups from which reliable causal connections can then be made.

19   The Freedom Revolution

The quarterly *Civil Rights Digest* (Spring 1968-   ) is published by the U.S. Commission on Civil Rights. In signed articles it gives broad coverage to problems encountered by blacks and other minority groups. Book reviews are a regular feature. The goals and day-to-day events of the Freedom Revolution can be traced from other publications: the monthly *SNCC Newsletter* issued by the Student Non-Violent Coordinating Committee in Atlanta; *Southern Patriot* (1942-   ), a monthly published by the Southern Conference Educational Fund, Louisville, Ky., and also available on microfilm; and *CORE-lator* (1965-1969?), an organ of the Congress on Racial Equality. The Southern Regional Council, Atlanta, issues pertinent reports and monographs on economic, political, and social problems in the journal, *New South* (1946-   ), an effectively illustrated monthly prior to 1966, now a quarterly. Volumes covering the period 1946-1967 are available on microfilm. New York-based *Freedomways: A Quarterly Review of the Negro Freedom Movement* contains thoughtful articles, occasional verse, and book reviews. *WCLC Newsletter* (1965-   ) is a monthly report of the Western Christian Leadership Council focusing on civil rights.

Alexander D. Brooks and Virginia H. Ellison's *Civil Rights and Liberties in the United States: An Annotated Bibliography* (New York: Civil Liberties Educational Foundation, 1962) includes a selection of general and scholarly works on Negro civil rights for the decade of the 1950's. Ann Pagenstecher's "Martin Luther King, Jr.: An Annotated Checklist," *Bulletin of Bibliography* 24 (January-April 1965):201-207, attempts to enumerate all works by and about King published in English, excepting newspapers and encyclopedias. The *Martin Luther King, Jr. Memorial Collection* and *Supplement 1* prepared by the San Francisco Theological Library (San Anselmo, California, 1969) merit attention.

Voices of resistance are sounded in *The Citizen* (1955-   ), earlier *The Citizens' Council,* the official journal of the Citizens' Councils of America,

Jackson, Miss. The Defenders of State Sovereignty and Individual Liberties, Richmond, Va., speak through *Defenders' News and Views* (1955-   ). *Thunderbolt: The White Man's Viewpoint* (1959-   ) is the monthly organ of the National States Rights Party, Savannah, Ga.

The involvement of the churches in civil rights is expressed in various serials. The National Conference for Interracial Justice, Chicago, publishes *Commitment* (1964-   ); *Church in Metropolis* is a quarterly publication of the Joint Urban Program of the Episcopal Church, New York; *SIP Newsletter* is a monthly bulletin of the Selma Inter-Religious Project of Tuscaloosa, Ala.; *Renewal* (1961-   ), issued monthly by the Chicago City Missionary Society, is largely concerned with urban problems and inequities of the black minorities.

20   Black Nationalism and Black Power

Rights & Reviews: A Magazine of the Black Power Movement in America (1964-   ) is issued with varying frequency by National CORE, New York; it is also available in microform. *Black Liberator* (1969-   ) is a monthly tabloid circulated by the Black Liberation Alliance, Chicago. *Black News* (1969-   ), Brooklyn, N.Y., is a bi-weekly voice of the ideology of black self-determination. The Muhammad Mosque No. 2, Chicago, publishes *Muhammad Speaks* (1960-   ), a weekly tabloid. *The Black Panther: Black Community News Service* is distributed weekly from San Francisco. Ernest Kaiser has written an extensive critical bibliographical essay, "Recent Literature on Black Liberation Struggles and the Ghetto Crisis," *Science and Society* 33 (Spring 1969): 168-196, tracing chronologically the black power movement from 1966 to date of issue. Richard Newman has compiled *Black Power* (Wakefield, Mass.: Community Change, 1969). Citations are generally to periodicals; they are not annotated. Despite limitations of date and format, Daniel T. Williams and Carolyn L. Redden's *Black Muslims in the United States: A Selected Bibliography* (Tuskegee: Tuskegee Institute, 1964) serves a useful purpose.

Church and Society (1970-   ) a bi-monthly journal of the United Presbyterian Church devotes considerable attention to church consciousness of minorities, reparations, and the Black Manifesto.

Index